DATA ANALYTICS USING R

About the Author

Seema Acharya is a Senior Lead Principal with the Education, Training and Assessment department of Infosys Limited. She is a technology evangelist, a learning strategist, and an author with over 15 years of information technology industry experience in learning/education services. She has designed and delivered several large-scale competency development programs across the globe involving organizational competency need analysis, conceptualization, design, development and deployment of competency development programs.

An educator by choice and vocation, her areas of interest and expertise are centered on Business Intelligence and Big Data, and Analytics Technologies such as Data Warehousing, Data Mining, Data Analytics, Text Mining and Data Visualization.

She has authored some other books as well on the subject and has co-authored a paper on *Collaborative Engineering Competency Development* for ASEE (American Society for Engineering Education). She holds the patent on *Method and system for automatically generating questions for a programming language*.

She is passionate about exploring new paradigms of learning and also dabbles into creating e-learning content to facilitate learning anytime and anywhere.

DATA ANALYTICS USING R

Seema Acharya
Senior Lead Principal
Infosys Limited

McGraw Hill Education (India) Private Limited

Published by McGraw Hill Education (India) Private Limited,
Registered Office: Anjana Complex No: 5/90 A, Butt Road, St. Thomas Mount, Chennai – 600016, Tamil Nadu, India.

Data Analysis using R

Tenth reprint 2025

Print Edition
ISBN-13: 978-93-5260-524-8
ISBN-10: 93-5260-524-1

E-book Edition
ISBN-13: 978-93-5260-525-5
ISBN-10: 93-5260-525-X

11 12 13 14 15 RAJ 29 28 27 26 25

Typeset at The Composers, 260 C.A Apt., Paschim Vihar, New Delhi 110063, and,
Printed and Bound in India at Rajkamal Electric Press, Kundli 131 028, Haryana.

Visit us at: www.mheducation.co.in
Toll free in India: 1800 103 5875
Write to us at: support.india@mheducation.com
CIN: U80302TN2010PTC111532

This book is dedicated to
my father who is and will always remain my beacon of righteous inspiration

Preface

Objective of this Book

We are in very exciting times! Statistical computing and high-scale data analysis tasks need a new category of computer language other than the procedural and object-oriented programming languages. The main objective of this category of language is to support various types of statistical analysis and data analysis tasks rather than developing new software. There are mounds of data available today which can be analyzed in different ways and can provide a wide range of useful insights for different operations in different industries. However, the problem was the lack of support, tools and techniques for data analysis for different purposes. R, a statistical and analytical language, has come to our rescue! To add to the benefits, it is an open source.

Target Audience

The audience for this book includes all levels of IT professionals, executives responsible for determining IT strategies, system administrators, data analysts and decision makers responsible for driving strategic initiatives, etc. It will help to chart your journey from a novice to a professional data analyst.

The book will also make for an interesting read for business users, management graduates, and business analysts.

Organization of the Book

The book has 12 chapters. Each chapter is organized in the following way:

Chapter 1 will help you learn the installation of R and R packages. It will get you comfortable working with any R package using functions such as `find.package()`, `install.packages()`, `library()`, `vignette()` and `packageDescription()`.

Chapter 2 will allow you to analyze directory content with commands such as `dir()` and `list()` and also easily analyze datasets using functions such as `str()`, `summary()`, `ncol()`, `nrow()`, `head()`, `tail()` and `edit()`.

Chapter 3 will familiarize with the processes for loading data from .csv, spreadsheets, web, Jason documents, XML, etc. It will acquaint the reader with usage of R with databases such as MySQL, PostgreSQL, SQLlite and JasperDB.

Chapter 4 is all about data frames. It will help you store data of varied data types into frames, retrieve data from data frames, execute R functions such as `dim()`, `nrow()`, `ncol()`, `str()`, `summary()`, `names()`, `head()`, `tail()` and `edit()` to understand the data in data frames. It will help you run descriptive statistics on the data (frequency, mean, median, mode, standard deviation, etc.).

Chapter 5 discusses regression analysis that is typically used to predict the value of an outcome (target or response) variable based on predictor variables.

Chapter 6 will explain logistic regression, binomial logistic regression model, and multinomial logistic regression model.

Chapter 7 is on Classification. It will help the learners induct a decision tree to perform classification and predict the value of the outcome variable using the created decision tree model.

Chapter 8 talks about exploring time series data. It will help you read time series data using `ts()` and `scan()` functions, apply linear filtering on it, and also decompose time series data. It will discuss visualizing time series data by plotting it appropriately.

Chapter 9 will help you with implementing clustering in R using `hclust()` function. It will also discuss k-means clustering in R.

Chapter 10 will help you determine the association rules given the transactions and itemsets and also evaluate the association rule using support, confidence and lift. It will discuss implementing association rule mining in R (create binary incidence matrix of the given itemsets, create item Matrix, determine item frequencies, use `apriori()` function and `eclat()` function.

Chapter 11 will assist you in performing text mining in R.

Chapter 12 will discuss parallel computing in R using the "doParallel" and "foreach" package.

Online Learning Centre

The book is accompanied by chapter wise power point presentations at *https://connect.mheducation.com* for instructors. Students will have access to question bank available through https://www.mheducation.co.in. See the back cover for more details.

How to Get the Most out of this Book?

It is easy to leverage the book to gain the maximum by religiously abiding by the following:

- Read up the chapters thoroughly. Perform hands-on by following the step-by-step instructions stated in demonstrations. Do NOT skip any demonstration. If required, repeat it a second time or till the time the concept is firmly etched.
- Explore the various options of all R functions and commands.
- Solve the review exercises given at the end of the chapters.
- Pick up public datasets and apply the data mining algorithms and analytical techniques that you learned in the various chapters of the book.

Where Next?

We have endeavored to unleash the power of R as a statistical data analytics and visualization tool and introduce you to several data mining algorithms and chart forms/visualizations. We recommend you to read the book from cover to cover, but if you are not that kind of person, we have made an attempt to keep the chapters self-contained so that you can go straight to the topics that interest you most.

Whichever approach you may choose, we wish you well!

A Quick Word for the Instructors' Fraternity

Attention has been paid in arriving at the sequence of chapters and also to the flow of topics within each chapter. This will assist our fellow instructors and academicians in carving out a syllabus from the Table of Contents (TOC) of the book. The complete TOC can qualify as the syllabi for a semester or if the college has an existing syllabus on Data Analysis or Data Science or Analytics and Visualization, a few chapters can be added to the syllabi to make it more robust. We leave it to your discretion on how you wish to use the same for your students.

We have ensured that each tool/component discussed in the book is with adequate hands-on content to enable you to teach better and provide ample hands-on practice to your students.

Happy Learning!!!

Seema Acharya

Acknowledgements

The making of this book was a journey that I am glad I undertook. The journey spanned a few months but the experience will last a lifetime. I had my family, friends, colleagues, and well-wishers onboard this journey and I wish to express my deepest gratitude to each one of them. Without their unflinching support and care, I could not have pulled it off.

I owe this book to the student and teacher's community who, with their continual bombardment of queries, impelled me to learn more, simplify my learnings and findings and place it neatly in the book. This book is for them.

I wish to thank my friends—the practitioners from the field for their good counsel and filling me in on the latest in the field of data analysis and sharing with me valuable insights on the best practices and methodologies followed therein.

A special thanks to the team of technical reviewers for their vigilant review and filling in with their expert opinion.

I have been fortunate to have the support of my team who sometimes, knowingly, and at other times, unknowingly, contributed to the making of the book by lending me their steady support.

I have been fortunate to have the awesome editorial assistance provided by McGraw Hill Education (India). I am thankful to Mohammed Salman Khurshid for signing me up for this wonderful creation. I wish to acknowledge and appreciate Ranjana Chaube and other team members who adeptly guided me through the entire process of preparation and publication and weathered delays in my submissions. Thanks a ton for your kind patience.

A special thanks to my sister, Sunita, who tirelessly egged me on, especially on days when my energy sagged. And finally, I can never sufficiently express my gratitude towards other members of my family and friends who patiently stomached my unavailability at events and my irrational schedules as I assembled the book. You make me what I am today. 'Thanks' sounds a small word for the unconditional support!

Seema Acharya

Acknowledgements

Contents

Chapter 1

Introduction to R

LEARNING OUTCOME

At the end of this chapter, you will be able to:

- Install R
- Install any R package
- Work with any R package using functions such as `find.package()`, `install.packages()`, `library()`, `vignette()` and `packageDescription()`

1.1 Introduction

Statistical computing and high-scale data analysis tasks needed a new category of computer language besides the existing procedural and object-oriented programming languages, which would support these tasks instead of developing new software. There is plenty of data available today which can be analysed in different ways to provide a wide range of useful insights for multiple operations in various industries. Problems such as the lack of support, tools and techniques for varied data analysis have been solved with the introduction of one such language called R.

1.1.1 What is R?

R is a scripting or programming language which provides an environment for statistical computing, data science and graphics. It was inspired by, and is mostly compatible with, the statistical language S developed at Bell laboratory (formerly AT & T, now Lucent technologies). Although there are some very important differences between R and S, much of the code written for S runs unaltered on R. R has become so popular that it is used as the single most important tool for computational statistics, visualisation and data science.

1.1.2 Why R?

R has opened tremendous scope for statistical computing and data analysis. It provides techniques for various statistical analyses like classical tests and classification, time-series analysis, clustering, linear and non-linear modelling and graphical operations. The techniques supported by R are highly extensible.

S is the pioneer of statistical computing; however, it is a proprietary solution and is not readily available to developers. In contrast, R is available freely under the GNU license. Hence, it helps the developer community in research and development.

Another reason behind the popularity and widespread use of R is its superior support for graphics. It can provide well-developed and high-quality plots from data analysis. The plots can contain mathematical formulae and symbols, if necessary, and users have full control over the selection and use of symbols in the graphics. Hence, other than robustness, user-experience and user-friendliness are two key aspects of R.

Why Learn R?

The following points describe why R language should be used (Figure 1.1):

- If you need to run statistical calculations in your application, learn and deploy R. It easily integrates with programming languages such as Java, C++, Python and Ruby.
- If you wish to perform a quick analysis for making sense of data.
- If you are working on an optimisation problem.
- If you need to use re-usable libraries to solve a complex problem, leverage the 2000+ free libraries provided by R.
- If you wish to create compelling charts.
- If you aspire to be a Data Scientist.
- If you want to have fun with statistics.

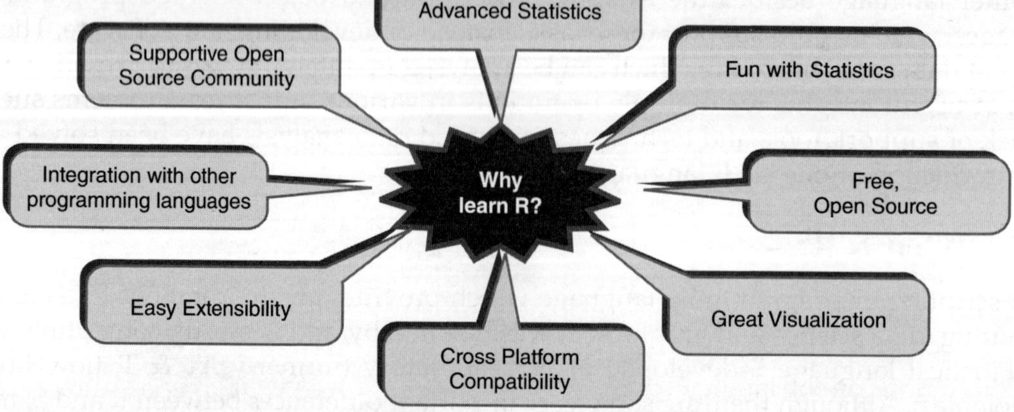

FIGURE 1.1 *Advantages of learning R language*

- R is free. It is available under the terms of the Free Software Foundation's GNU General Public License in source code form.
- It is available for Windows, Mac and a wide variety of Unix platforms (including FreeBSD, Linux, etc.).
- In addition to enabling statistical operations, it is a general programming language so that you can automate your analyses and create new functions.
- R has excellent tools for creating graphics such as bar charts, scatter plots, multi-panel lattice charts, etc.
- It has an object oriented and functional programming structure along with support from a robust and vibrant community.
- R has a flexible analysis tool kit, which makes it easy to access data in various formats, manipulate it (transform, merge, aggregate, etc.), and subject it to traditional and modern statistical models (such as regression, ANOVA, tree models, etc.)
- R can be extended easily via packages. It relates easily to other programming languages. Existing software as well as emerging software can be integrated with R packages to make them more productive.
- R can easily import data from MS Excel, MS Access, MySQL, SQLite, Oracle etc. It can easily connect to databases using ODBC (Open Database Connectivity Protocol) and ROracle package.

1.1.3 Advantages of R Over Other Programming Languages

Advanced programming languages like Python also support statistical computing and data visualisation along with traditional computer programming. However, R wins the race over Python and similar languages because of the following two advantages:

1. Python needs third party extensions and support for data visualisation and statistical computing. However, R does not require any such support extensively. For example, the lm function is present for linear regression analysis and data analysis in both Python and R. In R, data can be easily passed through the function and the function will return an object with detailed information about the regression. The function can also return information about the standard errors, coefficients, residual values and so on. When lm function is called in the Python environment, it will duplicate the functionalities using third party libraries such as SciPy, NumPy and so on. Hence, R can do the same thing with a single line of code instead of taking support from third party libraries.

> **TIP** *SciPy is used for performing data analysis tasks and NumPy is used for representing the data or objects.*

2. R has the fundamental data type, i.e., a vector that can be organised and aggregated in different ways even though the core is the same. Vector data type imposes some limitations on the language as this is a rigid type. However, it gives a strong logical base to R. Based on the vector data type, R uses the concept of data frames that are

like a matrix with attributes and internal data structure similar to spreadsheets or relational database. Hence, R follows a column-wise data structure based on the aggregation of vectors.

Just Remember

There are also some disadvantages of R. For example, R cannot scale efficiently for larger data sets. Hence, the use of R is limited to prototyping and sandboxing. It is rarely used for enterprise-level solutions. By default, R uses a single-thread execution approach while working on data stored in the RAM which leads to scalability issues as well. Developers from open source communities are working hard on these issues to make R capable of multi-threading execution and parallelisation. This will help R to utilise more than one core processor. There are big data extensions from companies like Revolution R and the issues are expected to be resolved soon. Other languages like SPlus can help to store objects permanently on disks, hence, supporting better memory management and analysis of high volume of massive datasets.

Check Your Understanding

1. What is R?

Ans: R is an open source programming language for data science and statistical computing.

2. What is the predecessor of R?

Ans: The statistical computing language, S is the predecessor of R.

3. What is the fundamental data type of R?

Ans: The fundamental data type of R is a vector.

4. What is the disadvantage of using R in enterprise-level large-scale solutions?

Ans: R language cannot scale up for large data sets. Hence, it is difficult to use R for large-scale data analysis tasks for enterprise-level solutions.

1.2 Downloading and Installing R

The integrated development suite for R language can be downloaded from the Comprehensive R Archive Network (CRAN)[1]. The network includes mirror websites for downloading the suite from different countries.

1.2.1 Downloading R

To download R, users need to visit the CRAN mirror page and click on the URL of the chosen mirror that will redirect them to the respective site (Figure 1.2).

[1] URL of CRAN—https://cran.r-project.org/mirrors.html

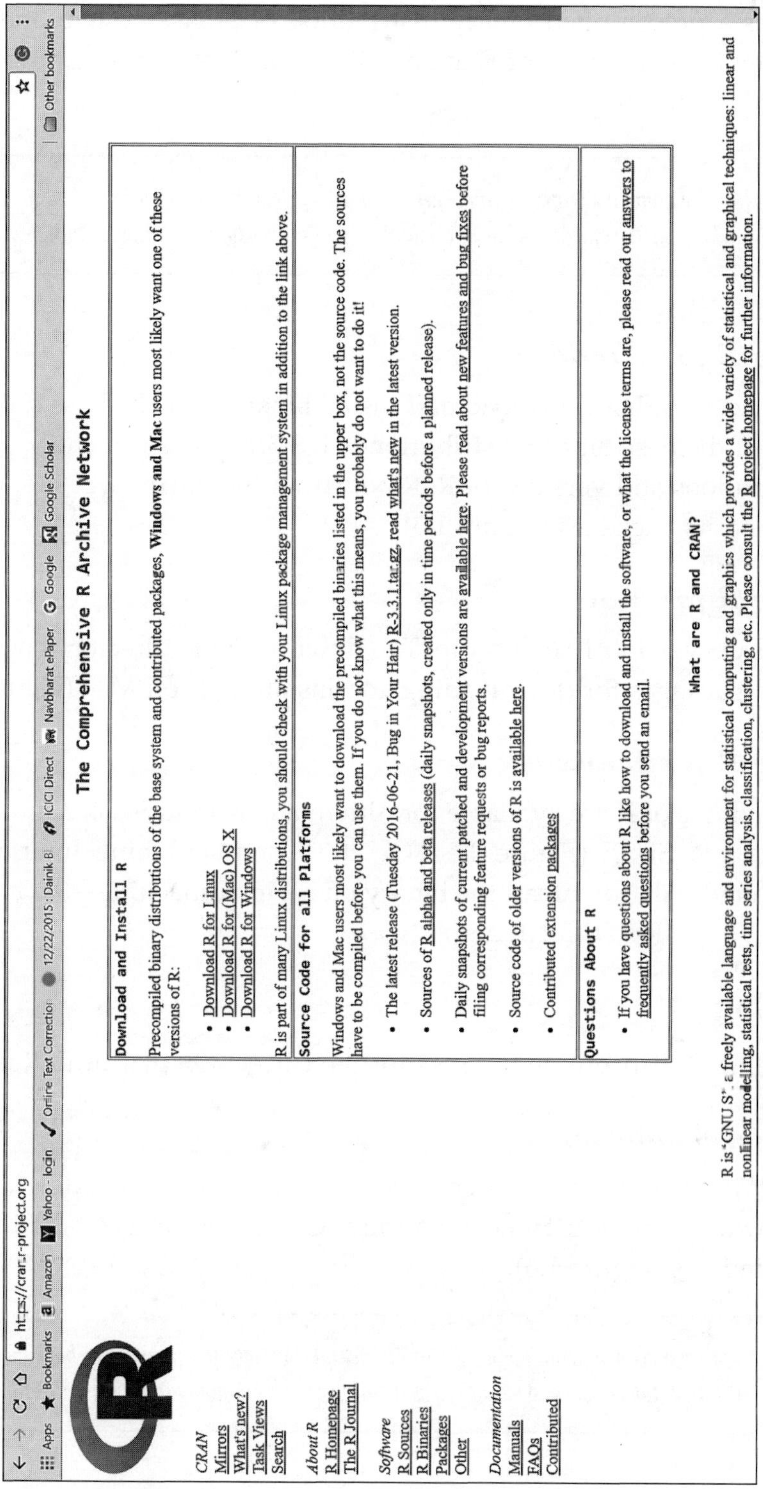

FIGURE 1.2 *CRAN website for downloading R*

R is offered as a precompiled binary distribution of a base system and contributing packages. Different distributions of R are available for different operating systems (OS) like Windows, Mac and Linux.

> **TIP** *In some Linux OS, R distributions are included by default. Hence, it is a good idea to check the package management system of a Linux OS platform before installing R on it.*

Downloading R for Windows

Windows users need to first download and install binaries for the base distribution. The current version of the base binary distribution is R 3.3.1. Users can check and download previous contributions and versions of R, Rtools from the mirror website. Rtools is used for building R and its packages (Figure 1.3).

Downloading R for Mac

R works on Mac OS version 10.6 or more. The downloadable directory contains the base distribution and packages for downloading and installing R on Mac (Figure 1.4).

Downloading R for Linux

Different distributions of R are available for different distributions of Linux like Ubuntu, Debian, RedHat and SUSE (Figure 1.5). On the Command Line Interface (CLI), the following command will download the binary on a Linux machine—$ wgethttp://cran.rstudio.com/src/base/R-3/R-3.1.1.tar.gz

1.2.2 Installing R

After downloading R distribution binaries for the correct OS platform, R is installed.

Installing R on Windows

Installing R on Windows is simple. Users need to double click on the downloaded binary, named R-3.3.1-win.exe, on a graphical interface. Command line installation options are available for Windows (Figure 1.6).

> **TIP** *Two versions are available for 32-bit and 64-bit Windows OS. By default, both the versions are installed. Hence, users need to select the desired version manually during installation.*

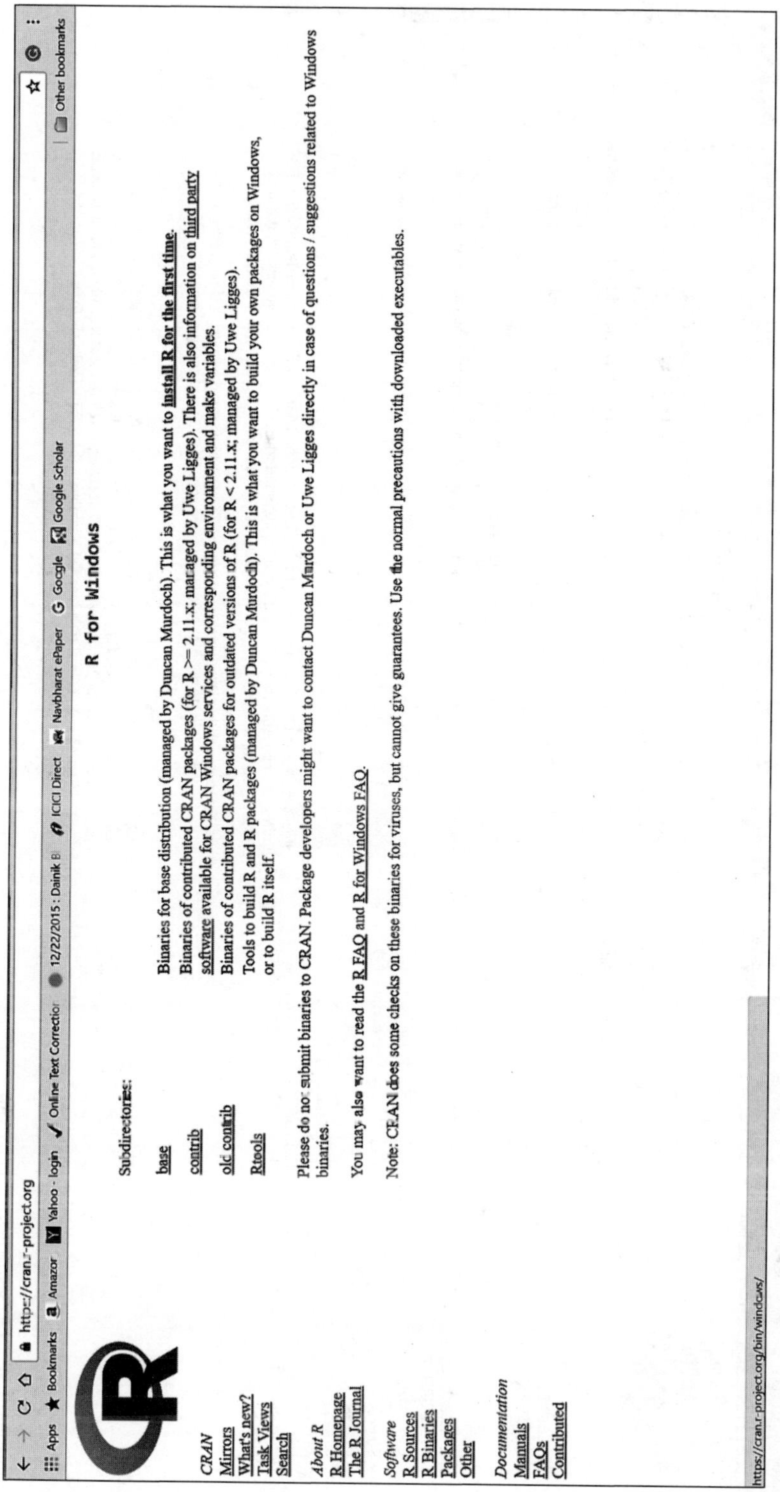

FIGURE 1.3 *Downloading R for Windows*

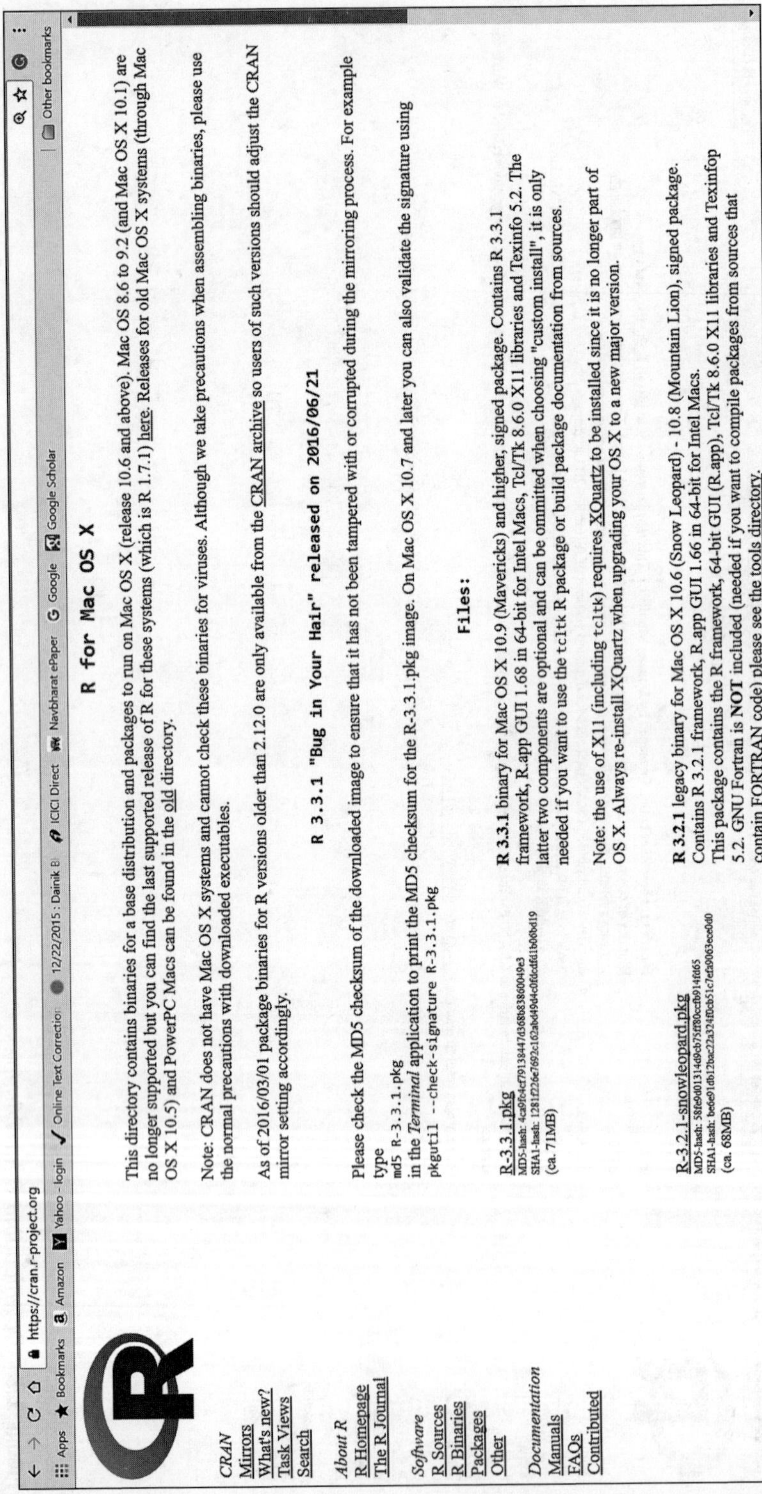

FIGURE 1.4 *Downloading R on Mac*

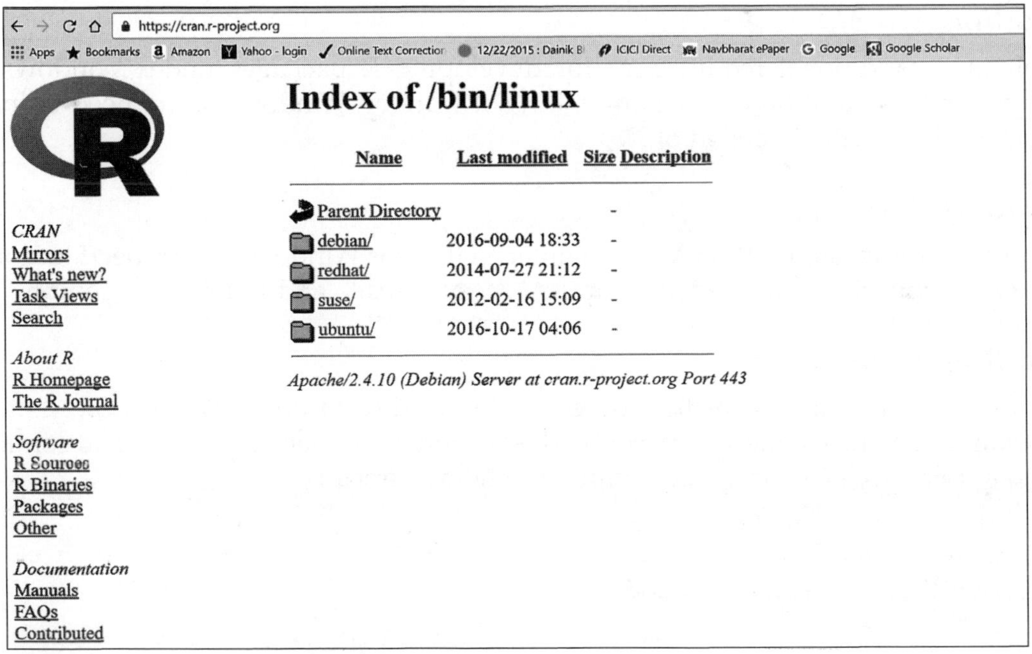

FIGURE 1.5 *Downloading R for Linux distributions*

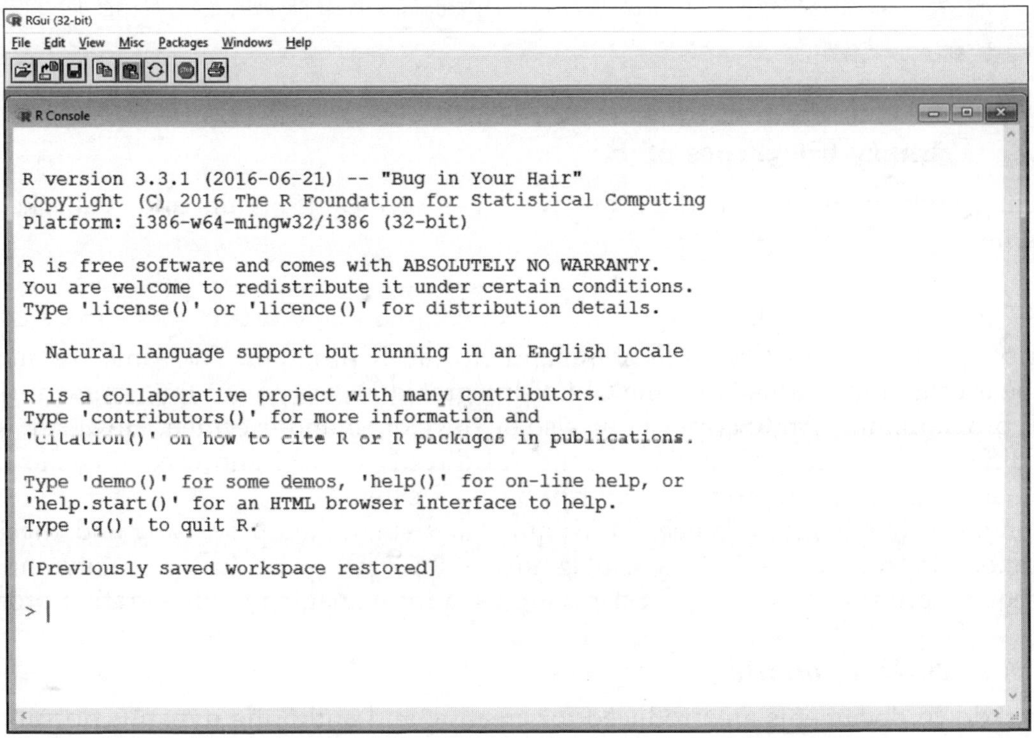

FIGURE 1.6 *R console on a 32-bit Windows PC*

Installing Rtools

Rtools is an additional requirement for developing R packages under Windows OS environment. In addition to installing the R software on Windows, users need to install Rtools for the installed version of R.

Installing R on Mac

The process for installing R on Mac is similar to that for Windows. Users need to double click on the binaries downloaded from the CRAN website and follow the prompts.

Installing R on Linux

Users need to install R from the source on Linux distributions. This can be done by following commands in the supervisor mode. The following steps will install and configure R into a user-specific subdirectory within the home directory:

```
$ tar xvf R-3.1.1.tar.gz
$ cd R-3.1.1
$ ./configure --prefix=$HOME/R
$ make && make install
```

> **TIP** *Setting the path on a Linux machine is very critical. Without the path, R and RScript do not work.*

1.2.3 Primary File Types of R

Working with R involves working on two types of files—RScripts and R markdown documents.

RScript

RScript is a text file that contains commands for an R program. The same commands can be executed individually on the CLI of Integrated Development Environment (IDE) for R programming. An RScript can be also be developed and executed. However, there is a difference between executing a command directly on CLI and executing the same command through an R script. An RScript has a .R extension.

Command line interface is needed for quick and small data processing and checking operations. In large-scale solutions, it integrates multiple programs during prototyping and subsequent phases. In that case, RScripts are used for managing the integration process.

Markdown Documents

R markdown documents are produced for creating and authoring dynamic documents, reports and presentations from R. R markdown documents have a set of markdown syntaxes derived from the core markdown syntaxes. These syntaxes are embedded into RScripts and codes. When these embedded codes and scripts are executed then the output is formatted based on the markdown syntaxes and hence becomes easily understandable. R markdown documents can be regenerated automatically if the underlying RScripts and codes or data are changed. The output format of an R markdown covers a wide range of formats including PDF, HTML, HTML5 slides, websites, dashboards, tufte handouts, notebooks, books, MS word, etc. The extension for R markdown document files is .rmd.

Check Your Understanding

1. How to locate an RScript file in a typical file system?

Ans: An RScript file can be located in a typical file system by verifying if the extension of the file is .R.

2. What is R markdown and how is it different from word documentation?

Ans: R markdown documents are dynamic and reproducible. Markdown files are used for making reports and documents with R. These markdown codes are embedded into files such as PDF, HTML, word files, etc. On the contrary, word files are text files only and do not support markdown.

1.3 IDEs and Text Editors

Various text editors can be used for writing RScripts and codes. Table 1.1 describes some popular IDEs and text editors for writing and executing R codes.

TABLE 1.1 Some IDEs and text editors for writing and executing R codes

Name	*Platform(s)*	*License*	*Details and Usage*
Notepad and Notepad++ to R	Windows, Linux and Mac	GNU GPL	Notepad++ to R is an editor for R that is simple and robust. It supports extensions like close passing to Notepad++ editor, R GUI editor and optionally to a PuTTY window on a remote machine. It supports batch processing using shortcuts, monitoring of execution of RScripts and so on.
Tinn-R	Windows	GNU GPL	Tinn-R is a word processor and text editor that can process generic ASCII and UNICODE on Windows OS. This is well integrated into R and supports GUI and IDE for R.
Revolution Productivity Enhancer (RPE)		Commercial	Revolution productivity enhancer is an R productivity or enhanced environment. However, it can work as an IDE for new users. The usability features of RPE are very supportive. It includes features like IntelliSense for detecting completion of word, code snippets, and so on. Hence, RPE is an integrated IDE and editor with built-in visual debugging tools.

There are various IDEs used in R language. You will learn about these IDEs in the following section.

1.3.1 R Studio

R studio is the most widely used IDE for writing, testing and executing R codes (Figure 1.7). This is a user-friendly and open source solution. There are various parts in a typical screen of an R studio IDE. These are:

- Console, where users write a command and see the output
- Workspace tab, where users can see active objects from the code written in the console
- History tab, which shows a history of commands used in the code
- File tab, where folders and files can be seen in the default workspace
- Plot tab, which shows graphs
- Packages tab, which shows add-ons and packages required for running specific process(s)
- Help tab, which contains the information on IDE, commands, etc.

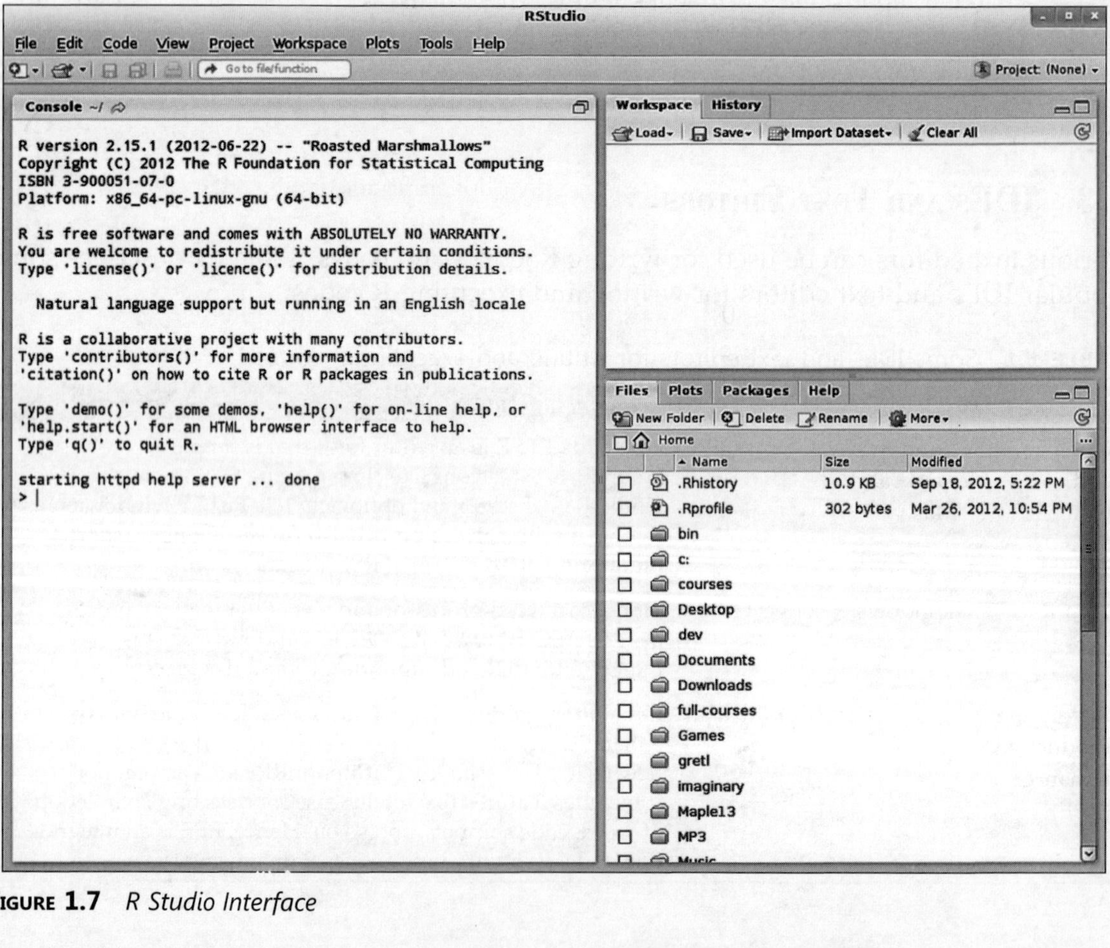

FIGURE 1.7 *R Studio Interface*

1.3.2 Eclipse with StatET

Eclipse is a well-known IDE for Java, C++, etc.; however, Eclipse can be used for statistical programming based on R also. The corresponding IDE is called Eclipse with StatET. Eclipse with StatET offers a set of tools that can be used for coding in R and building R packages. It supports one or more local and remote installations of R. Its functionalities can be expanded by using more add-ons like Sweave and Wikitext. Different parts of the IDE are given below:

- Console for R
- Object browser
- Package manager
- Debugger
- Data viewer
- R help system.

1.4 Handling Packages in R

A package in R is the fundamental unit of shareable code. It is a collection of the following elements:

- Functions
- Data sets
- Compiled code
- Documentation for the package and for the functions inside
- Tests – few tests to check if everything works as it should.

The directory where packages are stored is called a library. R comes with a standard set of packages. Others are available for download and installation as per requirement. As on date, there are over 10,000 plus packages available in CRAN. This is also one of the reasons behind the huge popularity and success of R.

Packages are used to share codes with others. One can develop their own R package. Any R user can then download, install and learn to use the package. Packages, therefore allow for an easy, transparent and cross-platform extension of the R base system.

R is an open source language; thus, new packages are being developed and updated by developers daily. Some of these packages may not work properly or may have bugs. Hence, it is not a good idea to use every new and updated package on R development environment. This can affect the stability of the development environment. A stable environment requires the *sandboxing technique* (a security mechanism often used to execute untested or untrusted programs or code from unverified or untrusted third parties, users, etc., without damaging/maligning the host machine or operating system or production environment) to test new packages or update a package before installing it in the development environment.

In general, there is a single package library with each installation of R on a computer. Users can change the path to that library to install a package on a different location other than the default package library. The command `.libPaths()` can be used to get or set the path of the package library.

Example

```
> .libPaths()
```

Output

```
C:/R/R-3.1.3/library
```

This is the default package library location. The following command will change it into another path:

Example

```
> .libPaths("~/R/win-library/3.1-mran-2016-07-02")
```

Output

```
C:/Users/User1/Documents/R/win-library/3.1-mran-2016-07-02
```

R can be extended easily with the help of a rich set of packages. There are more than 10,000 packages available for R. These packages are used for different purposes. Tables 1.2 and 1.3 list some commonly used R packages for different purposes.

TABLE 1.2 Commonly used R packages for different purposes

Data Management	*Data Visualisation*	*Data Products*	*Data Modelling and Simulation*
dplyr, tidyr, foreign, haven etc.	ggplot, ggvis, lattice, igraph etc.	shiny, slidify, knitr, markdown etc.	MASS, forecast, bootstrap, broom, nlme, ROCR, party etc.

TABLE 1.3 Commonly used packages in R

Author(s)	*Package Name*	*Description*	*Available At*
Andrew Gelman, et al.	arm	It is used for hierarchical or multi-level regression models.	http://cran.r-project.org/web/packages/arm/
Douglas Bates, Martin Maechler, and Ben Bolker	lme4	It contains functions for generating generalised and linear mixed-effects models.	http://cran.r-project.org/web/packages/lme4/
Duncan Temple Lang	Rcurl	It provides an interface of R to the package library, libcurl. The interface helps in interacting with the HTTP protocols for importing raw data from the web.	http://www.omegahat.org/RCurl/
Duncan Temple Lang	RJSONIO	It provides a set of functions to read and write JSON for analysing data from different web-based APIs.	http://www.omegahat.org/RJSONIO/
Duncan Temple Lang	XML	It provides functions and facilities for analysing HTML and XML documents to extract structured data from web-based sources.	http://www.omegahat.org/RSXML/

(Continued)

Author(s)	*Package Name*	*Description*	*Available At*
Gabor Csardi	igraph	It contains routines for network analysis and making simple graphs to represent social networks.	http://igraph.sourceforge.net/
Hadley Wickham	ggplot	It contains a set of grammar rules for implementing graphics in R. The package is used for creating high-quality graphics.	http://cran.r-project.org/web/packages/glmnet/index.html
Hadley Wickham	lubridate	The package provides functions to use dates in R in an easier way.	https://github.com/hadley/lubridate
Hadley Wickham	reshape	It contains a set of tools for manipulation, aggregation and management of data in R.	http://had.co.nz/plyr/
Ingo Feinerer	tm	It contains functions to perform text mining in R. Text mining helps to work with unstructured data.	http://www.spatstat.org/spatstat/
Jerome Friedman, Trevor Hastie, and Rob Tibshirani	glmnet	It helps to work with the elastic-net and also regularised and generalised linear models.	http://had.co.nz/ggplot2/

1.4.1 Installing an R Package

R comes with some standard packages that are installed when a user first installs R and additional packages can be installed separately. Users need to navigate through the package library and install a package in the desired location. Following commands are used for navigating through R package library and installing R package.

1. To start R, follow either Step 2 or 3. The assumption is that R is already installed on your machine.
2. If there is an "R" icon on the desktop of the computer that you are using, double click on the "R" icon to start R. If there is no "R" icon on the desktop then click on the "Start" button at the bottom left of your computer screen, and then choose "All programs", and start R by selecting "R" (or R X.X.X, where X.X.X gives the version of R, e.g. R 2.10.0) from the menu of programs.
3. The R console should show up.
4. Once you have started R, you can install an R package (e.g. the "ggplot2" package) by choosing "Install package(s)" from the "Packages" menu at the top of the R console. This will ask you for the website that you wish to download the package from. You can choose "Iceland" (or another country, if you prefer). It will also bring up a list of available packages that you can install, and you can choose the package that you want to install from that list (e.g. "ggplot2").
5. This will install the "ggplot2" package.
6. The "ggplot2" package is now installed. Whenever you want to use the "ggplot2" package after this, after having successfully started R, you first have to load the package by typing into the R console: library("ggplot2").
7. You can get help on a package by typing the following at the R prompt: help(package = "ggplot2")

1.4.2 Few Commands to Get Started

installed.packages()

A user can check for all installed packages on the machine by using the `installed.packages()` function.

```
> installed.packages()
             Package       LibPath                                           Version    Priority
arules       "arules"      "C:/Users/seema_acharya/Documents/R/win-library/3.2" "1.3-1"    NA
arulesViz    "arulesViz"   "C:/Users/seema_acharya/Documents/R/win-library/3.2" "1.1-0"    NA
assertthat   "assertthat"  "C:/Users/seema_acharya/Documents/R/win-library/3.2" "0.1"      NA
BH           "BH"          "C:/Users/seema_acharya/Documents/R/win-library/3.2" "1.62.0-1" NA
bit          "bit"         "C:/Users/seema_acharya/Documents/R/win-library/3.2" "1.1-12"   NA
bitops       "bitops"      "C:/Users/seema_acharya/Documents/R/win-library/3.2" "1.0-6"    NA
boot         "boot"        "C:/Users/seema_acharya/Documents/R/win-library/3.2" "1.3-18"   "recommended"
caTools      "caTools"     "C:/Users/seema_acharya/Documents/R/win-library/3.2" "1.17.1"   NA
class        "class"       "C:/Users/seema_acharya/Documents/R/win-library/3.2" "7.3-14"   "recommended"
coin         "coin"        "C:/Users/seema_acharya/Documents/R/win-library/3.2" "1.1-2"    NA
colorspace   "colorspace"  "C:/Users/seema_acharya/Documents/R/win-library/3.2" "1.2-6"    NA
corpcor      "corpcor"     "C:/Users/seema_acharya/Documents/R/win-library/3.2" "1.6.8"    NA
curl         "curl"        "C:/Users/seema_acharya/Documents/R/win-library/3.2" "2.3"      NA
DBI          "DBI"         "C:/Users/seema_acharya/Documents/R/win-library/3.2" "0.5-1"    NA
dendextend   "dendextend"  "C:/Users/seema_acharya/Documents/R/win-library/3.2" "1.1.8"    NA
DEoptimR     "DEoptimR"    "C:/Users/seema_acharya/Documents/R/win-library/3.2" "1.0-8"    NA
devtools     "devtools"    "C:/Users/seema_acharya/Documents/R/win-library/3.2" "1.12.0"   NA
dichromat    "dichromat"   "C:/Users/seema_acharya/Documents/R/win-library/3.2" "2.0-0"    NA
digest       "digest"      "C:/Users/seema_acharya/Documents/R/win-library/3.2" "0.6.9"    NA
doParallel   "doParallel"  "C:/Users/seema_acharya/Documents/R/win-library/3.2" "1.0.10"   NA
dplyr        "dplyr"       "C:/Users/seema_acharya/Documents/R/win-library/3.2" "0.5.0"    NA
ff           "ff"          "C:/Users/seema_acharya/Documents/R/win-library/3.2" "2.2-13"   NA
foreach      "foreach"     "C:/Users/seema_acharya/Documents/R/win-library/3.2" "1.4.3"    NA
foreign      "foreign"     "C:/Users/seema_acharya/Documents/R/win-library/3.2" "0.8-66"   "recommended"
FRB          "FRB"         "C:/Users/seema_acharya/Documents/R/win-library/3.2" "1.8"      NA
gclus        "gclus"       "C:/Users/seema_acharya/Documents/R/win-library/3.2" "1.3.1"    NA
gdata        "gdata"       "C:/Users/seema_acharya/Documents/R/win-library/3.2" "2.17.0"   NA
ggdendro     "ggdendro"    "C:/Users/seema_acharya/Documents/R/win-library/3.2" "0.1-20"   NA
ggfortify    "ggfortify"   "C:/Users/seema_acharya/Documents/R/win-library/3.2" "0.4.1"    NA
ggplot2      "ggplot2"     "C:/Users/seema_acharya/Documents/R/win-library/3.2" "2.0.0"    NA
git2r        "git2r"       "C:/Users/seema_acharya/Documents/R/win-library/3.2" "0.18.0"   NA
gplots       "gplots"      "C:/Users/seema_acharya/Documents/R/win-library/3.2" "2.17.0"   NA
gridBase     "gridBase"    "C:/Users/seema_acharya/Documents/R/win-library/3.2" "0.4-7"    NA
gridExtra    "gridExtra"   "C:/Users/seema_acharya/Documents/R/win-library/3.2" "2.2.1"    NA
gtable       "gtable"      "C:/Users/seema_acharya/Documents/R/win-library/3.2" "0.2.0"    NA
gtools       "gtools"      "C:/Users/seema_acharya/Documents/R/win-library/3.2" "3.5.0"    NA
```

....

`remove.packages()` can be used to uninstall a package.

packageDescription()

"DESCRIPTION" file has the basic information about a package. It has details such as what the package does, who is the author, what is the version for the documentation, the date, the type of license its use, and the package dependencies, etc. To access the description file inside R, use the function, packageDescription("package"). The same can also be accessed via the documentation of the package by using help(package = "package").

Let us look at the description for the "stats" package.

```
> packageDescription("stats")
Package: stats
Version: 3.2.3
Priority: base
Title: The R Stats Package
Author: R Core Team and contributors worldwide
Maintainer: R Core Team <R-core@r-project.org>
Description: R statistical functions.
License: Part of R 3.2.3
Suggests: MASS, Matrix, Suppdists, methods, stats4
Build: R 3.2.3; x86_64-w64-mingw32; 2015-12-10 13:03:29 UTC; windows

-- File: C:/Program Files/R/R-3.2.3/library/stats/Meta/package.rds
```

Or

```
> help(package="stats")
```

The output shown is partial.

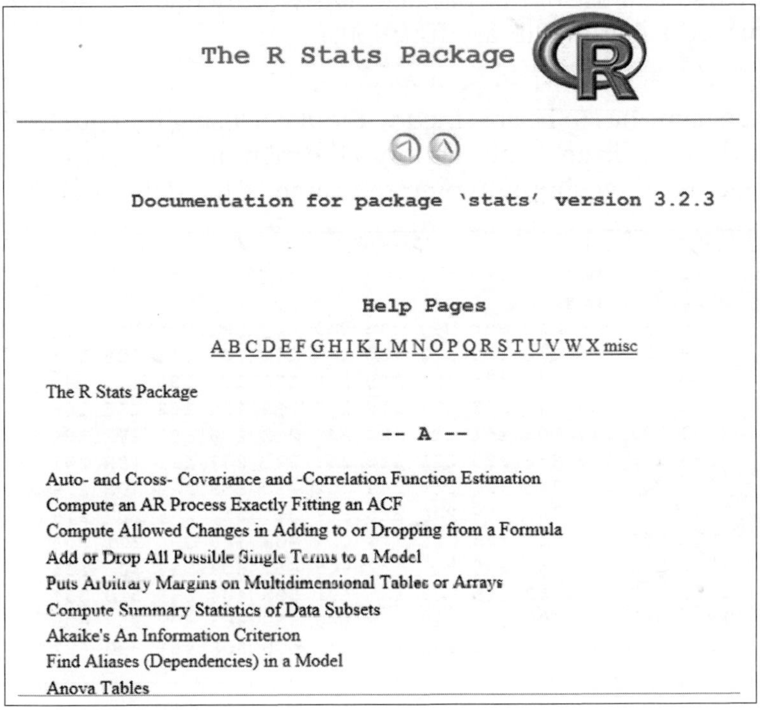

help(package = "package")

To get an overview of all the functions and datasets in an R package, use the help() function.

```
> help(package = "datasets")
```

The above will provide an overview of all functions and datasets inside the package, "datasets". One of the dataset available in "datasets" package is "AirPassengers". To access the dataset, "AirPassengers" inside the "datasets" package, use the code given below:

```
> datasets::AirPassengers
     Jan Feb Mar Apr May Jun Jul Aug Sep Oct Nov Dec
1949 112 118 132 129 121 135 148 148 136 119 104 118
1950 115 126 141 135 125 149 170 170 158 133 114 140
1951 145 150 178 163 172 178 199 199 184 162 146 166
1952 171 180 193 181 183 218 230 242 209 191 172 194
1953 196 196 236 235 229 243 264 272 237 211 180 201
1954 204 188 235 227 234 264 302 293 259 229 203 229
1955 242 233 267 269 270 315 364 347 312 274 237 278
1956 284 277 317 313 318 374 413 405 355 306 271 306
1957 315 301 356 348 355 422 465 467 404 347 305 336
1958 340 318 362 348 363 435 491 505 404 359 310 337
1959 360 342 406 396 420 472 548 559 463 407 362 405
1960 417 391 419 461 472 535 622 606 508 461 390 432
```

If there will be frequent use of this package, it is worthwhile to load it into the memory. This can be achieved using the library function:

```
> library (datasets)
```

Note: the package name has to be specified without enclosing it in quotes. The `library()` function will load the package, "datasets" into the memory. Then any dataset within this package can be accessed by simply typing the name of the dataset at the R prompt.

```
> library(datasets)
> AirPassengers
     Jan Feb Mar Apr May Jun Jul Aug Sep Oct Nov Dec
1949 112 118 132 129 121 135 148 148 136 119 104 118
1950 115 126 141 135 125 149 170 170 158 133 114 140
1951 145 150 178 163 172 178 199 199 184 162 146 166
1952 171 180 193 181 183 218 230 242 209 191 172 194
1953 196 196 236 235 229 243 264 272 237 211 180 201
1954 204 188 235 227 234 264 302 293 259 229 203 229
1955 242 233 267 269 270 315 364 347 312 274 237 278
1956 284 277 317 313 318 374 413 405 355 306 271 306
1957 315 301 356 348 355 422 465 467 404 347 305 336
1958 340 318 362 348 363 435 491 505 404 359 310 337
1959 360 342 406 396 420 472 548 559 463 407 362 405
1960 417 391 419 461 472 535 622 606 508 461 390 432
```

`find.package()` and `install.packages()` Command

`find.package()` and `install.packages()` commands will find and install specific R package(s). There are two versions of this command. The first helps in installing one package at a time and the other is used to install multiple packages at once using a single command—`install.packages()`. More details on commands like `find.package()` and `install.packages()` can be retrieved using the `help()` command. For example, help (installed.packages) can show details like the version number of a function.

Example

To install a single package, the command is:

```
>find.package("ggplot2")
>install.packages("ggplot2")
```

Output

The first command will help to find if there is any package named "ggplot2" installed in the system or not. Then the `install.packages()` function will install the package named "ggplot2" CLI (Figure 1.8). It will download and install the package and all the dependencies of the package.

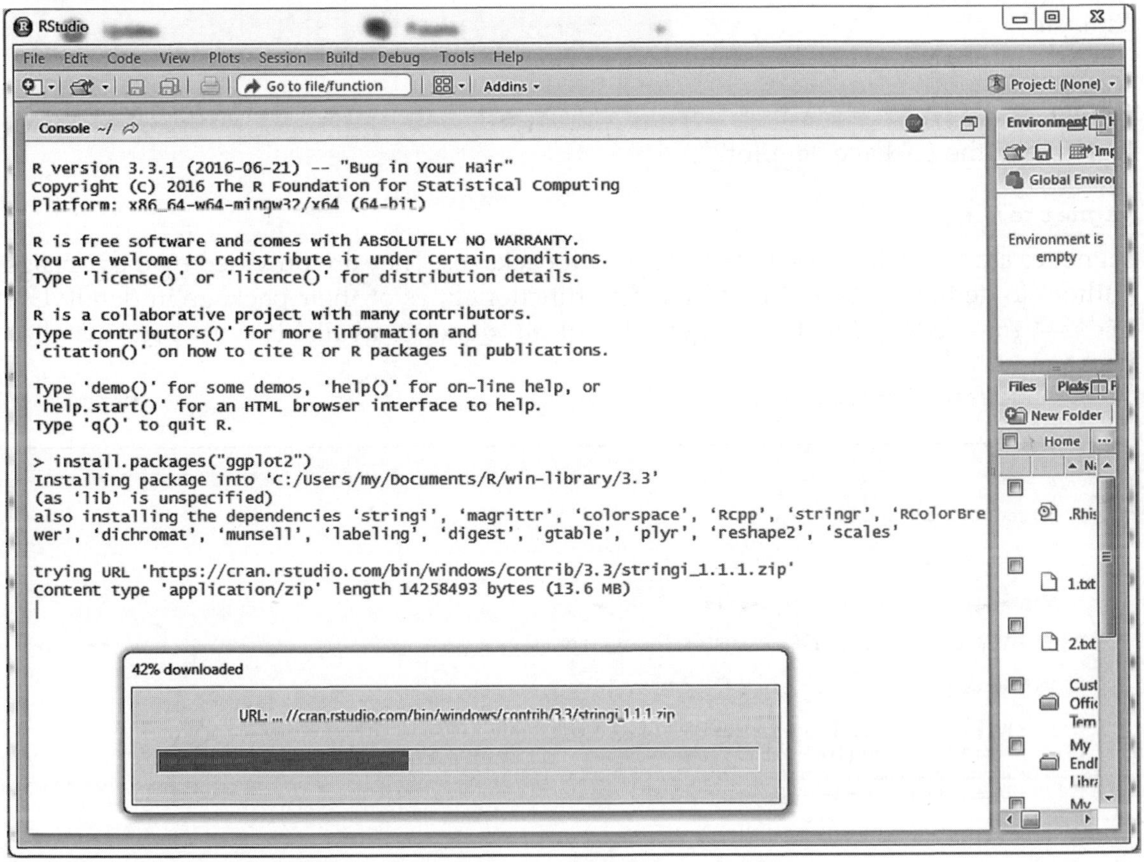

FIGURE 1.8 *Example of installing a package*

Example

To install more than one package(s) at a time, the `install.packages()` command will have the following format:

```
>install.packages(c("ggplot", "tidyr", "dplyr"))
```

Output

It will install packages ggplot, tidyr and dplyr.

> **TIP** *The command to check whether a package is installed or not is the 'if' condition checking. The command for checking whether the package "ggplot2" is installed or not can be done by using:*
>
> `>if (!require("ggplot2")){install.packages("ggplot2")}`

library()

`library()` command loads a package.

Example

```
>library(ggplot2)
```

Output

It will load the package "ggplot2".

vignette()

Vignettes are a very useful source of help with packages. They are provided by the package authors to demonstrate and highlight few functionalities of their package in detail. Use `browseVignettes()` function to get a list of all vignettes available with your installed packages.

```
> browseVignettes()
```

Vignettes found by "browseVignettes()"

Vignettes in package arules

- Introduction to arules - PDF source R code

Vignettes in package arulesViz

- Visualizing Association Rules: Introduction to arulesViz - PDF source R code

Vignettes in package coin

- A Lego System for Conditional Inference - PDF source R code
- coin: A Computational Framework for Conditional Inference - PDF source R code
- Implementing a Class of Permutation Tests: The coin Package - PDF source R code
- Order-restricted Scores Test - PDF source R code

Vignettes in package colorspace

- HCL-Based Color Palettes in R - PDF source R code

Vignettes in package curl

- The curl package: a modern R interface to libcurl - HTML source R code

Vignettes in package DBI

- A Common Database Interface (DBI) - HTML source
- A Common Interface to Relational Databases from R and S -- A Proposal - HTML source
- Implementing a new backend - HTML source R code

To view all vignettes for a specific package, e.g., "ggplot2", use the `vignette()` function.

```
Vignettes in package 'ggplot2':

ggplot2-specs                Aesthetic specifications (source, html)
extending-ggplot2            Extending ggplot2 (source, html)
```

Check Your Understanding

1. Name a few packages used for data management in R.

Ans: dplyr, tidyr, foreign, haven, etc.

2. Name a few packages used for data visualisation in R.

Ans: ggplot, ggvis, lattice, igraph, etc.

3. Name a few packages used for developing data produces in R.

Ans: shiny, slidify, knitr, markdown, etc.

4. Name a few packages used for data modelling and simulation in R.

Ans: MASS, forecast, bootstrap, broom, nlme, ROCR, party, etc.

5. How can the default path to package library be changed in R?

Ans: To change the default package library in R, users need to follow the following steps on the console of R IDE:

Step 1: Check the current path to the package library

```
> .libPaths()
```

Step 2: Change the path using the following command.

```
> .libPaths("write the desired path here")
```

6. What is the command to check and install the "dplyr" package?

Ans: `if (!require("dplyr ")) {install.packages("dplyr")}`

7. How can we install multiple packages in R?

Ans: To install multiple packages in R the command is, `>install.packages(c("ggplot","tidyr","dplyr"))`

Just Remember

To access help in RStudio, it can be accessed from the console and from the CLI (Figure 1.9). The command is `help()`.

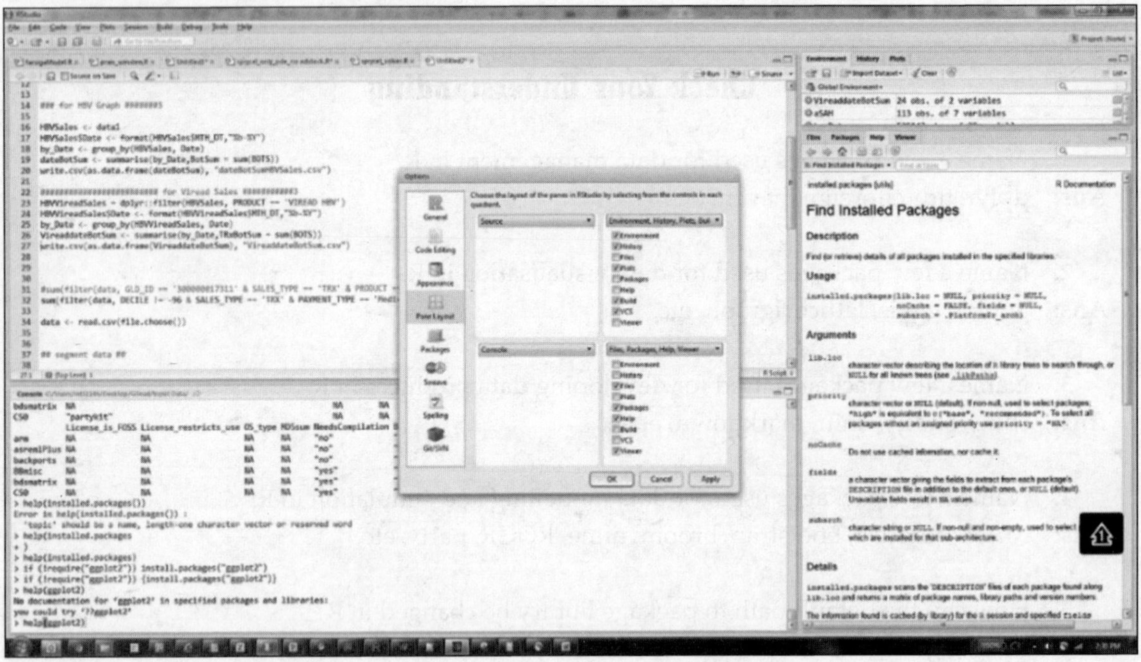

FIGURE 1.9 *Accessing `help()` command from the console and CLI*

Summary

- R is an open source and object-oriented programming language for statistical computing and data visualisation.
- R is a successor of the proprietary statistical computing programming language S.
- R can be downloaded and installed on different OS platforms like Windows, Linux and Mac.
- R has the fundamental data type of vector.
- Text editors like Notepad++ to R, Tinn-R and Rev R are more than just editors for R. These can support extended functionalities and IDE features.
- R has several IDEs like RStudio, Eclipse with StatET and so on.
- R has a rich library of more than 10,000 packages.
- R has two fundamental file types called RScripts and R markdown documents.
- R commands can be written in RScripts or through the command line interface.
- R has a rich collection of inbuilt data sets like mtcars, Biochemical Oxygen Demand (BOD), etc.

Key Terms

- **BOD:** An inbuilt data set in R, which contains data on the Biochemical Oxygen Demand.
- **CLI:** A console through which a user can interact with a computer. The interaction happens through successive lines of commands on the console.
- **IDE:** A special type of software that offers a set of comprehensive facilities to develop computer software. Usually, an IDE consists of a number of automation tools, a debugger and an editor for coding.
- **R:** An open source and object oriented programming language for statistical computing and data visualisation.

Multiple Choice Questions

1. What is R?
   (a) An object-oriented programming language
   (b) An open source project from CRAN
   (c) A programming language for statistical computing
   (d) All of these
2. Which one of the following programming languages is a dialect of R language?
   (a) Python (b) C
   (c) S (d) Q
3. Which one of the following is a text editor of R?
   (a) RStudio (b) Microsoft word
   (c) Notepad++ to R (d) Tableau
4. Which of the following are IDEs for R?
   (a) RStudio (b) Both a and c
   (c) Eclipse with StatET (d) None of these
5. What is the primary file type of R?
   (a) Vector (b) Text file
   (c) RScripts (d) Statistical file
6. R can be downloaded from:
   (a) CRAN website (b) Google PlayStore
   (c) None of these (d) All of these
7. Which one of the following R packages is used for data management?
   (a) haven (b) igraph
   (c) slidify (d) forecast

8. Which one of the following R packages is used for data visualisation?
   (a) haven (b) igraph
   (c) slidify (d) forecast
9. Which one of the following R packages is used for data products?
   (a) haven (b) igraph
   (c) slidify (d) forecast
10. Which one of the following R packages is used for data modelling and simulation?
   (a) haven (b) igraph
   (c) slidify (d) forecast
11. The functionalities of R are divided among:
   (a) Packages (b) Domains
   (c) Libraries (d) None of these

Short Questions

1. What is R? What are the advantages of R programming language over other general purpose programming languages?
2. How can we install a package on R?
3. Give examples of two IDEs for R.
4. Give detailed examples of three packages used in R.
5. Give a detailed description of head() command used in R.
6. How can we install multiple R packages with a single command?
7. State the difference(s) between `head()` and `tail()` commands used in R.
8. State the difference(s) between `ncol()` and `nrow()` commands used in R.

Answers to MCQs:

1. (d) 2. (c) 3. (c) 4. (b) 5. (c) 6. (a) 7. (a)
8. (b) 9. (c) 10. (d) 11. (a)

Chapter 2

Getting Started with R

LEARNING OUTCOME

At the end of this chapter, you will be able to:

- Analyse directory content with commands such as `dir()`, `list()`
- Analyse a dataset using functions such as `str()`, `summary()`, `ncol()`, `nrow()`, `head()`, `tail()`, `edit()`

2.1 Introduction

Data exploration in R is an approach to summarise and visualise important characteristics of a data set. An exploratory data analysis focusses on understanding the underlying variables and data structures to see how they can help in data analysis through various formal statistical methods.

2.2 Working with Directory

Before writing a program or code using R, it is important to find out the directory being used. This can be done using the `getwd()` function. If the current working directory is not as per preference, it can be changed using the `setwd()` function. The `dir()` or the `list.files()` functions give information about the files and directories in the current working directory or any other directory.

2.2.1 `getwd()` Command

`getwd()` command returns the absolute filepath of the current working directory. This function has no arguments.

Example

```
>getwd()
```

Output

```
[1] C:/Users/User1/Documents/R
```

Note the use of '/' as the file separator on Windows. The file path does not have a trailing '/' unless it is the root directory. The `getwd()` function can return NULL if the working directory is not available.

2.2.2 `setwd()` Command

`setwd()` command resets the current working directory to another location as per the user's preference.

Example

```
>setwd("C:/path/to/my_directory")
```

Output

It will change the path to the user specified directory.

2.2.3 `dir()` Function

This is equivalent to `list.files()` function.

This function returns a character vector of the names of files or directories in the named directory.

Syntax

```
dir(path = ".", pattern = NULL, all.files = FALSE,
           full.names = FALSE, recursive = FALSE,
           ignore.case = FALSE, include.dirs = FALSE, no.. = FALSE)
or

list.files(path = ".", pattern = NULL, all.files = FALSE,
           full.names = FALSE, recursive = FALSE,
           ignore.case = FALSE, include.dirs = FALSE, no.. = FALSE)
>dir()
character(0)

>list.files()
character(0)
```

The above command implies that there are no files or directories in the current directory.

Example 1

To display the files and directories in the current directory, use path= "." as an argument to `dir()`.

```
>dir(path=".")
 [1] "att connect"                   "BI_May_2015.pptx"       "BI_MetroMap-Final.png"        "BISkillMatrix-Final.xlsx"
 [5] "C"                             "cache"                  "Custom Office Templates"      "Dec2016-BroadbandBill.pdf"
 [9] "decision_tree.png"             "Default.rdp"            "desktop.ini"                  "DSS.wma"
[13] "ILP-AssociationRuleMining.pptx" "May-Broadband bill.pdf" "My Data Sources"             "My Music"
[17] "My Pictures"                   "My Shapes"              "My Tableau Repository"        "My Videos"
[21] "Northwind 2007 sample.accdt"   "Oct-Broadband bill.pdf" "OneNote Notebooks"            "Outlokk Files"
[25] "R"                             "Remote Assistance Logs" "samplelinearregression.png"   "SAP"
[29] "SQL Server Management Studio"  "Visual Studio 2005"     "Visual Studio 2008"           "Visual Studio 2010"
```

Example 2

To display the list of all files and directories in a specific path, use the command as follows:

```
> dir (path="C:/Users/Seema_acharya")
 [1] "AppData"
 [2] "Application Data"
 [3] "ATT_Connect_Setup.exe"
 [4] "CD95F661A5C444F5A6AAECDD91C2410a.TMP"
 [5] "Contacts"
 [6] "Cookies"
 [7] "Desktop"
 [8] "Documents"
 [9] "Downloads"
[10] "Favorites"
[11] "Links"
[12] "Local Settings"
[13] "Music"
[14] "My Documents"
[15] "NetHood"
[16] "NTUSER.DAT"
[17] "ntuser.dat.LOG1"
[18] "ntuser.dat.LOG2"
[19] "NTUSER.DAT{6cced2f1-6e01-11de-8bed-001e0bcd1824}.TM.blf"
[20] "NTUSER.DAT{6cced2f1-6e01-11de-8bed-001e0bcd1824}.
                              TMContainer00000000000000000001.regtrans-ms"
[21] "NTUSER.DAT{6cced2f1-6e01-11de-8bed-001e0bcd1824}.
                              TMContainer00000000000000000002.regtrans-ms"
[22] "ntuser.ini"
[23] "ntuser.pol"
[24] "Pictures"
[25] "PrintHood"
[26] "Recent"
[27] "Saved Games"
[28] "Searches"
[29] "SendTo"
[30] "Start Menu"
[31] "Templates"
[32] "Videos"
```

Example 3

To display the complete or absolute path of all files and directories in the specified path, use `dir()` as follows:

```
> dir(path="C:/Users/Seema_acharya", full.names=TRUE)
 [1] "C:/Users/Seema_acharya/AppData"
 [2] "C:/Users/Seema_acharya/Application Data"
 [3] "C:/Users/Seema_acharya/ATT_Connect_Setup.exe"
 [4] "C:/Users/Seema_acharya/CD95F661A5C444F5A6AAECDD91C2410A.TMP"
 [5] "C:/Users/Seema_acharya/Contacts"
 [6] "C:/Users/Seema_acharya/Cookies"
 [7] "C:/Users/Seema_acharya/Desktop"
 [8] "C:/Users/Seema_acharya/Documents"
 [9] "C:/Users/Seema_acharya/Downloads"
[10] "C:/Users/Seema_acharya/Favorites"
[11] "C:/Users/Seema_acharya/Links"
[12] "C:/Users/Seema_acharya/Local Settings"
[13] "C:/Users/Seema_acharya/Music"
[14] "C:/Users/Seema_acharya/My Documents"
[15] "C:/Users/Seema_acharya/NetHood"
[16] "C:/Users/Seema_acharya/NTUSER.DAT"
[17] "C:/Users/Seema_acharya/ntuser.dat.LOG1"
[18] "C:/Users/Seema_acharya/ntuser.dat.LOG2"
[19] "C:/Users/Seema_acharya/NTUSER.DAT{6cced2f1-6e01-11de-8bed-001e0bcd1824}.TM.blf"
[20] "C:/Users/Seema_acharya/NTUSER.DAT{6cced2f1-6e01-11de-8bed-001e0bcd1824}.TMContainer00000000000000000001.regtrans-ms"
[21] "C:/Users/Seema_acharya/NTUSER.DAT{6cced2f1-6e01-11de-8bed-001e0bcd1824}.TMContainer00000000000000000002.regtrans-ms"
[22] "C:/Users/Seema_acharya/ntuser.ini"
[23] "C:/Users/Seema_acharya/ntuser.pol"
[24] "C:/Users/Seema_acharya/Pictures"
[25] "C:/Users/Seema_acharya/PrintHood"
[26] "C:/Users/Seema_acharya/Recent"
[27] "C:/Users/Seema_acharya/Saved Games"
[28] "C:/Users/Seema_acharya/Searches"
[29] "C:/Users/Seema_acharya/SendTo"
[30] "C:/Users/Seema_acharya/Start Menu"
[31] "C:/Users/Seema_acharya/Templates"
[32] "C:/Users/Seema_acharya/Videos"
```

Example 4

To look for a specific pattern, e.g. file/directory names beginning with a "D", use the `dir()` command with a pattern = "^D" argument.

```
> dir(path="C:/Users/Seema_acharya", pattern="^D")
[1] "Desktop"  "Documents" "Downloads"
```

Example 5

To display a recursive list of files or directories in the specified path, use the `dir()` command as follows:

```
> dir(path="d:/data")
[1] "db"
> dir(path="d:/data", recursive=TRUE,include.dirs=TRUE)
[1] "db"  "db/Demo.0"  "db/Demo.ns"  "db/local.0"  "db/local.ns"
"db/mongod.lock"  "db/MyDB.0"  "db/MyDB.ns"
```

The options or arguments used with `dir()` can also be used with `list.files()`. Try it out and observe the output.

2.3 Data Types in R

R is a programming language. Like other programming languages, R also makes use of variables to store varied information. This means that when variables are created, locations are reserved in the computer's memory to hold the related values. The number of locations or size of memory reserved is determined by the data type of the variables. Data type essentially means the kind of value which can be stored, such as boolean, numbers, characters, etc. In R, however, variables are not declared as data types. Variables in R are used to store some R objects and the data type of the R object becomes the data type of the variable. The most popular (based on usage) R objects are:

- Vector
- List
- Matrix
- Array
- Factor
- Data Frames

A vector is the simplest of all R objects. It has varied data types. All other R objects are based on these atomic vectors. The most commonly used data types are listed as follows:

Data types supported by R are:

- Logical
- Numeric
    - Integer
- Character
- Double
- Complex
- Raw

`class()` function can be used to reveal the data type. Other R objects such as list, matrix, array, factor and data frames are discussed in detail in Chapter 3.

Logical

TRUE / T and FALSE / F are logical values.

```
> TRUE
[1] TRUE
> class(TRUE)
[1] "logical"

> T
[1] TRUE
> class(T)
[1] "logical"

> FALSE
[1] FALSE
> class(FALSE)
[1] "logical"

> F
[1] FALSE
> class(F)
[1] "logical"
```

Numeric

```
> 2
[1] 2
> class (2)
[1] "numeric"
> 76.25
[1] 76.25
> class(76.25)
[1] "numeric"
```

Integer

Integer data type is a sub class of numeric data type. Notice the use of "L" as a suffix to a numeric value in order for it to be considered an "integer".

```
> 2L
[1] 2
> class(2L)
[1] "integer"
```

Functions such as `is.numeric()`, `is.integer()` can be used to test the data type.

```
> is.numeric(2)
[1] TRUE
> is.numeric(2L)
[1] TRUE
> is.integer(2)
[1] FALSE
> is.integer(2L)
[1] TRUE
```

Note: Integers are numeric but NOT all numbers are integers.

Character

```
> "Data Science"
[1] "Data Science"
> class("Data Science")
[1] "character"
```

`is.character()` function can be used to ascertain if a value is a character.

```
> is.character ("Data Science")
[1] TRUE
```

Double (for double precision floating point numbers)

By default, numbers are of "double" type unless explicitly mentioned with an *L* suffixed to the number for it to be considered an integer.

```
> typeof (76.25)
[1] "double"
```

Complex

```
> 5 + 5i
[1] 5+5i
> class(5 + 5i)
[1] "complex"
```

Raw

```
> charToRaw("Hi")
[1] 48 69
> class (charToRaw ("Hi"))
[1] "raw"
```

`typeof()` function can also be used to check the data type (as shown).

```
> typeof(5 + 5i)
[1] "complex"
> typeof(charToRaw ("Hi")
+ )
[1] "raw"
> typeof ("DataScience")
[1] "character"
> typeof (2L)
[1] "integer"
> typeof (76.25)
[1] "double"
```

2.3.1 Coercion

Coercion helps to convert one data type to another, e.g. logical "TRUE" value when converted to numeric yields "1". Likewise, logical "FALSE" value yields "0 ".

```
> as.numeric(TRUE)
[1] 1

> as.numeric(FALSE)
[1] 0
```

Numeric 5 can be converted to character 5 using `as.character()`.

```
> as.character(5)
[1] "5"

> as.integer(5.5)
[1] 5
```

On converting characters, "hi" to numeric data type, the `as.numeric()` returns NA.

```
> as.numeric("hi")
[1] NA
Warning message:
NAs introduced by coercion
```

2.3.2 Introducing Variables and `ls()` Function

R, like any other programming language, uses variables to store information. Let us start by creating a variable "RectangleHeight" and assign the value 2 to it. Note the use of the operator "<-" to assign a value to the variable. Likewise, the variable "RectangleWidth" is defined and assigned the value 4. The area of the rectangle is computed using the formula "RectangleHeight * RectangleWidth". The computed value for the area of the rectangle is stored in the variable "RectangleArea".

```
> RectangleHeight <- 2
> RectangleWidth <- 4
> RectangleArea <- RectangleHeight * RectangleWidth
> RectangleHeight
[1] 2
> RectangleWidth
[1] 4
> RectangleArea
[1] 8
```

Note: When a value is assigned to a variable, it does not display anything on the console. To get the value, type the name of the variable at the prompt.

Use the `ls()` function to list all the objects in the working environment.

```
> ls()
[1] "RectangleArea" "RectangleHeight" "RectangleWidth"
```

ls() is also useful to clean the environment before running a code. Execute the rm() function as shown to clean up the environment.

```
> rm(list=ls())
> ls()
character(0)
```

2.4 Few Commands for Data Exploration

This section will use functions such as `summary()`, `str()`, `head()`, `tail()`, `view()`, `edit()`, etc., to explore a dataset. The dataset used in this section is "mtcars" from the "datasets" package.

Background to the mtcars dataset from R documentation:

This data was extracted from the 1974 Motor Trend US magazine. It comprises fuel consumption and 10 aspects of automobile design and performance for 32 automobiles (1973–74 models).

2.4.1 Load Internal Dataset

There are various inbuilt datasets in R, e.g. AirPassengers, mtcars, BOD, etc. A list of datasets is available at https://vincentarelbundock.github.io/Rdatasets/datasets.html

Let us load the mtcars dataset from the datasets package following the steps:

1. Check if the datasets package is already installed.

   ```
   >installed.packages()
   ```

2. If already installed and will be used frequently, load the package.

   ```
   >library(datasets)
   ```

3. Display the observations from the mtcars dataset.
mtcars is a dataset from the datasets package that has 32 observations on 11 variables. The 11 variables are described as follows:

[, 1]	mpg	Miles/(US) gallon
[, 2]	cyl	Number of cylinders
[, 3]	disp	Displacement (cu.in.)
[, 4]	hp	Gross horsepower
[, 5]	drat	Rear axle ratio
[, 6]	wt	Weight (1000 lbs)
[, 7]	qsec	1/4 mile time
[, 8]	vs	V/S
[, 9]	am	Transmission (0 = automatic, 1 = manual)
[,10]	gear	Number of forward gears
[,11]	carb	Number of carburetors

A subset of observations is given as follows:

```
> mtcars
                     mpg cyl  disp  hp drat    wt  qsec vs am gear carb
Mazda RX4           21.0   6 160.0 110 3.90 2.620 16.46  0  1    4    4
Mazda RX4 Wag       21.0   6 160.0 110 3.90 2.875 17.02  0  1    4    4
Datsun 710          22.8   4 108.0  93 3.85 2.320 18.61  1  1    4    1
Hornet 4 Drive      21.4   6 258.0 110 3.08 3.215 19.44  1  0    3    1
Hornet Sportabout   18.7   8 360.0 175 3.15 3.440 17.02  0  0    3    2
Valiant             18.1   6 225.0 105 2.76 3.460 20.22  1  0    3    1
Duster 360          14.3   8 360.0 245 3.21 3.570 15.84  0  0    3    4
Merc 240D           24.4   4 146.7  62 3.69 3.190 20.00  1  0    4    2
Merc 230            22.8   4 140.8  95 3.92 3.150 22.90  1  0    4    2
Merc 280            19.2   6 167.6 123 3.92 3.440 18.30  1  0    4    4
Merc 280C           17.8   6 167.6 123 3.92 3.440 18.90  1  0    4    4
Merc 450SE          16.4   8 275.8 180 3.07 4.070 17.40  0  0    3    3
Merc 450SL          17.3   8 275.8 180 3.07 3.730 17.60  0  0    3    3
Merc 450SLC         15.2   8 275.8 180 3.07 3.780 18.00  0  0    3    3
Cadillac Fleetwood  10.4   8 472.0 205 2.93 5.250 17.98  0  0    3    4
Lincoln Continental 10.4   8 460.0 215 3.00 5.424 17.82  0  0    3    4
Chrysler Imperial   14.7   8 440.0 230 3.23 5.345 17.42  0  0    3    4
Fiat 128            32.4   4  78.7  66 4.08 2.200 19.47  1  1    4    1
Honda Civic         30.4   4  75.7  52 4.93 1.615 18.52  1  1    4    2
Toyota Corolla      33.9   4  71.1  65 4.22 1.835 19.90  1  1    4    1
Toyota Corona       21.5   4 120.1  97 3.70 2.465 20.01  1  0    3    1
Dodge Challenger    15.5   8 318.0 150 2.76 3.520 16.87  0  0    3    2
AMC Javelin         15.2   8 304.0 150 3.15 3.435 17.30  0  0    3    2
```

`summary()` Command

`summary()` command includes functions like min, max, median, mean, etc., for each variable present in the given data frame.

Example

```
>summary(mtcars)
```

Output

The output shows a six-point summary of each of the column or variable of the dataset "mtcars". The summary points are min, 1st quartile, mean, median, 3rd quartile and max (Figure 2.1).

```
> summary(mtcars)
      mpg             cyl             disp             hp             drat             wt             qsec             vs               am              gear            carb
 Min.   :10.40   Min.   :4.000   Min.   : 71.1   Min.   : 52.0   Min.   :2.760   Min.   :1.513   Min.   :14.50   Min.   :0.0000   Min.   :0.0000   Min.   :3.000   Min.   :1.000
 1st Qu.:15.43   1st Qu.:4.000   1st Qu.:120.8   1st Qu.: 96.5   1st Qu.:3.080   1st Qu.:2.581   1st Qu.:16.89   1st Qu.:0.0000   1st Qu.:0.0000   1st Qu.:3.000   1st Qu.:2.000
 Median :19.20   Median :6.000   Median :196.3   Median :123.0   Median :3.695   Median :3.325   Median :17.71   Median :0.0000   Median :0.0000   Median :4.000   Median :2.000
 Mean   :20.09   Mean   :6.188   Mean   :230.7   Mean   :146.7   Mean   :3.597   Mean   :3.217   Mean   :17.85   Mean   :0.4375   Mean   :0.4062   Mean   :3.688   Mean   :2.812
 3rd Qu.:22.80   3rd Qu.:8.000   3rd Qu.:326.0   3rd Qu.:180.0   3rd Qu.:3.920   3rd Qu.:3.610   3rd Qu.:18.90   3rd Qu.:1.0000   3rd Qu.:1.0000   3rd Qu.:4.000   3rd Qu.:4.000
 Max.   :33.90   Max.   :8.000   Max.   :472.0   Max.   :335.0   Max.   :4.930   Max.   :5.424   Max.   :22.90   Max.   :1.0000   Max.   :1.0000   Max.   :5.000   Max.   :8.000
>|
```

FIGURE 2.1 *Example of* **`summary()`** *command*

`str()` Command

`str()` command displays the internal structure of a data frame. It can be used as an alternative to summary function. It is a diagnostic function and roughly displays one line per basic object.

Example 1

```
>str(str)
function(object,...)
```

The above example shows `str()` ***function itself serving as an argument. It displays compactly*** `str()` ***internal structure, stating that it is a function which takes an object as an argument.***

Example 2

```
str(ls)
function(name, pos = -1L, envir = as.environment(pos), all.names =
FALSE, pattern, sorted = TRUE)
```

Here, `ls()` is used as an argument to `str()` function. It provides a brief outline of the `ls()` function.

Example 3

```
>str(mtcars)
```

Output

When a data frame named "mtcars" is supplied, the command shows the internal structure of the data frame. The CLI is:

```
>str(mtcars)
"data.frame": 32 obs. of  11 variables:
 $ mpg :num  21 21 22.8 21.4 18.7 18.1 14.3 24.4 22.8 19.2 ...
 $ cyl :num  6 6 4 6 8 6 8 4 4 6 ...
 $ disp: num  160 160 108 258 360 ...
 $ hp  : num  110 110 93 110 175 105 245 62 95 123 ...
 $ drat: num  3.9 3.9 3.85 3.08 3.15 2.76 3.21 3.69 3.92 3.92 ...
 $ wt  : num  2.62 2.88 2.32 3.21 3.44 ...
 $ qsec: num  16.5 17 18.6 19.4 17 ...
 $ vs  :num  0 0 1 1 0 1 0 1 1 1 ...
 $ am  :num  1 1 1 0 0 0 0 0 0 0 ...
 $ gear: num  4 4 4 3 3 3 3 4 4 4 ...
 $ carb: num  4 4 1 1 2 1 4 2 2 4 ...
```

It shows the individual datatype of each column or variable of the mtcars dataset.

Example 4

Let us generate a vector of 100 normally distributed random numbers using the function `rnorm()`. To learn more about the `rnorm()` function, use help`(rnorm())` at the R prompt. However, for curious minds, remember to use help(rnorm()) at the R prompt. The standard mean and sd arguments used are 2 and 4, respectively.

```
> x<-rnorm(100,2,4)
> x
  [1] -3.34175887 -5.02883176  0.45095709  2.85552715  4.92674244 -4.41054919
  [7] -3.31820044 -0.80831621 -1.65448940  4.64511871  8.57459786  1.25646177
 [13]  6.87478751  2.64653705  1.91879015 -2.17452232  1.58073729  1.99871232
 [19] -3.88335858  2.82091957  3.90339039  6.21311421  2.66193705  1.78142291
 [25]  5.38151555  4.53184055  0.92504774  5.49552438 -0.54671622  4.01954453
 [31]  0.58261960  6.32910411 -1.77130695  3.77660052  3.55678634 -2.30606435
 [37]  2.06705854 -3.50544817  4.41538977  8.97132469 -0.50104855  9.55595510
 [43]  9.15602713 -5.36516159 -2.19773796 -1.62207865  4.28113440 -2.71814237
 [49] -0.01493734  6.40199661  5.32999450  4.74292147 -1.42301876  3.83878430
 [55]  8.32429912  0.27387502 -1.12127302  1.43047868  4.78700037  3.49284817
 [61]  7.67927741  8.70976443 -0.90567132  4.07628860 11.91775989  3.05700908
 [67]  0.40153453  5.16838083  1.50919970  4.73045804 -1.90190693 -0.91450400
 [73]  5.18817660  3.17153145  4.61942512  7.44159001  0.05577955  0.49172636
 [79]  5.22876321  0.17486091  3.01414795 -0.64969094  1.46025656  2.54332927
 [85] -1.25678091  2.82071806  5.45032052  7.68390297  6.58033732 -1.08314669
 [91] -1.08567254 -0.42997501  2.91873762  1.01037101 -5.46963909  2.37473930
 [97] -0.32233632 -3.09035251 -6.27470698  3.40189079
> summary(x)
   Min. 1st Qu.  Median    Mean 3rd Qu.    Max.
-6.2750 -0.8327  2.2210  2.0780  4.7340 11.9200
> str(x)
 num [1:100] -3.342 -5.029 0.451 2.856 4.927 ...
```

When we run the `summary()` function with "x" as the argument, we get the "minimum ", "1st quartile ", "Median ", "Mean ", "3rd Quartile" and "Maximum" for "x ".

Next, when we run `str()` on "x ", we get the information that "x" is a numeric vector consisting of 100 elements and it also returns the first 5 elements from the "x" vector.

Example 5

Let us now take it a step further by creating a 10 by 10 matrix, "m" and calling `str()` on it.

```
> m <- matrix(rnorm(100),10,10)
> str(m)
num [1:10, 1:10] -2.231 1.089 0.573 -0.183 0.964 …
> m[,1]
[1] -2.2310749 1.0885324 0.5730995 -0.1827884 0.9638976 1.2520684
-1.8088454 0.3247033 0.7654839 -0.31007222
```

The `str()` function tells us that *"m"* is a matrix of 10 rows and 10 columns and also displays the first 5 column values of the first row.

View() Command

`View()` command displays the given dataset in a spreadsheet-like data frame viewer.

Example

```
>View("mtcars")
```

Output

The output shows a tabular view of the content of the mtcars dataset (Figure 2.1).

head() Command

`head()` command displays the first *"n"* observations from the given data frame. The default value for *n* is 6. However, users can specify the value of *"n"* as per their requirement as well.

Example

```
>head(mtcars, n = 6)
```

Output

```
>head(mtcars, n = 6)
                   mpg cyl disp hp  drat wt    qsec  vs am gear carb
Mazda RX4          21.0  6  160 110 3.90 2.620 16.46  0  1   4    4
Mazda RX4 Wag      21.0  6  160 110 3.90 2.875 17.02  0  1   4    4
Datsun 710         22.8  4  108  93 3.85 2.320 18.61  1  1   4    1
Hornet 4 Drive     21.4  6  258 110 3.08 3.215 19.44  1  0   3    1
Hornet Sportabout  18.7  8  360 175 3.15 3.440 17.02  0  0   3    2
Valiant            18.1  6  225 105 2.76 3.460 20.22  1  0   3    1
>
```

The command shows the first 6 observations from mtcars.

tail() Command

`tail()` command displays the last *"n"* observations from a given data frame. The default value for *n* is 6. However, users can specify the value of *"n"* as per their requirement as well.

Example

```
>tail(mtcars, n = 5)
```

Output

```
> tail(mtcars, n = 5)
                mpg cyl disp  hp  drat   wt    qsec vs am  gear carb
Lotus Europa    30.4 4   95.1 113 3.77  1.513 16.9  1  1    5    2
Ford Pantera L  15.8 8  351.0 264 4.22  3.170 14.5  0  1    5    4
Ferrari Dino    19.7 6  145.0 175 3.62  2.770 15.5  0  1    5    6
Maserati Bora   15.0 8  301.0 335 3.54  3.570 14.6  0  1    5    8
Volvo 142E      21.4 4  121.0 109 4.11  2.780 18.6  1  1    4    2
```

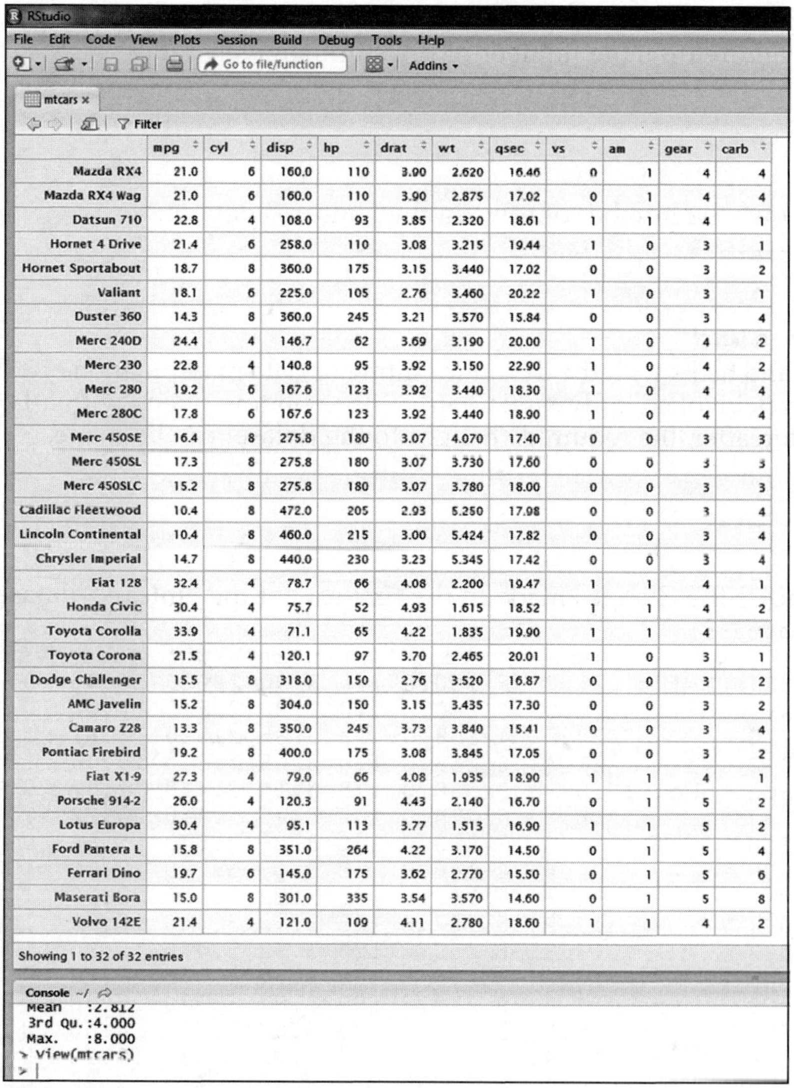

	mpg	cyl	disp	hp	drat	wt	qsec	vs	am	gear	carb
Mazda RX4	21.0	6	160.0	110	3.90	2.620	16.46	0	1	4	4
Mazda RX4 Wag	21.0	6	160.0	110	3.90	2.875	17.02	0	1	4	4
Datsun 710	22.8	4	108.0	93	3.85	2.320	18.61	1	1	4	1
Hornet 4 Drive	21.4	6	258.0	110	3.08	3.215	19.44	1	0	3	1
Hornet Sportabout	18.7	8	360.0	175	3.15	3.440	17.02	0	0	3	2
Valiant	18.1	6	225.0	105	2.76	3.460	20.22	1	0	3	1
Duster 360	14.3	8	360.0	245	3.21	3.570	15.84	0	0	3	4
Merc 240D	24.4	4	146.7	62	3.69	3.190	20.00	1	0	4	2
Merc 230	22.8	4	140.8	95	3.92	3.150	22.90	1	0	4	2
Merc 280	19.2	6	167.6	123	3.92	3.440	18.30	1	0	4	4
Merc 280C	17.8	6	167.6	123	3.92	3.440	18.90	1	0	4	4
Merc 450SE	16.4	8	275.8	180	3.07	4.070	17.40	0	0	3	3
Merc 450SL	17.3	8	275.8	180	3.07	3.730	17.60	0	0	3	3
Merc 450SLC	15.2	8	275.8	180	3.07	3.780	18.00	0	0	3	3
Cadillac Fleetwood	10.4	8	472.0	205	2.93	5.250	17.98	0	0	3	4
Lincoln Continental	10.4	8	460.0	215	3.00	5.424	17.82	0	0	3	4
Chrysler Imperial	14.7	8	440.0	230	3.23	5.345	17.42	0	0	3	4
Fiat 128	32.4	4	78.7	66	4.08	2.200	19.47	1	1	4	1
Honda Civic	30.4	4	75.7	52	4.93	1.615	18.52	1	1	4	2
Toyota Corolla	33.9	4	71.1	65	4.22	1.835	19.90	1	1	4	1
Toyota Corona	21.5	4	120.1	97	3.70	2.465	20.01	1	0	3	1
Dodge Challenger	15.5	8	318.0	150	2.76	3.520	16.87	0	0	3	2
AMC Javelin	15.2	8	304.0	150	3.15	3.435	17.30	0	0	3	2
Camaro Z28	13.3	8	350.0	245	3.73	3.840	15.41	0	0	3	4
Pontiac Firebird	19.2	8	400.0	175	3.08	3.845	17.05	0	0	3	2
Fiat X1-9	27.3	4	79.0	66	4.08	1.935	18.90	1	1	4	1
Porsche 914-2	26.0	4	120.3	91	4.43	2.140	16.70	0	1	5	2
Lotus Europa	30.4	4	95.1	113	3.77	1.513	16.90	1	1	5	2
Ford Pantera L	15.8	8	351.0	264	4.22	3.170	14.50	0	1	5	4
Ferrari Dino	19.7	6	145.0	175	3.62	2.770	15.50	0	1	5	6
Maserati Bora	15.0	8	301.0	335	3.54	3.570	14.60	0	1	5	8
Volvo 142E	21.4	4	121.0	109	4.11	2.780	18.60	1	1	4	2

FIGURE 2.1 *Example of* `View()` *command*

The command shows the last 5 observations from the data frame.

`ncol()` *Command*

`ncol()` command returns the number of columns in the given dataset.

Example

```
>ncol(mtcars)
```

Output

The output shows the number of columns in the "mtcars" dataset.

```
>ncol(mtcars)
[1] 11
```

nrow() Command

`nrow()` command returns the number of rows in the given dataset.

Example

```
>nrow(mtcars)
```

Output

The output shows the number of rows in the "mtcars" dataset.

```
>nrow(mtcars)
[1] 32
```

edit() Command

`edit()` command helps with the dynamic editing or data manipulation of a dataset. When this command is invoked, a dynamic data editor window opens with a tabular view of the dataset. Hereafter, the required changes to the dataset can be made.

Example

```
>edit(mtcars)
```

Output

The output shows the changes made in the first row of the "mtcars" dataset.

```
> edit(mtcars)
                     mpg cyl disp  hp drat    wt  qsec vs am gear carb
Mazda RX4 UPDATED   21.0   6 160.0 110 3.90 2.620 16.46  0  1    4    4
Mazda RX4 Wag       21.0   6 160.0 110 3.90 2.875 17.02  0  1    4    4
Datsun 710          22.8   4 108.0  93 3.85 2.320 18.61  1  1    4    1
Hornet 4 Drive      21.4   6 258.0 110 3.08 3.215 19.44  1  0    3    1
Hornet Sportabout   18.7   8 360.0 175 3.15 3.440 17.02  0  0    3    2
Valiant             18.1   6 225.0 105 2.76 3.460 20.22  1  0    3    1
Duster 360          14.3   8 360.0 245 3.21 3.570 15.84  0  0    3    4
Merc 240D           24.4   4 146.7  62 3.69 3.190 20.00  1  0    4    2
Merc 230            22.8   4 140.8  95 3.92 3.150 22.90  1  0    4    2
Merc 280            19.2   6 167.6 123 3.92 3.440 18.30  1  0    4    4
Merc 280C           17.8   6 167.6 123 3.92 3.440 18.90  1  0    4    4
Merc 450SE          16.4   8 275.8 180 3.07 4.070 17.40  0  0    3    3
Merc 450SL          17.3   8 275.8 180 3.07 3.730 17.60  0  0    3    3
Merc 450SLC         15.2   8 275.8 180 3.07 3.780 18.00  0  0    3    3
Cadillac Fleetwood  10.4   8 472.0 205 2.93 5.250 17.98  0  0    3    4
Lincoln Continental 10.4   8 460.0 215 3.00 5.424 17.82  0  0    3    4
Chrysler Imperial   14.7   8 440.0 230 3.23 5.345 17.42  0  0    3    4
Fiat 128            32.4   4  78.7  66 4.08 2.200 19.47  1  1    4    1
Honda Civic         30.4   4  75.7  52 4.93 1.615 18.52  1  1    4    2
Toyota Corolla      33.9   4  71.1  65 4.22 1.835 19.90  1  1    4    1
Toyota Corona       21.5   4 120.1  97 3.70 2.465 20.01  1  0    3    1
Dodge Challenger    15.5   8 318.0 150 2.76 3.520 16.87  0  0    3    2
AMC Javelin         15.2   8 304.0 150 3.15 3.435 17.30  0  0    3    2
Camaro Z28          13.3   8 350.0 245 3.73 3.840 15.41  0  0    3    4
Pontiac Firebird    19.2   8 400.0 175 3.08 3.845 17.05  0  0    3    2
Fiat X1-9           27.3   4  79.0  66 4.08 1.935 18.90  1  1    4    1
Porsche 914-2       26.0   4 120.3  91 4.43 2.140 16.70  0  1    5    2
Lotus Europa        30.4   4  95.1 113 3.77 1.513 16.90  1  1    5    2
Ford Pantera L      15.8   8 351.0 264 4.22 3.170 14.50  0  1    5    4
Ferrari Dino        19.7   6 145.0 175 3.62 2.770 15.50  0  1    5    6
Maserati Bora       15.0   8 301.0 335 3.54 3.570 14.60  0  1    5    8
Volvo 142E          21.4   4 121.0 109 4.11 2.780 18.60  1  1    4    2
```

> **TIP** *The modified dataset should be stored in a new variable. For example, it is a good practice to call the* `edit()` *method as mtcars_new = edit(mtcars).*

`fix()` Command

`fix()` command saves the changes in the dataset itself, so there is no need to assign any variable to it.

Example

```
> fix(mtcars)
> View(mtcars)
```

Output

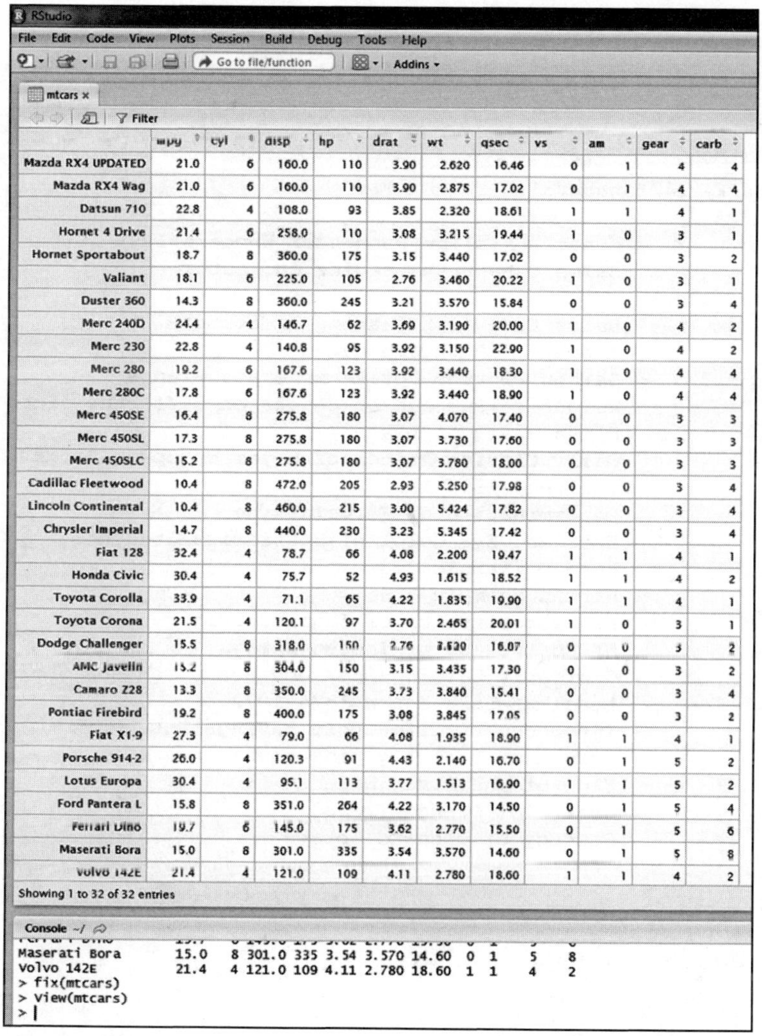

	mpg	cyl	disp	hp	drat	wt	qsec	vs	am	gear	carb
Mazda RX4 UPDATED	21.0	6	160.0	110	3.90	2.620	16.46	0	1	4	4
Mazda RX4 Wag	21.0	6	160.0	110	3.90	2.875	17.02	0	1	4	4
Datsun 710	22.8	4	108.0	93	3.85	2.320	18.61	1	1	4	1
Hornet 4 Drive	21.4	6	258.0	110	3.08	3.215	19.44	1	0	3	1
Hornet Sportabout	18.7	8	360.0	175	3.15	3.440	17.02	0	0	3	2
Valiant	18.1	6	225.0	105	2.76	3.460	20.22	1	0	3	1
Duster 360	14.3	8	360.0	245	3.21	3.570	15.84	0	0	3	4
Merc 240D	24.4	4	146.7	62	3.69	3.190	20.00	1	0	4	2
Merc 230	22.8	4	140.8	95	3.92	3.150	22.90	1	0	4	2
Merc 280	19.2	6	167.6	123	3.92	3.440	18.30	1	0	4	4
Merc 280C	17.8	6	167.6	123	3.92	3.440	18.90	1	0	4	4
Merc 450SE	16.4	8	275.8	180	3.07	4.070	17.40	0	0	3	3
Merc 450SL	17.3	8	275.8	180	3.07	3.730	17.60	0	0	3	3
Merc 450SLC	15.2	8	275.8	180	3.07	3.780	18.00	0	0	3	3
Cadillac Fleetwood	10.4	8	472.0	205	2.93	5.250	17.98	0	0	3	4
Lincoln Continental	10.4	8	460.0	215	3.00	5.424	17.82	0	0	3	4
Chrysler Imperial	14.7	8	440.0	230	3.23	5.345	17.42	0	0	3	4
Fiat 128	32.4	4	78.7	66	4.08	2.200	19.47	1	1	4	1
Honda Civic	30.4	4	75.7	52	4.93	1.615	18.52	1	1	4	2
Toyota Corolla	33.9	4	71.1	65	4.22	1.835	19.90	1	1	4	1
Toyota Corona	21.5	4	120.1	97	3.70	2.465	20.01	1	0	3	1
Dodge Challenger	15.5	8	318.0	150	2.76	3.520	16.87	0	0	3	2
AMC Javelin	15.2	8	304.0	150	3.15	3.435	17.30	0	0	3	2
Camaro Z28	13.3	8	350.0	245	3.73	3.840	15.41	0	0	3	4
Pontiac Firebird	19.2	8	400.0	175	3.08	3.845	17.05	0	0	3	2
Fiat X1-9	27.3	4	79.0	66	4.08	1.935	18.90	1	1	4	1
Porsche 914-2	26.0	4	120.3	91	4.43	2.140	16.70	0	1	5	2
Lotus Europa	30.4	4	95.1	113	3.77	1.513	16.90	1	1	5	2
Ford Pantera L	15.8	8	351.0	264	4.22	3.170	14.50	0	1	5	4
Ferrari Dino	19.7	6	145.0	175	3.62	2.770	15.50	0	1	5	6
Maserati Bora	15.0	8	301.0	335	3.54	3.570	14.60	0	1	5	8
Volvo 142E	21.4	4	121.0	109	4.11	2.780	18.60	1	1	4	2

FIGURE 2.2 *Viewing the "mtcars" dataset after the modifications using the* **`View()`** *command*

It shows the changes made to the first row of the dataset and the changes saved automatically rather than being discarded as in the `edit()` method (Figure 2.2).

> **TIP** *To read help on any command in R, the user can type "?" followed by the function name on the console.*

`data()` Function

The `data()` function lists the available datasets.

Syntax

```
> data()
```

Output

```
R data sets

Data sets in package 'datasets':

AirPassengers           Monthly Airline Passenger Numbers 1949-1960
BJsales                 Sales Data with Leading Indicator
BJsales.lead (BJsales)
                        Sales Data with Leading Indicator
BOD                     Biochemical Oxygen Demand
CO2                     Carbon Dioxide Uptake in Grass Plants
ChickWeight             Weight versus age of chicks on different diets
DNase                   Elisa assay of DNase
EuStockMarkets          Daily Closing Prices of Major European Stock
                        Indices, 1991-1998
Formaldehyde            Determination of Formaldehyde
HairEyeColor            Hair and Eye Color of Statistics Students
Harman23.cor            Harman Example 2.3
Harman74.cor            Harman Example 7.4
Indometh                Pharmacokinetics of Indomethacin
InsectSprays            Effectiveness of Insect Sprays
JohnsonJohnson          Quarterly Earnings per Johnson & Johnson Share
LakeHuron               Level of Lake Huron 1875-1972
LifeCycleSavings        Intercountry Life-Cycle Savings Data
Loblolly                Growth of Loblolly pine trees
Nile                    Flow of the River Nile
Orange                  Growth of Orange Trees
OrchardSprays           Potency of Orchard Sprays
```

data(trees) function loads the dataset, "trees".

Syntax

```
> data(trees)
```

Let us look at the data held in the trees dataset.

```
> trees
       Girth    Height   Volume
1      8.3      70       10.3
2      8.6      65       10.3
3      8.8      63       10.2
4      10.5     72       16.4
5      10.7     81       18.8
6      10.8     83       19.7
7      11.0     66       15.6
8      11.0     75       18.2
9      11.1     80       22.6
10     11.2     75       19.9
11     11.3     79       24.2
12     11.4     76       21.0
13     11.4     76       21.4
14     11.7     69       21.3
15     12.0     75       19.1
16     12.9     74       22.2
17     12.9     85       33.8
18     13.3     86       27.4
19     13.7     71       25.7
20     13.8     64       24.9
21     14.0     78       34.5
22     14.2     80       31.7
23     14.5     74       36.3
24     16.0     72       38.3
25     16.3     77       42.6
26     17.3     81       55.4
27     17.5     82       55.7
28     17.9     80       58.3
29     18.0     80       51.5
30     18.0     80       51.0
31     20.6     87       77.0
```

This dataset provides measurements of the girth, height and volume of timber in 31 felled blackberry trees.

Let us look at the summary of analysis on this dataset.

```
> summary(trees)
    Girth             Height           Volume
Min.    : 8.30    Min.    :63     Min.    :10.20
1st Qu. :11.05    1st Qu. :72     1st Qu. :19.40
Median  :12.90    Median  :76     Median  :24.20
Mean    :13.25    Mean    :76     Mean    :30.17
3rd Qu. :15.25    3rd Qu. :80     3rd Qu. :37.30
Max.    :20.60    Max.    :87     Max.    :77.00
```

Let us visualise this by plotting a scatter plot between the variables of the trees dataset (Figure 2.3).

```
>plot(trees, col="red", pch=16,main="scatter plot b/w variables of trees")
```

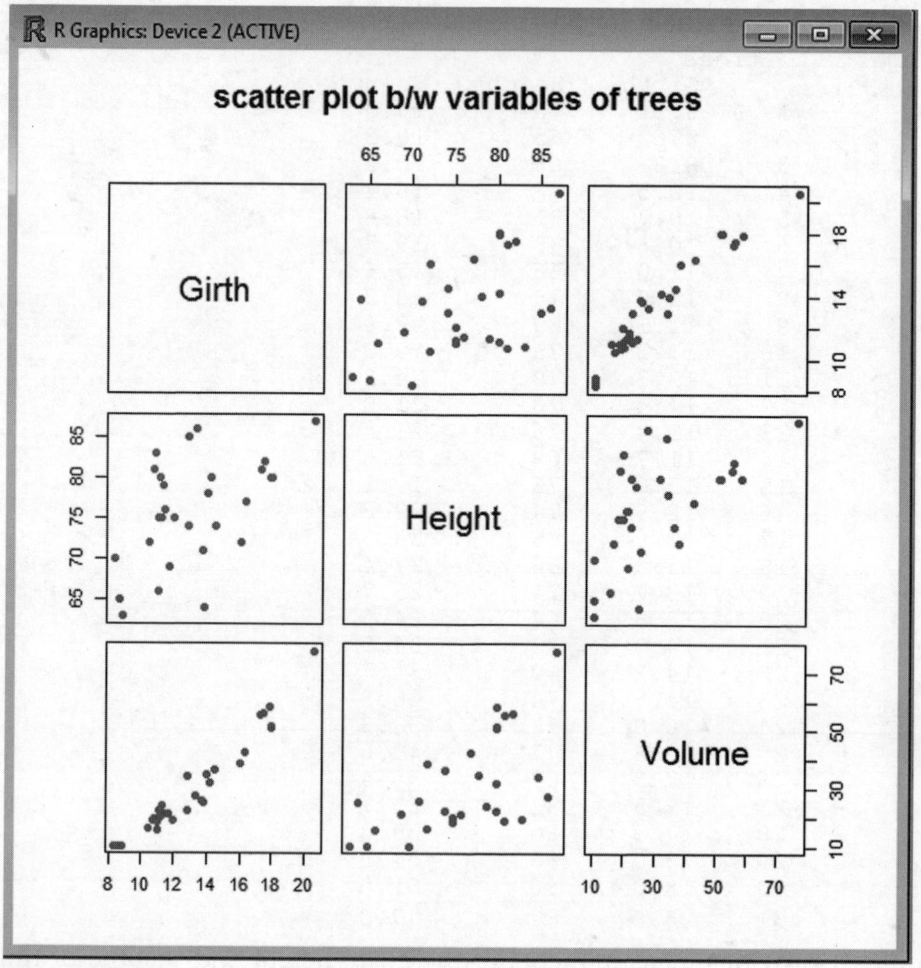

FIGURE 2.3 *Scatter plot between the variables of the trees dataset*

`save.image()` *Function*

`save.image()` function writes an external representation of R objects to the specified file. At a later point in time when it is required to read back the objects, one can use the load or attach function.

Syntax

save.image(file = ".RData", version = NULL, ascii = FALSE, safe = TRUE)

The file is to be given an extension of RData.

Note: The "R" and "D" in "RData" should be in capitals.

If ascii = TRUE, will save an ascii representation of the file. The default is ascii = FALSE. With ascii being set to false, a binary representation of the file is saved.

version is used to specify the current workspace format version. The value of NULL specifies the current default format.

safe is set to a logical value. A value of TRUE means that a temporary file is used to create the saved workspace. This temporary file is renamed to file if the save succeeds.

Check Your Understanding

1. What are the differences between the `head()` and `tail()` commands in R?

Ans: The `head()` command shows records from the start of the dataset, whereas the `tail()` command shows records from the end of the dataset.

2. What does the `data()` function help with?

Ans: The `data()` function lists the available datasets.

3. What is `nrow()` function?

Ans: `nrow()` command returns the number of rows in a given dataset.

Summary

- Data type essentially means the kind of value which can be stored, such as boolean, numbers, characters, etc. In R, however, variables are not declared as data types. Variables in R are used to store some R objects and the data type of the R object becomes the data type of the variable.
- `ls()` function lists all the objects in the working environment.
- `class()` function reveals the data type.
- `typeof()` function checks the data type.
- `data()` function lists the available datasets.

Key Terms

- **dir():** `dir()` function returns a character vector of the names of files or directories in the named directory.
- **getwd():** `getwd()` command returns the absolute file path of the current working directory. This function has no arguments.
- **setwd():** `setwd()` command resets the current working directory to another location as per the user's preference.
- **typeof():** `typeof()` function is used to check the data type.

PRACTICAL EXERCISES

1. BOD is an inbuilt data set in R. The output of the command `View(BOD)` is given below. What will be done by the code given below? Explain.

```
>View(BOD)
```

	Time	demand
1	1	8.3
2	2	10.3
3	3	19.0
4	4	16.0
5	5	15.6
6	7	19.8

```
>nrow(BOD)
```

2. What will be done by the following code?

```
>head(BOD, n=3)
```

3. What will be the output of the following codes?
   (a) The code is:
   ```
   > summary(mtcars$mpg)
   ```
   (b) The code is:
   ```
   >summary(c(3,2,1,2,4,6))
   ```
   (c) The code is:
   ```
   >str(c(1,2,3,4))
   ```
   (d) The code is:
   ```
   >str(c("Mon", "Tue","Wed","Thurs"))
   ```
   (e) The code is:
   ```
   >head(c("Mon", "Tue","Wed","Thurs"),2)
   ```
   (f) The code is:
   ```
   >tail(c("Mon", "Tue","Wed","Thurs"),2)
   ```
   (g) The code is:
   ```
   class(76.25L)
   ```

Chapter 3

Loading and Handling Data in R

LEARNING OUTCOME

At the end of this chapter, you will be able to:

- Store data of varied data types into vectors, matrixes, and lists
- Load data from .csv, spreadsheets, web, Jason documents, and XML
- Deal with missing or invalid values
- Run R functions on the data (`sum()`, `min()`, `max()`, `rep()`, `grep()`, `substr()`, `strsplit()`, etc.)
- Use R with databases such as MySQL, PostgreSQL, SQLlite, and JasperDB
- Create visualisations to help with deeper understanding of data

3.1 Introduction

Enterprise applications today generate a huge amount of data. This data is analysed to draw useful insights that can help decision makers make better and faster decisions. This chapter introduces the different data types such as numbers, text, logical values, dates, etc., supported in R. It also describes various R objects such as vector, matrix, list, dataset, etc., and how to manipulate data using R functions such as `sum()`, `min()`, `max()`, `rep()` and string functions such as `substr()`, `grep()`, `strsplit()`, etc. It explores import of data into R from .csv (comma separated values), spreadsheets, XML documents, JASON (Java Script Object Notation) documents, web data, etc., and interfacing R with databases such as MySQL, PostGreSQL, SQLlite, etc. There are quite a few challenges in analysing data. For instance, data is not always homogeneous, i.e. it comes from varied sources and in different formats. Ensuring data quality can pose several challenges. Stakeholders also view data from many perspectives and may have different requirements from it.

3.2 Challenges of Analytical Data Processing

Analytical data processing is a part of business intelligence that includes relational database, data warehousing, data mining and report mining. It is a computer processing technique that handles different types of business processing practices like sales, budgeting, financial reporting, management reporting, etc. All these processing techniques require big data.

Business analytics combines big data with technology. Different challenges occur during business data analytics. However, most of these challenges are mainly associated with data and they arise during the early stages of projects. Some of these challenges are explained ahead.

3.2.1 Data Formats

Data is the main element of business analytics. Business analytics uses sets of data to store a large amount of data. Selecting a data format is the first challenge in analytical data processing for researchers or developers. Analytical data processing requires a complete set of data, in the absence of which, developers can expect problems in further processing.

R is a well-documented programming language that stores data in the form of an object. It has a very simple syntax that helps in processing any type of data. R provides many packages and features such as open database connectivity (ODBC), which process different types of data formats. For example, ODBC supports data formats such as CSV, MS Excel, SQL, etc.

3.2.2 Data Quality

Maintaining data quality is another challenge in analytical data processing. Business analysts are required to deliver perfect information, inferences, outliers and output without any missing or invalid value. A data with inferior input or output is bound to give incorrect quality results.

With the help of R, business analysts can maintain data quality. Different tools of R help business analysts in removing invalid data, replacing missing values and removing outliers in data.

3.2.3 Project Scope

Projects based on analytical data processing are costly and time consuming. Hence, before starting a new project, business analysts should analyse the scope of the project. They should identify the amount of data required from external sources, time of delivery and other parameters related to the project.

3.2.4 Output Result via Stakeholder Expectation Management

In analytical data processing, analysts design projects that generate output with different types of values like p-value, the degree of freedom, etc. However, users or stakeholders prefer to see the output. The stakeholders do not want to see the constraints used in data processing, assumptions, hypothesis, p-values, chi-square value or any other value. Hence, an analytical project should try to fulfil all the expectations of the stakeholders.

Business analysts should use transparent methods and processes. They should also validate the data using cross validation. If business analysts use the standard steps of analytical data processing that generate the perfect output, they will not encounter any problems. Data input, processing, descriptive statistics, visualisation of data, report generation and output form the sequence of analytical data processing that analysts should follow while conducting business analysis for their project.

Check Your Understanding

1. What is analytical data processing?

Ans: Analytical data processing is a part of business intelligence that includes relational database, data warehousing, data mining and report mining.

2. List the challenges of analytical data processing.

Ans: Some challenges of analytical data processing are:

- Data formats
- Data quality
- Project scope
- Output results via stakeholder expectation management.

3. What are the common steps of analytical data processing?

Ans: Data input, processing, descriptive statistics, visualisation of data, report generation and output are the common steps of analytical data processing.

3.3 Expression, Variables and Functions

Let us get familiar with the R interface. We will start out by practicing expressions, variables and functions.

3.3.1 Expressions

Look at a few arithmetic operations such as addition, subtraction, multiplication, division, exponentiation, finding the remainder (modulus), integer division and computing the square root as given in Table 3.1.

TABLE 3.1 Arithmetic operations

Operation	*Operator*	*Description*	*Example*
Addition	*x* + *y*	*y* added to *x*	> 4 + 8 [1] 12
Subtraction	*x* − *y*	*y* subtracted from *x*	> 10 - 3 [1] 7
Multiplication	*x* * *y*	*x* multiplied by *y*	> 7 * 8 [1] 56
Division	*x* / *y*	*x* divided by *y*	< 8/3 [1] 2.666667
Exponentiation	*x* ^ *y* *x* ** *y*	*x* raised to the power *y*	> 2 ^ 5 [1] 32 **Or** >2 ** 5 [1] 32
Modulus	*x* %% *y*	Remainder of (*x* divided by *y*)	> 5 %% 3 [1] 2
Integer Division	*x*%/%*y*	*x* divided by *y* but rounded down	> 5 %/% 2 [1] 2
Computing the Square Root	sqrt(*x*)	Computing the square root of *x*	> sqrt (25) [1] 5

3.3.2 Logical Values

Logical values are TRUE and FALSE or T and F. Note that these are case sensitive. The equality operator is ==.

```
>  8 < 4
[1] FALSE
> 3 * 2 == 5
[1] FALSE
> 3 * 2 == 6
[1] TRUE
> F == FALSE
[1] TRUE
> T == TRUE
[1] TRUE
```

Guided Activity

Step 1: Create a vector, *x* consisting of 10 elements with values ranging from 1 to 10. Section 3.5 of this chapter deals with creation, accessing vector elements and vector arithmetic, etc.

```
>  x <- c(1:10)
```

Step 2: Display the contents of the vector, *x*.

```
> x
[1]  1  2  3  4  5  6  7  8  9  10
```

Step 3: Print the values of those elements whose values are either greater than 7 or less than 5.

'|' is the OR operator. Use the **OR** operator to display elements whose values are either greater than 7 or less than 10.

```
> x[(x>7) | (x<5)]
[1]  1  2  3  4  8  9 10
```

Explanation

Part (i) Display 'TRUE' for elements whose values are more than 7, else display 'FALSE'.

```
>  x>7
[1] FALSE FALSE FALSE FALSE FALSE FALSE FALSE TRUE TRUE TRUE
```

Part (ii) Display 'TRUE' for elements whose values are less than 5, else display 'FALSE'.

```
>  x<5
[1] TRUE TRUE TRUE TRUE FALSE FALSE FALSE FALSE FALSE FALSE
```

Step 4: Print the values of those elements whose values are greater than 7 and less than 10.

'&' is the AND operator. Use the **AND** operator to display elements whose values are greater than 7 and less than 10.

```
>  x[(x>7) & (x<10)]
[1]  8  9
```

3.3.3 Dates

The default format of date is YYYY-MM-DD.

(i) Print system's date.

```
> Sys.Date()
[1] "2017-01-13"
```

(ii) Print system's time.

```
> Sys.time()
[1] "2017-01-13 10:54:37 IST"
```

(iii) Print the time zone.

```
> Sys.timezone()
[1] "Asia/Calcutta"
```

(iv) Print today's date.

```
> today <- Sys.Date()
> today
[1] "2017-01-13"
> format (today, format = "%B %d %Y")
[1] "January 13 2017"
```

(v) Store date as a text data type.

```
> CustomDate = "2016-01-13"
> CustomDate
[1] "2016-01-13"
> class (CustomDate)
[1] "character"
```

(vi) Convert the date stored as text data type into a date data type.

```
> CustDate = as.Date(CustomDate)
> class(CustDate)
[1] "Date"
> CustDate
[1] "2016-01-13"
```

(vii) Find the difference between the following two dates.

```
>  strDates <- c("08/15/1947", "01/26/1950")
```

(viii) Convert strings into date format.

```
> dates = as.Date(strDates, "%m /%d /%Y")
> dates
[1] "1947-08-15" "1950-01-26"
```

(ix) Compute the difference between the two dates.

```
> dates[2] - dates[1]
Time difference of 895 days
```

3.3.4 Variables

(i) Assign a value of 50 to the variable called 'Var'.

```
> Var <-50
```

Or

```
> Var=5
```

(ii) Print the value in the variable, 'Var'.

```
> Var
[1] 50
```

(iii) Perform arithmetic operations on the variable, 'Var'.

```
> Var + 10
[1] 60
> Var / 2
[1] 25
```

Variables can be reassigned values either of the same data type or of a different data type.

(iv) Reassign a string value to the variable, 'Var'.

```
> Var <- "R is a Statistical Programming Language"
```

Print the value in the variable, 'Var'.

```
> Var
[1] "R is a Statistical Programming Language"
```

(v) Reassign a logical value to the variable, 'Var'.

```
> Var <- TRUE
> Var
[1] TRUE
```

3.3.5 Functions

In this section we will try out a few functions such as `sum()`, `min()`, `max()` and `seq()`.

`sum()` *function*

`sum()` function returns the sum of all the values in its arguments.

Syntax

```
sum(..., na.rm = FALSE)
```

where ... implies numeric or complex or logical vectors.

na,rm accepts a logical value. Should missing values (including NaN (Not a Number)) be removed?

Examples

(i) Sum the values '1', '2' and '3' provided as arguments to `sum()`

```
> sum(1, 2, 3)
[1] 6
```

(ii) What will be the output if NA is used for one of the arguments to `sum()`?

```
> sum(1, 5, NA, na.rm=FALSE)
[1] NA
```

If na.rm is FALSE, an NA or NaN value in any of the argument will cause NA or NaN to be returned.

(iii) What will be the output if NaN is used for one of the arguments to `sum()`?

```
> sum(1, 5, NaN, na.rm= FALSE)
[1] NaN
```

(iv) What will be the output if NA and NaN are used as arguments to `sum()`?

```
> sum(1, 5, NA, NaN, na.rm=FALSE)
[1] NA
```

(v) What will be the output if option, na.rm is set to TRUE?
If na.rm is TRUE, an NA or NaN value in any of the argument will be ignored.

```
> sum(1, 5, NA, na.rm=TRUE)
[1] 6
> sum(1, 5, NA, NaN, na.rm=TRUE)
[1] 6
```

min() function

`min()` function returns the minimum of all the values present in their arguments.

Syntax

```
min(..., na.rm=FALSE)
```

where … implies numeric or character arguments and na.rm accepts a logical value. Should missing values (including NaN) be removed?

Example

```
> min(1, 2, 3)
[1] 1
```

If na.rm is FALSE, an NA or NaN value in any of the argument will cause NA or NaN to be returned.

```
> min(1, 2, 3, NA, na.rm=FALSE)
[1] NA
> min(1, 2, 3, NaN, na.rm=FALSE)
[1] NaN
> min(1, 2, 3, NA, NaN, na.rm=FALSE)
[1] NA
```

If na.rm is TRUE, an NA or NaN value in any of the argument will be ignored.

```
> min(1, 2, 3, NA, NaN, na.rm=TRUE)
[1] 1
```

max() function

`max()` function returns the maximum of all the values present in their arguments.

Syntax

```
max(..., na.rm=FALSE)
```

where … implies numeric or character arguments
na.rm accepts a logical value. Should missing values (including NaN) be removed?

Example

```
> max(44, 78, 66)
[1] 78
```

If na.rm is FALSE, an NA or NaN value in any of the argument will cause NA or NaN to be returned.

```
> max(44, 78, 66, NA, na.rm=FALSE)
[1] NA
> max(44, 78, 66, NaN, na.rm=FALSE)
[1] NaN
> max(44, 78, 66, NA, NaN, na.rm=FALSE)
[1] NA
```

If na.rm is TRUE, an NA or NaN value in any of the argument will be ignored.

```
> max(44, 78, 66, NA, NaN, na.rm=TRUE)
[1] 78
```

seq() function

`seq()` function generates a regular sequence.

Syntax

```
seq(start from, end at, interval, length.out)
```

where,

Start from: It is the start value of the sequence.
End at: It is the maximal or end value of the sequence.
Interval: It is the increment of the sequence.
length.out: It is the desired length of the sequence.

Example

```
> seq(1, 10, 2)
[1]  1  3  5  7  9

> seq(1, 10, length.out=10)
 [1]  1  2  3  4  5  6  7  8  9  10

> seq(18)
[1]  1  2  3  4  5  6  7  8  9  10  11  12  13  14  15  16  17  18
```

Or

```
> seq_len(18)
 [1] 1  2  3  4  5  6  7  8  9  10  11  12  13  14  15  16  17  18
> seq(1, 6, by=3)
[1]  1  4
```

3.3.6 Manipulating Text in Data

There are many inbuilt string functions available in R that manipulate text or string. Finding a part of some text string, searching some string in a text or concatenating strings and other similar operations come under manipulating text operation. Table 3.2 explains some useful text manipulation operations.

Let us take a look at how R treats strings.

String values have to be enclosed within double quotes.

```
> "R is a statistical programming language"
[1] "R is a statistical programming language"
```

TABLE 3.2 Text manipulation of inbuilt functions of R

Functions	*Function Arguments*	*Description*
`substr(a, start stop)`	• *a* is a character vector. • Start and stop arguments contain a numeric value.	The function returns a part of the string beginning from the start argument and ending at the stop argument.
`strsplit(a, split, ...)`	• *a* is a character vector. • Split is also a character vector that contains a regular expression for splitting.	The function splits the given text string into substrings.
`paste(..., sep= '', ...)`	• The dots '...' define R objects. • sep argument is a character string for separating objects.	The function concatenates string vectors after converting the objects into strings.
`grep(pattern, a)`	• Pattern argument contains a matching pattern. • *a* is a character vector.	The function returns string after searching for a text pattern into a given text string.
`toupper(a)`	• *a* is a character vector.	The function converts a string into uppercase.
`tolower(a)`	• *a* is a character vector.	The function converts a string into lowercase.

Figure 3.1 describes the `strsplit()` and `grep()` in the R workspace

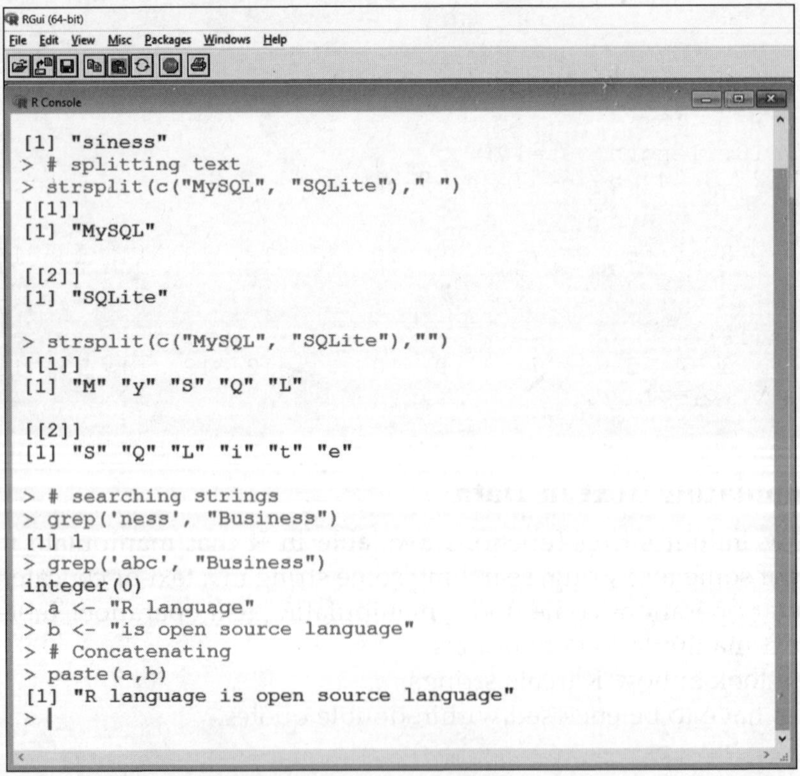

FIGURE 3.1 *Examples of string functions*

Few string functions are explained in detail as follows.

rep() function

rep() function repeats a given argument for a specified number of times. In the example below, the string, 'statistics' is repeated three times.

Example

```
> rep("statistics", 3)
[1]  "statistics"  "statistics"  "statistics"
```

grep() function

In the example below, the function grep() finds the index position at which the string, 'statistical' is present.

Example

```
> grep("statistical",c("R","is","a","statistical","language"),
fixed=TRUE)
[1]  4
```

toupper() function

toupper() function converts a given character vector into upper case.

Syntax

```
toupper(x)
```

x → is a character vector

Example

```
> toupper("statistics")
[1] "STATISTICS"
```

Or

```
> casefold ("r programming language", upper=TRUE)
[1] "R PROGRAMMING LANGUAGE"
```

tolower() function

tolower() function converts the given character vector into lower case.

Syntax

```
tolower(x)
```

x → is a character vector

Example

```
> tolower("STATISTICS")
[1]  "statistics"
```

Or

```
> casefold("R PROGRAMMING LANGUAGE", upper=FALSE)
[1] "r programming language"
```

substr() function

`substr()` function extracts or replaces substrings in a character vector.

Syntax

```
substr(x, start, stop)
```

x → character vector
start → start position of extraction or replacement
stop → stop or end position of extraction or replacement

Example

Extract the string 'tic' from 'statistics'. Begin the extraction at position 7 and continue the extraction till position 9.

```
> substr("statistics", 7, 9)
[1] "tic"
```

3.4 Missing Values Treatment in R

During analytical data processing, users come across problems caused by missing and infinite values. To get an accurate output, users should remove or clean the missing values. In R, NA (Not Available) represents missing values and Inf (Infinite) represents infinite values. R provides different functions that identify the missing values during processing (Table 3.3).

TABLE 3.3 Functions for handling missing values

Functions	*Function Arguments*	*Description*
`is.na(x)`	*x* is an R object to be tested.	The function checks the object and returns true if data is missing.
`na.omit (x, ...)`	*x* is an R object from which NA needs to be removed. The dots '...' define the other optional argument.	The function returns the object after removing missing values from it.
`na.exclude (x, ...)`	*x* is an R object from which NA needs to be removed. The dots '...' define the other optional argument.	The function returns the object after removing missing values from it.
`na.fail (x, ...)`	The package provides the functions for accessing all APIs.	The function will encounter an error if the object contains any missing values and will return the object if it does not contain any missing value.
`na.pass (x, ...)`	*x* is an R object from which NA needs to be removed. The dots '...' define the other optional argument.	The function returns the unchanged object.

The following example creates a vector 'A' with some missing values [10, 20, NA, 40] (Figure 3.2). The `is.na(A)` returns TRUE for the missing value. The `na.omit(A)` and `na.exclude(A)` removes the missing value and stores it into vector 'B' and 'D', respectively. The `na.fail(A)` generates an error if A has some missing value. The `na.pass(A)` returns the usual vector A.

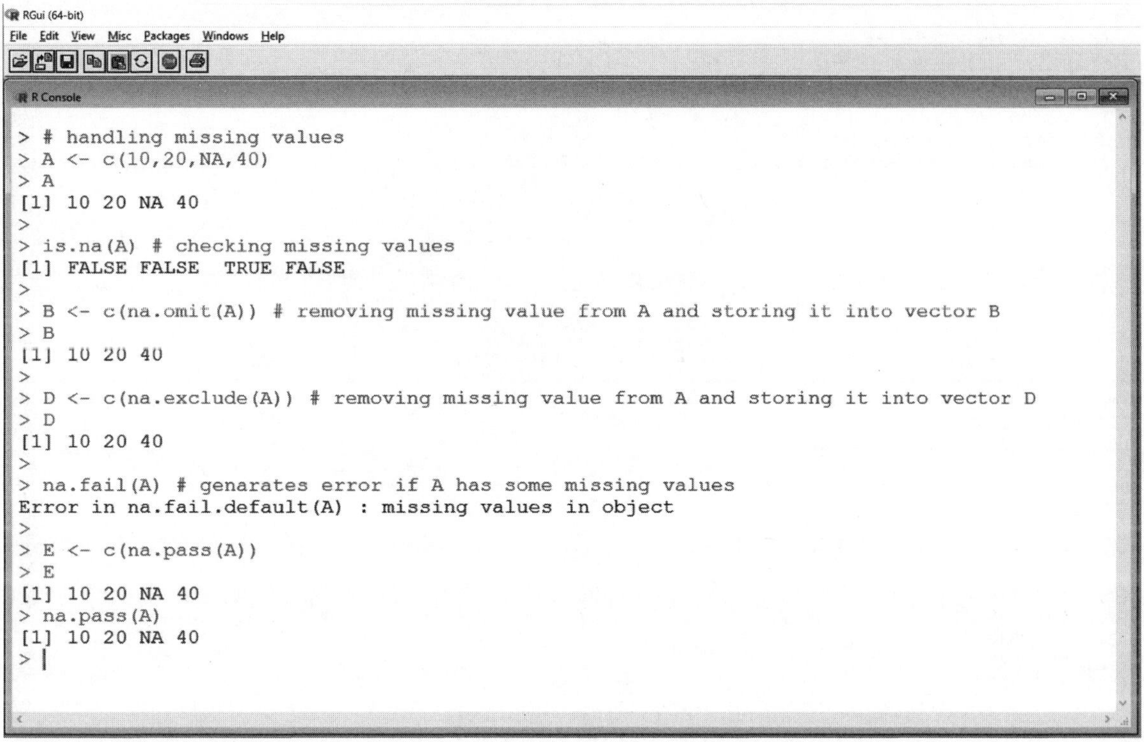

FIGURE 3.2 *Handling missing values*

3.5 Using the 'as' Operator to Change the Structure of Data

Sometimes analytical data processing requires data conversion from one data format into another. Generally, analytical data processing stores data in a table format, wherein it requires only some part of the table or another structure to store the table's data. In this case, R can convert the structure of the table into other structures like factor, list, etc.

The operator 'as' provides the facility to convert the structure of one dataset into another structure in R. The syntax of using this operator is

```
as.objecttype(objectname)
```

where,

objecttype is the type of object like data.frame, matrix, list, etc. and objectname is the name of the object that needs to be converted into another format.

Also, `as.numeric()` and `as.character()` functions convert characters and numbers, respectively.

The following example creates a data frame *D* using two vectors *a* and *b* (Figure 3.3). Now the command '`as.list(D)`' converts the data frame into list *B*. The command '`as.matrix(D)`' converts the data frame into a matrix.

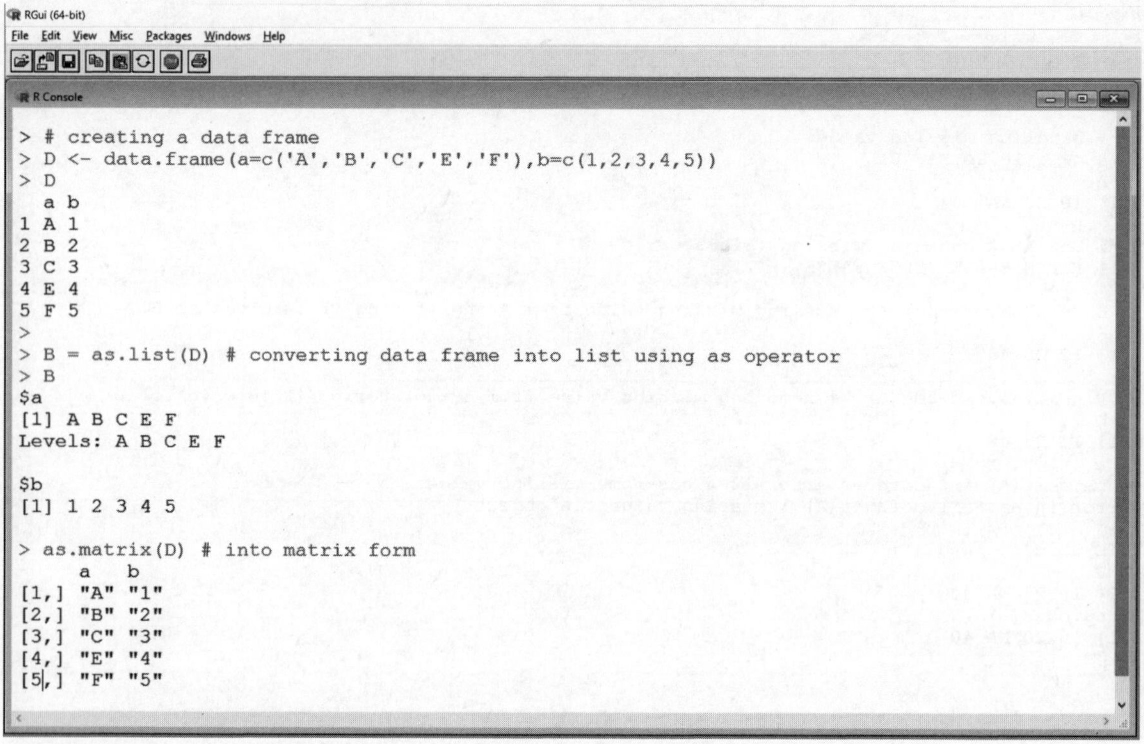

FIGURE 3.3 *Use of 'as' operator*

Check Your Understanding

1. What is the `na.omit()` function?

Ans: The `na.omit()` function is an inbuilt function of R that returns the object after removing missing values from it.

2. What is the `na.exclude()` function?

Ans: The `na.exclude()` function is an inbuilt function of R that returns the object after removing missing values from it.

(Continued)

3. What is `na.fail()` function?

Ans: The `na.fail()` function is an inbuilt function of R that shows an error if the object contains any missing value and returns the object if it does not contain any missing value.

4. Which function is used for checking missing values in an R object?

Ans: The `is.na()` is used for checking missing values in an R object. The function checks the object and returns true if data is missing.

5. What is the use of 'as' operator?

Ans: 'as' operator converts the structure of one dataset into another structure using R.

3.6 Vectors

A vector can have a list of values. The values can be numbers, strings or logical. All the values in a vector should be of the same data type.

A few points to remember about vectors in R are:

- Vectors are stored like arrays in C
- Vector indices begin at 1
- All vector elements must have the same mode such as integer, numeric (floating point number), character (string), logical (Boolean), complex, object, etc.

Let us create a few vectors.

1. Create a vector of numbers

```
> c(4, 7, 8)
[1]  4  7  8
```

The c function (c is short for combine) creates a new vector consisting of three values, viz. 4, 7 and 8.

2. Create a vector of string values.

```
> c("R", "SAS", "SPSS")
[1]  "R"    "SAS"    "SPSS"
```

3. Create a vector of logical values.

```
> c(TRUE, FALSE)
[1]   TRUE      FALSE
```

A vector cannot hold values of different data types. Consider the example below on placing integer, string and Boolean values together in a vector.

```
> c(4, 8, "R", FALSE)
[1]  "4" "8"   "R"   "FALSE"
```

TIP *All the values are converted into the same data type, i.e. 'character'.*

4. Declare a vector by the name, 'Project' of length 3 and store values in it.

```
> Project <- vector(length = 3)
> Project [1] <- "Finance Project"
> Project [2] <- "Retail Project"
> Project [3] <- "Energy Project"
```

Outcome

```
> Project
[1] "Finance Project" "Retail Project" "Energy Project"
> length (Project)
[1] 3
```

3.6.1 Sequence Vector

A sequence vector can be created with a start:end notation.

Objective

Create a sequence of numbers between 1 and 5 (both inclusive).

```
> 1:5
[1] 1 2 3 4 5
```

Or

```
> seq(1:5)
[1] 1 2 3 4 5
```

The default increment with seq is 1. However, it also allows the use of increments other than 1.

```
> seq (1, 10, 2)
[1] 1   3   5   7 9
```

Or

```
> seq (from=1, to=10, by=2)
[1] 1   3   5   7 9
```

Or

```
> seq (1, 10, by=2)
[1] 1 3 5 7 9
```

seq can also generate numbers in the descending order.

```
> 10:1
  [1]   10 9 8 7 6 5 4 3 2 1
> seq (10, 1, by=-2)
[1] 10 8 6 4 2
```

3.6.2 rep function

The rep function is used to place the same constant into long vectors. The syntax is rep (z,k), which creates a vector of k*length(z) elements, each equals to z.

Objective

Demonstrate rep function.

Act

```
> rep (3, 4)
[1] 3 3 3 3
```

Or

```
> x <-rep (3, 4)
> x
[1] 3 3 3 3
```

3.6.3 Vector Access

Objective

Let us create a variable, 'VariableSeq' and assign to it a vector consisting of string values.

```
> VariableSeq <- c ("R", "is", "a", "programming", "language")
```

Objective

To access values in a vector, specify the indices at which the value is present in the vector. Indices start at 1.

```
> VariableSeq[1]
[1] "R"
> VariableSeq[2]
[1] "is"
> VariableSeq[3]
[1] "a"
> VariableSeq[4]
[1] "programming"
> VariableSeq[5]
[1] "language"
```

Objective

Assign new values in an existing vector. For example, let us assign value, 'good programming' at indices 4 in the existing vector, 'VariableSeq'.

```
> VariableSeq[4] <- "good programming"
```

Outcome

```
> VariableSeq[4]
[1] "good programming"
```

Objective

To access more than one value from the vector.

(a) Access the first and the fifth element from the vector, 'VariableSeq'.

```
> VariableSeq[c(1, 5)]
[1] "R"      "language"
```

(b) Access first to the fourth element from the vector, 'VariableSeq'.

```
> VariableSeq[1:4]
[1] "R"    "is"    "a"    "good programming"
```

(c) Access the first, fourth and the fifth element from the vector, 'VariableSeq'.

```
> VariableSeq[c(1, 4:5)]
[1] "R"                "good programming" "language"
```

(d) Retrieve all the values from the variable, 'VariableSeq'

```
> VariableSeq
[1] "R"              "is"             "a"              "good programming"
[5] "language"
```

3.6.4 Vector Names

The `names()` function helps to assign names to the vector elements.
This is accomplished in two steps as shown:

```
> placeholder <- 1:5
> names(placeholder) <- c("r", "is", "a", "programming", "language")
```

The vector elements can then be retrieved using the indices position.

```
> placeholder
          r           is           a programming          language
          1            2           3           4                 5
> placeholder [3]
a
3
> placeholder [1]
r
1
> placeholder[4:5]
programming     language
          4            5
```

Or

```
> placeholder ["programming"]
programming
          4
```

Objective

Plot a bar graph using the barplot function. The barplot function uses a vector's values to plot a bar chart.

Act

The vector used is called BarVector.

```
> BarVector <- c(4, 7, 8)
> barplot(BarVector)
```

Outcome

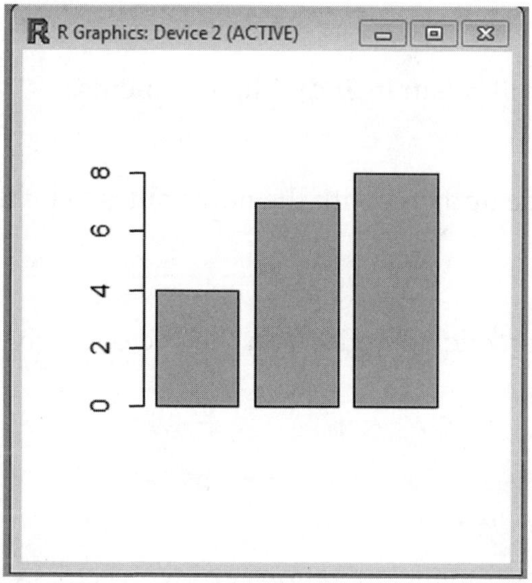

Let us use the name function to assign names to the vector elements. These names will be used as labels in the barplot.

```
> names(BarVector) <- c("India", "MiddleEast", "US")
> barplot(BarVector)
```

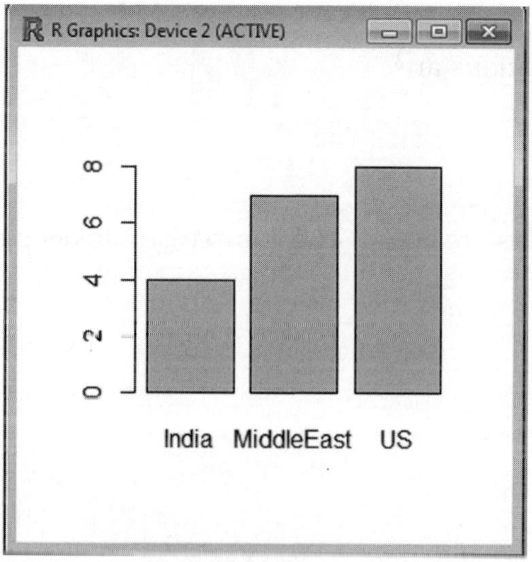

3.6.5 Vector Math

Let us define a vector, 'x' with three values. Let us add a scalar value (single value) to the vector. This value will get added to each vector element.

```
> x <- c(4, 7, 8)
> x +1
[1] 5 8 9
```

However, the vector will retain its individual elements.

```
> x
[1] 4 7 8
```

If the vector needs to be updated with the new values, type the statement given below.

```
> x <- x + 1
> x
[1] 5 8 9
```

We can run other arithmetic operations on the vector as given:

```
> x - 1
[1] 4 7 8
> x * 2
[1] 10 16 18
> x / 2
[1] 2.5 4.0 4.5
```

Let us practice these arithmetic operations on two vectors.

```
> x
[1] 5 8 9
> y <- c(1, 2, 3)
> y
[1] 1 2 3
> x + y
[1] 6 10 12
```

Other arithmetic operations are:

```
> x - y
[1] 4 6 6
> x * y
[1] 5 16 27
```

Check if the two vectors are equal. The comparison takes place element by element.

```
> x
[1] 5 8 9
> y
[1] 1 2 3
> x==y
[1] FALSE FALSE FALSE
> x < y
[1] FALSE FALSE FALSE
> sin(x)
[1] -0.9589243   0.9893582   0.4121185
```

3.6.6 Vector Recycling

If an operation is performed involving two vectors that requires them to be of the same length, the shorter one is recycled, i.e. repeated until it is long enough to match the longer one.

Objective

Add two vectors wherein one has length, 3 and the other has length, 6.

```
> c(1, 2, 3) + c(4, 5, 6, 7, 8, 9)
[1]  5  7  9  8  10  12
```

Objective

Multiply the two vectors wherein one has length, 3 and the other has length, 6.

```
> c(1, 2, 3) * c(4, 5, 6, 7, 8, 9)
[1]  4  10  18  7  16  27
```

Objective

Plot a Scatter Plot. The function to plot a scatter plot is 'plot'. This function uses two vectors, i.e. one for the x axis and another for the y axis. The objective is to understand the relationship between numbers and their sines. We will use two vectors. Vector, x which will have a sequence of values between 1 and 25 at an interval of 0.1 and vector, y which stores the sines of all values held in vector, x.

```
> x <-seq(1, 25, 0.1)
> y <-sin(x)
```

The plot function takes the values in the vector, x and plots it on the horizontal axis. It then takes the values in the vector, y and places it on the vertical axis (Figure 3.4).

```
> plot(x, y)
```

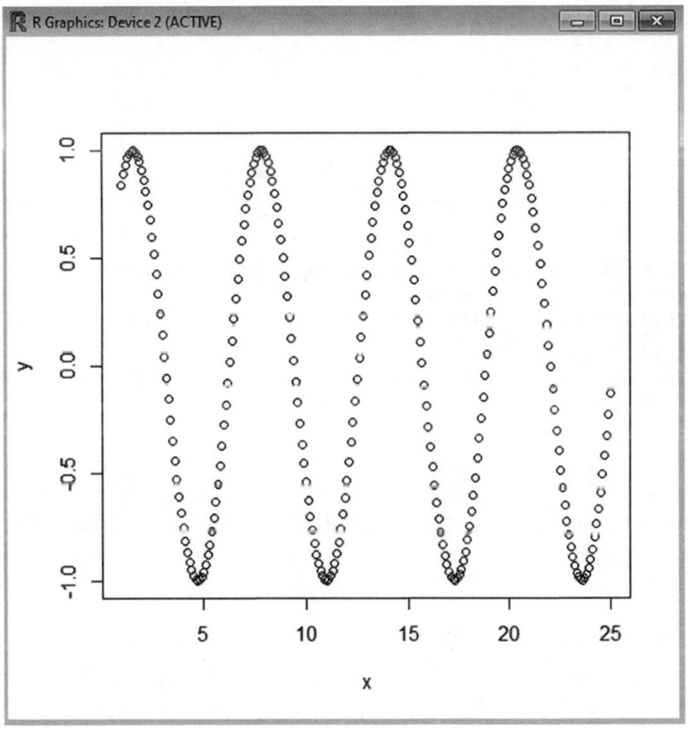

FIGURE 3.4 *Scatter plot*

3.7 MATRICES

Matrices are nothing but two-dimensional arrays.

Objective

Let us create a matrix which is 3 rows by 4 columns and set all its elements to 1.

```
> matrix (1, 3, 4)
         [, 1]   [, 2]   [, 3]   [, 4]
[1, ]      1       1       1       1
[2, ]      1       1       1       1
[3, ]      1       1       1       1
```

Objective

Use a vector to create an array, 3 rows high and 3 columns wide.

Step 1: Begin by creating a vector that has elements from 10 to 90 with an interval of 10.

```
> a <- seq(10, 90, by = 10)
```

Step 2: Validate by printing the value of vector a.

```
> a
[1]  10  20  30  40  50  60  70  80  90
```

Step 3: Call the matrix function with vector, 'a' the number of rows and the number of columns.

```
> matrix   (a, 3, 3)
          [, 1]     [, 2]     [, 3]
[1, ]       10        40        70
[2, ]       20        50        80
[3, ]       30        60        90
```

Objective

Re-shape the vector itself into an array using the dim function.

Step 1: Begin by creating a vector that has elements from 10 to 90 with an interval of 10.

```
> a <- seq (10, 90, by = 10)
```

Step 2: Validate by printing the value of vector, a.

```
> a
[1]  10   20   30   40   50   60   70   80   90
```

Step 3: Assign new dimensions to vector, a by passing a vector having 3 rows and 3 columns (c (3, 3)).

```
> dim(a)   <-   c(3, 3)
```

Step 4: Print the values of vector, a. You will notice that the values have shifted to form 3 rows by 3 columns. The vector is no longer one dimensional. It has been converted into a two-dimensional matrix that is 3 rows high and 3 columns wide.

```
> a
        [, 1]   [, 2]   [, 3]
[1, ]     10      40      70
[2, ]     20      50      80
[3, ]     30      60      90
```

3.7.1 Matrix Access

Objective

Access the elements of a 3 *4 matrix.

Step 1: Create a matrix, 'mat', 3 rows high and 4 columns wide using a vector.

```
> x <- 1:12
> x
[1]   1   2   3   4   5   6   7   8   9   10   11   12
> mat <- matrix (x, 3, 4)
> mat
          [, 1]   [, 2]   [, 3]   [, 4]
[1, ]       1       4       7      10
[2, ]       2       5       8      11
[3, ]       3       6       9      12
```

Step 2: Access the element present in the second row and third column of the matrix, 'mat'.

```
> mat [2, 3]
[1]  8
```

Objective

Access the third row of an existing matrix.

Step 1: Let us begin by printing the values of an existing matrix, 'mat'

```
> mat
          [, 1]   [, 2]   [, 3]   [, 4]
[1, ]       1       4       7      10
[2, ]       2       5       8      11
[3, ]       3       6       9      12
```

Step 2: To access the third row of the matrix, simply provide the row number and omit the column number.

```
> mat [3, ]
[1]     3    6    9    12
```

Objective

Access the second column of an existing matrix.

Step 1: Let us begin by printing the values of an existing matrix, 'mat'

```
> mat
          [, 1]   [, 2]   [, 3]   [, 4]
[1, ]       1       4       7      10
[2, ]       2       5       8      11
[3, ]       3       6       9      12
```

Step 2: To access the second column of the matrix, simply provide the column number and omit the row number.

```
> mat[, 2]
[1]  4  5  6
```

Objective

Access the second and third columns of an existing matrix.

Step 1: Let us begin by printing the values of an existing matrix, 'mat'.

```
> mat
        [, 1]    [, 2]    [, 3]    [, 4]
[1, ]      1        4        7       10
[2, ]      2        5        8       11
[3, ]      3        6        9       12
```

Step 2: To access the second and third columns of the matrix, simply provide the column numbers and omit the row number.

```
> mat[,2:3]
        [, 1]    [, 2]
[1, ]      4        7
[2, ]      5        8
[3, ]      6        9
```

Objective

Create a contour plot.

Create a matrix, 'mat' which is 9 rows high and 9 columns wide and assign the value '1' to all its elements.

```
> mat <- matrix(1, 9, 9)
```

Print all the values of the matrix, 'mat'.

```
> mat
      [, 1] [, 2] [, 3] [, 4] [, 5] [, 6] [, 7] [, 8] [, 9]
[1, ]    1     1     1     1     1     1     1     1     1
[2, ]    1     1     1     1     1     1     1     1     1
[3, ]    1     1     1     1     1     1     1     1     1
[4, ]    1     1     1     1     1     1     1     1     1
[5, ]    1     1     1     1     1     1     1     1     1
[6, ]    1     1     1     1     1     1     1     1     1
[7, ]    1     1     1     1     1     1     1     1     1
[8, ]    1     1     1     1     1     1     1     1     1
[9, ]    1     1     1     1     1     1     1     1     1
```

Assign '0' as the value to the element present in the third row and third column of the matrix, 'mat'.

```
> mat[3, 3] <-0
> mat
     [, 1] [, 2] [, 3] [, 4] [, 5] [, 6] [, 7] [, 8] [, 9]
[1, ]    1     1     1     1     1     1     1     1     1
[2, ]    1     1     1     1     1     1     1     1     1
[3, ]    1     1     0     1     1     1     1     1     1
[4, ]    1     1     1     1     1     1     1     1     1
[5, ]    1     1     1     1     1     1     1     1     1
[6, ]    1     1     1     1     1     1     1     1     1
[7, ]    1     1     1     1     1     1     1     1     1
[8, ]    1     1     1     1     1     1     1     1     1
[9, ]    1     1     1     1     1     1     1     1     1
```

Plot the contour chart using the `contour()` function (Figure 3.5). The `contour()` function creates a contour plot or adds contour lines to an existing plot. Look up the R documentation for a complete description of the `contour()` function.

```
>  contour(mat)
```

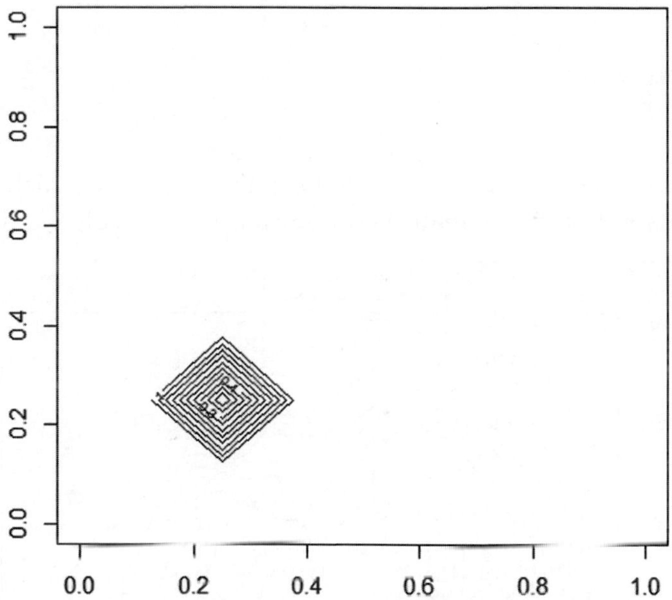

Figure 3.5 *Contour plot*

Objective

Create a 3D perspective plot with the `persp()` function (Figure 3.6). It provides a 3D wireframe plot most commonly used to display a surface.

```
>persp(mat)
```

We can add a title to our plot with the parameter '**main**'. Similarly, '**xlab**', '**ylab**' and '**zlab**' can be used to label the three axes. Coloring of the plot is done with parameter '**col**'. Similarly, we can add shading with the parameter '**shade**'.

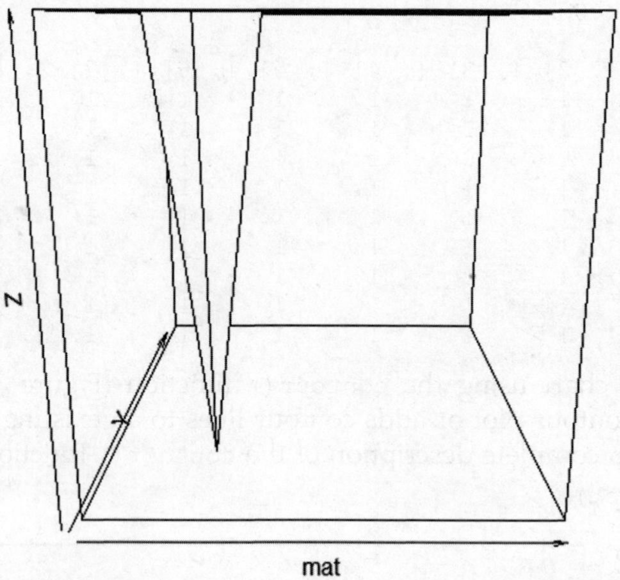

FIGURE 3.6 *3D perspective plot*

Objective

R includes some sample data sets. One of these is 'volcano', which is a 3D map of a dormant New Zealand volcano. Create a contour map of the volcano dataset (Figure 3.7).

```
> contour(volcano)
```

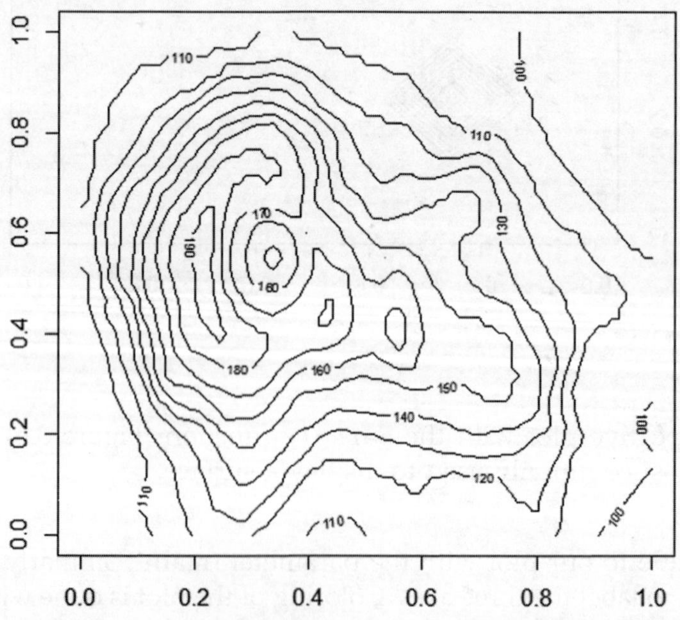

FIGURE 3.7 *Contour map*

Let us create a 3D perspective map of the sample data set, 'volcano' (Figure 3.8).

```
> persp(volcano)
```

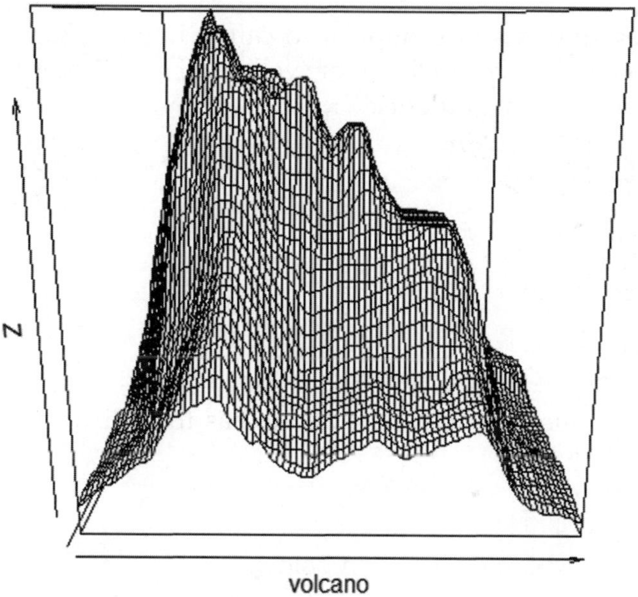

FIGURE 3.8 *3D perspective map of the sample data set, 'volcano'*

Objective

Create a heat map of the sample dataset, 'volcano' (Figure 3.9).

```
> image(volcano)
```

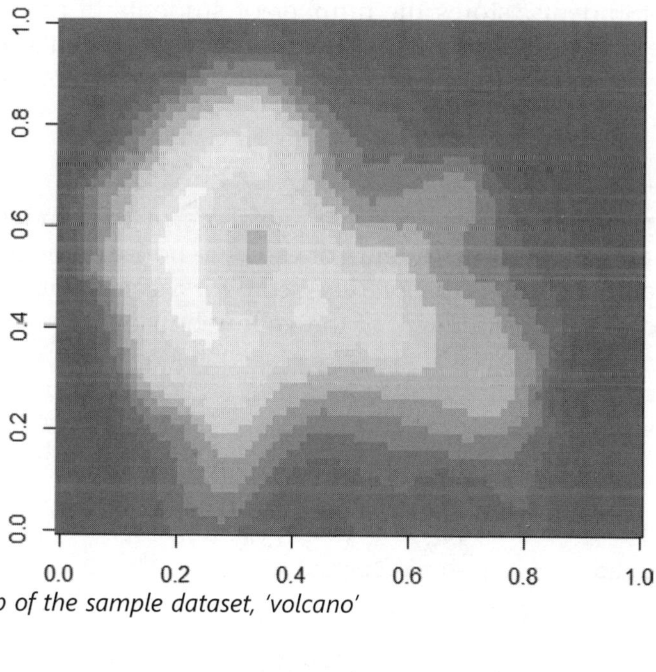

FIGURE 3.9 *Heat map of the sample dataset, 'volcano'*

3.8 Factors

3.8.1 Creating Factors

School, 'XYZ' places students in groups, also called houses. Each group is assigned a unique color such as 'red', 'green', 'blue' or 'yellow'. HouseColor is a vector that stores the house colors of a group of students.

```
> HouseColor <- c('red', 'green', 'blue', 'yellow', red', 'green', 'blue', 'blue')
> types <- factor(HouseColor)
> HouseColor
[1] "red" "green" "blue" "yellow" "red" "green" "blue" "blue"
> print(HouseColor)
[1] "red" "green" "blue" "yellow" "red" "green" "blue" "blue"
> print (types)
[1] red    green   blue   yellow   red   green   blue    blue
Levels:  blue   green   red  yellow
```

Levels denotes the unique values. The above has four distinct values such as 'blue', 'green', 'red' and 'yellow'.

```
> as.integer(types)
[1] 3 2 1 4 3 2 1 1
```

The above output is explained as given below.

1 is the number assigned to blue.
2 is the number assigned to green.
3 is the number assigned to red.
4 is the number assigned to yellow.

```
> levels(types)
[1]    "blue"     "green"     "red"     "yellow"
```

The vector 'NoofStudents' stores the number of students in each house/group with 12 students in blue house, 14 students in green house, 12 students in red house and 13 students in yellow house.

```
> NoofStudents <- c(12, 14, 12, 13)
> NoofStudents
[1]    12    14    12    13
```

The vector, 'AverageScore' stores the average score of the students of each house/group. 70 is the average score for students of the blue house, 80 is the average score for students of the green house, 90 is the average score for the students of the red house and 95 is the average score for the students of the yellow house.

```
> AverageScore(70, 80, 90, 95)
> AverageScore
[1] 70 80 90 95
```

Objective

Plot the relationship between NoofStudents and AverageScore (Figure 3.10).

```
> plot(NoofStudents, AverageScore)
```

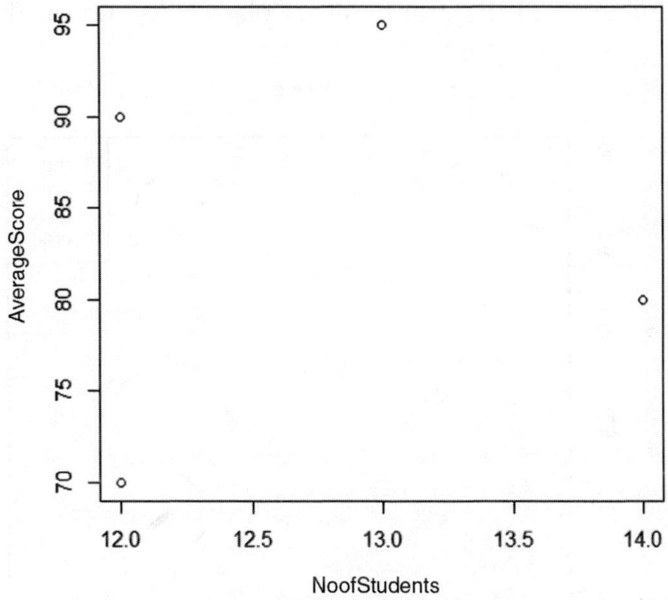

FIGURE 3.10 *Relationship between "NoofStudents" and "AverageScore"*

```
> plot (NoofStudents, AverageScore, pch=as.integer (types))
```

The above graph in Figure 3.10 displays 4 dots. Let us improve the graph by at least using different symbols to represent each house (Figure 3.11).

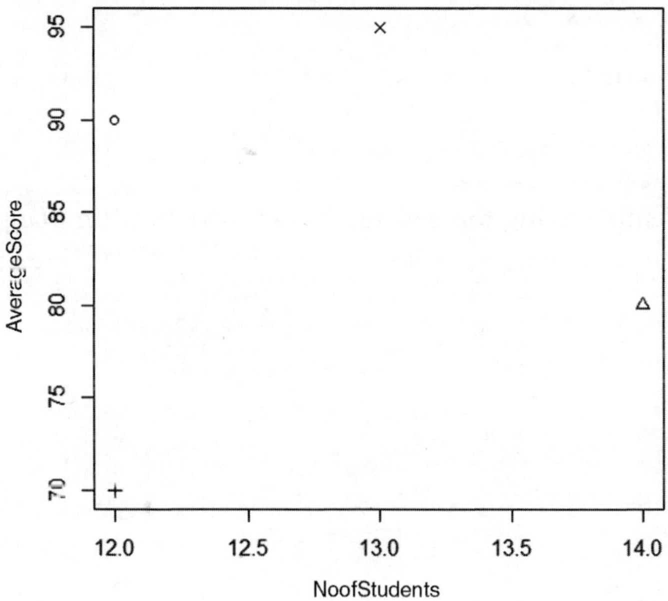

FIGURE 3.11 *Relationship between "NoofStudents" and "AverageScore" using different symbols.*

To add further meaning to the graph, let us place a legend on the top right corner (Figure 3.12).

```
> legend("topright", c("red", "green", "blue", "yellow"), pch=1:4)
```

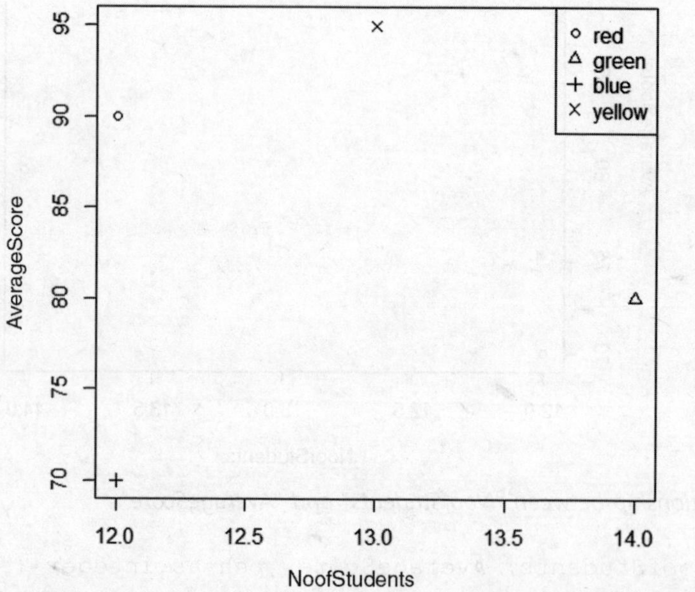

FIGURE 3.12 *Relationship between "NoofStudents" and "AverageScore" (with legends)*

3.9 LIST

List is similar to C Struct.

Objective

Create a list in R.

To create a list, 'emp' having three elements, 'EmpName', 'EmpUnit' and 'EmpSal'.

```
> emp <- list ("EmpName="Alex",  EmpUnit = "IT", EmpSal = 55000)
```

Outcome

To get the elements of the list, 'emp' use the command given below.

```
> emp
$EmpName
[1]   "Alex"

$EmpUnit
[1]    "IT"

$EmpSal
[1] 55000
```

Actually, the element names, e.g. 'EmpName', 'EmpUnit' and 'EmpSal' are optional. We could alternatively do this as shown below.

```
> EmpList <- list("Alex", "IT", 55000)
> EmpList
[[1]]
[1]  "Alex"

[[2]]
[1]  "IT"

[[3]]
[1]  55000
```

TIP *Here the elements of EmpList are referred to as 1, 2 and 3.*

3.9.1 List Tags and Values

A list has elements. The elements in a list can have names, which are referred to as tags. Elements can also have values.

For example, in the 'emp' list we have three elements, viz. EmpName, EmpUnit and EmpSal. The values are as follows. The element 'EmpName' has the value 'Alex', the element 'EmpUnit' has the value 'IT' and the element 'EmpSal' has the value 55000.

Let us look at the command to retrieve the names and values of the elements in a list.

Objective

Retrieve the names of the elements in the list 'emp'.

```
> names(emp)
[1]  "EmpName" "EmpUnit" "EmpSal"
```

Objective

Retrieve the values of the elements in the list 'emp'.

```
> unlist(emp)
EmpName    EmpUnit   EmpSal
 "Alex"       "IT"  "55000"
```

The command to retrieve the value of a single element in the list 'emp' is given below.

Objective

Retrieve the value of the element 'EmpName' in the list 'emp'.

```
> unlist(emp["EmpName"])
EmpName
"Alex"
```

The value of the other elements in the list can be checked in a similar manner.

```
> unlist(emp["EmpUnit"])
EmpUnit
  "IT"
> unlist(emp["EmpSal"])
EmpSal
  55000
```

Yet another way to retrieve the values of the elements in the list 'emp' is given as follows:

Objective

Retrieve the value of the element 'EmpName' in the list 'emp'.

```
> emp[["EmpName"]]
[1]  "Alex"
```

Or

```
> emp[[1]]
[1]  "Alex"
```

3.9.2 Add/Delete Element to or from a List

Before adding an element to the list 'emp', let us verify what elements exist in the list.

```
> emp
$EmpName
[1]   "Alex"

$EmpUnit
[1]  "IT"

$EmpSal
[1]  55000
```

Objective

Add an element with the name 'EmpDesg' and value 'Software Engineer' to the list, 'emp'.

```
> emp$EmpDesg = "Software Engineer"
```

Outcome

```
> emp
$EmpName
[1] "Alex"

$EmpUnit
[1] "IT"

$EmpSal
[1] 55000

$EmpDesg
[1] "Software Engineer"
```

Objective

Delete an element with the name 'EmpUnit' and value 'IT' from the list, 'emp'.

```
> emp$EmpUnit <- NULL
```

Outcome

```
> emp
$EmpName
[1]   "Alex"
$EmpSal
[1]  55000
$EmpDesg
[1]  "Software Engineer"
```

3.9.3 Size of a List

`length()` function can be used to determine the number of elements present in the list.

The list, 'emp' has three elements as shown:

```
> emp
$EmpName
[1] "Alex"

$EmpSal
[1] 55000

$EmpDesg
[1] "Software Engineer"
```

Objective

Determine the number of elements in the list, 'emp'.

```
> length(emp)
[1]  3
```

Recursive List

A recursive list means a list within a list.

Objective

Create a list within a list.

Let us begin with two lists, 'emp' and 'emp1'.

The elements in both the lists are as shown below.

```
> emp
$EmpName
[1]   "Alex"
```

```
$EmpSal
[1] 55000

$EmpDesg
[1] "Software Engineer"

> emp1
$EmpUnit
[1] "IT"

$EmpCity
[1] "Los Angeles"
```

We would like to combine both the lists into a single list called 'EmpList'.

```
> EmpList <- list(emp, emp1)
```

Outcome

```
> EmpList
[[1]]
[[1]] $EmpName
[1] "Alex"

[[1]]$EmpSal
[1]  55000

[[1]]$EmpDesg
[1] "Software Engineer"

[[2]]
[[2]]$EmpUnit
[1]  "IT"

[[2]]$EmpCity
[1] "Los Angeles"
```

3.10 Few Common Analytical Tasks

Reading, writing, updating and merging data are common operations in any programming language. These are used for processing data. All programming languages work with different types of data like numeric, characters, logical, etc. Just like any other processing, analytical data processing also requires general operations for complex processing. In the next section, you will learn about some common tasks of R that are required during analytical data processing.

3.10.1 Exploring a Dataset

Exploring a dataset means displaying the data of the dataset in a different form. Datasets are the main part of analytical data processing. It uses different forms or parts of the dataset. With the help of R commands, analysts can easily explore a dataset in different ways. Table 3.4 describes some functions for exploring a dataset.

TABLE 3.4 Functions for exploring a dataset

Functions	*Function Arguments*	*Description*
`names(dataset)`	• Dataset argument contains the name of the dataset.	The function displays the variables of the given dataset.
`summary(dataset)`	• Dataset argument contains the name of the dataset.	The function displays the summary of the given dataset.
`str(dataset)`	• Dataset argument contains the name of the dataset.	The function displays the structure of the given dataset.
`head(dataset, n)`	• Dataset argument contains the name of the dataset. • *n* is a numeric value to display the number of top rows.	The function displays the top rows according to the value of n. If the value of n is not provided in the function then by default the function displays the top 6 rows of the dataset.
`tail(dataset, n)`	• Dataset argument contains the name of the dataset. • *n* is a numeric value to display the number of bottom rows.	The function displays the top rows according to the value of n. If the value of n is not provided in the function then by default the function displays the bottom 6 rows of the dataset.
`class(dataset)`	• Dataset argument contains the name of the dataset.	The function displays the class of the dataset.
`dim(dataset)`	• Dataset argument contains the name of the dataset.	The function returns the dimension of the dataset which implies the total number of rows and columns of the dataset.
`table(dataset$variable names)`	• Dataset argument contains the name of the dataset. • Variable name contains the name of the variable names.	The function returns the number of categorical values after counting them.

The following example loads a matrix into the workspace. All the above commands are executed on the dataset, 'Orange' (Figures 3.13–3.15).

```
> library(Matrix)
> names(Orange) # displying the variables of the dataset Orange
[1] "Tree"          "age"           "circumference"
> summary(Orange) #displaying summary of the dataset Orange
 Tree       age          circumference
 3:7   Min.   : 118.0   Min.   : 30.0
 1:7   1st Qu.: 484.0   1st Qu.: 65.5
 5:7   Median :1004.0   Median :115.0
 2:7   Mean   : 922.1   Mean   :115.9
 4:7   3rd Qu.:1372.0   3rd Qu.:161.5
       Max.   :1582.0   Max.   :214.0
> str(Orange)
Classes 'nfnGroupedData', 'nfGroupedData', 'groupedData' and 'data.frame':      35 ob$
 $ Tree         : Ord.factor w/ 5 levels "3"<"1"<"5"<"2"<..: 2 2 2 2 2 2 2 4 4 4 ...
 $ age          : num  118 484 664 1004 1231 ...
 $ circumference: num  30 58 87 115 120 142 145 33 69 111 ...
 - attr(*, "formula")=Class 'formula'  language circumference ~ age | Tree
  .. ..- attr(*, ".Environment")=<environment: R_EmptyEnv>
 - attr(*, "labels")=List of 2
  ..$ x: chr "Time since December 31, 1968"
  ..$ y: chr "Trunk circumference"
 - attr(*, "units")=List of 2
  ..$ x: chr "(days)"
  ..$ y: chr "(mm)"
> |
```

FIGURE 3.13 *Exploring a dataset using* `names()`, `summary()` *and* `str()` *functions*

```
> head(Orange) # display top rows [ By default 6 rows]
  Tree  age circumference
1    1  118            30
2    1  484            58
3    1  664            87
4    1 1004           115
5    1 1231           120
6    1 1372           142
>
> head(Orange,2) # display top 2 rows
  Tree age circumference
1    1 118            30
2    1 484            58
>
> tail(Orange) # display bottom rows [By default 6 rows]
   Tree  age circumference
30    5  484            49
31    5  664            81
32    5 1004           125
33    5 1231           142
34    5 1372           174
35    5 1582           177
> tail(Orange,2) # display bottom 2 rows
   Tree  age circumference
34    5 1372           174
35    5 1582           177
```

FIGURE 3.14 *Exploring a dataset using* `head()` *and* `tail()` *functions*

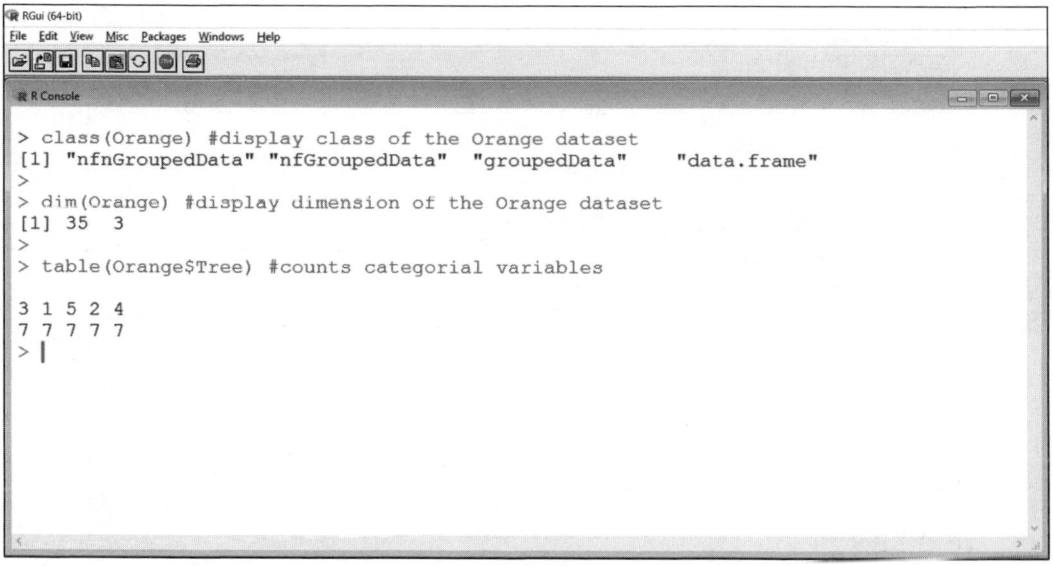

FIGURE 3.15 *Exploring a dataset using* **`class()`**, **`dim()`** *and* **`table()`** *functions*

3.10.2 Conditional Manipulation of a Dataset

Analytical data processing sometimes may require specific rows and columns of a dataset.

Table 3.5 lists commands that can be used for accessing specific rows and columns of a dataset.

TABLE 3.5 Commands for accessing specific rows and columns of a dataset

Commands	*Command Arguments*	*Description*
`Tablename[n]`	*n* is a numeric value.	The command displays the rows according to the given value of argument *n* of the table.
`Tablename[, n]`	*n* is a numeric value.	The command displays the columns according to the given value of argument *n* of the table.

The following example reads a table, 'Hardware.csv' into object, 'TD' on the R workspace. The TD[1] and TD[, 1] commands displays rows and columns (Figure 3.16).

3.10.3 Merging Data

Merging different datasets or objects is another common task used in most processing activities. Analytical data processing may also require merging two or more data objects. R provides a function `merge()` that merges data objects. The `merge()` function combines data frames by common columns or row names. It also follows the database join operations. The syntax of the `merge()` function is given as follows:

```
merge(x, y,…) OR
merge(x, y, by = intersect(names(x), names(y)), by.x = by, by.y =
by, all = FALSE, all.x = all, all.y = all, …)
```

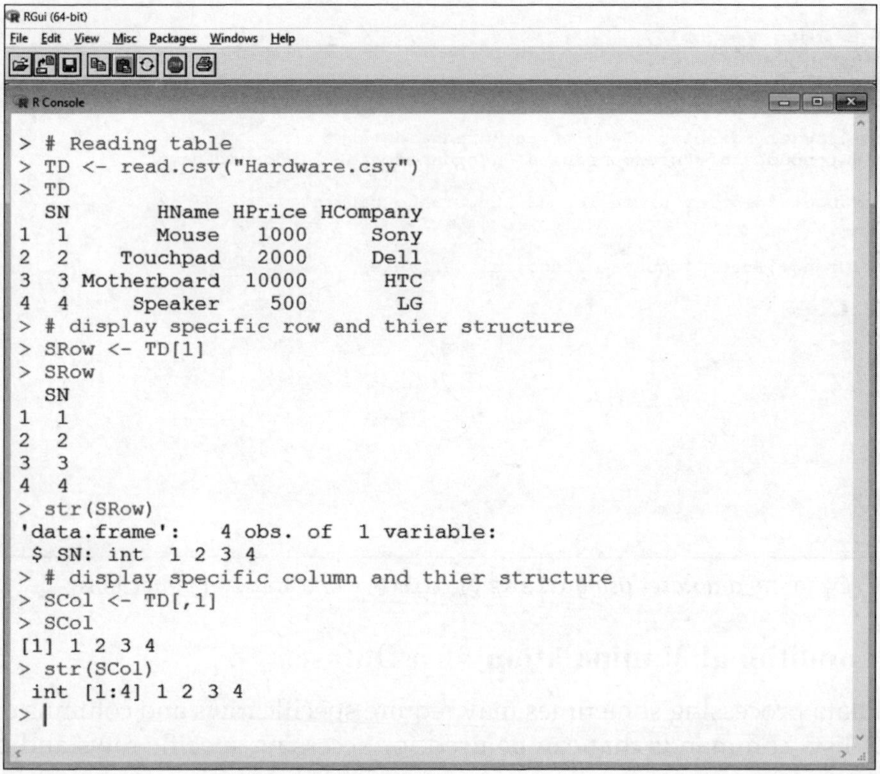

FIGURE 3.16 *Conditional manipulation of a dataset*

where, x is an object or data frame, y is an object or data frame and by, by.x, by.y arguments define the common columns or rows for merging. All arguments contain logical values 'TRUE' or 'FALSE'. If the value is TRUE then it returns the full outer join by adding all rows of x and y into the result object.

all.x argument contains logical values, 'TRUE' or 'FALSE'. If the value is TRUE then it returns the dataset as per left outer join after merging the objects by adding an extra row in x that is not matching with rows in y. If the value is FALSE then it merges the rows with the data from both x and y into the result object.

all.y argument contains logical values, 'TRUE' or 'FALSE'. If the value is TRUE then it returns the dataset as per right outer join after merging the objects by adding an extra row in y that is not matching with rows in x. If the value is FALSE then it merges the rows with data from both x and y into the result object.

The dots '…' define the other optional argument.

The following example creates two data frames, 'S' and 'T'. Then both the data frames are merged into a new data frame, 'E' (Figure 3.17).

In this example, two data frames, 'S' and 'T' are using different values to merge data. The merge command returns the data frames after merging them using the left and right outer join (Figure 3.18).

```
> S <- data.frame(RN = c('A','B','C'),RM =c(10,20,30))
> S
  RN RM
1  A 10
2  B 20
3  C 30
> T <- data.frame(TN = c('A','B','C'),TM =c(10,20,30))
> T
  TN TM
1  A 10
2  B 20
3  C 30
> E <- merge(S,T)
> E
  RN RM TN TM
1  A 10  A 10
2  B 20  A 10
3  C 30  A 10
4  A 10  B 20
5  B 20  B 20
6  C 30  B 20
7  A 10  C 30
8  B 20  C 30
9  C 30  C 30
>
```

FIGURE 3.17 *Merging data*

```
> S <- data.frame(RN = c('A','B'),RM =c(10,20))
> S
  RN RM
1  A 10
2  B 20
> T <- data.frame(TN = c('A','C'),TM =c(100,200))
> T
  TN  TM
1  A 100
2  C 200
> # Left outer join
> E <- merge(S,T,all.x = "TRUE")
> E
  RN RM TN  TM
1  A 10  A 100
2  B 20  A 100
3  A 10  C 200
4  B 20  C 200
> # right outer join
> E <- merge(S,T,all.y = "TRUE")
> E
  RN RM TN  TM
1  A 10  A 100
2  B 20  A 100
3  A 10  C 200
4  B 20  C 200
```

FIGURE 3.18 *Merging data using join condition*

3.11 AGGREGATING AND GROUP PROCESSING OF A VARIABLE

Aggregate and group operations aggregate the data of specific variables of a dataset after grouping variable data. Like merging, analytical data processing also requires aggregation and grouping operation on a dataset. R provides some functions for aggregation operation. The next section describes two functions `aggregate()` and `tapply()` of R.

3.11.1 `aggregate()` Function

The `aggregate()` function is an inbuilt function of R that aggregates data values. The function also splits data into groups after performing given statistical functions. The syntax of the `aggregate()` function is

```
aggregate(x, …) or
aggregate(x, by, FUN, …)
```

where, x is an object, by argument defines the list of group elements of the specific variable of the dataset, FUN argument is a statistic function that returns a numeric value after given statistic operations and the dots '…' define the other optional argument.

The following example reads a table, 'Fruit_data.csv' into object, 'S'. The `aggregate()` function computes the mean price of each type of fruit. Here by argument is list(Fruit.Name = S$Fruit.Name) that groups the Fruit.Name columns (Figure 3.19).

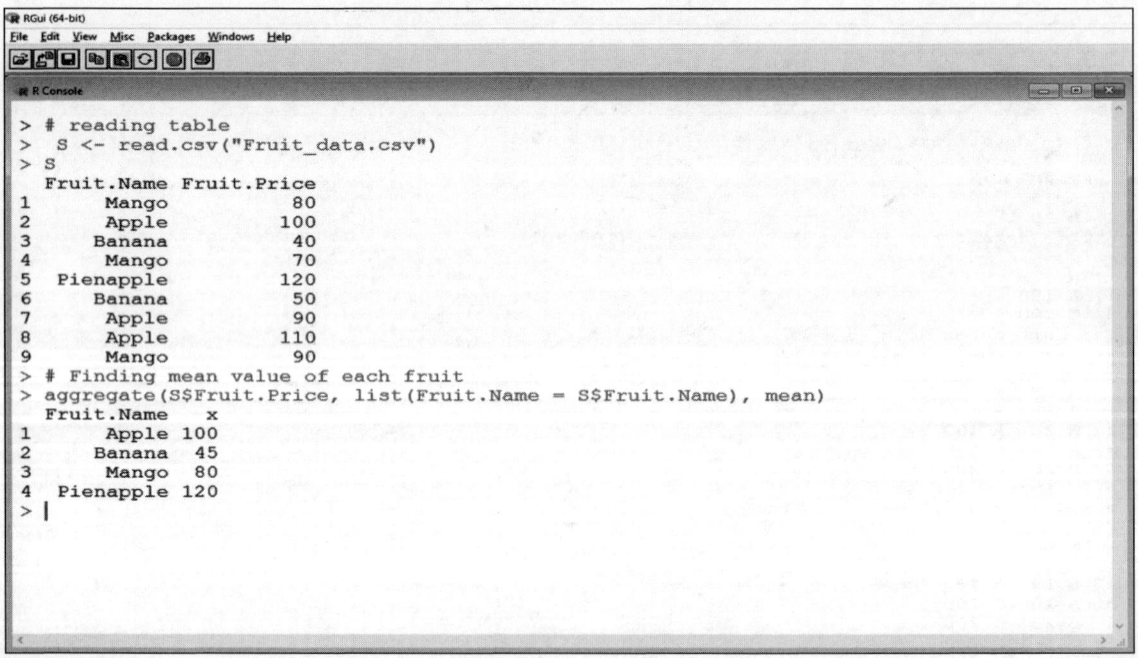

FIGURE 3.19 *Example of* `aggregate()` *function*

3.11.2 `tapply()` Function

The `tapply()` function is also an inbuilt function of R and works in a manner similar to the function `aggregate()`. The function aggregates the data values into groups after performing the given statistical functions. The syntax of the `tapply ()` function is

```
tapply (x, …) or
tapply(x, INDEX, FUN, …)
```

where, x is an object that defines the summary variable, INDEX argument defines the list of group elements—also called group variable, FUN argument is a statistic function that returns a numeric value after given statistic operations and the dots '…' define the other optional argument.

The following example reads the table, 'Fruit_data.csv' into object, 'A'. The `tapply()` function computes the sum and price of each type of fruit. Here Fruit.Price is a summary variable and Fruit.Name is a grouping variable. The FUN function is applied on the summary variable, Fruit.Price (Figure 3.20).

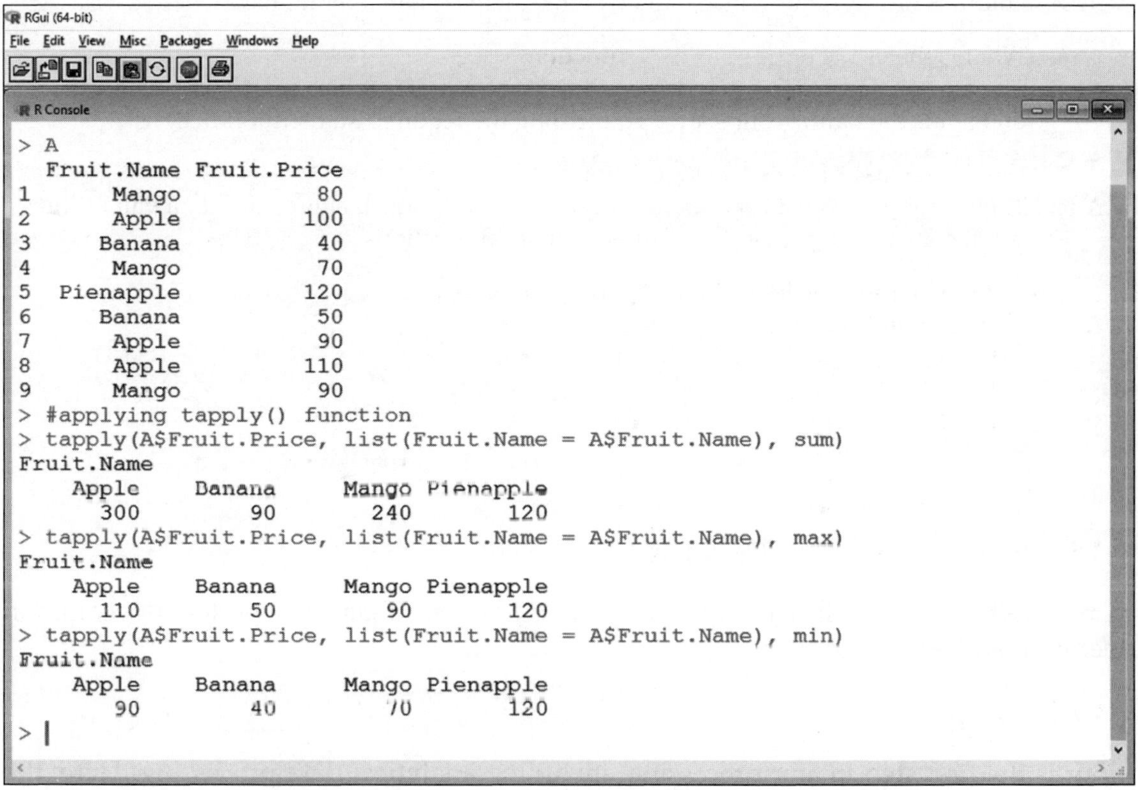

FIGURE 3.20 *Example of* `tapply()` *function*

Check Your Understanding

1. How do you define exploring a dataset?

Ans: Exploring a dataset implies display of data of a dataset in different forms.

2. Which function is used to display the summary of a dataset?

Ans: The `summary()` function is used to display the summary of a dataset.

3. What is the `head()` function?

Ans: The `head()` function is an inbuilt data exploring function that displays the top rows according to a given value.

4. What is the `tail()` function?

Ans: The `tail()` function is an inbuilt data exploring function that displays the bottom rows according to a given value.

5. What is the use of `merge()` function?

Ans: The `merge()` function is an inbuilt function of R. It combines data frames by common columns or row names. It also follows the database join operations.

6. What is the use of `aggregate()` function?

Ans: The `aggregate()` function is an inbuilt function of R which aggregates data values and splits data into groups after performing the required statistical functions.

7. What is the use of `tapply()` function?

Ans: The `tapply()` function is an inbuilt function of R which aggregates data values into groups after performing the required statistical functions.

8. List the inbuilt functions of R for manipulating text.

Ans: Some inbuilt functions of R for manipulating text are:

- `substr()`
- `strsplit()`
- `paste()`
- `grep()`

3.12 Simple Analysis Using R

In this section, you will learn how to read data from a dataset, perform a common operation and see the output.

3.12.1 Input

Input is the first step in any processing, including analytical data processing. Here, the input is dataset, 'Fruit'. For reading the dataset into R, use `read.table()` or `read.csv()` function. In Figure 3.21, the dataset, 'Fruit' is being read into the R workspace using the `read.csv()` function.

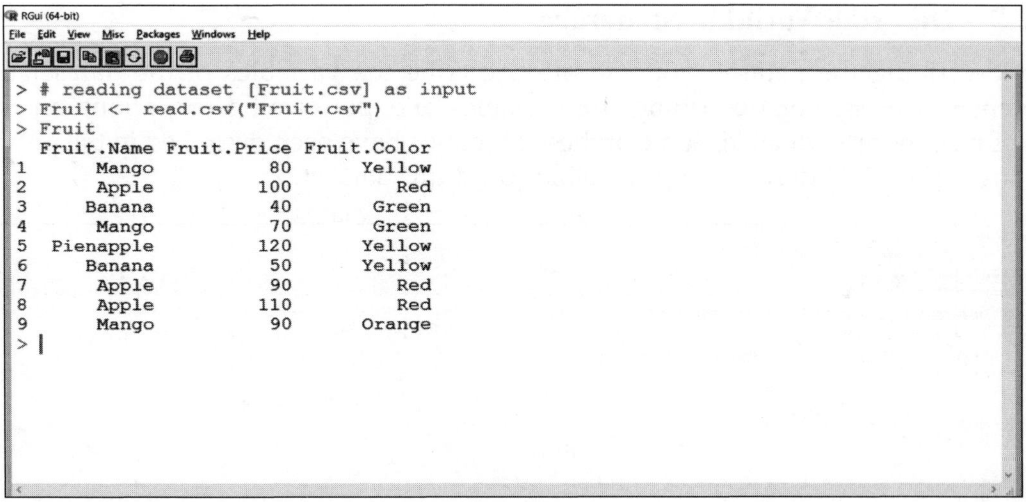

FIGURE 3.21 *Reading dataset as input into R workspace*

3.12.2 Describe Data Structure

After reading the dataset into the R workspace, the dataset can be described using different functions like `names()`, `str()`, `summary()`, `head()` and `tail()`. All these functions have been described in the previous sections. The following figure describes the 'Fruit' dataset using all these functions (Figure 3.22).

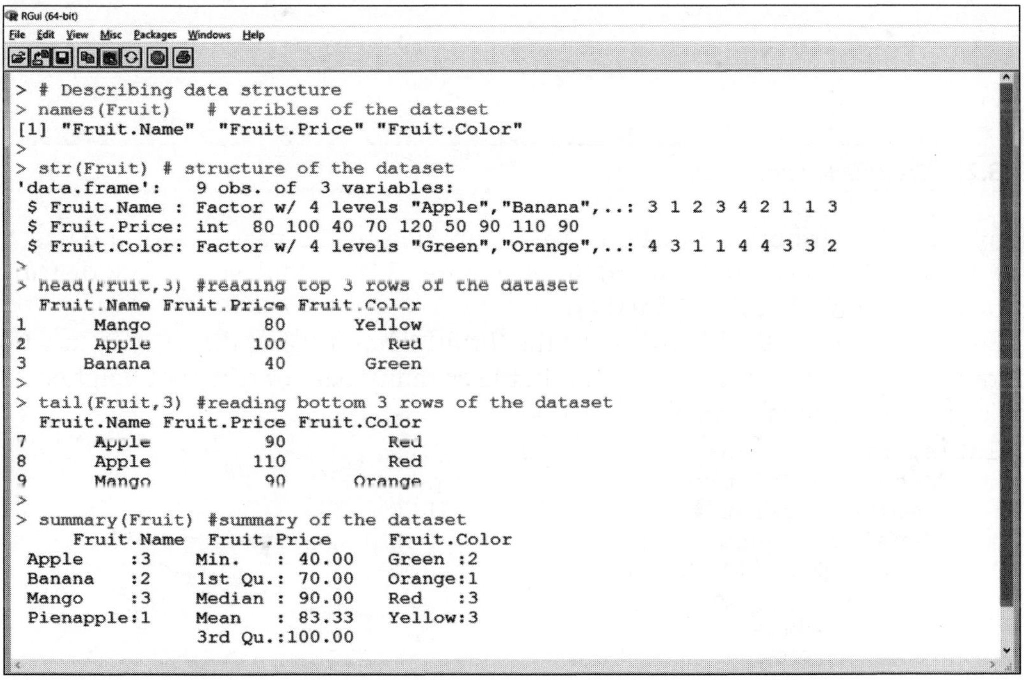

FIGURE 3.22 *Describing data structure*

3.12.3 Describe Variable Structure

After describing the dataset, you can also describe the variables of the dataset using different functions. For describing the variables and performing operations on them, many functions are available. Some of these functions have been described in the previous sections. Figure 3.23 describes the variables of 'Fruit' dataset.

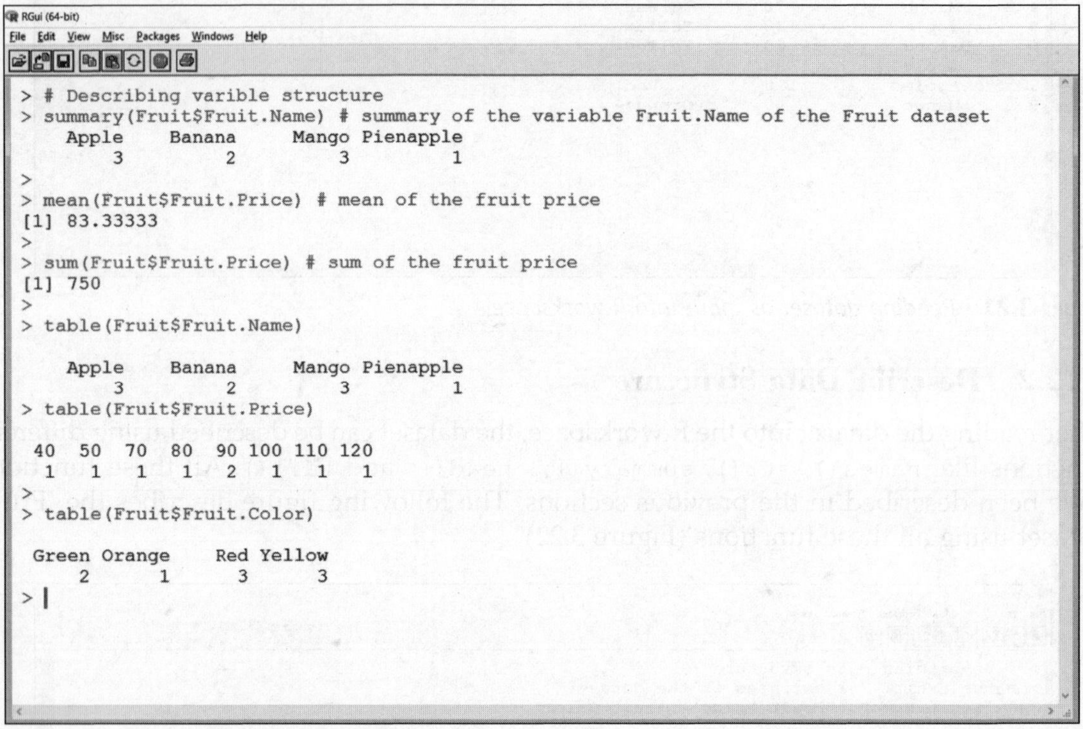

FIGURE 3.23 *Describing variable structure*

Many inbuilt distribution functions can be applied to the variables of a dataset that define the distribution of data in a dataset. Figures 3.24–3.26 describe few distribution functions applied on the 'Fruit' database.

Figure 3.24 describes the histogram of the 'Fruit' dataset using the `hist()` function. A histogram is a graphical display of data that uses many bars of different heights.

The complete syntax for `hist()` function is:

```
hist(x, breaks = 'Sturges',
     freq = NULL, probability = !freq,
     include.lowest = TRUE, right = TRUE,
     density = NULL, angle = 45, col = NULL, border = NULL,
     main = paste('Histogram of' , xname),
     xlim = range(breaks), ylim = NULL,
     xlab = xname, ylab,
     axes = TRUE, plot = TRUE, labels = FALSE,
     nclass = NULL, warn.unused = TRUE, ...)
```

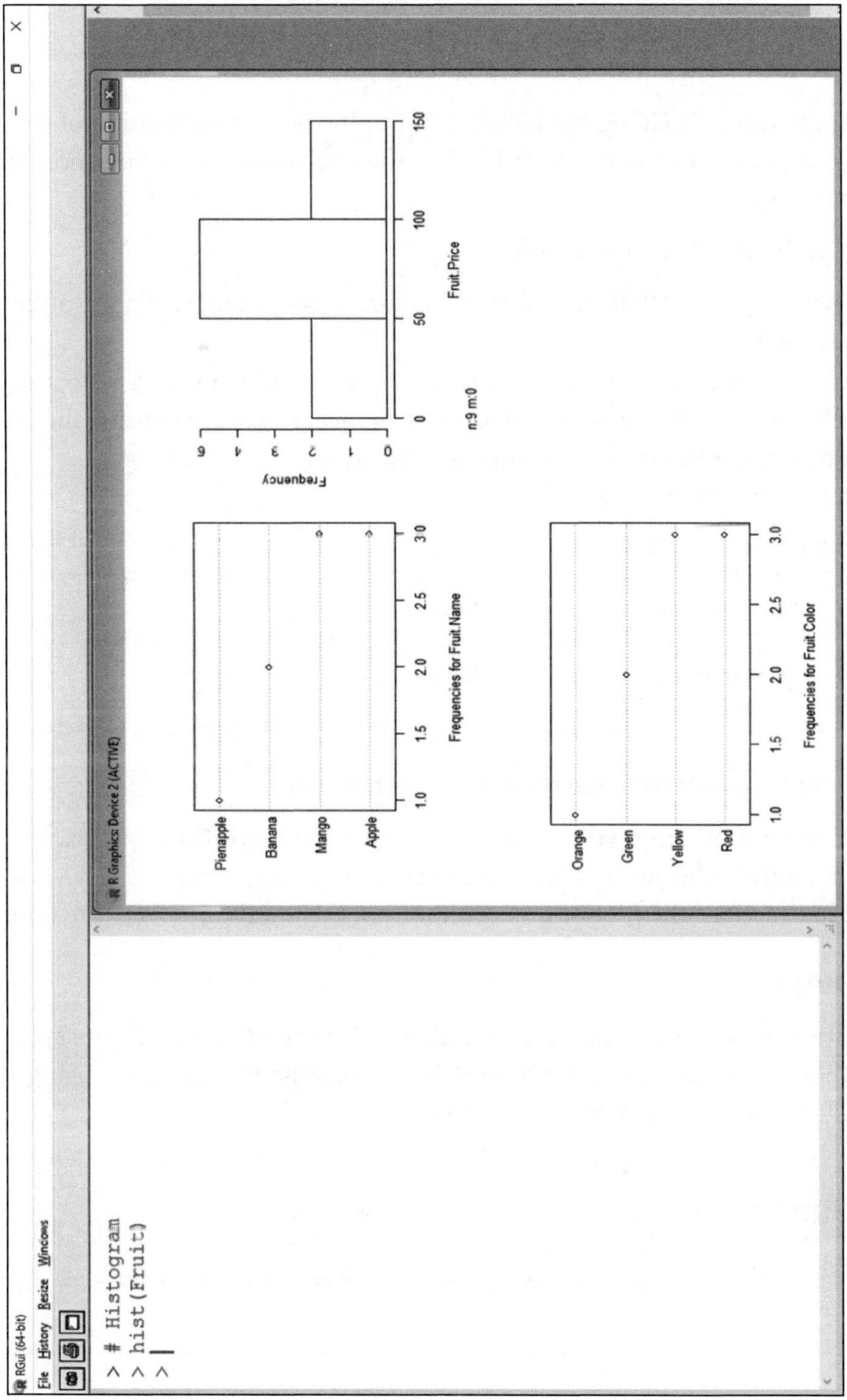

FIGURE 3.24 *Histogram of 'Fruit' dataset*

where,

x is the vector for which a histogram is required.

freq is a logical value. If TRUE, the histogram graphic is a representation of frequencies, the counts component of the result. If FALSE, the probability densities and component density are plotted.

main, xlab, ylab are arguments to title.

plot is a logical value. If TRUE (default), a histogram is plotted, else a list of breaks and counts is returned.

For explanation of other arguments in the `hist()` function, refer to R documentation.

Figure 3.25 describes the box-and-whisker plot of the 'Fruit' dataset using the `boxplot()` function. A box and whisker plot summarises the group values into boxes.

The syntax for `boxplot()` function is:

```
boxplot(x, ..., range = 1.5, width = NULL, varwidth = FALSE,
        notch = FALSE, outline = TRUE, names, plot = TRUE,
        border = par('fg'), col = NULL, log = '',
        pars = list(boxwex = 0.8, staplewex = 0.5, outwex = 0.5),
        horizontal = FALSE, add = FALSE, at = NULL)
```

where **x** is a numeric vector or a single list containing such vectors.

outline - If outline is not true, the outliers are not drawn.

range - This determines how far the plot whiskers extend out from the box.

For explanation of other arguments in the `boxplot()` function, refer to R documentation.

Figure 3.26 describes the plot of the 'Fruit' dataset using the `plot()` function.

3.12.4 Output

For storing the output, users may use .RData file. On the other hand, if users are using any GUIs then they can export the output into a specific file. Also, by using database functions like the write function, the output can be saved.

Just Remember

With the help of any R Graphical User Interface (GUI), users can execute all these commands. Some of the GUIs are described in the next section.

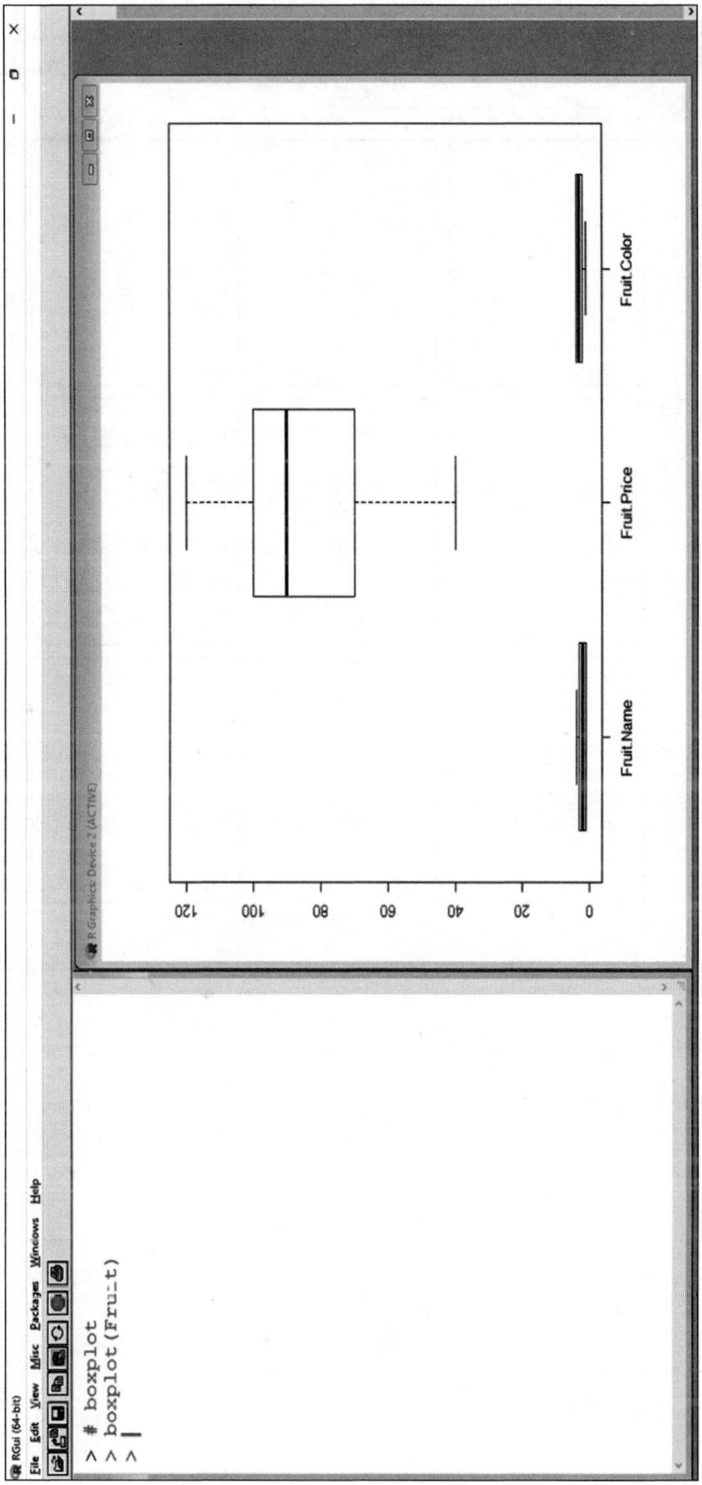

FIGURE 3.25 *Box-and-whisker plot of 'Fruit' dataset*

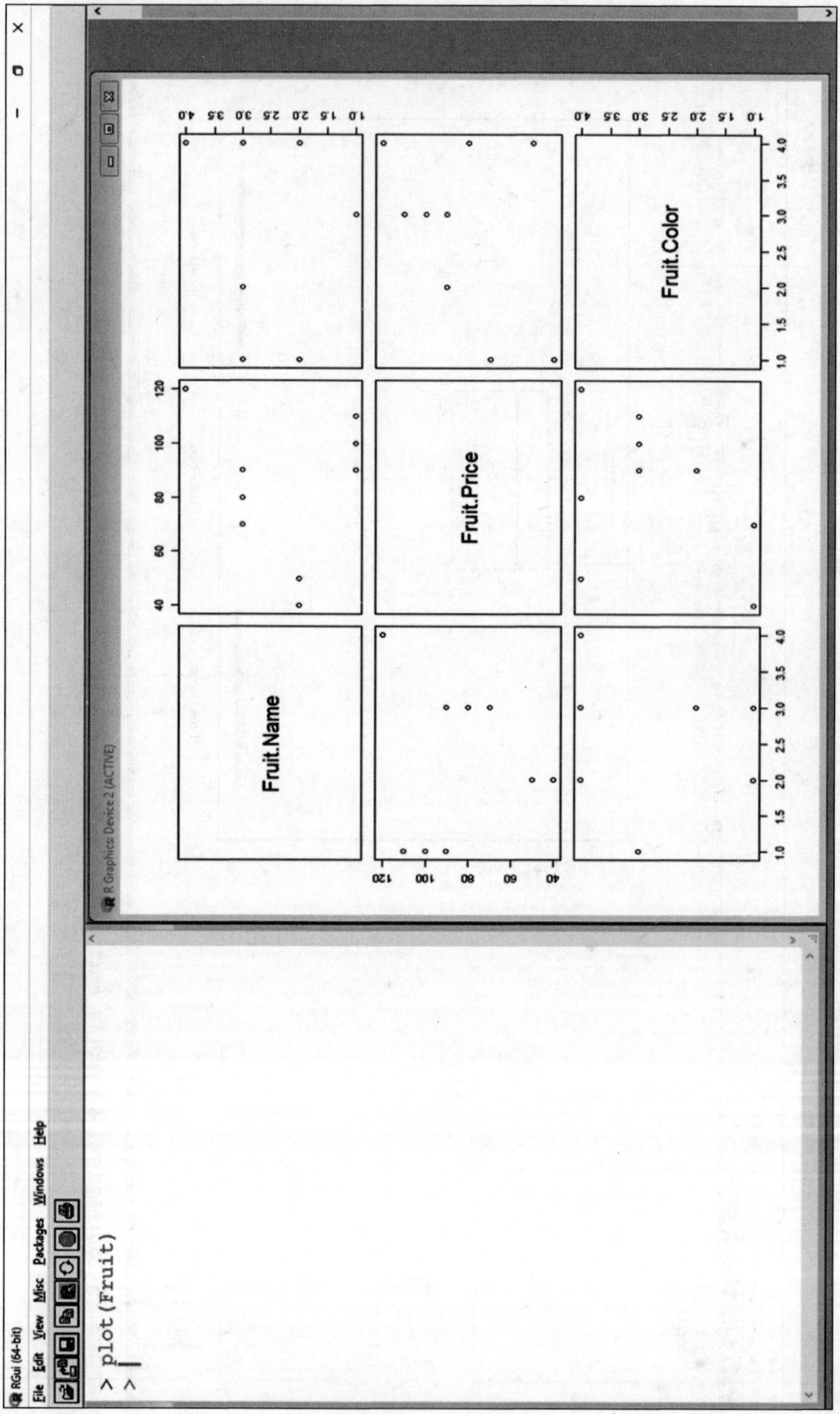

FIGURE 3.26 *'Fruit' dataset using* `plot()` *function*

Check Your Understanding

1. Write the names of the functions used for reading datasets or tables into the R workspace.

Ans: Functions used for reading datasets or tables into the R workspace are:
- `read.csv()`
- `read.table()`

2. List the inbuilt functions used for describing a dataset.

Ans: Some inbuilt functions used for describing a dataset are:
- `names()`
- `str()`
- `summary()`
- `head()`
- `tail()`

3. List the functions of R for describing variables.

Ans: Functions for describing variables are:
- `table()`
- `summary(tablename $ variablename)`
- `paste()`
- `grep()`
- `hist()`
- `plot()`

3.13 Methods for Reading Data

R supports different types of data formats related to a database. With the help of import and export utility of R, any type of data can be imported and exported into R. In this section, you will learn about the different methods used for reading data.

3.13.1 CSV and Spreadsheets

Comma separated value (CSV) files and spreadsheets are used for storing small size data. R has an inbuilt function facility through which analysts can read both types of files.

Reading CSV Files

A CSV file uses .csv extension and stores data in a table structure format in any plain text. The following function reads data from a CSV file:

```
read.csv('filename')
```

where,

filename is the name of the CSV file that needs to be imported.

The `read.table()` function can also read data from CSV files. The syntax of the function is

```
read.table('filename', header=TRUE, sep=',',...)
```

where,

filename argument defines the path of the file to be read, **header** argument contains logical values TRUE and FALSE for defining whether the file has header names on the first line or not, **sep** argument defines the character used for separating each column of the file and the dots '…' define the other optional arguments.

The following example reads a CSV file, 'Hardware.csv' using `read.csv()` and `read.table()` function (Figure 3.27).

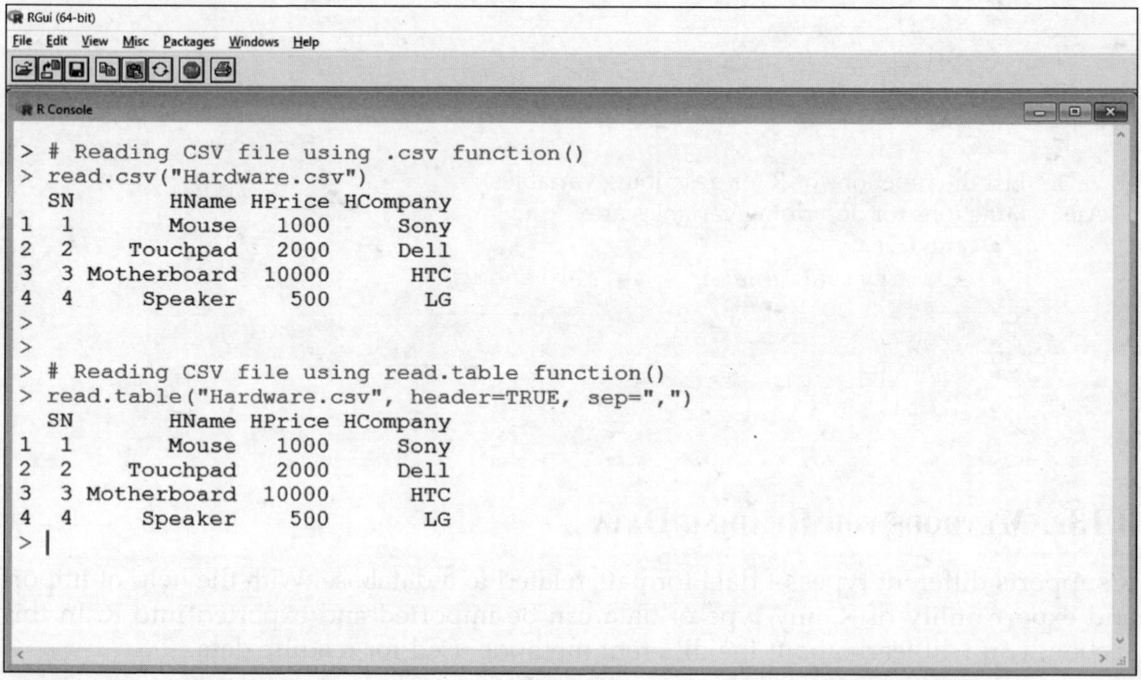

FIGURE 3.27 *Reading CSV file*

Reading Spreadsheets

A spreadsheet is a table that stores data in rows and columns. Many applications are available for creating a spreadsheet. Microsoft Excel is the most popular for creating an Excel file. An Excel file uses .xlsx extension and stores data in a spreadsheet.

In R, different packages are available such as gdata, xlsx, etc., that provide functions for reading Excel files. Importing such packages is necessary before using any inbuilt function of any package. The `read.xlsx()` is an inbuilt function of 'xlsx' package for reading Excel files. The syntax of the `read.xlsx()` function is

```
read.xlsx('filename',...)
```

where,

filename argument defines the path of the file to be read and the dots '…' define the other optional arguments.

In R, reading or writing (importing and exporting) data using packages may create some problems like incompatibility of versions, additional packages not loaded and so on. In order to avoid these problems, it is better to convert files into CSV files. After converting files into CSV files, the converted file can be read using the `read.csv()` function.

The following example illustrates creation of an Excel file, 'Softdrink.xlsx'. The 'Software.csv' file is the converted form of the 'Softdrink.xlsx' file (Figure 3.28). The function `read.csv()` is reading this file into R (Figure 3.29).

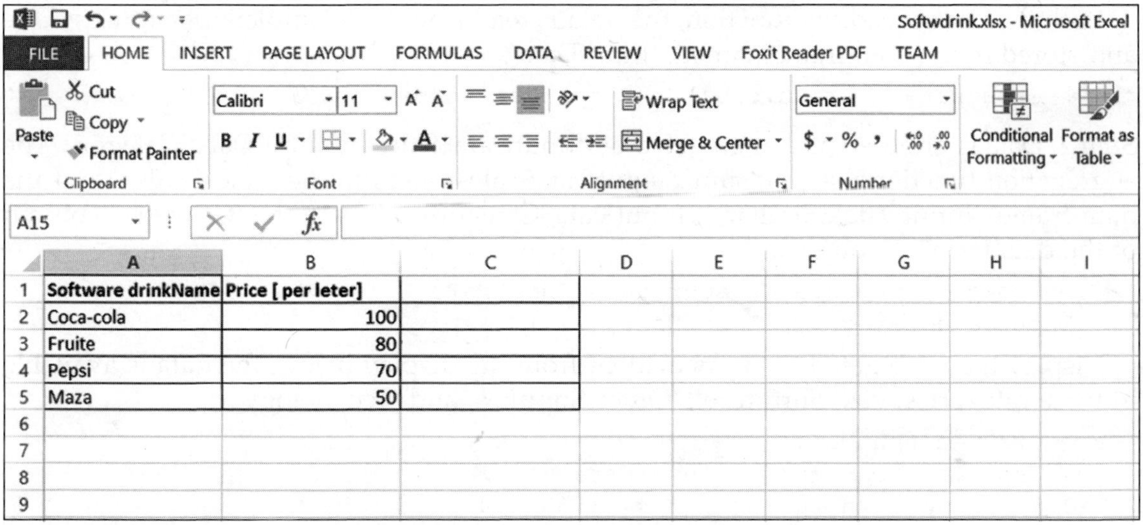

FIGURE 3.28 *Spreadsheet of Excel file*

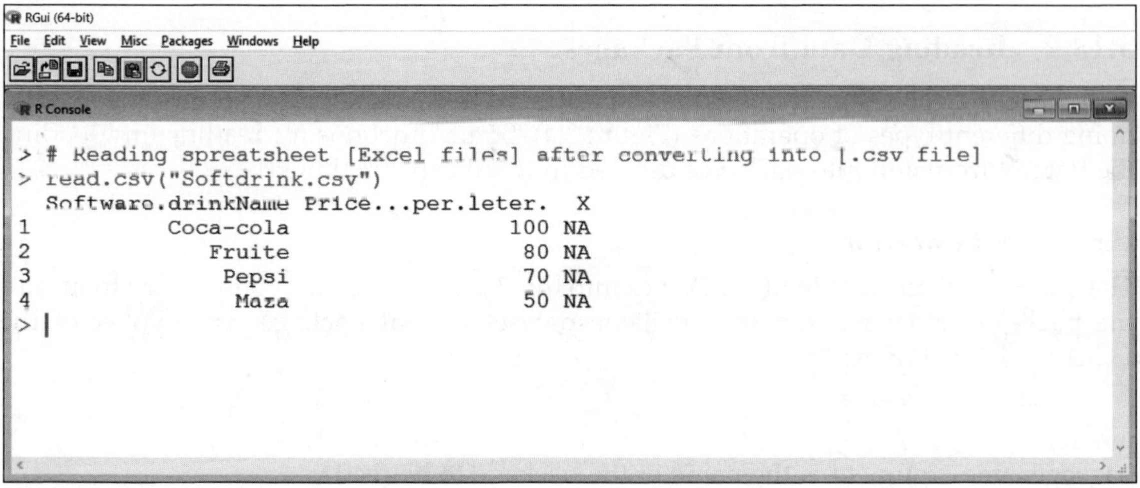

FIGURE 3.29 *Reading a converted CSV file*

Example: Reading the .csv file

To read the data from a .csv file (D:\SampleSuperstore.csv) into a data frame. The data should be grouped by 'Category'. The column on which grouping is done is 'Sales'. The aggregate function to be used is 'sum'.

Step 1: The data is stored in 'D:\SampleSuperstore.csv'. It is available under the following columns:

Row ID, Order ID, Order Date, Ship Date, Ship Mode, Customer ID, Customer Name, Segment, Country, State, City, Postal Code, Region, Product ID, Category, Sub-Category, Product Name, Sales, Quantity, Discount, Price.

A subset of the data is shown in Figure 3.30.

With the use of read.csv function, the data is read from 'D:\SampleSuperstore.csv' file and stored in the data frame named, 'InputData'.

```
> InputData <- read.csv("d:/SampleSuperstore.csv")
```

Step 2: Data is grouped and aggregated on InputData$Sales by InputData$Category. The aggregation function used is 'sum'. InputData$Sales refers to the 'Sales' column of the data frame, 'InputData'. Similarly, InputData$Category refers to the 'Category' column of the data frame, 'InputData'.

```
> GroupedInputData <- aggregate(InputData$Sales ~
InputData$Category, InputData, sum)
```

Display the aggregated data. As evident from the display below, the data is available in three categories, viz. 'Furniture', 'Office Supplies' and 'Technology'.

```
> GroupedInputData
  InputData$Category   InputData$Sales
1          Furniture          156514.4
2    Office Supplies          132600.8
3         Technology          168638.0
```

3.13.2 Reading Data from Packages

A package is a collection of functions and datasets. In R, many packages are available for doing different types of operations (Figure 2.4). Some functions for reading and loading the dataset from and into packages defined in R are explained next.

`library()` *Function*

The `library()` function loads packages into the R workspace. It is compulsory to import the package before reading the available dataset of that package. The syntax of the `library()` function is:

```
library(packagename)
```

where,
packagename argument is the name of the package to be read.

	A	B	C	D	E	F	G	H	I	J	K	L	M	N	O	P	Q	R	S	T	U
1	Row ID	Order ID	Order Date	Ship Date	Ship Mod	Customer	Customer	Segment	Country	City	State	Postal Coc	Region	Product IC	Category	Sub-Categ	Product N	Sales	Quant	Discou	Profit
2	1	CA-2013-1	11/9/2013	11/12/2013	Second Cl	CG-12520	Claire Gut	Consumer	United Sta	Henderso	Kentucky	42420	South	FUR-BO-1	Furniture	Bookcases	Bush Som	261.96	2	0	41.91
3	2	CA-2013-1	11/9/2013	11/12/2013	Second Cl	CG-12520	Claire Gut	Consumer	United Sta	Henderso	Kentucky	42420	South	FUR-CH-1	Furniture	Chairs	Hon Delux	731.94	3	0	219.6
4	3	CA-2013-1	6/13/2013	6/17/2013	Second Cl	DV-13045	Darrin Var	Corporate	United Sta	Los Angel	California	90036	West	OFF-LA-10	Office Sup	Labels	Self-Adhe	14.62	2	0	6.871
5	4	US-2012-1	10/11/2012	10/18/2012	Standard	SO-20335	Sean O'Dc	Consumer	United Sta	Fort Laude	Florida	33311	South	FUR-TA-1	Furniture	Tables	Bretford C	957.5775	5	0.45	-383
6	5	US-2012-1	10/11/2012	10/18/2012	Standard	SO-20335	Sean O'Dc	Consumer	United Sta	Fort Laude	Florida	33311	South	OFF-ST-10	Office Sup	Storage	Eldon Folc	22.368	2	0.2	2.516
7	6	CA-2011-1	6/9/2011	6/14/2011	Standard	BH-11710	Brosina Ho	Consumer	United Sta	Los Angel	California	90032	West	FUR-FU-1	Furniture	Furnishing	Eldon Exp	48.86	7	0	14.17
8	7	CA-2011-1	6/9/2011	6/14/2011	Standard	BH-11710	Brosina Ho	Consumer	United Sta	Los Angel	California	90032	West	OFF-AR-1	Office Sup	Art	Newell 32	7.28	4	0	1.966
9	8	CA-2011-1	6/9/2011	6/14/2011	Standard	BH-11710	Brosina Ho	Consumer	United Sta	Los Angel	California	90032	West	TEC-PH-10	Technolog	Phones	Mitel 5320	907.152	6	0.2	90.72
10	9	CA-2011-1	6/9/2011	6/14/2011	Standard	BH-11710	Brosina Ho	Consumer	United Sta	Los Angel	California	90032	West	OFF-BI-10	Office Sup	Binders	DXL Angle	18.504	3	0.2	5.783
11	10	CA-2011-1	6/9/2011	6/14/2011	Standard	BH-11710	Brosina Ho	Consumer	United Sta	Los Angel	California	90032	West	OFF-AP-1	Office Sup	Appliance	Belkin F5C	114.9	5	0	34.47
12	11	CA-2011-1	6/9/2011	6/14/2011	Standard	BH-11710	Brosina Ho	Consumer	United Sta	Los Angel	California	90032	West	FUR-TA-1	Furniture	Tables	Chromcra	1706.184	9	0.2	85.31
13	12	CA-2011-1	6/9/2011	6/14/2011	Standard	BH-11710	Brosina Ho	Consumer	United Sta	Los Angel	California	90032	West	TEC-PH-10	Technolog	Phones	Konftel 25	911.424	4	0.2	68.36
14	13	CA-2014-1	4/16/2014	4/21/2014	Standard	AA-10480	Andrew A	Consumer	United Sta	Concord	North Car	28027	South	OFF-PA-1	Office Sup	Paper	Xerox 196	15.552	3	0.2	5.443
15	14	CA-2013-1	12/6/2013	12/11/2013	Standard	IM-15070	Irene Mac	Consumer	United Sta	Seattle	Washingt	98103	West	OFF-BI-10	Office Sup	Binders	Fellowes	407.976	3	0.2	132.6
16	15	US-2012-1	11/22/2012	11/26/2012	Standard	HP-14815	Harold Pa	Home Off	United Sta	Fort Wort	Texas	76106	Central	OFF-AP-1	Office Sup	Appliance	Holmes R	68.81	5	0.8	-123.9
17	16	US-2012-1	11/22/2012	11/26/2012	Standard	HP-14815	Harold Pa	Home Off	United Sta	Fort Wort	Texas	76106	Central	OFF-BI-10	Office Sup	Binders	Storex Du	2.544	3	0.8	-3.816
18	17	CA-2011-1	11/11/2011	11/18/2011	Standard	PK-19075	Pete Kriz	Consumer	United Sta	Madison	Wisconsin	53711	Central	OFF-ST-10	Office Sup	Storage	Stur-D-Stc	665.88	6	0	13.32
19	18	CA-2011-1	5/13/2011	5/15/2011	Second Cl	AG-10270	Alejandro	Consumer	United Sta	West Jord	Utah	84084	West	OFF-ST-10	Office Sup	Storage	Fellowes	55.5	2	0	9.99
20	19	CA-2011-1	8/27/2011	9/1/2011	Second Cl	ZD-21925	Zuschuss	Consumer	United Sta	San Franci	California	94109	West	OFF-AR-1	Office Sup	Art	Newell 34	8.56	2	0	2.482

FIGURE 3.30 *Subset of the data from "SampleSuperstore.xls"*

`data()` *Function*

The `data()` function lists all the available datasets of the loaded package into the R workspace. For loading a new dataset into the loaded packages, users need to pass the name of the new dataset into `data()` function. The syntax of the `data()` function is:

```
data(datasetname)
```

where,

datasetname argument is the name of the dataset to be read.

The following example illustrates the loading of a matrix. The `data()` function lists all the available datasets of the loaded package. The ' > Orange ' command reads and displays the content of the dataset, 'Orange' into the workspace.

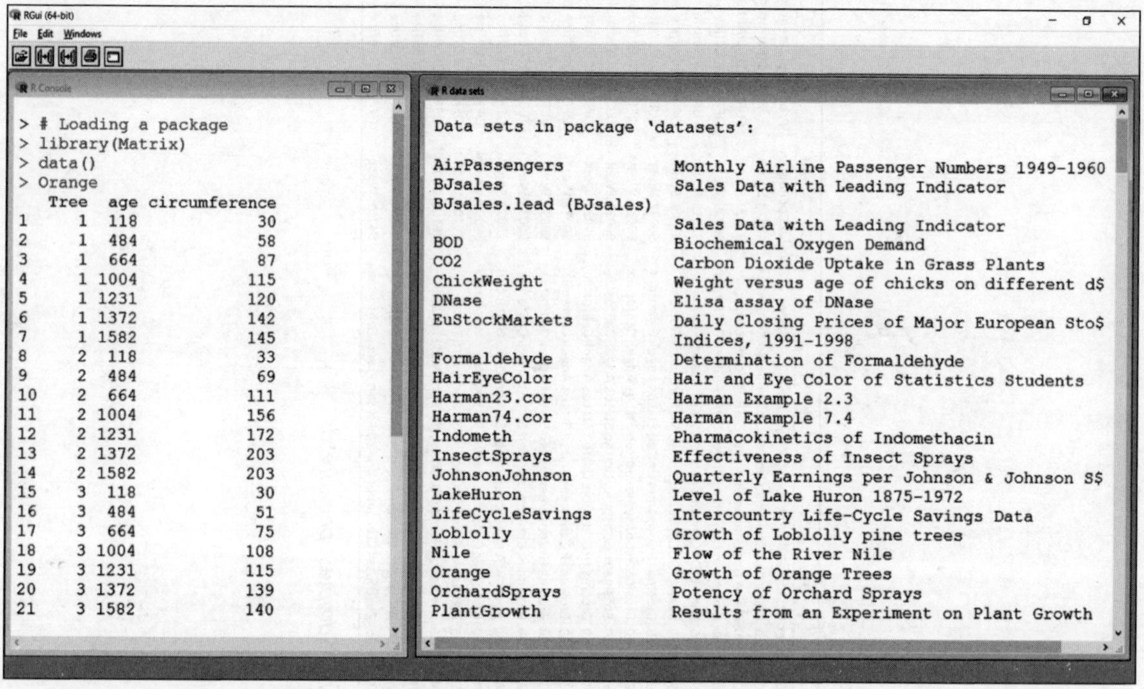

FIGURE 3.31 *Reading data from packages*

3.13.3 Reading Data from Web/APIs

Nowadays most business organisations are using the Internet and cloud services for storing data. This online dataset is directly accessible through packages and application programming interfaces (APIs). Different packages are available in R for reading from online datasets. Refer to Table 3.6 to view some packages.

TABLE 3.6 Packages for reading web data

Packages	*Description*	*Download Link*
RCurl	The package permits download of files from the web server and post forms.	https://cran.r-project.org/web/packages/RCurl/index.html
Google Prediction API	It allows uploading of data to Google storage and then training them for Google Prediction API.	http://code.google.com/p/r-google-predictionapi-v121
Infochimps	The package provides the functions for accessing all API.	http://api.infochimps.com
HttpRequest	The package reads the web data with the help of an HTTP request protocol and implements the GET, POST request.	https://cran.r-project.org/web/packages/httpRequest/index.html
WDI	The package reads all World Bank data.	http://cransprojectorg/web/packages/WD1/index.html
XML	The package reads and creates an XML and HTML document with the help of an HTTP or FTP protocol.	http://cransprojectorg/web/packages/XML/index.html
Quantmod	The package reads finance data from Yahoo finance.	http://crans-projectorg/web/packages/quantmodfindex.html
ScrapeR	The package reads online data.	http://crans-projectorg/web/packages/scrapeR/index.html

The following example illustrates web scraping. Web scraping extracts data from any webpage of a website. Here package 'RCurl' is used for web scraping (Figure 3.32). At first, the package, 'RCurl' is imported into the workspace and then `getURL()` function of the package, 'RCurl' takes the required webpage. Now `htmlTreeParse()` function parses the content of the webpage.

3.13.4 Reading a JSON (Java Script Object Notation) Document

Step 1: Install rjson package.

```
> install.packages("rjson")
Installing package into 'C:/Users/seema_acharya/Documents/R/win-
library/3.2'(as 'lib' is unspecified)
trying URL 'https://cran.hafro.is/bin/windows/contrib/3.2/
rjson_0.2.15.zip'
Content type 'application/zip' length 493614 bytes (482 KB)
downloaded 482 KB

package 'rjson' successfully unpacked and MD5 sums checked
```

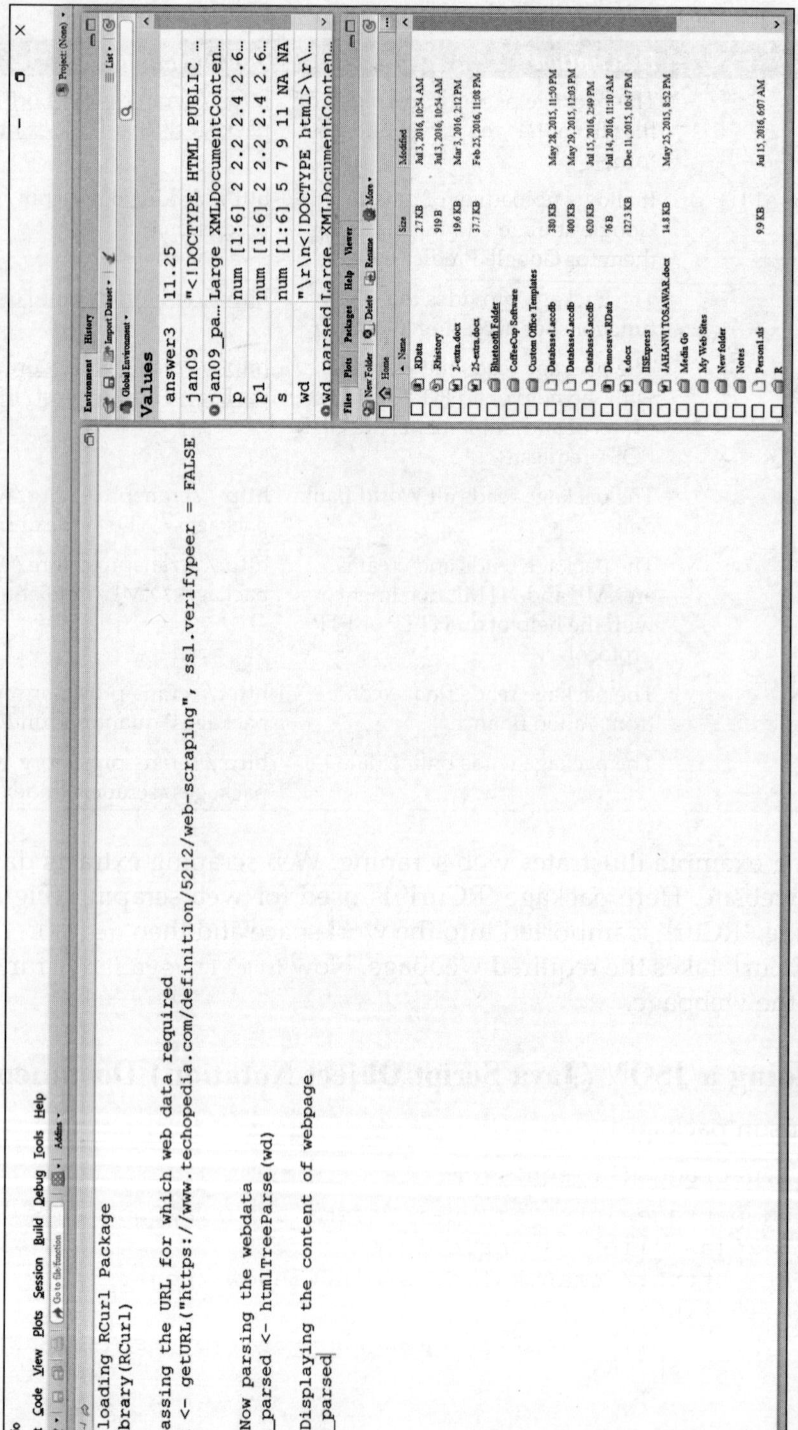

FIGURE 3.32 *Reading web data using the 'RCurl' package*

Step 2: Input data.
Store the data given below in a text file ('D:/Jsondoc.json'). Ensure that the file is saved with an extension of .json

```
{
   'EMPID':['1001','2001','3001','4001','5001','6001','7001','8001'
],
   'Name':['Ricky','Danny','Mitchelle','Ryan','Gerry','Nonita','Sim
on','Gallop' ],
   'Dept': ['IT','Operations','IT','HR','Finance','IT','Operations'
,'Finance']
}
```

A JSON document begins and ends with a curly brace ({}). A JSON document is a set of key value pairs. Each key:value pair is delimited using ',' as a delimiter.

Step 3: Read the JSON file, 'd:/Jsondoc.json'.

```
> output <- fromJSON(file = "d:/Jsondoc.json")
> output
$EMPID
[1] "1001"  "2001"  "3001"  "4001"  "5001"  "6001"  "7001"  "8001"

$Name
[1]  "Ricky"   "Danny"   "Mitchelle"   "Ryan"   "Gerry"   "Nonita"
[7]  "Simon"   "Gallop"

$Dept
[1]  "IT"        "Operations"  "IT"          "HR"          "Finance"
[6]  "IT"        "Operations"  "Finance"
```

Step 4: Convert JSON to a data frame.

```
> JSONDataFrame <- as.data.frame(output)
```

Display the content of the data frame, 'output'.

```
>  JSONDataFrame
   EMPID          Name         Dept
1   1001         Ricky           IT
2   2001         Danny   Operations
3   3001     Mitchelle           IT
4   4001          Ryan           HR
5   5001         Gerry      Finance
6   6001        Nonita           IT
7   7001         Simon   Operations
8   8001        Gallop      Finance
```

3.13.5 Reading an XML File

Step 1: Install an XML package.

```
> install.packages("XML")
Installing package into 'C:/Users/seema_acharya/Documents/R/win-library/3.2'(as 'lib' is unspecified)
trying URL 'https://cran.hafro.is/bin/windows/contrib/3.2/XML_3.98-1.3.zip'
Content type 'application/zip' length 4299803 bytes (4.1 MB)
downloaded 4.1 MB

package 'XML' successfully unpacked and MD5 sums checked
```

Step 2: Input data.
Store the data below in a text file (XMLFile.xml in the D: drive). Ensure that the file is saved with an extension of .xml.

```
<RECORDS>
   <EMPLOYEE>
      <EMPID>1001</EMPID>
      <EMPNAME>Merrilyn</EMPNAME>
      <SKILLS>MongoDB</SKILLS>
      <DEPT>Computer Science</DEPT>
   </EMPLOYEE>

   <EMPLOYEE>
      <EMPID>1002</EMPID>
      <EMPNAME>Ramya</EMPNAME>
      <SKILLS>People Management</SKILLS>
      <DEPT>Human Resources</DEPT>
   </EMPLOYEE>

   <EMPLOYEE>
      <EMPID>1003</EMPID>
      <EMPNAME>Fedora</EMPNAME>
      <SKILLS>Recruitment</SKILLS>
      <DEPT>Human Resources</DEPT>
   </EMPLOYEE>
</RECORDS>
```

Reading an XML File

The xml file is read in R using the function **`xmlParse()`**. It is stored as a list in R.

Step 1: Begin by loading the required packages.

```
> library("XML")
Warning message:
package 'XML' was built under R version 3.2.3
> library ("methods")
> output <- xmlParse(file = "d:/XMLFile.xml")

> print(output)
<?xml version="1.0"?>
<RECORDS>
     <EMPLOYEE>
          <EMPID>1001</EMPID>
          <EMPNAME>Merrilyn</EMPNAME>
          <SKILLS>MongoDB</SKILLS>
          <DEPT>ComputerScience</DEPT>
     </EMPLOYEE>
     <EMPLOYEE>
          <EMPID>1002</EMPID>
          <EMPNAME>Ramya</EMPNAME>
          <SKILLS>PeopleManagement</SKILLS>
          <DEPT>HumanResources</DEPT>
     </EMPLOYEE>
     <EMPLOYEE>
          <EMPID>1003</EMPID>
          <EMPNAME>Fedora</EMPNAME>
          <SKILLS>Recruitment</SKILLS>
          <DEPT>HumanResources</DEPT>
     </EMPLOYEE>
</RECORDS>
```

Step 2: Extract the root node from the XML file.

```
> rootnode <- xmlRoot(output)
```

Find the number of nodes in the root.

```
> rootsize <- xmlSize(rootnode)
> rootsize
[1]  3
```

Let us display the details of the first node.

```
> print (rootnode[1])
$EMPLOYEE
<EMPLOYEE>
     <EMPID>1001</EMPID>
     <EMPNAME>Merrilyn</EMPNAME>
     <SKILLS>MongoDB</SKILLS>
     <DEPT>ComputerScience</DEPT>
</EMPLOYEE>
attr(, "class")
[1] "XMLInternalNodeList"  "XMLNodeList"
```

Let us display the details of the first element of the first node.

```
> print(rootnode[[1]][[1]])
<EMPID>1001</EMPID>
```

Let us display the details of the third element of the first node.

```
> print(rootnode[[1]][[3]])
<SKILLS>MongoDB</SKILLS>
```

Next, display the details of the third element of the second node.

```
> print(rootnode[[2]][[3]])
<SKILLS>PeopleManagement</SKILLS>
```

We can also display the value of 2nd element of the first node.

```
> output <-xmlValue(rootnode[[1]][[2]])
> output
[1] "Merrilyn"
```

Step 3: Convert the input xml file to a data frame using the xmlToDataFrame function.

```
> xmldataframe <- xmlToDataFrame("d:/XMLFile.xml")
```

Display the output of the data frame.

```
>   xmldataframe
    EMPID    EMPNAME             SKILLS             DEPT
1    1001    Merrilyn           MongoDB  ComputerScience
2    1002       Ramya  PeopleMananement   HumanResources
3    1003      Fedora       Recruitment   HumanResources
```

Check Your Understanding

1. What is a CSV file?

Ans: A CSV file uses .csv extension and stores data in a table structure format in any plain text.

2. What is the use of `read.csv()` function?

Ans: A `read.csv()` function reads data from CSV files.

3. What is the use of `read.table()` function?

Ans: A `read.table()` function reads data from text files or CSV files.

4. What is the use of `read.xlsx()` function?

Ans: A `read.xlsx()` is an inbuilt function of 'xlsx' package for reading Excel files.

5. What is a package?

Ans: A package is a collection of functions and datasets. In R, many packages are available for doing different types of operations.

6. What is the use of the `library()` function?

Ans: The `library()` function loads packages into the R workspace. It is compulsory to import packages before reading the available dataset of that package.

7. What is the use of `data()` function?

Ans: The `data()` function lists all the available datasets of the loaded packages into the R workspace.

8. List five R packages for accessing web data.

Ans: Different packages are available in R for reading from an online dataset. These are:

- RCurl
- Google Prediction API
- WDI
- XML
- ScrapeR

9. What is web scraping?

Ans: Web scraping extracts data from any web page of a website.

3.14 Comparison of R GUIs for Data Input

R is mainly used for statistical analytical data processing. Analytical data processing needs a large dataset that is stored in a tabular form. Sometimes it is difficult to use inbuilt functions of R for doing such analytical data processing operations in R console. Hence, to overcome this problem, GUI is developed for R.

Graphical user interface is a graphical medium through which users interact with the language or perform operations. Different GUIs are available for data input in R. Each GUI has its own features. Table 3.7 describes some of the most popular R GUIs.

TABLE 3.7 Some popular R GUIs

GUI Name	*Description*	*Download Weblink*
RCommander (Rcmdr)	• RCommander was developed by John Fox and licensed under the GNU public license. • It comes with many plug-ins and has a very simple interface. • Users can install it like other packages of R within language.	http://socserv.mcmaster.ca/jfox/Misc/Rcmdr/ Or https://cran.r-project.org/web/packages/Rcmdr/index.html
Rattle	• Dr. Graham Williams developed the Rattle GUI package written in R. • Data mining operation is the main application area of Rattle. • It offers statistical analysis, validation, testing and other operations.	http://rattle.togaware.com/ Or http://rattle.togaware.com/rattle-install-mswindows.html
RKWard	• RKWard community developed the RKWard package. • It provides a transparent front end and supports different features for doing analytical operations in R. • It supports different platforms, such as Windows, Linux, BSD, and OS X.	https://rkward.kde.org/ Or http://download.kde.org/stable/rkward/0.6.5/win32/install_rkward_0.6.5.exe
JGR (Java GUI for R)	• Markus Helbig, Simon Urbanek, and lan Fellows developed JGR. • JGR is a universal GUI for R that supports cross platform. • Users can use it as a replacement for the default R GUI on Windows.	http://www.rforge.net/JGR/ Or https://cran.r-project.org/web/packages/JGR/
Deducer	• Deducer is another simple GUI that has a menu system for doing common data operations, analytical processing and other operations. • It is mainly designed to use it with the Java-based R Console [JGR].	http://www.deducer.org/pmwiki/pmwiki.php?n=Main.DeducerManual Or http://www.deducer.org/pmwiki/index.php?n=Main.DownloadingAndInstallingDeducer

Figure 3.33 shows the official screenshot of the RCommander (Rcmdr) GUI that is available in R.

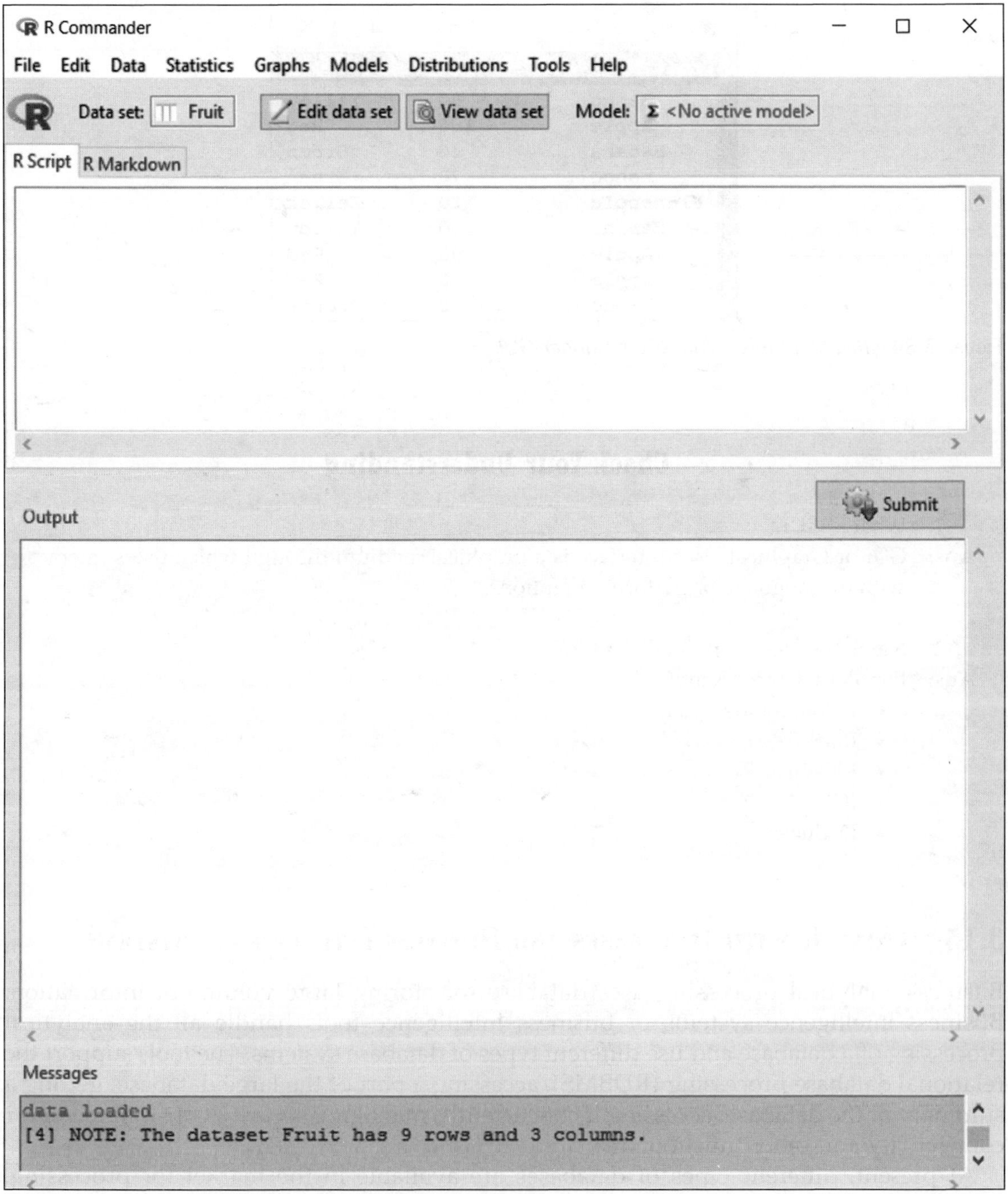

FIGURE 3.33 *RCommander GUI*

Figure 3.34 illustrates table, 'Fruit.csv' through Rcmdr GUI.

Fruit

	Fruit.Name	Fruit.Price	Fruit.Color
1	Mango	80	Yellow
2	Apple	100	Red
3	Banana	40	Green
4	Mango	70	Green
5	Pienapple	120	Yellow
6	Banana	50	Yellow
7	Apple	90	Red
8	Apple	110	Red
9	Mango	90	Orange

FIGURE 3.34 *Reading table using RCommander GUI*

Check Your Understanding

1. What is GUI?

Ans: GUI or Graphical User Interface is a graphical medium through which users interact with the language or perform operations.

2. Name the most popular GUIs for R.

Ans: Popular GUIs for R are:

- RCommander (Rcmdr)
- Rattle
- RKWard
- JGR
- Deducer

3.15 Using R with Databases and Business Intelligence Systems

Business analytical processing uses database for storing large volume of information. Business intelligence systems or business intelligence tools handle all the analytical processing of a database and use different types of database systems. The tools support the relational database processing (RDBMS), accessing a part of the large database, getting a summary of the database, accessing it concurrently, managing security, constraints, server connectivity and other functionality.

At present, different types of databases are available in the market for processing. They have many inbuilt tools, GUIs and other inbuilt functions through which database processing becomes easy. In this section, you will learn about database connection with SQL, MySQL, PostGreSQL and SQL Lite database as R provides inbuilt packages to access all of these. With the help of these packages, users can easily access a database since all the packages follow the same steps for accessing data from the database. In this section, you will go through a brief introduction on Jaspersoft and Pentaho with R.

3.15.1 RODBC

RODBC[1] is a package of languages that interacts with a database. Michael Lapsley and Brian Ripley developed this package.

RODBC helps in accessing databases such as MS Access and Microsoft SQL Server through an ODBC interface. Its package has many inbuilt functions for performing database operations on the database. Table 3.8 describes some major functions of RODBC packages used in database connectivity.

TABLE 3.8 Major functions of RODBC

Function	*Description*
`odbcConnect(dsn, uid= '', pwd= '')` where, dsn is domain name server, uid is the user ID and pwd is the password.	The function opens a connection to an ODBC database.
`sqlFetch(sqltable)` where, sqltable is name of the SQL table.	The function reads a table from an ODBC database into a data frame.
`sqlQuery(query)` where, query is the SQL query.	The function takes a query, sends to an ODBC database and returns its result.
`sqlSave(dataframe, tablename= 'sqltable')` where, data frame defines the data frame object and tablename argument is the name of the table.	The function writes or updates a data frame to a table in the ODBC database.
`sqlDrop(sqltable)` where, sqltable is the name of the SQL table.	The function removes a table from the ODBC database.
`odbcclose()`	The function closes the open connection.

Here is a sample code where package RODBC is used for reading data from a database.

```
># importing package
> library(RODBC)
> connect1 <- odbcConnect(dsn = 'servername', uid= '', pwd= '')
#Open connection
> query1 <- 'Select * from lib.table where…'
> Demodb <- sqlQuery(connect1, query1, errors = TRUE)
> odbcClose(connection)  #Close the connection
```

[1] To download RODBC—https://cran.r-project.org/web/packages/RODBC/index.html

3.15.2 Using MySQL and R

MySQL is an open source SQL database system. It is a small-sized popular database that is available for free download. For accessing MySQL database, users need to install the MySQL database system on their computers. MySQL database can be downloaded and installed from its official website.

R also provides a package, 'RMySQL' used for accessing the database from the MySQL database. Like other packages, RMySQL[2] has many inbuilt functions for interacting with a database.

Table 3.9 describes some major functions of RMySQL packages used in database connectivity.

TABLE 3.9 Major functions of RMySQL

Function	*Description*
`dbConnect(MySQL(), uid= '', pwd= '', dbname = '',…)` where, `MySQL()` is MySQL driver, uid is the user ID, pwd is the password and dbname is the database name.	The function opens a connection to the MySQL database.
`dbDisconnect(connectionname)` where, Connectionname defines the name of the connection.	The function closes the open connection.
`dbSendQuery(connectionname, sql)` where, connectionname defines the name of the connection.	The function runs the SQL queries of the open connection.
`dbListTables(connectionname)` where, connectionname defines the name of the connection.	The function lists the tables of the database of the open connection.
`dbWriteTable(connectionname, name = 'table name', value = data.frame.name)` where, connectionname defines the name of the connection.	The function creates the table and alternatively writes or updates a data frame in the database.

A sample code to illustrate the use of RMySQL for reading data from a database is given below.

```
># importing package
> library(RMySQL)
> connectm <- odbcConnect(MySQL(), uid= '', pwd= '',dbname = '',
host = '') #Open connection 'connectm'
> querym <- 'Select * from lib.table where…'
> Demom<- dbSendQuery(connectm, querym)
>dbDisconnect(connectm)  #Close the connection 'connect'
```

[2] To download RMySQL—https://cran.r-project.org/web/packages/RMySQL/

3.15.3 Using PostgreSQL and R

PostgreSQL is an open source and customisable SQL database system. After MySQL, PostgreSQL database is used for business analytical processing. For accessing the PostgreSQL database, users need to install the PostgreSQL database system on their computer system. Please note that it requires a server. Users can get a server on rent, download and install the MySQL database from its official website.[3]

R has a package, 'RPostgreSQL' that is used for accessing the database from the PostgreSQL database. Like other packages, RPostgreSQL[4] has many inbuilt functions for interacting with its database.

Table 3.10 describes open and close functions of RPostgreSQL packages used in database connectivity.

TABLE 3.10 Major functions of the RPostgreSQL

Function	*Description*
`dbConnect(driverobject, uid= '', pwd= '', dbname = '',...)` where, driverobject is an object of database driver, uid is the user ID, pwd is the password and dbname is the database name.	The function opens a connection to an RPostgreSQL database.
`dbDisconnect(connectionname)` where, Connectionname defines the name of the connection.	The function closes the open connection.

3.15.4 Using SQLite and R

SQLite is a server-less, self-contained, transactional and zero-configuration SQL database system. It is an embedded SQL database engine that does not require any server, due to which it is called a serverless database. The database also supports all business analytical data processing.

R has an RSQLite package that is used for accessing a database from the SQLite database. The RSQLite[5] has many inbuilt functions for working with the database.

Like other packages used for accessing a database, as explained in the previous sections, users can use the same methods—`dbconnect()` and `dbDisconnect()` for opening and closing the connection from the SQLite database, respectively. The only difference here is that users have to pass the SQLite database driver object in the `dbConnect()` function.

[3] https://www.postgresql.org/download/windows/

[4] To download RPostgreSQL—https://cran.r-project.org/web/packages/RPostgreSQL/index.html

[5] Users can use the following link for downloading RSQLite—https://cran.r-project.org/web/packages/RSQLite/index.html

3.15.5 Using JasperDB and R

JasperDB is another open source database system integrated with R. It was developed by the Jaspersoft community. It provides many business intelligence tools for analytical business processing. A Java library interface is used between JasperDB and R. It is called 'RevoConnectR for JasperReports Server'. The dashboard of the JasperReports Server provides many features through which R charts, an output of the RevoDeploy R, etc., are easily accessible.

Like other packages, JasperDB has a package or web service framework called 'RevoDeployR' developed by Revolution Analytics. RevoDeploy R[6] provides a set of web services with security features, scripts, APIs and libraries in a single server. It easily integrates with the dynamic R-based computations into web applications.

3.15.6 Using Pentaho and R

Pentaho is one of the most famous companies in the data integration field that develops different products and provides services for big data deployment and business analytics. The company provides different open source-based and enterprise-class platforms. Pentaho Data Integration (PDI) is one of the products of Pentaho[7] used for accessing database and analytical data processing. It prepares and integrates data for creating a perfect picture of any business. The tool provides accurate and analytics-ready data reports to the end users, eliminates the coding complexity and uses big data in one place.

R Script Executor is one of the inbuilt tools of the PDI tool for establishing a relationship between R and Pentaho Data Integration. Through R Script Executor, users can access data and perform analytical data operations. If users have R in their system already, then they just need to install PDI from its official website. The users need to configure environment variables, Spoon, DI Server, and Cluster nodes as well.

Although users can try PDI and transform a database using R Script Executor, PDI is a paid tool for doing analytical data integration operation. The complete installation process of the R Script Executor is available at http://wiki.pentaho.com/display/EAI/R+script+executor

Just Remember

During database access from MySQL, PostGreSQL and SQL Lite, users can use the same functions if their own driver object passes the same. For executing SQL queries, users can deploy the same functions for all the three databases.

[6] Users can download from the following link—http://community.jaspersoft.com/wiki/installation-steps-installer-distribution

[7] To download the Pentaho data integration tool—http://www.pentaho.com/download

Check Your Understanding

1. What is the RODBC?

Ans: RODBC is a package of R that interacts with a database. It provides database access to MS Access and Microsoft SQL server through an ODBC interface.

2. What is MySQL?

Ans: MySQL is an open source SQL database system. It is an Oracle product. MySQL is a popular small-sized database that is available for free download.

3. What is PostgreSQL?

Ans: PostgreSQL is another open source and customisable SQL database system. After MySQL, PostgreSQL database is used for business analytical processing.

4. What is RSQLite?

Ans: RSQLite is a package of R for accessing a database from the SQLite database.

5. What is RevoDeploy R?

Ans: RevoDeploy R provides a set of web services with security features, scripts, APIs and libraries for R in a single server.

6. What is the R Script Executor?

Ans: R Script Executor is one of the inbuilt tools of the Pentaho Data Integration tool for establishing the relationship between R and Pentaho Data Integration.

Case Study

Log Analysis

A log file is a file that stores events that occur in an operating system such as any source run in the system, messaging unit's different ways of communication, etc. Log files keep logs to be read in future, if required.

A transaction log is a file for communication between a server and users of that system or server or a data collection method that automatically captures the types, content or time of transaction made by a person from a terminal within that system. In web searches, a transaction log file is created which is an electronic record between interactions that have occurred during a search index between the web search engine and users searching for getting any information on that web.

(Continued)

Case Study

Many operating systems, software frameworks and progress include a logging system. It is easy for the reader or user to generate their own customised reports using R that can automatically analyse Apache log files and create reports automatically as compared to other software. Nowadays, R has become one of the most popular and powerful tool that can generate a model based on which, the requirements of the user can be tracked and searched.

Types of Log Files

Event Logs

Event logs record the events that are taking place in the execution of any system in order to provide an audit that can be used to enable the activities of the system and to diagnose problems or error in the system or servers. They are essential to analyse the activities of complex systems, particularly in the case of applications with little user interactions.

Transaction Logs

Every database system maintains some kind of transaction log which is not mainly stored as an audit trail for later analysis, and is not intended to be human-readable. These logs record changes to the stored data to allow database recovery from any failure or any other data error/loss and maintenance of the stored data in a consistent state.

Message Logs

In these types of log files, we can see multiple types of logs like the Internet Relay Chat (IRC), messaging programs, peer-to-peer file sharing clients with chat functions and multiplayer games commonly having the ability to automatically log textual communication, i.e. both public and private chat messages between users. Message logs may be referred to the third-party log storages from different channels. It builds a unique collective intelligence model where Rtool is the best tool to analyse the data and provide the model under any prediction/recommendations algorithms.

Internet Relay Chat (IRC)

Internet Relay Chat log files contain software and message logs. Message logs often include system/server messages and entries related to any resource which interacts with the servers. The user does some changes in the message logs by making them more like a combined message/event log file of the channel in question or for updating any information related to them. These are used to set the profile to access their details and enable the basic details. However, such a log is not comparable to a true IRC server event log file as it

(Continued)

Case Study

only records user-visible events for the period the user spent being connected to a certain channel.

Instant messaging (IM)

Instant messaging and VoIP chats often offer the chance to store encrypted log files to enhance the user's privacy to set the logs related to any user in the server/system as per the need of users. In this log file, the user can set priorities in the server files to set their needs and preferences. These logs require a password to be decrypted and viewed. These logs are often handled by the respective user-friendly application that is used in mobile application for getting information from the user and to check the interest of the users.

Transaction Log Analysis

Data stored in transaction logs of web search engines, intranets, and websites can provide valuable information into the understanding of information searching process of online searchers. This understanding can enlighten information designed system, interface development and devise the information architecture for content collections. The main role of these log files is to read the data provided by the user to get more information from them and set the records to identify the role and interest of different users. This is the main log files with the help of which we can track user preferences and their visits based on any transaction that they had done in the past.

Advantages of Rtool on Log File Analysis

Although R is not an easy to learn language, it has many advantages such as the fact that it can be used in UNIX scripts, it has several packages (CRAN) and outstanding graphical capabilities. It also has the ability to process lots of data with advanced statistical capabilities and connect to a database, making it one of the most powerful programming languages.

Getting the Data

Before being able to read the log file data, we must first import that data into R. The good thing is that R can parse log file without requiring any other additional work from the user. So, reading a Log file named log.log is as simple as executing the following:

```
> LOGS - read.table('log.log', sep=' ', header=F)
```

After executing the `read.table()` command, the logs variable holds all the information from log data from the log.log file. The head (logs) command illusrates the first few lines from the log variables to get an idea of how we are going to store this kind of data in R.

(Continued)

Case Study

Analysing the Data

Getting the data in R is not difficult for any user who has worked with R. However, the most important part is analysing the data. The most useful command we can run on a dataset with numeric values is the `summary()` command. The `summary()` command can give us better understanding of the output of the summary of the data.

By running the `summary()` command, we will get:

- *Min:* This is the minimum value of the whole dataset.
- *Median:* It is an element that divides the dataset into two subsets with the same number of elements. If the dataset has an odd number of elements, the median is part of the dataset of elements. If the dataset has an even number of elements, then the median is the mean values of the two center elements of the dataset. The median is the mean values of the two centre elements of the dataset.
- *Mean:* This is the mean value of the `data()`
- set, the sum of all values divided by the number of items in the datasets.
- *Max:* This is the maximum value found in the dataset.

Visualising the Data

To visualise the data, we need to run:

```
>barplot(table(logs[column name])
```

If we want to save the R bar plot to an image which is 1024 x 1024 pixels, we should run these lines in R commands:

```
>png('test.png', width=1024, height=1024)
>barplot(table(logs[,column name]))
>dev.off()
```

Similarly, we can visualise the number of requests per week day and per hour of the day.

The `pair()` command is especially useful since it gives a general overview of the data. Then `tempLOGS <- LOGS` command creates a copy of the LOGS variables into the tempLOGS variable.

Similarly, a user can implement and analyse other log files and get valuable output to generate any predictive model or recommendation engine.

Summary

- Analytical data processing is a part of business intelligence that includes relational database, data warehousing, data mining and report mining.
- Data formats, data quality, project scope and output results via stakeholder expectation management are the challenges faced during analytical data processing.
- Data input, processing, descriptive statistics, visualisation of data, report generation and output are the common steps of analytical data processing.

(Continued)

- R supports different types of data formats related to a database. With the help of import and export utility of R, any type of data can be imported and exported into R.
- A CSV file uses .csv extension and stores data in a table structure format in any plain text.
- A `read.csv()` function reads data from a CSV file.
- A `read.table()` function reads data from a text file or a CSV file.
- A package is a collection of functions and datasets. In R, many packages are available for doing different types of operations.
- A `read.xlsx()` is an inbuilt function of 'xlsx' package for reading Excel files.
- The `library()` function loads packages into the R workspace. It is compulsory to import the package before reading the available dataset of that package.
- The `data()` function lists all the available datasets of the loaded package in the R workspace.
- Different packages are available in R for reading from the online dataset or web data. RCurl, Google Prediction API, WDI, XML and ScrapeR are some such packages.
- Web scrapping extracts data from any webpage of a website.
- In R, NA (Not Available) represents the missing values and Inf (Infinite) represents the infinite values. R provides different functions that identify the missing values during processing.
- The `is.na()` function is used for checking missing values in an R object. The function checks an object and returns true if any data is missing.
- The `na.omit()` function is an inbuilt function of R that returns objects after removing missing values from the object.
- The `na.exclude()` function is an inbuilt function of R that returns objects after removing missing values from the object.
- The `na.fail()` function is an inbuilt function of R that detects an error, if any, and returns an object if an object does not contain any missing value.
- The operator 'as' converts the structure of one dataset into another structure in R.
- Exploring a dataset means displaying the data of a dataset in a different form.
- The `summary()` function is used for displaying the summary of a dataset.
- The `head()` function is an inbuilt data exploring function that displays the top rows according to a given value.
- The `tail()` function is an inbuilt data exploring function that displays the bottom rows according to a given value.
- The `merge()` function is an inbuilt function of R. The function combines the data frames by common columns or row names. It also follows the database join operations.
- Aggregate and group operations aggregate the data of specific variables of the dataset after the grouping of variable data.
- The `aggregate()` function is an inbuilt function of R. The function aggregates the data values. It also splits the data into groups after performing the required statistics function.
- The `tapply()` function is an inbuilt function of R. The function aggregates the data values into groups after performing the required statistics function.
- Manipulating text operation works on character strings and manipulating strings. There are many inbuilt string functions available in R that can manipulate text or string.
- The functions `read.csv()` and `read.table()` are used for reading datasets or tables into the R workspace.
- Graphical user interface (GUI) is a graphical medium through which users interact with a language or perform an operation.

(Continued)

- RCommander (Rcmdr), Rattle, RKWard, JGR, Deducer are some of the most popular GUIs for R.
- Business analytical processing uses a database for storing a large volume of information. Business intelligence systems or business intelligence tools handle all the business analytical processing of the database and uses different types of database systems.
- A database is a collection of values stored in a tabular form.
- RODBC is a package of R that interacts with a database. RODBC provides database accessing of MS Access and Microsoft SQL server through an ODBC interface.
- MySQL is an open source SQL database system and an Oracle product. MySQL is a popular small-sized database and is available for free download.
- RMySQL is a package of R that is used for accessing database from the MySQL database.
- PostgreSQL is another open source and customizable SQL database system. After MySQL, PostgreSQL database is used for business analytical processing.
- RPostgreSQL is a package of R for accessing database from the PostgreSQL database.
- SQLite is a server-less, self-contained, transactional, and zero-configuration SQL database system. It is an embedded SQL database engine that does not require any server, which is why it is called serverless database.
- RSQLite is a package of R for accessing database from the SQLite database.
- The 'RevoConnectR for JasperReports Server' is a java library interface between JasperReports Server and Revolution R Enterprise.
- The RevoDeploy R provides a set of web services for the security features, scripts, APIs, and libraries for the R into a single server.
- Pentaho Data Integration (PDI) is one of the products of Pentaho used for accessing the database and analytical data processing. It prepares and integrates data for creating a perfect picture of any business.
- R Script Executor is one of the inbuilt tools of the Pentaho Data Integration tool for establishing the relationship between R and Pentaho Data Integration.

Key Terms

- **CSV:** CSV is a file extension that stands for Comma Separated Values for creating CSV files.
- **Database:** A database is a collection of values stored in a tabular form.
- **GUI:** Graphical User Interface or GUI is a graphical medium through which users interact with a language or perform operations.
- **MySQL:** MySQL is an open source SQL database system and an Oracle product.
- **Package:** A package is a collection of functions and datasets.
- **PostgreSQL:** PostgreSQL is an open source and customisable SQL database system.
- **RODBC:** RODBC is a package of R that interacts with a database.
- **R Console:** R Console is a terminal where the command of R is executed.
- **RCommander:** RCommander is a famous R GUI.
- **RCurl:** RCurl is a package for reading data from online datasets or web data.
- **RMySQL:** RMySQL is a package of R for accessing database from the MySQL database.

- **RPostgreSQL:** RPostgreSQL is a package of R for accessing database from the PostgreSQL database.
- **RSQLite:** RSQLite is a package of R for accessing database from the SQLite database.
- **Spreadsheet:** A spreadsheet is a table that stores data in rows and columns.
- **SQLite:** SQLite is a server-less, self-contained, transactional and zero-configuration SQL database system.
- **Web scraping:** Web scraping extracts data from any webpage of a website.
- **Workspace:** Workspace is the current working environment of any software.

MULTIPLE CHOICE QUESTIONS

1. Which one of the following is not a challenge for analytical data processing?
   (a) Data Formats (b) Project Scope
   (c) Data Quality (d) Data Input
2. Which one of the following arguments of `read.table()` function contain logical values?
   (a) header (b) sep
   (c) filename (d) None of the above
3. Which one of the following functions loads a package into the R workspace?
   (a) `load()` (b) `library()`
   (c) `data()` (d) `install()`
4. Which one of the following functions lists all the available datasets of a loaded package into the R workspace?
   (a) `library()` (b) `data(datasetname)`
   (c) `data()` (d) `install()`
5. Which one of the following packages reads finance data from Yahoo finance?
   (a) Rcurl (b) XML
   (c) WDI (d) Quantmod
6. Which one of the following package reads all World Bank data?
   (a) RCurl (b) XML
   (c) WDI (d) Quantmod
7. Which one of the following packages is used for accessing web data?
   (a) ScrapeR (b) Stat
   (c) RSQLite (d) Matrix
8. Which one of the following commands converts a data frame into a matrix?
   (a) `as.Matrix(data frame)` (b) `.matrix(data frame)`
   (c) `as.numeric(data frame)` (d) None of the above
9. Which one of the following symbols is used by 'as' operator?
   (a) * (b) .
   (c) % (d) &

10. What is the correct output of the command `is.na( c(4,5,NA))`?
    (a) FALSE FALSE TRUE (b) FALSE TRUE TRUE
    (c) FALSE TRUE FALSE (d) TRUE FALSE TRUE
11. Which one of the following functions displays the variables of the given dataset?
    (a) `summary()` (b) `names()`
    (c) `str()` (d) `install()`
12. Which one of the following functions displays the structure of the given dataset?
    (a) `summary()` (b) `names()`
    (c) `str()` (d) `install()`
13. Which one of the following functions returns the number of categorical value after counting it?
    (a) `table(dataset$variablenames)` (b) `table(dataset.variablenames)`
    (c) `table(dataset)` (d) `table(variablenames)`
14. How many rows are returned by the `head()` or `tail()` function by default?
    (a) 1 (b) 4
    (c) 6 (d) 5
15. Which one of the following functions returns the bottom five rows of the dataset 'Mobile'?
    (a) `head(Mobile)` (b) `head(Mobile, 5)`
    (c) `tail(Mobile)` (d) `tail(Mobile,5)`
16. Which one of the following symbols is used for displaying specific rows and columns?
    (a) {} (b) *
    (c) [] (d) ()
17. Which one of the following functions contains the argument 'INDEX'?
    (a) `aggregate()` (b) `merge()`
    (c) `tapply()` (d) `sum()`
18. Which one of the following arguments is equal to 'Left Outer Join' operation in `merge()` function?
    (a) by.x (b) by.y
    (c) all.x (d) all.y
19. Which one of the following arguments is equal to 'Natural Join' operation in `merge()` function?
    (a) by.x (b) all.x
    (c) all (d) all.y
20. Which one of the following arguments is equal to 'Right Outer Join' operation in `merge()` function?
    (a) by.x (b) all.x
    (c) all (d) all.y

21. Which one of the following arguments is used for statistical operations?
    (a) INDEX (b) BY
    (c) FUN (d) ALL
22. What is the correct output of the command `substr('Programming Language',5,10)`?
    (a) 'rammin' (b) 'ramming'
    (c) 'amming' (d) Error
23. What is the correct output of the command `strsplit('Programming Language', ' ')`?
    (a) 'Programming Language' (b) 'Programming' 'Language'
    (c) Programming Language (d) Error
24. Which one of the following GUIs was developed by Dr. Graham Williams?
    (a) Rcmdr (b) Deducer
    (c) Rattle (d) JGR
25. Which one of the following GUIs is used with the Java-based R console (JGR)?
    (a) Rcmdr (b) Deducer
    (c) RKWard (d) Rattle

SHORT QUESTIONS

1. What do you mean by analytical data processing? What are the advantages of business analytics?
2. What is the difference between `read.csv()` and `read.table()` function?
3. How are packages in R read using the `library()` function?
4. What is the difference between the `library()` and `data()` functions?
5. How does web scraping use RCurl package?
6. What is the difference between `na.omit()` and `na.exclude()` functions?
7. What is the use of the 'as' operator in R? Explain with syntax and an example.
8. How can you explore a dataset in R?
9. What is the difference between `aggregate()` and `tapply()` functions?
10. What is the difference between `substr()` and `strsplit()` functions?
11. Which functions are used for describing a dataset? Explain with an example.
12. Which functions are used for describing variables? Explain with an example.

LONG QUESTIONS

1. Explain the methods of reading a dataset, along with an example and syntax.
2. Explain `read.xlsx()` function with an example and syntax.
3. Explain `data()` function with an example and syntax.
4. Explain the `is.na()` function with an example and syntax.
5. Explain the `na.omit()` function with an example and syntax.
6. Explain the `na.exclude()` function with an example and syntax.
7. Explain the `na.fail()` function with an example and syntax.
8. Explain the `na.pass()` function with an example and syntax.
9. Explain the `head()` function with an example and syntax.
10. Explain the `tail()` function with an example and syntax.
11. Explain the `merge()` function with an example and syntax.
12. Explain the `aggregate()` function with an example and syntax.
13. Explain the `tapply()` function with an example and syntax.
14. Explain text manipulation function with an example and syntax.
15. Explain RODBC package.
16. Explain RMySQL package.
17. Explain RPostGreSQL package.
18. Explain RSQLite package.
19. Explain Pentaho with R.
20. Create a table using a CSV file and read it into R using `read.csv()`.
21. Create a table and read it into R using `read.table()`.
22. Create a table in Excel and read it into R.
23. Create a data frame 'Book' that contains three vectors [Name, Price, Author]. Convert this data frame into a matrix and list the object using the operator 'as'.
24. Create a dataset or table ['Shop'] and apply all the data exploring functions on this table.
25. Create two data frames, 'Student' and 'Subject' with appropriate values. Merge both data frames using the merge function. Implement the left and right outer join operations on the data frames.
26. Create a dataset or table ['Smartphone'] that stores the mobile information [price, company name, model] of five different companies. Store at least 20 rows. Write the commands and find out the output for the following information:
    - Maximum price of mobile of each company

- Minimum price of mobile of each company
- Average price of mobile of each company
- Total price of mobile of each company

27. Create a dataset, 'Watch' and store the information about watches of four different companies. Explain all the steps of simple analytical data processing from input to output on this dataset.

Answers to MCQs:

1. (d)	2. (a)	3. (b)	4. (c)	5. (d)	6. (c)	7. (a)
8. (a)	9. (b)	10. (a)	11. (b)	12. (c)	13. (a)	14. (c)
15. (d)	16. (c)	17. (c)	18. (c)	19. (c)	20. (d)	21. (c)
22. (a)	23. (b)	24. (c)	25. (b)			

Chapter 4

Exploring Data in R

LEARNING OUTCOME

At the end of this chapter, you will be able to:

- **Store data of various types in frames, retrieve data from data frames, execute R functions such as `dim()`, `nrow()`, `ncol()`, `str()`, `summary()`, `names()`, `head()`, `tail()` and `edit()` to understand the data in data frames**
- **Load data from .csv, tab separated value file and table**
- **Handle missing values, invalid values and outliers**
- **Run descriptive statistics on the data, i.e. frequency, mean, median, mode, and standard deviation**
- **Create visualisations to promote deeper understanding of data**

4.1 Introduction

R provides interactive data visualisations to support analyses of statistical data. In R, data is usually stored in data frames owing to its ability to hold data of varied data types. These data frames are unlike the matrices, which can store data of only one type. In this chapter, we will begin by learning about data frames and gradually progress to read in data from .csv, tab separated value files, tables, etc., into data frames. Finally, we will explore data using various functions and interactive visualisations provided by R.

4.2 Data Frames

Imagine a data frame as something akin to a database table or an Excel spreadsheet. It has a specific number of columns, each of which is expected to contain values of a particular data type. It also has an indeterminate number of rows, i.e. sets of related values for each column.

Assume, we have been asked to store data of our employees (such as employee ID, name and the project that they are working on). We have been given three independent vectors, viz., namely, "EmpNo", "EmpName" and "ProjName" that holds details such as employee ids, employee names and project names, respectively.

```
>EmpNo <- c(1000, 1001, 1002, 1003, 1004)
>EmpName <- c("Jack", "Jane", "Margaritta", "Joe", "Dave")
>ProjName <- c("P01", "P02", "P03", "P04", "P05")
```

However, we need a data structure similar to a database table or an Excel spreadsheet that can bind all these details together. We create a data frame by the name, "Employee" to store all the three vectors together.

```
>Employee <- data.frame(EmpNo, EmpName, ProjName)
```

Let us print the content of the date frame, "Employee".

```
> Employee
  EmpNo    EmpName      ProjName
1 1000     Jack         P01
2 1001     Jane         P02
3 1002     Margaritta   P03
4 1003     Joe          P04
5 1004     Dave         P05
```

We have just created a data frame, "Employee" with data neatly organised into rows and the variable names serving as column names across the top.

4.2.1 Data Frame Access

There are two ways to access the content of data frames:

i. By providing the index number in square brackets
ii. By providing the column name as a string in double brackets.

By Providing the Index Number in Square Brackets

Example 1

To access the second column, "EmpName", we type the following command at the R prompt.

```
> Employee[2]
     EmpName
1       Jack
2       Jane
3 Margaritta
4        Joe
5       Dave
```

Example 2

To access the first and the second column, "EmpNo" and "EmpName", we type the following command at the R prompt.

```
> Employee[1:2]
  EmpNo    EmpName
1  1000       Jack
2  1001       Jane
3  1002 Margaritta
4  1003        Joe
5  1004       Dave
```

Example 3

```
> Employee [3,]
  EmpNo    EmpName     ProjName
3 1002     Margaritta  P03
```

Please notice the extra comma in the square bracket operator in the example. It is *not* a typo.

Example 4

Let us define row names for the rows in the data frame.

```
> row.names(Employee) <- c("Employee 1", "Employee 2", "Employee 3",
"Employee 4", "Employee 5")
> row.names (Employee)
[1] "Employee 1" "Employee 2" "Employee 3" "Employee 4" "Employee 5"
> Employee
           EmpNo     EmpName    ProjName
Employee 1  1000        Jack         P01
Employee 2  1001        Jane         P02
Employee 3  1002  Margaritta         P03
Employee 4  1003         Joe         P04
Employee 5  1004        Dave         P05
```

Let us retrieve a row by its name.

```
> Employee ["Employee 1",]
           EmpNo     EmpName    ProjName
Employee 1  1000        Jack         P01
```

Let us pack the row names in an index vector in order to retrieve multiple rows.

```
> Employee [c ("Employee 3", "Employee 5"),]
            EmpNo     EmpName    ProjName
Employee 3   1002  Margaritta         P03
Employee 5   1004        Dave         P05
```

By Providing the Column Name as a String in Double Brackets

```
> Employee [["EmpName"]]
[1]  Jack    Jane    Margaritta     Joe     Dave
Levels: Dave Jack Jane Joe Margaritta
```

Just to keep it simple (typing so many double brackets can get unwieldy at times), use the notation with the $ (dollar) sign.

```
> Employee$EmpName
[1]  Jack    Jane    Margaritta     Joe     Dave
Levels: Dave Jack Jane Joe Margaritta
```

To retrieve a data frame slice with the two columns, "EmpNo" and "ProjName", we pack the column names in an index vector inside the single square bracket operator.

```
> Employee[c("EmpNo", "ProjName")]
  EmpNo    ProjName
1  1000         P01
2  1001         P02
3  1002         P03
4  1003         P04
5  1004         P05
```

Let us add a new column to the data frame.

To add a new column, "EmpExpYears" to store the total number of years of experience that the employee has in the organisation, follow the steps given as follows:

```
> Employee$EmpExpYears <-c(5, 9, 6, 12, 7)
```

Print the contents of the date frame, "Employee" to verify the addition of the new column.

```
> Employee
  EmpNo      EmpName     ProjName      EmpExpYears
1  1000         Jack          P01                5
2  1001         Jane          P02                9
3  1002   Margaritta          P03                6
4  1003          Joe          P04               12
5  1004         Dave          P05                7
```

4.2.2 Ordering the Data Frames

Let us display the content of the data frame, "Employee" in ascending order of "EmpExpYears".

```
> Employee[order(Employee$EmpExpYears),]
  EmpNo    EmpName    ProjName    EmpExpYears
1  1000       Jack         P01              5
3  1002 Margaritta         P03              6
5  1004       Dave         P05              7
2  1001       Jane         P02              9
4  1003        Joe         P04             12
```

Use the syntax as shown next to display the content of the data frame, "Employee" in descending order of "EmpExpYears".

```
> Employee[order(-Employee$EmpExpYears),]
  EmpNo    EmpName    ProjName    EmpExpYears
4  1003        Joe         P04             12
2  1001       Jane         P02              9
5  1004       Dave         P05              7
3  1002 Margaritta         P03              6
1  1000       Jack         P01              5
```

4.3 R Functions for Understanding Data in Data Frames

We will explore the data held in the data frame with the help of the following R functions:

- `dim()`
  - `nrow()`
  - `ncol()`
- `str()`
- `summary()`
- `names()`
- `head()`
- `tail()`
- `edit()`

4.3.1 `dim()` Function

The `dim()` function is used to obtain the dimensions of a data frame. The output of this function returns the number of rows and columns.

```
> dim(Employee)
[1] 5 4
```

The data frame, "Employee" has 5 rows and 4 columns.

nrow() Function

The `nrow()` function returns the number of rows in a data frame.

```
> nrow(Employee)
[1] 5
```

The data frame, "Employee" has 5 rows.

ncol() Function

The `ncol()` function returns the number of columns in a data frame.

```
> ncol(Employee)
[1] 4
```

The data frame, "Employee" has 4 columns.

4.3.2 str() Function

The `str()` function compactly displays the internal structure of R objects. We will use it to display the internal structure of the dataset, "Employee".

```
> str (Employee)
'data.frame'  : 5 obs. of 4 variables:
$ EmpNo       : num 1000 1001 1002 1003 1004
$ EmpName     : Factor w/ 5 levels "Dave", "Jack", ..: 2 3 5 4 1
$ ProjName    : Factor w/ 5 levels "P01", "P02", "P03", ..: 1 2 3 4 5
$ EmpExpYears: num 5 9 6 12 7
```

4.3.3 summary() Function

We will use the `summary()` function to return result summaries for each column of the dataset.

```
> summary (Employee)
           EmpNo              EmpName    ProjName   EmpExpYears
Min.     : 1000    Dave          : 1    P01:1      Min.      :   5.0
1st Qu.  : 1001    Jack          : 1    P02:1      1st Qu.   :   6.0
Median   : 1002    Jane          : 1    P03:1      Median    :   7.0
Mean     : 1002    Joe           : 1    P04:1      Mean      :   7.8
3rd Qu.  : 1003    Margaritta    : 1    P05:1      3rd Qu.   :   9.0
Max.     : 1004                                   Max.      :  12.0
```

4.3.4 names() Function

The `names()` function returns the names of the objects. We will use the `names()` function to return the column headers for the dataset, "Employee".

```
> names (Employee)
[1]      "EmpNo"      "EmpName"    "ProjName"   "EmpExpYears"
```

In the example, names(Employee) returns the column headers of the dataset "Employee". The `str()` function helps in returning the basic structure of the dataset. This function provides an overall view of the dataset.

4.3.5 `head()` Function

The `head()` function is used to obtain the first *n* observations where *n* is set as 6 by default.

Examples

1. In this example, the value of *n* is set as 3 and hence, the resulting output would contain the first 3 observations of the dataset.

```
> head(Employee, n=3)
   EmpNo      EmpName  ProjName  EmpExpYears
1   1000         Jack       P01            5
2   1001         Jane       P02            9
3   1002   Margaritta       P03            6
```

2. Consider *x* as the total number of observations. In case of *any* negative values as input for *n* in the `head()` function, the output obtained is first *x+n* observations. In this example, *x*=5 and *n*= -2, then the number of observations returned will be $x + n = 5 + (-2) = 3$

```
> head(Employee, n=-2)
   EmpNo      EmpName  ProjName  EmpExpYears
1   1000         Jack       P01            5
2   1001         Jane       P02            9
3   1002   Margaritta       P03            6
```

4.3.6 `tail()` Function

The `tail()` function is used to obtain the last *n* observations where *n* is set as 6 by default.

```
> tail(Employee, n=3)
   EmpNo      EmpName  ProjName  EmpExpYears
3   1002   Margaritta       P03            6
4   1003          Joe       P04           12
5   1004         Dave       P05            7
```

Example

Consider the example, where the value of *n* is negative, and the output is returned by a simple sum up value of *x+n*. Here *x* = 5 and *n* =-2. When a negative input is given in the case of the `tail()` function, it returns the last x+*n* observations. The example given as follows returns the last 3 records from the dataset, "Employee".

```
> tail(Employee, n=-2)
     EmpNo      EmpName  ProjName  EmpExpYears
3     1002   Margaritta       P03            6
4     1003          Joe       P04           12
5     1004         Dave       P05            7
```

4.3.7 `edit()` Function

The `edit()` function will invoke the text editor on the R object. We will use the `edit()` function to open the dataset , "Employee" in the text editor.

```
> edit(Employee)
```

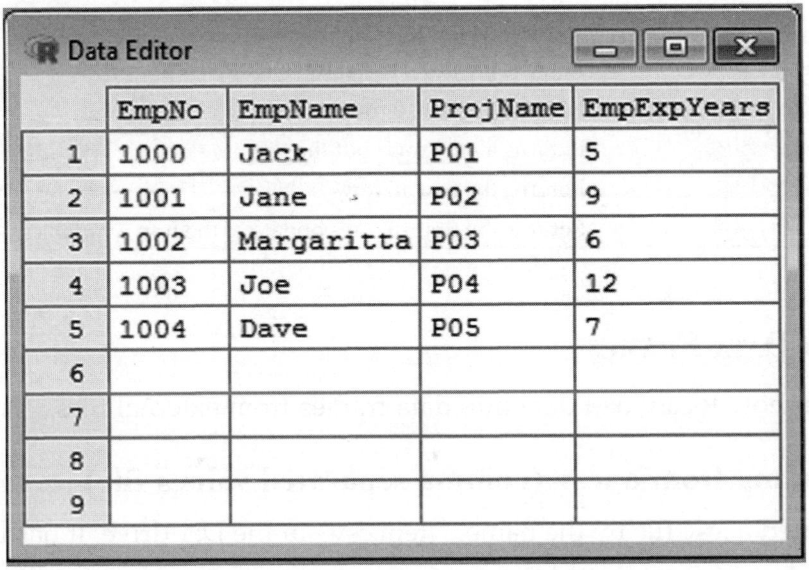

Data Editor

	EmpNo	EmpName	ProjName	EmpExpYears
1	1000	Jack	P01	5
2	1001	Jane	P02	9
3	1002	Margaritta	P03	6
4	1003	Joe	P04	12
5	1004	Dave	P05	7
6				
7				
8				
9				

To retrieve the first three rows (with all columns) from the dataset, "Employee", use the syntax given as follows:

```
> Employee[1:3,]
     EmpNo      EmpName  ProjName  EmpExpYears
1     1000         Jack       P01            5
2     1001         Jane       P02            9
3     1002   Margaritta       P03            6
```

To retrieve the first three rows (with the first two columns) from the dataset, "Employee", use the syntax given as follows:

```
> Employee[1:3, 1:2]
     EmpNo      EmpName
1     1000         Jack
2     1001         Jane
3     1002   Margaritta
```

TABLE 4.1 A brief summary of functions for exploring data in R

Function Name	*Description*
`nrow(x)`	Returns the number of rows
`ncol(x)`	Returns the number of columns
`str(mydata)`	Provides structure to a dataset
`summary(mydata)`	Provides basic descriptive statistics and frequencies
`edit(mydata)`	Opens the data editor
`names(mydata)`	Returns the list of variables in a dataset
`head(mydata)`	Returns the first *n* rows of a dataset. By default, *n* = 6
`head(mydata, n=10)`	Returns the first 10 rows of a dataset
`head(mydata, n= -10)`	Returns all the rows but the last 10
`tail(mydata)`	Returns the last *n* rows. By default, *n* = 6
`tail(mydata, n=10)`	Returns the last 10 rows
`tail(mydata, n= -10)`	Returns all the rows but the first 10
`mydata[1:10, ]`	Returns the first 10 rows
`mydata[1:10,1:3]`	Returns the first 10 rows of data of the first 3 variables

4.4 Load Data Frames

Let us look at how R can load data into data frames from external files.

4.4.1 Reading from a .csv (comma separated values file)

We have created a .csv file by the name, "item.csv" in the D:\ drive. It has the following content:

	A	B	C
1	**Itemcode**	**ItemCategory**	**ItemPrice**
2	I1001	Electronics	700
3	I1002	Desktop supplies	300
4	I1003	Office supplies	350

Let us load this file using the read.csv function.

```
> ItemDataFrame <- read.csv("D:/item.csv")
> ItemDataFrame
  Itemcode       ItemCategory  ItemPrice
1    I1001        Electronics        700
2    I1002   Desktop supplies        300
3    I1003    Office supplies        350
```

4.4.2 Subsetting Data Frame

To subset the data frame and display the details of only those items whose price is greater than or equal to 350.

```
> subset(ItemDataFrame, ItemPrice >=350)
  Itemcode        ItemCategory  ItemPrice
1    I1001         Electronics        700
3    I1003     Office supplies        350
```

To subset the data frame and display only the category to which the items belong (items whose price is greater than or equal to 350).

```
> subset(ItemDataFrame,ItemPrice >=350, select = c(ItemCategory))
      ItemCategory
1      Electronics
3 Office supplies
```

To subset the data frame and display only the items where the category is either "Office supplies" or "Desktop supplies".

```
> subset(ItemDataFrame, ItemCategory == "Office supplies" | ItemCat-
egory == "Desktop supplies")
  Itemcode        ItemCategory  ItemPrice
2    I1002    Desktop supplies        300
3    I1003     Office supplies        350
```

4.4.3 Reading from a Tab Separated Value File

For any file that uses a delimiter other than a comma, one can use the read.table command.

Example

We have created a tab separated file by the name, "item-tab-sep.txt" in the D:\ drive. It has the following content.

```
Itemcode       ItemQtyOnHand      ItemReorderLvl
I1001                     75                  25
I1002                     30                  25
I1003                     35                  25
```

Let us load this file using the read.table function. We will read the content from the file but will not store its content to a data frame.

```
> read.table("d:/item-tab-sep.txt",sep="\t")
        V1              V2                V3
1 Itemcode   ItemQtyOnHand    ItemReorderLvl
2    I1001              70                25
3    I1002              30                25
4    I1003              35                25
```

Notice the use of V1, V2 and V3 as column headings. It means that our specified column names, "Itemcode", ItemCategory" and "ItemPrice" are not considered. In other words, the first line is not automatically treated as a column header.

Let us modify the syntax, so that the first line is treated as a column header.

```
> read.table("d:/item-tab-sep.txt",sep="\t", header=TRUE)
  Itemcode     ItemQtyOnHand      ItemReorderLvl
1    I1001               70                   25
2    I1002               30                   25
3    I1003               35                   25
```

Now let us read the content of the specified file into the data frame, "ItemDataFrame".

```
> ItemDataFrame <- read.table("D:/item-tab-sep.txt",sep="\t",
header=TRUE)
> ItemDataFrame
  Itemcode     ItemQtyOnHand      ItemReorderLvl
1    I1001               70                   25
2    I1002               30                   25
3    I1003               35                   25
```

4.4.4 Reading from a Table

A data table can reside in a text file. The cells inside the table are separated by blank characters. An example of a table with 4 rows and 3 columns is given as follows:

1001	Physics	85
2001	Chemistry	87
3001	Mathematics	93
4001	English	84

Copy and paste the table in a file named "d:/mydata.txt" with a text editor and then load the data into the workspace with the function read.table.

```
> mydata = read.table("d:/mydata.txt")
> mydata
    V1          V2  V3
1 1001     Physics  85
2 2001   Chemistry  87
3 3001 Mathematics  93
4 4001     English  84
```

4.4.5 Merging Data Frames

Let us now attempt to merge two data frames using the merge function. The merge function takes an x frame (item.csv) and a y frame (item-tab-sep.txt) as arguments. By default, it joins the two frames on columns with the same name (the two "Itemcode" columns).

```
> csvitem <- read.csv("d:/item.csv")
> tabitem <- read.table("d:/item-tab-sep.txt",sep="\t",header=TRUE)
> merge (x=csvitem, y=tabitem)
  Itemcode      ItemCategory ItemPrice ItemQtyOnHand ItemReorderLvl
1    I1001       Electronics       700            70             25
2    I1002  Desktop supplies       300            30             25
3    I1003   Office supplies       350            35             25
```

4.5 Exploring Data

Data in R is a set of organised information. Statistical data type is more common in R, which is a set of observations where values for the variables are passed. These input variables are used in measuring, controlling or manipulating the results of a program. Each variable differs in size and type. R supports the following basic data types to explore:

- Integer
- Numeric
- Logical
- Character/string
- Factor
- Complex

Data types have been covered in Chapter 2. Based on the specific data characteristics in R, data can be explored in different ways. You will learn about these methods in the following section.

4.5.1 Exploratory Data Analysis

Exploratory data analysis (EDA) involves dataset analysis to summarise the main characteristics in the form of visual representations. Exploratory data analysis using R is an approach used to summarise and visualise the main characteristics of a dataset, which differs from initial data analysis. The main aim of EDA is to summarise and visualise the main characteristics of a dataset. It focuses on:

- Exploring data by understanding its structure and variables
- Developing an intuition about the dataset
- Considering how the dataset came into existence
- Deciding how to investigate by providing a formal statistical method
- Extending better insights about the dataset
- Formulating a hypothesis that leads to new data collection
- Handling any missing values
- Investigating with more formal statistical methods.

Some of the graphical techniques used by EDA are:

- Box plot
- Histogram
- Scatter plot
- Run chart
- Bar chart
- Density plots
- Pareto chart

Just Remember

In R, statistical data inputs are presented in a graphical form, which helps in improving insights gained from input data. The diagrams used in R are simple and can represent a large amount of data.

Check Your Understanding

1. Which function in R is used to obtain the values of dimension?

Ans: The `dim()` function is used to obtain the dimension of the dataset.

```
>dim(x)
[1] a b
```

where, *a* refers to the number of rows and *b* refers to the number of columns.

2. Which function in R is used to open the data editor?

Ans: The `edit(x)` function opens the data editor in R.

3. What is the default value of *n* in `head(mydata)` and `tail(mydata)` function?

Ans: The default value of *n* is 6.

4. State a few graphical techniques used by EDA in R.

Ans: The graphical techniques used by EDA in R are:

- Bar chart
- Histogram
- Scatter plot
- Density plot

4.6 Data Summary

Data summary in R can be obtained by using various R functions. Table 4.2 provides a brief overview of few R functions.

TABLE 4.2 Functions for obtaining data summary in R

Function Name	*Description*
`summary(x)`	Returns the min, max, median, and mean
`min(x)`	Returns the minimum value
`max(x)`	Returns the maximum value
`range(x)`	Returns the range of the given input
`mean(x)`	Returns the mean value
`median(x)`	Returns the median value
`mad(x)`	Returns the median absolute deviation value
`IQR(x)`	Returns the interquartile range
`quantile(x)`	Returns quartiles
`summary(x)`	Summarises the data frame
`apply(x,1,mean)`	Calculates the row mean value
`apply(x,2,mean)`	Calculates the column mean which is similar to the function of mean(x)

We will execute few R functions on the data set, "Employee". Let us begin by displaying the contents of the dataset, "Employee".

```
> Employee
   EmpNo       EmpName   ProjName   EmpExpYears
1   1000          Jack        P01             5
2   1001          Jane        P02             9
3   1002    Margaritta        P03             6
4   1003           Joe        P04            12
5   1004          Dave        P05             7
```

The summary(Employee[4]) function works on the fourth column, "EmpExpYears" and computes the minimum, 1st quartile, median, mean, 3rd quartile and maximum for its value.

```
> summary(Employee[4])
EmpExpYears
Min.    :  5.0
1st Qu. :  6.0
Median  :  7.0
Mean    :  7.8
3rd Qu. :  9.0
Max.    : 12.0
```

The min(Employee[4]) function works on the fourth column, "EmpExpYears" and determines the minimum value for this column.

```
> min(Employee[4])
[1] 5
```

The max(Employee[4]) function works on the fourth column, "EmpExpYears" and determines the maximum value for this column.

```
> max(Employee[4])
[1] 12
```

The range(Employee[4]) function works on the fourth column, "EmpExpYears" and determines the range of values for this column.

```
> range(Employee[4])
[1] 5 12
```

The Employee[,4] command at the R prompt displays the value of the column, "EmpExpYears" .

```
> Employee[,4]
[1] 5 9 6 12 7
```

The mean(Employee[,4]) function works on the fourth column, "EmpExpYears" and determines the mean value for this column.

```
> mean (Employee[,4])
[1] 7.8
```

The median(Employee[,4]) function works on the fourth column, "EmpExpYears" and determines the median value for this column.

```
> median(Employee[,4])
[1] 7
```

The mad(Employee[,4]) function returns the median absolute deviation value.

```
> mad (Employee[,4])
[1] 2.9652
```

The IQR(Employee[,4]) function returns the interquartile range.

```
> IQR (Employee[,4])
[1] 3
```

The quantile(Employee[,4]) function returns the quantile values for the column, "EmpExpYears".

```
> quantile(Employee[,4])
  0%   25%   50%   75%  100%
   5     6     7     9    12
```

The `sapply()` function is used to obtain the descriptive statistics with the specified input. With the use of this function, mean, var, min, max, sd, quantile and range can be determined.

The mean of the input data is found using:

```
sapply (sampledata, mean, na.rm=TRUE)
```

Similarly, other functions (such as mean, min, max, range and quantile) can be used with the `sapply()` function to obtain the desired output.

Consider the same data frame, Employee.

```
> sapply(Employee[4],mean)
EmpExpYears
  7.8

> sapply(Employee[4],min)
EmpExpYears
  5

> sapply(Employee[4],max)
EmpExpYears
  12

> sapply(Employee[4],range)
     EmpExpYears
[1,]           5
[2,]          12

> sapply(Employee[4],quantile)
     EmpExpYears
0%             5
25%            6
50%            7
75%            9
100%          12
```

TABLE 4.3 Function table to return the highest and lowest value in R matrix

Function Name	*Description*
`which.min()`	Returns the minimum position for each row in the matrix.
`which.max()`	Returns the maximum position for each row in the matrix.

```
> which.min(Employee$EmpExpYears)
[1] 1
```

At position 1, is the employee with the minimum years of experience, "5".

```
> which.max(Employee$EmpExpYears)
[1] 4
```

At position 4, is the employee with the maximum years of experience, "12".

For summarising data, there are three other ways to group the data based on some specific conditions or variables and subsequent to this, the `summary()` function can be applied. These are explained below.

- `ddply()` requires the "plyr" package

- `summariseBy()` requires doBy package
- `aggregate()` is included in base package of R.

A simple code to explain the `ddply()` function is:

```
data <- read.table(header= TRUE, text= 'no sex before after change
                                       1   M   54.2  5.2   -9.2
                                       2   F   63.2  61.0   1.1
                                       3   F   52    24.5   3.5
                                       4   F   25    55     2.5
                                       .
                                       .
                                       .
                                       .
                                       .
                                       .
                                       .
                                       54  M   54    45     1.2'
                                       )
```

When applying the `ddply()` function to the above input,

```
library(plyr)

#set the functions to run the length, mean, sd on the value based on
the "change" input for each group of inputs.

#Break down with the values of "no"

cdata <- ddply(data,c("no"),summarise,
      N=length(change),
     sd=sd(change),
mean=mean(change)
)
cdata
```

Output of the `ddply()` function is:

```
> no  N     sd    mean
   1  5     4.02  2.3
   2  14    5.5   2.1
   3  4     2.1   1.0
   .
   .
   .
   .
  54  9     2.0   0.9
```

4.7 Finding the Missing Values

In R, missing data is indicated as NA in the dataset, where NA refers to *"Not Available"*. It is neither a string nor a numeric value, but it is used to specify the missing data. Input vectors can be created with the missing values as follows:

```
x <- c(2,5,86,9,NA,45,3)
y <- c("red",NA,"NA")
```

In this case, *x* contains numeric values as the input. Here, NA can be used to avoid any errors or other numeric exceptions like infinity. In the second example, *y* contains the string values as the input. Here, the third value is a string 'NA' and the second value NA is a missing value. The function `is.na()` is used in R to identify the missing values. This function returns a Boolean value as either TRUE or FALSE.

```
> is.na(x)
[1] FALSE FALSE FALSE FALSE TRUE FALSE FALSE
```

```
> is.na(y)
[1] FALSE TRUE FALSE
```

The is.na function is used to find and create missing values.
`na.action` provides options for treating the missing data.
Possible `na.action` settings include:

- `na.omit, na.exclude`: This function returns the object by removing the missing values' observation.
- `na.pass`: This function returns object unchanged even with missing objects.
- `na.fail`: This function returns object if it has no missing values.

To enable the `na.action` in options, use getOption("na.action").

Examples

1. Populating the matrix with sample input values as follows:

```
> c <- as.data.frame (matrix(c(1:5,NA),ncol=2))
> c
  V1  V2
1  1   4
2  2   5
3  3  NA
```

`na.omit(c)` omits the NA missing values' row and returns the other object.

```
> na.omit(c)
  V1  V2
1  1   4
2  2   5
```

2. `na.exclude(c)` excludes the missing values and returns the object. A slight difference can be found in some residual and prediction functions.

```
> na.exclude(c)
  V1  V2
1  1   4
2  2   5
```

3. `na.pass(c)` returns the object unchanged along with the missing values.

```
> na.pass(c)
  V1  V2
1  1   4
2  2   5
3  3  NA
```

4. `na.fail(c)` returns an error when a missing value is found. It returns an object only when there is no missing value.

```
> na.fail(c)
Error in na.fail.default(c) : missing value in object
```

Basic commands that are used for finding missing data in the dataset are listed in Table 4.4.

TABLE 4.4 Function table for finding missing entities in a dataset in R

Function Name	*Description*

`sum(is.na(mydata))`
Example:
`> sum(is.na(c))`
`[1] 1`
	Number of missing data in dataset

`rowSums(is.na(data))`
Example:
`> rowSums(is.na(c));`
`[1] 0 0 1`
The third row has one missing value.
	Number of missing data per variable

`rowMeans(is.na(data))*length(data)`
Example:
`> rowMeans(is.na(c))*length(c)`
`[1] 0 0 1`
	Number of missing data per row

4.8 Invalid Values and Outliers

In R, special checks are conducted for handling invalid values. An invalid value can be NA, NaN, Inf or -Inf. Functions for these invalid values include `anyNA(x)` `anyInvalid(x)` and `is.invalid(x)`, where the value of x can be a vector, matrix or array. Here, `anyNA` function returns a TRUE value if the input has any Na or NaN values. Else, it returns a FALSE value. This function is equivalent to `any(is.na(x))`.

`anyInvalid` function returns a TRUE value, if the input has any invalid values. Else, it returns a FALSE value. This function is equivalent to `any(is.valid(x))`.

Unlike the other two functions, `is.invalid` returns an object corresponding to each input value. If the input is invalid, it returns TRUE, else it returns FALSE. This function is also equivalent to `(is.na(x) | is.infinite(x))`.

Few examples with the above functions are:

```
> anyNA(c(-9,NaN,9))
[1] TRUE

is.finite(c(-9, Inf,9))
> is.finite(c(-9, Inf,9))
[1] TRUE FALSE TRUE

is.infinite(c(-9, Inf,9))
> is.infinite(c(-9, Inf, 9))
[1] FALSE TRUE FALSE

is.nan(c(-9, Inf,9))
> is.nan(c(-9, Inf, 9))
[1] FALSE FALSE FALSE
> is.nan(c(-9, Inf, NaN))
[1] FALSE FALSE TRUE
```

The basic idea of invalid values and outliers can be explained with a simple example. Obtain the min, max, median mean, 1st quantile, 3rd quantile values using the `summary()` function.

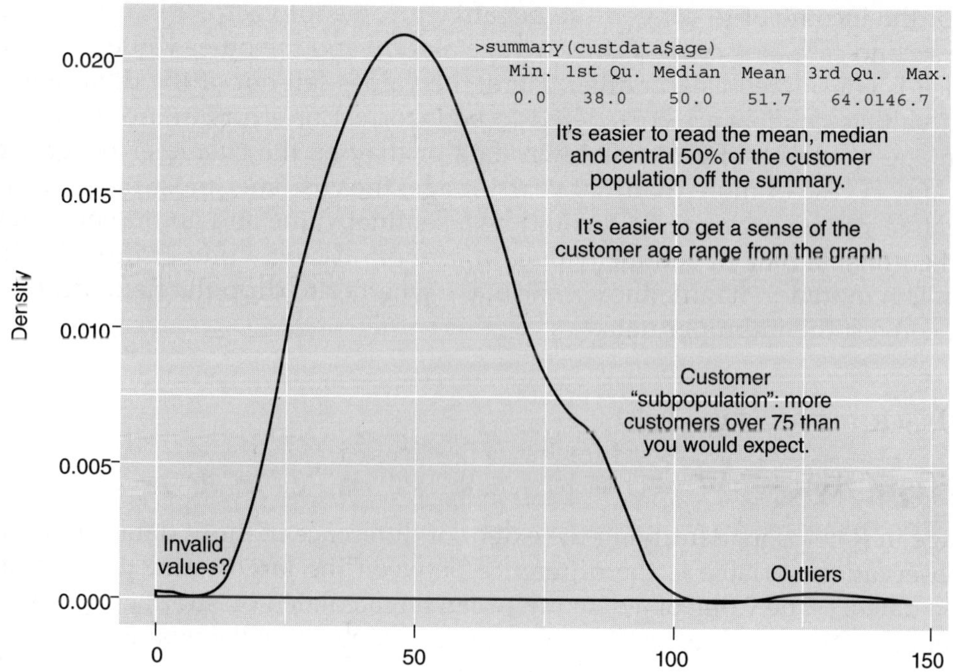

FIGURE 4.1 *Graphical representation of invalid values and outliers*

Figure 4.1 helps in understanding the difference between the invalid values and outliers in detail.

Figure 4.1 is explained as follows:

```
>summary(custdata$income)
```

#returns the minimum, maximum, mean, median, and quantile values of the 'income' from the 'custdata' input values.

Minimum	*1st Quantile*	*Median*	*Mean*	*3rd Quantile*	*Maximum*
-8700	14600	35000	53500	67000	615000

```
>summary(custdata$age)
```

#returns the minimum, maximum, mean, median, and quantile values of the 'age' from the 'custdata' input values.

Minimum	*1st Quantile*	*Median*	*Mean*	*3rd Quantile*	*Maximum*
0.0	38.0	50.0	51.7	64.0	146.7

The above two scenarios clearly explain the invalid and outlier values. In the first output, one of the values of 'income' is negative (-8700). Practically, a person cannot have negative income. Negative income is an indicator of debt. Hence, the income is given in negative values. However, such negative values are required to be treated effectively. A check is required on how to handle these types of inputs, i.e. either to drop the negative values for the income or to convert the negative income into zero.

In the second case, one of the values of 'age' is zero and the other value is greater than 120, which is considered as an outlier. Here, the values fall out of the data range of the expected values. Outliers are considered to be incorrect or errors in input data. In such cases, an age '0' could refer to unknown data or may be the customer never disclosed the age, and in case of more than 120 years of age, the customer must have lived long.

A negative value in the age field could be a sentinel value and an outlier could be an error data, unusual data or sentinel value. In case of missing a proper input to the field, an action is required to handle the scenario, i.e. whether to drop the field, drop the data input or convert the improper data.

4.9 Descriptive Statistics

4.9.1 Data Range

Data range in R helps in identifying the extent of difference in input data. The data range of the observation variable is the difference between the largest and the smallest data value in a dataset. The value of a data range can be calculated by subtracting the smallest value from the largest value, i.e. Range = Largest value – Smallest value.

For example, the range or the duration of rainfall can be computed as

```
# Calculates the duration.
>duration = time$rainfall
#Apply max and min function to return the range
>max(duration) - min(duration)
```

This sample code returns the range or duration by taking the minimum and maximum values. In the example above, time duration of rainfall is helpful in predicting the probability of duration of rainfall. Hence, there should be enough variation in the amount of rainfall and the duration of the rainfall.

4.9.2 Frequencies and Mode

Frequency

Frequency is a summary of data occurrence in a collection of non-overlapping types. In R, `freq` function can be used to find the frequency distribution of vector inputs. In the example given, consider sellers as the dataset and the frequency distribution of the shop variable is the summary of the number of sellers in each shop.

```
> head(subset(mtcars, select = 'gear'))
                     gear
Mazda RX4               4
Mazda RX4 Wag           4
Datsun 710              4
Hornet 4 Drive          3
Hornet Sportabout       3
Valiant                 3

> factor(mtcars$gear)
[1] 4 4 4 3 3 3 3 4 4 4 4 3 3 3 3 3 3 4 4 4 3 3 3 3 3 4 5 5 5 5 5 4
Levels: 3 4 5

> w = table(mtcars$gear)
> w
3      4       5
15     12      5


> t = as.data.frame(w)
> t
    Var1    Freq
1      3      15
2      4      12
3      5       5
```

```
> names(t) [1] = 'gear'
> t
    gear    Freq
1      3      15
2      4      12
3      5       5
```

The cbind() function can be used to display the result in column format.

```
> w
3       4       5
15     12       5
> cbind(w)
       w
3     15
4     12
5      5
```

Mode

Mode is similar to frequency, except that the value of mode returns the highest number of occurrences in a dataset. Mode can take both numeric and character as input data. Mode does not have any standard inbuilt function to calculate mode of the given inputs. Hence, a user-defined function is required to calculate mode in R. Here, the input is a vector value and the output is the mode value.

A sample code to return the mode value is

```
#Create the function
getmode <- function(y){
uniqy <- unique(y)
uniqy[which.max(tabulate(match(y,uniqy)))]
}
# Define the input vector values
v <- c(5,6,4,8,5,7,4,6,5,8,3,2,1)
#Calculate the mode with user-defined functions
resultmode<- getmode(v)
print(resultmode)
#Define characters as input vector values
charv <-c("as","is","is","it","in")
#Calculate mode using user-defined function
resultmode <-  getmode(charv)
print(resultmode)
```

Executing the above code will give the result as:

[1] 5

[1] "is"

```
> #Create the function
> getmode <- function(y) {
+ uniqy <- unique (y)
+ uniqy[which.max(tabulate(match(y, uniqy)))]
+ }
>

> v <- c(5,6,4,8,5,7,4,6,5,8,3,2,1)

> resultmode<- getmode(v)
> print(resultmode)
[1] 5

> charv <- c("as","is","is","it","in")
> resultmode <- getmode (charv)
> print (resultmode)
[1] "is"
```

4.9.3 Mean and Median

Statistical data in R is analysed using inbuilt functions. These inbuilt functions are found in the base R package. The functions take vector values as input with arguments and produce the output.

Mean

Mean is the sum of input values divided by the sum of the number of inputs. It is also called the average of the input values. In R, mean is calculated by inbuilt functions. The function `mean()` gives the output of the mean value in R.

Basic syntax for the `mean()` function in R is:

```
mean(x, trim=0, na.rm = FALSE,...)
```

where,
x is the input vector, trim specifies some drop in observations from both the sorted ends of the input vector and `na.rm` removes the missing values in the input vector.

Example 1

A sample code to calculate the mean in R is

```
#Define a vector
x<- c(15,54,6,5,9.2,36,5.3,8,-7,-5)
# Find the mean of the vector inputs
result.mean <- mean(x)
print(result.mean)
```

Output

On execution, it would produce an output value of `[1]12.65`.

```
> x<- c(15,54,6,5,9.2,36,5.3,8,-7,-5)
> result.mean <- mean(x)
> print (result.mean)
[1] 12.65
```

When the trim parameter is selected, it sorts the vector values first and drops the input values for calculating the mean based on the trim value from both the ends. Say trim = 0.4, 4 values from both the ends of sorted vector values are dropped. With the above sample, vector values (15,54,6,5,9.2,36,5.3,8,-7,-5) are sorted to (-7,-5,5,5.3,6,8,9.2,15,36,54) and 4 values are removed from both the ends, i.e. (-7,-5,5,5.3) from the left and (9.2,15,36,54) from the right.

Example 2

```
#Define a vector
x<- c(15,54,6,5,9.2,36,5.3,8,-7,-5)
# Find the mean of the vector inputs
result.mean <- mean(x, trim =0.3)
print(result.mean)
```

Output

On execution, it would produce an output value of `[1] 7.125`

```
> x<- c(15,54,6,5,9.2,36,5.3,8,-7,-5)
> result.means <- mean(x, trim =0.3)
> print(result.mean)
[1] 7.125
```

Example 3

In case of any missing value, the `mean()` function would return NA. In order to overcome such cases, na.rm = TRUE is used to remove the NA values from the list for calculating the mean in R.

```
#Define a vector
x<- c(15,54,6,5,9.2,36,5.3,8,-7,-5,NA)
# Find the mean of the vector inputs
result.mean <- mean(x)
print(result.mean)
#Dropping NA values from finding the mean
result.mean <- mean(x, na.rm=TRUE)
print(result.mean)
```

Output

On execution, it would produce an output value of

```
[1]NA
[1]12.65
```

```
> x<- c(15,54,6,5,9.2,36,5.3,8,-7,-5,NA)
> result.means <- mean (x)
> print (result.mean)
[1] NA
> result.mean <- mean (x, na.rm=TRUE)
> print (result.mean)
[1] 12.65
```

Example 4

Objective: To determine the mean of a set of numbers. To plot the numbers in a barplot and have a straight line run through the plot at the mean.

Step 1: To create a vector, "numbers".

```
> numbers <-c(1, 3, 5, 2, 8, 7, 9, 10)
```

Step 2: To compute the mean value of the set of numbers contained in the vector, "numbers".

```
> mean (numbers)
[1] 5.625
```

Outcome: The mean value for the vector, "numbers" is computed as 5.625.

Step 3: To plot a bar plot using the vector, "numbers".

```
> barplot (numbers)
```

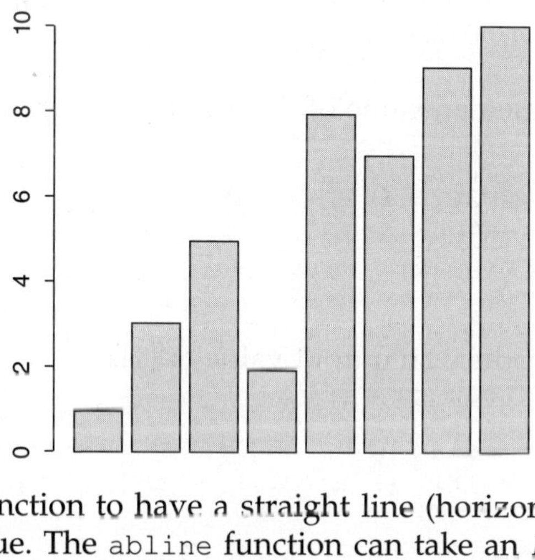

Step 4: Use the abline function to have a straight line (horizontal line) run through the bar plot at the mean value. The `abline` function can take an *h* parameter with a value to draw a horizontal line or a *v* parameter for a vertical line. When it's called, it updates the previous plot. Draw a horizontal line across the plot at the mean.

```
> barplot (numbers)
> abline (h = mean (numbers))
```

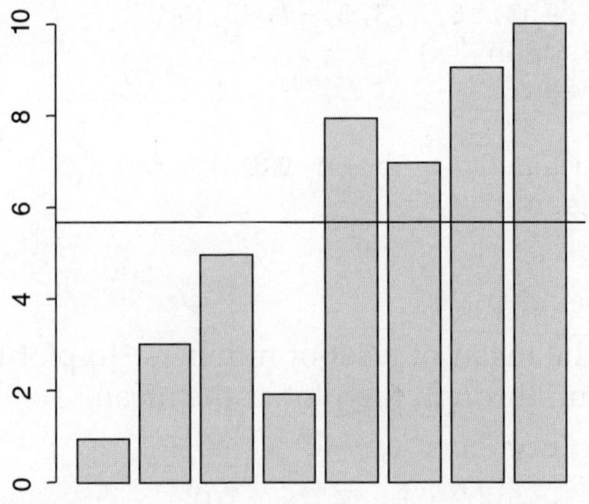

Outcome: A straight line at the computed mean value (5.625) runs through the bar plot computed on the vector, "numbers".

Median

Median is the middle value of the given inputs. In R, the median can be found using the `median()` function. Basic syntax for calculating the median in R is

```
median(x, na.rm=FALSE)
```

where,
x is the input vector value and na.rm removes the missing values in the input vector.

Example 1

A sample to find out the median value of the input vector in R is

```
#Define a vector
x<- c(15,54,6,5,9.2,36,5.3,8,-7,-5)
# Find the median value
median.result <-median(x)
print(median.result)
```

On execution, it would produce an output value of [1]7.

```
> x<- c(15,54,6,5,9.2,36,5.3,8,-7,-5)
> median.result <-median (x)
> print (median.result)
[1] 7
```

Example 2

Objective: To determine the median of a set of numbers. To plot the numbers in a bar plot and have a straight line run through the plot at the median.

Step 1: To create a vector, "numbers".

```
> numbers <- c(1, 3, 5, 2, 8, 7, 9, 10)
```

Step 2: To compute the median value of the set of numbers contained in the vector, "numbers".

```
> median(numbers)
[1] 6
```

Step 3: To plot a bar plot using the vector, "numbers". Use the abline function to have a straight line (horizontal line) run through the bar plot at the median.

```
> barplot (numbers)
> abline (h = median (numbers))
```

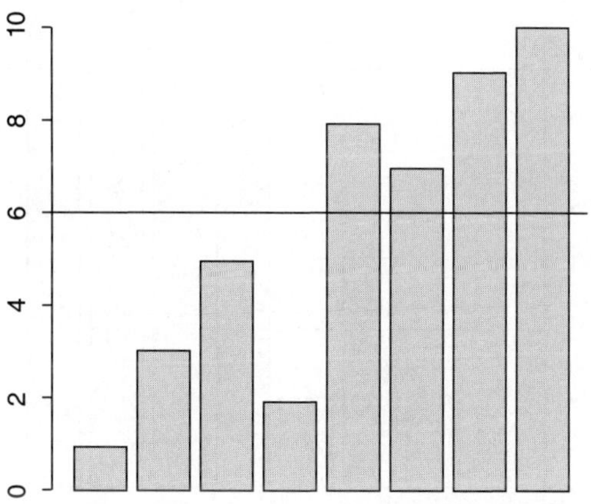

Outcome: A straight line at the computed median value (6.0) runs through the bar plot computed on the vector, "numbers".

4.9.4 Standard Deviation

Objective: To determine the standard deviation. To plot the numbers in a bar plot and have a straight line run through the plot at the mean and another straight line run through the plot at mean + standard deviation.

Step 1: To create a vector, "numbers".

```
> numbers <- c(1,3,5,2,8,7,9,10)
```

Step 2: To compute the mean value of the set of numbers contained in the vector, "numbers".

```
> mean(numbers)
[1] 5.625
```

Step 3: To determine the standard deviation of the set of numbers held in the vector, "numbers".

```
> deviation <- sd(numbers)
> deviation
[1] 3.377975
```

Step 4: To plot a bar plot using the vector, "numbers".

```
> barplot (numbers)
```

Step 5: Use the abline function to have a straight line (horizontal line) run through the bar plot at the mean value (5.625) and another straight line run through the bar plot at mean value + standard deviation (5.625 + 3.377975)

```
> barplot (numbers)
> abline (h=sd(numbers))
> abline (h=sd(numbers) + mean(numbers))
```

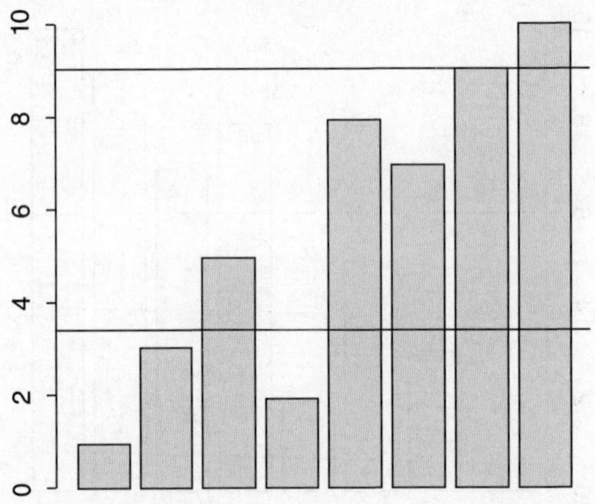

4.9.5 Mode

Objective: To determine the mode of a set of numbers. R does not have a standard inbuilt function to determine the mode. We will write out own, "Mode" function. This function will take the vector as the input and return the mode as the output value.

Step 1: Create a user-defined function, "Mode".

```
Mode <- function(v) {
        UniqValue <- unique(v)
        UniqValue[which.max(tabulate(match(v, UniqValue)))]
}
> Mode <-function(v) {
+ UniqValue <- unique(v)
+ UniqValue[which.max(tabulate(match(v, UniqValue)))]
+ }
```

While writing the above function, "Mode", we have used three other functions provided by R, viz. "unique", "tabulate" and "match".

unique function: The "unique" function will take the vector as the input and returns the vector with the duplicates removed.

```
> v
[1] 2 1 2 3 1 2 3 4 1 5 5 3 2 3
> unique(v)
[1] 2 1 3 4 5
```

match function: Takes a vector as the input and returns the vector that has the position of (first) match of its first arguments in its second.

```
> v
[1] 2 1 2 3 1 2 3 4 1 5 5 3 2 3
> UniqValue <- unique(v)
> UniqValue
[1] 2 1 3 4 5
> match(v,UniqValue)
[1] 1 2 1 3 2 1 3 4 2 5 5 3 1 3
```

tabulate function: Takes an integer valued vector as the input and counts the number of times each integer occurs in it.

```
> tabulate(match(v,UniqValue))
[1] 4 3 4 1 2
```

Going by our example, "2" occurs four times, "1" occurs three times, "3" occurs four times, "4" occurs one time and "5" occurs two times.

Step 2: Create a vector, "v".

```
> v <- c(2,1,2,3,1,2,3,4,1,5,5,3,2,3)
```

Step 3: Call the function, "Mode" and pass the vector, "v" to it.

```
> Output <- Mode(v)
```

Step 4: Print out the mode value of the vector, "v".

```
> print(Output)
[1] 2
```

Let us pass a character vector, "charv" to the "Mode" function.

Step 1: Create a character vector, "charv".

```
> charv <- c("o","it","the","it","it")
```

Step 2: Call the function, "Mode" and pass the character vector, "charv" to it.

```
> Output <- Mode(charv)
```

Step 3: Print out the mode value of the vector, "v".

```
> print(Output)
[1] "it"
```

Just Remember

In R, with basic inbuilt functions mean, median and range can be found out. But in case of finding mode, a user-defined function is needed to obtain the value of mode.

Check Your Understanding

1. What are the possible `na.action` settings?

Ans: The possible `na.action` settings are `na.omit`, `na.exclude`, `na.pass` and `na.fail`.

2. How are the missing values in the input vector removed?

Ans: `na.rm` removes the missing values in the input vector.

3. How is the data range obtained from a given input?

Ans: The value of the data range can be obtained by using the following formula:
Range = Largest value – Smallest value

4.10 Spotting Problems in Data with Visualisation

For a better understanding of input data, pictures or charts are preferred over text. Visualisation engages the audience well and numerical values, on comparison, cannot represent a big dataset in an engaging manner.

From Figure 4.1, we observe that the graph represents the density of data with respect to the age of the customers. The use of graphical representation to examine the given set of data is called *visualisation*. With this visualisation, it is easier to calculate the following:

- To determine the peak value of the age of the customers (maximum value)
- To estimate the existence of the sub-population
- To determine the outlier values.

The graphical representation displays the maximum available information from the lowest to the highest value. It also presents users with greater data clarity. For better usage of visualisation, the right aspect ratio and scaling of data is needed.

4.10.1 Visually Checking Distributions for a Single Variable

With R visualisation, one can answer the following questions:

- What is the peak value of the standard distribution?
- How many peaks are there in a distribution? (Basically bimodality vs unimodality)

- Is it normal data or lognormal data?
- How does the given data vary?
- Is the given data concerned in a certain interval or category?

Generally, visual representation of data is helpful to grasp the shape of data distribution. Figure 4.1 represents a normal distribution curve with an exception towards the right side of the figure. The summary statistics assumes that the data is more or less close to normal distribution.

Figure 4.2 represents a unimodal diagram with only one peak in the normal distribution diagram. It also represents the values in a more visually understandable way. It returns the mean customer age of about 51.7, which is nearly equal to 52.50% of the customers who fall in the age group of 38 to 64 years. With this statistical output, it can be concluded that the customer is a middle-aged person in the age range of 38–64 years.

The additional black curve in Figure 4.2 refers to a bimodal distribution. Usually, if a distribution contains more than two peaks, then it is considered a multimodal. The second black curve has the same mean age as that of the grey curve. However, here the curve concentrates on two sets of populations with younger ages between 20 and 30 and the older ages above 70.

These two sets of populations have different patterns in their behaviour and the probability of customers who have health insurance also differs. In such a case, using a logistic regression or linear regression fails to represent the current scenario. Hence,

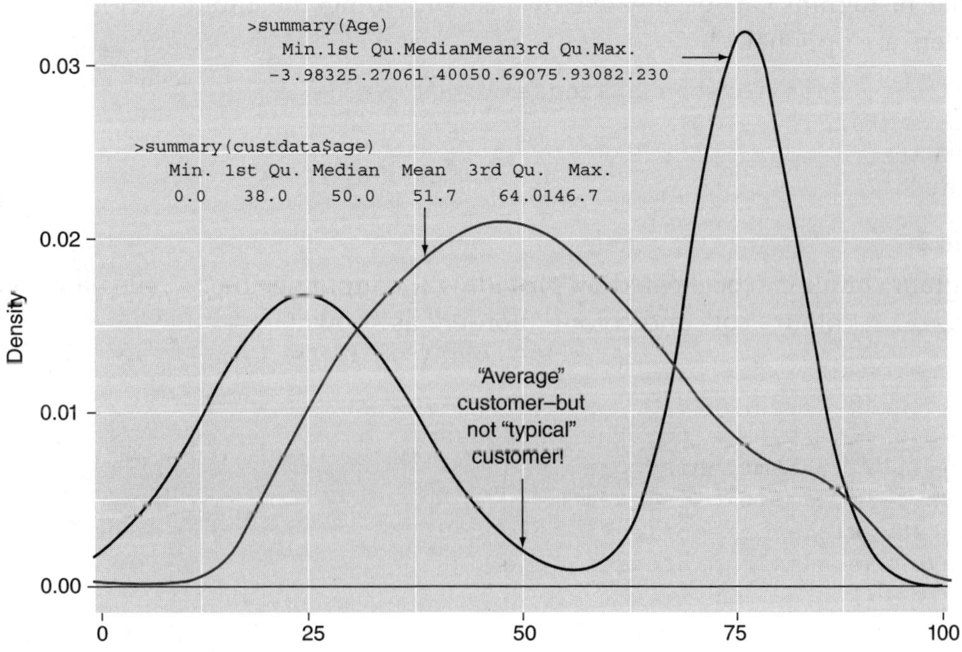

FIGURE 4.2 *Bimodal representation*

in order to overcome the difficulties faced for such representations, a density plot or histogram can examine the distribution of the input values. Moving forward, the histogram makes the representation simpler as compared to density plots and is the preferred method for presenting findings from quantitative analysis.

4.10.2 Histograms

A histogram is a graphical illustration of the distribution of numerical data in successive numerical intervals of equal sizes. It looks similar to a bar graph. However, values are grouped into continuous ranges in a histogram. The height of a histogram bar represents the number of values occurring in a particular range.

R uses `hist(x)` function to create simple histograms, where *x* is a numeric value to be plotted. Basic syntax to create a histogram using R is:

```
hist(v,main,xlab,xlim,ylim,breaks,col,border)
```

where,
v takes a vector that contains numeric values, 'main' is the main title of the bar chart, `xlab` is the label of the X-axis, `xlim` specifies the range of values on the X-axis, `ylim` specifies the range of values on the Y-axis, 'breaks' control the number of bins or mentions the width of the bar, 'col' sets the colour of the bars and 'border' sets the border colour of the bars.

Example 1

A simple histogram can be created by just providing the input vector where other parameters are optional.

```
# Create data for the histogram
h<- c (8,13,30,5,28)
#Create histogram for H
hist(h)
```

Example 2

A histogram simple can be created by providing the input vector "v", file name, label for X-axis "`xlab`", colour "col" and colour "border" as shown:

```
# Create data for the histogram
H <- c (8,13,30,5,28)
# Give a file name for the histogram
png(file = "samplehistogram.png")
#Create a sample histogram
hist(H, xlab="Categories", col="red")
#Save the sample histogram file
dev.off()
```

Executing the above code fetches the output as shown in Figure 4.3. It fills the bar with the 'col' colour parameter. And border to the bar can be done by passing values to the 'border' parameter.

```
> H <- c (8,13,30,5,28)
> hist(H, xlab="Categories", col="red")
```

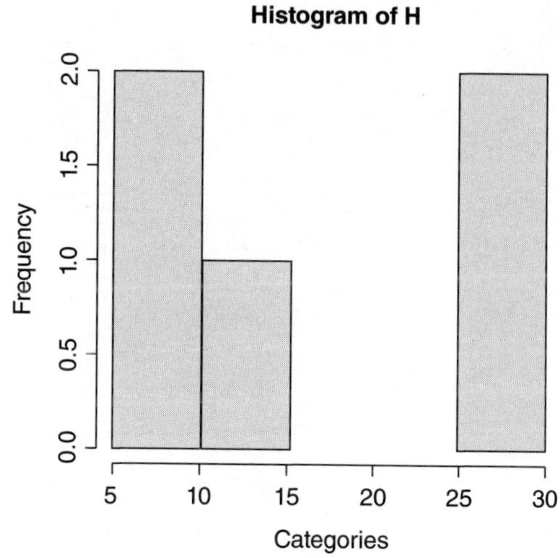

FIGURE 4.3 *Histogram*

Example 3

The parameters `xlim` and `ylim` are used to denote the range of values that are used in the X and Y axes. And *breaks* are used to specify the width of each bar.

```
#Create data for the histogram
H <- c (8,13,30,5,28)
# Give a file name for the histogram
png(file = "samplelimhistogram.png")
#Create a samplelimhistogram.png
hist(H, xlab ="Values", ylab= "Colours", col="green", xlim=c(0,30),
ylim=c(0,5), breaks= 5)
#Save the samplelimhistogram.png file
dev.off()
> H <- c (8,13,30,5,28)
> hist(H, xlab ="Values", ylab = "Colours", col= "green",
xlim=c(0,30), ylim=c(0,5), breaks=5)
```

Executing the above code will display the histogram as shown in Figure 4.4.

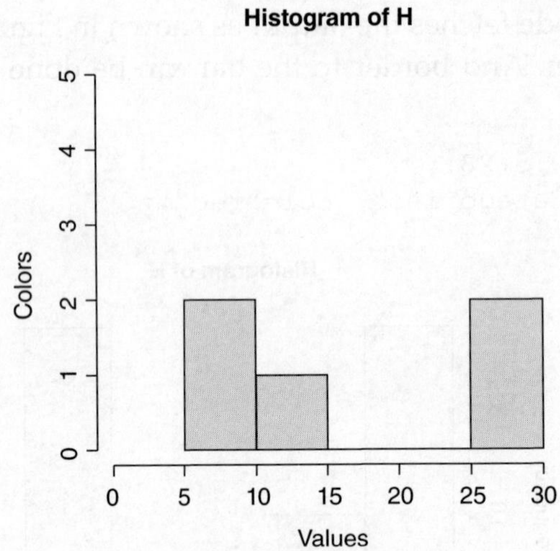

FIGURE 4.4 *Histogram with X and Y values*

```
> H <- c (8, 13, 30, 5, 28)
> bins <- c(0, 5, 10, 15, 20, 25, 30)
> bins
[1] 0 5 10 15 20 25 30
> hist(H, xlab ="Values", ylab=
"Colours", col="green", xlim=c(0,30),
ylim=c(0,5), breaks=bins)
```

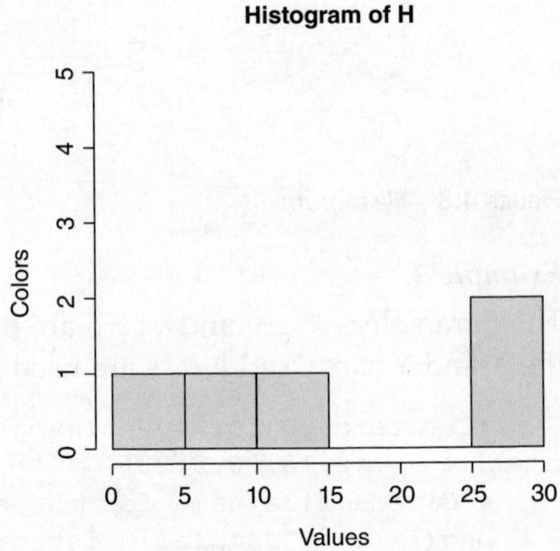

4.10.3 Density Plots

A density plot is referred to as a 'continuous histogram' of the given variable. However, the area of the curve under the density plot is equal to 1. Therefore, the point on the density plot diagram matches the fraction of the data (or the percentage of the data which is divided by 100 that takes a particular value). The resulting value of the fraction is very small.

A density plot is an effective way to assess the distribution of a variable. It provides a better reference in finding a parametric distribution. The basic syntax to create a plot is `plot(density(x)),` where *x* is a numeric vector value.

Example 1

A simple density plot can be created by just passing the values and using the `plot()` function (Figure 4.5).

```
# Create data for the density plot
h <- density (c(0.0, 38.0, 50.0, 51.7, 64.0, 146.0))
#Create density plot for h
plot(h)

> h <- density (c(0.0, 38.0, 50.0, 51.7, 64.0, 146.0))
> plot(h, xlab="Values", ylab="Density")
```

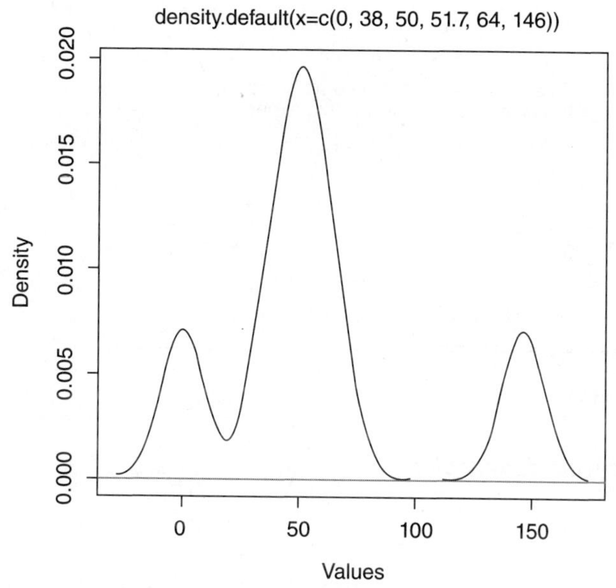

FIGURE 4.5 *Density plot*

When executing the above code, it displays the density plot for the given input values. The `plot()` function creates the density diagram. In case of widespread data range, the distribution of data is concentrated to one side of the curve. Here it is very complex to determine the exact value in the peak.

Example 2

In case of non-negative data, another way to plot the curve is using the distribution diagram on a logarithmic scale, which is equivalent to the plot the density plot of log10 (input value). For Figure 4.5 it is very hard to find out the peak value of the mass distribution. Hence, in order to simplify the visual representation log10 scale is used. In Figure 4.6 the peak value of the income distribution is clearly pictured as ~$40,000. In case of wide spread data this logarithmic approach can give a perfect result.

Figure 4.6 shows how the density plot is plotted in the logarithmic scale. Here, the logarithmic scale is given in both the ends of the X-axis where the Y-axis denotes the density values.

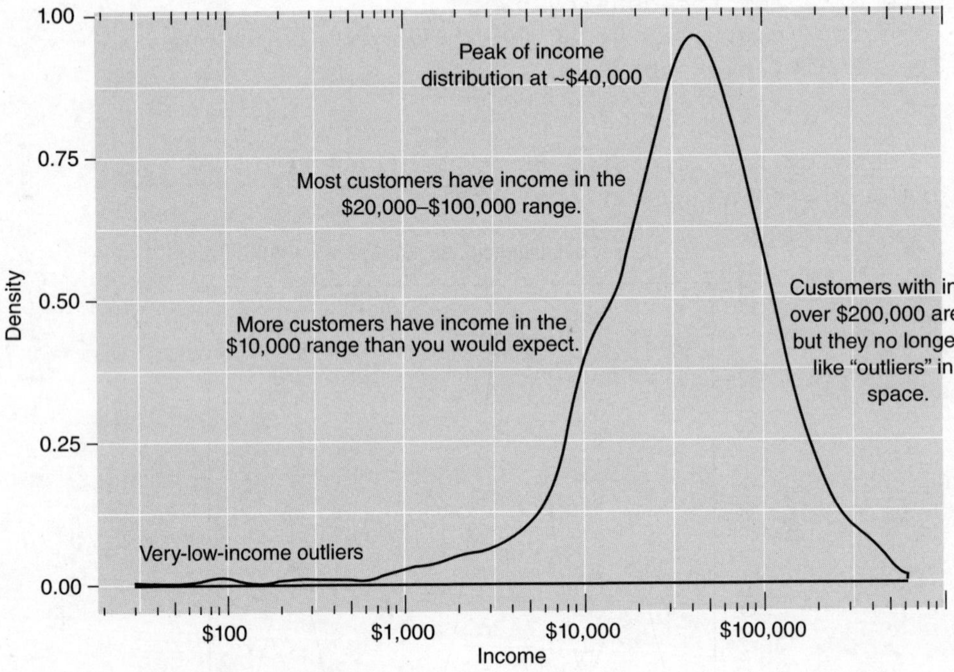

FIGURE 4.6 *Logarithmic scale density plot*

Example 3

The above sample code displays Figure 4.5 with the income of the customer on the X-axis and density on the Y-axis. To enable the dollar symbol in the input data labels=dollar parameter is passed. Hence, the amount is displayed with the dollar $ symbol (Figure 4.7).

```
library(scales)
barplot(custdata) + geom_density(aes(x=income)) + scale_x_
continuous(labels=dollar)
```

4.10.4 Bar Charts

A bar chart is a pictorial representation of statistical data. Both vertical and horizontal bars can be drawn using R. It also provides an option to colour the bars in different colours. The length of the bar is directly proportional to the values of the axes.

R uses the `barplot()` function to create a bar chart. The basic syntax for creating a bar chart using R is

```
barplot(H, xlab, ylab, main, names.arg, col)
```

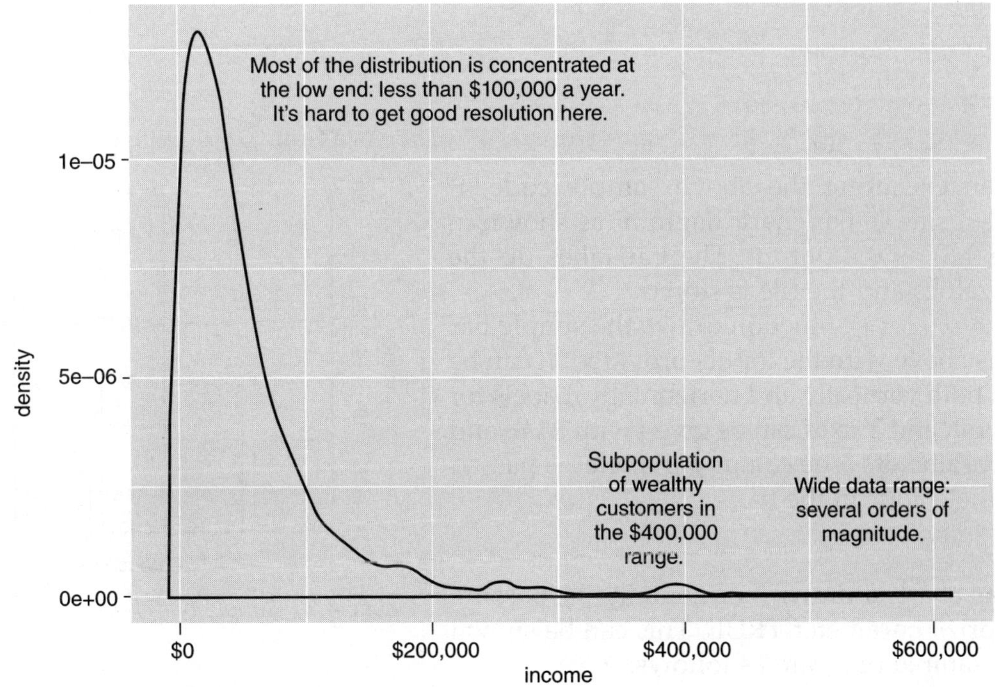

FIGURE 4.7 *Density function with symbol $*

where,

H is a matrix or a vector that contains the numeric values used in bar chart, `xlab` is the label of the X-axis, `ylab` is the label of the Y-axis, main is the main title of the bar chart, names.arg is the collection of names to appear under each bar and col is used to give colours to the bars.

Some basic bar charts commonly used in R are:

- Simple bar chart
- Grouped bar chart
- Stacked bar chart

1. Simple Bar Chart

A simple bar chart is created by just providing the input values and a name to the bar chart. The following code creates and saves a bar chart using the `barplot()` function in R.

Example 1

```
# Create data for the bar chart
H <- c (8,13,30,5,28)
#Give a name for the bar chart
png(file = "samplebarchart.png")
#Plot bar chart using barplot() function
barplot(H)
```

```
#Save the file
dev.off()

> H <- c (8,13,30,5,28)
> barplot (H, xlab = "Categories", ylab="Values", col="blue")
```

When executing the above sample code, it returns a simple bar chart diagram (as shown in Figure 4.8) as the output. The bar takes up the input values and the file is stored.

The `barplot()` function draws the simple bar chart as above with the inputs provided. It can be drawn both vertically and horizontally. Labels for both the X and Y axes can be given with `xlab` and `ylab` parameters. The colour parameter is passed to fill the colour in the bar.

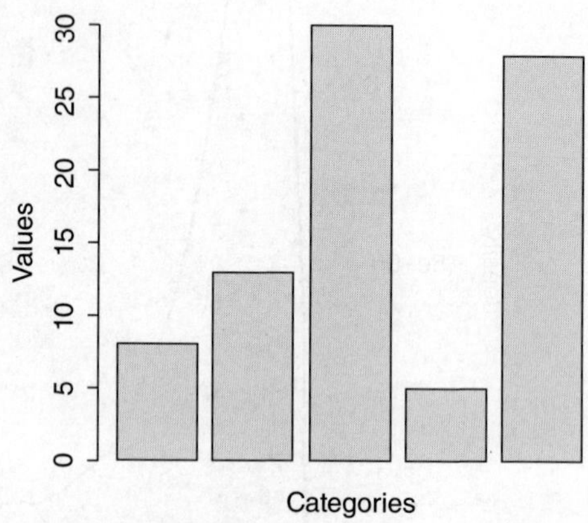

FIGURE 4.8 *Simple bar chart*

Example 2

The bar chart is drawn horizontally by passing the "horiz" parameter TRUE. This can be shown with a sample program as follows:

```
# Create data for the bar chart
H <- c (8,13,30,5,28)
#Give a name for the bar chart
png(file = "samplebarchart.png")
#Plot bar chart using barplot() function
barplot(H,  horiz=TRUE))
#Save the file
dev.off()

> barplot(H, xlab = "Values", ylab="Categories", col="blue",
horiz=TRUE)
```

Executing the above code in R will result in Figure 4.9 which takes up the input values and plots the bar using the `barplot()` function. Here when the "horiz" parameter is set to TRUE, it displays the bar chart in a horizontal position else it will be displayed as a default vertical bar chart.

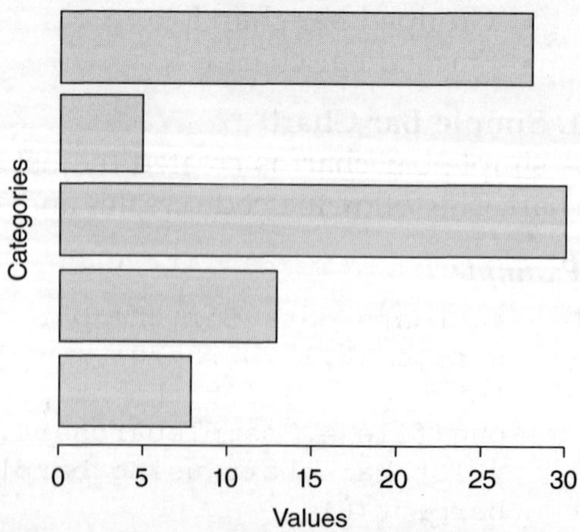

FIGURE 4.9 *Horizontal bar chart*

2. Group Bar Chart

A group data in R is used to handle multiple inputs and takes the value of the matrix. This group bar chart is created using the `barplot()` function and accepts the matrix inputs.

Example

```
> colors <- c("green","orange","brown")
> months <- c("Mar","Apr","May","Jun","Jul")
> regions <- c("East","West","North")
> Values <- matrix(c(2,9,3,11,9,4,8,7,3,12,5,2,8,10,11),nrow=3,ncol
= 5,byrow = TRUE)
> Values
      [,1]  [,2]  [,3]  [,4]  [,5]
[1,]     2     9     3    11     9
[2,]     4     8     7     3    12
[3,]     5     2     8    10    11
> rownames(Values) <- regions
> rownames(Values)
[1] "East" "West""North"
> Values
      [,1]  [,2]  [,3]  [,4]  [,5]
East     2     9     3    11     9
West     4     8     7     3    12
North    5     2     8    10    11

> colnames(Values) <- months
> Values
       Mar   Apr   May   Jun   Jul
East     2     9     3    11     9
West     4     8     7     3    12
North    5     2     8    10    11
> barplot(Values, col=colors, width=2, beside=TRUE, names.
arg=months, main="Total Revenue 2015 by month")
> legend("topleft", regions, cex=0.6, bty= "n", fill=colors);
```

In Figure 4.10, the matrix input is read and passed to the `barplot()` function to create a group bar chart. Here the legend column is included on the top right side of the bar chart.

3. Stacked Bar Chart

Stacked bar chart is similar to group bar chart where multiple inputs can take different graphical representations. Except by grouping the values, the stacked bar chart stacks each bar one after the other based on the input values.

Example

```
> days <- c("Mon","Tues","Wed")
> months <- c("Jan","Feb","Mar","Apr","May")
> colours <- c("red","blue","green")
> val <- matrix(c(2,5,8,6,9,4,6,4,7,10,12,5,6,11,13), nrow =3, ncol
=5, byrow =TRUE)
> barplot(val,main="Total",names.arg=months,xlab="Months",ylab="Day
s",col=colours)
> legend("topleft", days, cex=1.3,fill=colours)
```

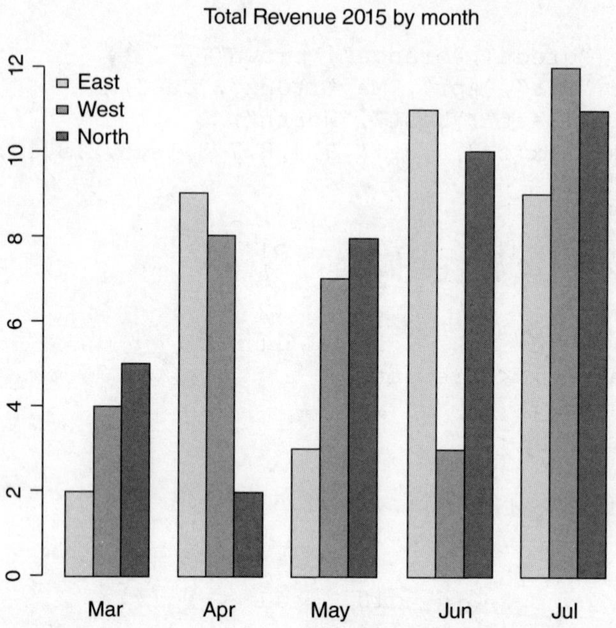

FIGURE 4.10 *Group bar chart*

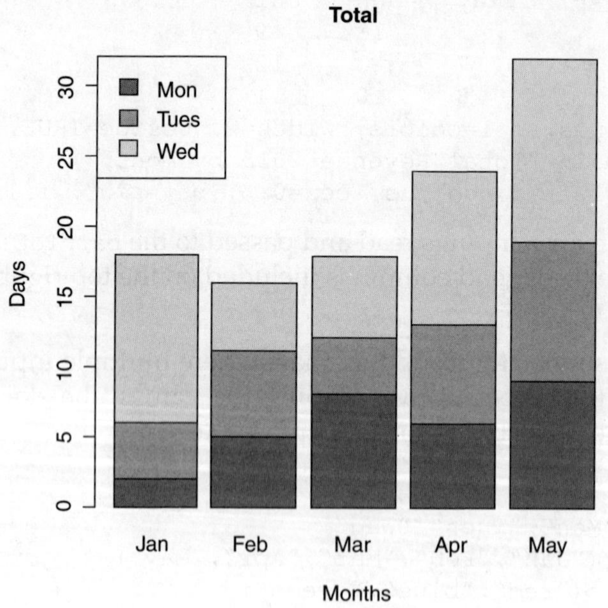

FIGURE 4.11 *Stacked bar chart*

In Figure 4.11, the 'Total' is set as the main title of the stack bar chart with 'Months' as the X-axis label and 'Season' as the Y-axis label. The code legend ("topleft", days, cex=1.3,fill=colours) specifies the legend to be displayed at the top right of the bar chart with colours filled accordingly.

Just Remember

Bar charts are an efficient way of presenting a huge collection of data. Here the values are represented in the X and Y axes and the legend function is used to summarise the data that is used in the chart, which can be positioned anywhere in the chart.

Check Your Understanding

1. What are the three types of bar charts used in R?

Ans: Simple bar chart, group bar chart and stacked bar chart are the three types of bar charts are used in R.

2. What are the advantages of using data visualisation?

Ans: The advantages of using data visualisation are:

- To determine the peak value of the age of the customer (maximum value)
- To estimate the existence of the subpopulation
- To determine the outliers easily.

3. Which function is used to create a bar chart?

Ans: The `barplot()` function is used to create a bar chart.
Syntax of `barplot()` is:
barplot(H, xlab, ylab, main, names.arg, col)

Summary

- Exploring data in R makes use of interactive data visualisations that further helps to analyse statistical data.
- `nrow(x)` and `ncol(x)` returns the number of rows and columns respectively of a given dataset.
- `dim(x)` is used to find the dimension of the given dataset.
- `summary(x)` provides basic descriptive statistics and frequencies.
- `edit(x)` opens the data editor.
- `head()` function is used to obtain the first *n* observations where n is set as 6 by default.
- `tail()` function is used to obtain the last *n* observations where *n* is set as 6 by default.
- Data in R, are sets of organised information. We deal more with statistical data type in R.
- Exploratory Data Analysis (EDA) involves analysing datasets in order to summarise the main characteristics in the form of visual representations.

(Continued)

- Some of the graphical techniques used by EDA are—box plot, histogram, scatter plot, Pareto chart, etc.
- Outliers are considered to be incorrect or error input data.
- In R, missing data is indicated as NA in the dataset, where NA refers to "Not Available". It is neither a string nor a numeric value but used to specify the missing data.
- Range = Largest value - Smallest value.
- Frequency is a summary of data occurrences in a collection of non-overlapping types.
- Mode is similar to the frequency except the value of mode returns the highest number of occurrences in the dataset.
- Mean is generally referred as summing up of input values and dividing the sum by the number of inputs.
- Median is the middle value of the given inputs.
- Histogram is a graphical illustration of the distribution of numerical data in successive numerical intervals of equal size.
- A bar chart is a pictorial representation of statistical data.
- A simple bar chart is created by just providing the input values and the name to the bar chart.
- Stacked bar chart is similar to group bar chart where multiple inputs can take different graphical representations.

KEY TERMS

- **Bar chart:** A bar chart is a pictorial representation of statistical data.
- **Data range:** Data range is the difference between the largest and smallest data values in a dataset.
- **Data visualisation:** The use of graphical representation to examine a given set of data is called data visualisation.
- **Density plot:** A density plot is otherwise referred to as a 'continuous histogram' of a given variable, except the area of the curve under the density plot is equal to 1.
- **EDA:** Exploratory Data Analysis (EDA) involves analysing datasets to summarise their main characteristics in the form of visual representations.
- **Frequency**: Frequency is a summary of data occurrences in a collection of non-overlapping types.
- **Histogram:** Histogram is a graphical illustration of the distribution of numerical data in successive numerical intervals of equal size.
- **Mean**: Mean is generally referred to as summing up of input values and dividing the sum by the number of inputs.
- **Median**: Median is the middle value of the given inputs.
- **Mode**: Mode is similar to frequency except the value of mode returns the highest number of occurrences in a dataset.
- **Outliers:** Outliers are considered to be incorrect or error input data.

MULTIPLE CHOICE QUESTIONS

1. How many numbers of columns are there in the given output?
```
>dim(Grades)
[1] 80 2
```
(a) 80 (b) 2
(c) NA (d) 0

2. What will be the output of the following code?
```
>head(dataset, n=5)
```
(a) returns first 5 observations (b) returns last 5 observations
(c) returns first 6 default observations (d) returns last 6 default observations

3. What will be the output of the following code:
`>tail(dataset, n=-55),` where there are total 70 observations?
(a) returns first 15 observations
(b) returns last 15 observations
(c) returns first 55 default observations
(d) returns last 55 default observations

4. What will be the output of the following code?
```
is.invalid(c(0,Inf,0))
```
(a) FALSE TRUE TRUE (b) FALSE FALSE FALSE
(c) FALSE TRUE FALSE (d) TRUE TRUE TRUE

5. Which function is used to open a data editor?
(a) `edit()` (b) `str()`
(c) `summary()` (d) `open()`

6. Which is not an invalid value in R?
(a) -inf (b) NA
(c) 0 (d) NaN

7. Which one of the following is used to drop missing values?
(a) na.rm=TRUE (b) na.rm=FALSE
(c) na.rm=0 (d) na.rm=NA

8. Which parameter is used to mention the width of each bar in a histogram?
(a) width (b) col
(c) breadth (d) xlab

9. Which parameter is used to give the border colour in a bar chart?
(a) col (b) border
(c) colour (d) fill

10. Which command is used to save a file in R?
(a) `dev.off()` (b) `dev.on()`
(c) `dev.save()` (d) `dev.close()`

SHORT QUESTIONS

1. List the differences between the `head()` and `tail()` functions?
2. What is EDA?
3. Differentiate between invalid values and outliers.
4. How are missing values treated in R?
5. What is data visualisation?
6. How to calculate a data range?
7. How to find a mode value?
8. Give contrast of mean and median.
9. What is density plot?
10. What is histogram?

LONG QUESTIONS

1. Explain the reason to use the trim parameter.
2. Create a histogram by filling the bar with 'blue' colour.
3. What is a bar chart? Describe the types of bar charts.
4. Create a horizontal bar chart.
5. Differentiate between a group and stacked bar chart.
6. Create and place a legend in bar chart.

Answers to MCQs:

1. (b) 2. (a) 3. (b) 4. (c) 5. (a) 6. (c) 7. (a)
8. (a) 9. (b) 10. (a)

Chapter 5

Linear Regression using R

LEARNING OUTCOME

At the end of this chapter, you will be able to:

- Explain regression analysis, which is typically used to predict the value of an outcome (target or response) variable based on predictor variables
- Create a simple linear regression model
- Validate a model using "residuals vs. fitted plot", "normal Q-Q plot", "scale location plot" and "residuals vs. leverage plot"

5.1 Introduction

Regression analysis is a statistical process for estimating relationships between variables. It includes many techniques for modelling and analysing several variables when the focus is on the relationship between a dependent variable (also called a target or response variable) and one or more independent variables (also called predictors). Simple linear regression is used to determine the extent of the linear relationship between a dependent variable and a single independent variable. Typically, regression analysis is used for one (or more) of the following three purposes: (1) prediction of the target variable (forecasting), (2) modelling the relationship between x and y and (3) testing of hypotheses.

5.2 Model Fitting

Models in R language are a representation of a sequence of data points, which has the look of noisy clouds of points. Model fitting refers to choosing the right model that best describes a set of data. R has different types of models. These are listed below along with their commands.

- ***Linear model (lm):*** lm() is a linear model function in R. It can be used to create a simple regression model.
- ***Generalised linear model (glm):*** It is specified by giving a symbolic description of a linear predictor and a description of the error distribution.
- ***Linear model for mixed effects (lme)***
- ***Non-linear least square (nls):*** It determines the non-linear (weighted) least-square estimate of the parameters of a non-linear model.
- ***Generalised additive models (GAM):*** GAMs are simply a class of statistical models in which the usual linear relationship between the response and predictors is replaced by several non-linear smooth functions to model and capture the non-linearities in the data.

Each model has a specific function and the data points are distributed based on the function that describes the model.

5.3 Linear Regression

Linear regression in R consists of two main variables that are related through an equation where exponent (power) of both the variables is 1. Mathematically a linear relationship represents a straight line when plotted as a graph. In case of a non-linear relationship, the exponent of the variables is not equal to 1 and it creates a curve on the graph.

General equation of linear regression is $y = ax + b$
where, y is a **response** variable, x is a **predictor** variable and a and b are constants called coefficients.

5.3.1 `lm()` function in R

```
lm(formula, data, subset, weights, na.action,
    method = "qr", model = TRUE, x = FALSE, y = FALSE, qr = TRUE,
    singular.ok = TRUE, contrasts = NULL, offset, ...)
```

where,

- "formula" represents the relation between x and y
- "data" contains the variable in the model
- "subset" is an optional vector that specifies a subset of observations used in model fitting

- "weights" is an optional vector that specifies the weight for the model fitting process. It takes a numeric vector value or NULL.
- "na.action" is an optional function that specifies the actions on how to react for data that contains NAs
- "method" is the method used in fitting
- model, *x*, *y*, *qr*—If this parameter is TRUE, then model matrix, model frame and QR decomposition are returned
- "singular.ok"— If this parameter is FALSE, then a singular fit is an error.
- "Contrasts" is an optional list offset used to specify prior known components that are to be included in the linear predictor.

Simple syntax of the `lm()` function in linear regression is lm(formula,data), where, the optional parameters can be omitted.

Let us determine the relationship model between the predictor and response variables for a student data set. The predictor vector stores the number of hours of study put in by the students, whereas the response vector stores the Freshmen score.

Check the Data in the Data Set

Consider the dataset given in Table 5.1, "D:\student.csv", indicating the number of hours of study put in by the students (NoOfHours) and their freshmen score (Freshmen_Score).

TABLE 5.1 Data in "student" data set

NoOfHours	*Freshmen_Score*
2	55
2.5	62
3	65
3.5	70
4	77
4.5	82
5	75
5.5	83
6	85
6.5	88

Read the Data from the Data Set into a Data Frame

Use the `read.table()` function to read the file D:\student.csv" in a table format and create a data frame, "HS" from it, with cases corresponding to lines and variables to fields in the file.

```
> HS <- read.table("D:/student.csv", sep=",",header=TRUE)
> HS
   NoOfHours      Freshmen_Score
1        2.0                  55
2        2.5                  62
3        3.0                  65
4        3.5                  70
5        4.0                  77
6        4.5                  82
7        5.0                  75
8        5.5                  83
9        6.0                  85
10       6.5                  88
```

Check the Result Summary of the Data Held in the Data Frame

Use the `summary()` to produce result summaries. Here minimum, 1st quartile, median, mean, 3rd quartile and maximum values are computed for all the numeric variables.

```
> summary(HS)
    NoOfHours            Freshmen_Score
Min.     : 2.000     Min.     : 55.00
1st Qu.  : 3.125     1st Qu.  : 66.25
Median   : 4.250     Median   : 76.00
Mean     : 4.250     Mean     : 74.20
3rd Qu.  : 5.375     3rd Qu.  : 82.75
Max.     : 6.500     Max.     : 88.00
```

Check the Internal Structure of the Data Frame

Display the internal structure of the R object, "HS". It shows that there are 10 observations of 2 variables, "NoOfHours" and "Freshmen_Score".

```
> str(HS)
'data.frame'       : 10 obs. of 2 variables:
 $ NoOfHours       : num  2 2.5 3 3.5 4 4.5 5 5.5 6 6.5
 $ Freshmen_Score  : int 55 62 65 70 77 82 75 83 85 88
```

Plot the R Object

Plot the R object, "HS" with "HS$NoOfHours" on the X-axis and "HS$Freshmen_Score" on the Y-axis. Refer Figure 5.1.

```
> plot (HS$NoOfHours, HS$Freshmen_Score)
```

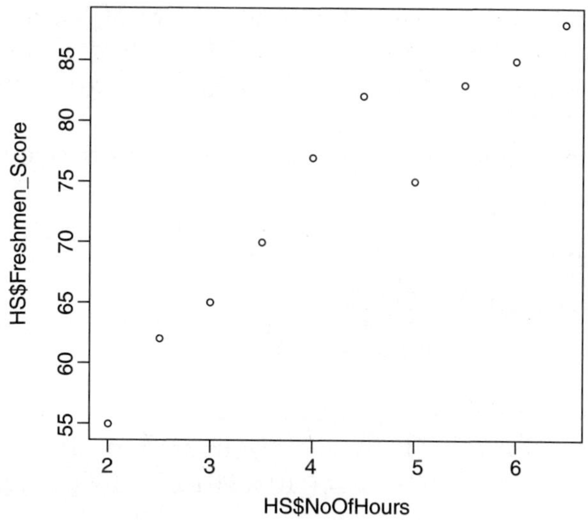

FIGURE 5.1 *Scatter plot of predictor vs. response variables*

Draw a horizontal line across the plot at the mean (mean of Freshmen_Score is 74.20) as indicated in Figure 5.2.

```
> abline (h=mean (HS$Freshmen_Score))
```

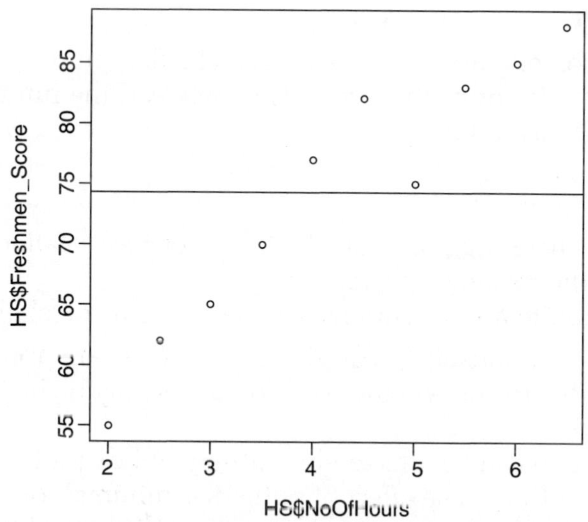

FIGURE 5.2 *Scatter plot of predictor vs. response variables with a straight line drawn at the mean*

When we use the mean to predict the Freshmen_Score score, at some instances we can observe a significant difference between the actual (observed) value and the predicted value.

For example, the first student has a Freshmen_Score of 55. If we used the mean to predict the score, we would have predicted it as 74.20. Here the observed score is lesser than the expected score. For the 10th student, the observed score is 88 which is larger than the predicted score of 74.20.

This indicates that to be able to predict the expected score, we may have to consider other factors as well.

Correlation Coefficient

$$r = \frac{n(\Sigma xy) - (\Sigma x)(\Sigma y)}{\sqrt{[n\Sigma x^2 - (\Sigma x)^2][n\Sigma y^2 - (\Sigma y)^2]}}$$

Solving this for the student data set,

$R = 10 \times (3295.5) - (42.5) \times (742)/\text{square root of}$
$([10 \times 201.25 - 1806.25]\ [10 \times 56130 - 550564])$

$= 32955 - 31545/1488.05$

$= 1410/1488.05$

$= 0.947548805$

$= 0.95$

Use the cor() Function in R to Determine the Degree and Direction of Linear Association

The degree and direction of a linear association can be determined using correlation. The Pearson correlation coefficient of the association between the number of hours studied and GPA score is shown as follows:

```
> cor(HS$NoOfHours, HS$Freshmen_Score)
[1] 0.9542675
```

The correlation value here suggests that there is a strong association between the number of hours studied and the freshmen score.

However, there are quite a few cautions associated with correlation:

1. For non-linear relationships, correlation is NOT an appropriate measure of association. To determine whether two variables may be linearly related, a scatter plot can be used.
2. Pearson correlation can be affected by outliers. A box plot can be used to identify the presence of outliers. The effect of outliers is minimal for Spearman correlation. Therefore, if outliers cannot be manipulated or eliminated from the analysis with proper justification, Spearman correlation is preferred.
3. A correlation value close to 0 indicates that the variables are not linearly associated. However, these variables may still be related. Thus, it is advised to plot the data.
4. Correlation does not imply causation, i.e. based on the value of correlation. It cannot be asserted that one variable causes the other.
5. Correlation analysis helps in determining the degree of association only.

Since correlation analysis may be inappropriate in determining the causation, we use regression techniques to quantify the nature of the relationship between the variables.

The regression model is represented using a mathematical model of form $y = f(X)$, where y is the dependent variable and X is the set of predictor variables ($x_1, x_2 \ldots x_n$).

In general, $f(X)$ may take linear or non-linear forms:

1. ***Linear form:*** $f(X) = \beta_0 + \beta_1 x_1 + \beta_2 x_2 + \ldots + \beta_n x_n + \varepsilon$
2. ***Non-linear form:*** $f(X) = \beta_0 + \beta_1 {x_1}^{p1} + \beta_2 {x_2}^{p2} + \ldots + \beta_n {x_n}^{pn} + \varepsilon$

Some commonly used linear forms are:

1. ***Simple linear form:*** There is one predictor and one dependent variable: $f(X) = \beta_0 + \beta_1 x_1 + \varepsilon$
2. ***Multiple linear form***: There are multiple predictor variables and one dependent variable:

$$f(X) = \beta_0 + \beta_1 x_1 + \beta_2 x_2 + \ldots + \beta_n x_n + \varepsilon$$

Some commonly used types of non-linear forms are:

1. ***Polynomial form:*** $f(X) = \beta_0 + \beta_1 {x_1}^{p1} + \beta_2 {x_2}^{p2} + \ldots + \beta_n {x_n}^{pn} + \varepsilon$
2. ***Quadratic form:*** $f(X) = \beta_0 + \beta_1 {x_1}^2 + \beta_2 x_1 + \varepsilon$
3. ***Logistic form:***

$$f(x) = \frac{1}{1 + e^{-(\beta_0 + \beta_1 x_1 + \beta_2 x_2 + \cdots + \beta_n x_n)}} + \varepsilon$$

where $\beta_0, \beta_1, \beta_2 \ldots \beta_n$ are said to be the regression coefficients and ε accounts for the error in prediction. The regression coefficients and the error in prediction are real numbers.

When a regression model is of a linear form, such a regression is called a linear regression. Similarly, when a regression model is of non-linear form, then such a regression is called a non-linear regression.

Since the scatter plot between the number of hours of study put in by students and the freshmen scores suggested a linear association, let us build a linear regression model to quantify the nature of this relationship.

Note: This chapter predominantly deals with linear regression.

In our example, we shall use the number of hours of study put in by a student to predict his/her freshmen score. Therefore, "Freshmen_Score" can be considered as the dependent variable, while the "NoOfHours" studied can be considered as the predictor variable. This is a case of simple linear regression because we have one predictor and one dependent variable.

Therefore, the regression model to predict the value of time taken to repair a computer could be expressed as Freshmen_Score = $\beta_0 + (\beta_1 \times \text{NoOfHours}) + \varepsilon$

Create the Linear Model Using `lm()`

Let us compute the coefficients:

(a) Intercept

(b) HS$NoOfHours

```
> x<-HS$NoOfHours
> y<-HS$Freshmen_Score
> n <- nrow (HS)
> xmean <- mean(HS$NoOfHours)
> ymean <- mean(HS$Freshmen_Score)
> xiyi <- x * y
> numerator <- sum(xiyi) - n * xmean * ymean
> denominator <- sum(x^2) - n * (xmean ^ 2)
> b1 <- numerator / denominator
> b0 <- ymean - b1 * xmean
> b1
[1] 6.884848
> b0
[1] 44.93939
```

Use the `lm()` to create the model. Here, "HS$Freshmen_Score" is the response or target variable and "HS$NoOfHours" is the predictor variable. Refer Figure 5.3 for visual representation of the model.

```
> model_HS <- lm(HS$Freshmen_Score ~ HS$NoOfHours)

> model_HS

Call:
lm(formula = HS$Freshmen_Score ~ HS$NoOfHours)

Coefficients:
 (Intercept) HS$NoOfHours
     44.939          6.885

> summary(model_HS)

Call:
lm(formula = HS$Freshmen_Score ~ HS$NoOfHours)

Residuals:
    Min       1Q   Median      3Q     Max
-4.3636  -1.5803  -0.3727  0.7712  6.0788

Coefficients
             Estimate Std. Error  t value  Pr(>|t|)
(Intercept)   44.9394     3.4210   13.136  1.07e-06 ***
HS$NoOfHours   6.8848     0.7626    9.028  1.81e-05 ***
---
Signif. codes:  0 '***' 0.001 '**' 0.01 '*' '0.05' '.' 0.1 '' 1

Residual standard error: 3.463 on 8 degrees of freedom
Multiple R-squared: 0.9106,  Adjusted R-squared:  0.8995
F-statistic: 81.51 on 1 and 8 DF, p-value: 1.811e-05
```

```
> plot(HS$NoOfHours, HS$Freshmen_Score, col="blue", main = "Linear
Regression",
+ abline(lm(HS$Freshmen_Score ~ HS$NoOfHours)), cex = 1.3, pch = 16,
xlab = "No of hours of study",
+ ylab = "Student Score")
```

Explanation of the Output

The first item shown in the output is the **formula** (lm(formula = HS$Freshmen_Score ~ HS$NoOfHours) that R uses to fit the data. `lm()` is a linear model function in R that is used to create a simple regression model. HS$NoOfHours is the predictor variable and HS$Freshmen_Score is the target/response variable.

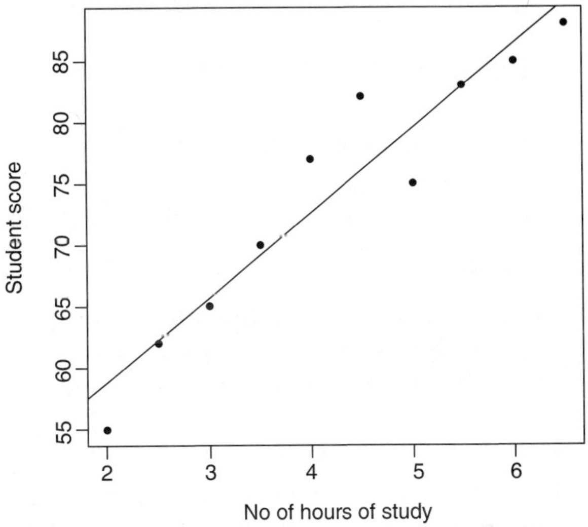

FIGURE 5.3 *Linear regression plot*

The next item in the model output describes **residuals**. What are "residuals"? The difference between the actual observed response values (HS$Freshmen_Score in our case) and the response values that the model predicted is called "residuals". The residuals section of the model output breaks it down into five summary points, viz., (Minimum, 1Q (first quartile), Median and 3Q (third quartile) and Maximum). When assessing how well the model fits the data, one should look for a symmetrical distribution across these points on the mean value zero (0).

NoOfHours	*Freshmen_Score*	*Predicted value*	*Residual Value (Actual Value – Estimated Value)*
2	55	58.70909	–3.70909
2.5	62	62.15152	–0.15152
3	65	65.59394	–0.59394
3.5	70	69.03636	0.96364
4	77	72.47879	4.52121
4.5	82	75.92121	6.07879 (maximum value)
5	75	79.36364	–4.36364 (minimum value)
5.5	83	82.80606	0.19394
6	85	86.24848	–1.24848
6.5	88	89.69091	–1.69091

To compute the five summary points, we write down the number in the ascending order.
(–4.36364, –3.70909, –1.69091, –1.24848, –0.59394, –0.15152, 0.19394, 0.96364, 4.52121, 6.07879)

Minimum: **–0.436364**

1Q: is at position 3.25.

To get the value at 3.5th position = (–1.69090 + –1.24848)/2 = **–1.46969**

To get the value at 3.25th position = (–1.69090 + –1,46969)/2 = **–1.580295**

Median: = (–0.59394 + –0.15152)/2 = **–0.37273**

(median is at position 5.5)

3Q: is at position 7.75

To get the value at 7.5th position = (0.19394 + 0.96364) / 2 = **0.57879**

To get the value at 7.75th position = (0.57879 + 0.96364) / 2 = **0.771215**

Maximum: **6.07879**

The next section in the model output describes the **coefficients** of the model. Theoretically, in simple linear regression, the coefficients are two unknown constants that represent the *intercept* and *slope* terms in a linear model.

Coefficient: Estimate

The coefficient, Estimate contains two rows. The first one is the intercept, which is the mean of the response *Y* when all predictors, all X = 0. Note, the mean is only useful if every *X* in the model actually has some values of zero. The second row in the Coefficients is the slope, or in our example, the effect HS_NoOfHours has on Freshmen_Score. The slope term in our model proves that for every hour increase in the NoOfHours, the required Freshmen_Score goes up by 6.8848 points.

Coefficient: Standard Error

The coefficient, Standard Error measures the average amount that the coefficient estimates vary from the actual average value of our response variable. Ideally this should be a lower number relative to its coefficients.

Coefficient: t-value

The coefficient, t-value is a measure of how many standard deviations our coefficient estimate is far away from 0. This should be far away from zero as this would enable us to reject the null hypothesis, i.e., we could declare that a relationship exists between HS_NoOfHours and Freshmen_Score. The t value is the coefficient divided by the standard error ((44.9394/3.4210) =13.1363). In general, *t*-values are also used to compute p-values.

Coefficient: Pr(>t)

The *Pr*(>*t*) acronym found in the model output relates to the probability of observing any value equal or larger than *t*. A small *p*-value indicates that it is unlikely we will observe a relationship between the predictor (HS_NoOfHours) and response (Freshmen_Score) variables due to chance. Typically, a *p*-value of 5% or less is a good cut-off point.

Note the 'signif. Codes' associated with each estimate.

Three stars (or asterisks) represent a highly significant *p*-value.

A coefficient marked *** is one whose p value < 0.001.

A coefficient marked ** is one whose p value < 0.01, and so on.

Residual Standard Error

Residual standard error is measure of the quality of a linear regression fit. Theoretically, every linear model is assumed to contain an error term, *E* which prevents us from perfectly predicting our response variable from the predictor one. Let us compute the Root Mean Squared Error (RMSE) which is the square root of the mean squared residual.

Let us consider the student data set given as follows:

NoOfHours	*Freshmen_ Score*	*Predicted value*	*Residual Value (Actual Value – Estimated Value)*	*Square of Residual*
2	55	58.70909	–3.70909	13.75734863
2.5	62	62.15152	–0.15152	0.02295831
3	65	65.59394	–0.59394	0.352764724
3.5	70	69.03636	0.96364	0.92860205
4	77	72.47879	4.52121	20.44133986
4.5	82	75.92121	6.07879	36.95168786
5	75	79.36364	–4.36364	19.04135405
5.5	83	82.80606	0.19394	0.037612724
6	85	86.24848	–1.24848	1.55870231
6.5	88	89.69091	–1.69091	2.859176628

Note: We will demonstrate how to compute the predicted and residual values using `predict()` and `resid()` functions in the following sections.

Residual Standard Error = Square root of (Sum of the squared residuals / Degrees of freedom in the model).

- Sum of the squared residuals = 95.95154715
- Degrees of freedom in the model = 8

Degree of freedom is given by number of rows in the dataset – Number of columns or variables. There are 10 rows in the student dataset and 2 columns HS$NoOfHours and HS$Freshmen_Score

i.e., 10 – 2 = 8

Degree of freedom in R can be computed using the `df.residual()` function.

```
>  df.residual (model_HS)
[1] 8
```

Residual Standard Error = Square root of (95.95154715/8)
Residual Standard Error = Square root of (11.99394339)
Residual Standard Error = 3.463227309

Multiple R-squared, Adjusted R-squared

Multiple R-squared The R-squared (R2R2) statistic provides a measure of how well the model fits the actual data. It takes the form of a proportion of variance. R2R2 is a measure of the linear relationship between our predictor variable (HS_NoOfHours) and our response/target variable (Freshmen_Score). It always lies between 0 and 1 (i.e., a number near 0 represents a regression that does not explain the variance in the response variable well and a number close to 1 does explain the observed variance in the response variable).

Multiple R-squared is also called "coefficient of determination". It gives an idea of how many data points fall within the results of the line formed by the regression equation. The higher the coefficient, the higher percentage of points the line passes through when the data points and line are plotted. If the coefficient is 0.80, then 80% of the points should fall within the regression line. Values of 1 or 0 would indicate that the regression line represents all or none of the data, respectively. A higher coefficient is an indicator of a better goodness of fit for the observations.

To compute multiple R-squared, square the correlation coefficient.

$$\text{Multiple R-squared} = (\text{correlation coefficient})^2$$
$$= (0.9542675)^2$$
$$= \mathbf{0.910626}$$

Adjusted R-squared Adjusted R-squared will decrease if more and more useless variables are added to a model. However, if you add more useful variables, the adjusted R-squared will increase. The adjusted R^2 will always be less than or equal to R^2.

$$R^2 \text{ adjusted} = 1 - \frac{(1-R^2)(N-1)}{N-p-1}$$

where

R^2 = sample R-square
p = Number of predictors
N = Total sample size.

R^2 = 0.910626
P = 1
N = 10
R^2 adjusted = 1 – ((0.089374 × 9) / 8)
R^2 adjusted = 1 – ((0.804366)/8)
R^2 adjusted = 1 – 0.10054575
R^2 adjusted = 0.8995

F-statistic

F-statistic is a good indicator of whether there is a relationship between predictor and response variables. The further the F-statistic is from 1, the better it is. However, both the number of data points and the number of predictors determine how large the F-statistic should be. Generally, when the number of data points is large, an F-statistic that is only slightly larger than 1 is sufficient to reject the null hypothesis (H0: There is no relationship between HS_NoOfHours and Freshmen_Score). The reverse is also true, i.e., if the number of data points is small, a large F-statistic is required to ascertain that there may be a relationship between the predictor and response variables. To compute the F statistic, the formula is

$$F = (\text{explained variation}/(k - 1))/(\text{unexplained variation}/(n - k))$$

where, k is the no. of variables in the dataset and n is the no. of observations.

$$F = (0.910626/1)/((1 - 0.910626)/8)$$
$$F = 0.910626/((0.089374)/8)$$
$$F= 0.910626/0.01117175$$
$$\mathbf{F = 81.51149103}$$

Use `predict()`

`predict()` is a generic function for making predictions from the results of various model fitting functions (Table 5.2).

```
> pred_HS <- predict(model_HS)
> pred_HS
       1        2        3        4        5        6        7        8
58.70909 62.15152 65.59394 69.03636 72.47879 75.92121 79.36364 82.80606
       9       10
86.24848 89.69091
```

TABLE 5.2 Data set with predicted/estimated values of freshmen score

	A	B	C
1	*NoOfHours*	*Freshmen_Score*	*Estimated Value*
2	2	55	58.70909
3	2.5	62	62.15152
4	3	65	65.59394
5	3.5	70	69.03636
6	4	77	72.47879
7	4.5	82	75.92121
8	5	75	79.36364
9	5.5	83	82.80606
10	6	85	86.24848
11	6.5	88	89.69091

Use `resid()`

Compute the residual values for the data set. The difference between the observed value of the dependent variable (y) and the predicted value ($\hat{y}$) is called the residual (e). Each data point has one residual. Both the sum and the mean of the residuals are equal to zero (Table 5.3).

```
> ResHS <- resid(model_HS)
> ResHS
         1          2          3         4         5         6          7
-3.7090909 -0.1515152 -0.5939394 0.9636364 4.5212121 6.0787879 -4.3636364
         8          9         10
 0.1939394 -1.2484848 -1.6909091
```

TABLE 5.3 Data set with residual values

	A	B	C	D
1	*NoOfHours*	*Freshmen_Score*	*Estimated Value*	*Residual value (Actual value – Estimated value)*
2	2	55	58.70909	–3.70909
3	2.5	62	62.15152	–0.15152
4	3	65	65.59394	–0.59394
5	3.5	70	69.03636	0.96364
6	4	77	72.47879	4.52121
7	4.5	82	75.92121	6.07879
8	5	75	79.36364	–4.36364
9	5.5	83	82.80606	0.19394
10	6	85	86.24848	–1.24848
11	6.5	88	89.69091	–1.69091

Compute the sum and mean of the residuals (Table 5.4).

TABLE 5.4 Sum and mean of residuals is zero

Residual Value (Actual Value – Estimated Value)
–3.70909
–0.15152
–0.59394
0.96364
4.52121
6.07879
–4.36364
0.19394
–1.24848
–1.69091
Sum = zero Mean = zero

A **residual** plot is a graph that shows the **residuals** on the vertical axis and the independent variable on the horizontal axis. If the points in a **residual** plot are randomly dispersed around the horizontal axis, a linear regression model is appropriate for the data; otherwise, a non-linear model is more appropriate (Figure 5.4).

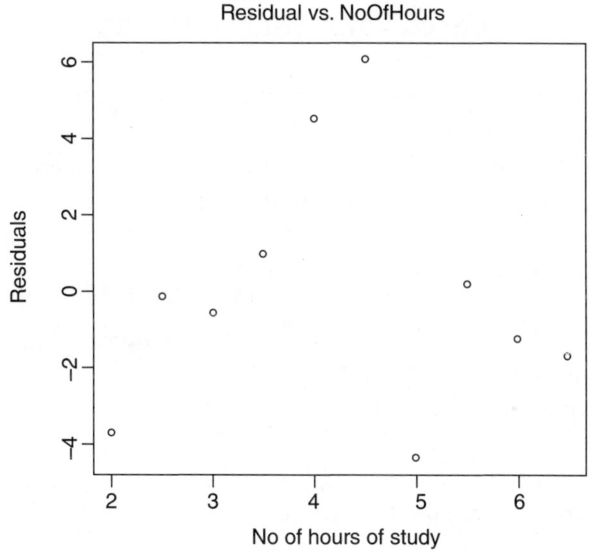

FIGURE 5.4 *Residual plot*

5.4 ASSUMPTIONS OF LINEAR REGRESSION

The model is validated based on the validation of the following assumptions of linear regression:

(1) *Assumptions about the form of the model* The linear regression model $Y = \beta_0 + \beta_1 x_1 + \beta_2 x_2 + \cdots + \beta_n x_n + \varepsilon$ that relates the response Y to the predictors $X_1, X_2 \cdots X_n$, is assumed to be linear in the regression coefficients $\beta_0, \beta_1 \cdots \beta_n$, if the relationship between the dependent and predictor variable(s) of the model is linear.

(2) *Assumptions about the errors:* The errors are assumed to be normally distributed with mean zero and a common variance σ^2.

This implies four assumptions:

1. The errors (also called as residues/residuals) of the model are normally distributed.
2. The errors of the model have a mean of zero.
3. The errors of the model have the same variance. This is also referred to as homoscedasticity principle.
4. The errors of the model should be statistically independent of each other.

These assumptions regarding errors are explained in detail in subsequent sections.

(3) ***Assumptions about the predictors:*** The predictor variables $x_1, x_2 \cdots x_n$ are assumed to be linearly independent of each other. If this assumption is violated, then the problem is called the *collinearity* problem.

Check Your Understanding

1. Which of the following are correct assumptions about errors?
   (a) The errors of the model are normally distributed.
   (b) The errors of the model should be statistically independent of each other.
   (c) The errors of the model have different variance.

2. The coefficient of determination is defined as:
   (a) SST/SSR (b) SSR/SST
   (c) SSE/SSR (d) SSR/SSE
   Note: SST is sum of squared total (SST), SSR is sum of squared regression (SSR) and SSE is sum of squared errors (SSE).

3. The adjusted R2 is preferred over R2 because R2 ______________________.
   (a) Can be inflated artificially by adding more and more predictors
   (b) Can be zero
   (c) Can take negative values

5.5 Validating Linear Assumption

5.5.1 Using Scatter Plot

The linearity of the relationship between the dependent and predictor variables of the model can be studied using scatter plots.

For the provided student data set (with variables, "NoOfHours" and "Freshmen_Score"), the scatter plot of number of hours of study put in by students (HS$NoOfHours) against Freshmen_Score (Freshmen_Score) is as shown in Figure 5.5.

It can be observed that the study time (in hours) exhibits a linear relationship with the score in the freshmen year.

If the relationship is not found to be linear in nature, then a non-linear regression analysis or a polynomial regression or data-transformation may be adopted for prediction.

5.5.2 Using Residuals vs. Fitted Plot

The assumption of linearity can also be validated using the residuals (errors) plotted against the fitted values. The fitted values are the predicted values of the dependent

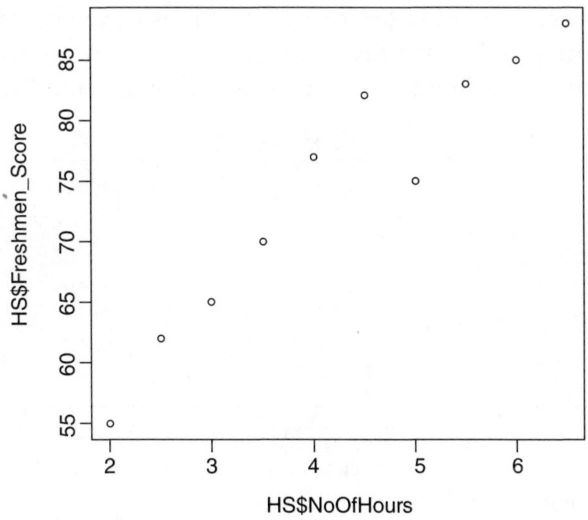

FIGURE 5.5 *Scatter plot*

variable. The plot of errors vs. fitted values for linear regression model for the student data set is given as:

$$\text{Freshmen\_Score} = \beta_0 + (\beta_1 \times \text{NoOfHours}) + \varepsilon$$
$$\text{Freshmen\_Score} = 44.9394 + (6.8848 \times \text{NoOfHours}) + \varepsilon$$

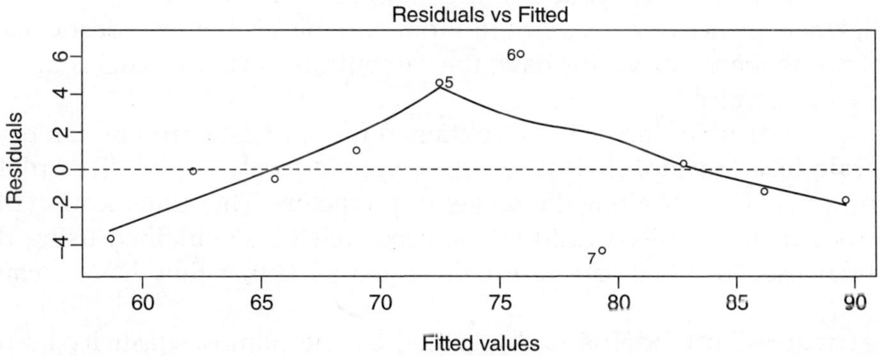

FIGURE 5.6 *Residuals vs. fitted plot*

It can be observed that the above plot does not follow any specific pattern. This is an indicator that the relationship between the dependent and predictor variables is linear in nature. If the residual vs. fitted values plot exhibits any pattern, then the relationship maybe non-linear.

5.5.3 Using Normal Q-Q Plot

A linear regression model is said to be valid if its errors (residuals) are normally distributed. A Normal Q-Q plot can be used to validate this assumption.

For the student data set, the Q-Q plot for the residuals of the best fit model (Figure 5.7), suggests that the residuals are normally distributed since the points lie close to normal line. It is good if residuals are lined well on the straight dashed line.

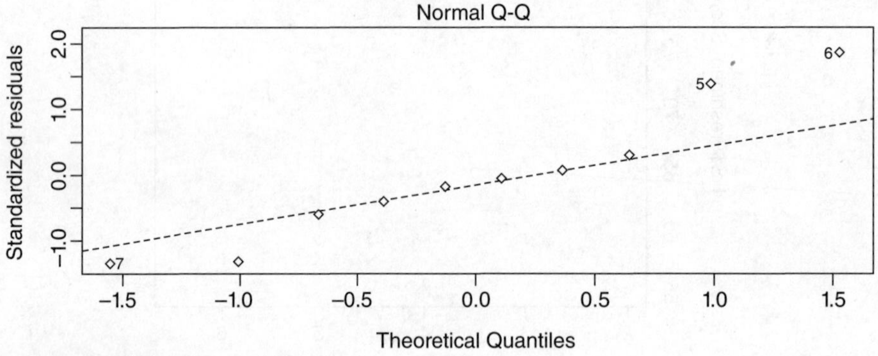

FIGURE 5.7 *Normal Q-Q plot*

5.5.4 Using Scale Location Plot

For a linear regression model to be valid for any statistical inference or prediction, it is essential that the errors (residuals) of the model be homoscedastic in nature. Homoscedasticity describes a situation in which the error term (i.e., the "noise" or random disturbance in the relationship between the independent variables and the dependent variable) is the same across all values of the independent variables.

In statistics, a sequence or a vector of random variables is homoscedastic if all random variables in the sequence or vector have the same finite variance. This is also known as homogeneity of variance.[1]

The homoscedasticity of the residuals obtained for our best fit model can be examined using the **scale-location plot**. It is also called **spread-location** plot. This plot shows if residuals are spread equally along the ranges of predictors. The scale-location plot depicts the square rooted standardised residual vs. predicted value obtained using the best fit model. Standardised residuals are residuals scaled such that they have mean of 0 and variance of 1.

The linear regression model is said to abide by the homoscedasticity assumption if there is no specific pattern observed in the scale-location plot. The scale-location plot of the best fit model for the student data set is as shown below (Figure 5.8).

It can be observed in the above plot that there is no specific pattern. In general, the homoscedasticity is said to be violated if:

- The residuals seem to increase or decrease in average magnitude with the fitted values. This is an indication that the variance of the residuals is not constant.
- The points in the plot lie on a curve around zero, rather than fluctuating randomly.
- A few points in the plot lie a long way from the rest of the points.

[1] Wikipedia: Homoscedasticity

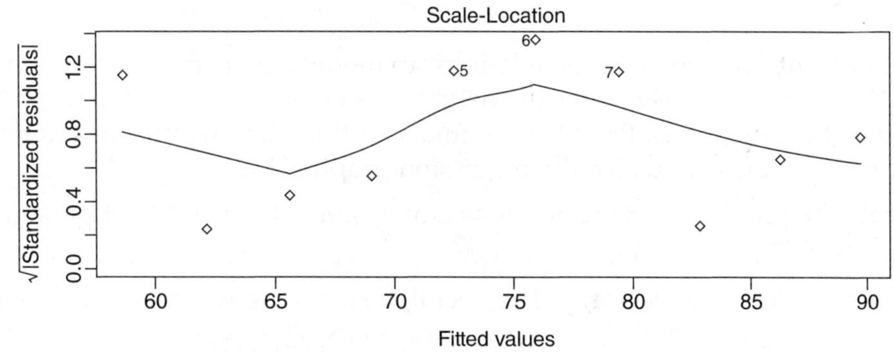

FIGURE 5.8 *Scale location plot*

5.5.5 Using Residuals vs. Leverage Plot

This plot is useful in determining the influential cases (i.e., subjects) if any. Not all outliers are influential in linear regression analysis. There could be a few outliers whose inclusion or exclusion from analysis would not affect the results a lot. They usually follow the trend in most cases and they do not really matter. On the other hand, there could be a few outliers which when excluded from analysis can significantly alter the results.

Here, plot patterns are not relevant. However, observe the outlying values at the upper right corner or at the lower right corner. These spots are the places where cases can be influential against a regression line. Look for cases outside of a dashed line, such as Cook's distance. Cook's distance can be defined as, *"Data points with large residuals (outliers) and/or high leverage may distort the outcome and accuracy of a regression. Cook's distance measures the effect of deleting a given observation. Points with a large Cook's distance are considered to merit closer examination in the analysis."*[2] Watch out for cases that are outside of Cook's distance (meaning they have high Cook's distance scores). These cases may influence the regression results. Exercise caution while excluding such cases as the regression results may be significantly altered if we exclude them. Refer Figure 5.9 for "Residuals vs Leverage" plot for the student data set.

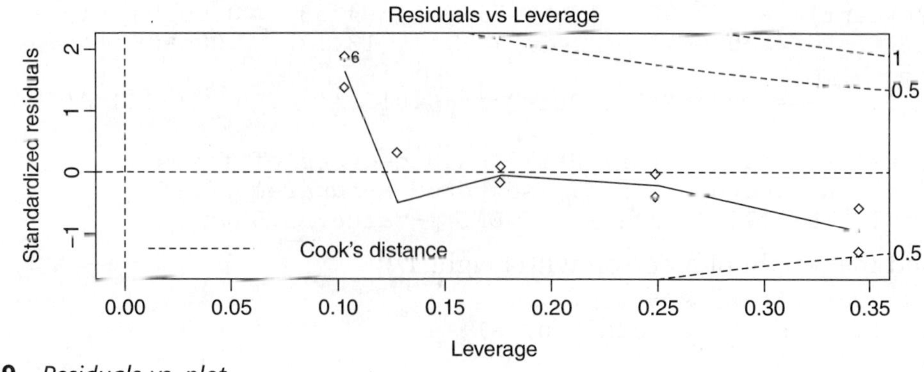

FIGURE 5.9 *Residuals vs. plot*

[2] Wikipedia: Cook's distance

Example 1

Problem statement: Demonstrate the relationship model between predictor and response variables. The predictor vector stores the heights of persons, whereas the response vector stores the weights of persons. Print the summary of the relationship. Also determine the weights of new persons. Visualise the regression graphically.

Step 1: Create the predictor vector, *x*. The vector, *x* stores the heights of persons.

```
> x <- c(152, 175, 139, 187, 129, 137, 180, 162, 151, 130)
```

Step 2: Create the response vector, y. The vector, y stores the weights of persons.

```
> y <- c(62, 80, 55, 90, 48, 56, 75, 73, 63, 49)
```

Step 3: Apply the `lm()` function.

```
> relation <- lm(y~x)
> print(relation)

Call:
lm(formula = y ~ x)

Coefficients:
(Intercept)  x
-34.7196     0.6473
```

Step 4: Print the summary of the relationship.

```
> print(summary(relation))

Call:
lm(formula = y ~ x)

Residuals:
    Min      1Q   Median     3Q    Max
-6.8013 -0.6989 -0.1445 1.8845 3.6673

Coefficients:
             Estimate Std. Error t Value Pr(>|t|)
(Intercept) -34.7196      7.6651   -4.53  0.00193   **
x             0.6473      0.0493   13.13  1.08e-06  ***
---
Signif. codes: 0 '***' 0.001 '**' 0.01 '*' 0.05 '.' 0.1 ' ' 1

Residual standard error: 3.117 on 8 degrees of freedom
Multiple R-squared: 0.9557, Adjusted R-squared: 0.9501
F-statistic: 172.4 on 1 and 8 DF, p-value: 1.076e-06
```

Step 5: Find the weight of a person with height 170.

```
> a <- data.frame(x = 170)
> result <- predict(relation, a)
> print(result)
       1
75.32795
```

Step 6: Visualise the regression graphically by plotting a chart.

```
> plot(y,x,col = "blue",main = "Height & Weight Regression",
+ abline(lm(x~y)),cex = 1.3,pch = 16,xlab = "Weight in Kg",ylab =
"Height in cm")
```

Example 2:

We will work with the "cars" dataset provided with R. This dataset can be accessed by typing "cars" at the R prompt. The dataset has 50 observations (rows) and 2 columns, viz., "dist" and "speed". Let us print out the first 6 rows of the car dataset using the head command.

```
> head(cars)
  speed  dist
1     4     2
2     4    10
3     7     4
4     7    22
5     8    16
6     9    10
```

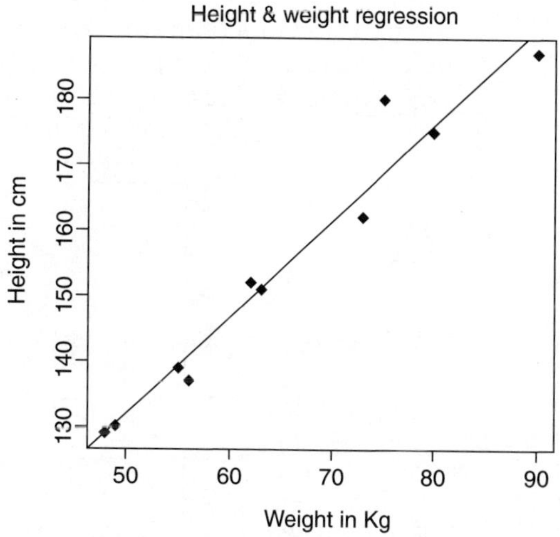

FIGURE 5.10 *Linear regression between predictor and response variables*

Problem statement: To be able to predict the distance (dist) by establishing a statistically significant linear relationship with the predictor variable (speed).

Step 1: Plot a scatter plot to visually understand the relationship between the predictor and response variables. The scatter plot indicates a linearly increasing relationship between the two variables (Figure 5.11).

```
> scatter.smooth(x=cars$speed, y=cars$dist, main="Dist ~ Speed")
```

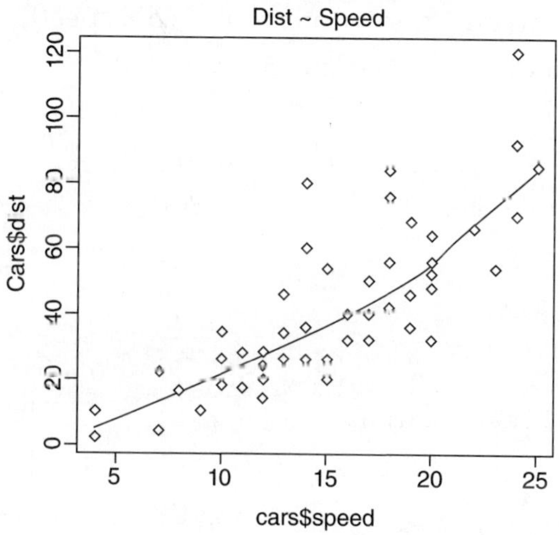

FIGURE 5.11 *Scatter plot for predictor vs. response variable for "cars" data set*

Step 2: Spot any outlier observations in the variable by plotting a box plot. We begin by dividing the graph area into two columns. One column contains the box plot for "speed" and the second column contains the box plot for "distance" (Figure 5.12).

```
> par(mfrow=c(1, 2)) # divide graph area in 2 columns
> boxplot(cars$speed, main="Speed", sub=paste("Outlier rows: ",
  boxplot.stats(cars$speed)$out)) #box plot for 'speed'
> boxplot(cars$dist, main="Distance", sub=paste("Outlier rows: ",
  boxplot.stats(cars$dist)$out)) # box plot for 'distance'
```

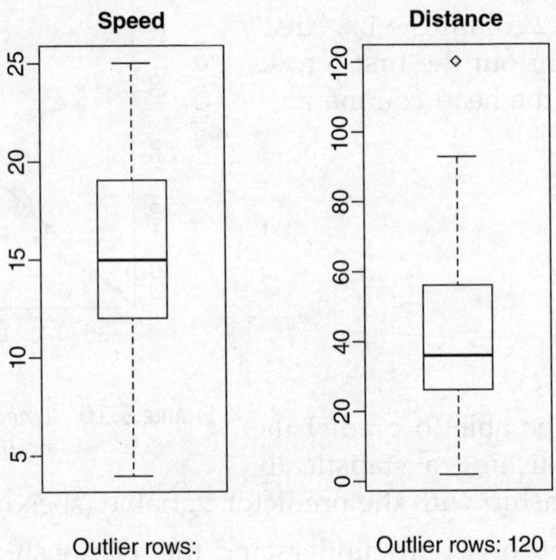

FIGURE 5.12 *Box plots*

Step 3: Build a linear relationship model. The "coefficients" part has two components, "intercept" (Intercept = -17.579) and "speed" (speed = 3.932). These are also called the beta coefficients. In other words, dist = Intercept + ($\beta \times$ speed).

```
> linearMod <- lm(dist ~ speed, data=cars)
> print(linearMod)

Call:
lm(formula = dist ~ speed, data = cars)

Coefficients:
(Intercept)      speed
-17.579          3.932

> print(summary(linearMod))

Call:
lm(formula = dist ~ speed, data = cars)
```

```
Residuals:
    Min       1Q  Median      3Q     Max
-29.069   -9.525  -2.272   9.215  43.201

Coefficients:
            Estimate Std.  Error t  value   Pr(>|t|)
(Intercept)  -17.5791     6.7584    -2.601    0.0123   *
speed          3.9324     0.4155     9.464  1.49e-12   ***
---
Signif. codes: 0 '***' 0.001 '**' 0.01 '*' 0.05 '.' 0.1 '' 1

Residual standard error: 15.38 on 48 degrees of freedom
Multiple R-squared: 0.6511, Adjusted R-squared: 0.6438
F-statistic: 89.57 on 1 and 48 DF, p-value: 1.49e-12
```

Step 4: Visualise the regression graphically by plotting a chart (Figure 5.13).

```
> plot(cars$dist, cars$speed, col = "blue", main = "Speed & Distance
Regression",
+ abline(lm(cars$speed ~ cars$dist)), cex = 1.3, pch=16, xlab =
"Distance", ylab = "Speed")
```

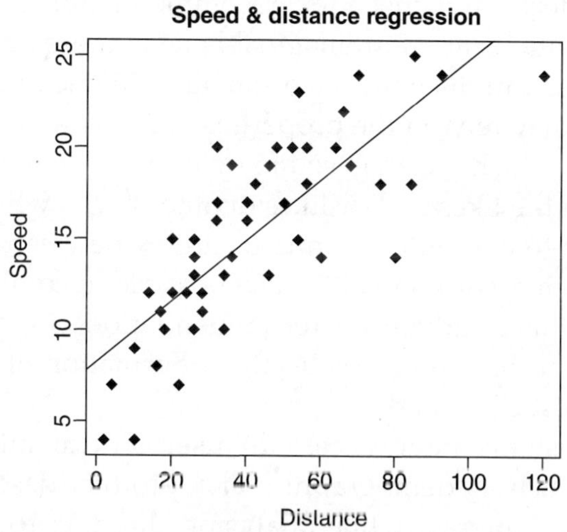

FIGURE 5.13 *Linear regression between predictor and response variables*

Check Your Understanding

1. Which plot is the most appropriate to examine the homoscedasticity of the residuals obtained for the best fit model?
   (a) Histogram
   (b) Bar Plot
   (c) Scale-location Plot
   (d) Heat Map

(Continued)

2. ________ link function is commonly used for generalised linear models with binomial distribution.
(a) Logit
(b) Inverse squared
(c) Inverse
(d) Identity

Case Study

Recommendation Engines

The term, 'recommender systems' is widely used nowadays. Recommender systems are composed of very simple algorithms that aim to provide the most relevant and accurate information to users by sorting/filtering useful information from very large databases. Recommendation engines discover data patterns from a given dataset by learning the consumers' information and then producing outcomes that correlate to their needs and interests. In addition, recommendation engines narrow down the risk that could become a complex decision to just a few recommendations search. Big data supports recommendations at an unimaginable level these days.

Recommendation engines work mainly in one of the following two ways, viz., either they rely on the properties of items with their bread crumps that a user likes, which are analysed to determine what else the user may like, or they rely on the likes and dislikes of other users, which the recommendation engine uses to compute a similarity index between users and recommends items to them accordingly. It is also possible to combine both these methods to build a highly-advanced recommendation engine. The main goal is to achieve the recommended collective information of users for the items that might interest customers.

These systems have access to user-centric information with profile attributes, such as demographics and product descriptions. They differ in the way they interact while analysing the data to develop affinity values between users and items, which can be used to identify well-matched pairs. A collaborative filtering system is used for matching and analysing historical interaction alone, while content-based filtering is used for profiling-based attributes.

Let us see how we can implement a recommendation engine with a collaborative memory-based recommendation engine. However, before that we must first understand the logic behind such a system. To this engine, each item and each user is nothing but an identifier or token element. Let us take the example of Netflix. Please note that we will not take any other attribute of

(Continued)

a movie, such as cast, director, genre, etc., into consideration while generating recommendations for users. The similarity between two users is represented by using a decimal number between -1.0 and 1.0. We will call this number, the *similarity index*. The possibility of a user liking a movie will be represented by using another decimal number between -1.0 and 1.0. Now that we have modelled the world around this system using simple terms, we can unleash a handful of elegant mathematical equations to define the relationship between these identifiers and numbers.

In our recommendation algorithm, we will maintain a number of sets, which should represent a member of supersets with all users and identifiers. Each user will have two sets, viz., a set of movies the user likes and a set of movies the user dislikes. Each movie will also have two sets associated with it, viz., a set of users who liked the movie and a set of users who disliked the movie. During the performance where recommendations start to generate, a number of sets will be produced, mostly unions or intersections of the other sets. We will also have ordered lists of suggestions and similar users for each user.

Similarly, like movies we can use the following recommendations.

Personalised Product Information E-commerce Sites

Such engines help in understanding customers' preferences on the basis of their visit on the website. They show the customers the most relevant recommendation-type products as per their needs or there likes in real time. Recommendations improve as the cognitive learning improves with regression about each visitor each time.

Website Personalisation

This is used by many organisations to calculate revenue on the basis of the number of hits from visitors. It increases their sales and targets new customers through segmentation into different clusters. It also allows getting in touch by message-centric methods.

Real-time Notifications

This is used by e-commerce for letting their customers know about the new top selling brands and available discounts. Such engines help brands build trust among their customers and create a sense of presence and urgency while showing real-time notifications of shoppers' activities on their website.

Summary

- Models in R are a representation of a sequence of data points.
- R has different types of models. These are listed below along with their commands:
  - Linear (lm)
  - Generalised linear models (glm)
  - Linear models for mixed effects (lme)
  - Non-linear least squares (nls)
  - Generalised additive models (gam)
- Linear regression relationship is represented by a straight line when plotted on a graph.
- General equation of linear regression is $y = ax + b$.
- Simple syntax of the `lm()` function in linear regression is lm(formula,data).
- F-statistics = $\dfrac{\text{explained variation}/(k-1)}{\text{unexplained variation}/(n-k)}$

  where, k is the number of variables in the dataset and n is the number of observations.
- Multiple R-squared = (correlation coefficient)^2
- Residual is computed by using the `resid()` function.
- The `predict()` function operates on any lm object and generates a vector of predicted values by default.
- Standardised residual in *R* is the ratio of normal residual to its standard deviation of residual.
- Cook's distance is used to identify the outliers in *X* values which are predictor variables.
- Standard error is the ratio of standard deviation to the square root of the sample size.
- The coefficient of determination r^2 is given as:

  $$r^2 = \frac{\Sigma(y_i - y')^2}{\Sigma(y_i - y')^2}$$
- Scatterplot in *R* can be created in many ways and the basic function is plot(*x*, *y*) where *x* and *y* are input vector values that are to be plotted.

Key Terms

- **Cook's distance:** Cook's distance is used to identify the outliers in X values, which are predictor variables.
- **Linear regression:** Linear regression is represented by a straight line when plotted on a graph.
- **Models:** Models in R are a representation of a sequence of data points.
- **Model fitting:** Model fitting is picking the right model that best describes the data.
- **`predict()`: `predict()`** is used to obtain the predicted values in R.
- **Residuals:** Residuals are the data of linear regression, which is the difference between the observed data of the independent variable y and the fitted values y^.
- **R-squared:** The coefficient of determination (R-squared) of linear regression model is the quotient of variances of the fitted values and the observed values of the dependent variables.
- **Scatterplot:** Scatterplot is used in displaying the relationship of the given input variables.

- **Standardised residual:** Standardised residual is the ratio of normal residual to its standard deviation of residual.
- **Studentised residuals:** Studentised residual is the ratio of the normal residual to its independent standard deviation of residual.

Multiple Choice Questions

1. What will be the response variable in the given equation?
   $y = ax + b$
   (a) a (b) b
   (c) x (d) y
2. Which function will compute the correlation of x and y, considering x and y are vectors?
   (a) `cor()` (b) `var()`
   (c) `cov()` (d) `dvar()`
3. Which function will be used to create a model as per linear regression in R?
   (a) `lm()` (b) `pp()`
   (c) `biglm()` (d) `glm()`
4. Which function will be used for making predictions from the results of various model fitting functions?
   (a) `compare()` (b) `contrasts()`
   (c) `predict()` (d) `resid()`
5. Residual is calculated as:
   (a) Residual = y - y^ (b) Residual = y^ - y
   (c) Residual = $y \sim x$ (d) Residual = $x \sim y$
6. The ratio of normal residual to its standard deviation of residual is:
   (a) Standardised residual (b) Studentised residual
   (c) Residual (d) R-squared

Short Questions

1. What is model fitting?
2. What is the general equation for computing linear regression?
3. What is a response and predictor variable?
4. What is the syntax of `lm()` function?
5. What is a residual?
6. What is leverage?

7. What is Cook's distance?
8. What is homoscedasticity?
9. How to find standard error?
10. How to plot a scatterplot?

Practical Exercises

1. Consider the "cars" data set. Assume "cars$dist" as the response variable and "cars$speed" as the predictor variable. Create a model using the `lm()` function. Explain the below plots with respect to residuals as per the model:

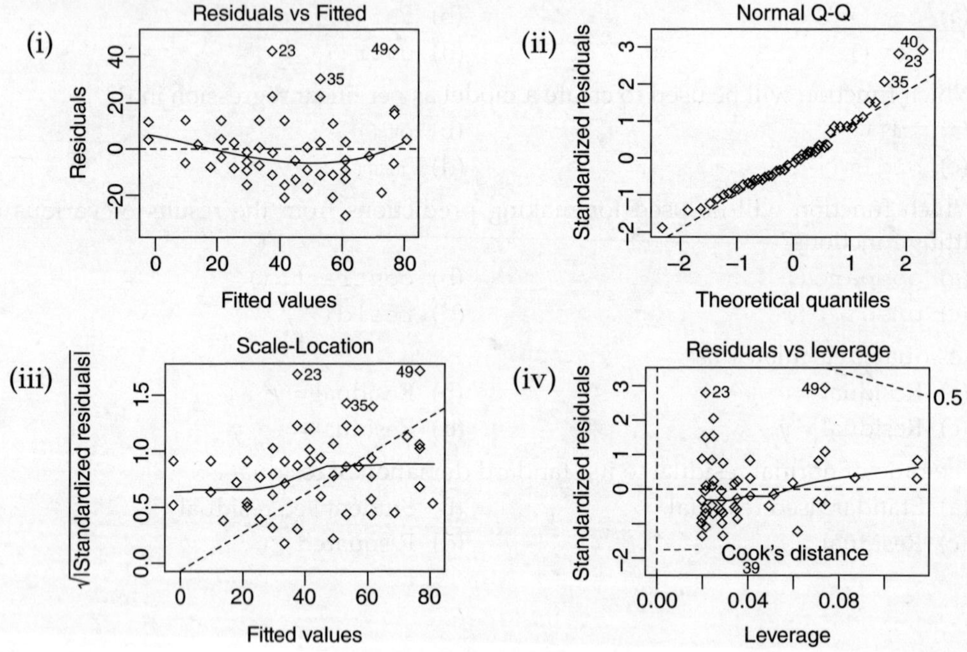

Chapter 6

Logistic Regression

LEARNING OUTCOME

At the end of this chapter, you will be able to:

- Select a suitable logistic regression technique for a problem statement
- Create binomial, multinomial and ordinal logistic regression models
- Determine the prediction accuracy of a logistic regression model
- Predict the outcome of a data point using a logistic regression model

6.1 Introduction

Logistic regression helps to describe the relationship between a dependent binary (dichotomous) variable and one or more nominal (also called as categorical variable. These variables have two or more categories without necessarily having any kind of natural order), ordinal (they have a clear ordering of the categories), interval (where the differences between values are meaningful and more often equally split) or ratio level independent variables (variables have a natural zero point).

In order to facilitate easy understanding, this section discusses the commonly asked questions in data science, explains regression, types of regression, significance of logistic regression and why we cannot stick to using only linear regression.

Let us ponder for a while on the commonly asked questions in data science (data science is also known as data-driven science. It is an interdisciplinary field that encompasses scientific methods, processes and systems with an intent to extract knowledge or gain insights from data in various forms, either structured or unstructured.)

Commonly asked questions in data science	*Algorithms used to provide the answers*
Is this A or B? Example: • Is this an apple or an orange? • Is this a pen or a pencil? • Is it sunny or overcast? • Email spam classification • A bank loan officer wants to determine which customers (loan applicants) are risky or which are safe based on the analysis of the data.	Classification algorithm
Is this weird? Example: • Fraud detection: Detecting credit card frauds • Surveillance	Anomaly detection algorithm. It is also referred to as outlier detection. These algorithms help with identifying items, events or observations that do not conform to an expected pattern or other items in a dataset.
Quantifiable questions such as, "How much or how many?" Examples: • Predicting house prices with increase in sizes of houses. • Determining relationship between the hours of study a student puts in, with respect to his/her exam results. • How many goals will be scored in the basketball match today? • What will be the day's temperature in the city tomorrow?	Regression algorithm (Refer chapter 5)
How is this organized?	Clustering algorithm (Refer chapter 9)
What should I do next? Example: • Robot uses deep reinforcement learning to pick a device from one box and put it in a container. Whether it succeeds or fails, it memorises the object and gains knowledge and train's itself to do this job with great speed and precision.	Reinforcement learning. It helps with making a decision. Reinforcement learning is a type of machine learning, and thereby also a branch of artificial intelligence. It allows machines and software agents to automatically determine the ideal behaviour within a specific context, in order to maximise its performance.

6.2 What is Regression?

Regression analysis is a predictive modeling technique. It estimates the relationship between a dependent (target) and an independent variable (predictor).

Example: A regression model can be used to predict the height of children with data given about their age, weight and other factors.

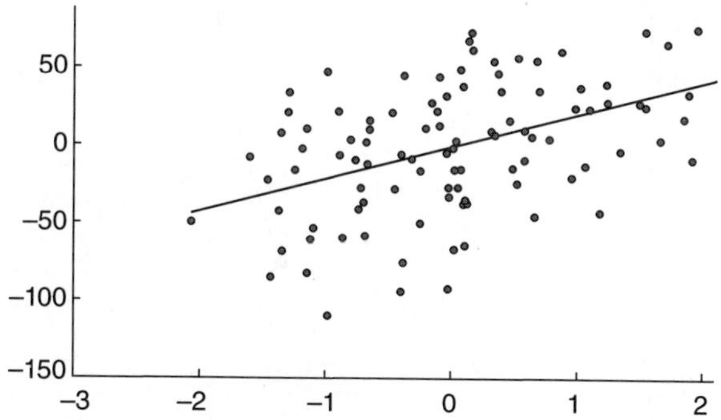

Figure 6.1 *Linear regression*

Refer Figure 6.1 and note that as X increases, Y also increases. X can increase independently of Y but Y will increase in accordance to X. So, X is the independent variable and Y is the dependent variable.

There are essentially three types of regression:

1. ***Linear regression:*** When there is a linear relationship between independent and dependent variables it is known as linear regression (Figure 6.1).
2. ***Logistic regression:*** When the dependent variable is categorical (0/1, True/False, Yes/No, A/B/C) in nature it is known as logistic regression (Figure 6.2).

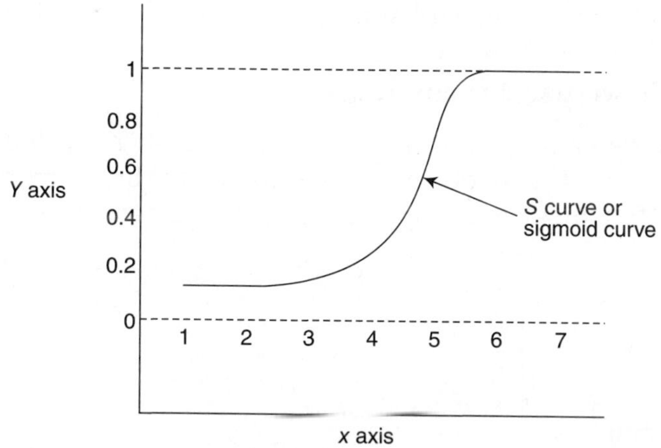

Figure 6.2 *Logistic regression*

As can be seen from Figure 6.2, Y's value is zero for certain values of X and Y's value is one for certain values of X. After the value 4 on the X-axis, the value of Y is becoming 1. We say it is undergoing a transition to become 1. This transition is the S or sigmoid curve.

3. ***Polynomial regression:*** When the power of the independent variable is more than 1 then it is referred as polynomial regression (Figure 6.3).

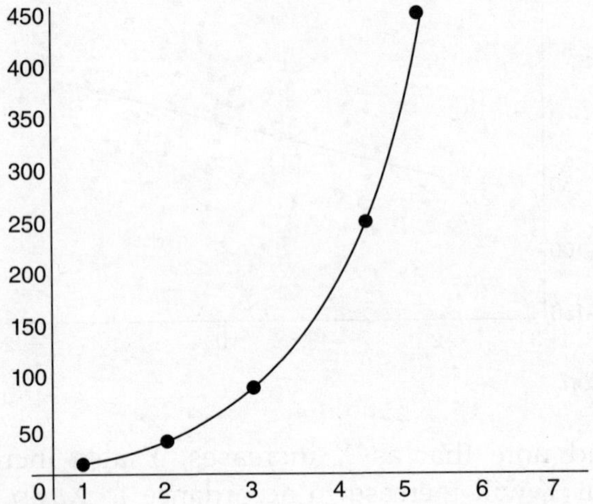

FIGURE 6.3 *Polynomial regression*

6.2.1 Why Logistic Regression?

Whenever the outcome of the dependent variable(y) is discrete, like 0/1, Yes/No, or A/B/C, we use logistic regression.

Example: Let us ask a question, "Is this animal a rat or an elephant?" The answer to this question is either a rat or an elephant. You cannot say it is a dog.

6.2.2 Why can't we use Linear Regression?

In linear regression *Y*'s value is in a range but in our case *Y*'s value is discrete, i.e., the value will either be 0 or 1. If you look at the best fit line for linear regression, it is crossing 1 and is also below 0. However, in logistic regression it cannot be below zero or above 1 (Figure 6.4).

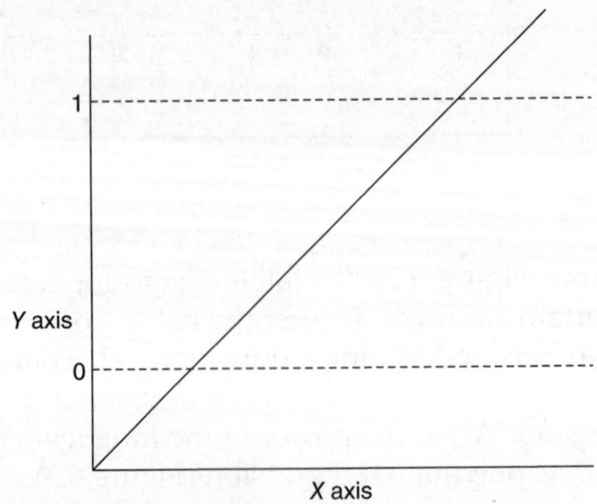

FIGURE 6.4 *Best fit line crosses 1 and is also below 0*

We will have to clip the best fit line of linear regression at 0 and 1 (Figure 6.5).

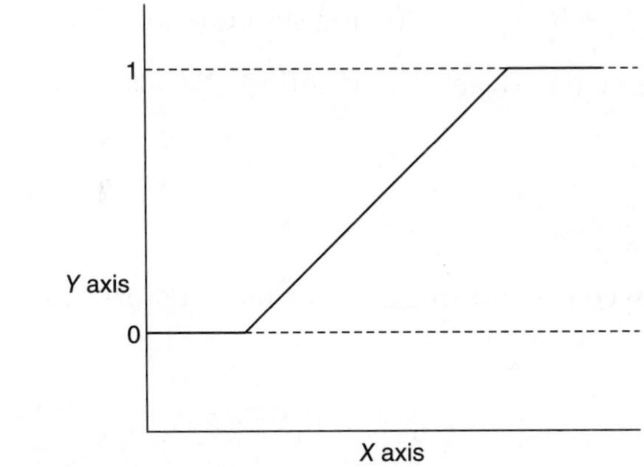

FIGURE 6.5 *Best fit line is clipped at 0 and 1*

The resulting curve cannot be formulated into a single formula. There is a need to find a new way to solve this problem. Therefore, logistic regression (Figure 6.6).

6.2.3 Logistic Regression

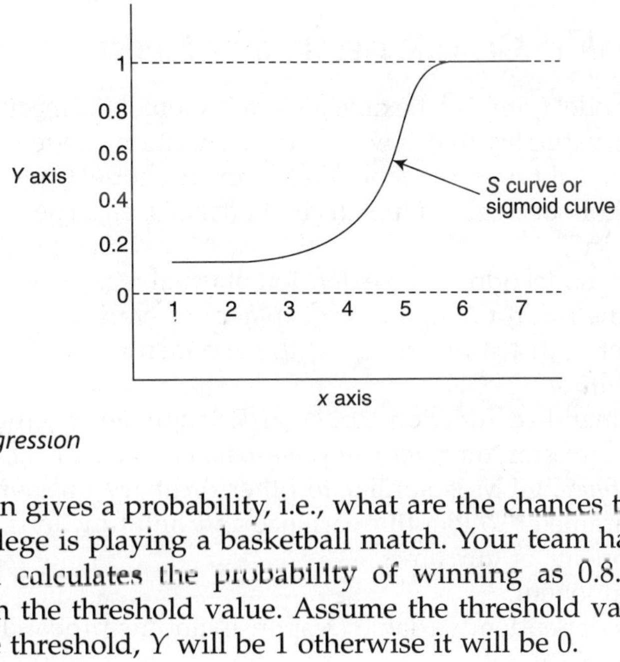

FIGURE 6.6 *Logistic regression*

Logistic regression gives a probability, i.e., what are the chances that Y will become 1.

Assume your college is playing a basketball match. Your team has scored 10 baskets. Assume the model calculates the probability of winning as 0.8. This probability is then compared with the threshold value. Assume the threshold value is fixed at 0.5. If probability is above threshold, Y will be 1 otherwise it will be 0.

Equation for a straight line:

$Y = C + B_1X_1 + B_2X_2 + \ldots$ Range of Y is from – (infinity) to infinity

Let us try to deduce the logistic regression equation from this equation.

$$Y = C + B_1X_1 + B_2X_2 + \dots \quad \text{(in logistic equation } Y \text{ can only be between 0 and 1)}$$

Now, to get the range of Y between 0 and infinity, let us transform Y.

$$\left.\frac{Y}{1-Y}\right\}^{Y=0|0}_{Y=1|\text{infinity}}$$

Now the range is between 0 and infinity. Let us transform it further to get the range between (infinity) and infinity.

$$\log\left(\frac{Y}{1-Y}\right) \rightarrow \log\left(\frac{Y}{1-Y}\right) = C + B_1X_1 + B_2X_2 + \dots$$

Thus, logistic regression is a regression model where the dependent variable is categorical.

Categorical → variables that can have only fixed values such as A/B/C or Yes/No

Dependent → $Y = f(X)$, i.e., Y is dependent on X.

The chapter presents detailed explanation of logistic regression, binary logistic regression and multinomial logistic regression.

6.3 Introduction to Generalised Linear Models

Generalised linear model (glm) is a flexible generalisation of ordinary linear regression that allows for response variables that have error distribution models other than a normal distribution. Several subtypes of generalised linear models are available. These are logistic regression, Poisson regression, survival analysis, etc. The focus of this chapter is on "logistic regression".

Generalised linear model (glm) is an extension of usual regression models through a link function. It allows the mean to depend on explanatory variables. The response variable is any member of set of distributions called the exponential family like normal, Poisson and binomial distributions.

The built-in command or function `glm()` of R language executes GLMs. The `glm()` function performs regression on *binary outcome data, probability data, count data, proportion data* and *other data types*. GLM is similar to other ordinary linear models except that it requires an extra parameter to identify variance and link functions.

The major components of glm are:

- A random component:
    - It identifies dependent variable (response) and its probability distribution.
    - This categorises the response variable Y and its probability distribution.
    - The random component of glm consists of a response variable Y with independent observations $(y_1, y_2 \dots y_n)$ from a distribution in the natural exponential family.

- A systematic component:
  - It identifies a set of explanatory variables that are used in a linear predictor function.
- A link function:
  - It defines the relationship between a random and systematic component.

The syntax of `glm()` command is:

```
glm(formula, family = family type(link = linkfunction), data,…)
```

where, "formula" argument defines the symbolic description of the model to be fitted, "data" argument is an optional argument that defines the dataset, the dots "…" define the other optional arguments, "family" argument defines the link function to be used in the model.

Table 6.1 describes the different types of families and their default link functions used in glm function.

TABLE 6.1 Types of families and their default link functions

Family	*Default link function*
Binomial	(link = "logit")
Gaussian	(link = "identity")
Gamma	(link = "inverse")
Inverse Gaussian	(link = "1/mu^2")
Poisson	(link = "identity", variance = "constant')
Quasi	(link = "logit")
Quasi Binomial	(link = "log")

Check Your Understanding

1. What do you mean by glm?

Ans: Generalised linear model (glm) is an extension of usual regression models through a link function.

2. What is the role of random components in the glm model?

Ans: A random component identifies the dependent variable (response) and its probability distribution in the glm model.

3. What is the role of the systematic component in the glm model?

Ans: A systematic component identifies a set of explanatory variables in the glm model.

4. What is the role of the link function in the glm model?

Ans: The link function defines the relationship between a random and systematic component in the glm model.

6.4 Logistic Regression

Logistic regression (LR) is an extension of linear regression to environments that contain a categorical dependent variable. LR is a part of GLM and uses the `glm()` command to fit the regression model. In LR, the parameter estimation is carried out through a maximum likelihood estimator. LR is derived from the logistic function given below:

$$P(Y=1)=\pi=\frac{e^Z}{1+e^Z}$$

The main objective of LR is to estimate how the probability of an event affects one or more explanatory variables. For LR, the following conditions are to be satisfied:

- An outcome variable with two categorical results, viz., 0 and 1.
- Proper estimation is required to know the probability P of an observed value of the outcome variable.
- The outcome variable must be related to the explanatory variables, which are done through logistic function.
- Proper estimation of coefficients of the regression equation must be developed.
- The regression model should be tested to check if it fits the intervals of the coefficients.

6.4.1 Use of Logistic Regression

Logistic regression is mostly used to solve classification problems, discrete choice models or to find the probability of an event.

- ***Classification problems:*** Classification problems are an important category of problems in which a decision maker classifies the customers into two or more categories. For example, customer churn is a very common problem that any industry or company faces. The reason why it is an important problem is that customer acquisition or acquisition of new customers and its costs are much higher than retaining existing customers or the cost of retaining existing customers. So many companies prefer to know customer churn or at least an early warning about a customer churn. Hence, LR is the best option to solve problems where the outcome is either binomial or multinomial.
- ***Discrete choice model:*** Discrete choice model (DCM) estimates the probability about customers who select a particular brand over several available alternative brands. For example, a company would like to know why customers opt for a particular brand and their motivation behind it. LR analyses such probabilities as well.
- ***Probability:*** Probability measures the possibility of the occurrence of any event. LR finds out the probability of an event.

6.4.2 Binomial Logistic Regression

Binomial or binary logistic regression (BLR) is a model in which the dependent variable is dichotomous. The expression is as follows:

$$P(Y=1)=\pi=\frac{e^Z}{1+e^Z}$$

where, Y can take two values, i.e., 0 or 1 and the independent variable can be of any type. Hence, the explanatory variables are either continuous or qualitative.

6.4.3 Logistic Function

Logistic function or sigmoidal function is a function that estimates various parameters and checks whether they are statistically significant and influence the probability of an event. The formula of the logistic function is as:

$$\pi(z)=\frac{e^z}{1+e^z}$$

$$z=\beta_0+\beta_1 x_1+\beta_2 x_2+\ldots+\beta_n x_n$$

where, $x_1, x_2 \ldots x_n$ are the explanatory variables.

The logistic function with one explanatory variable is given as:

$$P(Y=1|X=x)=\pi(x)=\frac{exp(\alpha+\beta x)}{1+exp(\alpha+\beta x)}$$

- When $\beta = 0$, it implies that $P(Y|x)$ is the same for each value of x, i.e., there is no statistically significant relationship between Y and X.
- When $\beta > 0$, it implies that $P(Y|x)$ increases as the value of X increases, i.e., the probability of the event increases as the value of X increases.
- When $\beta < 0$, it implies that $P(Y|x)$ decreases as the value of X increases, i.e., the probability of Y decreases as the value of X increases.

6.4.4 Logit Function

Logit function is the logarithmic transformation of the logistic function. It is defined as the natural logarithm of odds. Some logit models with only categorical variables have equivalent log-linear models. The formula of the logistic function is:

$$\text{Logit}(\pi)=1n\left(\frac{\pi}{1-\pi}\right)=\beta_0+\beta_1 X_1$$

Logit of a variable π is given by,

$$\frac{\pi}{1-\pi}=\text{odds}$$

Logistic Regression Parameters

Odds and odds ratio are two LR parameters. They are explained as given:

Odds is defined as the ratio of two probability values and is given as:

$$odds = \frac{\pi(x)}{1-\pi(x)}$$

Odds ratio (OR) is the ratio of two odds and as per the logit function it is given as:

$$\ln\left(\frac{\pi(x)}{1-\pi(x)}\right) = \beta_0 + \beta_1 x_1$$

Consider x to be an independent variable, i.e., covariate. Then the odds ratio OR is defined as the ratio of the odds for $x = 1$ to the odds for $x = 0$.

For $x = 0$,

$$\left(\frac{\pi(x)}{1-\pi(x)}\right) = \beta_0 \quad (1)$$

For $x = 1$,

$$\ln\left(\frac{\pi(1)}{1-\pi(1)}\right) = \beta_0 + \beta_1 \quad (2)$$

Subtracting equation (1) from equation (2), we get,

$$\beta_1 = \ln\left(\frac{\pi(1)/(1-\pi(1))}{\pi(0)/(1-\pi(0))}\right)$$

Hence, we can conclude that β_1 captures the change in the log odds ratio. The expression can be rewritten as

$$e^{\beta_1} = \frac{\pi(x+1)/(1-\pi(x+1))}{\pi(x)/(1-\pi(x+1))} = \text{Change in odds ratio}$$

Hence, a change in the explanatory variable also produces a change in the odds ratio. Suppose the value of odds ratio is 2, then the event is twice likely to occur when $x = 1$ compared to $x = 0$. Now, the x value changes when the odds ratio approximates the relative risk whether the risk increases or decreases.

6.4.5 Likelihood Function

Likelihood function [L(β)] represents the joint probability or likelihood of observing the collected data. This function also summarises the evidence of data about unknown parameters.

Consider the following n observations of a dataset: $x_1, x_2...x_n$. Their corresponding distribution is $f(x,\theta)$, where θ is the unknown parameter. Then, the likelihood function is $L(\theta) = f(x_1, x_2...x_n, \theta)$ which is the joint probability density function of the sample. The value of θ, θ^* which maximises $L(\theta)$ is called the *maximum likelihood estimator* of θ.

Take another example in which a dataset follows an exponential distribution with n observations $(x_1, x_2...x_n)$. For exponential distribution, the probability density is given by,

$$f(x, \theta) = \theta e^{-\theta x}$$

The equations below then represent the likelihood function as

$$L(x, \theta) = f(x_1, \theta) \cdot f(x_2, \theta) \ldots f(x_n, \theta)$$

By replacing the density function in the above expression, you will get an expression that represents the joint probability as:

$$\text{Joint probabilty} = \theta e^{-\theta x_1}\ X\ \theta e^{-\theta x_1}\ X \ldots \theta e^{-\theta x_n} = \theta^n e - \theta \sum_{i=1}^{n} x_i$$

Just Remember

Use log-likelihood function instead of handling the likelihood function. The log-likelihood function is given as

$$Ln(L(x, \theta)) = n1n\theta - \theta \sum_{i=1}^{n} x_i$$

Inbuilt R Language Function for Finding Likelihood Function

R language provides two functions, viz., `nlm()` and `optim()` for finding out the likelihood function.

nlm() Function

The `nlm()` function performs a non-linear minimisation and minimises the function using a Newton-type algorithm. In simple words, the `nlm()` function minimises arbitrariness of any user-defined function that is written in R and maximises its likelihood. Hence, to maximise the likelihood, the negative of the log likelihood is used. The syntax of the `nlm()` function is

```
nlm(f,p,…).
```

where, "*f*" argument defines a function to be minimised. The function should return a single value. "*P*" argument starts parameter values for minimisation and the dots "..." define the other optional arguments.

In the following example, a simple function *f* is finding the sum of (n-1)^2. The `nlm()` function estimates the likelihood function of *f* as shown in Figure 6.7.

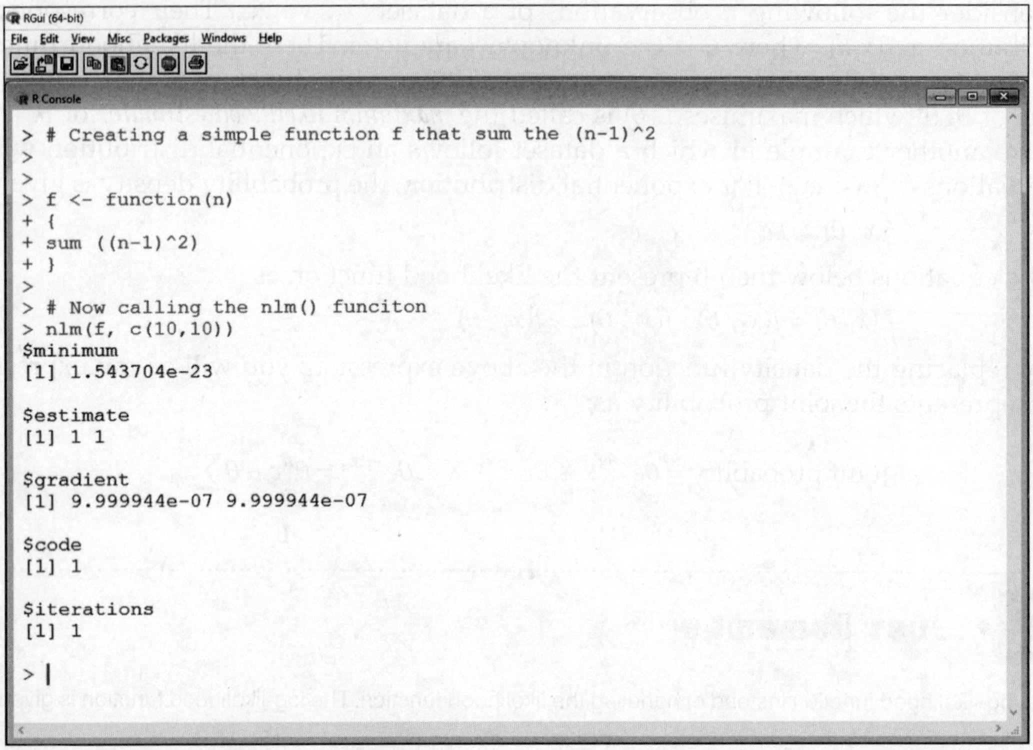

Figure 6.7 *Example of* `nlm()` *function*

`optim()` Function

The `optim()` function performs a general-purpose optimisation and optimises a function using a Nelder-Mead, conjugate-gradient and quasi-Newton algorithm. The syntax of the `optim()` function is `optim(par, fun,...)`

where, "par" argument defines the starting parameter values for optimisation and "fun" argument defines a function to be minimised or maximised. The function should return a scalar value. The dots "..." define the other optional arguments.

In the following example, the same function *f* from the previous example has been used. The `optim()` function performs the optimisation of the given function as shown in Figure 6.8.

6.4.6 Maximum Likelihood Estimator

Maximum likelihood estimator (MLE) estimates the parameters in LR. It is a statistical model to estimate model parameters of a function. For a given dataset, MLE chooses the values of model parameters that make the data 'more likely' than other parameter values. For finding out MLE, it is necessary to select a model that has one or more unknown parameters for the data.

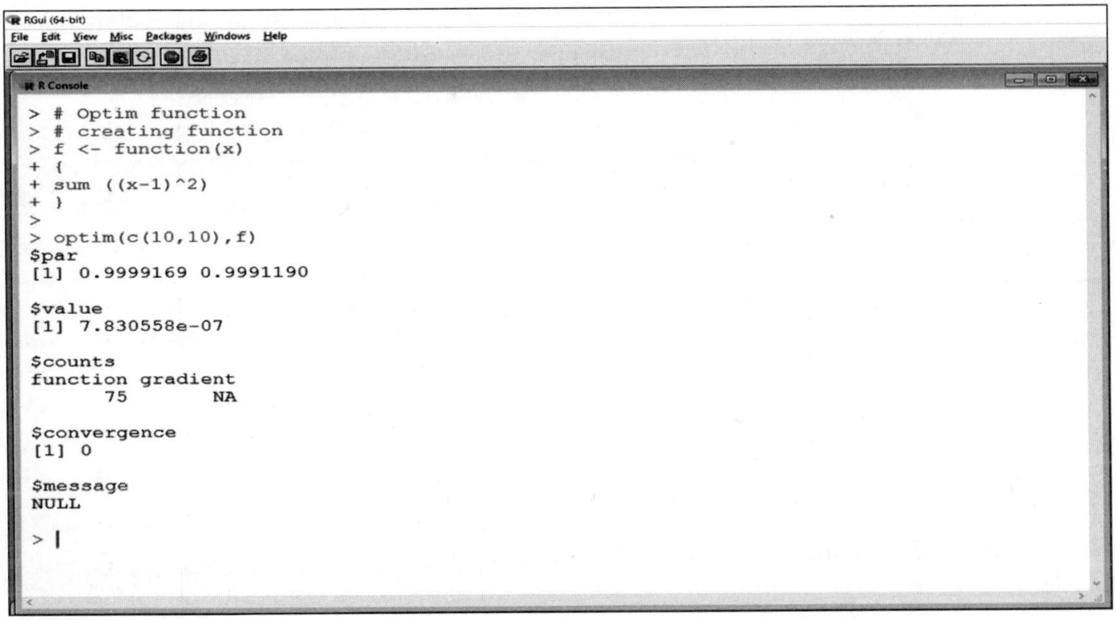

```
RGui (64-bit)
File Edit View Misc Packages Windows Help
R Console
> # Optim function
> # creating function
> f <- function(x)
+ {
+ sum ((x-1)^2)
+ }
>
> optim(c(10,10),f)
$par
[1] 0.9999169 0.9991190

$value
[1] 7.830558e-07

$counts
function gradient
      75       NA

$convergence
[1] 0

$message
NULL

> |
```

Figure 6.8 *Example of* **`optim()`** *function*

Inbuilt R Language Function `mle()` for Finding Maximum Likelihood Estimator

R language provides an inbuilt function `mle()` of the package 'stats4' for MLE. The `mle()` function finds or estimates the parameters by using the maximum likelihood method. The syntax of `mle()` function is:

```
mle(miunslogl, start = formals(minuslogl), method = "BFGS", ...)
```

where, "miunslogl" is a function to calculate negative log-likelihood, "start" argument contains the initial values for optimisers, "method" defines the optimisation method and the dots "..." define the other optional arguments.

The `mle()` function requires a function that calculates the negative log-likelihood. For this, the `mle()` function can use `nlm()` or `optim()` function.

In the following example, the `mle()` function is finding MLE of the simple function *f* (Figure 6.9).

Another Example for an LR Model

The following example defines MLE for an LR model. For fitting a logistic model, `optim()` or `nlm()` functions are required. Figure 6.10 describes the general code of the likelihood function, where log-likelihood function is used. Figure 6.11 is reading a table 'Student. data', where 'Annual.attendance' is a predictor that is predicting the column 'Eligible'. The `glm()` function implements this dataset. The `optim()` function is finding MLE of the table Studata.csv.

```
> # MLE function implementation
> f <- function(x)
+ {
+ sum ((x-1)^2)
+ }
>
> m <- mle(f, start= list(x=10))
> m

Call:
mle(minuslogl = f, start = list(x = 10))

Coefficients:
x
1
> summary(m)
Maximum likelihood estimation

Call:
mle(minuslogl = f, start = list(x = 10))

Coefficients:
  Estimate Std. Error
x        1  0.7071068

-2 log L: 7.987217e-30
>
```

FIGURE 6.9 *Example of* `mle()` *function*

```
mle.logreg = function(fmla, data)
{
    # Define the negative log likelihood function
    logl <- function(theta,x,y){
      y <- y
      x <- as.matrix(x)
      beta <- theta[1:ncol(x)]

      # Use the log-likelihood of the Bernouilli distribution, where p is
      # defined as the logistic transformation of a linear combination
      # of predictors, according to logit(p)=(x%*%beta)
      loglik <- sum(-y*log(1 + exp(-(x%*%beta))) - (1-y)*log(1 + exp(x%*%beta)))
      return(-loglik)
    }

    # Prepare the data
    outcome = rownames(attr(terms(fmla),"factors"))[1]
    dfrTmp = model.frame(data)
    x = as.matrix(model.matrix(fmla, data=dfrTmp))
    y = as.numeric(as.matrix(data[,match(outcome,colnames(data))]))

    # Define initial values for the parameters
    theta.start = rep(0,(dim(x)[2]))
    names(theta.start) = colnames(x)

    # Calculate the maximum likelihood
    mle = optim(theta.start,logl,x=x,y=y,hessian=T)
    out = list(beta=mle$par,vcov=solve(mle$hessian),ll=2*mle$value)
}
```

FIGURE 6.10 *Likelihood function definition for logistic regression model*

```
> mydata = read.csv("StuData.csv")
> fmla = as.formula("Eligible ~ Annual.attendance")
> mylogit = mle.logreg(fmla, mydata)
> mylogit
$beta
     (Intercept) Annual.attendance
    -1088.232500          6.377535

$vcov
                    (Intercept) Annual.attendance
(Intercept)         12384651237       -73613673.9
Annual.attendance     -73613674          849388.5

$ll
[1] 1.723595e-10

> summary(mylogit)
     Length Class  Mode
beta 2      -none- numeric
vcov 4      -none- numeric
ll   1      -none- numeric
> mylogit$ll
[1] 1.723595e-10
> |
```

FIGURE 6.11 *Maximum likelihood estimation of logistic regression model*

Check Your Understanding

1. What do you mean by LR?

Ans: Logistic regression (LR) is an extension of linear regression to environments that contain a categorical dependent variable.

2. Which function is used to implement LR?

Ans: The `glm()` function is used to implement LR.

3. What are the uses of LR?

Ans: Logistic regression is used to solve classification problems, discrete choice models and to find the probability of an event.

4. What is BLR?

Ans: Binomial or binary logistic regression (BLR) is a model in which the dependent variable is dichotomous.

(Continued)

5. What are the parameters of the logit function?

Ans: Odds and odds ratio are the two parameters of the logit function.

6. What is MLE?

Ans: Maximum likelihood estimator (MLE) estimates the parameters of a function in LR. For a given dataset, MLE chooses the values of model parameters that make the data 'more likely' than other parameter values.

7. What is a likelihood function?

Ans: Likelihood function [L(β)] represents the joint probability or likelihood of observing the collected data.

8. Which functions are used to find out the likelihood function?

Ans: The `nlm()` and `optim()` functions are used to find out the likelihood function.

9. Which function is used to find MLE?

Ans: The `mle()` of the package 'stats4' is used to find out MLE.

6.5 Binary Logistic Regression

This section will describe the concept of BLR, BLR with a single categorical predictor, three-way and *k*-way tables and continuous covariates.

6.5.1 Introduction to Binary Logistic Regression

Logistic regression is conducted if a dependent variable is binary and it is a predictive analysis. It also describes data and explains the relation between single binary and multiple independent variables (explanatory variables or predictors). Binary logistic regression is a type of LR that defines the relationship between a categorical response variable and one or more explanatory variables. These explanatory variables can be either continuous or categorical. It makes an explicit distinction between a response variable and explanatory variables.

In simple words, a BLR finds out the probability of success according to the given values of the explanatory variables. The following function defines the BLR model.

$$\text{Logit}(\pi_i) = 1n\left(\frac{\pi_i}{1-\pi_i}\right) = \beta_0 + \beta_1 x_i$$

or

$$\pi_i = \Pr(Y_i = 1 | X_i = x_i) = \frac{exp(\beta_0 + \beta_1 x_i)}{1+(\beta_0 + \beta_1 x_i)}$$

where, Y defines the binary response variable, $Y_i = 1$ defines the condition is true in observation i and $Y_i = 0$ defines the condition is not true in observation i, X defines the set of explanatory variables that can be either discrete, continuous or combination of both.

Model Fit

There are different types of statistical methods available, such as Pearson chi-square statistic [X^2], deviance [G^2], likelihood ratio test and statistic [ΔG^2] and Hosmer-Lemeshow test to check the goodness of statistics of the BLR model.

Parameter Estimation

Maximum likelihood estimator estimates the parameters in the binary logistic model. MLE uses some iterative algorithms like Newton-Raphson or iteratively re-weighted least squares (IRWLS) for estimating these variables. The following function describes the function that finds out parameters for the BLR model:

$$\text{Logit}(\beta_0, \beta_1) = \prod_{i=1}^{N} \pi_i^{y_i} (1 - \pi_i)^{n_i - y_i}$$

or

$$\prod_{i=1}^{N} \frac{\exp\{y_i(\beta_0 + \beta_1 x_i)\}}{1 + \exp(\beta_0 + \beta_1 x_i)}$$

Also, users can use `mle()`, `nlm()` or `optim()` functions for finding MLEs for any LR.

6.5.2 Binary Logistic Regression with a Single Categorical Predictor

Binary logistic regression with a single categorical predictor uses a categorical variable to fit data into the BLR model. When a single categorical variable is applied on the above-defined BLR model, the following model is obtained:

$$\pi = \Pr(Y = 1 \mid X = x)$$

where, Y is a response variable and X is an explanatory variable.

In the following example, a dummy data table 'Studata1.csv' explains the BLR with a single categorical predictor. The table contains information about annual attendance and annual scores of 15 students. The students are eligible to appear in the entrance exam if they clear both criteria, viz., annual score and annual attendance. Based on the annual score and annual attendance, the eligibility to appear or not for the entrance exam will be assessed. Table 6.2 puts the value 1 if students clear both criteria, otherwise 0. With the information of these tables, it is found that 6 out of 15 students clear the annual attendance and 5 out of 15 students clear the annual score. Table 6.2 summarises this data.

TABLE 6.2 Summarised data

	Clear [1]	*Not Clear[0]*
Attendance	6	9
Annual Score	5	10

Here, the annual score and annual attendance are response variables and eligibility is a single categorical variable. A response vector is created for Table 6.2. Also eligibility factor is created using the `as.factor()` function. The `glm()` command fills the data to the BLR model (Figure 6.12).

```
> # Defining the explanatory variable with 1 and 0 where 1 = eligible, 0 = not eligible
>
> Eligibility <- as.factor(c(1,0))
>
> # response vector that counts success and failure
> res <- cbind(clear = c(6,5), notclear = c(9,10))
> res
     clear notclear
[1,]     6        9
[2,]     5       10
>
> # fitting logistic model
> l <- glm(formula = res ~ Eligibility, family = binomial("logit"))
> l

Call:  glm(formula = res ~ Eligibility, family = binomial("logit"))

Coefficients:
 (Intercept)  Eligibility1
     -0.6931        0.2877

Degrees of Freedom: 1 Total (i.e. Null);  0 Residual
Null Deviance:        0.1437
Residual Deviance: 5.551e-15    AIC: 10.23
> |
```

FIGURE 6.12 *Binary logistic regression with a single categorical predictor*

Figure 6.13 provides a summary of the example. The information from the summary can be used to check the fitting of the model. The fitted model of the dummy data is:

$$\text{Logit}\ (\pi) = -0.6931 + 0.2877\ \text{el}$$

Here, el is a dummy variable that takes 1 if at least one student clears the eligibility criteria and 0 if no one clears the eligibility criteria. Also, users can use the `mle()` function for finding MLE of a given dataset, as described in *Section on Maximum Likelihood Estimator*.

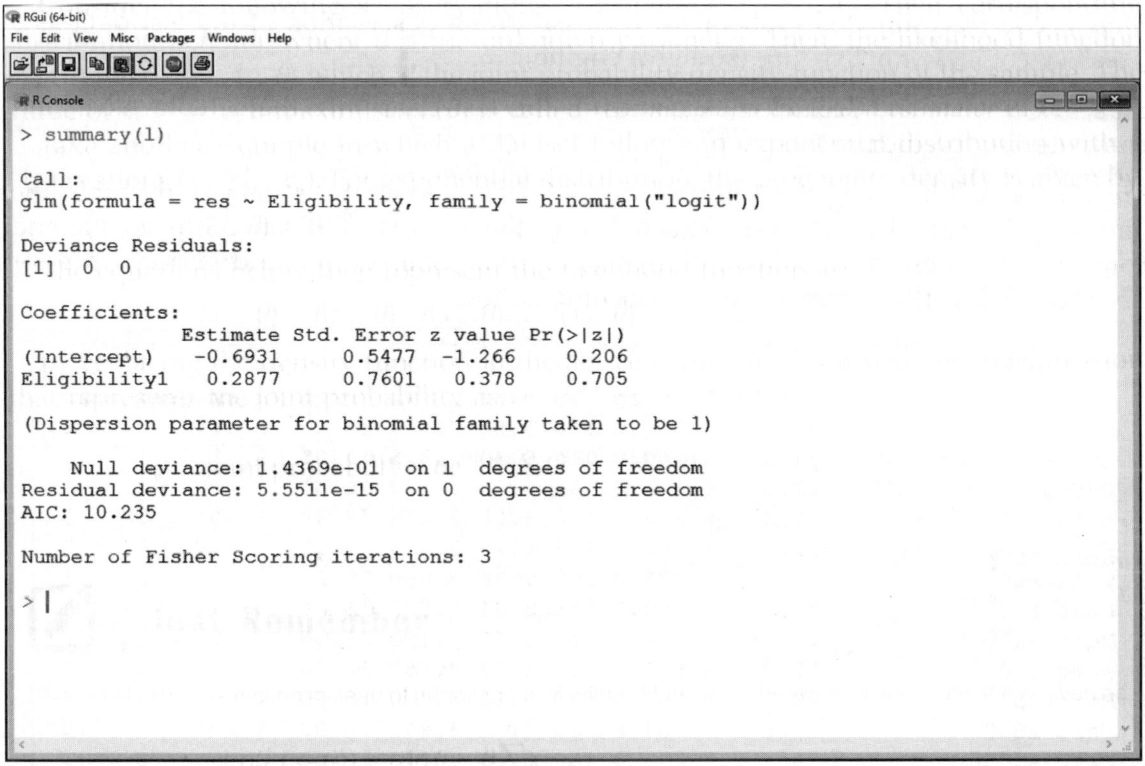

Figure 6.13 *Binary logistic regression summary*

Example:

Objective: To predict whether a car will have a *V*-engine or a straight engine based on our inputs.

Perform the following steps to build the model:

Step 1: Divide the data set into training data and testing data. We will use the variables "training" and "testing" to store the data subsets. The variable "training" will hold 80% of the data and the remaining 20% of the data will be stored in the "testing" variable.

Step 2: Build the model (i.e., estimate the regression coefficients) using the training data subset.

Step 3: Use the model to estimate the probability of a success, i.e., p = the probability that the car is likely to have a "V-engine".

Step 4: Determine a threshold probability based on domain knowledge (in this example we have assumed it to be 0.5).

Step 5: Use the estimated probability to classify each observation of the test data as a "Yes" (V-engine) or a "No" (S- (straight) engine).

Step 6: Compare the predicted outcomes of the test data with the actual values and compute the "prediction accuracy".

Step 7: We will be using the "mtcars" dataset. Let us look at the data held within the "mtcars" dataset. The data was extracted from the 1974 *Motor Trend* US magazine and comprises fuel consumption and 10 aspects of automobile design and performance for 32 automobiles (1973–74 models). – R documentation.

```
> mtcars
                     mpg cyl  disp  hp drat    wt  qsec vs am gear carb
Mazda RX4           21.0   6 160.0 110 3.90 2.620 16.46  0  1    4    4
Mazda RX4 Wag       21.0   6 160.0 110 3.90 2.875 17.02  0  1    4    4
Datsun 710          22.8   4 108.0  93 3.85 2.320 18.61  1  1    4    1
Hornet 4 Drive      21.4   6 258.0 110 3.08 3.215 19.44  1  0    3    1
Hornet Sportabout   18.7   8 360.0 175 3.15 3.440 17.02  0  0    3    2
Valiant             18.1   6 225.0 105 2.76 3.460 20.22  1  0    3    1
Duster 360          14.3   8 360.0 245 3.21 3.570 15.84  0  0    3    4
Merc 240D           24.4   4 146.7  62 3.69 3.190 20.00  1  0    4    2
Merc 230            22.8   4 140.8  95 3.92 3.150 22.90  1  0    4    2
Merc 280            19.2   6 167.6 123 3.92 3.440 18.30  1  0    4    4
Merc 280C           17.8   6 167.6 123 3.92 3.440 18.90  1  0    4    4
Merc 450SE          16.4   8 275.8 180 3.07 4.070 17.40  0  0    3    3
Merc 450SL          17.3   8 275.8 180 3.07 3.730 17.60  0  0    3    3
Merc 450SLC         15.2   8 275.8 180 3.07 3.780 18.00  0  0    3    3
Cadillac Fleetwood  10.4   8 472.0 205 2.93 5.250 17.98  0  0    3    4
Lincoln Continental 10.4   8 460.0 215 3.00 5.424 17.82  0  0    3    4
Chrysler Imperial   14.7   8 440.0 230 3.23 5.345 17.42  0  0    3    4
Fiat 128            32.4   4  78.7  66 4.08 2.200 19.47  1  1    4    1
Honda Civic         30.4   4  75.7  52 4.93 1.615 18.52  1  1    4    2
Toyota Corolla      33.9   4  71.1  65 4.22 1.835 19.90  1  1    4    1
Toyota Corona       21.5   4 120.1  97 3.70 2.465 20.01  1  0    3    1
Dodge Challenger    15.5   8 318.0 150 2.76 3.520 16.87  0  0    3    2
AMC Javelin         15.2   8 304.0 150 3.15 3.435 17.30  0  0    3    2
Camaro Z28          13.3   8 350.0 245 3.73 3.840 15.41  0  0    3    4
Pontiac Firebird    19.2   8 400.0 175 3.08 3.845 17.05  0  0    3    2
Fiat X1-9           27.3   4  79.0  66 4.08 1.935 18.90  1  1    4    1
Porsche 914-2       26.0   4 120.3  91 4.43 2.140 16.70  0  1    5    2
Lotus Europa        30.4   4  95.1 113 3.77 1.513 16.90  1  1    5    2
Ford Pantera L      15.8   8 351.0 264 4.22 3.170 14.50  0  1    5    4
Ferrari Dino        19.7   6 145.0 175 3.62 2.770 15.50  0  1    5    6
Maserati Bora       15.0   8 301.0 335 3.54 3.570 14.60  0  1    5    8
Volvo 142E          21.4   4 121.0 109 4.11 2.780 18.60  1  1    4    2
```

Step 8: Let us look at the structure of the dataset, "mtcars". This dataset has 32 observations of 11 variables.

```
> str(mtcars)
'data.frame':   32 obs. of  11 variables:
 $ mpg : num  21 21 22.8 21.4 18.7 18.1 14.3 24.4 22.8 19.2 ...
 $ cyl : num  6 6 4 6 8 6 8 4 4 6 ...
 $ disp: num  160 160 108 258 360 ...
 $ hp  : num  110 110 93 110 175 105 245 62 95 123 ...
 $ drat: num  3.9 3.9 3.85 3.08 3.15 2.76 3.21 3.69 3.92 3.92 ...
 $ wt  : num  2.62 2.88 2.32 3.21 3.44 ...
 $ qsec: num  16.5 17 18.6 19.4 17 ...
 $ vs  : num  0 0 1 1 0 1 0 1 1 1 ...
 $ am  : num  1 1 1 0 0 0 0 0 0 0 ...
 $ gear: num  4 4 4 3 3 3 3 4 4 4 ...
 $ carb: num  4 4 1 1 2 1 4 2 2 4 ...
```

Let us take a look at what these variables are:

mpg	Miles/(US) gallon
cyl	Number of cylinders
disp	Displacement (cu.in.)
hp	Gross horsepower
drat	Rear axle ratio
wt	Weight (1000 lbs)
qsec	1/4 mile time
vs	V/S
am	Transmission (0 = automatic, 1 = manual)
gear	Number of forward gears
carb	Number of carburetors

Step 9: Let us load the package "caTools". This package has the "`sample.split()`" function. This function will be used to split the data into test and train subsets.

```
> library(caTools)
```

Step 10: Use the `sample.split()` function to split the data into test and train subsets. The splitting ratio is 0.8, i.e., 80:20 ratio. We plan to use 80% of the data as training data to train the model and the remaining 20% of the data as testing data to test the model.

```
> split <-sample.split(mtcars, SplitRatio = 0.8)
> split
[1] TRUE TRUE TRUE TRUE TRUE FALSE TRUE TRUE FALSE FALSE TRUE
```

The "TRUE" represents 80% of the data and "FALSE" represents the remaining 20% of the data.

Step 11: Store 80% of the data into the variable "training".

```
> training <- subset(mtcars, split == "TRUE")
> training
                     mpg cyl  disp  hp drat    wt  qsec vs am gear carb
Mazda RX4           21.0   6 160.0 110 3.90 2.620 16.46  0  1    4    4
Mazda RX4 Wag       21.0   6 160.0 110 3.90 2.875 17.02  0  1    4    4
Datsun 710          22.8   4 108.0  93 3.85 2.320 18.61  1  1    4    1
Hornet 4 Drive      21.4   6 258.0 110 3.08 3.215 19.44  1  0    3    1
Hornet Sportabout   18.7   8 360.0 175 3.15 3.440 17.02  0  0    3    2
Duster 360          14.3   8 360.0 245 3.21 3.570 15.84  0  0    3    4
Merc 240D           24.4   4 146.7  62 3.69 3.190 20.00  1  0    4    2
Merc 280C           17.8   6 167.6 123 3.92 3.440 18.90  1  0    4    4
Merc 450SE          16.4   8 275.8 180 3.07 4.070 17.40  0  0    3    3
Merc 450SL          17.3   8 275.8 180 3.07 3.730 17.60  0  0    3    3
Merc 450SLC         15.2   8 275.8 180 3.07 3.780 18.00  0  0    3    3
Cadillac Fleetwood  10.4   8 472.0 205 2.93 5.250 17.98  0  0    3    4
Lincoln Continental 10.4   8 460.0 215 3.00 5.424 17.82  0  0    3    4
Fiat 128            32.4   4  78.7  66 4.08 2.200 19.47  1  1    4    1
Honda Civic         30.4   4  75.7  52 4.93 1.615 18.52  1  1    4    2
Dodge Challenger    15.5   8 318.0 150 2.76 3.520 16.87  0  0    3    2
AMC Javelin         15.2   8 304.0 150 3.15 3.435 17.30  0  0    3    2
Camaro Z28          13.3   8 350.0 245 3.73 3.840 15.41  0  0    3    4
Pontiac Firebird    19.2   8 400.0 175 3.08 3.845 17.05  0  0    3    2
Fiat X1-9           27.3   4  79.0  66 4.08 1.935 18.90  1  1    4    1
Porsche 914-2       26.0   4 120.3  91 4.43 2.140 16.70  0  1    5    2
Ford Pantera L      15.8   8 351.0 264 4.22 3.170 14.50  0  1    5    4
Ferrari Dino        19.7   6 145.0 175 3.62 2.770 15.50  0  1    5    6
```

Step 12: Store the remaining 20% of the data into the variable "testing".

```
> testing <- subset(mtcars, split == "FALSE")
```

```
> testing
                   mpg cyl  disp  hp drat    wt  qsec vs am gear carb
Valiant           18.1   6 225.0 105 2.76 3.460 20.22  1  0    3    1
Merc 230          22.8   4 140.8  95 3.92 3.150 22.90  1  0    4    2
Merc 280          19.2   6 167.6 123 3.92 3.440 18.30  1  0    4    4
Chrysler Imperial 14.7   8 440.0 230 3.23 5.345 17.42  0  0    3    4
Toyota Corolla    33.9   4  71.1  65 4.22 1.835 19.90  1  1    4    1
Toyota Corona     21.5   4 120.1  97 3.70 2.465 20.01  1  0    3    1
Lotus Europa      30.4   4  95.1 113 3.77 1.513 16.90  1  1    5    2
Maserati Bora     15.0   8 301.0 335 3.54 3.570 14.60  0  1    5    8
Volvo 142E        21.4   4 121.0 109 4.11 2.780 18.60  1  1    4    2
```

Step 13: Use the `glm()` function to create the model. `glm` is used to fit generalised linear models. A typical predictor has the form response ~ terms where response is the (numeric) response vector and terms is a series of terms which specifies a linear predictor for response. For binomial and quasibinomial families the response can also be specified as a factor (when the first level denotes failure and all others success) or as a two-column matrix with the columns giving the numbers of successes and failures. A terms specification of the form first plus second indicates all the terms in the first together with all the terms in the second and any duplicates removed. – R documentation.

```
>model<-glm(formula=vs~wt+disp, family="binomial", data=training)
> model

Call: glm(formula = vs ~ wt + disp, family = "binomial", data = training)

Coefficients:
(Intercept)             wt              disp
   1.15521         1.29631          -0.03013
Degrees of Freedom: 22 Total  (i.e. Null);    20 Residual
Null Deviance:          28.27
Residual Deviance: 15.77        AIC  21.77
```

Here, "Null Deviance" shows how well the response variable is predicted by a model that includes only the intercept (grand mean). "Residual deviance" shows how well the response variable is predicted with inclusion of the independent variables.

Step 14: Use the predict function. `predict()` is a generic function for predictions from the results of various model fitting functions.

```
> res <- predict(model, testing, type="response")
> res
        Valiant          Merc 230          Merc 280 Chrysler Imperial
    0.242712021       0.730443537       0.637708248       0.005644668
 Toyota Corolla     Toyota Corona      Lotus Europa     Maserati Bora
    0.800910919       0.675354954       0.562561393       0.036094938
     Volvo 142E
    0.752824025
```

Step 15: Check the accuracy of the model by using the `table()` function. `table()` uses the cross-classifying factors to build a contingency table of the counts at each combination of factor levels. Here, the "ActualValue" represents the values as how it appears in the dataset. The "PredictedValue" is the value predicted by our model. Let us try and explain this. When the actual value in the dataset for the variable, "vs" was "0", our model also predicted "0". However, when the actual value in the dataset was "1", our model predicted "1" six times correctly but also reported "0" incorrectly once.

```
> (table (ActualValue=testing$vs, PredictedValue=res>0.5))
           PredictedValue
ActualValue  FALSE  TRUE
          0      2     0
          1      1     6
```

Step 16: The equation below shows that our model is accurate 88.9% times. This is definitely good accuracy for the model.

```
> (2+6) / (2+0+1+6)
[1] 0.8888889
```

6.5.3 Binary Logistic Regression for Three-way and k-way Tables

A three-way contingency table contains cross-classification of observations using the level of three categorical variables. Just like three-way contingency table, k-way contingency table contains cross-classification of observations and uses k-way categorical variables. Binary logistic regression for three-way and k-way contingency tables uses three or k-categorical variables for fitting data to BLR model. When these tables are applied on the above defined BLR model, the following model is obtained:

$$\text{Logit}(\pi) = \left(\frac{\pi}{1-\pi}\right) = \beta_0 + \beta_1 X_1 + \beta_2 X_2$$

where, X is the explanatory variable.

The following example uses the same dummy data table "Studata1.csv" used in the previous example with an additional column. A new table "Studata1.csv" stores all the new information. The new column stores the information about the internal exams indicating whether students clear the internal exam or not. Table 6.3 summarises this data.

TABLE 6.3 Summary data with additional new data

	Clear	*Not Clear*
Attendance	6	9
Annual Score	5	10
Internal Exam	15	0

The `glm()` command is also fitting the table to the BLR model. Figure 6.14 describes the model fitting while Figure 6.15 describes the result.

```
RGui (64-bit)
File Edit View Misc Packages Windows Help
R Console
> # Binary Logistic model for 3-way tables
> E = factor(c("NA","C","N"))
>
> # three categorical response variables that counts success and failure
> res <- cbind(clear = c(6,5,10), notclear = c(9,10,0))
> res
     clear notclear
[1,]     6        9
[2,]     5       10
[3,]    10        0
> EN = (E =="N")
> EC = (E =="C")
>
> # fitting the Binary Logistic model
> bl <- glm(formula = res ~ EC + EN, family = binomial("logit"))
> bl

Call:  glm(formula = res ~ EC + EN, family = binomial("logit"))

Coefficients:
(Intercept)       ECTRUE       ENTRUE
    -0.4055      -0.2877      25.5238

Degrees of Freedom: 2 Total (i.e. Null);  0 Residual
Null Deviance:      16.07
Residual Deviance: 2.467e-10    AIC: 12.23
> |
```

FIGURE 6.14 *Binary logistic regression for the three-way table*

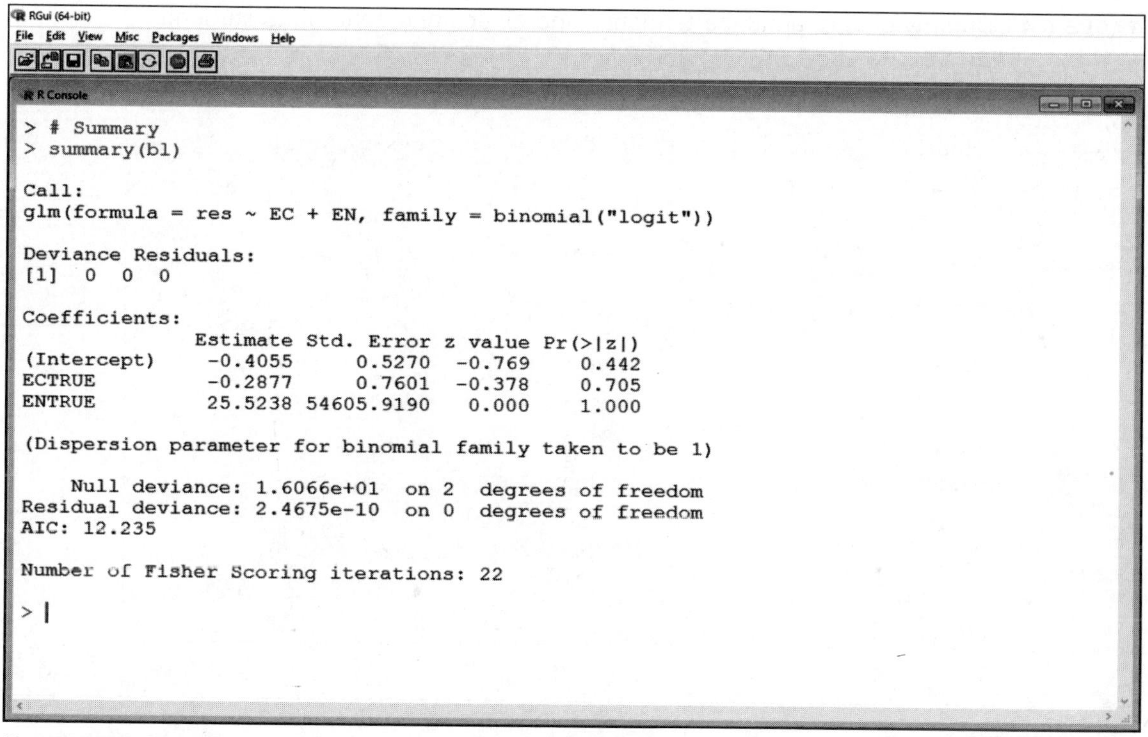

FIGURE 6.15 *Summary of the model for the three-way table*

6.5.4 Binary Logistic Regression with Continuous Covariates

A covariate variable is a simple variable that predicts the outcome of another variable. Explanatory, independent and predictor are some of the other names of a covariate variable. A covariate variable may either be discrete or continuous. The BLR with continuous covariates follows the general concept of the LR where a predictor variable predicts the outcome of the response variable. Users may make some adjustments for getting a more accurate answer.

The following example is reading a table "Studata.csv" that contains two columns described in Table 6.4. The column "annual attendance" stores the annual attendance. There is another column "eligibility". Here "annual attendance" is a covariate (predictor) that predicts the values of the "eligibility" column (response). If the "annual attendance" is less than 175, then "eligibility" is 0 else 'annual attendance' is 1. The `glm()` function is implementing this data and is described in Figure 6.16 while a summary of the same is described in Figure 6.17.

TABLE 6.4 Dummy data of annual attendance and eligibility criteria of 15 students

Student Name	*Annual Attendance*	*Eligibility*
Student1	256	1
Student2	270	1
Student3	150	0
Student4	200	1
Student5	230	1
Student6	175	1
Student7	140	0
Student8	167	0
Student9	230	1
Student10	180	1
Student11	155	0
Student12	210	1
Student13	160	0
Student14	155	0
Student15	260	1

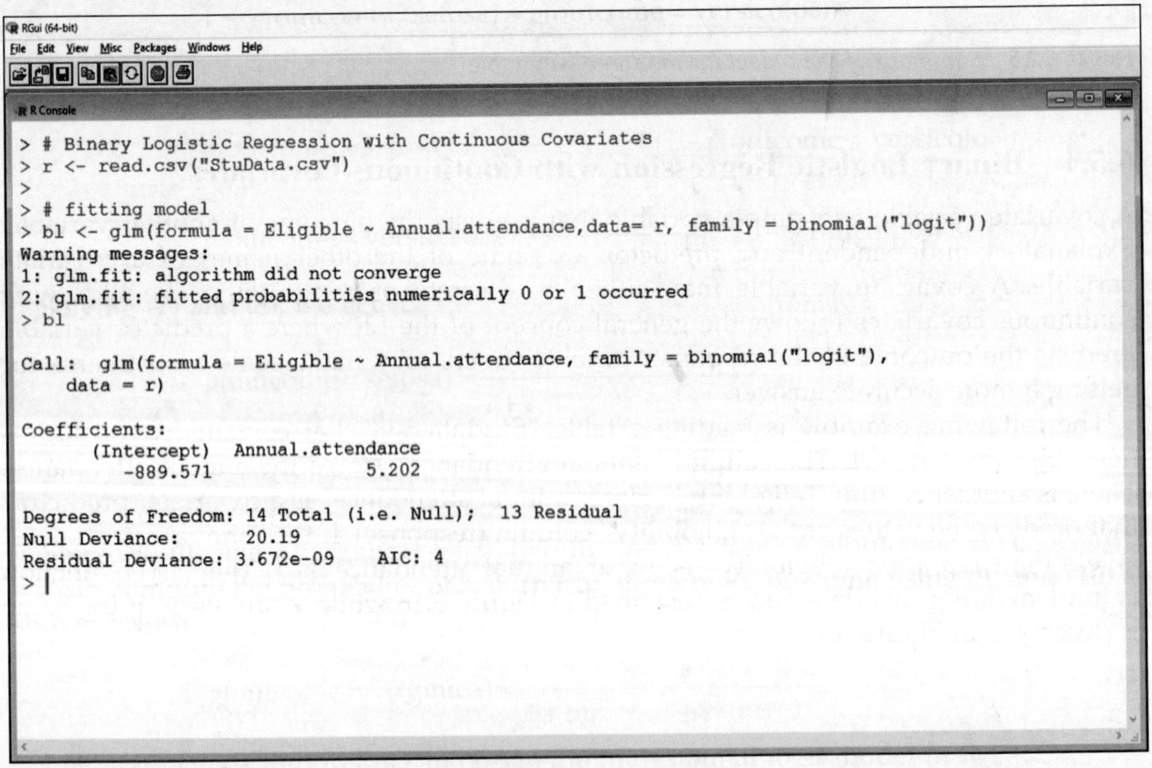

FIGURE 6.16 *Binary logistic regression with continuous covariate*

```
> # Summary
> summary(bl)

Call:
glm(formula = Eligible ~ Annual.attendance, family = binomial("logit"),
    data = r)

Deviance Residuals:
       Min          1Q      Median          3Q         Max
-4.371e-05  -2.100e-08   2.100e-08   2.100e-08   4.197e-05

Coefficients:
                  Estimate Std. Error z value Pr(>|z|)
(Intercept)       -889.571 605216.133  -0.001    0.999
Annual.attendance    5.202   3541.670   0.001    0.999

(Dispersion parameter for binomial family taken to be 1)

    Null deviance: 2.0190e+01  on 14  degrees of freedom
Residual deviance: 3.6721e-09  on 13  degrees of freedom
AIC: 4

Number of Fisher Scoring iterations: 25

>
```

FIGURE 6.17 *Binary logistic regression with continuous covariate summary*

Use cases

- "Customer loyalty" is of utmost importance to any business. Businesses the world over execute several programs/schemes to retain their customers. One such business firm wants to arrange for an early intervention process or processes to reduce customer churn. This is possible if they are able to predict when a customer is likely to churn, much ahead of time.
- Banks stores the transaction records for each customer. They study these transaction records in order to determine if a transaction is fraudulent.
- Logit analysis is used by marketers to assess customer acceptance of a new product. It attempts to determine the intensity or magnitude of customers' purchase intentions and translates that into a measure of actual buying behavior. Many e-commerce websites assess this behavior using this model.

Check Your Understanding

1. Which function is used by BLR?

Ans: BLR uses the following function:

(Continued)

$$\text{Logit}(\pi_i) = \ln\left(\frac{\pi_i}{1-\pi_i}\right) = \beta_0 + \beta_1 x_i$$

or

$$\pi_i = \Pr(Y_i = 1 | X_i = x_i) = \frac{\exp(\beta_0 + \beta_1 x_i)}{1 + (\beta_0 + \beta_1 x_i)}$$

where,

Y defines the binary response variable, $Y_i = 1$ defines the condition is true in observation i, $Y_i = 0$ defines the condition is not true in observation i and X defines the set of explanatory variables that can be either discrete, continuous or a combination of both.

2. What is a three-way contingency table?

Ans: A three-way contingency table contains cross-classification of observations that use the level of three categorical variables.

3. What is a covariate variable?

Ans: A covariate variable is a simple variable that predicts the outcome of another variable.

4. List the names of major statistical methods used to check the goodness of statistics of the BLR model.

Ans: Some major statistical methods used to check the goodness of statistics of the BLR model are:

- Pearson chi-square statistic [X^2]
- Deviance [G^2]
- Likelihood ratio test and statistic [ΔG^2]
- Hosmer-Lemeshow test and statistic

6.6 Diagnosing Logistic Regression

After fitting the model, it is necessary to check the model. Different types of diagnostic methods are available for checking the logistics model. According to the type of dataset and research, users can select diagnostic methods and interpret the output. R provides an inbuilt package 'LogisticDx' that provides various methods for diagnosing the logistics regression model. The `dx()`, `gof()`, `or()`, and `plot.glm()` are the major diagnostic functions of the 'LogisticDx' package. Some major diagnostics are explained ahead.

6.6.1 Residual

Residual is a common measure influence that identifies potential outliers. Pearson and deviance residual are two common residuals. Pearson residual assesses how predictors are transformed during the fitting process. It uses *mean* and *standard deviation* for assessment. Deviance residual is a best diagnostic measure when individual points are not fitting well by the model. One of the functions `dx()` of the package 'LogisticDx' performs the diagnosis of the model. After passing the logistics regression model object into the function `dx()`, it returns the Pearson and deviance residual, along with the other parameters. Figure 6.18 describes all return values of the `dx()` function.

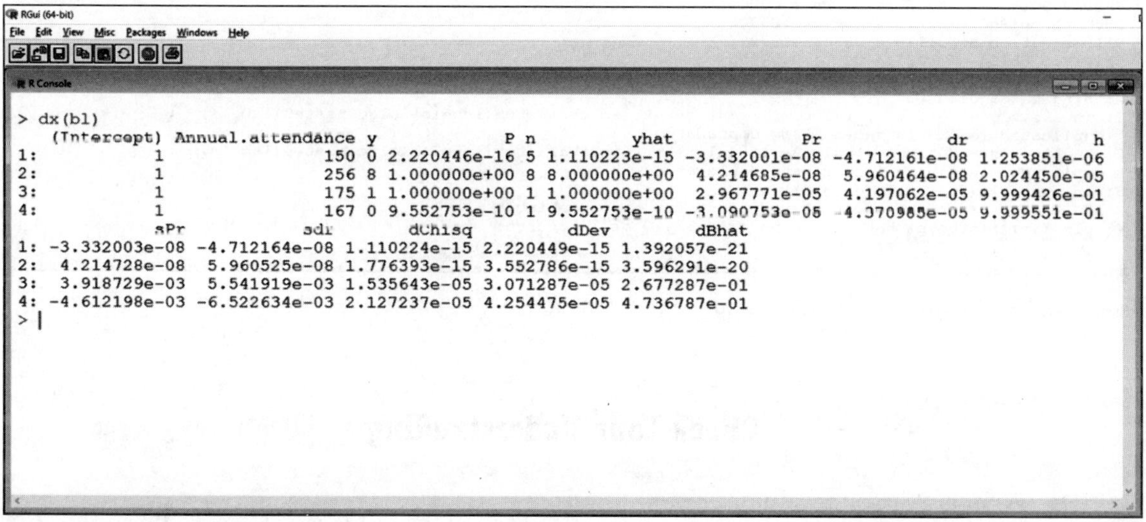

FIGURE 6.18 *Diagnosis of model using* `dx()` *function*

6.6.2 Goodness-of-Fit Tests

Different methods check the goodness of statistics of the BLR model. It is best to use the inbuilt function `gof()` of the package 'LogisticDx' to check the goodness-of-fit tests for the logistics regression model. Figure 6.19 describes the generated output of the `gof()` function.

6.6.3 Receiver Operating Characteristic Curve

Receiver operating characteristic curve is a plot of specificity (False positive rate) against sensitivity (True positive rate). The area under the ROC curve quantifies the predictive ability of the model. If the value under the curve is equal to 0.5, then the model can randomly predict. If the value is close to 1, then the model can do a good prediction.

```
> gof(bl)
         chiSq df pVal
PrI  1.8360e-09 13    1
drI  3.6721e-09 13    1
PrG  1.8360e-09  2    1
drG  3.6721e-09  2    1
PrCT 1.8360e-09  2    1
drCT 3.6721e-09  2    1
                         val df    pVal
HL chiSq          1.8360e-09  8 1.00000
mHL F                     NA  3      NA
OsRo Z                    NA NA 1.00000
SstPgeq0.5 Z      6.5860e-07 NA 1.00000
SstPl0.5 Z        6.5371e-07 NA 1.00000
SstBoth chiSq     8.6109e-13  2 1.00000
SllPgeq0.5 chiSq  3.1167e-09  1 0.99996
SllPl0.5 chiSq    3.2871e-09  1 0.99995
SllBoth chiSq     3.4058e-09  2 1.00000
Warning messages:
1: In `levels<-`(`*tmp*`, value = if (nl == nL) as.character(labels) else paste0(labels,  :
  duplicated levels in factors are deprecated
2: In `levels<-`(`*tmp*`, value = if (nl == nL) as.character(labels) else paste0(labels,  :
  duplicated levels in factors are deprecated
3: In anova.lm(stats::lm(dr ~ G)) :
  ANOVA F-tests on an essentially perfect fit are unreliable
4: glm.fit: fitted probabilities numerically 0 or 1 occurred
```

FIGURE 6.19 *Diagnosis of model using* `gof()` *function*

Check Your Understanding

1. What is Pearson residual?

Ans: Pearson residual assesses how predictors are transformed during the fitting process. It uses mean and standard deviation for assessment.

2. What is deviance residual?

Ans: Deviance residual is the best diagnostic measure when individual points are not fitting well by the model.

3. What is 'LogisticDx'?

Ans: 'LogisticDx' is an R package that provides functions for diagnosing the LR model.

4. What are the major diagnostic functions of the 'LogisticDx' package?

Ans: `dx()`, `gof()`, `or()`, and `plot.glm()` are some major diagnostic functions of the 'LogisticDx' package.

5. What is the use of `gof()`?

Ans: The `gof()` function of 'LogisticDx' package checks the goodness-of-fit tests for the LR model.

6.7 Multinomial Logistic Regression Models

Multinomial logistic regression (MLR) is a type of linear regression where more than two levels of independent variables (predictors) predict the outcome of the dependent variable (response variable). MLA uses a dependent variable as a nominal variable because a nominal variable has no intrinsic ordering. For example, strong performance, average performance or weak performance has no ordering, instead each one represents a different category.

MLP is an extension of the BLR that describes the relationship between these nominal dependent variables and one or more levels of independent variables. It estimates a different BLR model for each variable that defines the success of that model.

R provides many options to implement MLR. One of the methods is using an inbuilt function, `multinom()` of the packages 'nnet'. The nnet package is a neural network package. Before using this package, it is necessary to install and load the package into the R workspace. The `multinom()` function implements MLR. The syntax of the `multinom()` function is:

```
multinom(formula,, data,…)
```

where, "formula" argument defines the symbolic description of the model to be fitted, "data" argument is an optional argument that defines the dataset and the dots "…" define the other optional arguments.

In the following example, a dummy table 'Icecream.csv' is created to store information about the test of flavours of ice cream. With the help of MLR, the table analyses which flavours of ice cream are 'most likely', 'likely', 'not likely' and 'other' by children. Each child is asked to put a number on each flavour. Then the `multinom()` function implements MLR of this data as described in Figure 6.20. Figure 6.21 describes the summary of the output.

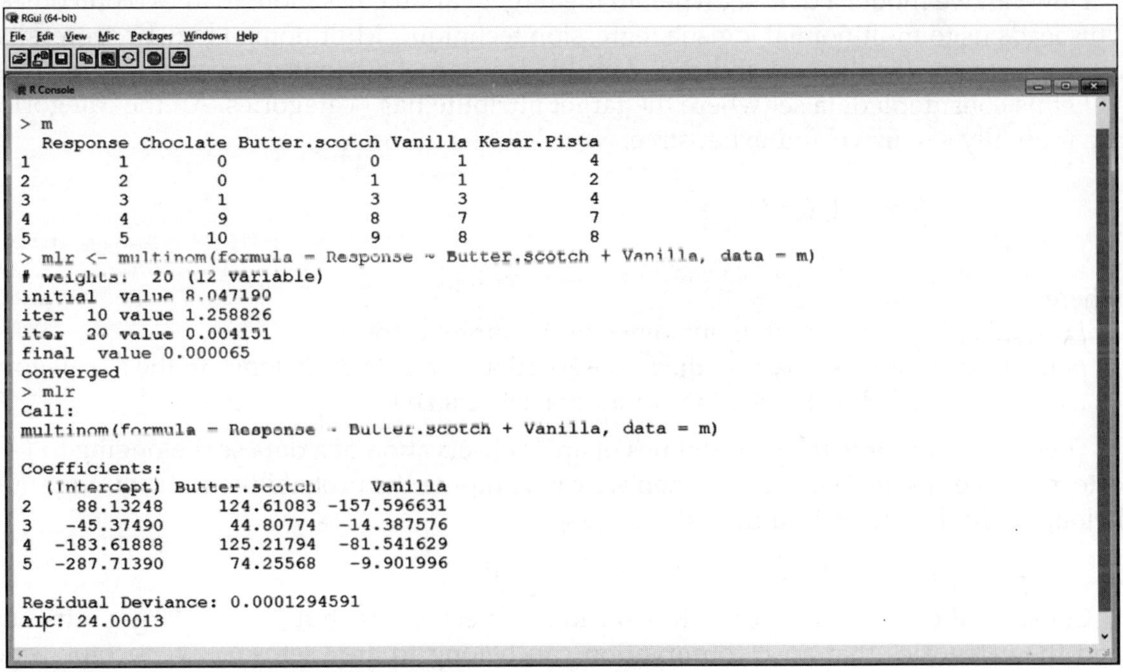

Figure 6.20 *Multinomial logistic regression*

```
5  -287.71390      74.25568    -9.901996

Residual Deviance: 0.0001294591
AIC: 24.00013
> summary(mlr)
Call:
multinom(formula = Response ~ Butter.scotch + Vanilla, data = m)

Coefficients:
  (Intercept) Butter.scotch      Vanilla
2    88.13248     124.61083 -157.596631
3   -45.37490      44.80774  -14.387576
4  -183.61888     125.21794  -81.541629
5  -287.71390      74.25568   -9.901996

Std. Errors:
   (Intercept) Butter.scotch      Vanilla
2 1.521140e-17           NaN          NaN
3 5.658746e-08  4.525448e-07 3.961739e-07
4 6.634308e+02  2.696999e+02 3.937780e+02
5 6.634308e+02  2.696999e+02 3.937780e+02

Residual Deviance: 0.0001294591
AIC: 24.00013
Warning message:
In sqrt(diag(vc)) : NaNs produced
> |
```

FIGURE 6.21 *Summary of MLR*

How can we model a data set wherein the target variable has more than two outcomes? This leads us to multinomial logistic regression technique. Multinomial logistic regression allows us to predict the probabilities of multi-class target attributes, given the predictors.

Let us consider a data set where the target attribute has *J* categories. All the categories are mutually exclusive and exhaustive,

$$\sum_{j=1}^{J} p_{ij} = 1, \text{ for each } i$$

where,

$j = 1, 2, ..., J$ are the possible outcomes of the target attribute
p_{ij} denotes the probability that the ith observation of a data set belongs to the jth category
$i = 1, 2, ..., k$ are the observations of a data set of size k.

Thus, if we compute the probabilities of an ith observation of a data set belonging to $J - 1$ categories, i.e., $p_{i1}, p_{i2}, p_{i3}, ..., p_{i(J-1)},$ then we can compute the probability of the observation belonging to the one remaining category as

$$p_{iJ} = 1 - (p_{i1} + p_{i2} + p_{i3} + ... + p_{i(J-1)})$$

Consider the "iris" data set in R. Consider "Species" attribute as the target attribute and the categories that an ith observation can belong to are "setosa", "versicolor" and "virginica". Assume the categories are indexed as 1, 2 and 3, respectively, and the probability of an ith observation belonging to either of these three categories will sum up to 1. This can be depicted as shown below.

$$p_{i\ \text{setosa}} + p_{i\ \text{versicolor}} + p_{i\ \text{virginica}} = 1$$

Now, once we determine the probability of an ith observation belonging to say "setosa" and "versicolor", we can compute the probability of it belonging to "virginica" as:

$$p_{i\ \text{virginica}} = 1 - (p_{i\ \text{setosa}} + p_{i\ \text{versicolor}})$$

Recall, in binomial logistic regression, since the target attribute had only two possible outcomes, it was sufficient to set up a single logit function as

$$\ln\left(\frac{p}{1-p}\right) = \beta_0 + \beta_1 x_1 + \beta_2 x_2 + \cdots + \beta_n x_n$$

However, in multinomial logistic regression, the target attribute has more than two possible outcomes. Hence, we adopt an approach wherein we nominate one of the outcomes as a pivot/baseline/reference outcome and then calculate log odds for all the other remaining outcomes relative to the reference outcome. Suppose, if the nominal target attribute has J possible outcomes, then we need to determine J - 1 individual binomial logistic regression models.

For the iris data set, since Species is the target attribute with 3 possible outcomes ("setosa", "virginica" and "versicolor"), we need to set up 3 - 1 = 2 logit models. Let us assume "virginica" as the reference outcome. Then the two logit models are as shown below.

$$\ln\left(\frac{p(\text{outcome} = \text{setosa})}{p(\text{outcome} = \text{virginica})}\right) = \begin{matrix}\beta_0^{\text{setosa}} + \beta_1^{\text{setosa}} * \text{Sepal. Length} + \beta_2^{\text{setosa}} * \text{Sepal. Width} + \\ \beta_3^{\text{setosa}} * \text{Petal. Length} + \beta_4^{\text{setosa}} * \text{Petal. Width}\end{matrix}$$
$$= g_{\text{setosa}}(X) \qquad (1)$$

$$\ln\left(\frac{p(\text{outcome} = \text{versicolor})}{p(\text{outcome} = \text{virginica})}\right) = \begin{matrix}\beta_0^{\text{versicolor}} + \beta_1^{\text{versicolor}} * \text{Sepal. Length} + \beta_2^{\text{versicolor}} \\ * \text{Sepal. Width} + \beta_3^{\text{versicolor}} * \text{Petal. Length} + \\ \beta_4^{\text{versicolor}} * \text{Petal. Width}\end{matrix}$$
$$= g_{\text{versicolor}}(X) \qquad (2)$$

In general, the logit model for a jth category for a data set with n predictors is:

$$\ln\left(\frac{p(\text{outcome} = j^{th}\ \text{category})}{p(\text{outcome} = \text{reference category})}\right) = \beta_0^j + \beta_1^j * x_1 + \beta_2^j * x_2 + \beta_3^j * x_3 + \cdots + \beta_n^j * x_n$$
$$= g_j(X)$$

where,

$\beta_0, \beta_1, ..., \beta_n$ are the regression coefficients
$x_1, x_2, ..., x_n$ are the predictor variables
$j = 1, 2, ..., J-1$

To estimate the probabilities associated with each outcome, let us perform the following steps.

The logit models (1) and (2) can be rewritten as shown:

$$\frac{p(\text{outcome} = \text{setosa})}{p(\text{outcome} = \text{virginica})} = e^{g_{\text{setosa}}(X)} \quad (3)$$

$$\frac{p(\text{outcome} = \text{versicolor})}{p(\text{outcome} = \text{virginica})} = e^{g_{\text{versicolor}}(X)} \quad (4)$$

Since, $p(\text{outcome} = \text{virginica}) = 1 - (p(\text{outcome} = \text{setosa}) + p(\text{outcome} = \text{versicolor}))$, we can rewrite (3) and (4) as shown:

$$\frac{p(\text{outcome} = \text{setosa})}{1 - (p(\text{outcome} = \text{setosa}) + p(\text{outcome} = \text{versicolor}))} = e^{g_{\text{setosa}}(X)} \quad (5)$$

$$\frac{p(\text{outcome} = \text{versicolor})}{1 - (p(\text{outcome} = \text{setosa}) + p(\text{outcome} = \text{versicolor}))} = e^{g_{\text{versicolor}}(X)} \quad (6)$$

Rewriting (5) and (6), we get,

$$p(\text{outcome} = \text{setosa}) = \frac{e^{g_{\text{setosa}}(X)}}{1 + e^{g_{\text{setosa}}(X)}} * (1 - p(\text{outcome} = \text{versicolor})) \quad (7)$$

$$p(\text{outcome} = \text{versicolor}) = \frac{e^{g_{\text{versicolor}}(X)}}{1 + e^{g_{\text{versicolor}}(X)}} * (1 - p(\text{outcome} = \text{setosa})) \quad (8)$$

Solving (7) and (8), we get,

$$p(\text{outcome} = \text{setosa}) = \frac{e^{g_{\text{setosa}}(X)}}{1 + e^{g_{\text{setosa}}(X)} + e^{g_{\text{versicolor}}(X)}} \quad (9)$$

$$p(\text{outcome} = \text{versicolor}) = \frac{e^{g_{\text{versicolor}}(X)}}{1 + e^{g_{\text{setosa}}(X)} + e^{g_{\text{versicolor}}(X)}} \quad (10)$$

Since, $p(\text{outcome} = \text{virginica}) = 1 - (p(\text{outcome} = \text{setosa}) + p(\text{outcome} = \text{versicolor}))$, we can compute the probability of occurrence of reference outcome using (9) and (10) as shown below.

$$p(\text{outcome} = \text{virginica}) = \frac{1}{1 + e^{g_{\text{setosa}}(X)} + e^{g_{\text{versicolor}}(X)}} \quad (11)$$

Let us now look at how we can obtain the multinomial logit model in R.

Let us first observe the levels of the target attribute (i.e., before setting the reference outcome) using the code shown:

Step 1: Assign the "iris" dataset to a variable "IrisDataset". The "iris" dataset provides the measurement in centimeters of the variables, sepal length and width, petal length and width for 50 flowers from each of the three species of "iris", viz., "setosa", "versicolor" and "virginica".

```
> IrisDataset <- iris
```

Step 2: Determine the levels of the "Species" column. "levels" provides access to the levels attribute of a variable.

```
> levels(IrisDataset$Species)
[1] "setosa"          "versicolor"      "virginica"
```

Notice that the species, "setosa" is placed as the first level.

Step 3: Set the pivot/baseline/reference outcome as "virginica" using the `relevel()` function. "relevel" levels of a factor are re-ordered so that the level specified by `ref` is first and the others are moved down.

```
> IrisDataset$SpeciesReleveled <- relevel(IrisDataset$Species, ref =
"virginica"
> levels(IrisDataset$SpeciesReleveled)
[1] "virginica"   "setosa"          "versicolor"
```

Note that the reference outcome is always placed as the first level of the factor, i.e., the target attribute.

The new column "SpeciesReleveled" is added to the "IrisDataset" data set as shown.

Let us display a subset of the IrisDataset. Few row nos. (1, 2, 51, 52, 101, 102) have been selected to display rows corresponding to each of the three species.

```
> print(IrisDataset[c(1,2,51,52,101,102),], row.names = F)
Sepal.Length Sepal.Width Petal.Length Petal.Width Species SpeciesReleveled
         5.1         3.5          1.4         0.2 setosa            setosa
         4.9         3.0          1.4         0.2 setosa            setosa
         7.0         3.2          4.7         1.4 versicolor    versicolor
         6.4         3.2          4.5         1.5 versicolor    versicolor
         6.3         3.3          6.0         2.5 virginica      virginica
         5.8         2.7          5.1         1.9 virginica      virginica
```

Let us use "SpeciesReleveled" as the new target attribute and proceed with fitting a model to the above data.

Step 4: To build the multinomial logistic regression classifier, let us perform the following steps.

1. Divide the "IrisDataset" data set into training data and testing data: Load the package "caTools". This package has the "`sample.split()`" function. This function will be used to split the data into test and train subsets.

Use the `sample.split()` function to split the data into test and train subsets. The splitting ratio is 0.6, i.e., 60:40 ratio. We plan to use 60% of the data as training data to train the model and the remaining 40% of the data as testing data to test the model.

```
> split <- sample.split(IrisDataset, SplitRatio = 0.6)
> split
[1] FALSE  TRUE  TRUE  FALSE  TRUE  FALSE
```

The "TRUE" represents 60% of the data and "FALSE" represents the remaining 40% of the data.

```
> training <- subset(IrisDataset[c(-5)], split == "TRUE")
> testing <- subset(IrisDataset[c(-5)], split == "FALSE")
```

2. ***Build the model using the training data:*** Let us use the training data to build the multinomial logistic regression classifier. To estimate the regression coefficients of the two logit models, let us use the `multinom()` function which belongs to the **nnet** package in R, as shown in the code below. `multinom()` fits multinomial log-linear models via neural networks.

```
> library(nnet)

> model <- multinom(formula = SpeciesReleveled ~ .,data = training)
# weights:  18 (10 variable)
initial  value 82.395922
iter  10 value 5.860978
iter  20 value 0.257840
iter  30 value 0.014877
iter  40 value 0.010180
iter  50 value 0.010030
iter  60 value 0.009509
iter  70 value 0.006793
iter  80 value 0.006383
iter  90 value 0.006283
iter 100 value 0.006136
final  value 0.006136
stopped after 100 iterations
> print(model)
Call:
multinom(formula = SpeciesReleveled ~ ., data = training)

Coefficients:
           (Intercept)  Sepal.Length Sepal.Width  Petal.Length Petal.Width
setosa        14.44179      73.60551    76.35325    -129.66718   -94.38017
versicolor 101.91660      47.96270    62.77323     -95.03296   -68.56682

Residual Deviance: 0.01227198
AIC: 20.01227
```

3. Use the model to estimate the probability of a success: Let us estimate the probabilities of a few random observations from testing data as shown:

```
> random_test_obs <- testing[c(6,13,22,34,49,53),]
> print(random_test_obs, row.names = F)
  Sepal.Length Sepal.Width Petal.Length Petal.Width SpeciesReleveled
           4.8         3.4          1.6         0.2           setosa
           4.8         3.4          1.9         0.2           setosa
           4.4         3.2          1.3         0.2           setosa
           5.6         3.0          4.5         1.5       versicolor
           5.7         2.9          4.2         1.3       versicolor
           7.6         3.0          6.6         2.1        virginica
```

Let us now use the `predict()`. It is a generic function for predictions from the results of various model fitting functions.) function in R, to estimate the probabilities of the above observations. Note, that **type = "prob"** argument allows us to compute the probabilities associated with each of the three outcomes of the target attribute.

```
> predicted_probability <- data.frame(predict(model, random_test_
obs, type = "prob"))
> print(predicted_probability, row.names = F)
    virginica        setosa   versicolor
7.005010e-175  1.000000e+00 6.174970e-10
5.489360e-158  9.999799e-01 2.009373e-05
2.343326e-172  1.000000e+00 8.172575e-09
 4.976749e-13  3.677291e-43 1.000000e+00
 1.006545e-30  6.981706e-36 1.000000e+00
 1.000000e+00 8.900046e-110 2.655813e-51
```

Let us try to sum the probabilities of the three outcomes for each random observation, as shown below.

```
> predicted_probability <- data.frame(predicted_probability,apply
(predicted_probability,1,sum))
> colnames(predicted_probability)[4] <- "sum"
> print(predicted_probability, row.names = F)
    virginica        setosa   versicolor  sum
7.005010e-175  1.000000e+00 6.174970e-10    1
5.489360e-158  9.999799e-01 2.009373e-05    1
2.343326e-172  1.000000e+00 8.172575e-09    1
 4.976749e-13  3.677291e-43 1.000000e+00    1
 1.006545e-30  6.981706e-36 1.000000e+00    1
 1.000000e+00 8.900046e-110 2.655813e-51    1
```

Observe that for each observation above, the sum of probabilities of the outcomes is 1.

Next, let us determine the outcomes associated with each of the random observation selected above.

4. Use the estimated probability to classify the observations

Let us once again use the `predict()` function in R. This time let us use **type = "class"** argument, which allows us to predict the most probable outcome associated with each observation, as shown in the code below.

```
> predicted_class <- data.frame(predict(model, random_test_obs, type
= "class"))
> colnames(predicted_class) <- c("predicted class")
> predicted_probability <- subset(predicted_probability, select =
c(-4))
> predicted_class <- data.frame(predicted_probability, predicted_
class)
> print(predicted_class, row.names = F)
    virginica         setosa     versicolor   predicted.class
 7.005010e-175   1.000000e+00   6.174970e-10            setosa
 5.489360e-158   9.999799e-01   2.009373e-05            setosa
 2.343326e-172   1.000000e+00   8.172575e-09            setosa
  4.976749e-13   3.677291e-43   1.000000e+00        versicolor
  1.006545e-30   6.981706e-36   1.000000e+00        versicolor
  1.000000e+00  8.900046e-110   2.655813e-51         verginica
```

Observe that the outcome with the highest probability has been chosen as the most probable outcome, i.e., the predicted class.

5. Compare the predicted outcomes with the actual values

Let us now compare the actual values with the predicted outcomes for the sample of random observations from the testing data, as shown:

```
> actual_class <- random_test_obs$SpeciesReleveled
> #Compare the actual values with predicted outcomes for the random
observations from testing data
> predicted_class <- subset(predicted_class, select = c(4))
> comparison_data <- data.frame(actual_class, predicted_class)
> print(comparison_data, row.names = F)
 actual_class predicted.class
       setosa          setosa
       setosa          setosa
       setosa          setosa
   versicolor      versicolor
   versicolor      versicolor
    virginica       virginica
```

Note that in the above comparison data, none of the observation is misclassified.

Let us determine and compare the predicted outcomes for all test data points to compute the prediction accuracy.

Let us estimate the predicted outcomes for each observation in the testing data and create a confusion matrix to compute the prediction accuracy of the model, as shown:

```
> predicted_class <- predict(model, testing_data, type = "class")
> #Extract the actual values from the testing data
> actual_class <- testing_data$SpeciesReleveled
> #Create a confusion matrix
> addmargins(table(actual_class,predicted_class))
               predicted_class
actual_class  virginica  setosa  versicolor  Sum
  virginica          25       0           0   25
  setosa              0      12           0   12
  versicolor          1       0          22   23
  Sum                26      12          22   60
```

From the above results, we can observe that an instance (i.e., 1) from the testing data has been misclassified. In other words, out of 60 instances, 59 instances (i.e., 25+ 12 + 22) have been predicted correctly. Therefore,

Prediction accuracy = 59 / 60 i.e. 98.33%

Use cases:

- During the testing phase of a software application, the testing team classifies the source of the detected bugs into one of the three categories, viz., requirement analysis, design or code bugs.
- Based on the complexity level of the questions, the assessment team of the college classifies the questions into three categories, viz., simple, medium and complex.

Check Your Understanding

1. What do you mean by MLR?

Ans: MLR or multinomial logistic regression is a type of linear regression where more than two levels of independent variables predict the outcome of the dependent variable.

2. What is the use of `multinom()` function?

Ans: The `multinom()` function is an inbuilt function of the 'nnet' package of R that implements MLR.

Case Study

Audience/ Customer Insights Analysis

Audience insight is very helpful and is used in hospitals, social network, e-commerce, biomedical, pharmachemicals, bioinformatics and many other industries.

This case study is used by companies to indicate the level of growth and predict new user behaviour. This case study uses complex algorithms like time series, neural network, graph exploration data analysis (EDA), graph search mapping, regression model, pattern recognition, data mapping, social analysis mapping, clustering, etc., to analyse the behaviour of users and clients.

In this case study, a regression model is used to find the audiences' insight on different parameters. Other models can be used as well to conclude other things. As the data, we collected for this problem involves many parameters and each parameter provides detailed information on other parameters, it is difficult to ignore any parameter without analysing its data.

Logistic algorithm is one of the most popular statistical algorithms used for probability discrete variables. If properly applied, a logistic algorithm can give the most powerful insight on the attributes of dependent variables. The logistic function maps or translates changes in the values of continuous or dichotomous independent variables on the right-hand side of the logistic equation to increase or decrease the probability of the event modelled by dependent variables or the left-hand side variables. The implementation of logistic regression techniques includes a wealth of tools for the analysts to first construct a model, then test its ability to perform good in terms of data (*audience insight data*) from which real data goes to analysis again and this data is assumed to be a random sample from a really large database.

Before moving further, a clarification is warranted regarding the nature of dependent variables. In many analytics, customers (unit of data) may have more than one choice. For example, during online shopping, customers may opt for costlier items with low price with some offers. In such situations, the MLR model might be useful rather than a binary or dichotomous logistic regression model, while multinomial models can be implemented in R.

The parameter estimated from the logistic regression model can be applied to a simple data step to the 'interest of customer', this 'score' or creating a group of customers of event outcome for each member of the customer group. This 'score' can be used to select subsets of the customers to the substantive issue under analysis.

(Continued)

Case Study

Construction of Dependent Variables

These variables may give the result of some natural information of data with their behaviour of the units under the analysis. This information from each variable identifies the dependent and independent variables for analysis. From a statistical point of view, the dichotomous, nominal level dependent variable must have both *discriminating* and *exhaustive* nature.

Selecting the 'Optimal Subset' of Independent Variables

In many different models, the main task is to find the optimal subset from data as this will give us information on how to optimise the algorithm to get more accurate results. The substantive variables are required to get the backward, forward, stepwise generation of information for selecting the covariance errors. This information in optimal subset plots the ROC as this can indicate the past behaviour of customers in time series of their activities.

The optimal subset helps us design the segmentation of different kinds of users. Each segment stores information on customers' activities. It is used to provide more effective product recommendations to customers. To select the optimum subset, the percentage change in the agglomerative coefficient variables is observed, which indicates precisely the heterogeneity within the segments with 'point and distance'[1] in the form of small cluster segments, along with producing a graphical analysis of the results.

Past Behaviour

Past behaviour is the widely used dependent variable that predicts future predictive behaviour of customers. To do so, the past trends in customers' behaviour are observed to analyse if there is a cyclical pattern in forecasting customer activities. To assess the nature of variables to be forecasted, the basic premise is to use past behaviour to predict future behaviour.

Information about past activities (behaviour) of the customers is divided into three categories, viz., acquisition, use and possession. This classification into behavioural subsets helps to determine some information about customers as per their behaviour. This data helps to determine future needs of customers.

In general, the identification of consumer segments is useful in marketing with the subset information as long as the following four statements apply:

(Continued)

[1] Point and distance will be discussed in detail in *Chapter 9: Clustering*.

Case Study

1. ***Substantial:*** The value in terms of potentially increased sales makes it worthwhile to do so.
2. ***Differentiable:*** There are practical means of differentiating purchase behaviour among market segments. There is homogeneity within and heterogeneity between segments.
3. ***Operational:*** There is a cost-effective method of reaching the targeted market segment.
4. ***Responsive:*** The differentiated market segments respond differently to marketing offerings tailored to meet their needs.

The above four parameters help create patterns and subsets for getting the dependent and independent variables in time series of past customer behaviours. Besides these parameters, another main parameter is customer cognitive behaviour in terms of their satisfaction with a product.

Implicit expectations represent the norms of performance that reflect accepted standards established by business in general. This is calculated by the mean of inverse matrix for checking the fitness in the way business behaves towards the customer and vice versa.

Static performance expectations address how performance and quality for a specific application are defined. Performance measures for each application are unique, though general expectations relate to the quality of outcome. This outcome is plotted in the ROC curve to check the variable fitness and also for correcting the inaccuracies of the algorithm. This helps in designing the covariance matrix to get the accurate distance in measurements with fitness parameters.

Dynamic performance expectations indicate how products or services evolve over time and include the changes in support offered. These also include product and service enhancement offered to meet future business needs. Such requirements are detected on the basis of the research data on past customer activities, behaviour towards products and their availability in the market. Dynamic performance expectations may help to produce 'static' performance expectations. New users, integrations or system requirements develop and become more stable and this stable model is checked by the fitness of algorithm in past and future predictors in patterns.

Interpersonal expectations reflect the relationship between the customers and the products or service providers. Person-to-person relationships are important, especially where support services are required. Expectations for interpersonal support include technical knowledge, ability to solve problems, ability to communicate, time taken to resolve problems, etc.

Summary

- The generalised linear model (glm) is an extension of usual regression models through a link function.
- The inbuilt command `glm()` of R implements the GLMs and performs the regression on different data like binary, probability, count data, proportion data, etc.
- A random component, a systematic component and a link function are the main components of the glm model.
- A random component identifies the dependent variable (response) and its probability distribution in the glm model.
- A systematic component identifies a set of explanatory variables in the glm model.
- A link function defines the relationship between a random and systematic component in the GLM model.
- Logistic regression is an extension of linear regression to environments that contain a categorical dependent variable. The `glm()` function is used to implement LR.
- Logistic regression is used to solve classification problems, discrete choice models or to find out the probability of an event.
- Binomial logistic regression is a model in which the dependent variable is dichotomous.
- Logistic or sigmoidal function estimates the parameters, checks whether they are statistically significant and whether they influence the probability of an event.
- Logit function is the logarithmic transformation of the logistic function. It is defined as the natural logarithm of odds.
- Odds and odds ratio are two parameters of the logit function.
- Odds is one of the parameters of the logit function defined as the ratio of two probability values.
- Odds ratio is another parameter of the logit function defined as the ratio of two odds.
- Maximum likelihood estimator (MLE) estimates the parameters of a function in LR. For a given dataset, MLE chooses the values of model parameters that make the data 'more likely' than other parameter values.
- Likelihood function [$L(\beta)$] represents the joint probability or likelihood of observing the collected data.
- R provides two functions, viz., `nlm()` and `optim()` for finding out the likelihood function.
- The `nlm()` function performs a non-linear minimisation and minimises the function using a Newton-type algorithm.
- The `optim()` function performs a general purpose optimisation and optimises the function using a Nelder-Mead, conjugate-gradient and quasi-Newton algorithm.
- Binary logistic regression is a type of LR that defines the relationship between a categorical response variable and one or more explanatory variables.
- A three-way contingency table contains a cross-classification of observation using the level of three categorical variables.
- A covariate variable is a simple variable that predicts the outcome of another variable.
- Binary logistic regression with a single categorical predictor uses only a single categorical variable to fit data to the BLR model.
- Binary logistic regression for three-way and k-way contingency table uses three or k categorical variable for fitting the data to the BLR model.
- The BLR with continuous covariates follows the general concept of logistic regression where a predictor variable predicts the outcome of the response variable.

(Continued)

- Pearson chi-square statistic [X^2], deviance [G^2], likelihood ratio test and statistic [ΔG^2], and Hosmer-Lemeshow test and statistic are available to check the goodness of statistics of the BLR model.
- Residuals, goodness-of-fit tests and receiver operating characteristic curve are major diagnostics used for diagnosing the logistics regression model.
- Residual is a common measure influence that identifies potential outliers.
- Pearson and deviance residuals are two common types of residuals.
- The Pearson residual assess how predictors are transformed during the fitting process. It uses mean and standard deviation for assessment.
- The deviance residual is the best diagnostic method when individual points are not fitting well by the model.
- The 'LogisticDx' is an R package that provides functions for diagnosing the logistics regression model.
- The `dx()`, `gof()`, `or()` and `plot.glm()` are major diagnostic functions of the 'LogisticDx' package.
- The `gof()` function of the 'LogisticDx' package checks the goodness-of-fit tests for the logistics regression model.
- Receiver operating characteristic (ROC) curve is a plot of specificity (False positive rate) against sensitivity (True positive rate). The area under the ROC curve quantifies the predictive ability of the model.
- Multinomial logistic regression (MLR) is a type of linear regression where more than two levels of independent variables predict the outcome of the dependent variable.
- The `multinom()` function is an inbuilt function of the 'nnet' package of R that implements MLR.

Key Terms

- **Binomial logistic regression:** Binomial or binary logistic regression (BLR) is a model in which the dependent variable is dichotomous.
- **Covariate variable:** A covariate variable is a simple variable that predicts the outcome of another variable.
- **Deviance residual:** Deviance residual is the best diagnostic measure when individual points are not fitting well by the model.
- **GLM:** The generalised linear model (GLM) is an extension of usual regression models through a link function.
- **Likelihood function:** Likelihood function [$L(\beta)$] represents the joint probability or likelihood of observing collected data.
- **Link function:** It defines the relationship between a random and a systematic component.
- **LogisticDx:** The 'LogisticDx' is an R package that provides functions for diagnosing the logistics regression model.
- **Logistic function:** Logistic function or sigmoidal function is a function that estimates the parameters, checks whether they are statistically significant and whether they influence the probability of an event.
- **Logit function:** Logit function is the logarithmic transformation of the logistic function.
- **Logistics regression:** Logistic regression (LR) is an extension of linear regression to environments that contain a categorical dependent variable. The `glm()` function is used to implement logistics regression.
- **Maximum likelihood estimator:** Maximum likelihood estimator (MLE) estimates the parameters of a function in LR. For a given

dataset, MLE chooses the values of model parameters that make the data *more likely* than other parameter values.

- **Multinomial logistic regression:** Multinomial logistic regression (MLR) is a type of linear regression where more than two levels of independent variables predict the outcome of the dependent variable.
- **`nlm()`:** The `nlm()` function is an inbuilt function of R that finds the likelihood estimation using nonlinear minimisation.
- **nnet:** The 'nnet' is a neural network package of R that provides a function `multinom()` to implement MLR.
- **Odds:** Odds is one of the parameters of the logit function defined as the ratio of two probability values.
- **Odds ratio:** Odds ratio is another parameter of the logit function defined as the ratio of two ODDS.
- **`optim()`:** The `optim()` function is an inbuilt function of R that finds the likelihood estimation using general purpose optimisation.
- **Pearson residual:** Pearson residual assess how the predictors are transformed during the fitting process. It uses the mean and standard deviation for assessment.
- **Predictor:** Predictor is an independent variable in regression analysis.
- **Residual:** Residual is a common measure influence that identifies potential outliers.
- **Response variable:** Response variables are dependent variables in regression analysis.
- **ROC Curve:** Receiver operating characteristic (ROC) curve is a plot of specificity against sensitivity. The area under the ROC curve quantifies the predictive ability of a model.
- **stats4:** The 'stats4' is a package of R that provides a function `mle()` to implement the maximum likelihood estimation.
- **Three-way contingency table:** A three-way contingency table contains cross-classification of observations using the level of three categorical variables.

Multiple Choice Questions

1. From the given options, which of one the following is another name for a dependent variable?
   (a) Explanatory variable (b) Independent variable
   (c) Response variable (d) Predictor
2. From the given options, which regression type is an extension of the linear regression model that uses a link function?
   (a) Generalised linear model (b) Non-linear regression model
   (c) Logistics regression model (d) None of the above
3. From the given options, which one of the following functions defines the relationship between a random and a systematic component?
   (a) Logit function (b) User-defined function
   (c) Link function (d) None of the above

4. From the given options, which regression is an extension of linear regression to environments that contain a categorical dependent variable?
   (a) Generalised linear model (b) Non-linear regression
   (c) Logistics regression (d) None of the above
5. From the given options, which one of the following functions implements binary logistic regression?
   (a) `glm()` (b) `multinom()`
   (c) `nls()` (d) `lm()`
6. From the given options, which one of the following functions implements multinomial logistic regression?
   (a) `glm()` (b) `lm()`
   (c) `nls()` (d) `multinom()`
7. From the given options, which one of the following tables contains cross-classification of observations that uses the level of three categorical variables?
   (a) A k-way contingency (b) A two-way contingency
   (c) A four-way contingency (d) A three-way contingency
8. From the given options, which one of the following packages contains the diagnosis functions for the diagnosis of logistic regression?
   (a) nnet (b) stat
   (c) LogisticDx (d) party
9. The binomial family argument of the glm() function uses which one of the following link functions?
   (a) logit (b) identity
   (c) inverse (d) log
10. The `glm()` or `multinom()` function uses which one of the following symbols for defining formula mode?
    (a) $ (b) ~
    (c) * (d) #
11. The Gaussian family argument of the `glm()` function uses which one of the following link functions?
    (a) logit (b) identity
    (c) inverse (d) log
12. From the given options, which one of the following packages contains a function that implements the multinomial logistic regression?
    (a) nnet (b) stat
    (c) LogisticDx (d) party
13. From the given options, which one of the following functions returns Pearson and deviance residuals?
    (a) `gof()` (b) `dx()`
    (c) `or()` (d) `plot.glm()`

14. From the given options, which one of the following is a common measure influence that identifies potential outliers?
    (a) Over-dispersion
    (b) Goodness-of-fit tests
    (c) ROC curve
    (d) Residual

15. From the given options, which one of the following functions is a logarithmic transformation of the logistic function?
    (a) Logit function
    (b) Link function
    (c) Likelihood function
    (d) None of the above

16. From the given options, which one of the following functions estimates the parameters and checks significance statistics?
    (a) Logit function
    (b) Link function
    (c) Likelihood function
    (d) Logistic function

17. From the given options, which one of the following functions represents joint probability or likelihood of observing the collected data?
    (a) Logit function
    (b) Link function
    (c) Likelihood function
    (d) Logistic function

18. The ratio of two probability values is called:
    (a) ODDS
    (b) OR
    (c) ODDP
    (d) ODDL

19. The ratio of two ODDS is called:
    (a) ODDP
    (b) OR
    (c) ODDL
    (d) None of the above

20. What is the full form of MLE?
    (a) Minimum likelihood estimator
    (b) Maximum likelihood estimation
    (c) Minimum likelihood estimation
    (d) Maximum likelihood estimator

21. What is the full form of nlm used in the `nlm()` function?
    (a) Non-linear minimisation
    (b) Non log-linear minimisation
    (c) Non-linear maximisation
    (d) Non log-linear maximisation

22. From the given options, which one of the following functions determines the maximum likelihood estimators?
    (a) nlm()
    (b) optim()
    (c) mle()
    (d) glm()

23. From the given options, which ine of the following functions determines the likelihood function?
    (a) nlm()
    (b) lm()
    (c) mle()
    (d) glm()

24. From the given options, which one of the following packages contains the `mle()` function?
    (a) nnet
    (b) stats4
    (c) LogisticDx
    (d) party

25. From the given options, which one of the following functions determines the likelihood function using the Nelder-Mead algorithm?
    (a) `nlm()` (b) `optim()`
    (c) `mle()` (d) `glm()`

Short Questions

1. What is GLM regression? What are its components?
2. What are the applications of logistic regression?
3. What are independent and dependent variables in regression?
4. What is the difference between the logistic and logit functions?
5. What is the difference between `nlm()` and `optim()` functions?
6. What is the difference between Pearson and deviance residuals?
7. What is the difference between residual and goodness-of-fit tests?

Long Questions

1. Which function implements the GLM model in R? Explain with an example and syntax.
2. Explain the `nlm()` function with syntax and an example.
3. Explain the `optim()` function with syntax and an example.
4. Explain the `mle()` function with syntax and an example.
5. Explain binary logistic regression with a single categorical variable.
6. Explain binary logistic regression with a contingency table.
7. Explain binary logistic regression with a covariate variable.
8. Explain the `multinom()` function with syntax and an example.
9. Create a table with an 'employee' column that stores the necessary information including each employee's performance scores. Implement logistic regression to check whether an employee is eligible for promotion or not based on his/her performance score. Also, implement the `mle()` function for defining the maximum likelihood estimation.
10. Create a table with a 'person' column that stores the information like name, age, gender, annual income and other. Implement the binary logistic regression with single categorical and three-way contingency table after placing the required information on the table.
11. Create a table with a 'pizza' column that stores the information that is necessary to implement multinomial logistics regression. After placing the information, implement multinomial logistics regression on this table.

Answers to MCQs:

1. (c)	2. (a)	3. (c)	4. (c)	5. (a)	6. (d)	7. (d)
8. (c)	9. (a)	10. (b)	11. (b)	12. (a)	13. (b)	14. (d)
15. (a)	16. (d)	17. (c)	18. (a)	19. (b)	20. (d)	21. (a)
22. (c)	23. (a)	24. (b)	25. (b)			

Chapter 7

Decision Tree

LEARNING OUTCOME

At the end of this chapter, you will be able to:

- Induct a decision tree to perform classification
- Explain the various attribute selection measures used to split data while inducting a decision tree for classification
- Predict the value of the outcome variable using the created decision tree model

7.1 Introduction

Decision trees are being extensively used in many classification and prediction applications. Sometimes they are also called classification and regression trees (CART or C&RT). Key advantages of using decision trees in decision making are:

- Decision trees are known to clearly lay out the problem so that every possible outcome of a decision can be challenged. They enable analysts to completely analyse all possible consequences of a decision and quantify the values of outcomes and the probabilities of achieving them.
- Decision trees are very intuitive and easy to explain.
- Decision trees require minimum data preparation from users. Missing values do not prevent splitting of the data to build the trees. They are also not sensitive to the presence of outliers.

Decision trees are being used in varied areas to arrive at business decisions. Some areas are:

- To increase capacity vs outsourcing to fulfil demand
- To purchase cars for company car fleet or to get them on lease
- Deciding when to launch a new product
- Deciding which celebrity to invite to endorse your product

This chapter discusses appropriate problems for decision making, the ID3 algorithm, the importance of measuring entropy and information gains and issues in decision tree learning such as over fitting, handling missing attributes and handling attributes with different costs.

7.2 What is a Decision Tree?

In the previous chapter, you learnt about the relationship between different variables of business data using R. In this chapter, you will learn about the graphical representation of such types of business data using R. Decision tree is one of the methods of graphical representation of data. Business analytics involves big data and requires suitable representation for it for which decision tree is the best method.

Decision tree is a part of machine learning and it is mostly used in data mining applications. It is a type of undirected graph (an undirected graph is a graph in which edges have no orientation, i.e., the edge (x, y) is identical to the edge (y, x) that represents the decisions and their outcomes in a tree structure or hierarchal form. In other words, an undirected graph is a group of nodes and edges where there is no cycle in the graph and there is a path between every two nodes of the graph. In a decision tree graph, a node represents the events or choices and edges represent the decision rules.

Decision tree is a type of supervised learning algorithm. In supervised learning, we make predictions using a known dataset, often called the training dataset. Supervised learning problems are classified into "regression" or "classification" problem. In "**regression**" problem, we predict the results within a continuous output. This implies that we map input variables to some continuous function. For example, predict the price of a house based on the size of the house in the real estate market. Here, the price as a function of house size is a continuous output.

In "**classification**" problem, we predict the results within a discrete output. This implies that we map input variables into discrete categories.

Examples of classification task are:

- Determine whether the house sells for more than or less than the asking price. Here, we classify the house based on the price into two discrete categories.
- Classify a loan applicant as "low", "medium" or "high" credit risks.
- Categorise news stories as finance, weather, entertainment, sports, etc.
- Classify credit card transactions as legitimate or fraudulent.
- Predict whether tumour cells are benign or malignant.

Many data mining applications use decision trees for making various kinds of decisions. A decision tree classifies data by partitioning attribute space and tries to find the axis-parallel decision boundaries for some criteria.

Consider the following scenario. You have been asked to explore the "iris" dataset. This dataset has measurements in centimetres for the variables "Sepal.Length", "Sepal.Width", "Petal.Length" and "Petal.Width" for 50 flowers from each of the three species of iris, viz., "setosa", "versicolor" and "virginica". A subset of the data is given as follows:

```
Sepal.Length  Sepal.Width   Petal.Length   Petal.Width   Species
7.4           2.8           6.1            1.9           virginica
7.9           3.8           6.4            2.0           virginica
6.4           2.8           5.6            2.2           virginica
6.3           2.8           5.1            1.5           virginica
6.1           2.6           5.6            1.4           virginica
7.7           3.0           6.1            2.3           virginica
6.3           3.4           5.6            2.4           virginica
6.4           3.1           5.5            1.8           virginica
6.0           3.0           4.8            1.8           virginica
6.9           3.1           5.4            2.1           virginica
6.7           3.1           5.6            2.4           virginica
6.9           3.1           5.1            2.3           virginica
5.8           2.7           5.1            1.9           virginica
6.8           3.2           5.9            2.3           virginica
6.7           3.3           5.7            2.5           virginica
6.7           3.0           5.2            2.3           virginica
6.3           2.5           5.0            1.9           virginica
6.5           3.0           5.2            2.0           virginica
6.2           3.4           5.4            2.3           virginica
5.9           3.0           5.1            1.8           virginica
```

The values that the "Species" attribute holds are called class labels or classes and the attribute itself is called class label attribute. The class label of a new instance can be predicted by studying the patterns in the previously processed data. The previously processed data is referred to as historical data. The attributes that are used in order to predict the value of the class label attribute are called the predictor attributes.

Your supervisor checks on you if you have studied the data set. He poses a question, "If I were to provide you with the values for "Sepal.Length", "Sepal.Width", "Petal.Length" and "Petal.Width" for a particular flower, will you be able to state the species to which it belongs?

Sepal.Length	*Sepal.Width*	*Petal.Length*	*Petal.Width*	*Species*
5.1	3.5	1.4	0.2	?

Likewise, study the "readingSkills" data set. This data set has variables "age", "shoeSize", "score" and "nativeSpeaker". A subset of the data is given as follows:

```
> readingSkills[c(1:100),]
      nativeSpeaker  age   shoesize   score
1     yes            5     24.83189   32.29385
2     yes            6     25.95238   36.63105
3     no             11    30.42170   49.60593
4     yes            7     28.66450   40.28456
5     yes            11    31.88207   55.46085
6     yes            10    30.07843   52.83124
7     no             7     27.25963   34.40229
8     yes            11    30.72398   55.52747
9     yes            5     25.64411   32.49935
10    no             7     26.69835   33.93269
11    yes            11    31.86645   55.46876
12    yes            10    29.15575   51.34140
13    no             9     29.13156   41.77098
14    no             6     26.86513   30.03304
15    no             5     24.23420   25.62268
16    yes            6     25.67538   35.30042
17    no             5     24.86357   25.62843
18    no             6     26.15357   30.76591
19    no             9     27.82057   41.93846
20    yes            5     24.86766   31.69986
21    no             6     25.21054   30.37086
22    no             6     27.36395   29.29951
23    no             8     28.66429   38.08837
24    yes            9     29.98455   48.62986
25    yes            10    30.84168   52.41079
26    no             7     26.80696   34.18835
27    yes            6     26.88768   35.34583
28    yes            8     28.42650   43.72037
29    no             11    31.71159   48.67965
30    yes            8     27.77712   44.14728
31    yes            9     28.88452   48.69638
32    yes            7     26.66743   39.65520
33    no             9     28.91362   41.79739
34    no             9     27.88048   42.42195
35    yes            7     25.46581   39.70293
```

If the age, shoeSize and score for a child is provided, then will you be able to state if the child is a native speaker of the language in the reading test?

age	*shoeSize*	*score*	*nativeSpeaker*
11	30.63692	55.721149	?

"Decision tree" helps to answer these questions and several more similar ones. The answer to the stated questions is provided in Section 7.2, "Decision tree representation in R".

7.2.1 Terminologies Associated with Decision Tree

Various terminologies associated with decision tree are depicted in Figure 7.1 and are described as follows:

- ***Root node:*** It represents the entire population or sample. It gets divided into two or more homogeneous sets.
- ***Decision node:*** It is a subnode that can be split into further subnodes.
- ***Leaf or terminal node:*** It is a node that does not split further into subnodes.
- ***Splitting:*** It is a process of dividing a node into subnodes.
- ***Pruning:*** It is a process of removing subnodes of a decision node.
- ***Branch or subtree:*** It is a subsection of the entire tree.
- Depth of a node is the minimum number of steps required to reach the node from the root.

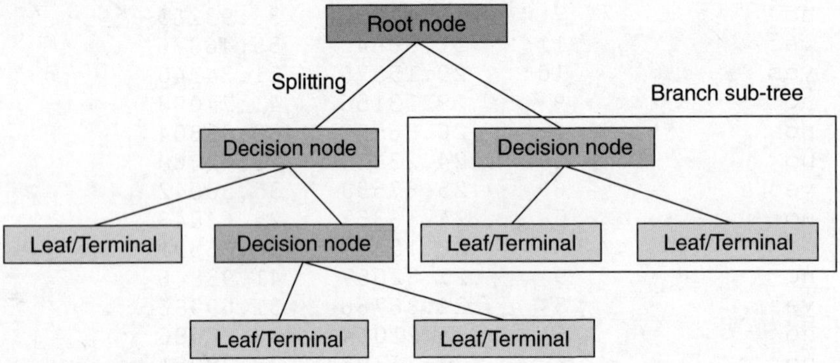

FIGURE 7.1 *Decision Tree*

Definition of a Decision Tree

A decision tree is a tree-like structure in which an internal node (decision node) represents a test on an attribute. A branch represents the outcome of the test. Each leaf/terminal node represents a class label. A path from the root to leaf represents classification rules.

Example of a Decision Tree

Assume we would like to take a decision based on the gender of the employee. If it is a male employee, perform a further check on the income scale and then decide appropriately. If it is a female employee, check on the age. For female employees <= 30 follow the branch that leads to "Yes" (this could be a certain policy applicable to employees <= 30 years of age), else follow the branch that leads to "No" (Figure 7.2).

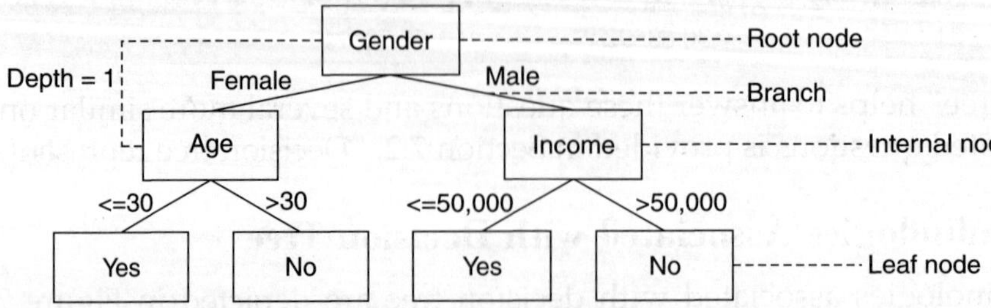

FIGURE 7.2 *An example of a decision tree*

Advantages of a Decision Tree

- Does not require domain knowledge/expertise
- Is easy to comprehend
- The classification steps of a decision tree are simple and fast
- Works with both numerical as well as categorical data
- Able to handle both continuous and discrete attributes
- Scales to big data
- Requires very little data preparation (as it works with NAs, no need for normalisation, etc.).

Disadvantages of a Decision Tree

- Easy to overfit the tree
- Complex "if then" relationships inflates tree size
- Decision boundaries are rectilinear
- Small variations in the data can imply that very different looking trees are generated.

Check Your Understanding

1. What is a decision tree?

Ans: A decision tree is a part of machine learning and it is mostly used in data mining applications. It is a type of undirected graph that represents the decisions and their outcomes in a tree structure or hierarchal form.

2. What is an undirected graph?

Ans: An undirected graph is a group of nodes and edges where there is no cycle in the graph and there is one path between every two nodes of the graph.

3. What represents the node and edges in a decision tree?

Ans: In a decision tree graph, a node represents the events or choices and edges represent the decision rules.

7.3 Decision Tree Representation in R

R has features for tree-based modelling and generates various types of trees like regression tree, classification tree, recursive tree, etc. R represents the decision tree just as it is generally represented by the graph where the internal or non-leaf node represents a choice or options between available alternatives and the leaf or terminal node represents the decisions. It provides different packages, such as party, rpart, maptree, tree, partykit, and randomforest that create different types of such trees. The most popular packages are 'party' and 'rpart'. A brief introduction to both packages is given ahead.

7.3.1 Representation using 'party' Package

The party package contains many functions but the core function is the `ctree()` function. It follows the concept of recursive partitioning and embeds the tree-structured models into conditional inference procedures. Actually, conditional inference tree (ctree) is a non-parametric class of regression tree that solves various regression problems, such as nominal, ordinal, univariate and multivariate response variables or numbers. The basic syntax of the `ctree()` function is:

```
ctree(formula, data, controls =  ctree_control ()...)
```

where, "formula argument" defines a symbolic description of the model to be fit using the "~" symbol, "data argument" defines the data frame that contains the variables in the selected model and "controls argument" is an optional argument that contains an object of class TreeControl. It is obtained using ctree_control and the dots "..." define other optional arguments.

Example 1

This example takes a vector "a" and binds it into a data frame "cb". For creating a recursive decision tree, the 'party' package is loaded. The `ctree()` function creates a recursive tree "*t*" and four terminal nodes. Using the `plot()` function, Figure 7.3 defines this tree.

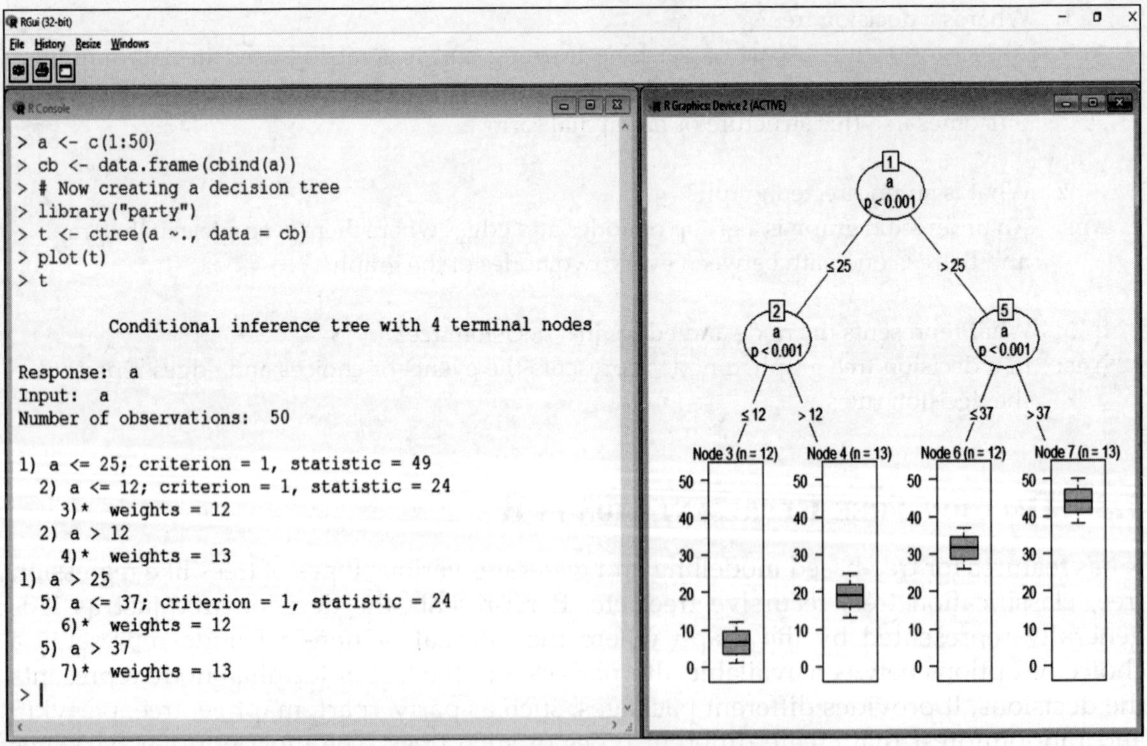

FIGURE 7.3 *A simple decision tree of a vector using the* `ctree()` *function*

Example 2

This example takes an inbuilt dataset "cars" that contains two variables, viz., "speed" and "dist". Here, variable "dist" is taken as a predictor and variable "speed" as a response. The `ctree()` function creates a recursive tree t using the formula "speed~dist". In Figure 7.4, it can be seen that the function generates three terminal nodes.

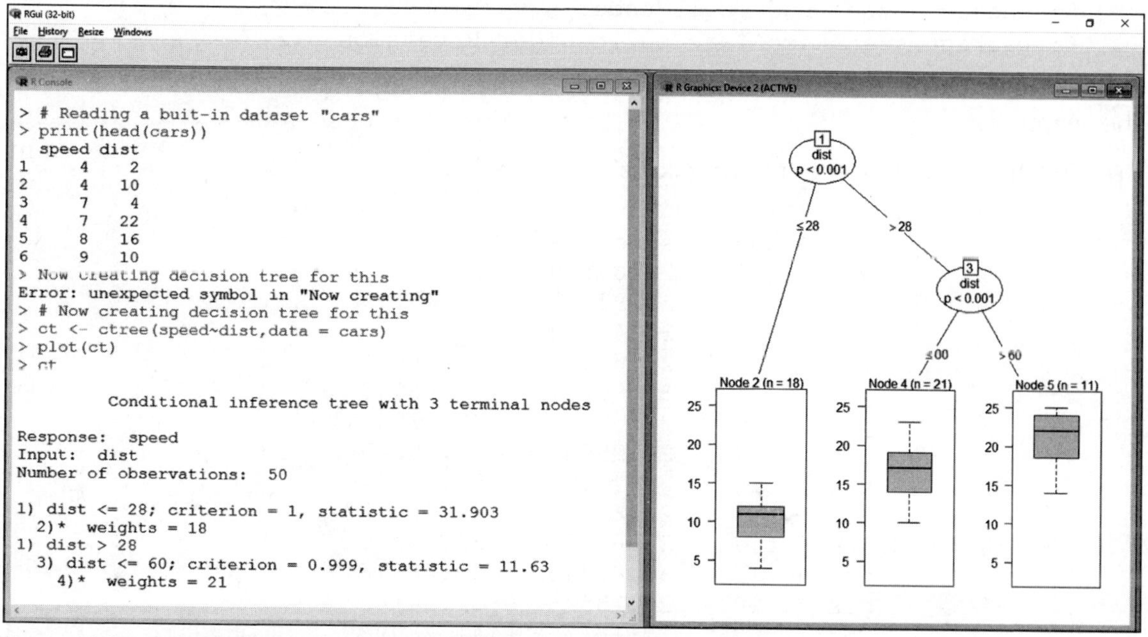

FIGURE 7.4 *A simple decision tree of an inbuilt dataset 'cars' using the* `ctree()` *function*

Example 3

To determine whether a child is a native speaker or not based on his/her age and scores in the reading test.

Step 1: Load the party package.

```
> library(party)
Loading required package: grid
Loading required package: mvtnorm
Loading required package: modeltools
Loading required package: stats4
Loading required package: strucchange
Loading required package: zoo

Attaching package: 'zoo'

The following objects are masked from 'package:base':
  as.Date, as.Date.numeric
```

```
Loading required package: sandwich
Warning messages:
1: package 'party' was built under R version 3.2.3
2: package 'mvtnorm' was built under R version 3.2.3
3: package 'modeltools' was built under R version 3.2.3
4: package 'strucchange' was built under R version 3.2.3
5: package 'zoo' was built under R version 3.2.3
6: package 'sandwich' was built under R version 3.2.3
```

The above command loads the namespace of the package, "party" and attaches it on the search list.

Step 2: Check the data set "readingSkills".

```
> readingSkills[c(1:100),]
  nativeSpeaker  age   shoeSize     score
1           yes    5   24.83189  32.29385
2           yes    6   25.95238  36.63105
3            no   11   30.42170  49.60593
4           yes    7   28.66450  40.28456
5           yes   11   31.88207  55.46085
6           yes   10   30.07843  52.83124
7            no    7   27.25963  34.40229
8           yes   11   30.72398  55.52747
9           yes    5   25.64411  32.49935
10           no    7   26.69335  33.93269
11          yes   11   31.86645  55.46876
12          yes   10   29.15575  51.34140
13           no    9   29.13156  41.77098
14           no    6   26.86513  30.03304
15           no    5   24.23420  25.62268
16          yes    6   25.67538  35.30042
17           no    5   24.86357  25.62843
18           no    6   26.15357  30.76591
19           no    9   27.82057  41.93846
20          yes    5   24.86766  31.69986
21           no    6   25.21054  30.37086
22           no    6   27.36395  29.29951
23           no    8   28.66429  38.08837
24          yes    9   29.98455  48.62986
25          yes   10   30.84168  52.41079
26           no    7   26.80696  34.18835
27          yes    6   26.88768  35.34583
28          yes    8   28.42650  43.72037
29           no   11   31.71159  48.67965
30          yes    8   27.77712  44.14728
31          yes    9   28.88452  48.69638
32          yes    7   26.66743  39.65520
33           no    9   28.91362  41.79739
34           no    9   27.88048  42.42195
```

35	yes	7	28.46581	39.70293
36	yes	8	27.71701	44.06255
37	no	7	25.18567	34.27840
38	yes	11	30.78970	55.98101
39	yes	11	30.75664	55.86037
40	yes	11	30.51397	56.60820
41	no	5	26.23732	26.18401
42	no	5	24.36030	25.36158
43	no	7	27.60571	32.88146
44	no	10	29.64754	45.76171
45	yes	8	29.49313	43.48726
46	yes	7	26.92283	38.91425
47	yes	8	28.35511	44.99324
48	no	6	26.10433	29.35036
49	yes	8	29.63552	43.66695
50	yes	8	27.25306	43.68387
51	no	8	26.22137	37.74103
52	yes	6	26.12942	36.26278
53	no	9	30.46199	42.50194
54	no	7	27.81342	34.33921
55	yes	10	29.37199	52.83951
56	yes	10	29.34344	51.94718
57	yes	7	25.46308	39.52239
58	no	10	28.77307	45.85540
59	no	11	30.35263	50.02399
60	no	8	29.32793	37.52172
61	yes	10	28.87461	51.53771
62	no	7	26.62042	33.96623
63	no	7	28.11487	33.39622
64	no	11	30.98741	50.28310
65	yes	10	29.25488	50.80650
66	yes	5	24.54372	31.95700
67	no	8	26.99163	37.61791
68	no	11	30.26624	50.22454
69	no	7	27.86489	34.20965
70	yes	10	30.16982	52.16763
71	yes	7	25.53495	40.24965
72	no	7	26.75747	34.72458
73	yes	10	29.62773	51.47984
74	no	5	24.41493	25.32841
75	no	9	30.64056	42.88392
76	yes	7	26.78045	39.36539
77	yes	8	28.51236	43.69140
78	yes	5	23.68071	32.33290
79	no	7	26.75671	33.12978
80	no	10	29.65228	47.08507
81	no	9	29.33337	41.29804
82	no	6	26.47543	29.52375
83	no	9	28.35927	41.92929

```
84            no     8   27.15459   38.30587
85            no    10   30.58496   45.20211
86           yes     9   30.08234   48.72401
87            no     9   28.34494   42.42763
88           yes    11   29.25025   55.98533
89           yes     9   28.21583   48.18957
90            no     8   28.10878   37.39201
91            no     8   26.78507   37.40460
92           yes    10   31.09258   51.95836
93            no     5   24.29214   26.37935
94            no     7   27.03635   33.52986
95           yes     7   24.92221   40.19923
96            no     6   27.22615   29.54096
97           yes     7   25.61014   41.15145
98           yes    10   28.44878   52.57931
99           yes     7   27.60034   40.01064
100          yes    11   31.97305   56.71151
```

"readingSkills" is a toy dataset which exhibits a spurious/false correlation between a child's shoe size and the score in his/her reading skills. It has a total of 200 observations on four variables, viz., nativeSpeaker, age, shoeSize and score. The explanation for the variables is given as follows:

- Nativespeaker: It is a factor that can have a value of yes or no. "yes" indicates that the child is a native speaker of the language in the reading test.
- age: It is the age of the child.
- shoeSize: This variable stores the shoe size of the child in cm.
- score: This variable has the raw score of the child in the reading test.

Step 3: Create a data frame, "Inputdata" and have it store from 1 to 105 records of the "readingSkills" data set.

```
> InputData <-readingSkills[c(1:105),]
```

The above command extracts out a subset of the observations in "readingSkills" and places it in the data frame "InputData".

Step 4: Give the chart file a name.

```
> png(file = "decision_tree.png")
```

"decision_tree.png" is the name of the output file. With this command, a plot device is opened and nothing is returned to the R interpreter.

Step 5: Create the tree.

```
> OutputTree <-ctree(
+ nativeSpeaker ~ age + shoeSize + score
+ data = InputData)
```

ctree is the conditional inference tree. We have supplied two inputs. The first being the formula that is a symbolic description of the model to be fit and the second input "data" is to specify the data frame containing the variables in the model.

Step 6: Check out the content of "OutputTree".

```
> OutputTree
  Conditional inference tree with 4 terminal nodes
Response: nativeSpeaker
Inputs: age, shoeSize, score
Number of observations: 105
1) score <= 38.30587; criterion = 1, statistic = 24.932
   2) age <= 6; criterion = 0.993, statistic = 9.361
      3) score <= 30.76591; criterion = 0.999, statistic = 14.093
         4)* weights = 13
      3) score > 30.76591
         5)* weights = 9
   2) age > 6
      6)* weights = 21
1) score > 38.30587
   7)* weights = 62
```

Step 7: Save the file.

```
> dev.off()
null device
          1
```

This command is to shut down the specified device "png" in our example.

The output from the whole exercise is shown in Figure 7.5.

The inference is that anyone with a reading score <= 38.306 and age greater than 6 is NOT a native speaker.

Let us go back to the question asked in Section 7.1. "If the age, shoeSize and score for a child is provided, will you be able to state if the child is a native speaker of the language in the reading test?"

Let us try answering this question.

Step 1: Load the "rpart" package. A detailed explanation of "rpart" package is provided in Section 7.2.2 "Representation using "rpart" Package".

```
> library(rpart)
```

Step 2: Specify the values for "age", "shoeSize" and "score" for a child for whom we wish to determine if he/she is a native speaker of the language or not.

```
> nativeSpeaker_find <-data.frame("age" = 11, "shoeSize" = 30.63692,
"score" = 55.721149)
```

Step 3: Create an rpart object "fit".

```
> fit <-rpart(nativeSpeaker ~ age + shoeSize + score, data=readingSkills)
```

Step 4: Use predict function. predict is a generic function for predictions from the results of various model fitting functions.

```
> prediction <-predict(fit, newdata=nativeSpeaker_find, type = "class")
```

Step 5: Print the returned value from predict function. The inference is, for the child aged 11 with shoe size = 30.63692 and a score of 55.721149, he/she is a native speaker of the language in the reading test.

```
> print(prediction)
  1
yes
Levels: no    yes
```

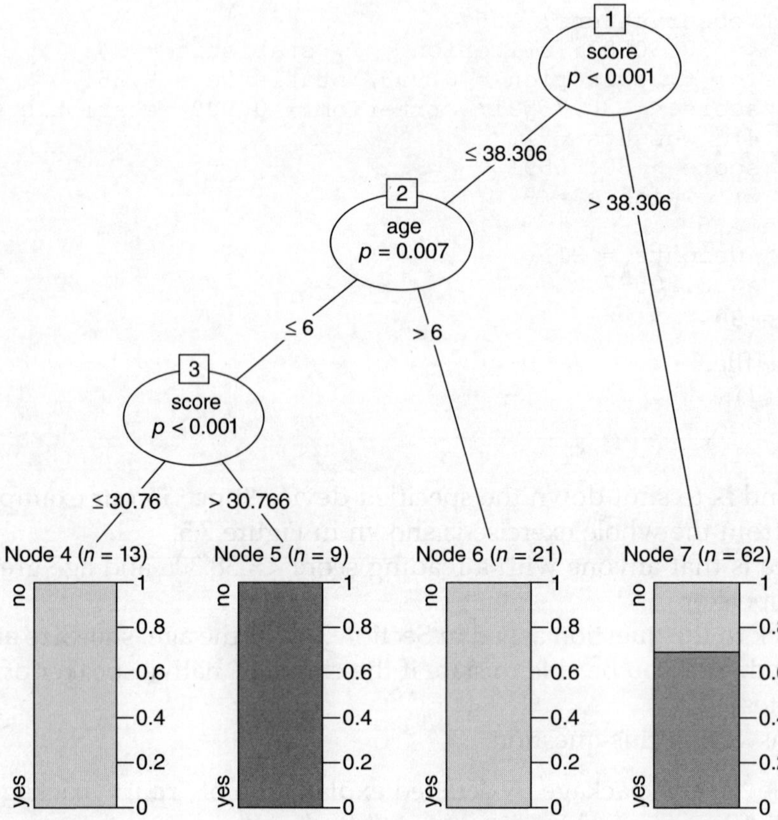

FIGURE 7.5 *A simple decision tree of an inbuilt dataset 'readingSkills' using the* `ctree()` *function*

Example 4

We will work with the "airquality" data set. This data set has data of "daily air quality measurements in New York from May to September 1973".

The data set has 154 observations on six variables.

Variable	*Data type*	*Meaning*
Ozone	numeric	Ozone in parts per billion
Solar.R	numeric	Solar radiation in Langleys
Wind	numeric	Average wind speed in miles per hour
Temp	numeric	Maximum daily temperature in degrees Fahrenheit
Month	numeric	Month (1—12)
Day	numeric	Day (1—31)

Step 1: Print the first 6 entries of the data set "airquality".

```
> head(airquality)
    Ozone    Solar.R      Wind    Temp    Month   Day
1   41       190          7.4     67      5       1
2   36       118          8.0     72      5       2
3   12       149          12.6    74      5       3
4   18       313          11.5    62      5       4
5   NA       NA           14.3    56      5       5
6   28       NA           14.9    66      5       6
```

Step 2: Remove the records with missing "ozone" data.

```
> airq <-subset(airquality, !is.na(Ozone))
```

Step 3: Print the first six entries of the cleaned-up dataset "airq".

```
> head(airq)
    Ozone    Solar.R      Wind    Temp    Month   Day
1   41       190          7.4     67      5       1
2   36       118          8.0     72      5       2
3   12       149          12.6    74      5       3
4   18       313          11.5    62      5       4
6   28       NA           14.9    66      5       6
7   23       299          8.6     65      5       7
```

Step 4: Use ctree to construct a model of Ozone as a function of all other covariates.

```
> air.ct <-ctree(Ozone ~ ., data = airq, controls = ctree_
control(maxsurrogate = 3))
> air.ct
      Conditional inference tree with 5 terminal nodes
Response: Ozone
Inputs: Solar.R, Wind, Temp, Month, Day
Number of observations: 116

1) Temp <= 82; criterion = 1, statistic = 56.086
   2) Wind <= 6.9; criterion = 0.998, statistic = 12.969
      3) *  weights = 10
   2) Wind > 6.9
      4) Temp <= 77; criterion = 0.997, statistic = 11.599
         5) *  weights = 48
      4) Temp > 77
         6) *  weights = 21
1) Temp > 82
   7) Wind <= 10.3; criterion = 0.997, statistic = 11.712
      8) *  weights = 30
   7) Wind > 10.3
      9) *  weights = 7
```

Step 5: Plot a decision tree.

```
> plot (air.ct)
```

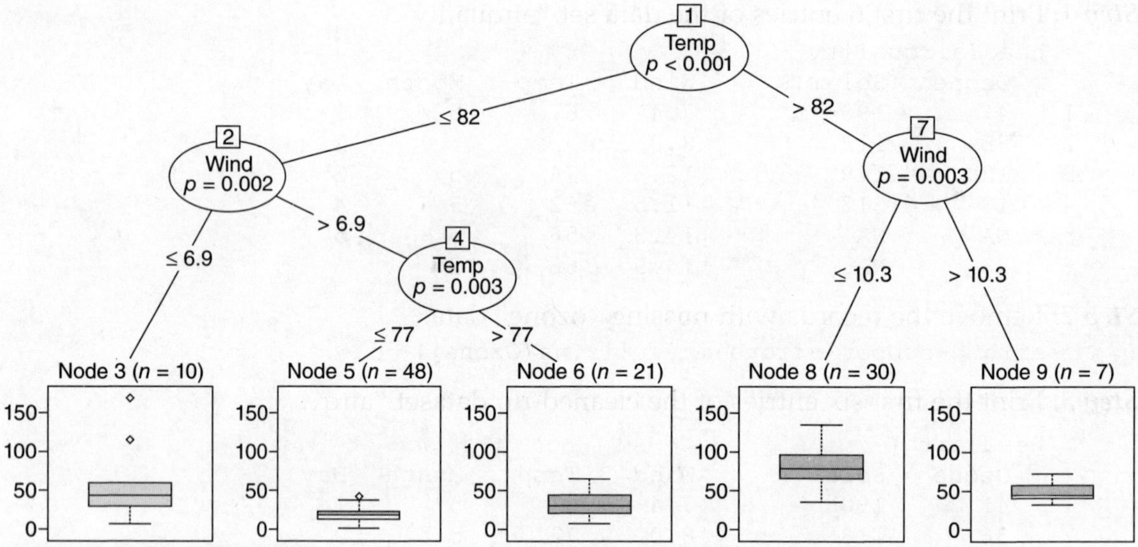

FIGURE 7.6 *A simple decision tree of an inbuilt dataset 'airquality' using the* `ctree()` *function*

Data is divided into five classes (as seen in Figure 7.6, in nodes labelled 3, 5, 6, 8 and 9). To understand the meaning of the plot, let us consider a measurement with temperature of 70 and wind speed of 12. At the highest level the data is divided into two categories according to temperature, i.e., either ≤ 82 or > 82. Our measurement follows the left branch (temperature ≤ 82). The next division is made according to wind speed, by giving two categories according to wind speed, i.e., either ≤ 6.9 or > 6.9. Our measurement follows the right branch (speed > 6.9). We arrive at the final division, which once again depend sup on the temperature and has two categories: either ≤ 77 or > 77. Our measurement has temperature ≤ 77, so it gets classified in node 5. Let us look at the boxplot for Ozone in node 5. It suggests that we expect the conditions for our measurement to be associated with a relatively low level of ozone.

Example 5

We will work with the "iris" data set. The iris data set gives data on the dimensions of sepals and petals measured on 50 samples of three different species of iris (setosa, versicolor and virginica).

Step 1: Print the first six entries of the data set "iris".

```
> head (iris)
     Sepal.Length  Sepal.Width  Petal.Length  Petal.Width  Species
1    5.1           3.5          1.4           0.2          setosa
2    4.9           3.0          1.4           0.2          setosa
3    4.7           3.2          1.3           0.2          setosa
4    4.6           3.1          1.5           0.2          setosa
5    5.0           3.6          1.4           0.2          setosa
6    5.4           3.9          1.7           0.4          setosa
```

Step 2: Use ctree to construct a model of iris "Species" as a function of all other covariates.

```
> iris.ct <- ctree(Species ~ ., data=iris, controls = ctree_
control(maxsurrogate =3))
> iris.ct

        Conditional interference tree with 4 terminal nodes

Response: Species
Inputs: Sepal.Length, Sepal.Width, Petal.Length, Petal.Width
Number of observations: 150

1) Petal.Length <= 1.9; criterion = 1, statistic = 140.264
  2)* weights = 50
1) Petal.Length > 1.9
  3) Petal.Width <=1.7; criterion = 1, statistic = 67.894
    4) Petal.Length <= 4.8; criterion = 0.999, statistic = 13.865
      5)* weights = 46
    4) Petal.Length > 4.8
      6)* weights = 8
3) Petal.Width > 1.7
    7)* weights = 46
```

Step 3: Plot a decision tree.

```
> plot(iris.ct)
```

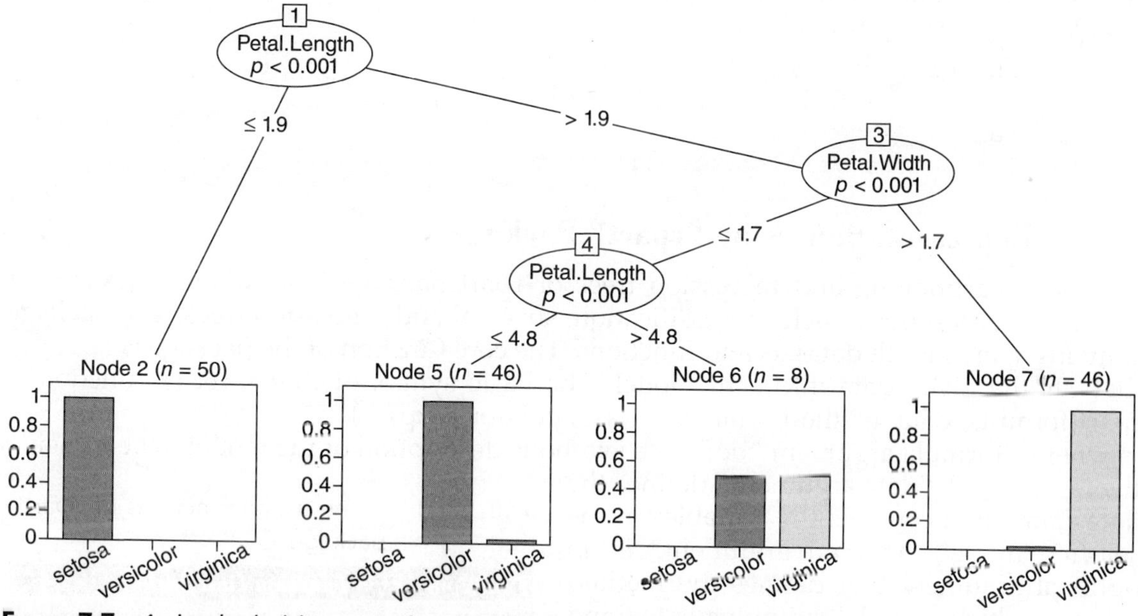

FIGURE 7.7 *A simple decision tree of an inbuilt dataset 'iris' using* `ctree()` *function*

The structure of the tree is essentially the same as with "airquality" data set. The only difference is the representation of the nodes wherein "ozone" is a continuous numerical variable and "iris Species" is a categorical variable. The nodes are thus represented as bar plots. As evident from the plot in Figure 7.7, Node 2 is predominantly "setosa", node 5 is mostly "versicolor" and node 7 is almost all "viriginica". Node 6 is half "versicolor" and half "virginica" and corresponds to a category with long, narrow petals. An interesting observation is that the model depends only on the dimensions of the petals and not on those of the sepals.

Let us go back to the question asked in Section 7.1, i.e., "If I were to provide you with the values for "Sepal.Length", "Sepal.Width", "Petal.Length" and "Petal.Width" for a particular flower, will you be able to state the species to which it belongs?

Step 1: Load the "rpart" package.

```
> library(rpart)
```

Step 2: Specify the values for "Sepal. Length", "Sepal.Width", "Petal.Length" and "Petal. Width" of the flower for whom we wish to determine the species.

```
> new_species <-data.frame ("Sepal.Length" = 5.1, "Sepal.Width" = 3.5,
+                            "Petal.Length" = 1.4, "Petal.Width" = 0.2)
```

Step 3: Create an rpart object "fit".

```
> fit <-rpart(Species ~ Sepal.Length + Sepal.Width + Petal.Length +
Petal.width, data = iris)
```

Step 4: Use the predict function. predict is a generic function for predictions from the results of various model fitting functions.

```
> prediction <-predict(fit, newdata = new_species, type = "class")
```

Step 5: Print the returned value from the predict function. The inference is, for a flower with values ("Sepal.Length" = 5.1, "Sepal.Width" = 3.5, "Petal.Length" = 1.4, "Petal.Width" = 0.2), the species is "setosa".

```
> print(prediction)
   1
setosa
Levels: setosa versicolor virginica
```

7.3.2 Representation using "rpart" Package

Recursive partitioning and regression trees or rpart package is a famous package for creating decision trees, such as classification, survival and regression trees. The package contains many inbuilt datasets and functions. The core function of the package is `rpart()` that fits the given data into a fit model. The basic syntax of the `rpart()` function is rpart(formula, data, method = (anova/class/poisson/exp)...)

where, "formula argument" defines a symbolic description of the model to be fit using the "~" symbol, "data argument" defines the data frame that contains the variables in the selected model, "method argument" is an optional argument that defines the method through which a model is implemented and the dots "..." define other optional arguments.

Along with this, the 'rpart' package contains many useful functions for decision trees. These functions are also used during the pruning of decision trees. Table 7.1 describes some other major functions of the package.

TABLE 7.1 Some useful functions of 'rpart' package

Functions	*Function Description*
`plotcp(tree)`	It plots the cross-validation output.
`printcp(tree)`	It prints the complexity parameter.
`text()`	It labels the decision tree plot.
`post()`	It creates postscript plot of decision tree.

The following example takes an inbuilt dataset 'cars' that was used in the previous example. It contains two variables, viz., 'speed' and 'dist'. The `rpart()` function creates a recursive tree *t* using the 'speed~dist' formula. In Figure 7.8, it can be seen that the function generates the following decision tree. Along with this, Figure 7.9 shows the cross-validation result of the decision tree.

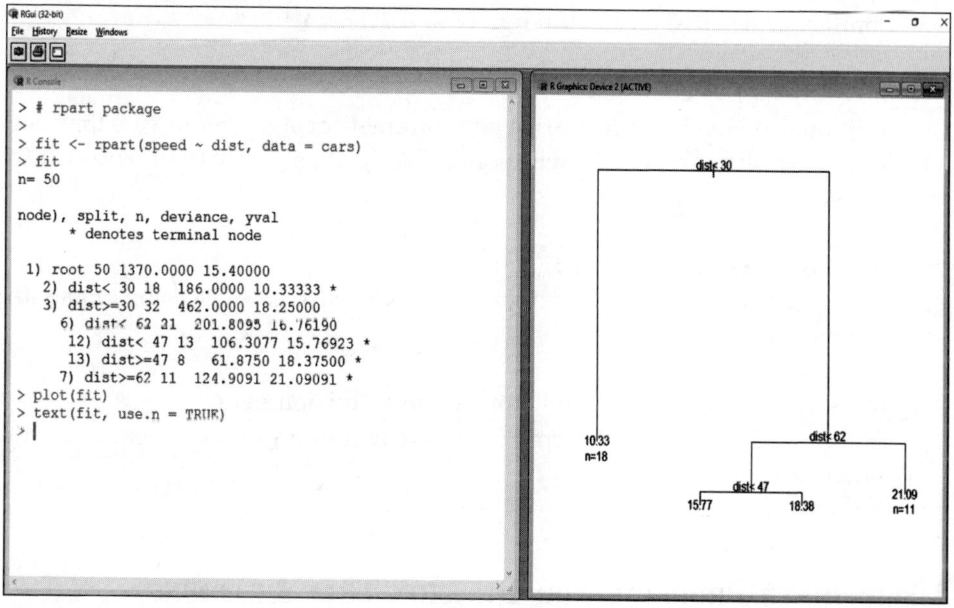

FIGURE 7.8 *A simple decision tree of an inbuilt dataset 'cars' using the* `rpart()` *function*

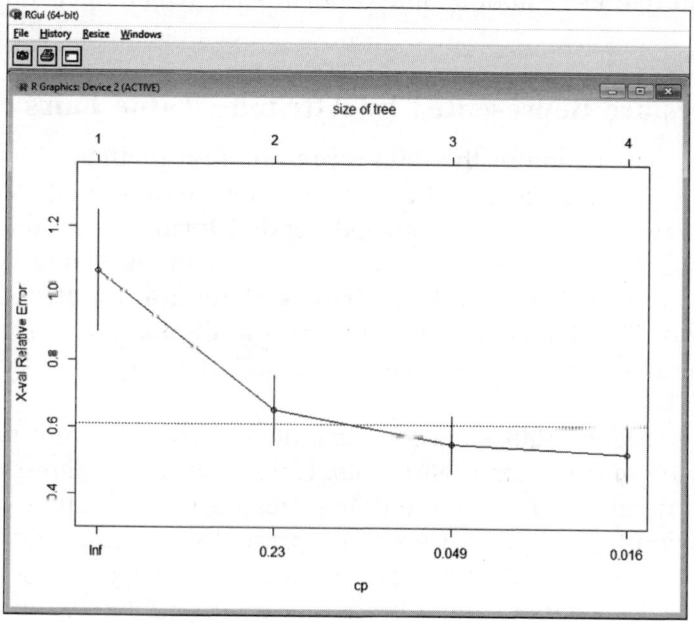

FIGURE 7.9 *Cross-validation result using the* `plotcp()` *function*

Check Your Understanding

1. Which packages build decision trees in R?

Ans: R language provides different packages, such as party, rpart, maptree, tree, partykit, randomforest, etc., that create different types of trees.

2. What is a ctree?

Ans: A conditional inference tree (ctree) is a non-parametric class of regression tree that solves various regression problems such as nominal, ordinal, univariate and multivariate response variables or numbers.

3. What is the use of the `rpart()` function?

Ans: `rpart()` is a function of the 'rpart' package that also creates decision or classification trees of the given dataset.

4. What is the use of the `printcp()` function in a decision tree?

Ans: `printcp()` is a function of the 'rpart' package that prints the complexity parameter of the generated decision tree.

7.4 Appropriate Problems for Decision Tree Learning

In this section, you will learn about some problems for which decision trees provide the best solutions.

7.4.1 Instances are Represented by Attribute-Value Pairs

An attribute-value pair is one of the data-representation methods in computer science. Name-value pair, field-value pair and key-value pair are other names of attribute-value pair. This method represents data in an open-ended form so that the user can modify the data and extend it in future as well. Different applications, such as general metadata, Windows registry, query strings and database systems use an attribute-value pair for storing information. The database uses it for storing the real data. If any problem uses attribute-value pairs for storing data, then a decision tree is a good choice for representing it.

For example, a student database needs attributes, such as student name, student age, class, etc., for storing information of students. Here, a student's name is stored using the attribute "student name" and the value pair stores the actual values of the students. In this case, the decision tree is the best way to represent this information.

In the following example, attribute-pair values are created using two vectors, viz., "snames" and "sage". A data frame *d* binds these vectors. Now, the `ctree()` function creates a decision tree using this data. Since this data is dummy data and contains only eight rows, the `ctree()` function creates a single parent-child node (Figure 7.10).

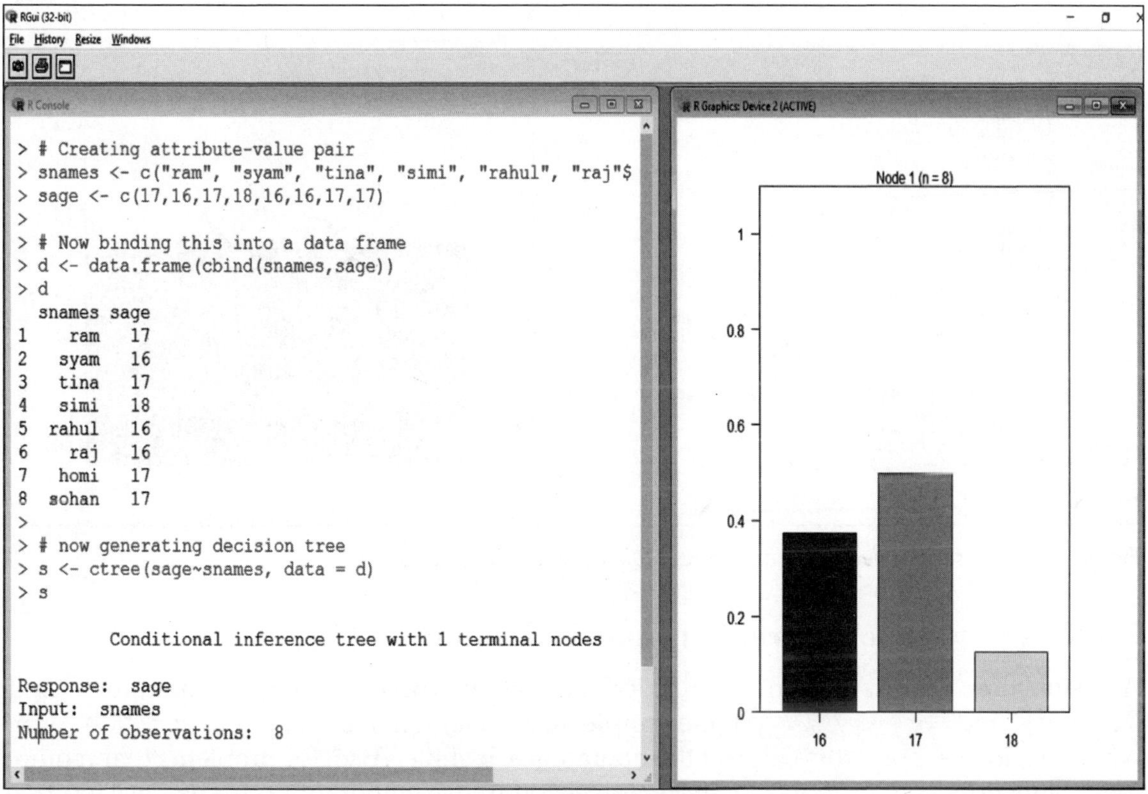

FIGURE 7.10 *A simple decision tree that contains attribute-pair values*

7.4.2 Target Function has Discrete Output Values

For any problem that needs discrete output values, such as [yes/no], [true/false], [positive/negative], etc., for representing data or solving problems, a decision tree is preferred. A decision tree generates a tree with a finite number of terminal and non-terminal nodes. These nodes are also properly labelled so that they're easier to read. Along with this, the function helps to label any terminal node as an output value.

The following example takes a dummy dataset "student" that contains a few data means storing annual attendance and the score of 15 students only. The column "Eligible" contains only "yes" or "no" values according to the attendance and score information. It means column "Eligible" contains discrete output values. The `ctree()` function creates a decision tree "fit" that generates only one terminal node. It is because there are only 15 rows. If you increase the number of rows, then it will create a recursive tree with more than one level (Figure 7.11).

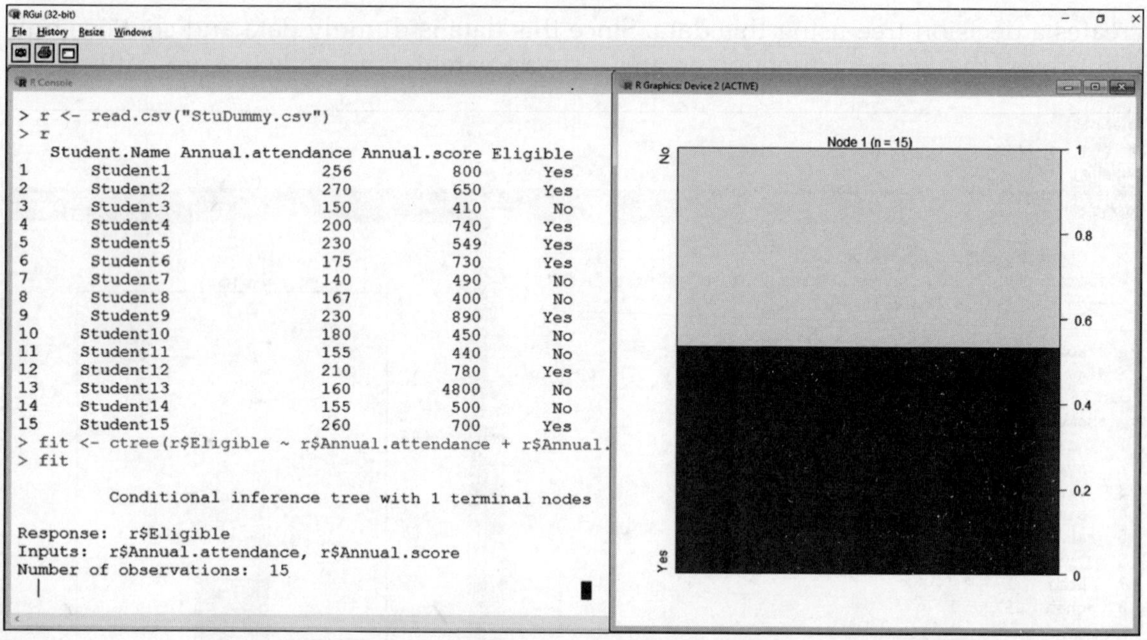

FIGURE 7.11 *A simple decision tree that contains discrete output values*

7.4.3 Disjunctive Descriptions may be Required

A disjunction form is a sum of products of operands that use logical operators "and [& / + /]" and "or [| | /*/V"]. For example, (a ∧ b ∧ c) ∨ (a ∧ b ∧ c) is a disjunction form, where the logical operators connect the operands a, b and c. Also, for problems that require the disjunction form of representation, a decision tree is a good option. The decision tree uses nodes and edges for representing a dataset in disjunction form. The `ctree()` function that creates the decision tree also uses these disjunction forms for data representation.

The following example takes an inbuilt dataset "mtcars" that contains many features. The `ctree()` function creates a recursive tree "mt" using the formula "am~disp+hp+mpg". In this formula, predictors are in the disjunctive form. In Figure 7.12, it can be seen that the function is generating the following decision tree.

7.4.4 Training Data May Contain Errors or Missing Attribute Values

Training data is a type of data that is used to design learning algorithms. Machine learning algorithms use training data and testing data. Such algorithms perform classification, clustering, partitioning and other similar tasks on this data. While designing training data, some values can be mislabelled for an attribute or there might be training data with errors in it. In such cases, the decision tree is a robust method for representing training data. Using pruning techniques, these errors can be easily resolved. This is discussed in the later sections of this chapter. It is also possible that training data may have some missing values. In such a case, decision trees can efficiently represent the training data.

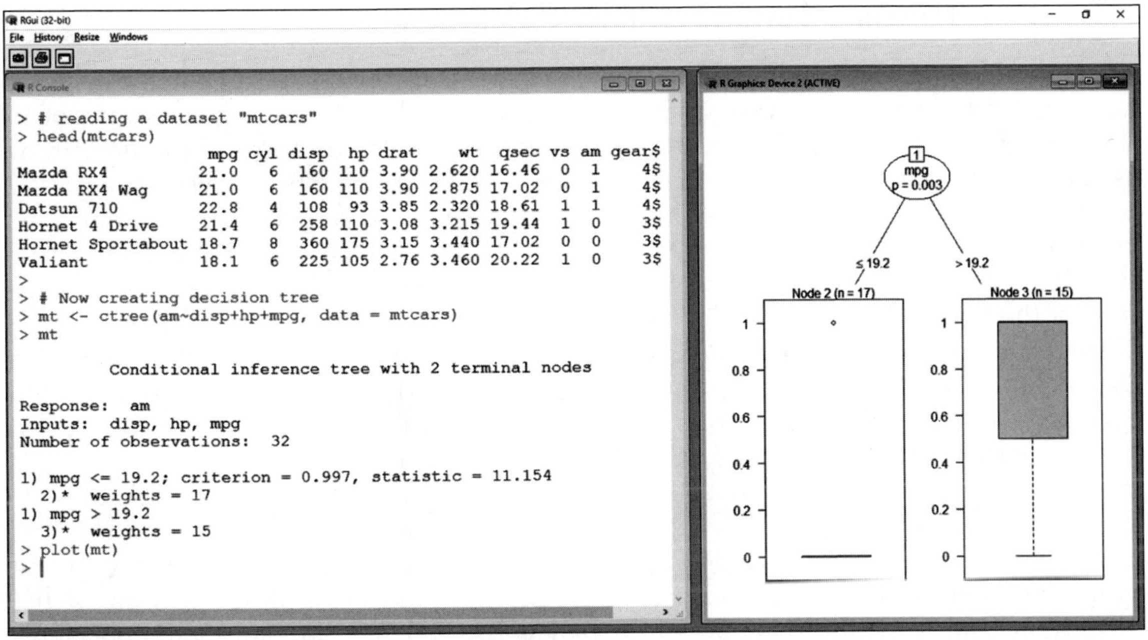

FIGURE 7.12 *A simple decision tree of a built-in dataset "mtcars"*

Check Your Understanding

1. What do you mean by an attribute-value pair?

Ans: An attribute-value pair is one of the data-representation methods in computer science. Name-value pair, field-value pair and key-value pair are some other names of the attribute-value pair.

2. What is the use of an attribute-value pair?

Ans: Different applications, such as general metadata, Windows registry, query strings and database systems use an attribute value pair for storing their information.

3. What do you mean by discrete value?

Ans: Discrete value is a type of value that contains two values such as [yes/no], [true/false], [positive/negative], etc.

4 What do you mean by the disjunction form?

Ans: A disjunction form is a sum of products of operands using logical operators "and [& / + /]" and "or [| | / * / V"]. For example, $(a \wedge b \wedge c) \vee (a \wedge b \wedge c)$ is a disjunction form where the logical operators connect the operands a, b and c.

7.5 Basic Decision Tree Learning Algorithm

After learning the basics of the decision tree, this section will explain some of the decision tree learning algorithms. These algorithms use inductive methods on the given values of an attribute of an unknown object for finding an appropriate classification. These algorithms use decision trees to do the same. The main objective of creating these trees is to classify any unknown instances in the training dataset. These trees traverse from the root node to the leaf node and test the attributes of the nodes. After which, they move down to the branch of the tree according to the attribute value of the dataset. It is repeated at each level of the tree.

There are different algorithms defined for creating decision trees, such as ID3 (Iterative Dichotomiser 3), C4.5 (C4.5 is an extension of Quinlan's earlier ID3 algorithm. The decision trees generated by C4.5 can be used for classification, and for this reason, C4.5 is often referred to as a statistical classifier.), CART (Classification and Regression Tree), etc. ID3 is the first decision-tree learning algorithm. The C4.5 and C5.0 came after ID3 for improving the ID3 algorithm.

In all algorithms, features have a major role in classifying trees. Information gain and entropy are two major metrics for finding the best attributes or features of trees. Metric entropy measures the impurity of data, whereas the information gain metric measures the features by reducing the entropy. Section 7.5 discusses the details of these metrics.

Along with this, speed and memory consumption are used to measure how the algorithm will perform and accurately construct the final tree. The subsection explains the ID3 algorithm in detail.

7.5.1 ID3 Algorithm

ID3 algorithm is one of the most used basic decision tree algorithm. In 1983, Ross Quinlan developed this algorithm. The basic concept of ID3 is to construct a tree by following the top-down and greedy search methodology. It constructs a tree that starts from the root and moves downwards from it. In addition, for performing the testing of each attribute at every node, the greedy method is used. The ID3 algorithm does not require any backtracking for creating a tree.

In other words, the ID3 algorithm classifies the given objects according to the characteristics of the dataset called *features*. Such a model creates a tree where each node of the tree works as a router. The training and prediction process predicts the particular feature using this tree. The pseudocode of the ID3 algorithm is given below.

1. If the dataset is pure, then
   (i) construct a leaf having the name of the class,
2. else
   (i) choose the feature with the highest information gain, and
   (ii) for each value of that feature
      (a) take the subset of the dataset having that feature value,
      (b) construct a child node having the name of that feature value and
      (c) call the algorithm recursively on the child node and the subset.

R provides a package "data.tree" for implementing the ID3 algorithm. The package "data.tree" creates a tree from the hierarchical data. It provides many methods for traversing the tree in different orders. After converting the tree data into a data frame, any operation like print, aggregation can be applied on it. Due to this, many applications like machine learning and financial data analysis use this package. In the package "data.tree", the ID3 algorithm is implemented with an inbuilt dataset "mushroom". The dataset "mushroom" contains the features of the mushrooms.

The following example creates a dummy dataset "Mango.csv" that contains the features of mangos. The ID3 algorithm is implementing this dummy dataset in Figure 7.13 using a function called "TrainID3". Figure 7.14 describes the pseudo code of the function "TrainID3". In Figure 7.13, the function `Node$new()` is used to create the root node for the dataset. Along with this, the classification of the mango dataset is done using the feature "taste". If the taste of the mango is sweet, then it is edible but if it is sour, then it is toxic.

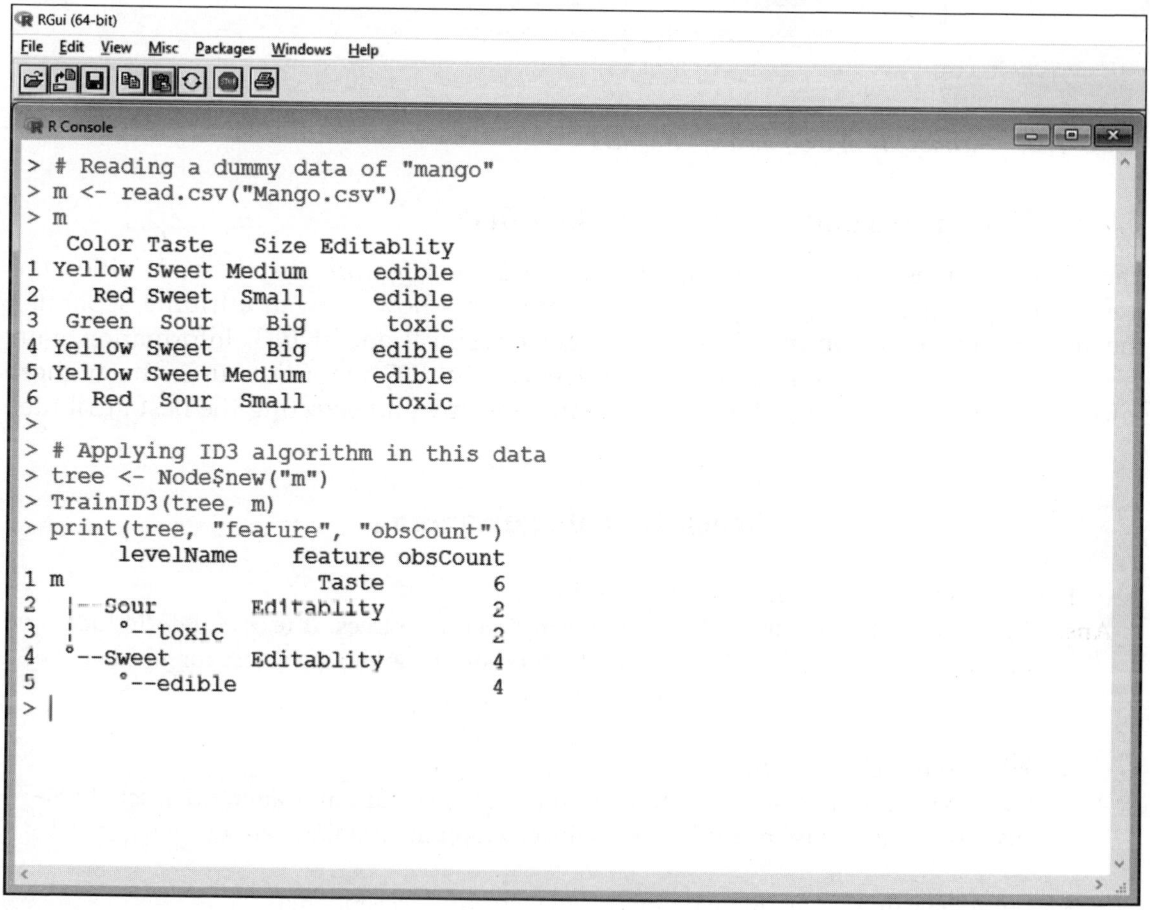

FIGURE 7.13 *Implementing the ID3 using the package "data.tree"*

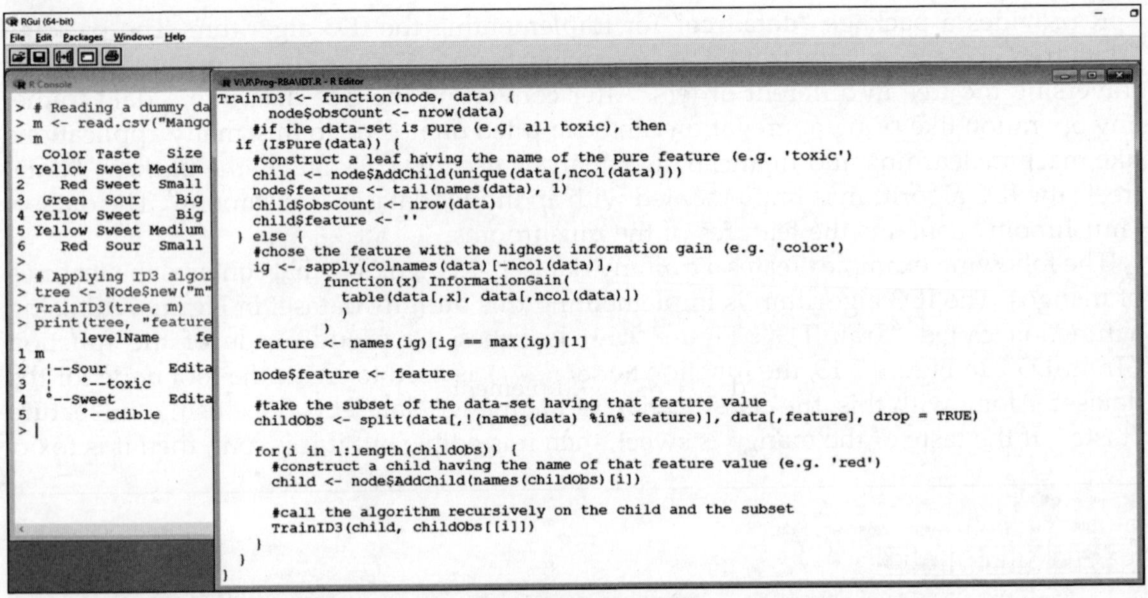

FIGURE 7.14 *Pseudocode of the function "TrainID3"*

7.5.2 Which Attribute is the Best Classifier?

Each algorithm uses a particular metric for finding a feature that best classifies the tree. During classification, information gain measures how a given attribute separates the training examples according to the target classification. In ID3, information gain is measured as the reduction in entropy. Hence, the ID3 algorithm uses the highest information gain for making the decision using entropy and selecting the best attribute.

Check Your Understanding

1. What is the decision-tree learning algorithm?

Ans: The decision-tree learning algorithm creates recursive trees. It uses certain inductive methods on the given values of an attribute of an unknown object for finding the appropriate classification using decision tree rules.

2. What is the need of learning algorithms?

Ans: Learning algorithms generate different types of trees for any training dataset. These trees are used to classify any unknown instances in the training dataset.

3. Write the names of learning algorithms that create a decision tree.

Ans: Different algorithms such as ID3, C4.5, CART, etc., are used to create decision trees. ID3 is the first decision-tree learning algorithm.

4. Write the names of two metrics that find the best attributes of a decision tree.
Ans: Information gain and entropy are two major metrics for finding the best attributes or features of trees.

5. What is ID3?
Ans: The ID3 algorithm is one of the most used basic decision tree algorithm. In 1983, Ross Quinlan developed this algorithm. The basic concept of ID3 is to construct a tree by following the top-down and greedy search methodology.

6. What is data.tree?
Ans: R provides a package "data.tree" for implementing the ID3 algorithm. The package "data.tree" creates a tree from the hierarchical data.

6. What is the best classifier of the ID3 algorithm?
Ans: The highest information gain of the ID3 algorithm is the best classifier for making decisions using entropy.

7.6 Measuring Features

In this section, we will discuss entropy and information gain in detail and how they are calculated.

7.6.1 Entropy—Measures Homogeneity

Entropy measures the impurity of collected samples that contain positive and negative labels. A dataset is pure if it contains only a single class; otherwise, the dataset is impure. Entropy calculates the information gain for an attribute of a tree. In simple words, entropy measures the homogeneity of the dataset. ID3 algorithm uses entropy to calculate the homogeneity of a sample. The entropy is zero if the sample is completely homogeneous and if the sample is equally divided (i.e., 50% on each side) it has an entropy of one.

Example

Let us look at the two nodes below and answer a simple question. Which node can we describe easily (Figure 7.15)?

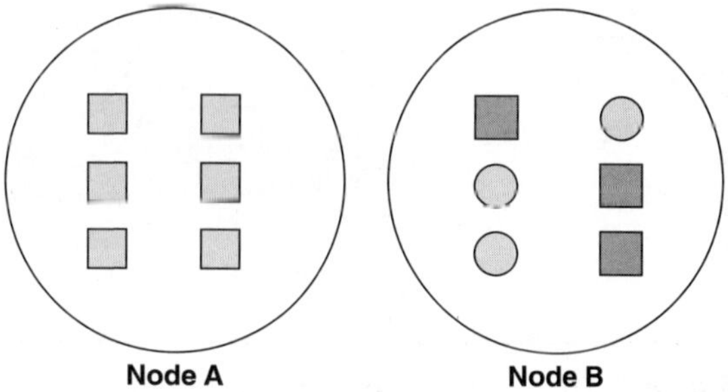

Figure 7.15

The answer is Node A. Why? Because it requires less information as all the values are similar. On the other hand, Node B requires more information to be able to completely describe it. In other words, we can say, Node A is pure, and Node B is impure. Thus, the inference is that less impure or pure nodes require less information and impure nodes require more information. Entropy is a measure of this disorganisation in a system.

Let us consider a set S that contains the positive label "$P(+)$" and the negative label "$P(-)$". The entropy is defined by the formula,

$$\text{Entropy } (S) = -P(+) \log_2 P(+) - P(-)\log_2 P(-)$$

where, $P(+)$ = Proportion of positive examples in S and $P(-)$ = Proportion of negative examples in S.

For example, the set S contains the positive and negative labels 0.5+ and 0.0–, respectively. Now put these values to the given formula as:

$$\text{Entropy } (S) = -0.5 \log_2 0.5 - 0.5\log_2 0.5 = 1$$

Hence, after calculation, the entropy of set S is 1.

Please note that the entropy of a pure dataset is always zero. If the dataset contains equal numbers of positive and negative labels, then the entropy is always 1.

Example: Calculating Impurity

In the following example, the same dataset "Mango.csv" is considered to check its purity using a function "IsPure". A dataset is pure if it contains only a single class. Since the given dataset contains two classes, it is not a pure dataset. Hence, the function "IsPure" returns false, as shown in Figure 7.16.

```
> m
   color taste   size ediblity
1 Yellow Sweet Medium   edible
2    Red Sweet  Small   edible
3  Green  Sour    Big    toxic
4 Yellow Sweet    Big   edible
5 Yellow Sweet Medium   edible
6    Red  Sour  Small    toxic
>
> # Measuring impuring using ImPure function
>
> IsPure <- function(data) {
+   length(unique(data[,ncol(data)])) == 1
+ }
>
> # checking impuring
> IsPure(m)
[1] FALSE
>
```

FIGURE 7.16 *Checking impurity using the* `IsPure()` *function*

Example: Calculating Entropy

In the following example, the same dataset "Mango.csv" is read and its entropy is calculated using the function "Entropy". It returns the entropy of the dataset "m" 0.9182958 (Figure 7.17).

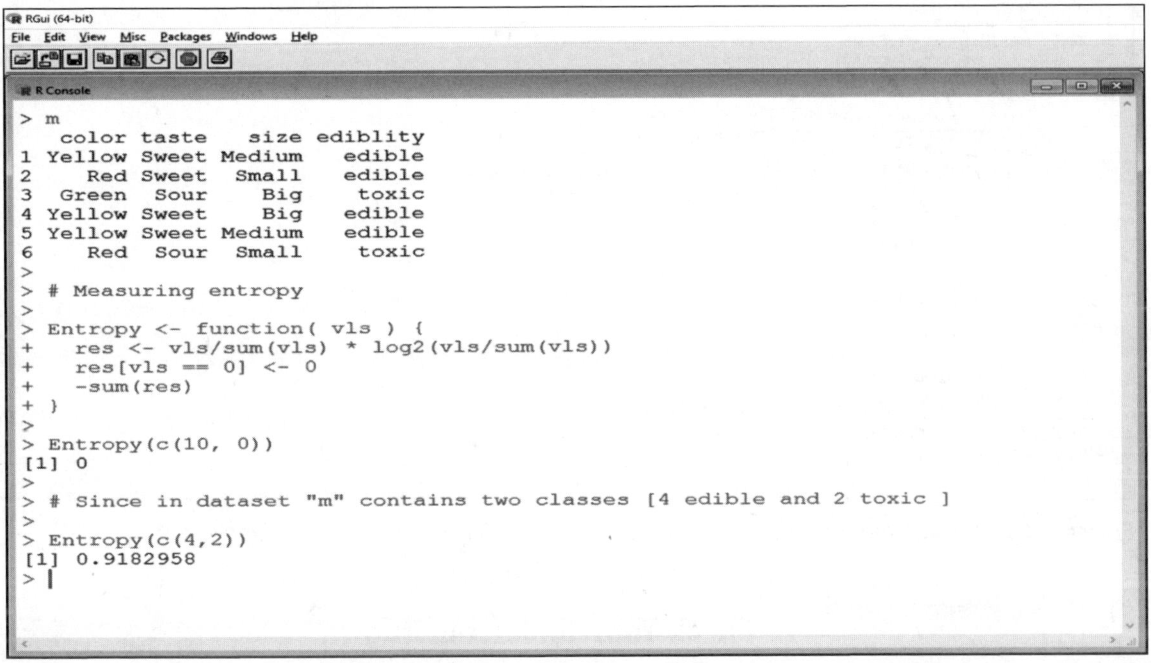

FIGURE 7.17 *Calculating entropy using the* `Entropy()` *function*

7.6.2 Information Gain—Measures the Expected Reduction in Entropy

Information gain is another metric that is used to select the best attribute of a decision tree. Information is a metric that minimises decision tree depth. In tree traversing, an optimal attribute that can split the tree node is required. Information gain easily does this and also finds out the best attribute with the most entropy reduction.

The expected reduction of the entropy that is related to the specified attribute during the splitting of decision tree node is called *information gain*. Let the Gain(S, A) be the information gain of an attribute A. Then the information gain is defined by the formula

$$\text{Gain}(S, A) = \text{Entropy}(S) - \sum_{v \in \text{Values}(A)} \frac{|S_v|}{|S|} \text{Entropy}(S_v)$$

The following example reads the same dataset "Mango.csv" and calculates the information gain using the `InformationGain()` function where the function "Entropy" is also used. For all the three features colour, taste and size, the function returns values 0.5849625, 0.9182958 and 0.2516292, respectively. Here, the information gain of the "taste" is maximum. Hence, it will be selected as the best feature (Figure 7.18).

```
1 Yellow Sweet Medium    edible
2    Red Sweet  Small    edible
3  Green  Sour    Big     toxic
4 Yellow Sweet    Big    edible
5 Yellow Sweet Medium    edible
6    Red  Sour  Small     toxic
> # information gain
> InformationGain <- function( tble ) {
+   tble <- as.data.frame.matrix(tble)
+   entropyBefore <- Entropy(colSums(tble))
+   s <- rowSums(tble)
+   entropyAfter <- sum (s / sum(s) * apply(tble, MARGIN = 1, FUN = Entropy ))
+   informationGain <- entropyBefore - entropyAfter
+   return (informationGain)
+ }
> mt <- table(m[,c('color', 'edibility')])
> mt
        edibility
color    edible toxic
  Green       0     1
  Red         1     1
  Yellow      3     0
> InformationGain(mt)
[1] 0.5849625
> mt <- table(m[,c('size', 'edibility')])
> InformationGain(mt)
[1] 0.2516292
```

FIGURE 7.18 *Calculating information gain using the* `InformationGain()` *function*

Check Your Understanding

1. What is entropy?

Ans: Entropy is a metric for selecting the best attribute that measures the impurity of collected samples containing positive and negative labels.

2. What is a pure dataset?

Ans: A dataset is pure if it contains only a single class; otherwise, the dataset is impure. The entropy of a pure dataset is always zero and if the dataset contains equal number of positive and negative labels, then the entropy is always 1.

3. What is the formula for calculating entropy?

Ans: The formula for calculating entropy is $\text{Entropy}(S) = -P(+)\log_2 P(+) - P(-)\log_2 P(-)$, where

$P(+)$ defines the proportion of positive examples in S and $P(-)$ is the proportion of negative examples in S.

4. What is the formula of calculating information gain?

Ans: The formula for calculating information gain is $\text{Gain}(S, A) = \text{Entropy}(S) - \sum_{v \in \text{Values}(A)} \frac{|S_v|}{|S|} \text{Entropy}(S_v)$ where A is an attribute of S.

7.7 Hypothesis Space Search in Decision Tree Learning

Hypothesis space search is a set of all the possible hypotheses that are retuned by it. In simple words, it contains a complete space of finite discrete-valued functions. In hypothesis space search, a hypothesis language is used for defining it in conjunction with the restriction bias. Hypothesis space search is used by machine learning algorithms.

The ID3 algorithm uses simple to complex *hill climbing search* methods for doing hypothesis space search that maintains only a single current hypothesis. Along with this, during hill climbing search, no backtracking is used. For measuring attributes, information gain metric is used. Here a pseudocode of the hypothesis space search [ID3] is written as:

1. Do the complete hypothesis space search. It should contain all finite discrete-valued functions [there should be one target function in these functions]
2. Output a single hypothesis
3. No backtracking that can create some local minima
4. Now use statistically-based search choices so that noisy data can be easily managed
5. Do inductive bias by using short trees.

Check Your Understanding

1. What is a hypothesis space search?
Ans: A hypothesis space search is a set of all possible decision trees.

2. Which search is used by ID3 algorithm for hypothesis space search?
Ans: The ID3 algorithm uses simple to complex hill climbing search methods for doing hypothesis space search.

7.8 Inductive Bias in Decision Tree Learning

Inductive bias is a set of assumptions that includes training data for predicting the output from the given input data. It is also called learning bias; whose main objective is to design an algorithm that can learn and predict an outcome. For this, learning algorithms use training examples that define the relationship between input and output. Each algorithm has different inductive biases.

The inductive bias of the ID3 decision tree learning is the shortest tree. Hence, when ID3 or any other decision tree learning classifies the tree, then the shortest tree is preferred over larger trees for the induction bias. Also, the trees that place high information gain attributes that are close to the root are also preferred over those that are not close and they are used as inductive bias.

7.8.1 Preference Biases and Restriction Biases

The ID3 decision tree learning search is a complete hypothesis space. It becomes incomplete when the algorithm finds a good hypothesis and it stops the search. The *candidate-elimination* search is an incomplete hypothesis space search because it contains only some hypotheses. It also becomes complete when the algorithm finds a good hypothesis and stops the search.

Preference Biases

A type of inductive bias where some hypotheses are preferred over others is called *preference bias or search bias*. For example, the bias of ID3 decision tree learning is an example of the preference bias. This bias is solely a consequence of ordering of the hypothesis search and different from the type of bias used by the candidate-elimination algorithm. The LMS algorithm for parameter tuning is another example of preference bias.

Restriction Biases

A type of inductive bias where some hypothesis is restricted to a smaller set is called *restriction bias or the language bias*. For example, the bias of the candidate-elimination algorithm is an example of the restriction bias. This bias is solely the consequence of the expressive power of its presentation of hypothesis. Linear function is another example of restriction bias.

Check Your Understanding

1. What is inductive bias?
Ans: Inductive bias is a set of assumptions that also includes training data for the prediction of the output from the given input data. It is also called learning bias.

2. What is the inductive bias of the ID3 decision tree learning?
Ans: The inductive bias of the ID3 decision tree learning is the shortest tree.

3. What is a candidate-elimination search?
Ans: A candidate-elimination search is an incomplete hypothesis space search because it contains only some hypotheses.

4. What is preference bias?
Ans: A type of inductive bias where some hypothesis is preferred over others is called the preference bias or search bias.

5. What is restriction bias?
Ans: A type of inductive bias where some hypothesis is restricted to a smaller set is called the restriction bias or language bias.

7.9 WHY PREFER SHORT HYPOTHESES

Occam's razor is a classic example of inductive bias. It prefers the simplest and shortest hypothesis that fits the data. The philosopher, William of Occam proposed it in 1320.

Physicists prefer providing simple explanations for the motion of planets. According to Occam, because there are fewer short hypotheses than longer hypotheses, it is less likely that one will find a short hypothesis that coincidentally fits the training data. Occam's razor argument became a successful strategy in experiments.

7.9.1 Reasons for Selecting Short Hypothesis

Some reasons that answer the question, "Why prefer short hypotheses?" as the induction bias of a decision tree are given below.

- During decision tree learning, let us assume there are few simple trees and many complex trees. A simple tree that fits the data is more likely to be the correct one. Hence, anyone will prefer a simple tree to a more complex tree. However, sometimes it can also create problems.
- Another reason is that anyone might accept a simple and general tree for the prediction. In machine learning, learning is the process of generalisation where a simple tree is likely to be more general than a complex tree. A general tree accurately gives the output on the population. Hence, Occam's razor prefers short hypotheses and states that when two hypotheses equally explain a training set, then always select the general hypothesis.
- Another reason for selecting the short hypothesis is that it takes lesser space. For example, in report party with space constraints and in data compression, a small hypothesis may accurately define the data as compared to a more complex hypothesis.

7.9.2 Problems with Argument

Some problems that may occur when applying the argument, "Why prefer short hypotheses?" as the induction bias of a decision tree are:

- The argument, "Why prefer short hypotheses?" can be made about many other constraints. It puts many questions in front of others like 'Why is short description constraint more relevant than others?"
- Along with this, it is based on the internal representation of the learner.

Check Your Understanding

1. What is an Occam's razor?

Ans: Occam's razor is a classic example of the inductive bias. It prefers the simplest and short hypothesis that fits the data. The philosopher, William of Occam proposed it in 1320.

2. Why does decision tree prefer short hypotheses?

Ans: A decision tree prefers short hypotheses as it takes less space. Moreover, it efficiently represents the data.

7.10 Issues in Decision Tree Learning

Decision trees and their algorithms are one of the best tools for machine learning tasks. Many issues arise during the use of the learning algorithm. Hence, it is good to understand the issues and resolve them. The following subsection explains these issues.

7.10.1 Overfitting

Overfitting is one of the major issues in decision tree learning. The decision tree grows each ranch deeply to classify the training data and instance. However, in case the training data is small, or the data is noisy, then the overfitting problem occurs. In simple words, a decision tree is perfect to classify training data, but it does not perform well on unknown real-world instances. It happens due to noise in the training data and a number of training instances that are too small to fit. This type of issue is called overfitting training data. Here is a simple definition of overfitting.

Definition of Overfitting

"Given a hypothesis space H, a hypothesis h in H is said to overfit the training data if there exists some alternative hypothesis h' in H, such that h has smaller error than h' over the training examples, but h' has a smaller error than h over the entire distribution of instances."

Overfitting can decrease the accuracy of the decision tree on any real-world instance; hence, it is necessary to resolve the problem of overfitting. Avoiding overfitting, reduced error pruning and rule-post pruning are some methods for resolving the problem of overfitting. Here is a brief introduction of all these three aspects.

Avoiding Overfitting the Data

Overfitting occurs when a training instance is too small to fit a model. Hence, try to use a training instance that is big in size. Avoiding overfitting is one of the simple solutions, but it is not a standard way to overcome the problem. Some methods to avoid overfitting are:

- Stop growing the tree earlier. If the tree stops growing, then the problem automatically resolves; since the obtained training set is already small, it easily fits into the model.
- This method uses a separate set of examples that do not include any training data. It is the training and validation set method. This method works even if the training set is misled due to random errors. The validation set exhibits the same random fluctuations by 2/3 training set and 1/3 validation set.
- Use a statistical test. It estimates whether to expand a node of a tree or not. In addition, the test that expands a node improves performance beyond the training set.
- The last method is to explicitly measure the complexity for encoding training examples and the decision tree. When the encoding size is minimised, then stop measuring. For this, the minimum description length principle can be used.

Reduced Error Pruning

Pruning or reduced error pruning is another method for resolving overfitting problems. The simple concept of pruning is to remove subtrees from a tree. The reduced error pruning algorithm goes through the entire tree and removes the nodes, including the subtree of that node that has no negative effect on the accuracy of the decision tree. It turns the subtree into a leaf node with the most common label.

Removing the redundant subtrees does not provide an accurate answer. Instead, it provides the same answer as the original tree. In this case, using a validation test instead of using a testing set is good for deciding how accurate the subtree is. The validation test can be taken from the training set. The pseudocode of the reduced error pruning algorithm is:

1. Split the dataset into training and validation sets
2. Consider a node for pruning
3. Perform pruning by removing the subtree at that node and make it a leaf. Assign the most common class at that node.
4. A node is removed if the resulting tree performs no worse than the original tree on the validation sets. It removes the coincidences and errors.
5. Nodes of the tree are removed iteratively by selecting the node whose removal mostly increases the decision tree accuracy on the graph.
6. Pruning process continues until further pruning is harmful.

R provides inbuilt features for pruning decision trees. The packages 'rpart' and 'tree' provide functions to perform pruning on the decision tree. Pruning gives the best result when the dataset is big. If the size of the dataset is small, then pruning generates the same result. Here, pruning is discussed with the 'rpart' package. The `prune()` function of the 'rpart' package determines a nested sequence of subtrees of the given rpart object. The function recursively snips or trims off the least important splits according to the complexity parameter [cp].

For finding out the complexity parameter, the `printcp()` function of the package can be used. Through this, the size of a tree can be selected to minimise the cross-validated error. The "xerror" column is used to find the minimum cross-validated error. Along with this, fit$cptable[which.min(fit$cptale[,"xerror"]), "CP"] can also be used with the prune function.

The basic syntax of the `prune()` function is:

```
prune(tree, cp, …)
```

where, the tree argument contains the fitted model object of the class 'rpart', the cp argument contains the complexity parameter to which the tree will be trimmed and the dots "…" define other optional arguments.

The following example takes an inbuilt dataset "cars" that contains two variables, viz., "speed" and "dist". The `rpart()` function creates a recursive tree *t* using the formula "speed~dist". In Figure 7.19 shows a decision tree before pruning. In Figure 7.20, the `printcp()` function is used for finding out the complexity parameter. The minimum value for the column xerror is 0.58249, which is also taken as the CP value in the prune function. Figure 7.20 shows the same decision tree as there are only 50 rows in the dataset.

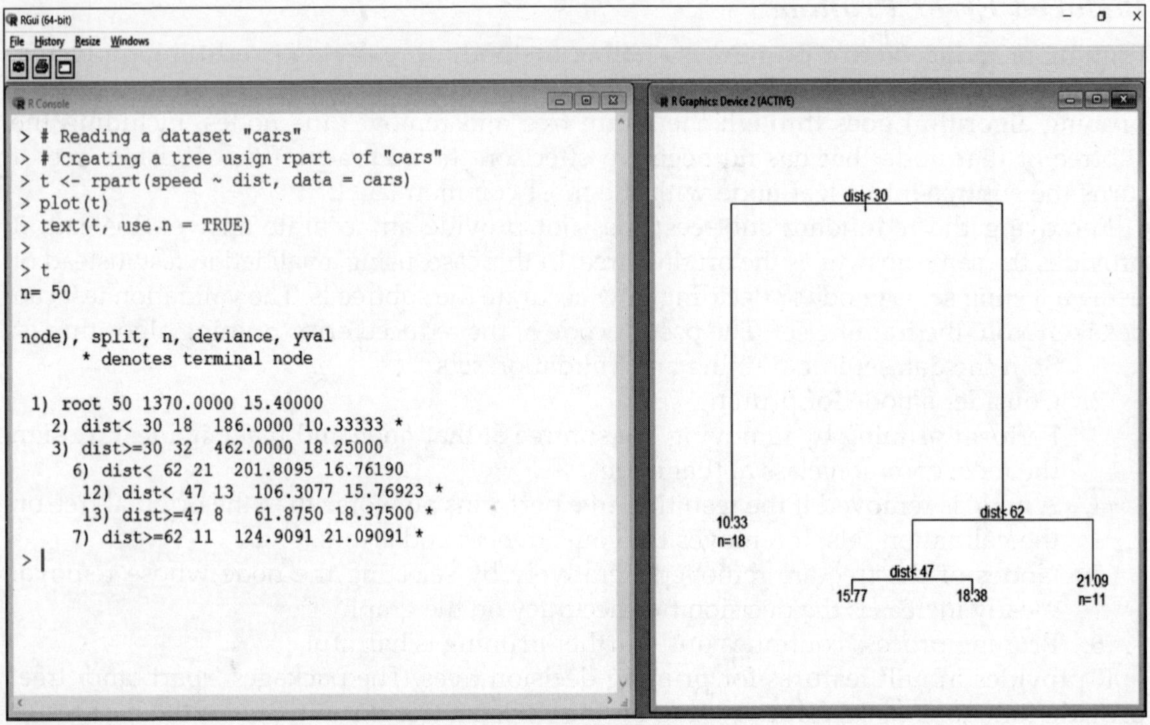

FIGURE 7.19 *Decision tree before pruning*

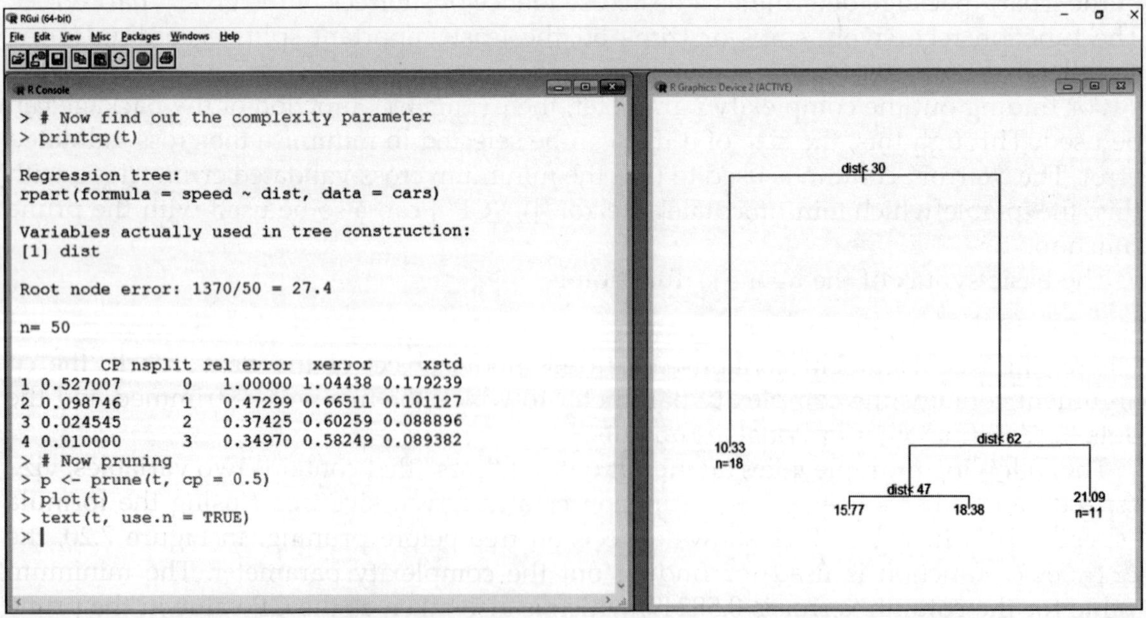

FIGURE 7.20 *Decision tree after pruning*

Rule Post-Pruning

Rule post-pruning is the best method for resolving the overfitting problem that gives high accuracy hypotheses. This method prunes the tree and reduces the overfitting problem. The steps of the rule post-pruning method are:

1. Infer the decision tree from the training set and grow the tree until the training data is fitted as well as possible. It allows overfitting to happen.
2. Now convert the learned tree into an equivalent set of rules by creating one rule for each path from the root node to the leaf node.
3. Prune each rule by removing any precondition that results in improving its estimates accuracy.
4. At last, sort the pruned rules by their estimates accuracy and consider them in this sequence when classifying subsequent instances.

Rule post-pruning can improve the estimated accuracy by calculating the rule accuracy over training data or by calculating the standard deviation that assumes a binomial distribution. A large dataset estimates accuracy very closely and uses lower bound for the measurement of rule performance.

7.10.2 Incorporating Continuous-Values Attributes

Sometimes it is possible that attributes of some learning data contain continuous values instead of discrete values which means these attributes do not contain yes/no, true/false or similar values. The attributes containing continuous values create problems during learning. In this case, Boolean value attribute is useful. For this, follow the steps as mentioned below.

1. Reduce the continuous value attribute to the Boolean value attribute through some threshold value.
2. Sort the examples according to the continuous values for selecting the threshold value.
3. Identify adjacent examples that differ in classification for reaching candidate threshold values.
4. In the end, select the attribute whose information gain value is maximum and take it as an ideal threshold value.

Along with this method of the threshold value, another method is also used for handling continuous values attribute. In this method, split the continuous values into multiple intervals instead of two.

7.10.3 Alternative Measures for Selecting Attributes

A problem in decision tree also occurs when an attribute has many values. These values separate the training examples into very small subsets that give a high information gain when Gain is used. To avoid this problem, GainRatio is used instead of Gain. Let the GainRatio (S, A) be a GainRatio of an attribute A. Then it is defined by the formula

$$\text{GainRatio}(S, A) = \frac{\text{Gain}(S, A)}{\text{SplitInformation}(S, A)}$$

where,

$$\text{SplitInformation}(S, A) = -\sum_{i=1}^{c} \frac{|S_i|}{|S|} \log_2 \frac{|S_i|}{|S|}$$; Si is the subset of S for which A has values v_i.

Sometimes, GainRatio also creates a problem when Si is nearly equal to S. In this case, GainRatio is not defined or very large. Hence, to avoid this, calculate the GainRatio only on attributes with above average Gain and then select the best GainRatio.

7.10.4 Handling Training Examples with Missing Attributes Values

A problem in decision trees occurs when the training examples contain missing attribute values. Some methods for handling the missing values of attributes are given below.

- One of the simplest methods is to sort the training examples. Select the most common value of that attribute and use it in another training example. For instance, in some training examples, if the attribute A contains some missing values in a node *n*, then continue calculating gain and assigning the most common value of A in another training example.
- Another method is to assign the most common value of the attribute at the node. For example, assign the missing value of an attribute A to the node *n*.
- Another complex method for handling missing values is to assign the probability to each possible value of the attribute that contains the missing values. These probability values are used to calculate the Gain. In case, if more missing values are there, then further sub-divide the probability values at subsequent branches of the tree.

7.10.5 Handling Attributes with Different Costs

The last problem occurs in the decision tree when the attributes have different costs. These different costs affect the overall cost of the learning process. Some medical diagnosis tasks, such as blood test, biopsy result and temperature contain significant cost values that make the learning task more expensive for patients.

To overcome such problems, use decision trees that contain low-cost attributes. The ID3 algorithm uses a cost term in attribute selection method for considering the attribute costs for its modification. Another method is to divide the Gain by the cost of the attribute and replace Gain(S,A) by the formula:

$$\frac{\text{Gain}^2(S, A)}{\text{Cost}(A)} \quad \text{or} \quad \frac{2^{\text{Gain}(S,A)} - 1}{\text{Cost}(A) + 1^{\omega}}$$

Where $\omega \in [0, 1]$ that determines the importance of cost.

Check Your Understanding

1. What is the definition of overfitting?

Ans: The definition of overfitting is, 'Given a hypothesis space H, a hypothesis h in H is said to overfit the training data if there exists some alternative hypothesis h' in H, such that h has smaller error than h' over the training examples, but $h`$ has a smaller error than h over the entire distribution of instances.'

2. What do you mean by pruning or reduced error pruning?

Ans: Pruning or reduced error pruning is another method for resolving the overfitting problem. The simple concept of pruning is to remove the subtrees from a tree.

3. What is the use of the `prune()` function?

Ans: The `prune()` function of the 'rpart' package determines a nested sequence of subtrees of the given rpart object. The function is recursively snipping or trimming off the least important splits according to the complexity parameter [cp].

4. What is the use of the `printcp()` function?

Ans: For finding out the complexity parameter, the `printcp()` function of the package can be used. Through this, the size of tree is selected as such that it minimises the cross-validated error. The "xerror" column is used to find out the minimum cross-validated error.

5. What is the use of the GainRatio in decision tree?

Ans: The GainRatio is used to overcome the problem of the attributes that contains many values in decision tree.

6. What is the formula of the GainRatio?

Ans: The formula of the GainRatio is $\text{GainRatio}(S, A) = \dfrac{\text{Gain}(S, A)}{\text{SplitInformation}(S, A)}$

where, $\text{SplitInformation}(S, A) = -\sum_{i=1}^{c} \frac{|S_i|}{|S|} \log_2 \frac{|S_i|}{|S|}$ and S_i is the subset of S for which A has values v_i.

Case Study

Helping Retailers Predict In-store Customer Traffic

In the internet era, prediction of customer behaviour is a very valuable insight, since it helps a marketer to analyse its products' value and send updates for selling its products. The online market depends on the history of its customers. Devising new strategies for markets and attracting customers to stores and trying to convert the incoming traffic into sales profitably are all vital to the financial health of retailers.

Every retailer uses different strategies to increase store traffic and convert traffic into profits. They invest in prime real estate with desirable properties such as high foot-traffic of their targeted customer segments, customer populations, customer convenience and visibility. Once they determine a location, retailers drive store traffic in a variety of ways such as spending on advertising, offering loss-leader about the products with various discounts or conducting various promotional events in local markets, such as offering discounts at various levels or price deductions.

Whenever customers visit a store, retailers try to convert the customers profitably through several means. They ensure that the right product is available at the right place, at the right time and at the right price. They invest in store labour to ensure that customers experience a good and competitively priced shopping service that would encourage them to purchase and return to the store in future as well.

Such relationships are critical to retailers for the following reasons. First, they get to know the feedback of other stores and requirements of the customers. Financial data of the local customers can be calculated using time-series data. Decision tree is very important for this type of problem as we can calculate the risk factors in the local market and understand the needs of the customers from their previous behaviour. This is also known as learning the cognitive behaviour of the customer. Let us take the example of iPhone 7 that was launched recently. This brand also uses time-series analysis for understanding the behaviour of their customers by means of data gathered from the earlier models like iPhone 6 and iPhone 6s. How the customer used these earlier models and what features they look for in competitive products provides important insights for product development.

Decision tree is very useful for gathering information about new market values as these depend on the time series that comes from historical data. Using such data, we can analyse information from new products as well. We can analyse customer behaviour in conjunction with their financial status and give them best discounts for their needs.

If we analyse historical data, many products have failed badly because they were not able to understand the requirements of the market at that time.

(Continued)

Case Study

So, to play it safe, every company nowadays tries to understand the market and its needs as per the market values, thus, creating a decision tree from the time-series data is an essential task for them.

Decision trees can help in reducing errors by means of information gain from the parent to the child. Tree biased induction in ID3 helps to generate a recommendation engine. Such an engine is a powerful tool to understand the needs of the market and help companies choose profitable markets.

Decision trees have many features that are very helpful to retailers and companies for offering discounts by comparing the information gain and loss in the market. This is also done by understanding the behaviour of the customer with regards to the new product and older products—iPhone 6 and 6s being pertinent examples here because after launching iPhone 7 and 7s the prices of iPhone 6 and 6s were reduced by 20k in the Indian Market.

Using decision tree and its properties in data mining, we can increase the profits for retailers and help companies convert customer traffic into profits. Data mining is presented in more detail in the next few chapters.

Summary

- A decision tree is a type of undirected graph that represents decisions and their outcomes in a tree structure or hierarchal form. It is a part of machine learning and it is mostly used in data mining applications.
- R provides different packages, such as party, rpart, maptree, tree, partykit and randomforest that create different types of trees.
- Ctree is a non-parametric class of regression tree that solves various regression problems such as nominal, ordinal, univariate and multivariate response variables or numbers.
- An attribute-value pair is one of the data-representation methods in computer science. Name-value pair, field-value pair and key-value pair are other names of the attribute-value pair.
- During the design of training data, some values may be mislabelled for an attribute, some data may be missing in the attribute or there may be some errors in the training data. In such cases, a decision tree is a robust method to represent training data.
- The decision-tree learning algorithms create recursive trees. They use some inductive methods on the given values of an attribute of an unknown object for finding the appropriate classification using decision tree rules.
- Learning algorithms generate different types of trees for any training dataset. These trees are used to classify any unknown instances in the training dataset.
- The ID3 algorithm is one of the most commonly used basic decision tree algorithms. In 1983, Ross Quinlan developed this algorithm. The basic concept of the ID3 is to construct a tree by following the top-down and greedy search methodology.
- R provides a package "data.tree" for implementation of the ID3 algorithm. The package "data.tree" creates a tree from the hierarchical data.
- Information gain is another metric that is used to select the best attribute of the decision tree. Information gain is a metric that minimises the decision tree depth.

(Continued)

- The formula of calculating information gain is

  $$\text{Gain}(S, A) = \text{Entropy}(S) - \sum_{v \in \text{Values}(A)} \frac{|S_v|}{|S|} \text{Entropy}(S_v)$$, where A is an attribute of S.

- The candidate-elimination search is an incomplete hypothesis space search because it contains only some hypothesis.
- A type of inductive bias where some hypothesis is preferred over others is called the preference bias or search bias.
- The `prune()` function of the 'rpart' package determines a nested sequence of subtrees of the given rpart object. The function recursively snips or trims off the least important splits according to the complexity parameter [cp].
- Incorporating continuous-values attributes, alternative measures for selecting attributes, handling training examples with missing attributes values and handling attributes with different costs are some issues with decision trees.
- The formula of the GainRatio is $\text{GainRatio}(S, A) = \frac{\text{Gain}(S, A)}{\text{SplitInformation}(S, A)}$

  where $\text{SplitInformation}(S, A) = -\sum_{i=1}^{c} \frac{|S_i|}{|S|} \log_2 \frac{|S_i|}{|S|}$ and S_i is the subset of S for which A has values v_i.

- By sorting training examples using the most common value or using probability values, the problem of missing attribute values can be resolved in the decision tree.
- By using a decision tree that contains low-cost attributes in the decision tree, the problem of attribute with different cost can be resolved in the decision tree.

KEY TERMS

- **Continuous value:** Continuous value is a type of value that contains many values.
- **ctree:** ctree is a non-parametric class of regression tree that solves various regression problems such as nominal, ordinal, univariate and multivariate response variables or numbers.
- **data.tree:** data.tree is a package of R used for implementing the ID3 algorithm.
- **Edge:** In the decision tree graph, an edge represents the decision rules.
- **Entropy:** Entropy is a metric for selecting the best attribute that measures the impurity of collected samples containing positive and negative labels.
- **Hypothesis space search:** A hypothesis space search is a set of all possible hypotheses.
- **ID3:** The ID3 is the first decision-tree learning algorithm. In 1983, Ross Quinlan developed this algorithm. The basic concept of ID3 is to construct a tree by following the top-down and greedy search methodology.
- **Information gain:** Information gain is a metric that is used to select the best attribute of a decision tree. Information gain is a metric that minimises decision tree depth.
- **Inductive bias:** Inductive bias is a set of assumptions that includes training data for the prediction of the output from the given input data.
- **mushroom:** mushroom is an inbuilt dataset of the package "data.tree".
- **Overfitting:** Overfitting is one of the major issues in decision tree learning. It happens

due to the noise in training data and the number of training instances that are too small to fit.

- **party:** party is a package for creating a decision tree in R.
- **Preference bias:** Preference bias is a type of inductive bias where some hypothesis is preferred over other hypotheses.
- **Pruning:** Pruning or reduced error pruning is a method for resolving overfitting problems. The simple concept of pruning is to remove subtrees from a tree.
- **Pure dataset:** A pure dataset contains only a single class and entropy of a pure dataset is always zero.
- **Restriction bias:** Restriction bias is a type of inductive bias where some hypothesis is restricted to a smaller set.
- **rpart:** rpart is a package for creating a decision tree or a regression tree in R.
- **Undirected graph:** An undirected graph is a group of nodes and edges where there is no cycle in the graph and there is one path between every two nodes of the graph.

Multiple Choice Questions

1. Which one of the following packages is different from the others?
   (a) rpart (b) party
   (c) tree (d) stats
2. Which one of the following packages contains the `ctree()` function?
   (a) rpart (b) tree
   (c) party (d) data.tree
3. Which one of the following options represents events in a decision tree?
   (a) Edge (b) Graph
   (c) Node (d) None of the above
4. Which one of the following arguments is a part of the `rpart()` function?
   (a) method (b) controls
   (c) cp (d) use.n
5. Which one of the following arguments is a part of the `ctree()` function?
   (a) method (b) controls
   (c) cp (d) use.n
6. Which one of the following arguments is a part of the `prune()` function?
   (a) method (b) controls
   (c) cp (d) use.n
7. Which one of the following arguments is a part of the `text()` function?
   (a) method (b) controls
   (c) cp (d) use.n
8. Which one of the following packages contains the `prune()` function?
   (a) rpart (b) partykit
   (c) party (d) data.tree

9. Which one of the following functions plots the cross-validation output in the generated decision tree?
   (a) `plotcp()` (b) `printcp()`
   (c) `prune()` (d) `text()`
10. Which one of the following functions prints the complexity parameter in the generated decision tree?
   (a) `plotcp()` (b) `printcp()`
   (c) `prune()` (d) `text()`
11. Which one of the following functions performs pruning of a decision tree?
   (a) `plotcp()` (b) `printcp()`
   (c) `prune()` (d) `text()`
12. Which one of the following functions prints the labels on a plotted decision tree?
   (a) `plotcp()` (b) `printcp()`
   (c) `prune()` (d) `text()`
13. Which one of the following is the best classifier of a decision tree?
   (a) Highest information gain (b) Entropy
   (c) Inductive bias (d) None of the above
14. What is the entropy value of a pure dataset?
   (a) 2 (b) 3
   (c) 1 (d) 0
15. How many number of classes is used in a pure dataset?
   (a) 1 (b) 2
   (c) 3 (d) 4
16. Which one of the following is the inductive bias of the ID3 decision tree learning?
   (a) Linear function (b) Shortest tree
   (c) Minimum (d) Maximum
17. Which one of the following is the preference bias?
   (a) Linear function (b) Shortest tree
   (c) Minimum (d) Maximum
18. Which one of the following is the restriction bias?
   (a) LMS algorithm (b) Shortest tree
   (c) Linear function (d) Maximum
19. Which one of the following is a classic example of inductive bias?
   (a) LMS algorithm (b) Shortest tree
   (c) Linear function (d) Occam's razor
20. Which one of the following is the correct full form of "cp"?
   (a) Common parameter (b) Classic parameter
   (c) Complexity parameter (d) Complexity point

Short Questions

1. What is the role of decision trees in machine learning? How many types of trees are used in machine learning?
2. Write about the packages, 'rpart' and 'party'.
3. What is the difference between CTree and `ctree()` in R?
4. What is the decision-tree learning algorithm?
5. What are the applications of the decision-tree learning algorithm?
6. What is hypothesis space search? List its steps.
7. What are the methods to resolve "the missing attributes value problem" in the decision tree?

Long Questions

1. Think of a problem statement and represent it using a decision tree.
2. Explain the packages data.tree, entropy and information gain with examples.
3. Explain "Occam's razor".
4. What is pruning? Why it is used in a decision tree?
5. Explain the `prune()` function with syntax and an example.
6. Create a dataset and generate the decision tree for it using the `ctree()` function.
7. Create a dataset that contains attribute-value pairs. Generate the decision tree for it using the `ctree()` function.
8. Create a dataset that contains attribute-value pairs. Generate the decision tree for it using the `ctree()` function.
9. Create a dataset that contains discrete values. Generate the decision tree for it using the `ctree()` function.
10. Create a dataset that contains the data in disjunction form. Generate the decision tree for it using the `ctree()` function.
11. Take any inbuilt dataset from R and explain pruning in this dataset.
12. Create a dataset that contains the features of apples. Now find out the "entropy" and "information gain" for this dataset. Also, find out the best feature of the apple dataset.

Practical Exercise

1. Visit the UCI Machine Learning Repository site (https://archive.ics.uci.edu/ml/datasets.html). Look up the bank marketing dataset (http://archive.ics.uci.edu/ml/machine-learning-databases/00222/ - (use bank-additional-full.csv)). Induct a decision tree to predict whether the client will subscribe a term deposit or not (predict the value of variable *y*).

   A sample of the data is shown as follows:

```
  age       job marital    education default housing loan   contact month day_of_week campaign pdays
1  56 housemaid married     basic.4y      no      no   no telephone   may         mon        1   999
2  57  services married high.school unknown      no   no telephone   may         mon        1   999
3  37  services married high.school      no     yes   no telephone   may         mon        1   999
4  40    admin. married     basic.6y      no      no   no telephone   may         mon        1   999
5  56  services married high.school      no      no  yes telephone   may         mon        1   999
6  45  services married     basic.9y unknown      no   no telephone   may         mon        1   999
  previous    poutcome emp.var.rate cons.price.idx cons.conf.idx euribor3m nr.employed  y
1        0 nonexistent          1.1         93.994         -36.4     4.857        5191 no
2        0 nonexistent          1.1         93.994         -36.4     4.857        5191 no
3        0 nonexistent          1.1         93.994         -36.4     4.857        5191 no
4        0 nonexistent          1.1         93.994         -36.4     4.857        5191 no
5        0 nonexistent          1.1         93.994         -36.4     4.857        5191 no
6        0 nonexistent          1.1         93.994         -36.4     4.857        5191 no
```

Note: As recommended on the UCI Machine Learning website, avoid using the 'duration' column as a predictor.

Chapter 8

Time Series in R

LEARNING OUTCOME

At the end of this chapter, you will be able to:

- Read time series data using `ts()` and `scan()` functions
- Apply linear filtering on time series data
- Apply Simple, Holt and Holt-winters exponential smoothing to time series data
- Decompose time series data
- Fit time series data into the ARIMA model
- Plot time series data

8.1 Introduction

Success in business today relies profoundly on timely, informed decisions. Business houses have realised the importance of analysing time series data that helps them to analyse and predict sales numbers for the next fiscal year, predict and take proactive measures to deal with overwhelming website traffic, monitor competition position and much more. Several methods have evolved over time that help with prediction and forecasting. One such method, which makes use of time-based data is *time series modelling*. Time series modelling involves working on time (years, days, hours and minutes) based data, to derive hidden insights, which then lead to informed decision making.

This chapter will help answer the following questions with regard to time series data:

- Is there a *trend*? Do the measurements tend to increase (or decrease) over time?

- Is there *seasonality*? Does the data regularly exhibit repeating pattern of highs and lows related to calendar time such as seasons, quarters, months, days of the week and so on?
- Are their *outliers* in the data?
- Is there *variance* over time, either constant or non-constant?
- Are there *abrupt* changes to either the level of the series or the variance?

Time series data finds typical uses with the following:

- Trend analysis
- Cyclical fluctuation analysis
- Variance analysis

The chapter begins with sections on basic R commands for data visualisation and data manipulation and then delves deeper into reading time series data, plotting it, decomposing it, performing regression analysis and exponential smoothing and then carries a detailed explanation of the ARIMA model.

8.2 What is Time Series Data?

Time series analysis plays a major role in business analytics. Time series data can be defined as quantities that trace the values taken by a variable over a period such as month, quarter or year. For example, in share market, the price of shares changes every second. Another example of time series data is measuring the level of unemployment each month of the year.

Univariate and multivariate are two types of time series data. When time series data uses a single quantity for describing values, it is termed univariate. However, when time series data uses more than a single quantity for describing values, it is called multivariate. Time series analysis performs the analysis of both types of time series data. R provides a feature for performing time series analysis. The following subsections discuss the basic commands of R that are necessary for time series analysis.

8.2.1 Basic R Commands for Data Visualisation

R language provides many commands that plot the given data, such as `plot()`, `hist()`, `pie()`, `boxplot()`, `stripchart()`, `curve()`, `abline()`, `qqnorm()`, etc. of which `plot()` and `hist()` commands are mostly used in time series analysis. Here is a brief introduction to some of these commands.

plot() Function

The `plot()` command of R helps to create different types of charts. It has many options for visualising data in different forms. Along with this, the graphical parameters such as col, font, lwd, lty, cex, etc., can also use the plot command for enhancing the visualisation of time series data. The basic syntax of the `plot()` command is:

```
plot(x, y, type, main, sub, xlab, ylab,…)
```

where, "x" argument defines the coordinates of points in the plot that can be any R objects, "y" argument is an optional argument that contains y coordinates of points if the X-axis is used and "type" argument defines which type of plot is to be drawn. Table 8.1 describes the different values of "type" argument, "main" argument defines the title of the plot, "sub" argument defines the subtitle of the plot, "xlab" argument defines the title for the X-axis, "ylab" argument defines the title for the Y-axis and the dots "..." define the other optional arguments.

TABLE 8.1 Values of "type" argument of plot command

Type Value	*Graph Type*
p	Points on plot
l	Lines on plot
b	Both points and lines
c	For the lines part alone of b
o	Overplotting of lines and points
h	Histogram like vertical lines on plot
s	Stair steps on plot
S	Other steps on plot
n	No plotting

The following example creates an object named "s" and the `plot()` function creates a histogram of this object. Along with this the parameters, "main" (overall title for the plot), "col" (plotting colour) and "lwd" (line width) customise the plot (Figure 8.1).

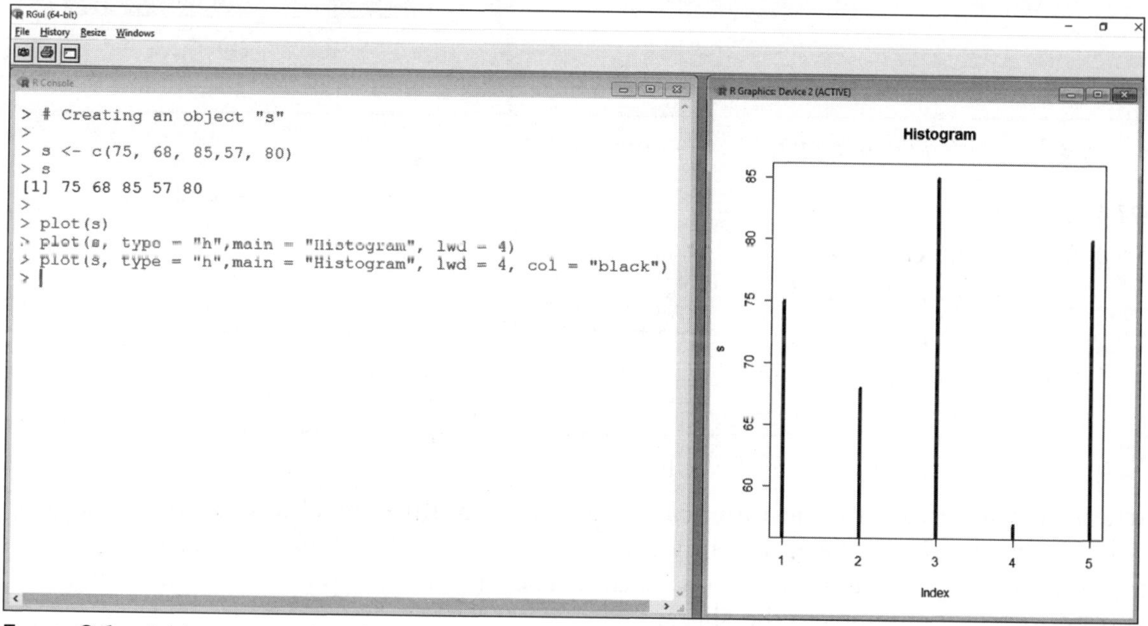

FIGURE 8.1 *A histogram using the* `plot()` *command*

hist() Function

R provides the `hist()` command for creating the histogram of any data set. A histogram is a type of plot that uses different bars for the graphical representation of a data set. It divides the data set into certain ranges and creates bars of different heights. The basic syntax of the `hist()` function is `hist(x, … )`

where, "x" is a vector of values for which the histogram is to be drawn and the dots "…" define the other optional arguments.

The following example reads a table "StuAt.csv". The object *h* stores the attendance for January. The `hist()` function creates the histogram of this object *h* (Figure 8.2).

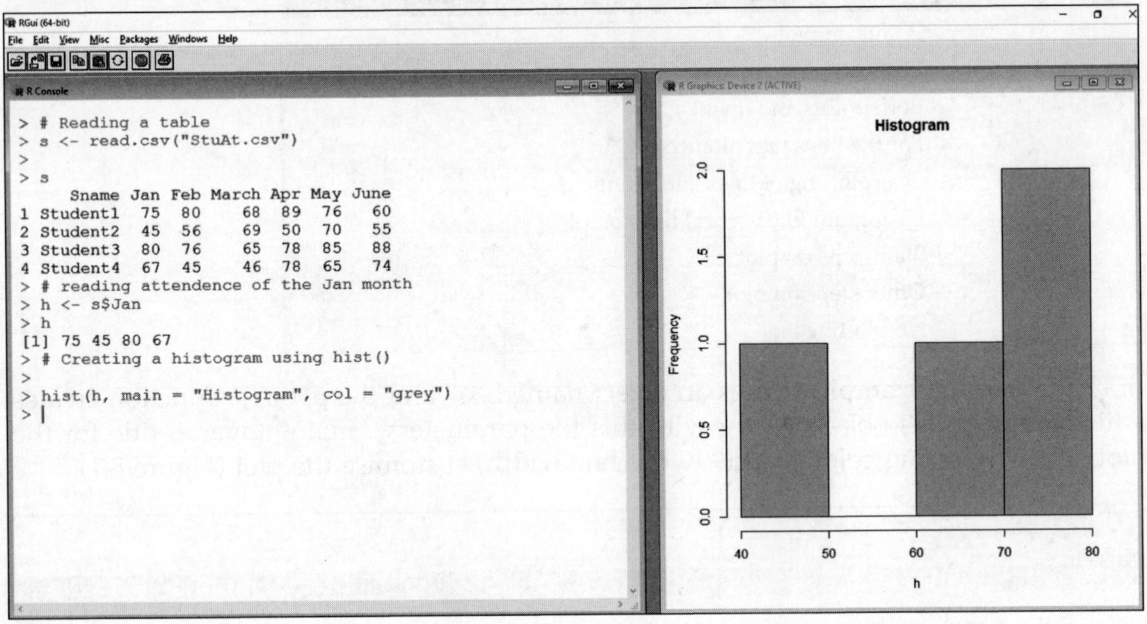

Figure 8.2 *A histogram using the* `hist()` *command*

pie() Function

Step 1: Create a vector "B".

```
> B <- c(2, 4, 5, 7, 12, 14, 16)
```

Step 2: Plot the pie chart using the pie function. The syntax for `pie()` is:

```
pie(x, labels = names(x), edges = 200, radius = 0.8,
    clockwise = FALSE, init.angle = if(clockwise) 90 else 0,
    density = NULL, angle = 45, col = NULL, border = NULL,
    lty = NULL, main = NULL, ...)
```

where, *x* is a vector of non-numerical numerical quantities, clockwise accepts a logical value indicating if the slices are drawn clockwise or counter-clockwise, main is used to provide the overall title of the pie chart, col is used to state the plotting colour and labels is used to provide names to the slices.

```
> pie(B)
```

Note: Refer to the R documentation for definition and explanation of other parameters.

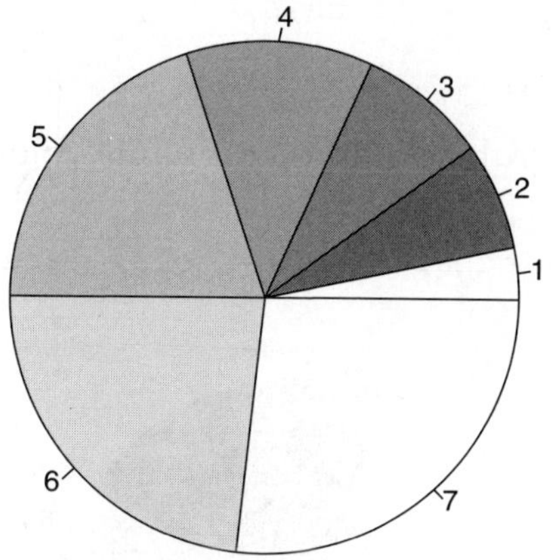

FIGURE 8.3 *Pie chart*

Step 3: Plot the pie chart with values provided for parameters such as main, col, labels, etc.

```
> pie(B, main="My Piechart", col=rainbow(length(B)),
+ labels=c("Mon", "Tue", "Wed", "Thu", "Fri", "Sat", "Sun"))
```

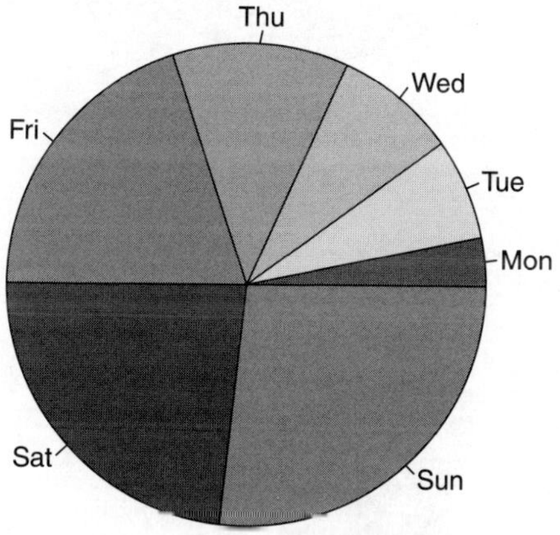

FIGURE 8.4 *My Piechart*

Let us see how to set up black, grey and white colour for clear printing.

```
> cols <- c("grey90", "grey50", "black", "grey 30", "white", "grey
70", "grey 50")
```

Let us calculate the percentage for each day, using one decimal place.

```
> percentlabels<- round(100*B/sum(B), 1)
> percentlabels
[1] 3.3  6.7  8.3   11.7  20.0  23.3  26.7
```

Now, add a '%' sign to each percentage value using the paste command.

```
> pielabels<- paste(percentlabels, "%", sep="")
> pielabels
[1] "3.3%"  "6.7%"  "8.3%"  "11.7%"  "20.0%"  "23.3%"  "26.7%"
```

Finally, plot the pie chart in black, grey and white colour with values displayed in percentage for labels.

```
> pie (B, main="My Piechart", col= cols, labels=pielabels, cex=0.8)
```

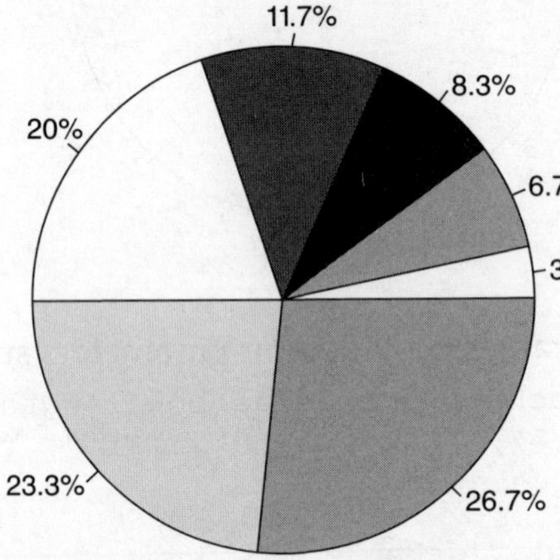

FIGURE 8.5 *My Piechart*

Add a legend to the right.

```
> legend("topright", c("Mon", "Tue", "Wed", "Thu", "Fri", "Sat",
"Sun")), cex=0.8, fill=cols)
```

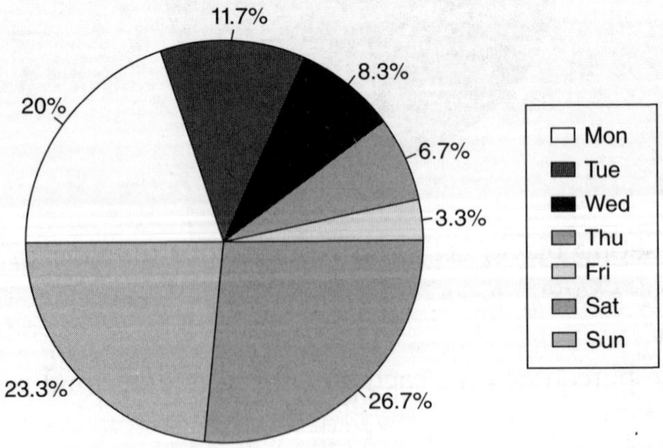

FIGURE 8.6 *My Piechart*

boxplot() Function

The boxplot is also referred to as box and whiskers plot. It was invented in 1977 by John Tukey, who is also known as the father of exploratory data analysis. The purpose of a boxplot is to efficiently display the following five magic numbers or statistical measures:

- Minimum or low value
- Lower quartile or 25th percentile
- Median or 50th percentile
- Upper quartile or 75th percentile
- Maximum or high value

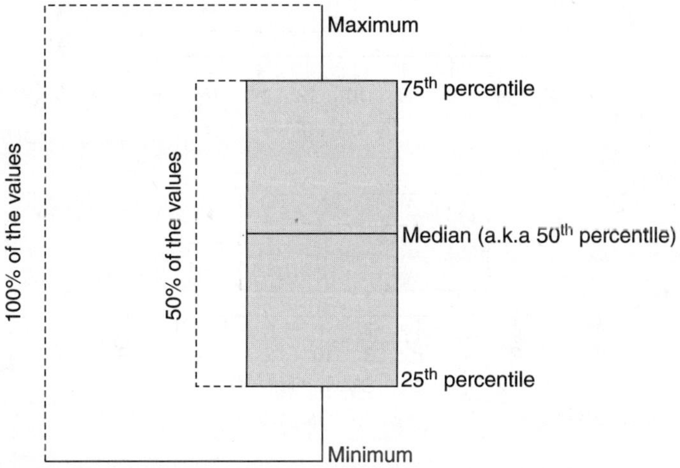

FIGURE 8.7 *Boxplot*

A boxplot can be drawn either vertically or horizontally and is often used in conjunction with a histogram.

Advantages of Boxplot

- Provides a fair idea about the data's symmetry and skewness (skewness is asymmetry in statistical distribution).
- It shows outliers.
- It allows for an easy comparison of data sets.

Steps to Create a Boxplot

Step 1: We will use the "trees" dataset. This data set provides measurements of the girth (diameter in inches), height and volume of timber in 31 felled black cherry trees. Use the `head()` function to view the top six rows from the data set.

```
> head(trees)
    Girth   Height   Volume
1   8.3     70       10.3
2   8.6     65       10.3
3   8.8     63       10.2
4   10.5    72       16.4
5   10.7    81       18.8
6   10.8    83       19.7
```

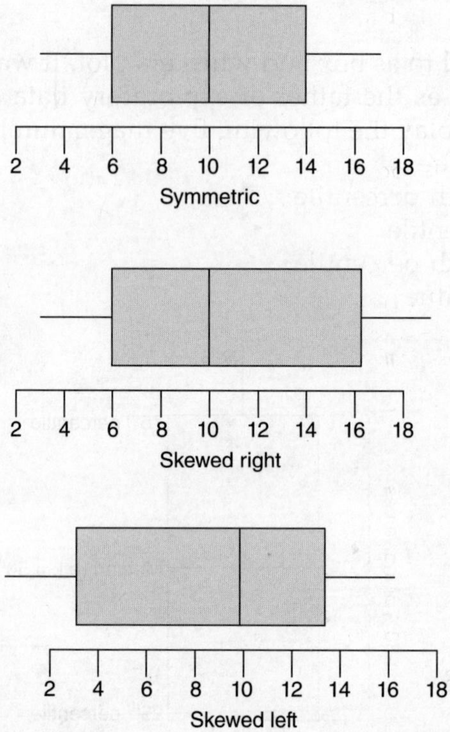

FIGURES 8.8 (A TO C) *Boxplots*

Step 2: Plot the boxplot using the `boxplot()` function. Boxplot is used to show the five magic numbers, viz., minimum, maximum, median, lower quartile and upper quartile.

```
> boxplot(trees)
```

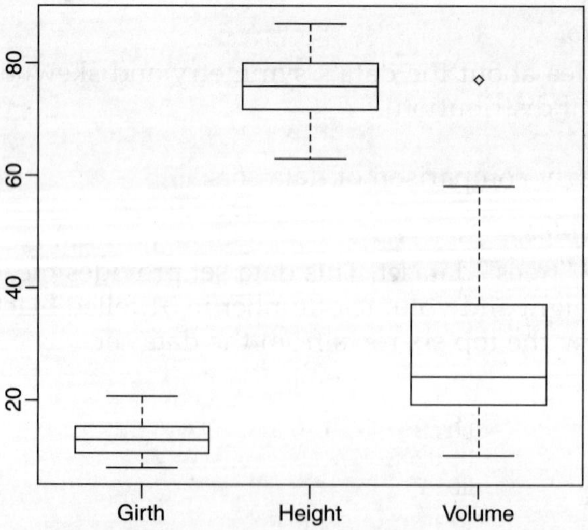

FIGURE 8.9 *Boxplot for "tree" dataset.*

The complete syntax of the `boxplot()` function is:

```
boxplot(x, ..., range = 1.5, width = NULL, varwidth = FALSE,
        notch = FALSE, outline = TRUE, names, plot = TRUE,
        border = par("fg"), col = NULL, log = "",
        pars = list(boxwex = 0.8, staplewex = 0.5, outwex = 0.5),
        horizontal = FALSE, add = FALSE, at = NULL)
```

where, *x* is a numeric vector or a single list containing such vectors.

> **TIP** *Refer to the R documentation for definition and explanation of other parameters.*

Step 3: Use parameters such as "main" to provide an overall title to the plot and "ylab" to provide label to the Y-axis, etc.

```
> boxplot(trees$Height, main="Height of Trees", ylab="Tree height in
feet")
```

FIGURE 8.10 *Boxplot with parameter values*

stripchart() Function

The `stripchart()` function helps to create one-dimensional scatter plots (or dot plots) of the given data. These plots are a good alternative to boxplots when sample sizes are small.

Consider the "airquality" data set. It is a data frame with 153 observations on six variables (Ozone, Solar.R, Wind, Temp, Month and Day).

Step 1: Check the internal structure of the R object "airquality" using `str()`.

```
> str(airquality)
'data.frame': 153 obs. Of 6 variables:
$ Ozone: int 41 36 12 18 NA 28 23 19 8 NA ...
$ Solar.R: int 190 118 149 313 NA NA 299 99 19 194 ...
$ Wind: num 7.4 8 12.6 11.5 14.3 14.9 8.6 13.8 20.1 8.6 ...
$ Temp: int 67 72 74 62 56 66 65 59 61 69 ...
$ Month: int 5 5 5 5 5 5 5 5 5 5 ...
$ Day: int 1 2 3 4 5 6 7 8 9 10...
```

Step 2: Let us make a strip chart for the ozone readings.

```
> stripchart(airquality$Ozone)
```

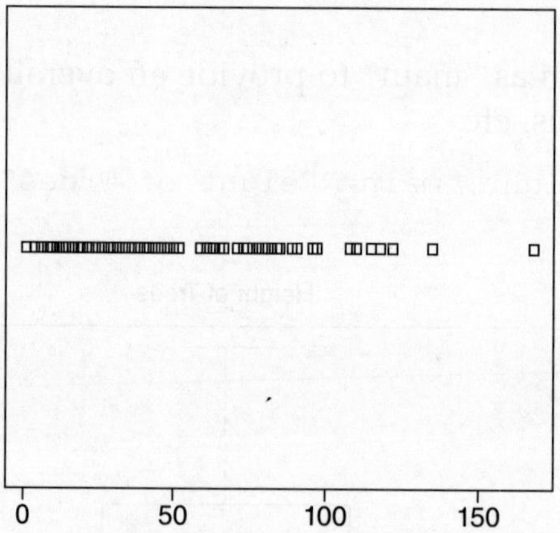

FIGURE 8.11 *Stripchart*

We can see that the data is mostly cluttered below 50 with one falling outside 150. The syntax for `stripchart()` is:

```
stripchart(x, method = "overplot", jitter = 0.1, offset = 1/3,
           vertical = FALSE, group.names, add = FALSE,
           at = NULL, xlim = NULL, ylim = NULL,
           ylab = NULL, xlab = NULL, dlab = "", glab = "",
           log = "", pch = 0, col = par("fg"), cex = par("cex"),
           axes = TRUE, frame.plot = axes, ...)
```

where,

- x: the data from which the plots are to be produced. It can be a single numeric vector or a list of numeric vectors.
- main: main title (on top)
- xlab: X-axis label
- ylab: Y-axis label
- method: method used to separate coincident points, "overplot" causes such points to be overplotted, "jitter" to jitter the points or "stack" to have the coincident points stacked.

- col: default plotting colour
- pch: either an integer specifying a symbol or a single character to be used as the default in plotting points.

Refer to the R documentation for definition and explanation of other parameters.

Step 3: Plot the stripchart using the parameters such as main, xlab, ylab, method, col, pch, etc.

```
> stripchart(airquality$Ozone,
+ main="Mean ozone in parts per billion at Roosevelt Island",
+ xlab="Parts Per Billion",
+ ylab="Ozone",
+ method="jitter",
+ col="orange",
+ pch=1
+ )
```

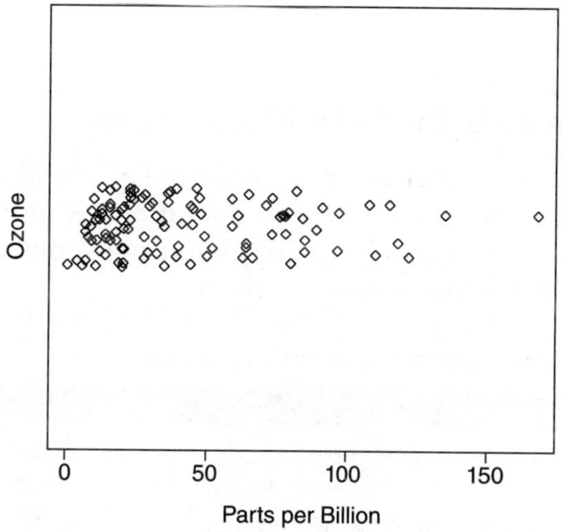

FIGURE 8.12 *Mean ozone in parts per billion at Roosevelt Island*

curve () Function

It draws a curve corresponding to a function over the interval `[from, to]`. `curve()` can also plot an expression in the variable `xname`, default `x`. The syntax for `curve()` is:

```
curve(expr, from = NULL, to = NULL, n = 101, add = FALSE,
      type = "l", xname = "x", xlab = xname, ylab = NULL,
      log = NULL, xlim = NULL, ...)
```

where, *x* is a 'vectorising' numeric R function and
from, to provided the range over which the function will be plotted.

Refer to the R documentation for definition and explanation of other parameters.

```
> curve(x^2, from=1, to=50, , xlab="x", ylab="y")
```

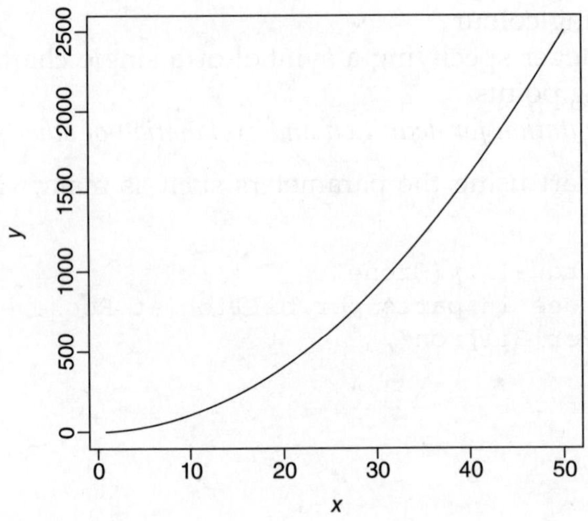

FIGURE 8.13 *A curve*

8.2.2 Basic R Commands for Data Manipulation

Time series analysis most often requires arithmetic mean, standard deviation, difference, probability distribution, density and other such operations. R provides various commands that perform these operations and help manipulate time series data. Table 8.2 describes some common commands for time series analysis.

TABLE 8.2 Some major manipulation commands/functions

Functions	*Function arguments*	*Description*
`mean(x)`	*x* argument defines any *r* object.	The function returns the arithmetic mean of the given object.
`diff(x)`	*x* argument contains either any numeric vector or matrix.	The function returns the lagged and iterated difference.
`sd(x)`	*x* argument contains either any numeric vector or any *r* object.	The function returns the standard deviation of the given object.
`log(x)`	*x* argument contains either any numeric vector or any *r* object.	The function returns the logarithms of the given object.
`pnorm(x)`	*x* argument contains either any numeric vector or any *r* object.	The function returns the normal distribution function.
`dnorm(x)`	*x* argument contains either any numeric vector or any *r* object.	The function returns the density of the object.

The following example creates an object *"d"*. The functions described above generate different values used during time series analysis. For example, the `pnorm()` and `qnorm()` functions define the distribution properties of the data (Figure 8.14) explains this.

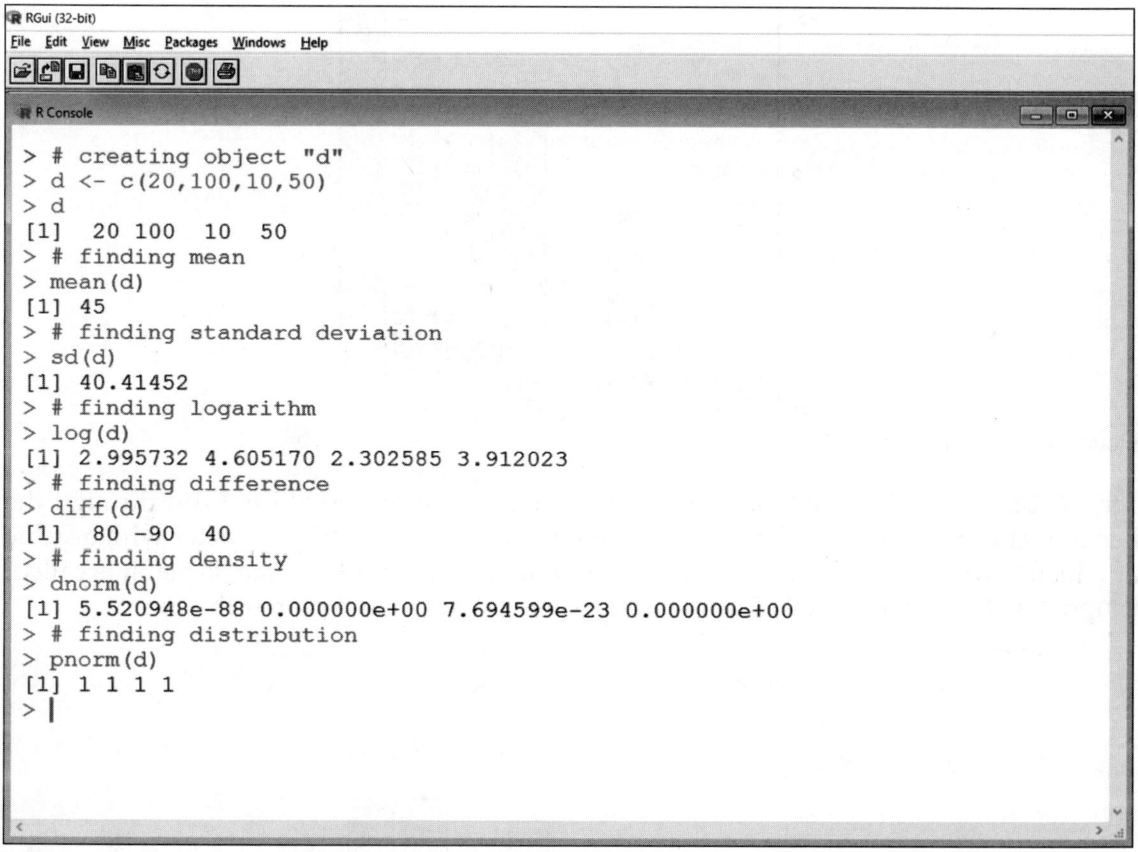

RGui (32-bit)
File Edit View Misc Packages Windows Help
R Console

```
> # creating object "d"
> d <- c(20,100,10,50)
> d
[1]  20 100  10  50
> # finding mean
> mean(d)
[1] 45
> # finding standard deviation
> sd(d)
[1] 40.41452
> # finding logarithm
> log(d)
[1] 2.995732 4.605170 2.302585 3.912023
> # finding difference
> diff(d)
[1]  80 -90  40
> # finding density
> dnorm(d)
[1] 5.520948e-88 0.000000e+00 7.694599e-23 0.000000e+00
> # finding distribution
> pnorm(d)
[1] 1 1 1 1
> |
```

FIGURE 8.14 *Some manipulation commands*

`mean()` *Function*

Objective: To determine the mean of a set of numbers. Plot the numbers in a bar plot and have a straight line run through the plot at the mean.

Step 1: Create a vector "numbers".

```
> numbers <- c(1, 3, 5, 2, 8, 7, 9, 10)
```

Step 2: Compute the mean value of the set of numbers contained in the vector "numbers".

```
> mean(numbers)
[1] 5.625
```

Outcome: The mean value for the vector "numbers" is computed as 5.625.

Step 3: Plot a bar plot using the vector "numbers".

```
> barplot(numbers)
```

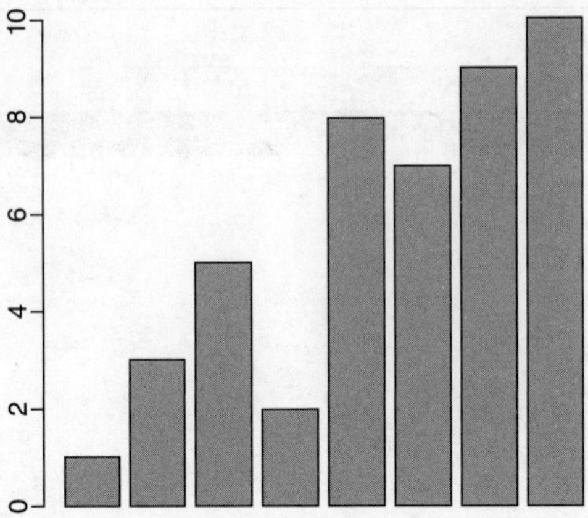

FIGURE 8.15 *A Barplot*

Step 4: Use the abline function to have a straight line (horizontal line) run through the bar plot at the mean value. The `abline` function can take an "*h*" parameter with a value at which to draw a horizontal line or a "*v*" parameter for a vertical line. When it is called, it updates the previous plot. Draw a horizontal line across the plot at the mean:

```
> barplot(numbers)
> abline(h= mean(numbers))
```

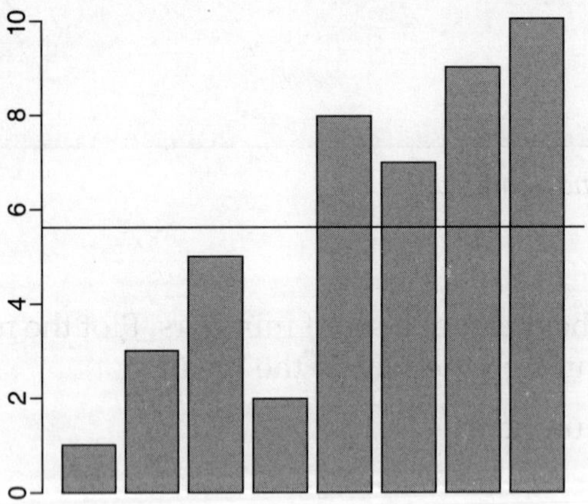

FIGURE 8.16 *A bar plot with a straight line at the computed mean value*

Outcome: A straight line at the computed mean value (5.625) runs through the bar plot computed on the vector "numbers".

`median()` *Function*

Objective: To determine the median of a set of numbers. Plot the numbers in a bar plot and have a straight line run through the plot at the median.

Step 1: Create a vector "numbers".

```
> numbers <- c(1,3,5,2,8,7,9,10)
```

Step 2: Compute the median value of the set of numbers contained in the vector "numbers".

```
> median(numbers)
[1] 6
```

Step 3: Plot a bar plot using the vector "numbers". Use the abline function to have a straight line (horizontal line) run through the bar plot at the median.

```
> barplot(numbers)
> abline(h = median(numbers))
```

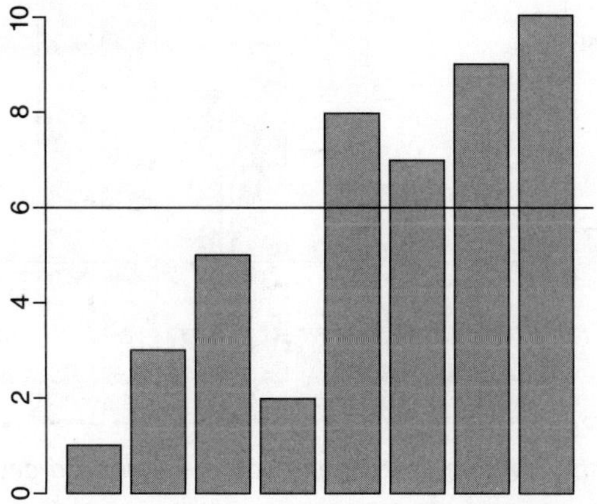

FIGURE 8.17 *A bar plot with a straight line at the computed median value*

Outcome: A straight line at the computed median value (6.0) runs through the bar plot computed on the vector "numbers".

sd() Function

Objective: To determine the standard deviation. Plot the numbers in a bar plot and have a straight line run through the plot at the mean and another straight line run through the plot at mean + standard deviation.

Step 1: Create a vector "numbers".

```
> numbers <-c(1,3,5,2,8,7,9,10)
```

Step 2: Compute the mean value of the set of numbers contained in the vector "numbers".

```
> mean(numbers)
[1] 5.625
```

Step 3: Determine the standard deviation of the set of numbers held in the vector "numbers".

```
> deviation <- sd(numbers)
> deviation
[1] 3.377975
```

Step 4: Plot a bar plot using the vector "numbers".

```
> barplot(numbers)
```

Step 5: Use the abline function to have a straight line (horizontal line) run through the bar plot at the mean value (5.625) and another straight line run through the bar plot at mean value + standard deviation (5.625 + 3.377975)

```
> barplot(numbers)
> abline(h=sd(numbers))
> abline(h=sd(numbers) + mean(numbers))
```

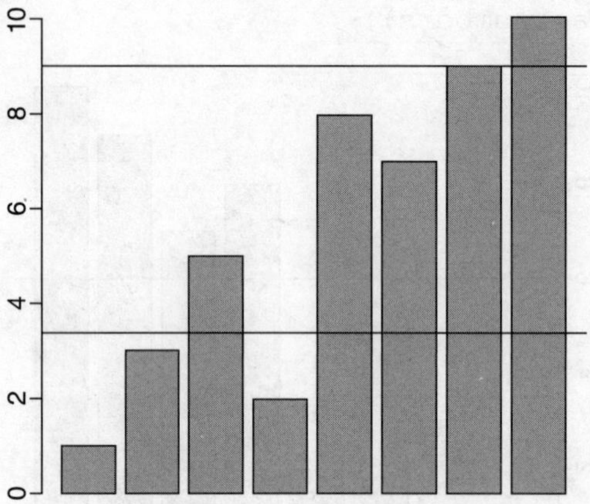

FIGURE 8.18 *A bar plot with straight line at its mean value + standard deviation*

Mode Function

Objective: To determine the mode of a set of numbers.

R does not have a standard inbuilt function to determine the mode. We will write our own "mode" function. This function will take the vector as the input and return the mode as the output value.

Step 1: Create a user-defined function "Mode".

```
Mode <- function(v) {
  UniqValue <- unique(v)
  UniqValue[which.max(tabulate(match(v,UniqValue)))]
}
```

On execution of the above code,

```
>  Mode <- function(v) {
+ UniqValue <-unique(v)
+ UniqValue [which.max(tabulate(match(v,UniqValue)))]
+}
```

While writing the above function "Mode", we have used three other functions provided by R, viz., "unique", "tabulate" and "match".

unique function: The "unique" function will take a vector as the input and return the vector with the duplicates removed.

```
> v
[1] 2 1 2 3 1 2 3 4 1 5 5 3 2 3
> unique(v)
[1] 2 1 3 4 5
```

match function: Takes a vector as the input and return the vector that has the positions of (first) matches of its first arguments in its second.

```
> v
[1] 2 1 2 3 1 2 3 4 1 5 5 3 2 3
> UniqValue <-unique(v)
> UniqValue
[1] 2 1 3 4 5
> match(v,UniqValue)
[1] 1 2 1 3 2 1 3 4 2 5 5 3 1 3
```

tabulate function: Takes an integer valued vector as the input and counts the number of times each integer occurs in it.

```
> tabulate(match(v,UniqValue))
1] 4 3 4 1 2
```

Going by our example, "2" occurs 4 times, "1" occurs 3 times, "3" occurs 4 times, "4" occurs 1 time and "5" occurs 2 times.

Step 2: Create a vector "v".

```
> v <- c(2,1,2,3,1,2,3,4,1,5,5,3,2,3)
```

Step 3: Call the function "Mode" and pass the vector "v" to it.

```
> Output <- Mode(v)
```

Step 4: Print the mode value of the vector "v".

```
> print (Output)
[1] 2
```

Let us pass a character vector "charv" to the "Mode" function.

Step 1: Create a character vector "charv".

```
> charv <- c("o", "it", "the", "it", "it")
```

Step 2: Call the function "Mode" and pass the character vector "charv" to it.

```
> Output <- Mode(charv)
```

Step 3: Print out the mode value of the vector "v".

```
> print(Output)
[1] "it"
```

`log()` Function

The following are the variants of the `log()` function:

- `log()` computes the natural logarithms (Ln) for a number or vector
- `log10()` computes common logarithms (Lg)
- `log2()` computes binary logarithms (Log2)
- `log(x,b)` computes logarithms with base b.

```
> log (5)
[1] 1.609438
> log10(5)
[1] 0.69897
> log2(5)
[1]2.321928
>log(9,base=3)
[1] 2
```

Using log functions with a vector.

```
> x <- rep(1:10)
> x
 [1] 1 2 3 4 5 6 7 8 9 10
> log(6)
 [1] 1.791759
> log (x)
 [1] 0.0000000  0.6931472  1.0986123  1.3862944  1.6094379
     1.7917595  1.9459101
 [8] 2.0794415  2.1972246  2.3025851
> log (x,6)
 [1] 0.0000000  0.3868528  0.6131472  0.7737056  0.8982444
     1.0000000  1.0860331
 [8] 1.1605584  1.2262944  1.2850972
```

diff() Function

`diff()` function returns suitably lagged and iterated differences. The syntax is:

```
diff(x, lag = 1, differences = 1, ...)
```

where,

- *x* is a numeric vector or matrix containing the values to be differenced
- lag is an integer indicating which lag to use
- differences is an integer indicating the order of the difference.

Example

```
> temp <-c(10,1,1,1,1,1,1,2,1,1,1,1,1,1,1,3,10)
> temp
[1] 10  1  1  1  1  1  1  2  1  1  1  1  1  1  1  3  10
> diff(temp)
[1] -9  0  0  0  0  0  1 -1  0  0  0  0  0  0  2  7
> diff(diff(temp))
[1]  9  0  0  0  0  1 -2  1  0  0  0  0  0  2  5
> diff(temp, differences=2)
[1]  9  0  0  0  0  1 -2  1  0  0  0  0  0  2  5
```

Note: Output of diff(diff(temp)) and diff(temp, differences=2) is the same.

dnorm() and pnorm() Function

The syntax, purpose and examples of `dnorm()` and `pnorm()` functions are given in Table 8.3.

TABLE 8.3 `dnorm()` and `pnorm()` functions

Function	*Purpose*	*Syntax*	*Example*
`dnorm()`	Probability Density Function (PDF)	`dnorm(x, mean, sd)`	`dnorm(0, 0, 0.5)` Gives the density (height of the PDF) of the normal with mean=0 and sd=0.5.
`pnorm()`	Cumulative Distribution Function (CDF)	`pnorm(q, mean, sd)`	`pnorm(1.96, 0, 1)` Gives the area under the standard normal curve to the left of 1.96, i.e., ~0.975.

Example

Step 1: Create a sequence xseq.

```
> xseq <- seq(-4, 4, .01)
> xseq
```

```
  [1] -4.00 -3.99 -3.98 -3.97 -3.96 -3.95 -3.94 -3.93 -3.92 -3.91 -3.90 -3.89
 [13] -3.88 -3.87 -3.86 -3.85 -3.84 -3.83 -3.82 -3.81 -3.80 -3.79 -3.78 -3.77
 [25] -3.76 -3.75 -3.74 -3.73 -3.72 -3.71 -3.70 -3.69 -3.68 -3.67 -3.66 -3.65
 [37] -3.64 -3.63 -3.62 -3.61 -3.60 -3.59 -3.58 -3.57 -3.56 -3.55 -3.54 -3.53
 [49] -3.52 -3.51 -3.50 -3.49 -3.48 -3.47 -3.46 -3.45 -3.44 -3.43 -3.42 -3.41
 [61] -3.40 -3.39 -3.38 -3.37 -3.36 -3.35 -3.34 -3.33 -3.32 -3.31 -3.30 -3.29
 [73] -3.28 -3.27 -3.26 -3.25 -3.24 -3.23 -3.22 -3.21 -3.20 -3.19 -3.18 -3.17
 [85] -3.16 -3.15 -3.14 -3.13 -3.12 -3.11 -3.10 -3.09 -3.08 -3.07 -3.06 -3.05
 [97] -3.04 -3.03 -3.02 -3.01 -3.00 -2.99 -2.98 -2.97 -2.96 -2.95 -2.94 -2.93
[109] -2.92 -2.91 -2.90 -2.89 -2.88 -2.87 -2.86 -2.85 -2.84 -2.83 -2.82 -2.81
[121] -2.80 -2.79 -2.78 -2.77 -2.76 -2.75 -2.74 -2.73 -2.72 -2.71 -2.70 -2.69
[133] -2.68 -2.67 -2.66 -2.65 -2.64 -2.63 -2.62 -2.61 -2.60 -2.59 -2.58 -2.57
[145] -2.56 -2.55 -2.54 -2.53 -2.52 -2.51 -2.50 -2.49 -2.48 -2.47 -2.46 -2.45
[157] -2.44 -2.43 -2.42 -2.41 -2.40 -2.39 -2.38 -2.37 -2.36 -2.35 -2.34 -2.33
[169] -2.32 -2.31 -2.30 -2.29 -2.28 -2.27 -2.26 -2.25 -2.24 -2.23 -2.22 -2.21
[181] -2.20 -2.19 -2.18 -2.17 -2.16 -2.15 -2.14 -2.13 -2.12 -2.11 -2.10 -2.09
[193] -2.08 -2.07 -2.06 -2.05 -2.04 -2.03 -2.02 -2.01 -2.00 -1.99 -1.98 -1.97
[205] -1.96 -1.95 -1.94 -1.93 -1.92 -1.91 -1.90 -1.89 -1.88 -1.87 -1.86 -1.85
[217] -1.84 -1.83 -1.82 -1.81 -1.80 -1.79 -1.78 -1.77 -1.76 -1.75 -1.74 -1.73
[229] -1.72 -1.71 -1.70 -1.69 -1.68 -1.67 -1.66 -1.65 -1.64 -1.63 -1.62 -1.61
[241] -1.60 -1.59 -1.58 -1.57 -1.56 -1.55 -1.54 -1.53 -1.52 -1.51 -1.50 -1.49
[253] -1.48 -1.47 -1.46 -1.45 -1.44 -1.43 -1.42 -1.41 -1.40 -1.39 -1.38 -1.37
[265] -1.36 -1.35 -1.34 -1.33 -1.32 -1.31 -1.30 -1.29 -1.28 -1.27 -1.26 -1.25
[277] -1.24 -1.23 -1.22 -1.21 -1.20 -1.19 -1.18 -1.17 -1.16 -1.15 -1.14 -1.13
[289] -1.12 -1.11 -1.10 -1.09 -1.08 -1.07 -1.06 -1.05 -1.04 -1.03 -1.02 -1.01
[301] -1.00 -0.99 -0.98 -0.97 -0.96 -0.95 -0.94 -0.93 -0.92 -0.91 -0.90 -0.89
[313] -0.88 -0.87 -0.86 -0.85 -0.84 -0.83 -0.82 -0.81 -0.80 -0.79 -0.78 -0.77
[325] -0.76 -0.75 -0.74 -0.73 -0.72 -0.71 -0.70 -0.69 -0.68 -0.67 -0.66 -0.65
[337] -0.64 -0.63 -0.62 -0.61 -0.60 -0.59 -0.58 -0.57 -0.56 -0.55 -0.54 -0.53
[349] -0.52 -0.51 -0.50 -0.49 -0.48 -0.47 -0.46 -0.45 -0.44 -0.43 -0.42 -0.41
[361] -0.40 -0.39 -0.38 -0.37 -0.36 -0.35 -0.34 -0.33 -0.32 -0.31 -0.30 -0.29
[373] -0.28 -0.27 -0.26 -0.25 -0.24 -0.23 -0.22 -0.21 -0.20 -0.19 -0.18 -0.17
[385] -0.16 -0.15 -0.14 -0.13 -0.12 -0.11 -0.10 -0.09 -0.08 -0.07 -0.06 -0.05
[397] -0.04 -0.03 -0.02 -0.01  0.00  0.01  0.02  0.03  0.04  0.05  0.06  0.07
[409]  0.08  0.09  0.10  0.11  0.12  0.13  0.14  0.15  0.16  0.17  0.18  0.19
[421]  0.20  0.21  0.22  0.23  0.24  0.25  0.26  0.27  0.28  0.29  0.30  0.31
```

(Continued)

```
[433] 0.32 0.33 0.34 0.35 0.36 0.37 0.38 0.39 0.40 0.41 0.42 0.43
[445] 0.44 0.45 0.46 0.47 0.48 0.49 0.50 0.51 0.52 0.53 0.54 0.55
[457] 0.56 0.57 0.58 0.59 0.60 0.61 0.62 0.63 0.64 0.65 0.66 0.67
[469] 0.68 0.69 0.70 0.71 0.72 0.73 0.74 0.75 0.76 0.77 0.78 0.79
[481] 0.80 0.81 0.82 0.83 0.84 0.85 0.86 0.87 0.88 0.89 0.90 0.91
[493] 0.92 0.93 0.94 0.95 0.96 0.97 0.98 0.99 1.00 1.01 1.02 1.03
[505] 1.04 1.05 1.06 1.07 1.08 1.09 1.10 1.11 1.12 1.13 1.14 1.15
[517] 1.16 1.17 1.18 1.19 1.20 1.21 1.22 1.23 1.24 1.25 1.26 1.27
[529] 1.28 1.29 1.30 1.31 1.32 1.33 1.34 1.35 1.36 1.37 1.38 1.39
[541] 1.40 1.41 1.42 1.43 1.44 1.45 1.46 1.47 1.48 1.49 1.50 1.51
[553] 1.52 1.53 1.54 1.55 1.56 1.57 1.58 1.59 1.60 1.61 1.62 1.63
[565] 1.64 1.65 1.66 1.67 1.68 1.69 1.70 1.71 1.72 1.73 1.74 1.75
[577] 1.76 1.77 1.78 1.79 1.80 1.81 1.82 1.83 1.84 1.85 1.86 1.87
[589] 1.88 1.89 1.90 1.91 1.92 1.93 1.94 1.95 1.96 1.97 1.98 1.99
[601] 2.00 2.01 2.02 2.03 2.04 2.05 2.06 2.07 2.08 2.09 2.10 2.11
[613] 2.12 2.13 2.14 2.15 2.16 2.17 2.18 2.19 2.20 2.21 2.22 2.23
[625] 2.24 2.25 2.26 2.27 2.28 2.29 2.30 2.31 2.32 2.33 2.34 2.35
[637] 2.36 2.37 2.38 2.39 2.40 2.41 2.42 2.43 2.44 2.45 2.46 2.47
[649] 2.48 2.49 2.50 2.51 2.52 2.53 2.54 2.55 2.56 2.57 2.58 2.59
[661] 2.60 2.61 2.62 2.63 2.64 2.65 2.66 2.67 2.68 2.69 2.70 2.71
[673] 2.72 2.73 2.74 2.75 2.76 2.77 2.78 2.79 2.80 2.81 2.82 2.83
[685] 2.84 2.85 2.86 2.87 2.88 2.89 2.90 2.91 2.92 2.93 2.94 2.95
[697] 2.96 2.97 2.98 2.99 3.00 3.01 3.02 3.03 3.04 3.05 3.06 3.07
[709] 3.08 3.09 3.10 3.11 3.12 3.13 3.14 3.15 3.16 3.17 3.18 3.19
[721] 3.20 3.21 3.22 3.23 3.24 3.25 3.26 3.27 3.28 3.29 3.30 3.31
[733] 3.32 3.33 3.34 3.35 3.36 3.37 3.38 3.39 3.40 3.41 3.42 3.43
[745] 3.44 3.45 3.46 3.47 3.48 3.49 3.50 3.51 3.52 3.53 3.54 3.55
[757] 3.56 3.57 3.58 3.59 3.60 3.61 3.62 3.63 3.64 3.65 3.66 3.67
[769] 3.68 3.69 3.70 3.71 3.72 3.73 3.74 3.75 3.76 3.77 3.78 3.79
[781] 3.80 3.81 3.82 3.83 3.84 3.85 3.86 3.87 3.88 3.89 3.90 3.91
[793] 3.92 3.93 3.94 3.95 3.96 3.97 3.98 3.99 4.00
```

Step 2: Compute the probability density and cumulative distribution using `dnorm()` and `pnorm()`.

```
> densities <- dnorm(xseq,0,1)
> cumulative <- pnorm(xseq,0,1)
> plot(xseq, densities, col="darkgreen", xlab="", ylab="Density",
type="l", lwd=2, cex=2, main="PDF of Standard Normal", cex.axis=.8)
> plot(xseq, cumulative, col="darkorange", xlab="", ylab="Cumulative
Probability", type="l", lwd=2, cex=2, main="CDF of Standard Normal",
cex.axis=.8)
```

8.2.3 Linear Filtering of Time Series

A part of simple component analysis, the linear filter divides the data by applying the linear filtering process. A simple component analysis divides the data into four main components called trend, seasonal, cyclical and irregular. Each component has its own special feature. For example, the trend, seasonal, cyclical and irregular components define the long-term progression, the seasonal variation, the repeated but non-periodic fluctuations, and the random or irregular components of any time series, respectively.

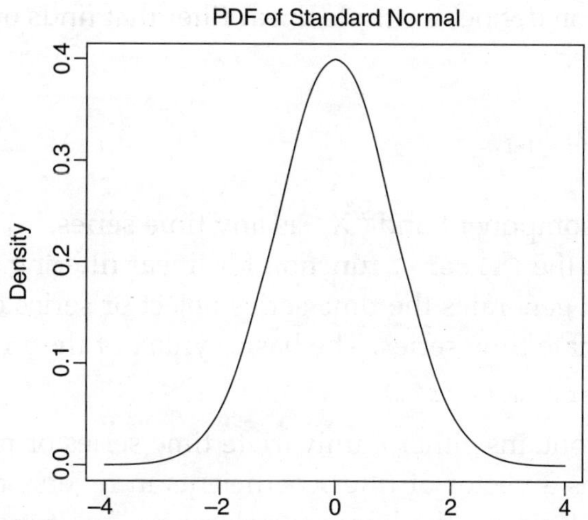

FIGURE 8.19 *PDF of Standard Normal*

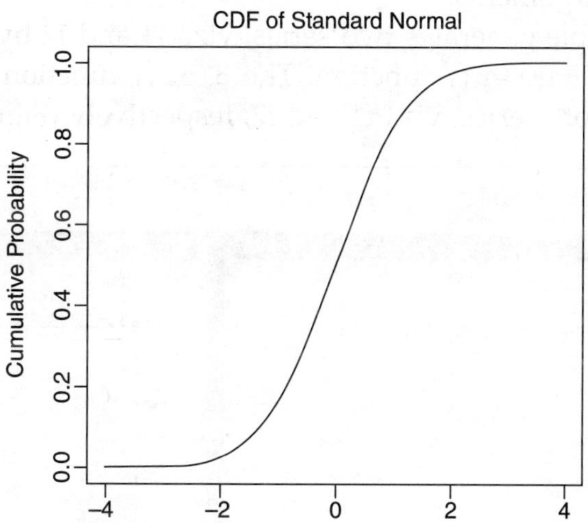

FIGURE 8.20 *CDF of Standard Normal*

The simple process of linear filtering converts the time series input data in linear output in traditional time series analysis. Different classes of linear filters are available. The moving averages with equal weights are a simple class of a linear filter. The following equation defines this simple class of linear filter:

$$T_t = \frac{1}{2a+1}\sum_{i=-a}^{a} X_{t+i}$$

where, "T_t" is a trend component, "X_t" is any time series, "a" defines the moving average and "i" represents counter variable.

The following equation defines a simple linear filter that finds out the trend component on the given time series:

$$T_t = \sum_{i=-\infty}^{\infty} \lambda_i \, X_{t+i}$$

where, "T_t" is a trend component and "X_t" is any time series.

R language provides the `filter()` function for linear filtering on time series analysis. The `filter()` function generates the time series object or series of any given univariate time series or multivariate time series. The basic syntax of the `filter()` function is:

```
filter(x, filter, method,…)
```

where, "x" argument contains either a univariate time series or multivariate time series, filter argument contains a vector of filter coefficients in reverse time order and method argument defines a method for the linear filtering process. It can be either convolution (for moving average or MA) or recursive (for auto regression or AR) and the dots "…" define other optional arguments.

The following example generates two series, viz., f1 and f2 by incrementing 1 and 2, respectively, using the `filter()` function. The `plot()` function is used to create solid and dashed lines for both series, viz., f1 and f2, respectively (Figure 8.4).

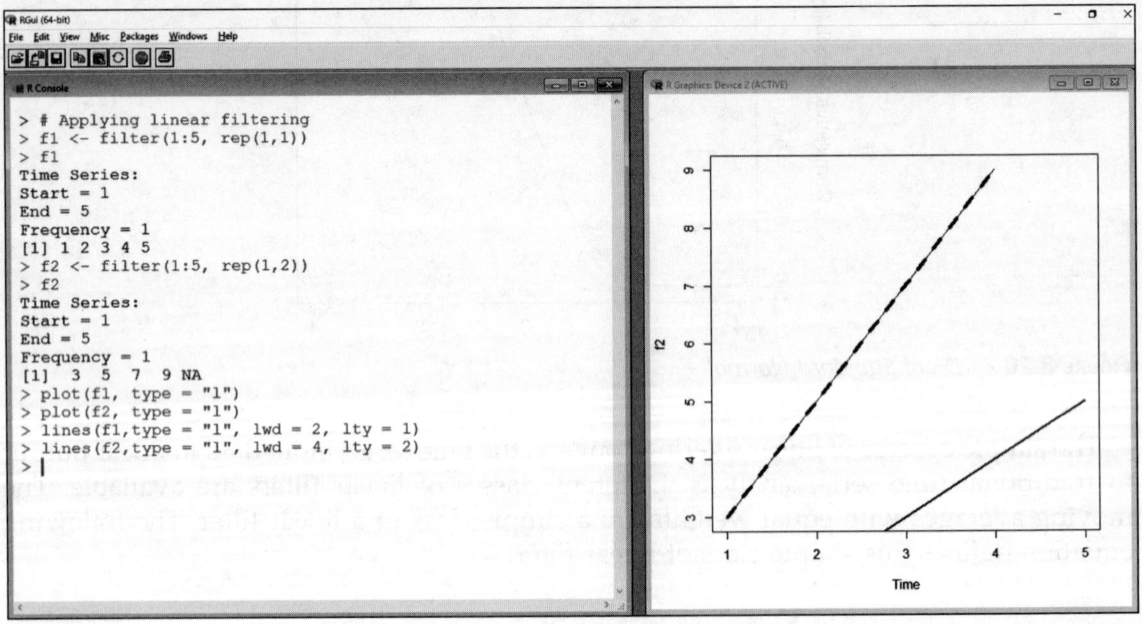

FIGURE 8.21 *Linear filtering using the* `filter()` *command*

Check Your Understanding

1. What is the difference between univariate and multivariate time series?

Ans: A univariate time series is a type of time series that uses a single quantity for describing values. A multivariate time series is a type of time series that uses more than a single quantity for describing values.

2. List the names of some basic R commands used for visualisation of time series data.

Ans: `plot()`, `hist()`, `boxplot()`, `pie()`, `abline()`, `qqnorm()`, `stripchart()`, and `curve()` are some R commands used for visualisation of time series data.

3. List the names of some basic R commands used for the manipulation of time series data.

Ans: `means()`, `sd()`, `log()`, `diff()`, `pnorm()`, and `qnorm()` are some R commands used for the manipulation of time series data.

4. What is `filter()` function?

Ans: The `filter()` function performs the linear filtering of time series data and generates the time series of the given data.

8.3 Reading Time Series Data

For the analysis of time series data, it is necessary to read and store time series data into some objects. R provides functions `scan()` and `ts()` for this. A brief introduction of each function is given as follows.

8.3.1 `scan()` Function

The `scan()` function reads the data from any file. Since time series data contains data with respect to a successive time interval, it is the best function for reading it. The basic syntax of the `scan()` function is `scan(filename)`

where, Filename argument contains the name of the file to be read.

The following example is reading a file "Attendance.txt". The file contains the attendance of a month of class (Figure 8.22).

8.3.2 `ts()` Function

The `ts()` function stores time series data and creates the time series object. Sometimes, data may be stored in a simple object. In such a case the `as.ts()` function can convert a simple object into a time series object. In addition, R also provides a function `is.ts()` that checks whether an object is a time series object or not. The basic syntax of the `ts()` function is

```
ts(data, start, end, frequency, class, …)
```

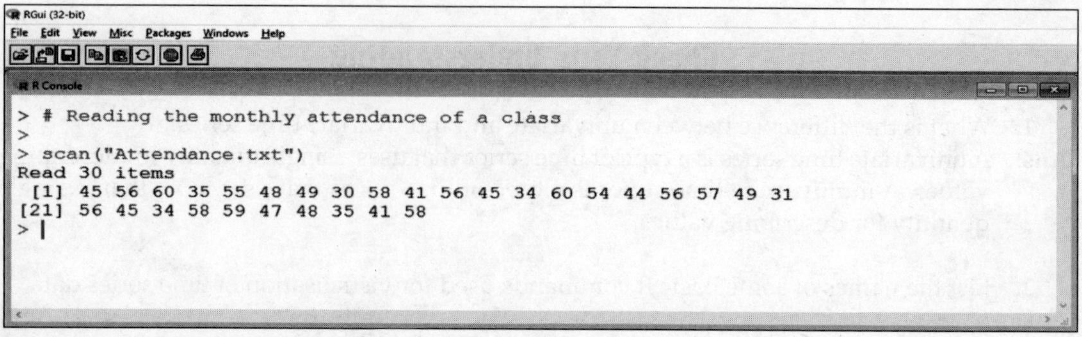

FIGURE 8.22 *Reading time series data using the* `scan()` *function*

where, "data" argument contains time series values stored in any vector or matrix, "start" argument contains a single number or a vector of two integers that defines the time of the first observation, "end" argument contains a single number or a vector of two integers that defines the time of the last observation, "frequency" argument contains a single number that defines the number of observations per unit of time and "class" is an optional argument that defines the class for the output. The default class is "ts" for a single series; classes such as "mts", "ts", "matrix", etc., are used for multiple series; and the dots "…" define other optional arguments.

In the following example described in Figure 8.23, the `ts()` function stores the object *s* that contains the attendance of one month which has been read with the use of the `scan()` function.

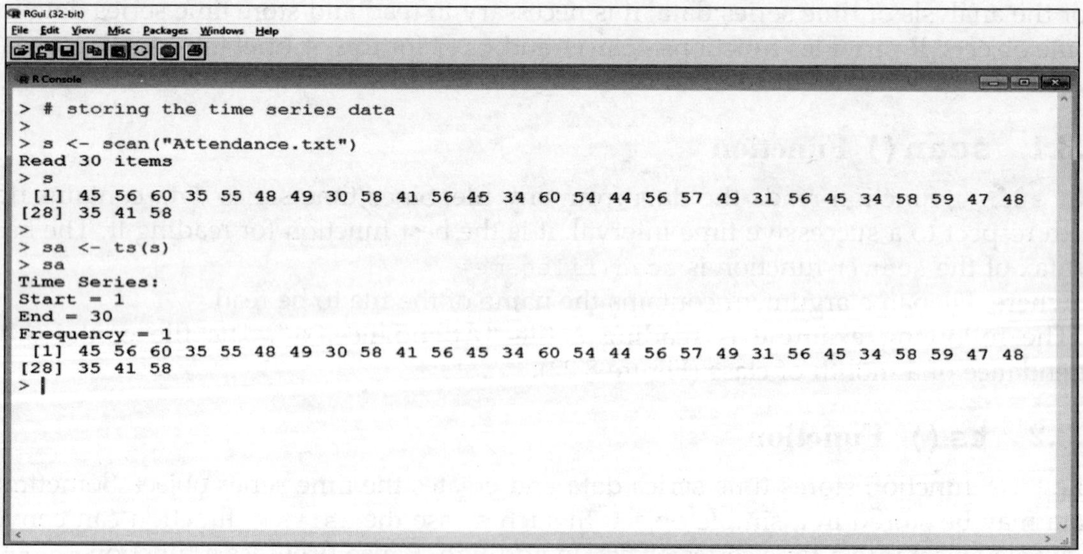

FIGURE 8.23 *Storing time series data using the* `ts()` *function*

Time series analysis also stores daily, monthly, quarterly or yearly data. For this, the frequency argument of the `ts()` function is used. In the following example, the `scan()`

function is reading a file into an object *s*. The `ts()` function creates a time series object *t* using the frequencies 12 and 4. The frequency 12 stores the object in yearly form and frequency 4 stores the object quarterly. Along with this, the start *c* = (2011, 1) argument defines that time series analysis is starting from January 2011 (Figure 8.24).

```
> s <- scan("SA.dat")
Read 24 items
> s
 [1] 75 80 68 89 76 60 45 56 69 50 70 55 80 76 65 78 85 88 67 45 46 78 65 74
> # Now storing this data into yearly using start and end argument
> t <- ts(s, frequency=12, start=c(2011,1), end = c(2012,12))
> t
     Jan Feb Mar Apr May Jun Jul Aug Sep Oct Nov Dec
2011  75  80  68  89  76  60  45  56  69  50  70  55
2012  80  76  65  78  85  88  67  45  46  78  65  74
>
> # Now storing this data into quaterly
> t <- ts(s, frequency=4, start=c(2011,1))
> t
     Qtr1 Qtr2 Qtr3 Qtr4
2011   75   80   68   89
2012   76   60   45   56
2013   69   50   70   55
2014   80   76   65   78
2015   85   88   67   45
2016   46   78   65   74
> |
```

FIGURE 8.24 *`ts()` function with frequency parameter*

Check Your Understanding

1. What is `scan()` function?

Ans: The `scan()` function reads the data from any file. Since time series data contains data with respect to a successive time interval, it is the best function for reading it.

2. What is the `ts()` function?

Ans: The `ts()` function stores time series data and creates the time series object.

3. What is `as.ts()` and `is.ts()` function?

Ans: The `as.ts()` function converts a simple object into a time series object and the `is.ts()` function checks whether an object is a time series object or not.

8.4 Plotting Time series Data

In time series analysis, plotting time series data is the next basic task after reading and storing time series data. A plotting task represents time series data graphically that is easily understandable by anyone. For plotting time series data, the `plot()` function of

R is the best function (described in Section 8.1). The basic syntax for plotting time series data is `plot.ts(x)`

where, "x" is any time series object.

The following example creates a plot of simple time series object *t* that contains time series data regarding attendance. The plot in Figure 8.25 describes the additive model because there are random fluctuations in the attendance data.

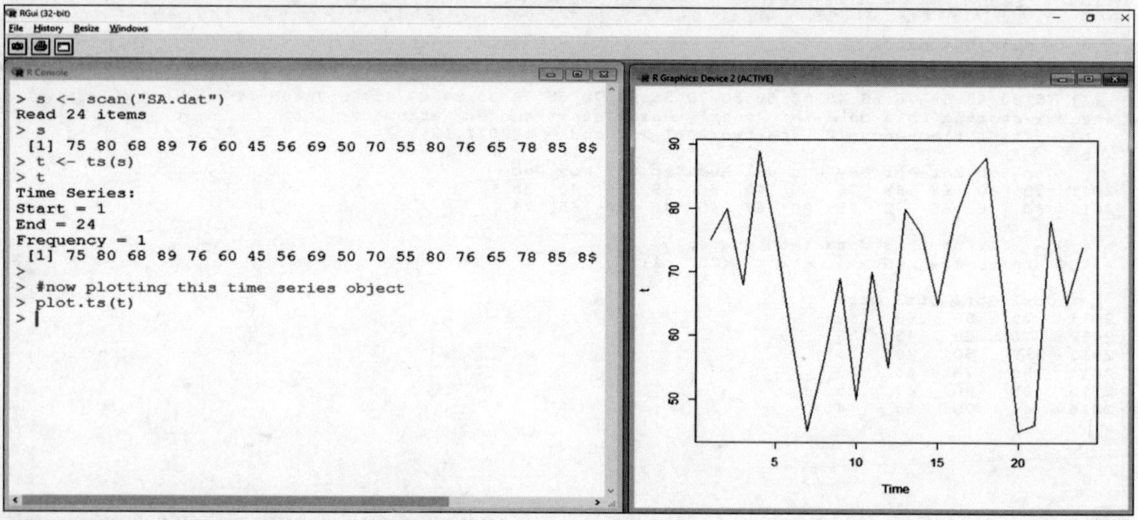

FIGURE 8.25 *Plotting simple time series data*

The following example creates plots of the attendance data of some students over six months. An object *s* stores the time series data and the `ts()` function creates the time series object *t* for this object *s* (Figure 8.26).

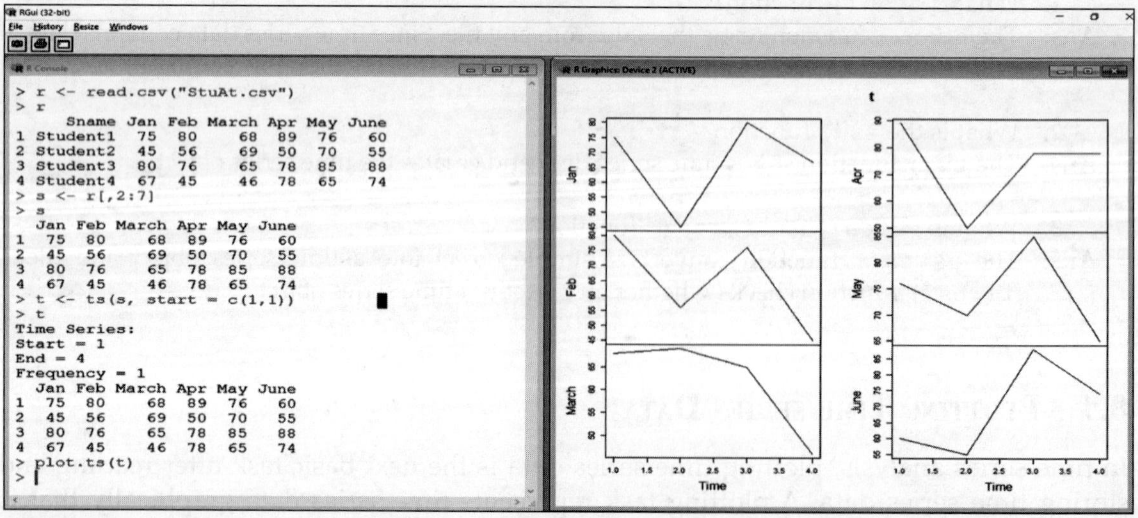

FIGURE 8.26 *Another example of plot of time series data*

8.5 Decomposing Time Series Data

Decomposing time series data is also a part of the simple component analysis that defines four components, viz., trend, seasonal, cyclical and irregular. A time series changes because of seasonal, cyclical or irregular events; hence, the need for generating these four components. The seasonal component contains the data that occurs seasonally every year. For example, fruit prices change according to the season. The cyclical component contains data that changes daily, weekly, monthly or annually. For example, share prices change daily. The irregular component contains the data that occurred at a specific time point but was not related to a season or a cycle. For example, a natural incident or any political event is an example of this sort of irregular data that happens at a specific time.

Decomposing time series data refers to a process that decomposes the given time series data into different components. In business analytics, decomposing is used to find out a particular component of seasonal or non-seasonal time series data. The following subsections describe different methods of decomposition available in R.

8.5.1 Decomposing Non-Seasonal Data

A non-seasonal time series contains the trends and the irregular components; hence, the decomposition process converts the non-seasonal data into these components. An additive model is used for finding out these components of the non-seasonal time series. This additive model uses a smoothing method by calculating the moving average of the time series.

R provides a function `SMA()` that smooths time series data by calculating the moving average and estimates trend and irregular component. The package "TTR" defines this function. The basic syntax of the `SMA()` function is:

```
SMA(x,n,…)
```

where, "x" argument contains the series that defines time series data like price, volume, etc.; the "n" argument contains a numeric value for calculating the average and the dots "…" define other optional arguments.

The following example takes the same time series data that is stored in the file "SA.dat". The time series object *t* stores this data. Figure 8.27 describes the plotting of this time series data. It can be seen from the plot that there are random fluctuations in the attendance data over time. Now `SMA()` uses this data to estimate the trend component of the time series. For this, the function smooths the data using a simple moving average of order 4. Now this smoothed time series data is plotted using the `plot()` function. Figure 8.28 displays the smoothed time series data or the trend component of the time series data, which is smoother than that displayed in Figure 8.27.

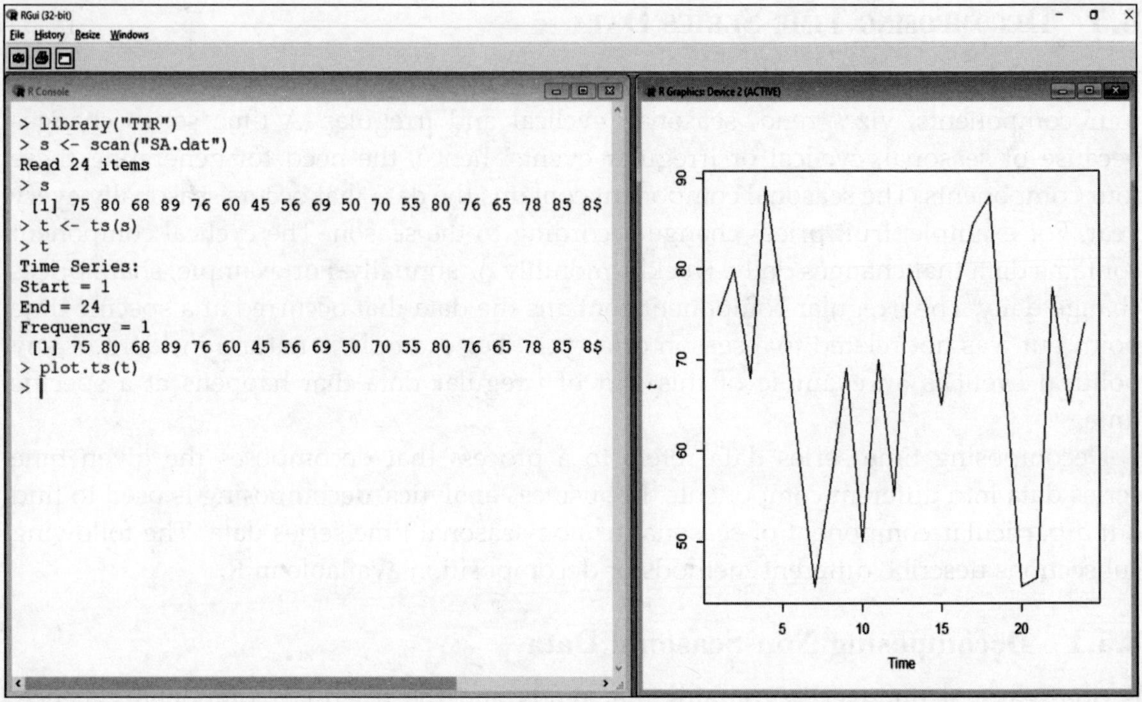

FIGURE 8.27 *Normal plotting of time series data*

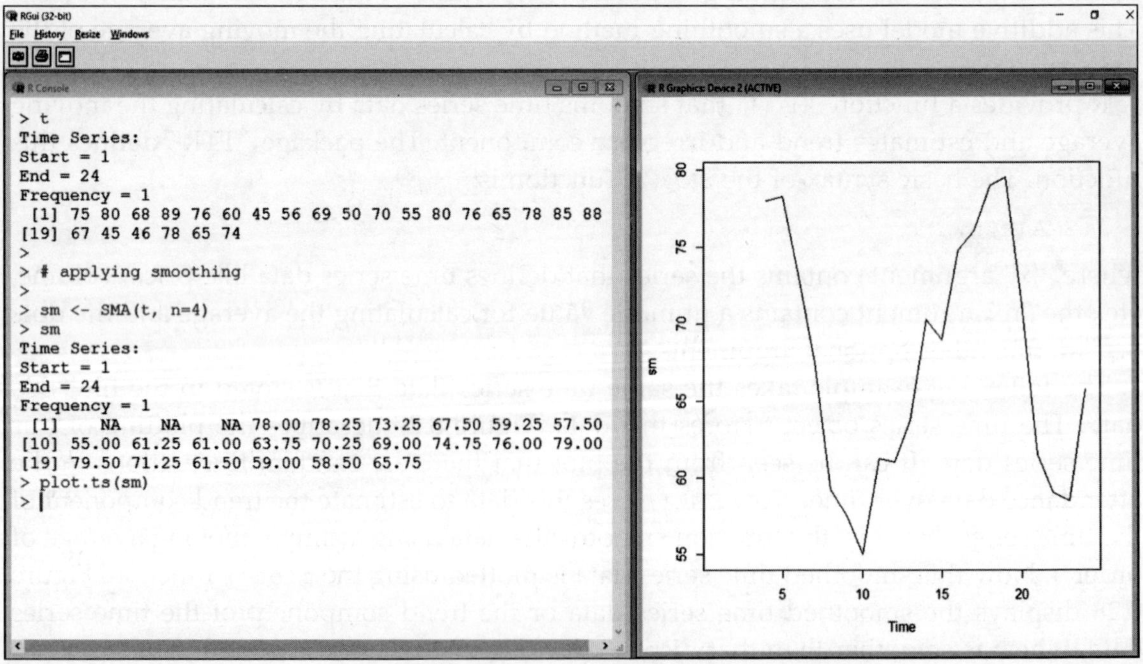

FIGURE 8.28 *Decomposition of the non-seasonal data using the* `SMA()` *function*

If the value of the order argument increases, it will plot more smoothed time series plot. In simple words, a higher value generates the trend component more accurately. Figure 8.29 defines the trend component of time series data using a high order value.

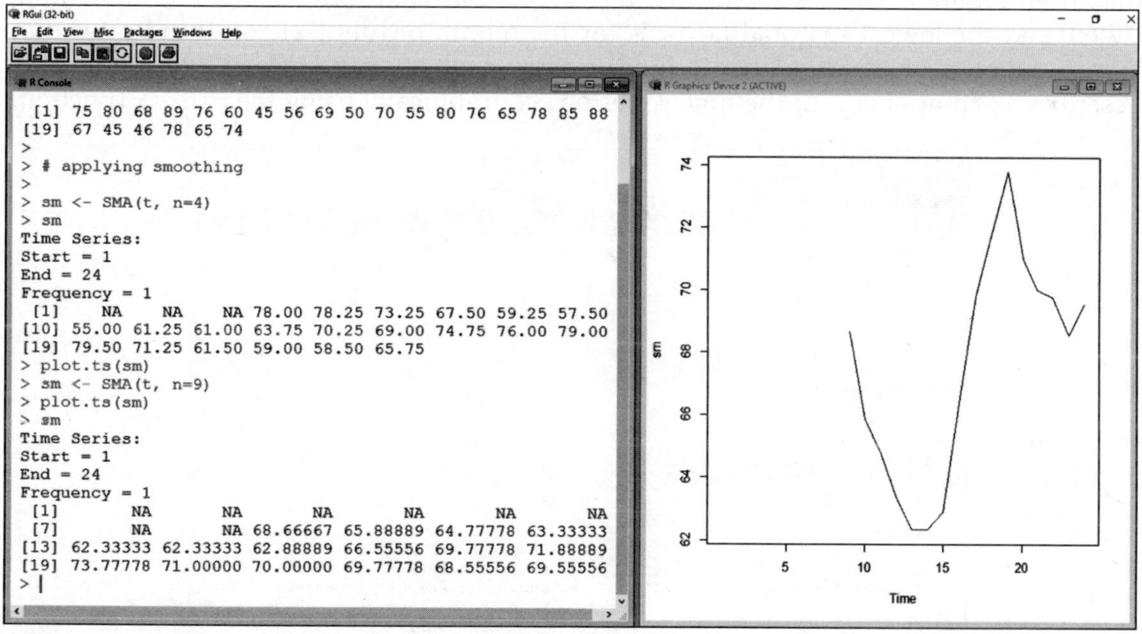

FIGURE 8.29 *Decomposition using* `SMA()` *with high value order for smoothness*

8.5.2 Decomposing Seasonal Data

A seasonal time series contains the seasonal, trend and irregular components; hence, the decomposition process converts the seasonal data into these three components. It also uses an additive model for finding out these components. The additive model calculates the moving average of the time series and smooths the models.

R provides two functions, viz., `decompose()` and `stl()` for the decomposition of seasonal data. A brief introduction to both functions is given as follows.

`decompose()` Function

The `decompose()` function decomposes the time series into seasonal, trend and irregular components. The function also smooths time series data by calculating moving averages. The basic syntax of `decompose()` function is:

```
decompose(x, type, …)
```

where, "x" argument contains a time series object for which components are to be estimated, "type" is an optional argument that defines the type of component to be estimated and the dots "…" define other optional arguments.

The following example creates a time series object *t* of the time series data regarding attendance that is stored in the file "SA.dat". The `decompose()` function returns all these components of this time series object *t* into a form of list objects (Figure 8.30). Along with this, from Figure 8.30, it is found that the largest seasonal factor is for month of June [17.63] and the lowest seasonal factor is for the month of July [-21.86]. It indicates that there is a high peak of attendance in June and low peak of attendance in July. Figure 8.31 describes all components of the time series object graphically using the `plot()` function.

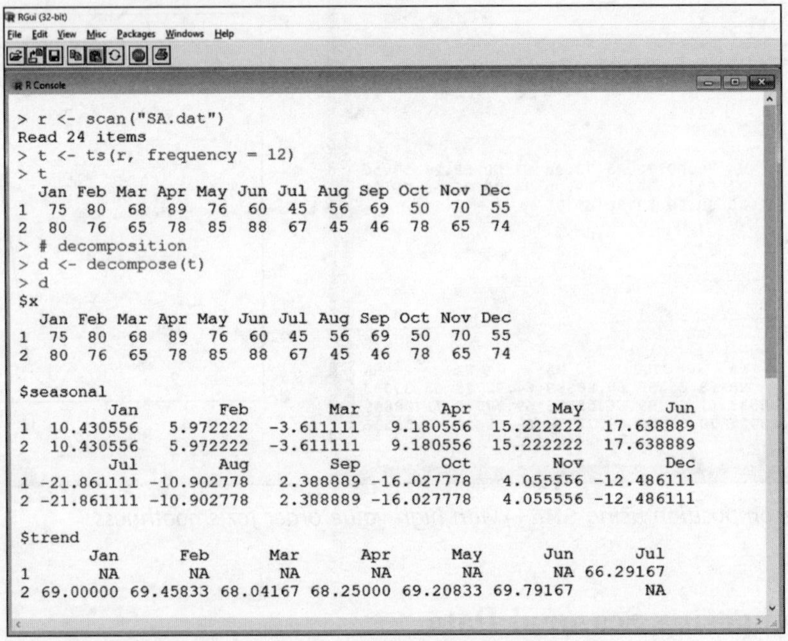

```
RGui (32-bit)
File Edit View Misc Packages Windows Help
R Console
> r <- scan("SA.dat")
Read 24 items
> t <- ts(r, frequency = 12)
> t
  Jan Feb Mar Apr May Jun Jul Aug Sep Oct Nov Dec
1  75  80  68  89  76  60  45  56  69  50  70  55
2  80  76  65  78  85  88  67  45  46  78  65  74
> # decomposition
> d <- decompose(t)
> d
$x
  Jan Feb Mar Apr May Jun Jul Aug Sep Oct Nov Dec
1  75  80  68  89  76  60  45  56  69  50  70  55
2  80  76  65  78  85  88  67  45  46  78  65  74

$seasonal
        Jan        Feb        Mar        Apr        May        Jun
1 10.430556   5.972222  -3.611111   9.180556  15.222222  17.638889
2 10.430556   5.972222  -3.611111   9.180556  15.222222  17.638889
        Jul        Aug        Sep        Oct        Nov        Dec
1 -21.861111 -10.902778   2.388889 -16.027778   4.055556 -12.486111
2 -21.861111 -10.902778   2.388889 -16.027778   4.055556 -12.486111

$trend
       Jan      Feb      Mar      Apr      May      Jun      Jul
1       NA       NA       NA       NA       NA       NA 66.29167
2 69.00000 69.45833 68.04167 68.25000 69.20833 69.79167       NA
```

FIGURE 8.30 *Decomposing seasonal data using the* `decompose()` *function*

`stl()` Function

The seasonal trend decomposition (STL) is an algorithm that uses non-parametric regression methods for calculating the components. R provides the function `stl()` for decomposing seasonal data using "loess" regression. The function estimates the seasonal and trend components of the given time series data. The basic syntax of the `stl()` function is:

```
stl(x, s. Window,...)
```

where, "x" argument contains a time series object for which components are to be estimated, "s. Window" contains either the character string "periodic" or numeric number (which should be odd and at least contain the value 7) and the dots "..." define the other optional arguments.

The following example creates a time series object *t* of the time series data stored in the file "SA.dat". The `stl()` function returns all seasonal, trend and remainder components of this time series object t into a form of list objects (Figure 8.32). Figure 8.33 describes all these components of the time series objects graphically using the `plot()` function.

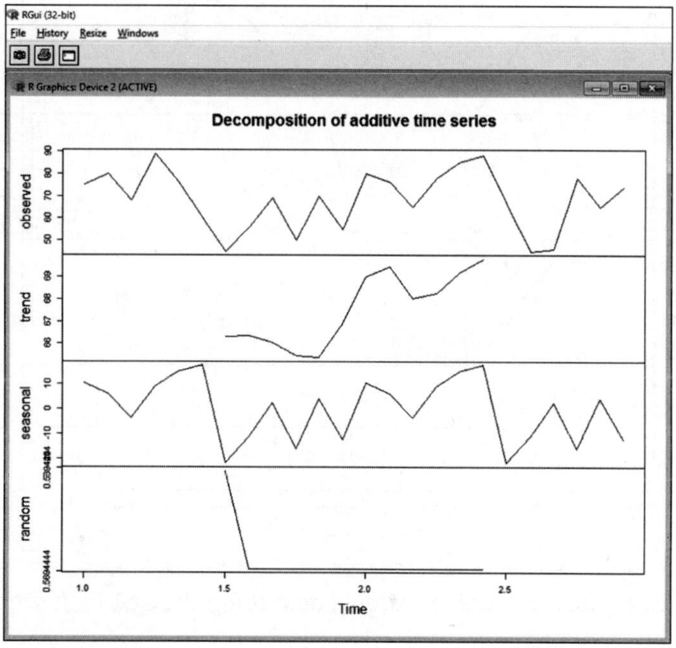

FIGURE 8.31 *Generated components of the seasonal data*

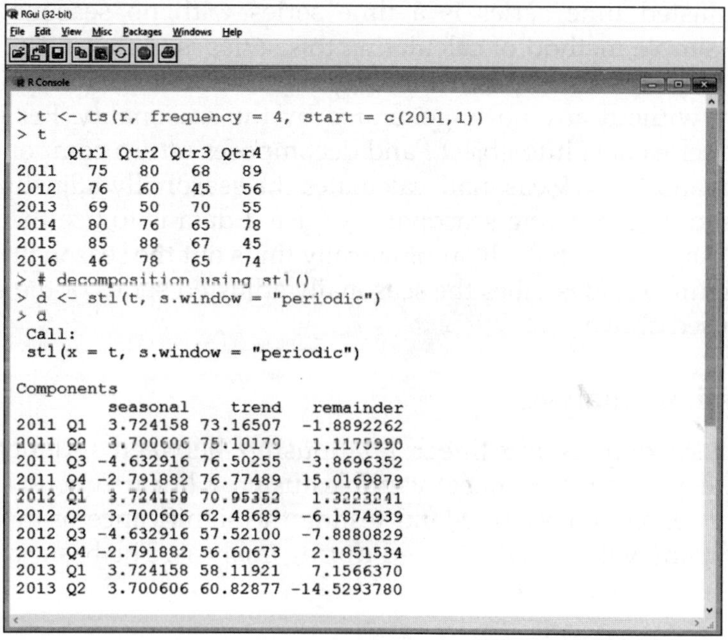

```
> t <- ts(r, frequency = 4, start = c(2011,1))
> t
     Qtr1 Qtr2 Qtr3 Qtr4
2011   75   80   68   89
2012   76   60   45   56
2013   69   50   70   55
2014   80   76   65   78
2015   85   88   67   45
2016   46   78   65   74
> # decomposition using stl()
> d <- stl(t, s.window = "periodic")
> d
 Call:
 stl(x = t, s.window = "periodic")

Components
         seasonal    trend   remainder
2011 Q1  3.724158 73.16507  -1.8892262
2011 Q2  3.700606 75.10179   1.1175990
2011 Q3 -4.632916 76.50255  -3.8696352
2011 Q4 -2.791882 76.77489  15.0169879
2012 Q1  3.724158 70.95352   1.3223241
2012 Q2  3.700606 62.48689  -6.1874939
2012 Q3 -4.632916 57.52100  -7.8880829
2012 Q4 -2.791882 56.60673   2.1851534
2013 Q1  3.724158 58.11921   7.1566370
2013 Q2  3.700606 60.82877 -14.5293780
```

FIGURE 8.32 *Decomposing seasonal data using the* `stl()` *function*

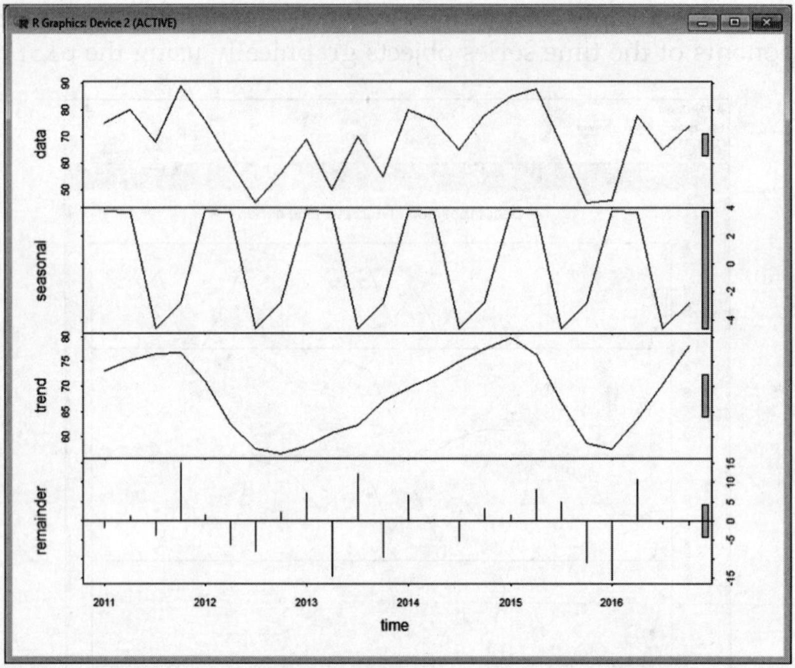

FIGURE 8.33 *Generated components of the seasonal data using the* `stl()` *function*

8.5.3 Seasonal Adjustment

A seasonally adjusted time series is a time series with no seasonality or seasonal component. The simple method of calculating this series is to first calculate the seasonal component and then remove it from the original time series. This series provides the trend component without any noise generated by the seasonality. For example, Figure 8.34 reads a time series data into object *t* and decomposes return components in an object *d*. Now the command "t – d$seasonal" calculates the seasonally adjusting component.

Another method of generating seasonally adjusted data is to use the inbuilt function `seas()` of the package "seasonal". It automatically finds out the seasonally adjusted series. The following Figure 8.35 describes the seasonally adjusted series of the same time series data as the one used above.

8.5.4 Regression Analysis

Regression analysis defines the linear relationship between independent variables (predictors) and dependent (response) variables using a linear function. R provides the `lm()` function for regression analysis and testing the significance of the coefficient. The function returns many values that are used during analysis. The basic syntax of function `lm()` is:

```
lm(formula, data, …)
```

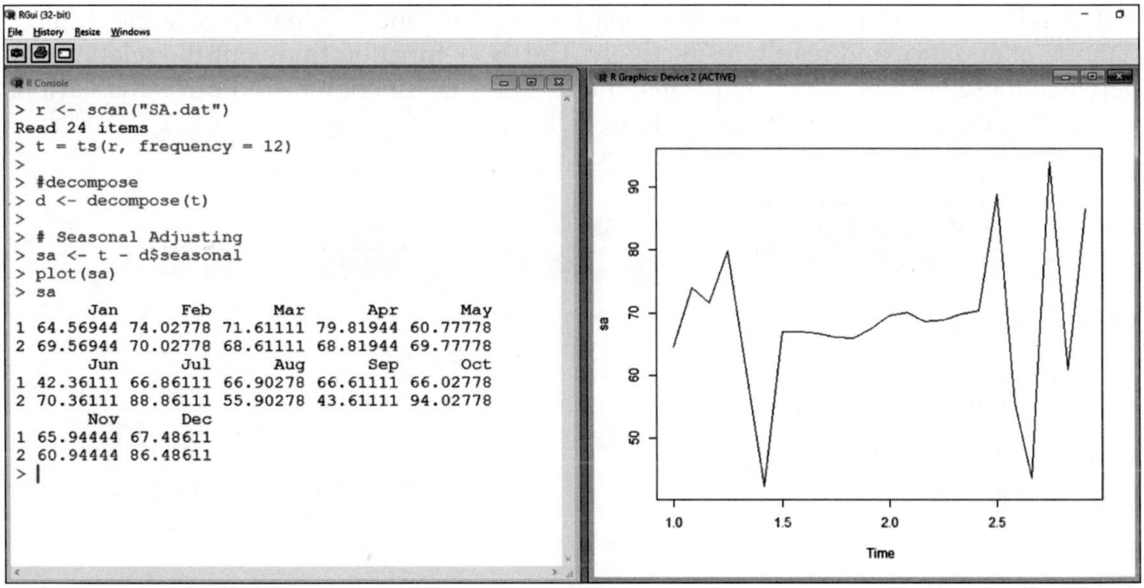

FIGURE 8.34 *Seasonally adjusting data using difference method*

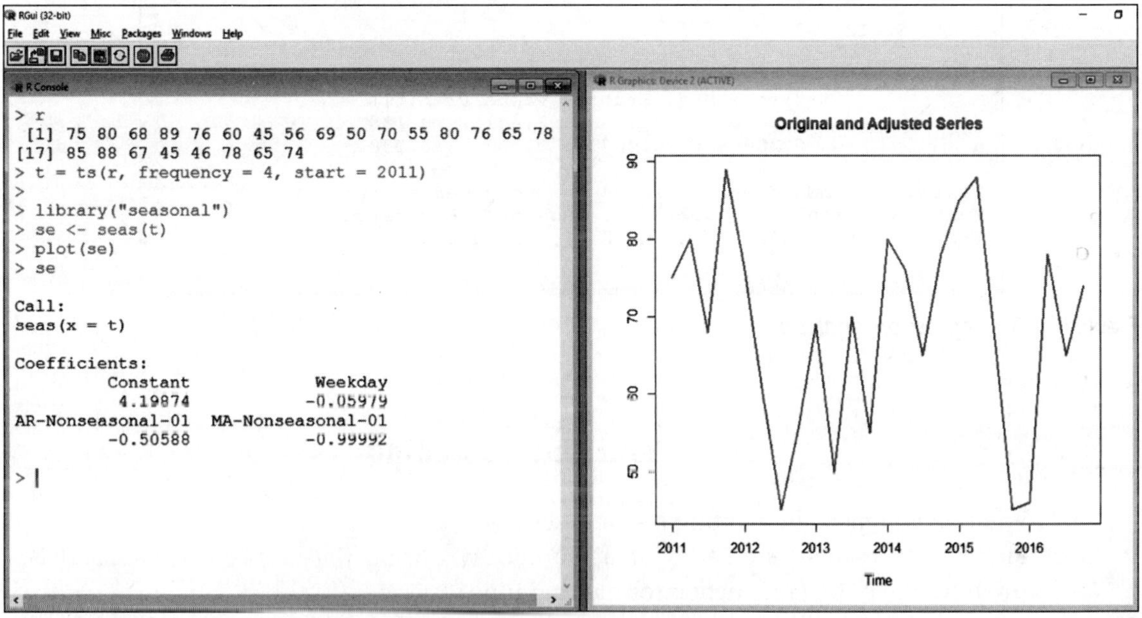

FIGURE 8.35 *Seasonally adjusting using the* `seas()` *function*

where, "formula" argument represents an object of class "formula" and defines the symbolic description of the model to be fitted; "data" is an optional argument that may be a data frame, list or an object and the dots "…" define the other optional arguments.

The following example creates two vectors, viz., "a" and "r" that store some dummy data on attendance and result, respectively. The `lm()` function finds out the relationship between these vectors. Along with this, the `summary()` function also returns the various values that describe the coefficient (Figure 8.36).

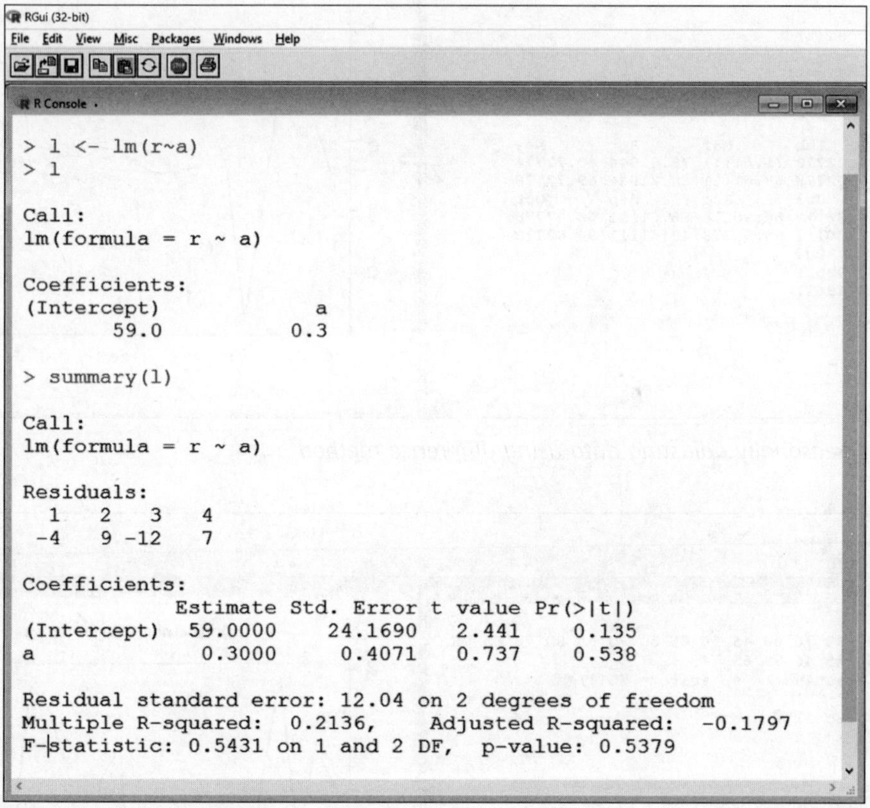

FIGURE 8.36 *Regression analysis*

Check Your Understanding

1. What do you mean by plotting the time series?

Ans: Plotting represents time series data graphically during time series analysis and R provides the `plot()` function for plotting time series data.

2. What do you mean by decomposing a time series?

Ans: Decomposing a time series is a process that decomposes the given time series data into different components.

(Continued)

3. What is the `SMA()` function ?

Ans: The `SMA()` function is used for the decomposition of the non-seasonal time series. It smooths time series data by calculating the moving average and estimates the trend and irregular components. The function is available in the package "TTR".

4. What is the `decompose()` function?

Ans: The `decompose()` function is used for the decomposition of the seasonal time series. It decomposes the time series into the seasonal, trend and irregular components and smooths time series data by calculating the moving averages.

5. What is the use of the `lm()` function?

Ans: The `lm()` function is used for regression analysis and for testing the significance of the coefficient. The function returns many values that are useful for time series analysis.

8.6 Forecasts Using Exponential Smoothing

Forecasts are a type of prediction that predict future events from past data. Here, the forecast process uses exponential smoothing for making predictions. An exponential smoothing method finds out the changes in time series data by ignoring the irrelevant fluctuations and makes the short-term forecast prediction for time series data.

The following subsection describes three types of exponential smoothing. All of them use a common inbuilt function `HoltWinters()` of R but with different parameters. The basic syntax of the `HoltWinters()` function is:

```
HoltWinters(x, alpha = NULL, beta = NULL, gamma = NULL, ...)
```

where, "x" argument contains any time series object, "alpha" argument defines the alpha parameter of Holt-Winters Filter, "beta" argument defines the beta parameter of the Holt-winters Filter (For exponential smoothing, it is set to FALSE), "gamma" argument defines the seasonal component (for non-seasonal model, it is set to FALSE) and the dots "..." define the other optional arguments.

The `HoltWinters()` function returns a value between 0 and 1 of all three parameters (alpha, beta and gamma). If the value is near zero, then it indicates that forecasts are done on less recent observation and if the value is near to one, then it indicates that forecasts are done on the most recent observation. Brief introductions to each type of exponential smoothing are given ahead.

8.6.1 Simple Exponential Smoothing

A simple exponential smoothing estimates the level at the current time point and performs the short-term forecast. The alpha parameter of the `HoltWinters()` function controls the simple exponential smoothing. To implement simple exponential smoothing, it is necessary to set the beta and gamma parameters to FALSE in the `HoltWinters()` function.

In the following example, the `ts()` function creates a time series object a of time series data stored in the file "Attendance.txt". The `HoltWinters()` function implements the exponential smoothing without any trend and seasonal component. The value of the alpha parameter is 0.030. Since this value is near to zero, we know that forecasts are done on both recent and less recent observations. Along with this, in the generated plot, the vertical zigzag lines represent the original time series and the single horizontal vertical line represents the forecast. The forecast line is smoother than the original time series (Figure 8.37).

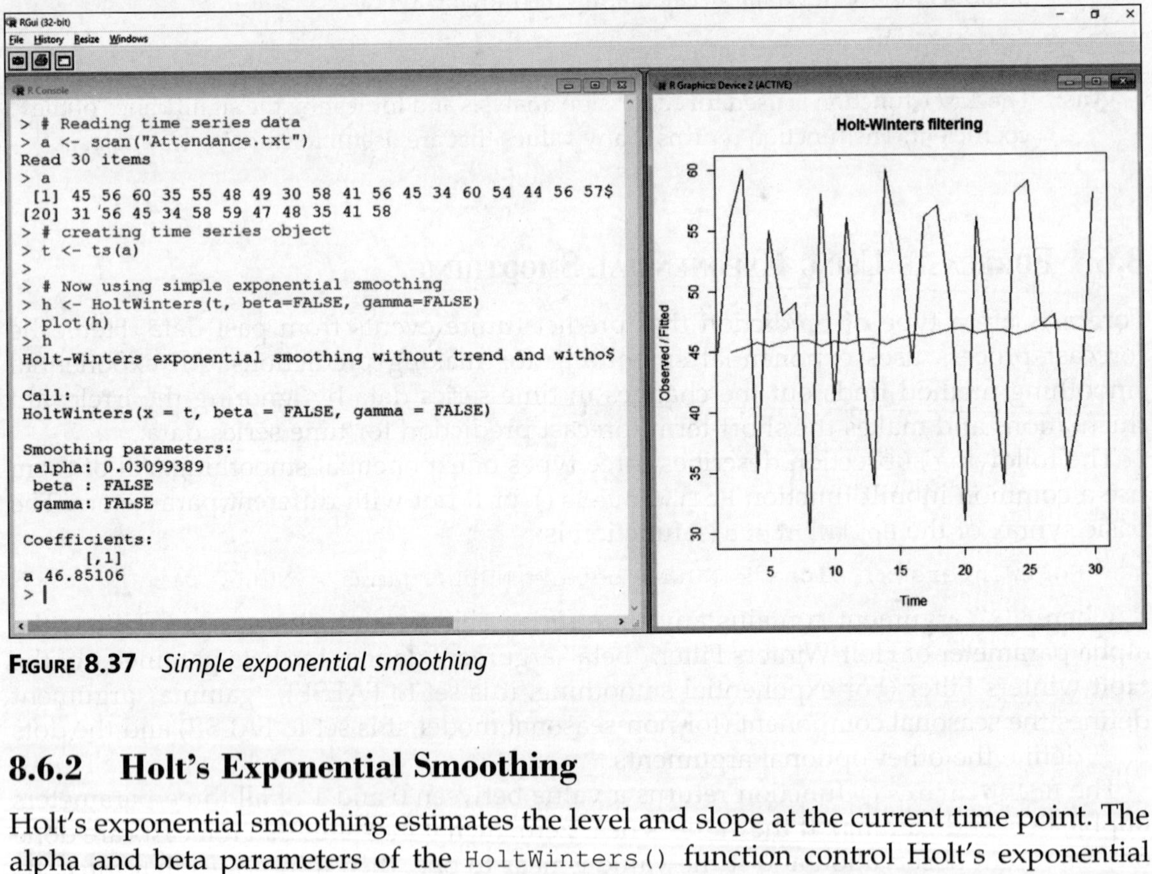

FIGURE 8.37 *Simple exponential smoothing*

8.6.2 Holt's Exponential Smoothing

Holt's exponential smoothing estimates the level and slope at the current time point. The alpha and beta parameters of the `HoltWinters()` function control Holt's exponential smoothing and estimate the level and slope, respectively. It is the best method for time series containing trend components. To implement this smoothing, it is necessary to set the gamma parameter to FALSE in the `HoltWinters()` function.

In the following example, the `ts()` function creates a time series object *a* of time series data stored in the file "Attendance.txt". The `HoltWinters()` function implements Holt's exponential smoothing with trend components but does not contain any seasonal component. The values of alpha and beta parameters are near to zero, indicating forecasts are done on less recent observations in the time series. In the generated plot, the black vertical zigzag lines represent the original time series and the grey vertical zigzag lines represent the forecast. Since both the lines are not smooth, the forecast agrees with the observed original time series (Figure 8.38).

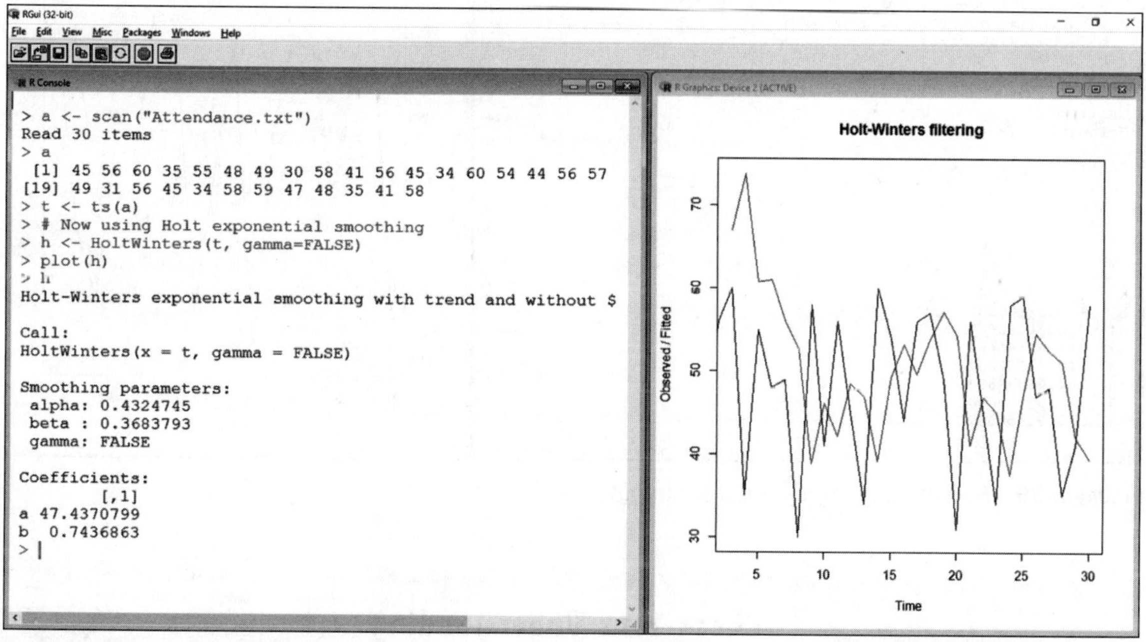

FIGURE 8.38 *Holt's exponential smoothing*

8.6.3 Holt-Winters Exponential Smoothing

Holt-Winters exponential smoothing estimates the level, slope and seasonal component at the current time point. The alpha, beta and gamma parameters of the `HoltWinters()` function controls the Holt-Winters exponential smoothing and estimates the level, slope of trend component and seasonal component, respectively. It is the best smoothing method for time series containing trend and seasonal components. To implement this smoothing, only time series objects need to pass in the `HoltWinters()` function.

In the following example, the `ts()` function creates a time series object *a* of time series data stored in the file "Attendance.txt". The `HoltWinters()` function implements the Holt-Winters exponential smoothing with trend and seasonal components. The values of all parameters are zero, indicating that forecasts are done on less recent observations in the time series. Just like the above example, in the following generated plot, the black vertical zigzag lines represent the original time series and the grey vertical zigzag lines represent the forecast (Figure 8.39).

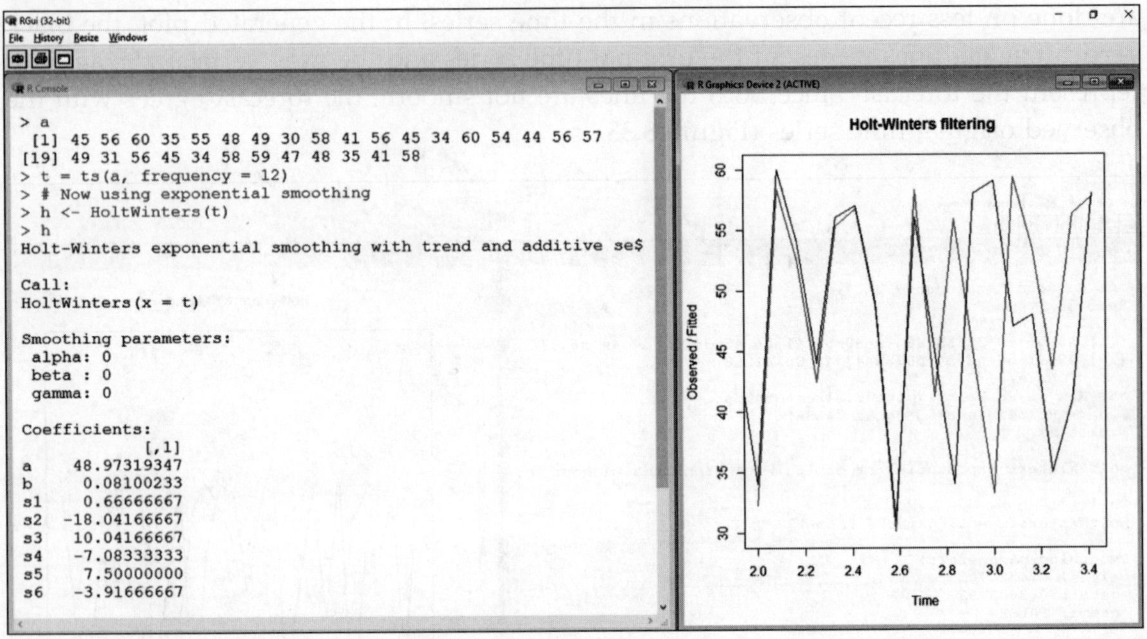

FIGURE 8.39 *Holt-Winters exponential smoothing*

Check Your Understanding

1. What do you mean by exponential smoothing?

Ans: Exponential smoothing method finds out the changes in time series data by ignoring the irrelevant fluctuations and makes the short-term forecast prediction for time series data.

2. What is the `HoltWinters()` function?

Ans: The `HoltWinters()` function is an inbuilt function, commonly used for finding exponential smoothing. All three types of exponential smoothing use the `HoltWinters()` function but with different parameters. The `HoltWinters()` function returns a value between 0 and 1 for all the three parameters, viz., alpha, beta and gamma.

3. What is the function of Holt's exponential smoothing?

Ans: Holt's exponential smoothing estimates the level and slope at the current time point. The alpha and beta parameters of the `HoltWinters()` function controls it and estimates the level and slope, respectively.

8.7 ARIMA Models

ARIMA (Autoregressive Integrated Moving Average) is another method of time series forecasting. The exponential models make short-term forecasts without using correlation between the successive values of the time series. However, sometimes a correlation requires forecasting some irregular components. In this case, the ARIMA model is best suited for forecasting. The ARIMA model explicitly defines the irregular components of a stationary time series with non-zero autocorrelation.

The ARIMA model is represented by ARIMA(p,d,q) where parameters p, d and q defines the autoregression (AR) order, the degree of differencing and the moving average (MA) order, respectively. It follows some stages such as model estimation, parameter checking, forecasting, analysis and diagnostic for finding a suitable model for any time series data. A brief introduction to each stage is given ahead.

8.7.1 Differencing a Time Series

Differencing a time series is the first step for finding an appropriate ARIMA model. The ARIMA model is basically used for a stationary time series; hence, for a non-stationary time series it is necessary to difference the time series until a stationary time series is not obtained. R provides a `diff()` function for finding out the difference. For obtaining a stationary time series, it is necessary to pass the value of difference variable (d) of the ARIMA model in the `diff()` function. The basic syntax of the `diff()` function is:

```
diff(x, differences, …)
```

where, "x" argument contains an object to differentiate, "differences" argument contains a numeric value that defines the order of difference and the dots "…" define the other optional arguments.

In the following example, the `ts()` function creates a time series object "ax" of the time series data stored in the file "Attendance.txt". The `diff()` function performs difference on this object "ax" where the order of the difference is 2. After placing several values for the difference argument, 2 is taken for the order of difference since it appears stationary in mean and variance (Figure 8.41).

8.7.2 Selecting a Candidate ARIMA Model

Now the next step in finding an appropriate ARIMA model is to analyse the autocorrelation and partial autocorrelation of the stationary time series. This analysis helps to find the most appropriate values of p and q for an ARIMA(p, d, q) model. R language provides the `acf()` and `pacf()` functions for finding the actual values of the autocorrelation [q] and the partial autocorrelation [p] of the time series, respectively. The basic syntax of the `acf()` and `pacf()` functions are:

```
acf(x,lag.max = NULL, …)
pacf(x, lag.max = NULL,…)
```

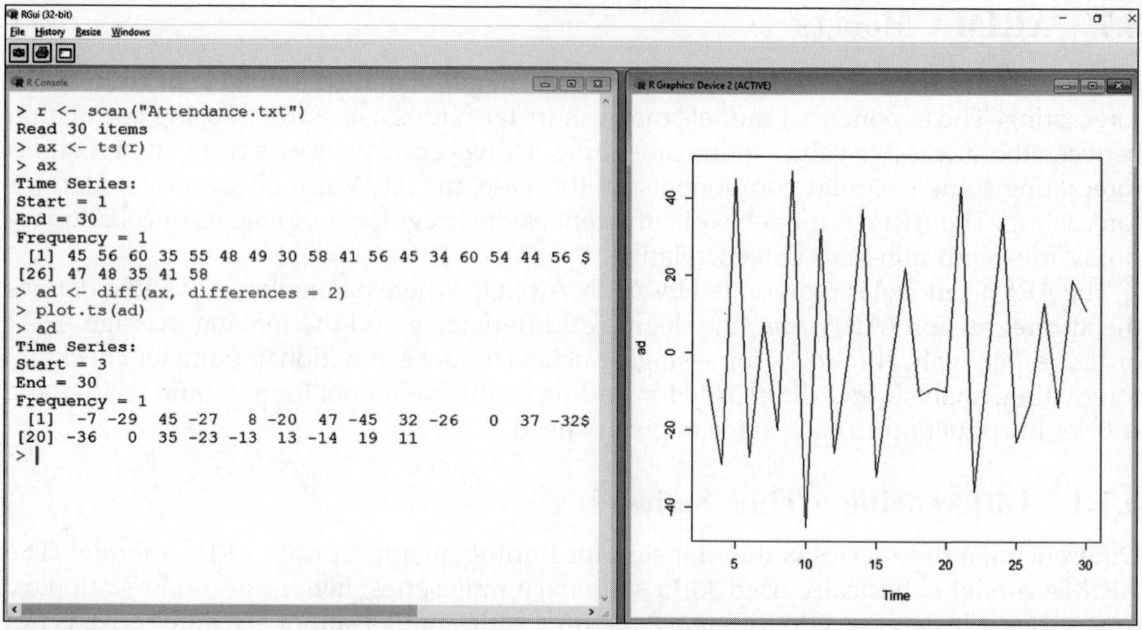

FIGURE 8.41 *Differencing a time series using the* `diff()` *function*

where, "x" argument contains any time series object or vector, lag.max is an optional argument that defines the maximum lag at which to calculate ACF or PACF and the dots "..." define the other optional arguments.

In the following example, we see the differentiated time series object "ad" that was generated by the `diff()` function in the example given in the previous subsection. The `acf()` and `pacf()` functions calculate the actual values of the autocorrelation and partial autocorrelation of the differentiated time series, respectively. Figure 8.42 is describing the ACF and in the generated plot, since the line at lag 1 goes beyond the dotted line; hence, the value of the autocorrelation at lag 1 exceeds the significance bounds. Figure 8.43 is describing the partial ACF and in the generated plot, since all lines at lags 1, 2 and 3 are going beyond the dotted line; hence, the value of the partial autocorrelation at these lags exceeds the significance bounds.

According to the value of autocorrelation and partial correlation, a suitable ARIMA(p, d, q) model is selected. Along with this, R also provides an inbuilt function `auto.arima()` that automatically returns the best candidate ARIMA(p, d, q) model for the given time series.

8.7.3 Forecasting Using an ARIMA Model

After selecting the suitable candidate ARIMA(p, d, q) model, parameters of the selected ARIMA(p, d, q) model is found out. These values are also used for defining the predictive model that makes the forecasts for the time series. R provides the `arima()` function that finds out the parameters of the selected ARIMA(p, d, q) model. The basic syntax of the `arima()` function is:

```
arima(x, order(0L, 0L, 0L), …)
```

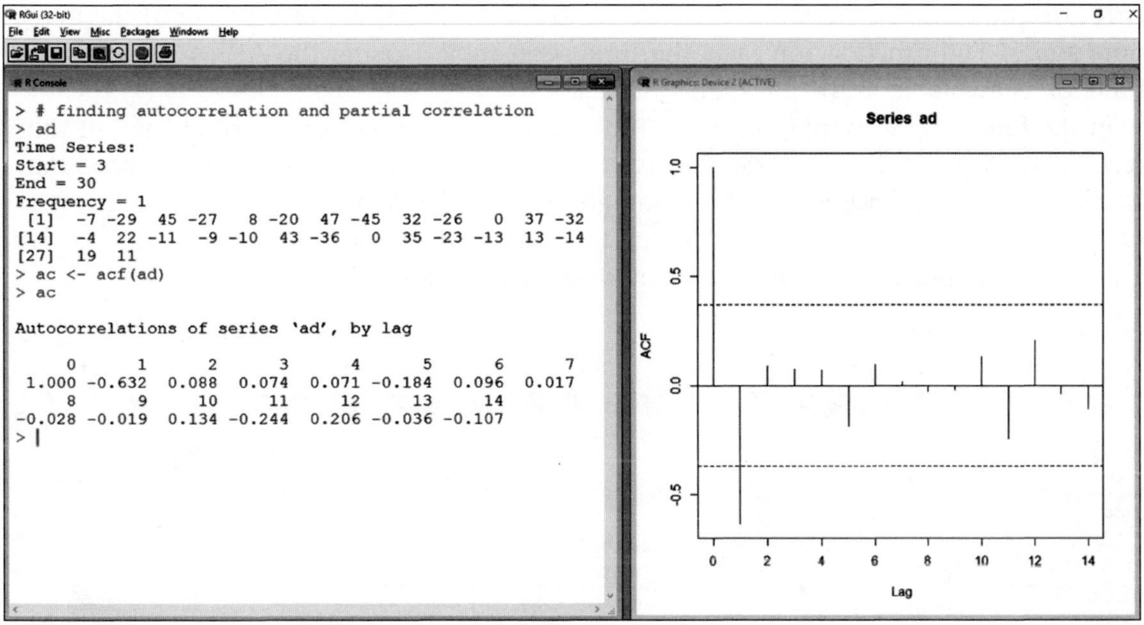

FIGURE 8.42 *Autocorrelation using the* `acf()` *function*

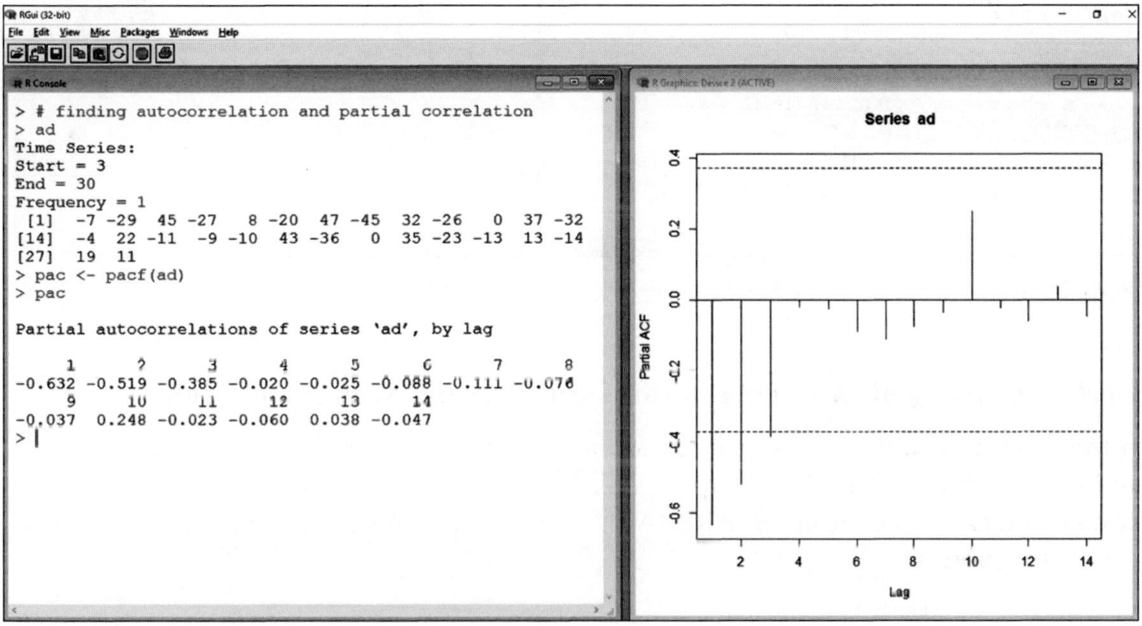

FIGURE 8.43 *Partial autocorrelation using the* `pacf()` *function*

where, "x" argument contains a time series object, order argument defines the order component of ARIMA(p, d, q) model and the dots "…" define the other optional arguments.

R also provides the function `forecast.Arima()` for making forecasting of the given time series. The function forecasts the time series object using the ARIMA model. The function is available in the package "forecast".

In the following example, the `ts()` function creates a time series object "ax" of time series data stored in the file "Attendance.txt". Here ARIMA(0,2,1) is selected as a candidate ARIMA model for finding out the parameters of the ARIMA model using the `arima()` function. The `forecast.Arima()` forecasts the output of ARIMA model ["af"]. Figure 8.44 also describes the plot of the obtained forecast values.

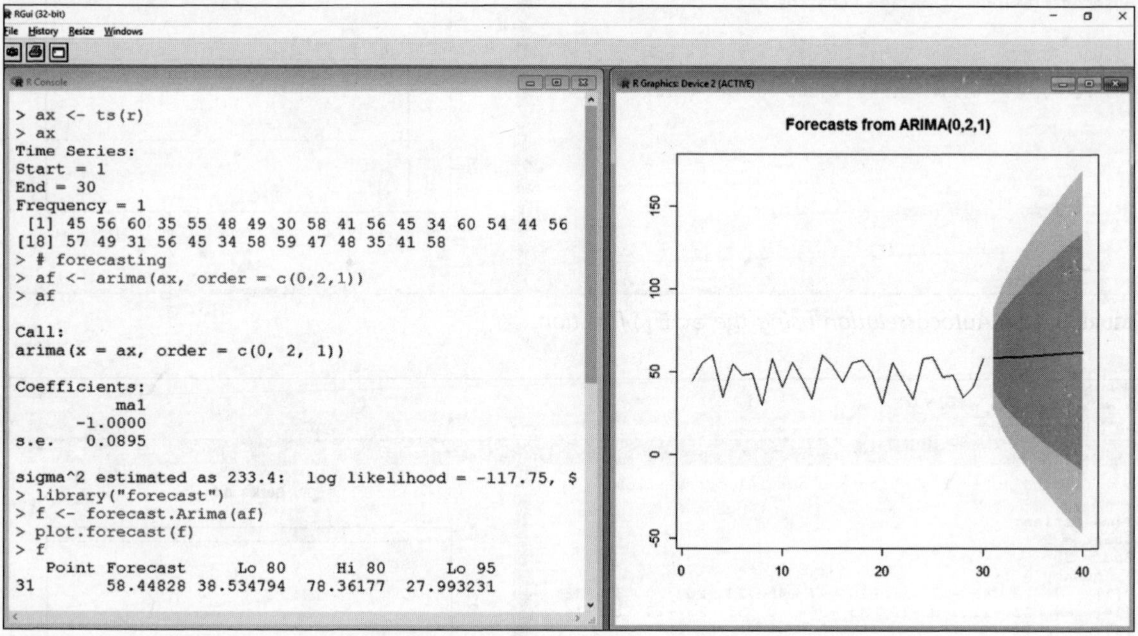

Figure 8.44 *Forecasting using ARIMA model*

8.7.4 Analysis of Autocorrelations and Partial Autocorrelations

In this step, the values of autocorrelation and partial autocorrelation are analysed and simulated from an ARIMA(p, d, q) model. R provides the function `arima.sim()` that simulates these values from an ARIMA(p, d, q) model. The basic syntax of the `arima.sim()` function is:

```
arima.sim(model, n, …)
```

where, "model" argument contains a list that defines the coefficients of the component AR and/or MA. In addition, an optional component order can also be used, "n" argument contains a positive value for defining the number of output series and the dots "..." define the other optional arguments.

In the following example, some dummy values of AR and MA coefficients are taken according to the calculation done in the previous subsections. The `arima.sim()` function now simulates it into an object "as". Figure 8.45 also gives a corresponding plot of this object.

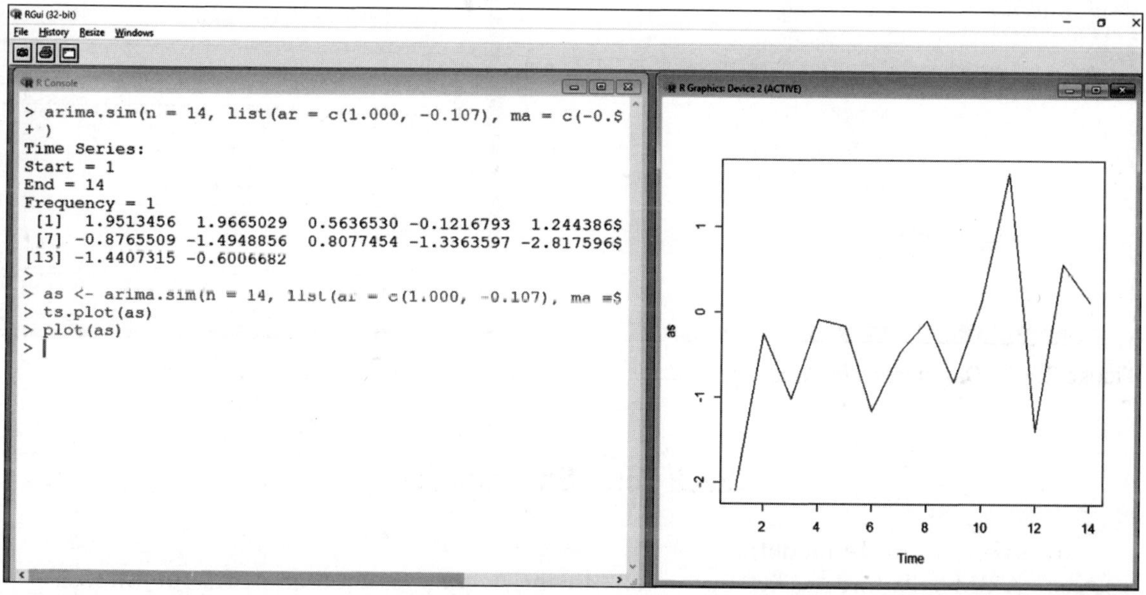

FIGURE 8.45 *Analysis of ACF and PACF using the* `arima.sim()` *function*

8.7.5 Diagnostic Checking

Diagnostic checking is the last step in fitting an ARIMA model process. It checks the residuals from the fit model. R provides the function `tsdiag()` that creates a diagnostic plot for the time series fitted model. The function returns three plots, viz., "Standardised residuals plot", "ACF of residuals plot" and "plot defining the p-values of the Ljung-Box statistic". The basic syntax of the `tsdiag()` function is:

```
tsdiag(object, ...)
```

where, "object" argument contains a time series fitted model and the dots "..." define the other optional arguments.

In the following example, the `tsdiag()` function takes a fitted model "af" obtained in the previous subsection. Figure 8.46 describes all three plots of the corresponding fitted model.

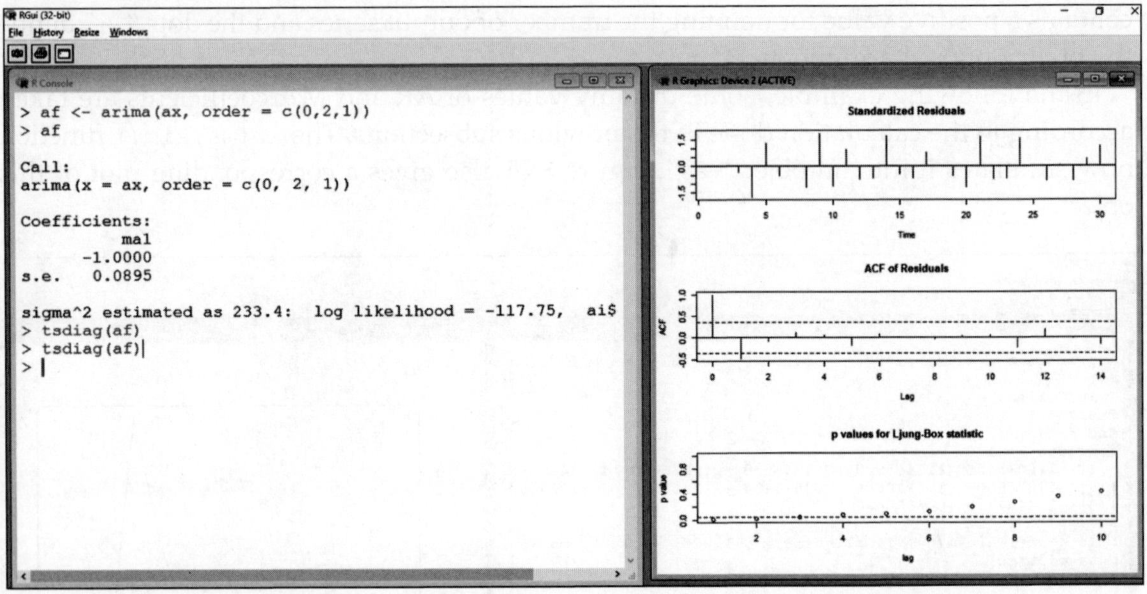

FIGURE 8.46 *Diagnostic checking and plot for fitted model using the* `tsdiag()` *function*

Check Your Understanding

1. What is ARIMA model?

Ans: ARIMA (Autoregressive Integrated Moving Average) is another method of time series forecasting. The ARIMA model explicitly defines the irregular component of a stationary time series with non-zero autocorrelation. It is represented by ARIMA(p,d,q) where parameters p, d and q define the autoregression (AR) order, the degree of differencing and the moving average (MA) order, respectively.

2. What is the use of `acf()` and `pacf()` functions in ARIMA modelling?

Ans: The `acf()` and `pacf()` functions determine the actual values of the autocorrelation [q] and partial autocorrelation [p] of the time series, respectively, for an ARIMA(p, q, r) model.

3. What is the use of the `forecast.Arima()` function?

Ans: The `forecast.Arima()` function makes the forecasting of the given time series using an ARIMA model. The function is available in the package "forecast".

4. What is the use of the `tsdiag()` function?

Ans: The `tsdiag()` function creates a diagnostic plot for the time series fitted model and checks the residuals from the fit model. It returns three plots, viz., "Standardised residuals plot", "ACF of residuals plot" and "plot defining the p-values of the Ljung-Box statistic".

Practical Assignment

Let us analyse the "AirPassengers" data set. It is a classic Box and Jenkins airline data. The data set has monthly airline passenger numbers from 1st January, 1949 to 31st December, 1960.

Step 1: Display the data stored in the data set "AirPassengers".

```
> AirPassengers
     Jan Feb Mar Apr May Jun Jul Aug Sep Oct Nov Dec
1949 112 118 132 129 121 135 148 148 136 119 104 118
1950 115 126 141 135 125 149 170 170 158 133 114 140
1951 145 150 178 163 172 178 199 199 184 162 146 166
1952 171 180 193 181 183 218 230 242 209 191 172 194
1953 196 196 236 235 229 243 264 272 237 211 180 201
1954 204 188 235 227 234 264 302 293 259 229 203 229
1955 242 233 267 269 270 315 364 347 312 274 237 278
1956 284 277 317 313 318 374 413 405 355 306 271 306
1957 315 301 356 348 355 422 465 467 404 347 305 336
1958 340 318 362 348 363 435 491 505 404 359 310 337
1959 360 342 406 396 420 472 548 559 463 407 362 405
1960 417 391 419 461 472 535 622 606 508 461 390 432
```

Step 2: Decompose the time series "AirPassengers" into three components, viz., trend, seasonal and irregular. The function "decompose()" returns a list object, where the estimates of the seasonal, trend and irregular components are stored in named elements of that list objects, called "seasonal", "trend", and "random", respectively.

```
> passengers <- decompose(AirPassengers)
> passengers
$x
     Jan Feb Mar Apr May Jun Jul Aug Sep Oct Nov Dec
1949 112 118 132 129 121 135 148 148 136 119 104 118
1950 115 126 141 135 125 149 170 170 158 133 114 140
1951 145 150 178 163 172 178 199 199 184 162 146 166
1952 171 180 193 181 183 218 230 242 209 191 172 194
1953 196 196 236 235 229 243 264 272 237 211 180 201
1954 204 188 235 227 234 264 302 293 259 229 203 229
1955 242 233 267 269 270 315 364 347 312 274 237 270
1956 284 277 317 313 318 374 413 405 355 306 271 306
1957 315 301 356 348 355 422 465 467 404 347 305 336
1958 340 318 362 348 363 435 491 505 404 359 310 337
1959 360 342 406 396 420 472 548 559 463 407 362 405
1960 417 391 419 461 472 535 622 606 508 461 390 432

$seasonal
            Jan        Feb        Mar        Apr        May        Jun
1949 -24.748737 -36.188131  -2.241162  -8.036616  -4.506313  35.402778
1950 -24.748737 -36.188131  -2.241162  -8.036616  -4.506313  35.402778
1951 -24.748737 -36.188131  -2.241162  -8.036616  -4.506313  35.402778
1952 -24.748737 -36.188131  -2.241162  -8.036616  -4.506313  35.402778
1953 -24.748737 -36.188131  -2.241162  -8.036616  -4.506313  35.402778
1954 -24.748737 -36.188131  -2.241162  -8.036616  -4.506313  35.402778
1955 -24.748737 -36.188131  -2.241162  -8.036616  -4.506313  35.402778
```

```
1956 -24.748737 -36.188131  -2.241162  -8.036616  -4.506313  35.402778
1957 -24.748737 -36.188131  -2.241162  -8.036616  -4.506313  35.402778
1958 -24.748737 -36.188131  -2.241162  -8.036616  -4.506313  35.402778
1959 -24.748737 -36.188131  -2.241162  -8.036616  -4.506313  35.402778
1960 -24.748737 -36.188131  -2.241162  -8.036616  -4.506313  35.402778
            Jul        Aug        Sep        Oct        Nov        Dec
1949  63.830808  62.823232  16.520202 -20.642677 -53.593434 -28.619949
1950  63.830808  62.823232  16.520202 -20.642677 -53.593434 -28.619949
1951  63.830808  62.823232  16.520202 -20.642677 -53.593434 -28.619949
1952  63.830808  62.823232  16.520202 -20.642677 -53.593434 -28.619949
1953  63.830808  62.823232  16.520202 -20.642677 -53.593434 -28.619949
1954  63.830808  62.823232  16.520202 -20.642677 -53.593434 -28.619949
1955  63.830808  62.823232  16.520202 -20.642677 -53.593434 -28.619949
1956  63.830808  62.823232  16.520202 -20.642677 -53.593434 -28.619949
1957  63.830808  62.823232  16.520202 -20.642677 -53.593434 -28.619949
1958  63.830808  62.823232  16.520202 -20.642677 -53.593434 -28.619949
1959  63.830808  62.823232  16.520202 -20.642677 -53.593434 -28.619949
1960  63.830808  62.823232  16.520202 -20.642677 -53.593434 -28.619949

$trend
          Jan      Feb      Mar      Apr      May      Jun      Jul      Aug
1949       NA       NA       NA       NA       NA       NA 126.7917 127.2500
1950 131.2500 133.0833 134.9167 136.4167 137.4167 138.7500 140.9167 143.1667
1951 157.1250 159.5417 161.8333 164.1250 166.6667 169.0833 171.2500 173.5833
1952 183.1250 186.2083 189.0417 191.2917 193.5833 195.8333 198.0417 199.7500
1953 215.8333 218.5000 220.9167 222.9167 224.0833 224.7083 225.3333 225.3333
1954 228.0000 230.4583 232.2500 233.9167 235.6250 237.7500 240.5000 243.9583
1955 261.8333 266.6667 271.1250 275.2083 278.5000 281.9583 285.7500 289.3333
1956 309.9583 314.4167 318.6250 321.7500 324.5000 327.0833 329.5417 331.8333
1957 348.2500 353.0000 357.6250 361.3750 364.5000 367.1667 369.4583 371.2083
1958 375.2500 377.9167 379.5000 380.0000 380.7083 380.9583 381.8333 383.6667
1959 402.5417 407.1667 411.8750 416.3333 420.5000 425.5000 430.7083 435.1250
1960 456.3333 461.3750 465.2083 469.3333 472.7500 475.0417       NA       NA
          Sep      Oct      Nov      Dec
1949 127.9583 128.5833 129.0000 129.7500
1950 145.7083 148.4167 151.5417 154.7083
1951 175.4583 176.8333 178.0417 180.1667
1952 202.2083 206.2500 210.4167 213.3750
1953 224.9583 224.5833 224.4583 225.5417
1954 247.1667 250.2500 253.5000 257.1250
1955 293.2500 297.1667 301.0000 305.4583
1956 334.4583 337.5417 340.5417 344.0833
1957 372.1667 372.4167 372.7500 373.6250
1958 386.5000 390.3333 394.7083 398.6250
1959 437.7083 440.9583 445.8333 450.6250
1960       NA       NA       NA       NA

$random
             Jan         Feb         Mar         Apr         May         Jun
1949          NA          NA          NA          NA          NA          NA
1950   8.4987374  29.1047980   8.3244949   6.6199495  -7.9103535 -25.1527778
1951  12.6237374  26.6464646  18.4078283   6.9116162   9.8396465 -26.4861111
1952  12.6237374  29.9797980   6.1994949  -2.2550505  -6.0770202 -13.2361111
1953   4.9154040  13.6881313  17.3244949  20.1199495   9.4229798 -17.1111111
1954   0.7487374  -6.2702020   4.9911616   1.1199495   2.8813131  -9.1527778
1955   4.9154040   2.5214646  -1.8838384   1.8282828  -3.9936869  -2.3611111
1956  -1.2095960  -1.2285354   0.6161616  -0.7133838  -1.9936869  11.5138889
1957  -8.5012626 -15.8118687   0.6161616  -5.3383838  -4.9936869  19.4305556
```

```
1958 -10.5012626 -23.7285354 -15.2588384 -23.9633838 -13.2020202  18.6388889
1959 -17.7929293 -28.9785354  -3.6338384 -12.2967172   4.0063131  11.0972222
1960 -14.5845960 -34.1868687 -43.9671717  -0.2967172   3.7563131  24.5555556
            Jul         Aug         Sep         Oct         Nov         Dec
1949 -42.6224747 -42.0732323  -8.4785354  11.0593434  28.5934343  16.8699495
1950 -34.7474747 -35.9898990  -4.2285354   5.2260101  16.0517677  13.9116162
1951 -36.0808081 -37.4065657  -7.9785354   5.8093434  21.5517677  14.4532828
1952 -31.8724747 -20.5732323  -9.7285354   5.3926768  15.1767677   9.2449495
1953 -25.1641414 -16.1565657  -4.4785354   7.0593434   9.1351010   4.0782828
1954  -2.3308081 -13.7815657  -4.6868687  -0.6073232   3.0934343   0.4949495
1955  14.4191919  -5.1565657   2.2297980  -2.5239899 -10.4065657   1.1616162
1956  19.6275253  10.3434343   4.0214646 -10.8989899 -15.9482323  -9.4633838
1957  31.7108586  32.9684343  15.3131313  -4.7739899 -14.1565657  -9.0050505
1958  45.3358586  58.5101010   0.9797980 -10.6906566 -31.1148990 -33.0050505
1959  53.4608586  61.0517677   8.7714646 -13.3156566 -30.2398990 -17.0050505
1960          NA          NA          NA          NA          NA          NA

$figure
 [1] -24.748737 -36.188131  -2.241162  -8.036616  -4.506313  35.402778
 [7]  63.830808  62.823232  16.520202 -20.642677 -53.593434 -28.619949

$type
[1] "additive"

attr(,"class")
[1] "decomposed.ts"
```

Step 3: Plot the trend component as stored in "passengers$trend".

```
> plot(passengers$trend, col = ("dodgerblue3", main="Trend", xlab=
"Jan 1949 to Dec 1960", ylab = "No. of passengers")
```

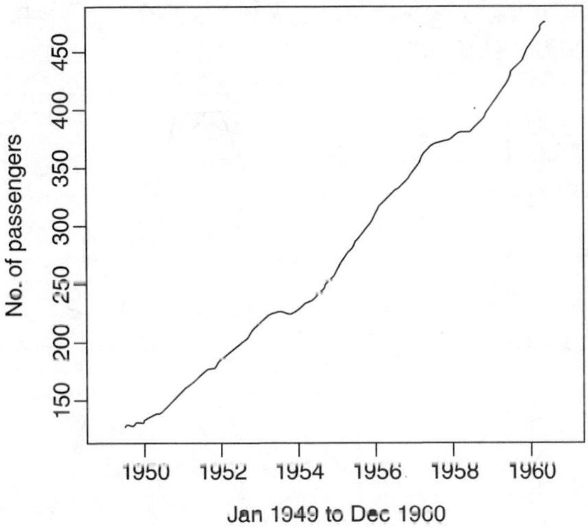

Figure 8.47

Step 4: Plot the seasonal component as stored in "passengers$seasonal".

```
> plot(passengers$seasonal, col = ("dodgerblue3", main="Seasonal",
xlab= "Jan 1949 to Dec 1960", ylab = "No. of passengers")
```

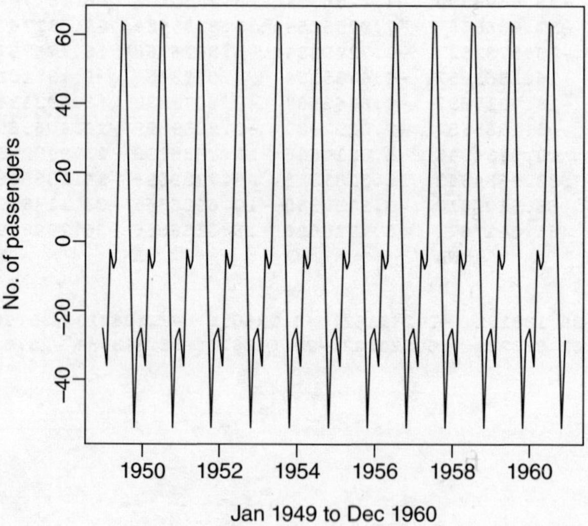

FIGURE 8.48

Step 5: Plot the seasonal monthly data for 1949 (January 1949 to December 1949).

```
> plot(ts(passengers$seasonal[1:12]), col = ("dodgerblue3"),
main="Seasonal monthly data for 1949",xlab= "Jan 1949 to Dec 1949",
ylab = "No. of passengers")
```

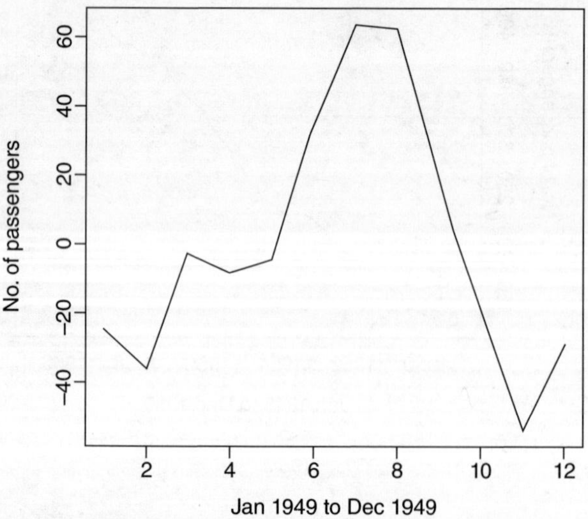

FIGURE 8.49 *Seasonal monthly data for 1949*

Let us further explore the time series data.

Step 6: Check the class of the data set "AirPassengers".

```
> data(AirPassengers)
> class(AirPassengers)
[1] "ts"
```

The above states that data series "AirPassengers" is in a time series format.

Step 7: Use `start()` and `end()` to extract and encode the times the first and last observations were taken.

```
> start(AirPassengers)
[1]    1949  1
```

The above states that the time series data starts in January 1949.

```
> end(AirPassengers)
[1]     1960  12
```

The time series ends in December 1960.

Step 8: Use the `frequency()` function to return the number of samples per unit time.

```
> frequency(AirPassengers)
[1]   12
```

Step 9: Let us take a look at the summary data.

```
> summary(AirPassengers)
      Min.      1st Qu.     Median     Mean       3rd Qu.     Max.
      104.0     180         265.5      280.3      360.5       622.0
> plot(AirPassengers)
```

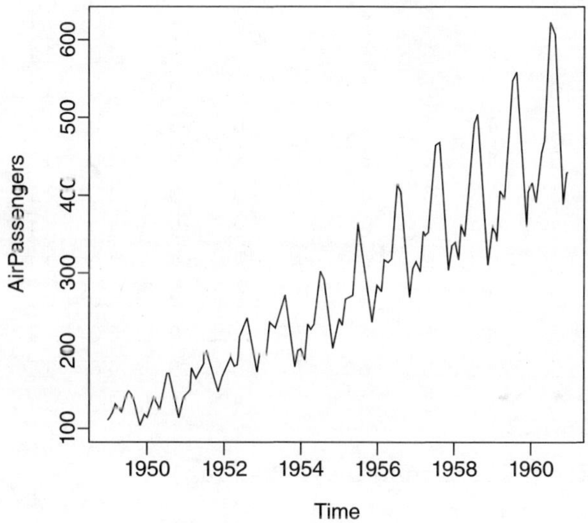

FIGURE 8.50

The above plot shows the distribution of data.

```
> abline(reg=lm(AirPassengers~time(AirPassengers)))
```

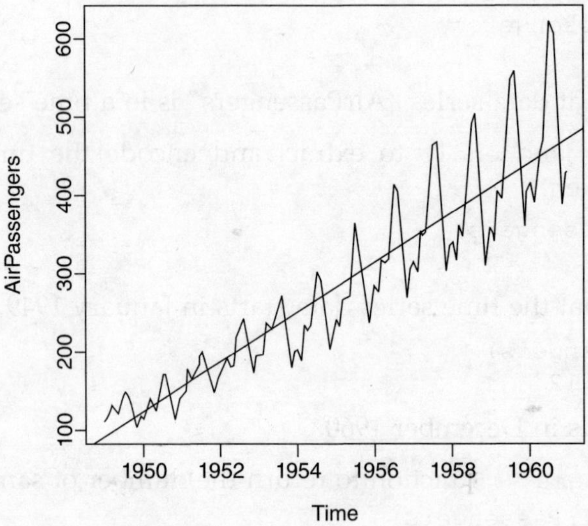

FIGURE 8.51

This will fit in a line.

Step 10: The function `cycle()` gives the positions in the cycle of each observation.

```
> cycle(AirPassengers)
     Jan Feb Mar Apr May Jun Jul Aug Sep Oct Nov Dec
1949   1   2   3   4   5   6   7   8   9  10  11  12
1950   1   2   3   4   5   6   7   8   9  10  11  12
1951   1   2   3   4   5   6   7   8   9  10  11  12
1952   1   2   3   4   5   6   7   8   9  10  11  12
1953   1   2   3   4   5   6   7   8   9  10  11  12
1954   1   2   3   4   5   6   7   8   9  10  11  12
1955   1   2   3   4   5   6   7   8   9  10  11  12
1956   1   2   3   4   5   6   7   8   9  10  11  12
1957   1   2   3   4   5   6   7   8   9  10  11  12
1958   1   2   3   4   5   6   7   8   9  10  11  12
1959   1   2   3   4   5   6   7   8   9  10  11  12
1960   1   2   3   4   5   6   7   8   9  10  11  12
```

```
> plot(aggregate(AirPassengers,FUN=mean))
```

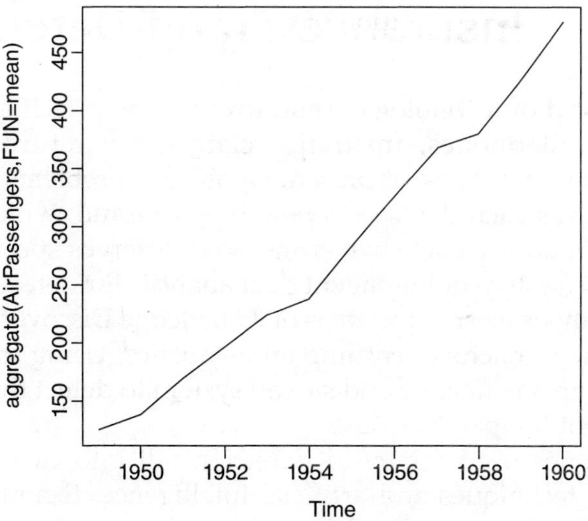

FIGURE 8.52

Aggregates the data and displays a year-on-year trend. The year-on-year trend clearly shows that the #passengers have been increasing without fail.

Step 11: Plot a box and whiskers plot.

```
> boxplot(AirPassengers~cycle(Airpassengers))
```

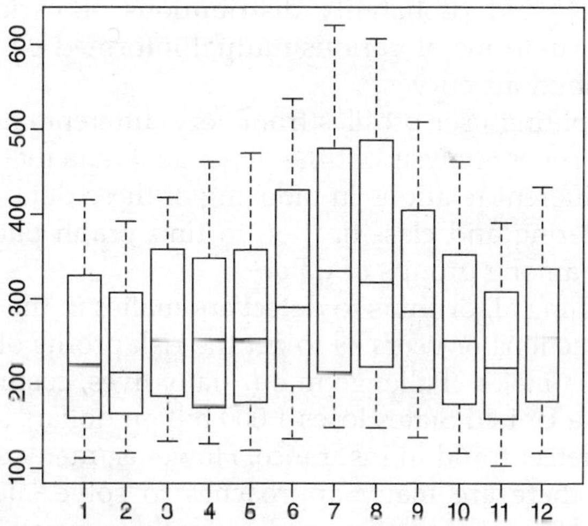

FIGURE 8.53

Inferences

- The variance and the mean value in July and August is much higher than other months.
- Even though the mean value of each month is quite different, its variance is small. Hence, we have a strong seasonal effect with a cycle of 12 months or less.

Case Study

Insurance Fraud Detection

In the world of technology, fraud involves high-tech gadgets and processes such as cell phones, insurance claims, tax return claims, credit card transactions, etc. These represent significant problems for governments and businesses as each day sees a new type of fraud, which these bodies fail to predict. Fraud is a collective crime, so it deserves special treatment with the help of the system of intelligent data analysis for detecting and preventing it. These methods exist in the areas of Knowledge Discovery in Databases (KDD), data mining, machine learning and statistics. Using intelligent systems, we can develop an effective and steady system to detect these frauds and ensure they do not happen in future.

Techniques used for fraud detection fall into two primary classes, viz., statistical techniques and artificial intelligence. Examples of statistical data analysis techniques include the following:

- Data pre-processing techniques that include the means pair wise, list wise missing data finding properties for detection, validation, error correction and filling up of missing or incorrect data by the means pair wise, list wise missing data finding properties.
- Calculation of various random statistical parameters such as mean, performance metrics, statistical probability distributions charts and so on.
- Models and probability distributions of various business activities either in terms of various mutual informed parameters or probability distributions curves.
- Computing user profiles from very different channels.
- Time series analysis of time-dependent data that uses loops of variables on different relations in indexing of these data.
- Clustering and classification to find graph patterns and associations rules among groups of data.
- Matching algorithms to detect anomalies in the behaviour of customer transactions or users as to get the risk profile of the customer.

Fraud is a major challenge in our daily lives, costing us billions. In many surveys, the United States loses 1,000 billion dollars every year because of a failure to detect fraud in insurance. However, many companies are working on it and there are many approaches to solve such prediction lacunae. According to many scientists and researchers, neural network is one of the best approaches to solve the problem of predicting fraud. In this case study, we will try to throw some light on the neural network approach though there are other effective approaches as well.

(Continued)

Case Study

Neural Network

Similar to a living neuron circuit, the neural network depends on the information of its nodes and their weights. These weights are changeable, as are the layers and dynamic properties of hidden neural network variables.

To understand this type of problem let us consider survey information pertaining to US. Until 2009, car companies in the US faced nearly 9.1 billion USD in loss but in 2016 this figure neared 150 billion USD. To reduce this sort of loss, what is needed is a very good analytical and statistical approach that uses historical data to predict the current and future output. For these kinds of problems, the neural network is useful, especially back-propagate neural network algorithm.

Use of Neural Network

The dataset was adjusted before the beginning of training with many time series data as per the insurance claims in day-to-day life and this data was stored according to the nature of claim by the customers. In time related column we used a single node, which is days related to accident and type of claim column. Then we converted this data into binary variants and time variant as integers.

However, there are many complexities in neural networks and one of them has to do with minimising the nodes and layers. To reduce the number of input nodes required, variants are grouped under the following labels—timing, demographics, policy, rating and customer social status. Each node of the neural network takes inputs and has a weight for each input. Now, the weights are in the range of -1 and 1 to reflect how certain factors can increase or decrease the detection of fraud. These weights are interpreted in the light of the importance of each input and larger weights are more significant.

To check the accuracy of the neural network we need to check the co-variance and error, and for this root square mean (RSE) is a good algorithm to use. For the errors, there are many RSE algorithms that we can use but the choice depends on the variables and types of errors we get from the node information and mutual information. Through these processes, we can create a neural network model to predict frauds.

Summary

- Time series data is a type of data that is stored at regular intervals or follows the concept of time series. According to the statistic, a time series defines the sequence of numerical data points in successive order.

(Continued)

- A multivariate time series is a type of time series that uses more than a single quantity for describing the values. The `plot()`, `hist()`, `boxplot()`, `pie()`, `abline()`, `qqnorm()`, `stripcharts()` and `curve()` are some R commands used for visualisation of time series data.
- The `mean()`, `sd()`, `log()`, `diff()`, `pnorm()` and `qnorm()` are some R commands used for manipulation of time series data.
- The simple component analysis divides the data into four main components named trend, seasonal, cyclical and irregular. The linear filter is a part of simple component analysis.
- Linear filtering of time series uses linear filters for generating the different components of the time series. Time series analysis mostly uses a moving average as a linear filter.
- A `filter()` function performs linear filtering of time series data and generates the time series of the given data.
- A `scan()` function reads the data from any file. Since time series data contains data with respect to a successive time interval, it is the best function for reading it.
- A `ts()` function stores time series data and creates a time series object.
- The `as.ts()` function converts a simple object into time series object and the `is.ts()` function checks whether an object is a time series object or not.
- The plotting task represents time series data graphically during time series analysis and R provides the `plot()` function for plotting of time series data.
- A non-seasonal time series contains the trend and irregular components; hence, the decomposition process converts the non-seasonal data into these components.
- The `SMA()` function is used for decomposition of non-seasonal time series. It smooths time series data by calculating the moving average and estimates the trend and irregular components. The function is available in the package "TTR".
- A seasonal time series contains the seasonal, trend and irregular component; hence, the decomposition process converts the seasonal data into these three components.
- The `seas()` function automatically finds out the seasonally adjusting series. The function is available in the "seasonal" package.
- Regression analysis defines the linear relationship between independent variables (predictors) and dependent (response) variables using a linear function.
- Forecasts are a type of prediction that predicts the future events from the past data.
- Simple exponential smoothing estimates the level at the current time point and performs the short-term forecast. The alpha parameter of the `HoltWinters()` function controls the simple exponential smoothing.
- Holt's exponential smoothing estimates the level and slope at the current time point. The alpha and beta parameters of the `HoltWinters()` function controls it and estimates the level and slope, respectively.
- Holt-Winters exponential smoothing estimates the level, slope and seasonal component at the current time point. The alpha, beta and gamma parameters of the `HoltWinters()` function controls it and estimates the level, slope of trend component and seasonal component, respectively.
- The ARIMA (Autoregressive Integrated Moving Average) is another method of time series forecasting. The ARIMA model explicitly defines the irregular component of a stationary time series with non-zero autocorrelation. It is represented by ARIMA(p, d, q) where parameters p, d and q define the autoregression (AR) order, the degree of differencing and the moving average (MA) order, respectively.

(Continued)

- A `diff()` function is differencing a time series for finding an appropriate ARIMA model. It helps to obtain a stationary time series for an ARIMA model and also finds out the value of 'd' parameter of an ARIMA(p, q, r) model.
- An `auto.arima()` function automatically returns the best candidate ARIMA(p, d, q) model for the given time series.
- An `arima()` function finds out the parameters of the selected ARIMA(p, d, q) model.
- The `arima.sim()` function simulates the values of the autocorrelation and partial autocorrelation from an ARIMA(p, d, q) model.

KEY TERMS

- **ARIMA:** The ARIMA (Autoregressive Integrated Moving Average) is a method of time series forecasting.
- **Decomposing time series:** Decomposing time series is a process that decomposes a given time series data into different components.
- **Exponential smoothing:** The exponential smoothing method finds out the changes in time series data by ignoring irrelevant fluctuation and making a short-term forecast prediction for time series data.
- **Forecasts:** Forecasts are a type of prediction that predict future events from past data.
- **Holt's exponential smoothing:** Holt's exponential smoothing estimates the level and slope at the current time point.
- **Holt-Winters exponential smoothing:** Holt-Winters exponential smoothing estimates the level, slope and seasonal component at the current time point.
- **`HoltWinters()` function:** The `HoltWinters()` function is a common inbuilt function for finding exponential smoothing. All three exponential smoothing use it.
- **Linear filtering:** Linear filtering of time series uses linear filters for generating different components of the time series.
- **Multivariate time series:** A multivariate time series is a type of time series that uses more than a single quantity for describing the values.
- **Non-seasonal time series:** A non-seasonal time series contains the trend and irregular components.
- **Plotting:** Plotting task represents time series data graphically during time series analysis.
- **Regression analysis:** Regression analysis defines the linear relationship between independent variables (predictors) and dependent (response) variables using a linear function.
- **Seasonal adjusting series:** A seasonally adjusting time series is a time series with no seasonality or seasonal component.
- **Seasonal time series:** A seasonal time series contains the seasonal, trend and irregular components.
- **Simple component analysis:** Simple component analysis divides data into four main components, viz., trend, seasonal, cyclical and irregular.
- **Simple exponential smoothing:** Simple exponential smoothing estimates the level at the current time point and does the short-term forecast.
- **Time series data:** Time series data is a type of data that is stored at regular intervals or follows the concept of time series.
- **Univariate time series:** A univariate time series is a type of time series that uses a single quantity for describing the values.

MULTIPLE CHOICE QUESTIONS

1. Which one of the following commands is used for visualisation in time series analysis?
   (a) `diff()` (b) `sd()`
   (c) `plot()` (d) `means()`
2. Which one of the following commands is used for manipulation in time series analysis?
   (a) `plot()` (b) `pnorm()`
   (c) `qqnorm()` (d) `hist()`
3. Which one of the following commands is different from others?
   (a) `qnorm()` (b) `pnorm()`
   (c) `qqnorm()` (d) `log()`
4. Which one of the following commands stores the time series object?
   (a) `as.ts()` (b) `is.ts()`
   (c) `ts()` (d) `scan()`
5. Which one of the following commands reads the time series object?
   (a) `plot()` (b) `is.ts()`
   (c) `ts()` (d) `scan()`
6. Which one of the following commands plots the time series object?
   (a) `as.ts()` (b) `plot()`
   (c) `ts()` (d) `scan()`
7. Which one of the following commands implements linear filtering?
   (a) `ts()` (b) `decompose()`
   (c) `filter()` (d) `scan()`
8. Which one of the following commands decomposes non-seasonal time series?
   (a) `seas()` (b) `stl()`
   (c) `decompose()` (d) `SMA()`
9. Which one of the following commands decomposes seasonal time series data?
   (a) `seas()` (b) `ts()`
   (c) `decompose()` (d) `SMA()`
10. Which one of the following commands is used for seasonally adjusting time series?
    (a) `seas()` (b) `stl()`
    (c) `decompose()` (d) `SMA()`
11. Which one of the following components are used by non-seasonal time series data?
    (a) Trend and seasonal (b) Irregular and trend
    (c) Seasonal and Irregular (d) Cyclical and trend
12. Which one of the following components are used by seasonal time series data?
    (a) Trend, irregular and seasonal (b) Irregular, cyclical and trend
    (c) Seasonal, cyclical and irregular (d) Cyclical, trend, and seasonal

13. Which one of the following packages contains the `SMA()` function?
    (a) Forecast (b) Seasonal
    (c) TTR (d) Graphics
14. Which one of the following packages contains the `seas()` function?
    (a) Forecast (b) Seasonal
    (c) TTR (d) Graphics
15. Which one of the following packages contains the `forecast()` function?
    (a) Forecast (b) Seasonal
    (c) TTR (d) Graphics
16. Which one of the following functions implements regression analysis?
    (a) `ts()` (b) `lm()`
    (c) `seas()` (d) `decompose()`
17. Which one of the following functions implements exponential smoothing?
    (a) `HoltWinters()` (b) `seas()`
    (c) `arima()` (d) `plot()`
18. Which one of the following functions is used for differencing a time series object?
    (a) `HoltWinters()` (b) `acf()`
    (c) `diff()` (d) `pacf()`
19. Which one of the following functions estimates the autocorrelation for time series object?
    (a) `acf()` (b) `diff()`
    (c) `arima()` (d) `pacf()`
20. Which one of the following functions estimates the partial autocorrelation for time series object?
    (a) `acf()` (b) `diff()`
    (c) `arima()` (d) `pacf()`
21. Which one of the following functions automatically returns a candidate ARIMA model?
    (a) `HoltWinters()` (b) `auto.arima()`
    (c) `arima()` (d) `arima.sim()`
22. Which one of the following functions finds out the parameters of a candidate ARIMA model?
    (a) `HoltWinters()` (b) `auto.arima()`
    (c) `arima()` (d) `arima.sim()`
23. Which one of the following function simulates an ARIMA model?
    (a) `HoltWinters()` (b) `auto.arima()`
    (c) `arima()` (d) `arima.sim()`
24. Which one of the following functions forecasts an ARIMA model?
    (a) `arima()` (b) `auto.arima()`
    (c) `forecast.Arima()` (d) `arima.sim()`

25. Which one of the following function creates a diagnostic plot for an ARIMA model?
    (a) `arima()` (b) `auto.arima()`
    (c) `tsdiag()` (d) `ts()`
26. Which one of the following is not a parameter of an ARIMA model?
    (a) Moving average (b) Difference
    (c) Auto regression (d) Lag
27. How many plots are generated by the `tsdiag()` function?
    (a) 2 (b) 3
    (c) 4 (d) 5
28. Which one of the following is not a parameter of the `HoltWinters()` function?
    (a) Alpha (b) Gamma
    (c) Beta (d) Lambda
29. Which one of the following parameters of the `HoltWinters()` function controls simple exponential smoothing?
    (a) Alpha (b) Gamma
    (c) Beta (d) Lambda
30. Which one of the following parameters of the `HoltWinters()` function controls Holt's exponential smoothing?
    (a) Alpha and beta (b) Gamma and beta
    (c) Beta and lambda (d) None of the above
31. Which one of the following parameters of the `HoltWinters()` function controls Holt-Winters exponential smoothing?
    (a) Alpha and beta (b) Alpha, beta, and gamma
    (c) Beta, gamma and lambda (d) None of the above

SHORT QUESTIONS

1. Describe time series data with respect to time series analysis.
2. What is the difference between univariate and multivariate time series?
3. What are the basic R commands for visualisation of time series data?
4. What is basic R commands for the manipulation of time series data?
5. What is linear filtering in time series analysis?
6. What is simple component analysis?
7. What is plotting in time series analysis?
8. What is decomposing in time series analysis?
9. What is the difference between non-seasonal and seasonal time series?

10. What is exponential smoothing in time series analysis?
11. What steps are used for fitting an appropriate ARIMA model?
12. How does one analyse the autocorrelation and partial correlation for fitting an ARIMA model?
13. How does one forecast an ARIMA model in time series analysis?

LONG QUESTIONS

1. Explain the `plot()` function with syntax and an example.
2. Explain the `hist()` function with syntax and an example.
3. Explain the `filter()` function with syntax and an example.
4. Explain the `scan()` function with syntax and an example.
5. Explain the `ts()` function with syntax and an example.
6. Explain the `SMA()` function with syntax and an example.
7. Explain the `decompose()` function with syntax and an example.
8. Explain the `stl()` function with syntax and an example.
9. Explain seasonally adjusting series and decompose it without using any function.
10. Explain the `seas()` function with syntax and an example.
11. Explain the `lm()` function with syntax and an example.
12. Explain forecasting in time series analysis.
13. Explain the `HoltWinters()` function.
14. Explain simple exponential smoothing with an example.
15. Explain Holt's exponential smoothing with an example.
16. Explain Holt-Winters exponential smoothing with an example.
17. Explain ARIMA model.
18. Explain the `diff()` function with syntax and an example.
19. Explain the `acf()` function with syntax and an example.
20. Explain the `pacf()` function with syntax and an example.
21. Explain the `arima()` function with syntax and an example.
22. Explain the `tsdiag()` function with syntax and an example.
23. Create and read a time series data for changing prices of shares using `ts()` and `scan()` functions. Also, plot the time series data.
24. Create time series data and apply linear filtering on it. Interpret the output.
25. Create time series data and decompose it. Interpret the output.

26. Create time series data that applies all the three exponential smoothing on it. Also, interpret the output.
27. Create time series data and fit it into an ARIMA model by following all the steps used during fitting an ARIMA model.

Answers to MCQs:

1. (c)	2. (b)	3. (c)	4. (c)	5. (d)	6. (b)	7. (c)
8. (d)	9. (c)	10. (a)	11. (a)	12. (b)	13. (c)	14. (b)
15. (a)	16. (b)	17. (a)	18. (c)	19. (a)	20. (d)	21. (b)
22. (c)	23. (d)	24. (c)	25. (c)	26. (d)	27. (b)	28. (d)
29. (a)	30. (a)	31. (b)				

Chapter 9

Clustering

LEARNING OUTCOME

At the end of this chapter, you will be able to:

- Create a distance matrix using the `dist()` function
- Implement clustering in R using `hclust()` function
- Implement k-means clustering in R

9.1 Introduction

Clustering analysis has widespread application in areas such as data analysis, market research, pattern recognition, etc. It is extensively used to:

- Classify documents on the web for information discovery;
- Detect credit card frauds in outlier detection applications; and
- Gain insight into the distribution of data to observe characteristics of each cluster, etc.

This chapter deals with hierarchical clustering in both Euclidean and non-Euclidean spaces. It also discusses partitioning clustering k-means algorithm. Hierarchical and partitioning clustering is demonstrated using R. The chapter also deliberates on few other algorithms such as BFR (Bradley, Fayyad, and Reina) algorithm, a variant of the k-means algorithm that performs clustering in a high-dimensional Euclidean space, the CURE (**C**lustering **U**sing **RE**presentatives) algorithm, the GRGPF algorithm that uses non-Euclidean space, the BDMO algorithm, stream-clustering algorithms (B. Babcock, M. Datar, R. Motwani, L. O'Callaghan), etc.

9.2 WHAT IS CLUSTERING?

Clustering techniques are the most important techniques with respect to business analytics and data mining. Clustering is a process that examines given data and partitions this data into many groups on the basis of their similarities or features. These groups of data are called *clusters*.

Given a set of points, group the points into some number of clusters, so that:

- Members of a cluster are close/similar to each other
- Members of different clusters are dissimilar

Usually points are in a high dimensional space and similarity is defined using a distance measure (such as Euclidean/Cosine/Jaccard distance measure, etc.)

Cluster analysis divides data into groups (clusters) that are meaningful and useful. Let us look at an example of clustering. Assume you fire a query of "movie" in a search engine. The query returns a number of web pages. These web pages are then grouped into categories such as "movie reviews", "star cast", "theatres", "trailers", etc. Each of the category (cluster) can further be broken into a number of "sub-categories" (sub-clusters) to form a hierarchical structure that aids a user's comprehension of the query results.

Clustering can also be expressed as a technique that examines a collection of points and groups them into clusters based on their distance. Figure 9.1 shows three clusters and two outliers. Data points in a cluster are closer to each other by their Euclidean distance than they are to data points outside the group.

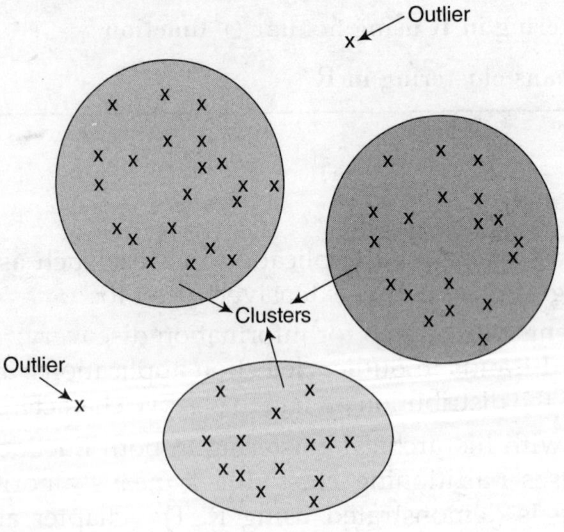

FIGURE 9.1 *Clusters and outliers*

Clustering in two dimensions is easy. Clustering small amounts of data also looks easy. However, clustering is not always easy especially when applications involve not two but 10 or 100 or 10,000 dimensions. In high dimensional spaces, almost all pairs of points are at approximately the same distance from each other and it is not intuitively clear how to group them.

The main objective of clustering is to find points in the same cluster having a small distance from each other along with points in different clusters where points have a larger distance from each other. In general, there are different types of clustering available in statistics that are used during data mining.

Nowadays, several fields make use of clustering algorithms to implement different applications in their respective fields. Data mining, information retrieval, search engines, academics, psychology and medical, machine learning, computer graphics, pattern recognition, etc., are few of the major application areas of clustering.

The field of business data analytics deals with huge mounds of data and requires the use of different types of algorithms to implement clustering. R provides different packages to implement clustering. Each package has different inbuilt functions to implement clustering and to determine the clusters.

9.3 Basic Concepts in Clustering

Before learning clustering in R, comprehension of few basic concepts (points, spaces and distances) is important. You will learn about these basic concepts in this section.

9.3.1 Points, Spaces, and Distances

Points, spaces, and distances are some of the most important concepts in clustering.

Points and Spaces

Clustering is a data mining process where data are viewed as points in a multi-dimensional space. The collection of points stored in a single place is called space. These points are said to belong to the same space. In other words, space is a universe of a set of points from where points are drawn in the dataset. "Euclidean space" is one of the famous and useful spaces.

In the Euclidean space, points are vectors of real numbers. The number of dimensions of the space is the length of the vector, and the coordinates of the represented points are the components of the vector.

Distances

Distance is another important metric used in clustering. The difference between any two points is called *distance*. All spaces have a distance measure and they have to follow the following properties of distance:

- Distance must be non-negative.
- Distance should be symmetric where the order of points does not matter during distance computing.
- Distance measures should also follow the triangle inequality rule which means the distance from x to y to z is never less than the distance from x to z directly.

Clustering uses different types of distance according to the need of application. The most common types of distance measures are Euclidean distance, Manhattan distance, Hamming distance, Maximum norm, L1 distance, etc., which are used for finding distance between the points.

R language provides a `dist()` function for measuring distance by using different types of methods. The function calculates the distance and returns the distance matrix. This distance matrix is calculated by using the specified distance measure that computes the distance between rows of a data matrix. The basic syntax of `dist()` is as follows:

```
dist(x, method = "Euclidean",…)
```

where,

x argument defines a numeric matrix, or an object that can be converted to a matrix or a data frame; method argument defines the name of the method for measuring the distance measure. Table 9.1 shows the names of the distance measure; the dots, "…" define the other optional arguments.

TABLE 9.1 Different distance measures

Distance Measure Method	*Description*
Euclidean	It calculates the distance by taking the square root of sums of the squares of the differences between the coordinates of the points in each dimension.
Manhattan	It returns the absolute distance by the sum of the magnitudes of the differences in each dimension
Binary	The binary bits are either 0 (zero) or 1 (non-zero). The zero and non-zero elements are represented by 'Off' and 'On'. The binary distance is the proportion of bits where only one bit should be 'On' bit.
Maximum	It returns the maximum distance between two vectors.
Canberra	It works with non-negative values where terms with zero numerators and denominators are omitted from the sum and treated as if the values are missing.
Minkowski	It represents the *p* norm where the pth root of the sum of the pth powers of the differences of the components.

Example 1

The `dist()` function is creating distance matrices of a matrix "m" of 4 by 4 using *Euclidean* and *Manhattan method* (Figure 9.2).

Example 2

The `dist()` function is creating distance matrices of a matrix "m" of 4 by 4 using the methods "binary", "maximum", "Canberra", and "Minkowski" (Figure 9.3).

```
> # Finding different distance of matrix m
> m
     [,1] [,2] [,3] [,4]
[1,]    1    5    9   13
[2,]    2    6   10   14
[3,]    3    7   11   15
[4,]    4    8   12   16
>
> # the Euclidean distance
> dist(m,method="euclidean")
  1 2 3
2 2
3 4 2
4 6 4 2
>
> # Manhattan distance
> dist(m,method="manhattan")
   1  2  3
2  4
3  8  4
4 12  8  4
>
```

FIGURE 9.2 *Distance matrices using Euclidean and Manhattan method*

```
> # the Jaccard method for binary data
> dist(m,method="binary")
  1 2 3
2 0
3 0 0
4 0 0 0
>
> # maximum distance
> dist(m,method="maximum")
  1 2 3
2 1
3 2 1
4 3 2 1
>
> # canberra distance
> dist(m,method="canberra")
          1         2         3
2 0.5139110
3 0.8380952 0.3590249
4 1.0770746 0.6337662 0.2852601
>
> # minkowski distance
> dist(m,method="minkowski")
  1 2 3
2 2
3 4 2
4 6 4 2
```

FIGURE 9.3 *Distance matrices using remaining methods*

Example 3

Let us take a look at the "mtcars" dataset. "mtcars" data set is a data frame with 32 observations (for 32 automobiles) on 11 variables (fuel consumption and 10 aspects of automobile design).

```
> mtcars
```

```
                     mpg cyl  disp  hp drat    wt  qsec vs am gear carb
Mazda RX4           21.0   6 160.0 110 3.90 2.620 16.46  0  1    4    4
Mazda RX4 Wag       21.0   6 160.0 110 3.90 2.875 17.02  0  1    4    4
Datsun 710          22.8   4 108.0  93 3.85 2.320 18.61  1  1    4    1
Hornet 4 Drive      21.4   6 258.0 110 3.08 3.215 19.44  1  0    3    1
Hornet Sportabout   18.7   8 360.0 175 3.15 3.440 17.02  0  0    3    2
Valiant             18.1   6 225.0 105 2.76 3.460 20.22  1  0    3    1
Duster 360          14.3   8 360.0 245 3.21 3.570 15.84  0  0    3    4
Merc 240D           24.4   4 146.7  62 3.69 3.190 20.00  1  0    4    2
Merc 230            22.8   4 140.8  95 3.92 3.150 22.90  1  0    4    2
Merc 280            19.2   6 167.6 123 3.92 3.440 18.30  1  0    4    4
Merc 280C           17.8   6 167.6 123 3.92 3.440 18.90  1  0    4    4
Merc 450SE          16.4   8 275.8 180 3.07 4.070 17.40  0  0    3    3
Merc 450SL          17.3   8 275.8 180 3.07 3.730 17.60  0  0    3    3
Merc 450SLC         15.2   8 275.8 180 3.07 3.780 18.00  0  0    3    3
Cadillac Fleetwood  10.4   8 472.0 205 2.93 5.250 17.98  0  0    3    4
Lincoln Continental 10.4   8 460.0 215 3.00 5.424 17.82  0  0    3    4
Chrysler Imperial   14.7   8 440.0 230 3.23 5.345 17.42  0  0    3    4
Fiat 128            32.4   4  78.7  66 4.08 2.200 19.47  1  1    4    1
Honda Civic         30.4   4  75.7  52 4.93 1.615 18.52  1  1    4    2
Toyota Corolla      33.9   4  71.1  65 4.22 1.835 19.90  1  1    4    1
Toyota Corona       21.5   4 120.1  97 3.70 2.465 20.01  1  0    3    1
Dodge Challenger    15.5   8 318.0 150 2.76 3.520 16.87  0  0    3    2
AMC Javelin         15.2   8 304.0 150 3.15 3.435 17.30  0  0    3    2
Camaro Z28          13.3   8 350.0 245 3.73 3.840 15.41  0  0    3    4
Pontiac Firebird    19.2   8 400.0 175 3.08 3.845 17.05  0  0    3    2
Fiat X1-9           27.3   4  79.0  66 4.08 1.935 18.90  1  1    4    1
Porsche 914-2       26.0   4 120.3  91 4.43 2.140 16.70  0  1    5    2
Lotus Europa        30.4   4  95.1 113 3.77 1.513 16.90  1  1    5    2
Ford Pantera L      15.8   8 351.0 264 4.22 3.170 14.50  0  1    5    4
Ferrari Dino        19.7   6 145.0 175 3.62 2.770 15.50  0  1    5    6
Maserati Bora       15.0   8 301.0 335 3.54 3.570 14.60  0  1    5    8
Volvo 142E          21.4   4 121.0 109 4.11 2.780 18.60  1  1    4    2
```

Since there are 11 measurement attributes (mpg, cyl, disp, hp, drat, wt, etc.) for each automobile, the data set can be seen as a collection of 32 sample vectors in an 11-dimensional space. In order to determine the dissimilarity between two automobiles, say Honda Civic and Camaro Z28, let us calculate the distance between them using the dist function:

Step 1: Create a data frame, "x" and assign it the details of the car, "Honda Civic".

```
> x <- mtcars["Honda Civic",]
> x
             mpg  cyl disp hp drat wt    qsec  vs am gear carb
Honda Civic  30.4 4    75.7 52 4.93 1.615 18.52 1  1  4    2
```

Step 2: Create a data frame, "y" and assign it the details of the car, "Camaro Z28".

```
> y <- mtcars["Camaro Z28",]
> y
             mpg  cyl disp hp  drat wt   qsec  vs am gear carb
Camaro Z28   13.3 8   350  245 3.73 3.84 15.41 0  0  3    4
```

Step 3: Use the `rbind()` function to take data-frames, "x" and "y" as arguments and combine by *rows*. Use the `dist()` function to compute and return the distance matrix (computed by using the specified distance measure to compute the distances between the rows of a data matrix).

```
> dist(rbind(x, y))
                Honda Civic
Camaro Z28      335.8883
```

Likewise, we can compute the distance between Camaro Z28 and Pontiac Firebird:

```
> z <- mtcars["Pontiac Firebird",]
> dist(rbind(y, z)
                      Camaro Z28
Pontiac Firebird      86.26658
```

Conclusion

As the distance between Camaro Z28 and Pontiac Firebird (86.267) is smaller than the distance between Camaro Z28 and Honda Civic (335.89), we conclude that Camaro Z28 is more similar to Pontiac Firebird than to Honda Civic.

Let us now compute the distance matrix. We will apply the same distance computation between all possible pairs of automobiles in mtcars, and arrange the result into a 32x32 symmetric matrix, with the element at the *i*-th row and *j*-th column being the distance between the *i*-th and *j*-th automobiles in the data set.

```
> dist(as.matrix(mtcars))
```

	Mazda RX4	Mazda RX4 Wag	Datsun 710	Hornet 4 Drive
Mazda RX4 Wag	0.6153251			
Datsun 710	54.9086059	54.8915169		
Hornet 4 Drive	98.1125212	98.0958939	150.9935191	
Hornet Sportabout	210.3374396	210.3358546	265.0831615	121.0297564
Valiant	65.4717710	65.4392224	117.7547018	33.5508692
Duster 360	241.4076490	241.4088680	294.4790230	169.4299647
Merc 240D	50.1532711	50.1146059	49.6584796	121.2739722
Merc 230	25.4683117	25.3284509	33.1803843	118.2433145
Merc 280	15.3641921	15.2956865	66.9363534	91.4224033
Merc 280C	15.6724727	15.5837744	67.0261397	91.4612914
Merc 450SE	135.4307018	135.4254826	189.1954941	72.4964325
Merc 450SL	135.4014424	135.3960351	189.1631745	72.4313532
Merc 450SLC	135.4794674	135.4723157	189.2345426	72.5718466
Cadillac Fleetwood	326.3395903	326.3355070	381.0926242	234.4403876
Lincoln Continental	318.0469808	318.0429333	372.8012090	227.9726091
Chrysler Imperial	304.7203408	304.7169175	359.3014906	218.1548299
Fiat 128	93.2679950	93.2530993	40.9933763	184.9689734
Honda Civic	102.8307567	102.8230713	52.7704607	191.5510700
Toyota Corolla	100.6040368	100.5887588	47.6535017	192.6714187
Toyota Corona	42.3075233	42.2659224	12.9654743	138.5304725
Dodge Challenger	163.1150750	163.1134210	217.7795805	72.4403915
AMC Javelin	149.6047203	149.6014522	204.3188913	61.3601899
Camaro Z28	233.2228758	233.2248748	286.0049209	163.6632641
Pontiac Firebird	248.6780270	248.6762035	303.3583889	156.2240346

9.3.2 Clustering Strategies

Clustering strategies are techniques that define the way of performing clustering on any dataset. Hierarchical and partitioning are two major and fundamental categories of clustering strategies. The clustering algorithms follow the techniques according to the need of the application.

Hierarchical Clustering Strategy

Hierarchical clustering strategy defines a hierarchical structure of objects of a dataset and their clusters. The main strategy of the Hierarchical algorithm is to start with each point in its own cluster and then combine the clusters according to their "closeness" by using the appropriate definition of "close". After this, it stops combining the clusters when some clusters become undesirable. For example, the user can stop combining the clusters after getting the predetermined number of clusters or sometimes the user can also stop combining the clusters based on the compactness measures of clusters.

The hierarchical clustering strategy can be either agglomerative or divisive.

- Agglomerative hierarchical clustering:
  - Bottom up
  - Initially, each point is a cluster
  - Repeatedly combine the two nearest clusters into one
- Divisive hierarchical clustering:
  - Top down
  - Start with one cluster and recursively split it

The key operation in agglomerative hierarchical clustering is to "repeatedly combine two nearest clusters".

There are three important questions to answer as we go about building the hierarchical algorithm:

- How do you represent a cluster of more than one point?
- How do you determine the "nearness" of clusters?
- When do you stop combining clusters?

We will answer the above three questions in Section 9.2, *Hierarchical Clustering*.

Partitioning Clustering Strategy

The main strategy of partitioning clustering is to divide or partition the dataset of n objects or tuples of a dataset into k partitions. After partitioning the dataset, each partition represents a cluster, where $k \leq n$. In simple words, it classifies the given datasets into k different groups that satisfies the following conditions:

- Each group should contain at least one object.
- Each object should belong to exactly one group.

The cluster algorithms also use the concept of point assignment, Euclidean space, density-based methods, grid-based methods, model-based methods, or fit the data into main memory for doing clustering.

- The main strategy of the point assignment clustering is to consider points in some order and then assign each point to the cluster where it best fits. In this strategy, initial clusters are estimated in a short phase. In some applications, these points are not assigned if they are too far from the current clusters, i.e. outliers.
- In Euclidean space strategy, clustering algorithms use an arbitrary distance measure. The algorithms can use centroids (average of points) in the Euclidean space. In the non-Euclidean space, the algorithms need to develop their method to summarise the clusters.
- Some algorithms use the size of the data for clustering. These algorithms assume that the data is small enough to fit in main memory for clustering. Alternatively, the algorithms assume whether the data must reside in the secondary memory for clustering. In applications, where the data size is too big then it is not feasible to put all pairs of points in main memory. In such a case, not all the points of the clusters can be placed in main memory at the same time.

9.3.3 Curse of Dimensionality

Analysis and organisation of data in high-dimensional spaces (over hundreds of dimensions) that cannot fit in low-dimensional settings are called the curse of dimensionality. Normally a Euclidean space contains two dimensions but the high-dimensional Euclidean space contains many dimensions and defines different unintuitive properties. These properties also come under the curse of dimensionality. The *curse* in the curse of dimensionality indicates that all pairs of points are equally far away from each other and two vectors are mostly orthogonal.

In high-dimensional spaces, there are huge points to distribute the distances among these points. For this, consider a d-dimensional Euclidean space and select n random points in the unit cube.

- When $d = 1$, then place random points on a line of length equal to 1. In this case, some pairs of points are very close on the line or some points are very far away on the line. Hence, the average distance between a pair of points will be 1/3.
- When d is very large, then the Euclidean distance between two random points $[x_1, x_2 \dots x_d]$ and $[y_1, y_2 \dots y_d]$ on a line is as follows:

$$\text{Distance} = \sqrt{\sum_{i=1}^{d}(x_i - y_i)^2}$$

where,

x_i and y_i = random variables between 0 to 1

9.3.4 Angles Between Vectors

An angle between two vectors defines a single point or the shortest angle, where one vector turns around to another vector. But, in high-dimensional spaces, there are a number of vectors. For finding angles between vectors, take any three random points P, Q, and R in a d-dimensional space (high-dimensional space).

$P = [x_1, x_2 ... x_d]$
$R = [y_1, y_2 ... y_d]$
$Q = \text{origin}$

The shortest angle between *P*, *Q*, and *R* is the cosine of the angle *PQR* that is the dot product of *P* and *R* divided by the product of lengths of the vectors *P* and *Q*. The following formula defines the angle:

$$\text{Angles between vectors} = \frac{\sum_{i=1}^{d} x_i y_i}{\sqrt{\sum_{i=1}^{d} x_i^2}\sqrt{\sum_{i=1}^{d} y_i^2}}$$

As soon as *d* grows, the denominator grows linearly in *d*, whereas the numerator is a sum of random values that can be positive or negative. Hence, the expected value of the numerator is 0 and for the large values of *d*, the cosine of the angle between any two vectors is almost 0. It indicates that the angle is close to 90 degrees.

Check Your Understanding

1. What is a cluster in cluster analysis?

Ans: A cluster is a group of data in cluster analysis.

2. What is space in clustering?

Ans: A collection of points stored in a single place is called *space*. These points are said to belong to the same space.

3. What is a `dist()` function?

Ans: R language provides a `dist()` function for measuring the distance using different methods. The function calculates the distance and returns the distance matrix.

4. What are clustering strategies?

Ans: Clustering strategies are the techniques that define the way of performing clustering on any dataset. Hierarchical and partitioning are two major and fundamental categories of clustering strategies.

5. What is a hierarchical clustering strategy?

Ans: Hierarchical clustering strategy defines a hierarchical structure of the objects of a dataset and their clusters. The hierarchical clustering strategy can be either agglomerative or divisive.

6. What is partitioning clustering strategy?

Ans: Partitioning clustering strategy divides or partitions the dataset of *n* objects or tuples into *k* partitions of the dataset.

9.4 Hierarchical Clustering

Hierarchical clustering organises a set of nested clusters as a tree. Each cluster (node) of the tree, excluding the leaf nodes, is the union of its sub-clusters (children) and the root of the tree is the cluster that contains all the objects. In both types of hierarchical clustering techniques, agglomerative clustering is the most common clustering.

Hierarchical clustering generates either dendrogram (tree-like diagram) or nested cluster diagram (clusters into other clusters). Figure 9.4 defines four points generated after hierarchical clustering.

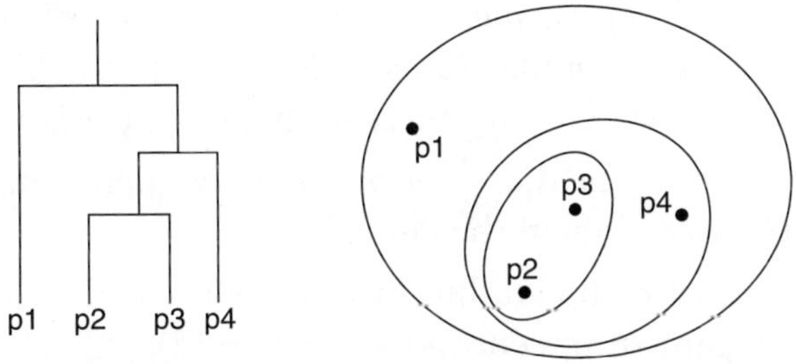

(a) Dendrogram. (b) Nested cluster diagram.

Figure 9.4 *Dendrogram and nested cluster diagram*

During hierarchical clustering, it is necessary to find how to represent the clusters, how to merge any two clusters, and how to stop merging clusters. Here is the pseudocode of the hierarchical algorithm:

1. While it is not time to stop Do
   a. Find and select the best two clusters to merge;
   b. Combine those two clusters into one cluster;
2. End;

   In Figure 9.4, cluster $p2$ and $p3$ are merged to give one cluster ($p2$, $p3$) which then is merged with cluster $p4$. This cluster, comprising $p2$, $p3$ and $p4$, is then merged with cluster $p1$.

9.4.1 Hierarchical Clustering in Euclidean Space

Euclidean space contains two dimensions with one centre point. For performing hierarchical clustering on this space, it is necessary to represent a cluster by its centroid or average of the points in the cluster. Since a Euclidean space has only one centre point, it becomes the centroid. By applying the above pseudocode of hierarchical clustering algorithm on the space, we get:

1. The algorithm initialises the cluster (centre point of space).
2. Find the Euclidean distance between their centroids, i.e. the distance between any two clusters.

3. Select two clusters with the shortest distance and merge them.
4. Let us consider Euclidean space. We have four basic questions to answer.
   - How do you represent a cluster of more than one point?
   - How do you represent the location of each cluster, to tell which pair of clusters is closest?

     Represent each cluster by its centroids. A centroid here is the average of its points.
   - How do you determine the "nearness" of clusters?

     Measure cluster distances by distances of centroids
   - When do you stop combining clusters?

     Pick a number "k" upfront and stop when you have "k" clusters or stop when the next merge would create a bad cluster. A bad cluster is a cluster with low "cohesion". "Cohesion" can be measured by any of the below approaches.

     Approach 1: measure the diameter of the merged cluster. Diameter = maximum distance between points in the cluster.

     Approach 2: measure the radius of the merged cluster. Radius = maximum distance of a point from centroid (or clustroid). "Clustroid" will be explained when we discuss clustering in non-Euclidean space.

     Approach 3: measure the density. Density = number of points per unit volume. E.g. divide the number of points in the cluster by the diameter or radius of the c luster.

In the Figure 9.5, *o* represents the data points whereas *x* represents the centre point. We have three data points with coordinates (0, 0), (2, 1) and (1, 2). Let us begin by assuming that points (1, 2) and (2, 1) are the closest. Compute the centroid of the two points by averaging its *x* and *y* coordinates to give *x* = (1.5, 1.5). Then consider the clusters, one with centroid (0, 0) and another with centroid (1.5, 1.5). Combine the three points (0, 0), (1, 2) and (2, 1) into a single cluster with centroid (1, 1). The centroid was computed by averaging the *x* coordinates for all the three data points ((0 + 2 + 1) / 3) and likewise averaging the *y* coordinates for all the three data points ((0 + 1 + 2) /3).

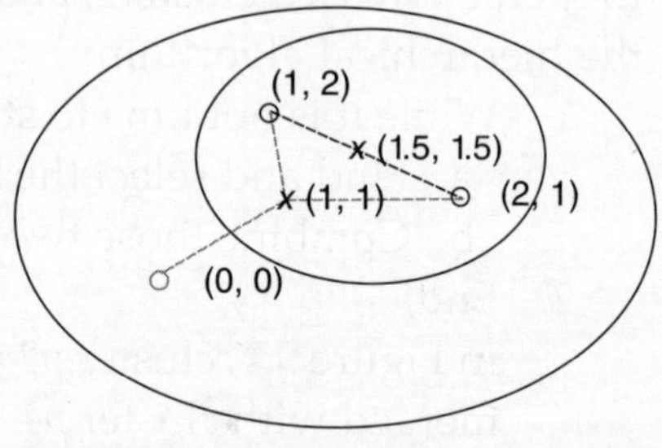

Figure 9.5 *Centroid in a Euclidean space*

Implementation of Hierarchical Clustering in R

R language provides a function `hclust()` that performs hierarchical clustering on a distance matrix. For finding the distance matrix, `dist()` function is used that generates the distance matrix. The basic syntax of `hclust()` is as follows:

```
hclust(d, method,...)
```

where,

"*d*" argument defines a dissimilar structure such as dissimilar matrix generated by `dist()` function; "method" argument defines the type of method used for clustering. This can be "ward.D", "ward.D2", "single", "complete", "average", "median", "centroid", "mcquitty"; the dots "..." define the other optional arguments.

In the following example, `matrix()` function creates a 10 by 10 matrix. The `dist()` function creates a dissimilar matrix "ed" using the Euclidean method. Now the `hclust()` function generates the dendrogram of this matrix (Figure 9.6).

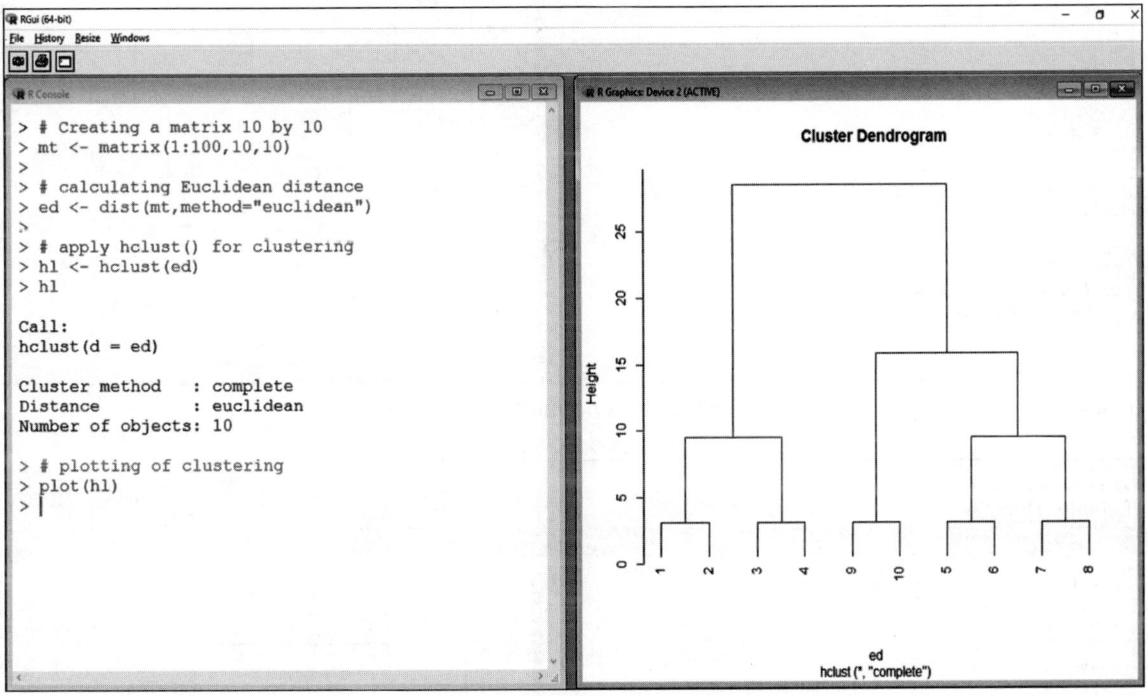

FIGURE 9.6 *Generating dendrogram using hclust() function for clustering*

Example 1

In this example, a sample dataset "DemoSample.csv" is taken for clustering that contains two columns, "Sample1" and "Sample2". `as.matrix() function is` used to convert the dataset, "r" into a matrix, "dc". The `dist()` function creates a dissimilar matrix "dm" using the Euclidean method. Now, the `hclust()` function generates different types of dendrogram for this sample dataset using different methods. Figures 9.7–9.9 shows the dendrograms generated using the method "complete", "average", and "single" respectively. All the three dendrograms are different.

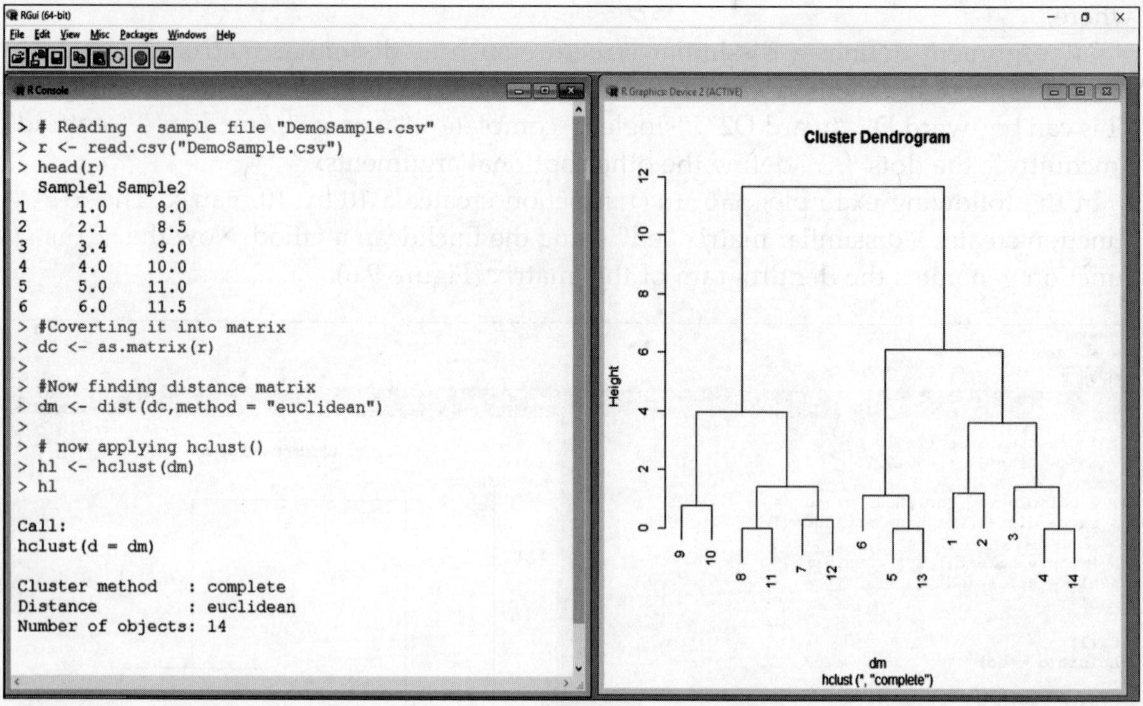

FIGURE 9.7 *Dendrogram for the sample data using method "complete"*

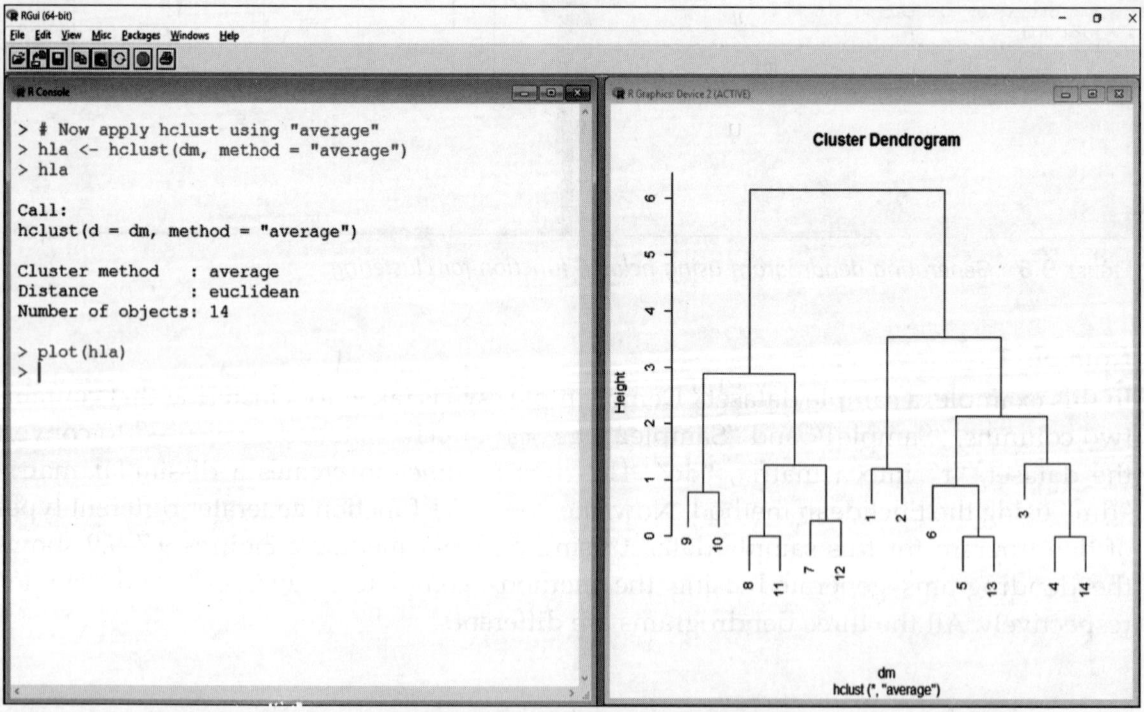

FIGURE 9.8 *Dendrogram for the sample dataset using method "average"*

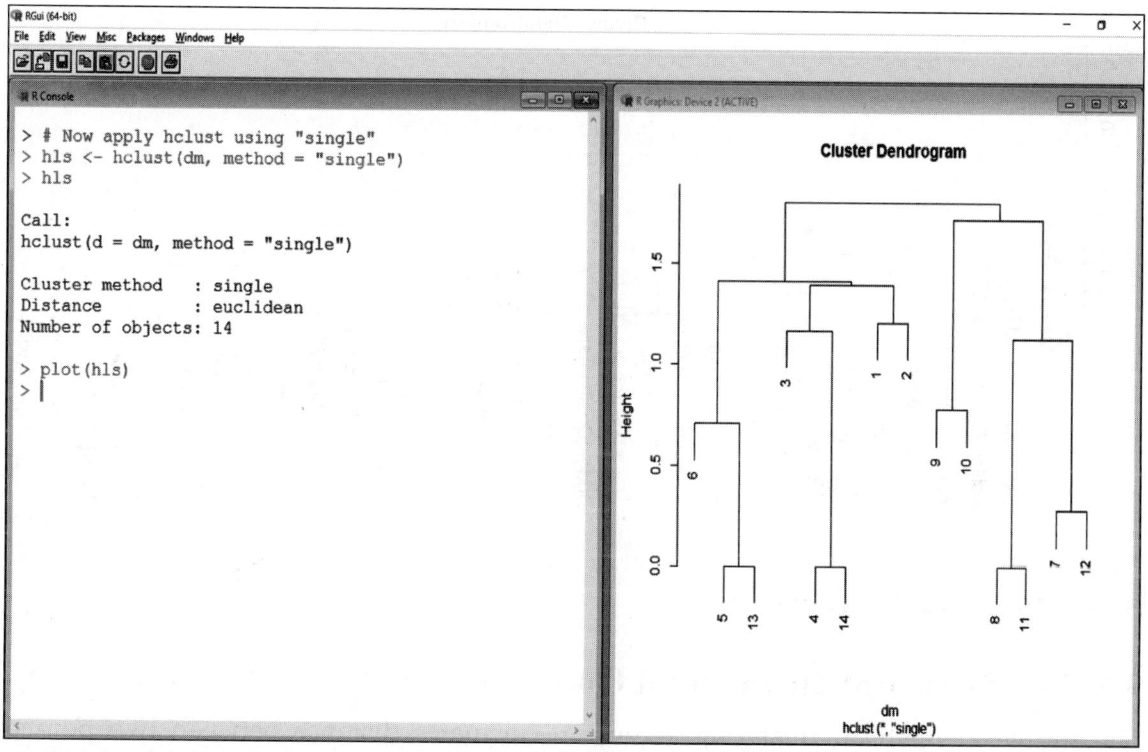

FIGURE 9.9 *Dendrogram for the sample dataset using method "single"*

Example 2

For the data set mtcars, we can run the distance matrix with hclust, and plot a dendrogram that displays a hierarchical relationship among the vehicles.

Step 1: Find the distance matrix.

```
> d <- dist(as.matrix(mtcars))
```

Step 2: Apply hierarchical clustering.

```
> hc <- hclust (d)
```

Step 3: Plot the dendrogram (Figure 9.10).

```
> plot (hc)
```

Careful inspection of the dendrogram shows that 1974 Pontiac Firebird and Camaro Z28 are classified as close relatives as expected.

Similarly, the dendrogram shows that the 1974 Honda Civic and Toyota Corolla are close to each other.

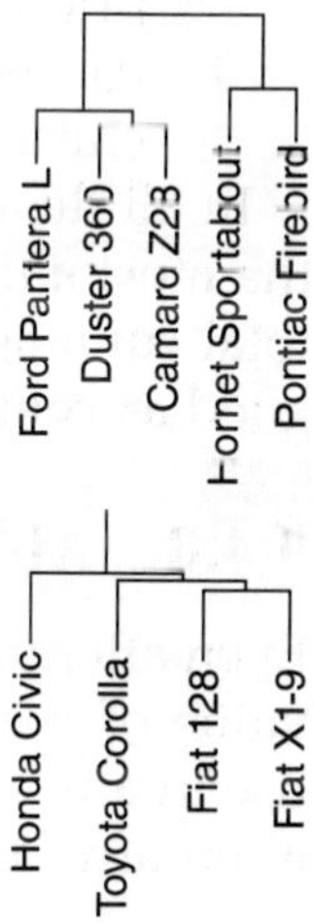

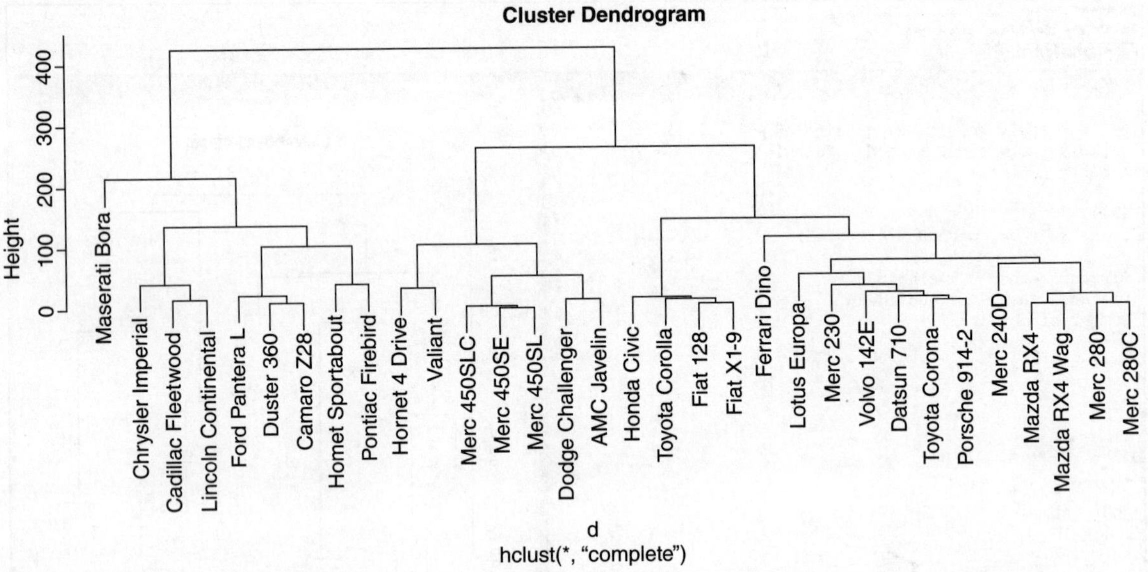

FIGURE 9.10 *Cluster dendrogram*

9.4.2 Efficiency of Hierarchical Clustering

The simple hierarchical clustering algorithm calculates distance between two points, which is not very efficient. Hence, to improve the efficiency of hierarchical clustering it is necessary to calculate distances between every pair of cluster for finding the best merger. In this case, the hierarchical clustering should use the following steps:

1. At first, calculate the distances between every pair of points that takes time $O(n^2)$.
2. Now, find the smallest distance from the pairs and arrange their distances into a priority queue. It also takes time $O(n^2)$.
3. After this, remove all entries of the two clusters that are to be merged from the priority queue. It takes time O(nlogn).
4. At last, calculate all the distances between the new cluster and the remaining clusters. It takes time O(nlogn).

In all the four steps, the last two steps execute in O(nlogn) time which means that at the most *n* times, whereas the first two steps execute only once in $O(n^2)$ time, hence the total running time complexity of the hierarchical clustering is $O(n^2 logn)$ which is very good as compared to $O(n^3)$.

9.4.3 Alternative Rules for Controlling Hierarchical Clustering

Even after improving the efficiency of the algorithm, there are still some limitations. The value of *n* is very large, which should not be, because a large value is not feasible to use in any application through clustering approach. To overcome such a problem, some alternative rules are available that can control hierarchical clustering.

1. Find out the distance between the two clusters that is a minimum of all distances between any two points where each point should be selected from each cluster. It generates an entirely different cluster that is obtained using the distance-of-centroid rule. For example, in Figure 9.11, it is good to select the next cluster point (10, 5) with the cluster of two points as (10, 5) has distance *p*2 and there is no other pair of unclustered points that is this close.

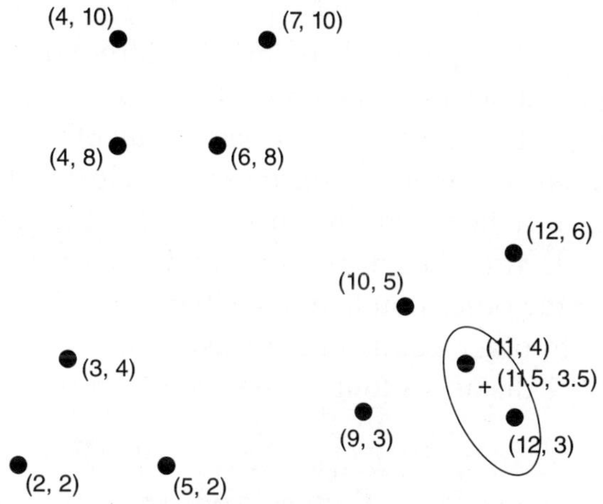

FIGURE 9.11 *Points in the space for finding clusters*

2. Another rule is to find out the distance between the two clusters that is to be the average distance of all pairs where each point should be selected from each cluster.
3. The third rule is to calculate the radius of a cluster. The radius is the maximum distance between all the points and the centroid. For this, combine two clusters whose resulting cluster has the lowest radius. In this case, another method is to use the sum of squares of the distances between the points and the centroid.
4. The last rule is to calculate the diameter of a cluster. The diameter of a cluster is the maximum distance between any two points of the cluster.

9.4.4 Hierarchical Clustering in Non-Euclidean Space

In the non-Euclidean space, the only "locations" that we can talk about are the points themselves, i.e. there is no "average" of two points. The question is then, "how to represent a cluster of many points?" The answer is to compute a "clustroid". A "clustroid" is a data point "closest" to other points. The other question is "how does one determine the "nearness" of clusters?" The simple answer is to treat clustroid as if it were centroid when computing intercluster distances.

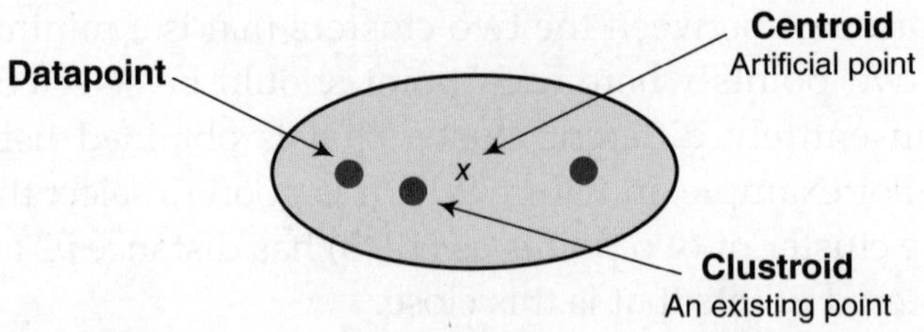

FIGURE 9.12 *A cluster with clustroid*

In Figure 9.12, we have a cluster on three data points. A centroid here is an average of all data points in the cluster. This implies that the centroid is an artificial point. On the other hand, a clustroid is an existing data point that is "closest" to all other points in the cluster.

There are different methods available for selecting the clustroid. Each clustroid is designed to minimise the distance between the clustroid and other points in the cluster. Some common methods for selecting the clustroid that minimises are as follows:

- The average distance to the other points in the cluster.
- The maximum distance to other points in the cluster.
- The sum of squares of the distances to the other points in the cluster.

Check Your Understanding

1. What do you mean by hierarchical clustering?

Ans: Hierarchical clustering organises the set of nested clusters as a tree. Each cluster [node] of the tree, excluding the leaf nodes, is the union of its sub-clusters [children] and the root of the tree is the cluster that contains all the objects.

2. What is a Euclidean space?

Ans: A Euclidean space contains two dimensions with one centre point.

9.5 k-MEANS ALGORITHM

k-means algorithm is one of the famous partitioning clustering algorithm. This section explains the basics of the k-means algorithm, the number of clusters for this, and its right value. Along with this, the BFR algorithm is also described in this section.

9.5.1 k-means Basics

k-means algorithm is an unsupervised clustering method that assigns different data objects into a number of clusters. It takes the input dataset (k), partitions it into a set of *n* objects, and assigns them to *k* clusters. Due to this, the similarity of the resulting intra-cluster is high, whereas the similarity of the inter-cluster is low. The mean value of the objects (cluster's centroid or centre of gravity) in a cluster finds the cluster similarity.

The main strategy of k-means algorithm is that it first randomly selects k number of objects, where each object initially represents a cluster mean or centre. After this, for each remaining object, the object is assigned to its similar cluster according to the distance between the object and the cluster mean. Now the algorithm calculates the new mean for each cluster and this process is repeated until the defined function converges. The pseudocode of the k-means algorithm is given below:

k-means algorithm

(k = number of clusters, D = a dataset containing n objects):

1. Initially choose k points from the dataset, D that are likely to be in different clusters as the initial cluster centres;
2. Make these points the centroids of their clusters;
3. For each of the remaining points p:
   - Find the centroid to which p is closest;
   - Add p to the cluster of that centroid;
   - Adjust the centroid of that cluster to account for p;
4. End;

To fix the centroid of the clusters, the algorithm may add an optional step where it reassigns each point, including the k initial points, to the k clusters.

Implementation of k-means Clustering in R

R language provides a function `k-means()` that performs the k-means clustering on a data matrix. The basic syntax of `k-means()` is as follows:

```
k-means(x, centers, iter.max= 10, nstart = 1, algorithm =
c("Hartigan-Wong", "Lloyd", "Forgy", "MacQueen"),…)
```

where,

"x" argument defines a numeric matrix of the data or an object that can be converted to a matrix; "centers" argument contains either the number of clusters (k) or a set of initial (distinct) cluster centers; "iter.max" argument defines the maximum number of iterations; "nstart" argument defines the number of random sets that should be chosen if centers is a number; "algorithm" defines the type of algorithm used for clustering; the dots, "…" defines the other optional arguments.

Example 1

`matrix()` function is used to create a 4 by 4 matrix. The `k-means()` function takes value 3 for "centers" argument to create the number of clusters of the matrix (Figure 9.13). It is necessary that the value of the "centers" argument is less than the value of the column value of the matrix. The function returns the cluster means of all three clusters along with cluster components and vector. Figure 9.14 defines the corresponding plot for the given clusters of the matrix.

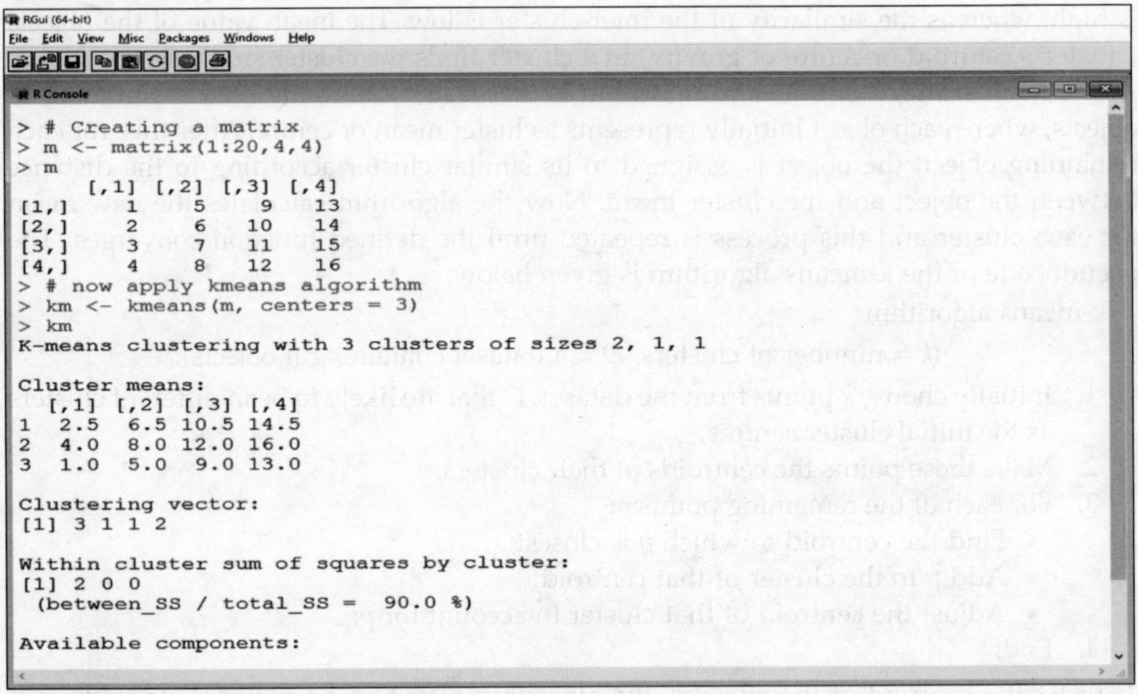

FIGURE 9.13 *Use of* `k-means()` *function for clustering*

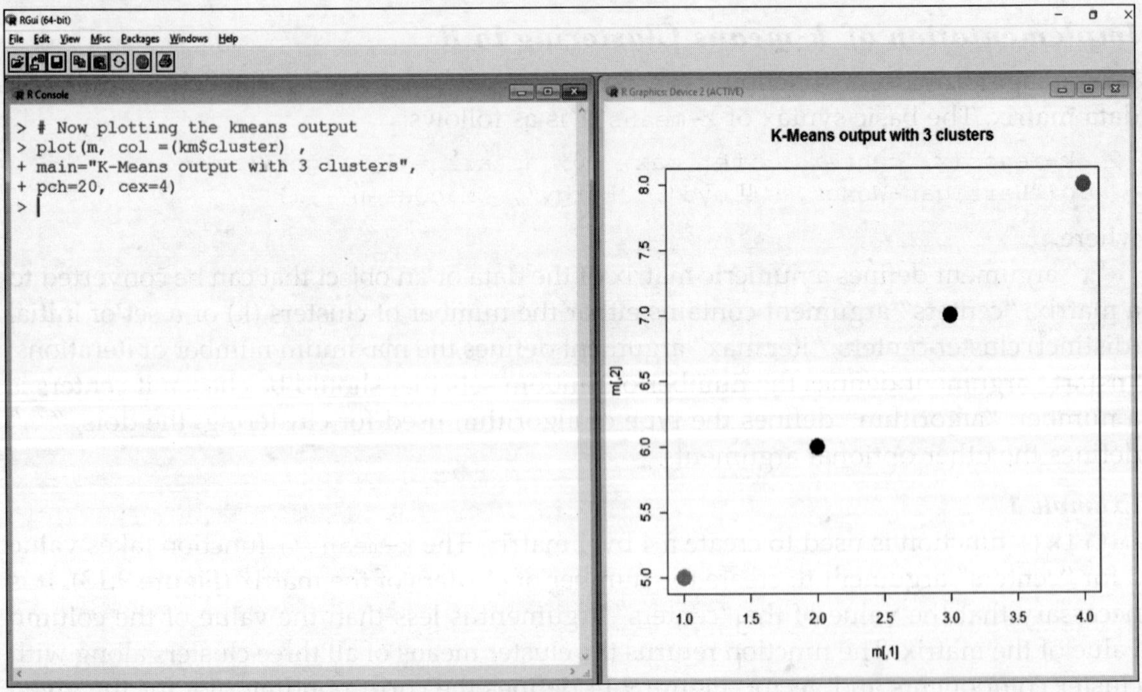

FIGURE 9.14 *Plot of clusters or* `k-means()` *function output*

Example 2

This demonstration uses the iris dataset. This dataset gives the measurements in centimeters of the variables, sepal length and width, petal length and width of 50 flowers of each of the three species of iris. The species are *Iris setosa, versicolor,* and *virginica.*

Let us start by looking at the first 6 records (there are a total of 150 rows) of the iris dataset. Data is available under five columns (variables), "Sepal.Length", "Sepal.Width", "Petal.Length", "Petal.Width" and "Species".

```
> head(iris)
    Sepal.Length  Sepal.Width  Petal.Length  Petal.Width  Species
1   5.1           3.5          1.4           0.2          setosa
2   4.9           3.0          1.4           0.2          setosa
3   4.7           3.2          1.3           0.2          setosa
4   4.6           3.1          1.5           0.2          setosa
5   5.0           3.6          1.4           0.2          setosa
6   5.4           3.9          1.7           0.4          setosa
```

Step 1: Copy the dataset, "iris" into a data frame, "newiris".

```
> newiris <- iris
> head(newiris)
    Sepal.Length  Sepal.Width  Petal.Length  Petal.Width  Species
1   5.1           3.5          1.4           0.2          setosa
2   4.9           3.0          1.4           0.2          setosa
3   4.7           3.2          1.3           0.2          setosa
4   4.6           3.1          1.5           0.2          setosa
5   5.0           3.6          1.4           0.2          setosa
6   5.4           3.9          1.7           0.4          setosa
```

Step 2: Set the "Species" column of the data frame, "newiris" to NULL.

```
> newiris$Species <- NULL
```

Note: The "Species" column is no longer present in the data frame, "newiris".

```
> head(newiris)
    Sepal.Length  Sepal.Width  Petal.Length  Petal.Width
1   5.1           3.5          1.4           0.2
2   4.9           3.0          1.4           0.2
3   4.7           3.2          1.3           0.2
4   4.6           3.1          1.5           0.2
5   5.0           3.6          1.4           0.2
6   5.4           3.9          1.7           0.4
```

Step 3: Apply k-means to the data frame, "newiris", and store the clustering result in "kc". The cluster number is set to 3.

```
> (kc <- kmeans(newiris, 3))
k-means clustering with 3 clusters of sizes 50, 62, 38

Cluster means:
  Sepal.Length   Sepal.Width   Petal.Length   Petal.Width
1     5.006000      3.428000       1.462000      0.246000
2     5.901613      2.748387       4.393548      1.433871
3     6.850000      3.073684       5.742105      2.071053
Clustering vector:
 [1] 111111111111111111111111111111111111111111111111112232
     222222222222222222222223222
[82] 222222222222222222232333323333332233332323223333332
     333323332332332

Within cluster sum of squares by cluster:
[1] 15.15100 39.82097 23.87947
 (between_SS / total_SS = 88.4%)

Available components:

[1] "cluster" "centers" "totss" "withinss" "tot.withinss" "be-
tweenss" "size" "iter" "ifault"
```

Compare the "Species" label with the clustering result.

```
> table (iris$Species, kc$cluster)
              1     2      3
setosa        50    0      0
versicolor    0     48     2
virginica     0     14     36
```

Step 4: Let us plot the clusters and their centres. Note that there are four dimensions ("Sepal.Length", "Sepal.Width", "Petal.Length" and "Petal.Width") in the data. We will use only two dimensions ("Sepal.Length" and "Sepal.Width") to draw the plot as follows (Figure 9.15):

```
> plot(newiris[c("Sepal.Length", "Sepal.Width")], col=kc$cluster)
$Species, kc$cluster)
> points(kc$centers[,c("Sepal.Length", "Sepal.Width")], col=1:3,
pch=8, cex=2)
```

"Points" is a generic function to draw a sequence of points at the specified coordinates. The argument, "pch" is to plot "character", i.e. "symbol to use", "col" specifies the color code to use and "cex" is for "character or symbol expansion" (Figure 9.16).

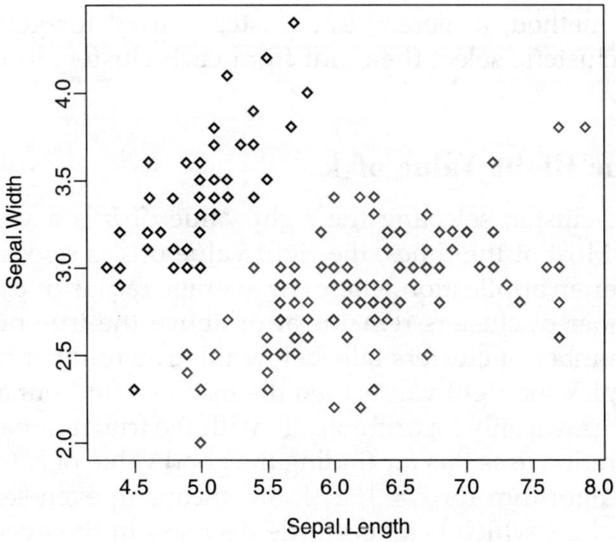

FIGURE 9.15

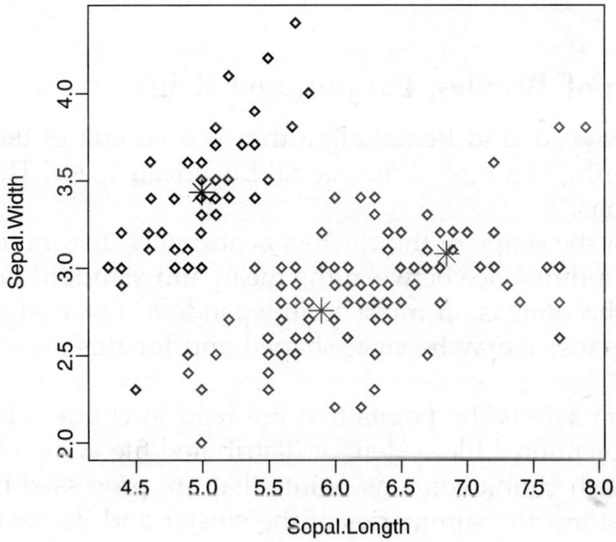

FIGURE 9.16

9.5.2 Initialising Clusters for k-means

In the k-means algorithm, selecting the initial *k* points is a very critical task. For this, the following methods can be used:

- In the first method, select the points that are as far away from one another as possible. In this case, it is good to select the points randomly. If there are points fewer than *k* points, then add the points with minimum distance from the selected points.

- In the second method, a hierarchical cluster is used for getting a sample of the data. In the *k* clusters, select the point from each cluster closest to the centroid of the cluster.

9.5.3 Picking the Right Value of k

After initialising the cluster, selecting the right value of *k* is a very tough task in the k-means algorithm. Most of the times, the right value of *k* is selected based on guesses. For example, consider an application where the average radius or diameter values grows slowly and the number of clusters remains at or above the true number of clusters. In simple words, the number of clusters falls below the true number present in the data.

If it is difficult to pick the right value, then the user can find out a good value. A good value of *k* is one that grows only logarithmically with the true number. A different number of the clustering operation uses this for finding the good value of *k*. For this, it is necessary to run the k-means algorithm for $k = 1, 2, 4, 8\ldots$ means in even series. It will give two values between v and $2v$, which is a very little decrease in the average diameter that is justified by the data that lies between $v/2$ and v. In this case, using the binary search is the best method for finding the correct value of *k*. In conclusion, selecting the logarithmic value for *k* is best.

9.5.4 Algorithm of Bradley, Fayyad, and Reina

The BFR (Bradley, Fayyad, and Reina) algorithm is a variant of the k-means algorithm that performs clustering in a high-dimensional Euclidean space. The algorithm uses the following assumptions:

- It assumes that the shape of the clusters is normally distributed about a centroid.
- There may be a difference between the mean and standard deviation for a cluster and for this, the dimension must be independent. For example, in two different dimensions, a cluster may be cigar-shaped and for this, the cigar must not rotate on the axes.

The BFR algorithm selects the points that are read in chunks. These chunks may be obtained from a conventional file system or distributed file system that partitions it into appropriate sizes. Each chunk contains points that are processed in the main memory. The main memory stores the summaries of the cluster and its data. The main memory data contains three other objects (Discard, Compressed, and Retained) with the chunks from the input.

Discard Set

Discard set is a summary of the clusters themselves. Actually, these cluster summaries are a very essential part. However, the points that the summary represents are discarded and have no representation in main memory other than through this summary.

Compressed Set

A compressed set is also the summary of the clusters but for sets of points that are found close to one another and not close to any other cluster. The points represented by the compressed set are also discarded implying that they do not appear explicitly in the main memory. These represented sets of points are known as miniclusters.

Retained Set

Retained set contains points that can neither be assigned to a cluster nor are they sufficiently close to any other points that allow them to be represented by a compressed set. These points are held in main memory exactly as they appear in the input file.

If the data is d-dimensional then the discard and compressed set are represented by *2d+1* values. In simple words, it represents a set of points by their count, their centroid, and the standard deviation in each dimension. Along with this, it is good to use N (count), SUM (sum of dimension-divided by N), SUMSQ (square root of variance) instead of using count, their centroid, and the standard deviation respectively.

Figure 9.17 defines all the three sets: discard, compressed, and retained.

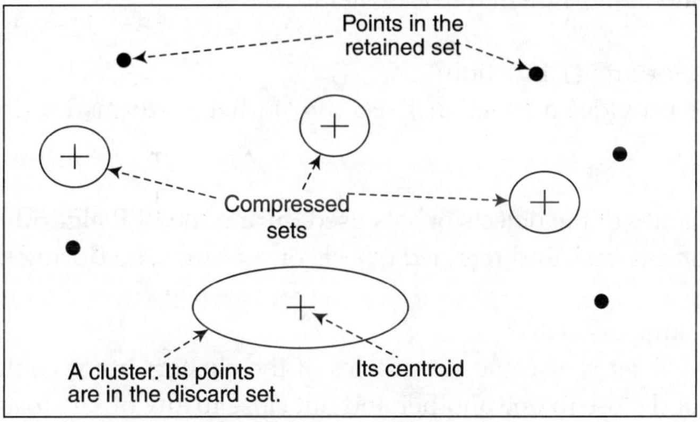

FIGURE 9.17 *Discard set, compressed set, and retained set*

9.5.5 Processing Data in the BFR Algorithm

The BFR (Bradley, Fayyad, and Reina) algorithm processes a chunk of points of any dataset by using the following steps:

1. First, it finds all points that are sufficiently close to the centroid of a cluster. It is simple to add the point to the N, SUM, and SUMSQ that represent the cluster. After this, it discards the points.
2. In the second step, it finds all points that are not sufficiently close to any centroid. These points are clustered along with the points that are in the retained set. For this, it uses any main-memory clustering algorithm such as hierarchical clustering. Then it is summarised and adds the clusters of more than one point to the compressed set, so singleton clusters become the retained set of points.

3. Then it obtains the miniclusters from the old compressed set and from our attempts to cluster new points and the old retained set. Although none of these miniclusters can be merged with one of the *k* clusters, they might merge with one another.
4. In the next step, points that are assigned to clusters or miniclusters and are not in the retained set are then written out to the secondary memory with their assignment.
5. In the final step, if this happens to be the last chunk of input data then we can either treat the compressed and retained set as outliers and never cluster them or assign each point in the retained set to the cluster of the nearest centroid and merge each minicluster with the cluster whose centroid is closest to the centroid of the minicluster.

Check Your Understanding

1. What is a k-means algorithm?

Ans: k-means algorithm is an unsupervised clustering method that assigns different data objects into a number of clusters. It takes the input dataset (k), partitions it into a set of *n* objects, and assigns them into *k* clusters.

2. What is a `k-means()` function?

Ans: R language provides a function `k-means()` that performs k-means clustering on a data matrix.

3. Write the names of the objects or sets used during the BFR algorithm.

Ans: Discard, compressed, and retained objects or sets are used during the BFR algorithm.

4. What is a compressed set?

Ans: A compressed set is also the summaries of the clusters but it contains a set of points that are found close to one another and not close to any other cluster.

9.6 CURE ALGORITHM

The CURE (Clustering Using **RE**presentatives) algorithm is another large-scale clustering algorithm.

9.6.1 Initialisation in CURE

The CURE algorithm follows the concept of Euclidean space and does not consider the shape of clusters. The algorithm represents the clusters using a collection of representative points. Due to this, the algorithm is called the Clustering Using **RE**presentatives.

The CURE algorithm uses the following steps for clustering during the initialisation phase of the algorithm:

1. It takes a small sample from the dataset and clusters it into the main memory. For this, it is good to use the hierarchical method that merges the clusters having a close pair of points.
2. Then it selects a small set of points from each cluster as representative points. These points should be selected in such a way that they are as far from one another as possible.
3. After this, it moves each representative point to a fixed fraction of the distance between its location and the centroid of its cluster. Most often 20% is selected as a good fraction. In this step, it also uses Euclidean space for finding the distance between two points.

9.6.2 Completion of the CURE Algorithm

In this section, completion stage of the CURE algorithm is discussed, which is the last step of the algorithm. In this step, the algorithm merges two clusters if they have a pair of representative points, one from each cluster and are close to each other. The algorithm continues merging until there are no more sufficiently close clusters.

In the last step of the algorithm, points are assigned. For this, each point p is brought from secondary storage and compared with the representative points. After this, p is assigned to the cluster of the representative point that is closest to the point p.

Figure 9.18 represents two different clusters with different shapes by following the concept of the CURE algorithm.

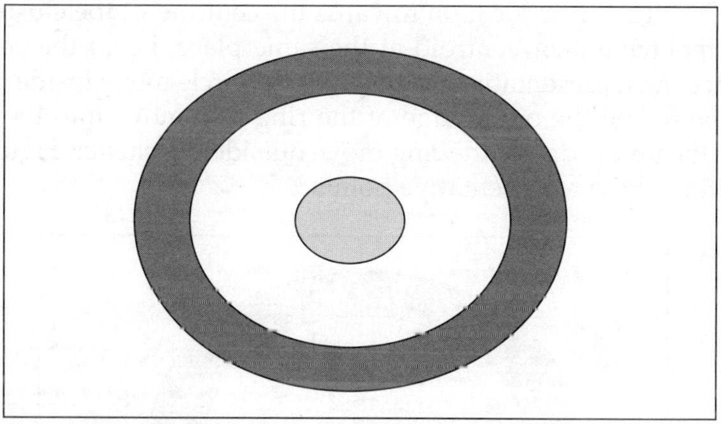

FIGURE 9.18 *Representation of two clusters using CURE algorithm*

In two circles, the inner cluster is an ordinary circle, while the outer cluster is a ring around the circle. The three steps of the algorithm are as follows:

1. In the first step, hierarchical clustering algorithm can be used on some sample data based on Figure 9.18. The distance taken between two clusters is the shortest distance between any pair of points, one from each cluster. It easily generates the two clusters, meaning pieces of the ring would stick together and pieces of the

inner circle would stick together but pieces of the ring would be far away from the pieces of the circle.

2. In the second step, representative points are selected from the sample data. If the sample data is large enough then it is easy to count the sample points of the cluster at the greatest distance from one another that are lying on the boundary of the cluster. Figure 9.19 defines the representative points.

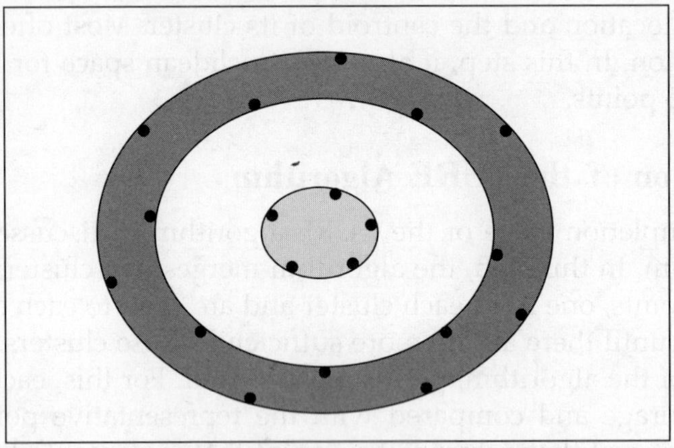

FIGURE 9.19 *Selecting representative points that are far from one another*

3. In the third and last step, move the representative points with a fixed fraction of the distance from their true location towards the centroid of the cluster. In Figure 9.19, both clusters have their centroid at the same place, i.e. at the centre of the inner circle hence the representative points from the circle move inside the cluster. Along this, the points on the outer edge of the ring also move into their cluster but the points on the inner edge of the ring move outside the cluster. Figure 9.20 shows the final location of the representative points.

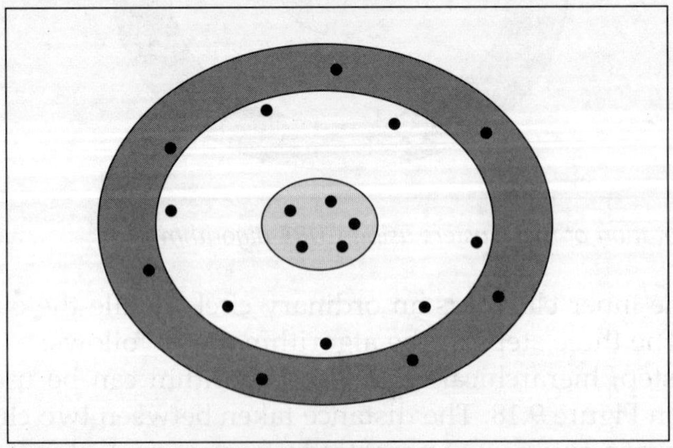

FIGURE 9.20 *Final location of the representative points*

9.7 Clustering in Non-Euclidean Space

This section discusses the clustering algorithm in non-Euclidean space to handle non-main memory data. The GRGPF algorithm is one of the clustering algorithm that uses non-Euclidean space. Its name comes from the name of its authors V. Ganti, R. Ramakrishnan, J. Gehrke, A. Powell, and J. French. It follows the concept of hierarchical and partitioning methods and represents the clusters using sample points in the main memory.

The algorithm organises the clusters in a hierarchical form (tree) so that it is easy to assign the new points to the appropriate cluster by passing it down the tree. The leaves of the tree contain the summaries of some clusters and the interior nodes of the tree contain subsets of the cluster information that makes it possible to describe the clusters that are reachable through that node. Along with this, it also groups the clusters using their distance from one another. In this case, the clusters at a leaf are close and the clusters reachable from one interior node are relatively close as well.

The major steps of the GRGPF algorithm are as follows:

- Representing the clusters
- Initialising the cluster tree
- Adding points in the clusters
- Merging and Splitting the clusters

The following subsections describe the steps.

9.7.1 Representing Clusters in the GRGPF Algorithm

Clusters grow in size as points are assigned to it. Some points in clusters are stored on disk and not used in guiding the assignment of points. The representation of a cluster in main memory involves several features. Before getting to understand the features, it is important to consider the below:

Assume p is any point in the cluster, then ROWSUM(p) is the sum of the squares of the distances from p to each of the other points in the cluster and d is the distance measure

The following features form the representation of the cluster:

1. N defines the number of points in the cluster.
2. The clustroid is the point in the cluster with the smallest ROWSUM. It minimises the sum of the squares of the distances to the other points.
3. The k points of the clusters closest to the clustroid and their rowsums also come under representation of cluster except when the addition of points to the cluster causes the clustroid to change. For this, it is assumed that the new clustroid would be one of these k points near the old clustroid.
4. The k points of the clusters furthest from the clustroid and their rowsums also come under representation of cluster. Through this, it can be considered whether two clusters are close enough for merging. For this, it is assumed that if two clusters are close then a pair of points distant from their respective clustroids would be close.

9.7.2 Initialising the Cluster Tree

After representing the clusters in main memory, the GRGPF algorithm initialises the cluster tree. In the algorithm, the clusters are organised into a tree. Every cluster representation has a size that does not depend on the number of points in the clusters.

In the cluster tree, each leaf of the tree holds as many cluster representations as can fit whereas the interior node contains a sample of the clustroids of the clusters. Each subtree of the interior node represents these clusters along with the pointer to the roots of those subtrees.

The algorithm initialises the cluster tree by taking a main memory sample of the dataset and performs hierarchical clustering on it. It generates a tree *T* that is not exactly the tree used by the GRGPF algorithm. The algorithm selects from *T* and few nodes that represent the clusters according to the desired size *n*. These clusters work as initial clusters for the algorithm and their representations are placed at the leaf of the cluster-representing tree.

Now the algorithm groups the clusters using one common ancestor in *T* into the interior nodes of the cluster-representing tree. By doing this, clusters descended from one interior node are as close as possible. For getting more efficient output, it is good to rebalance the cluster-representing tree.

9.7.3 Adding Points in the GRGPF Algorithm

Adding points is the next step in the GRGPF algorithm after initialisation. The algorithm reads points from the disk (secondary storage) and inserts each point into the nearest cluster. For this, the algorithm uses the following steps:

1. The algorithm starts at the root and looks at the sample of clustroids for each of the children of the root.
2. During this, examine the next child that has the clustroid closest to the new point *p*. It repeats this process for each node in the tree.
3. Some sample clustroids at a node may have been seen at a higher level but each level provides more details about the clusters that are lying below it, so we see many new sample clustroids each time we go a level down the tree.
4. After reaching a leaf that contains the cluster features for each cluster represented by that leaf. At last, that cluster is selected whose clustroid is closest to point *p*.

The algorithm adds 1 to *N* or add the square of the distance between *p* and each of the nodes *q* used in the representation to ROWSUM(q). These points *q* includes the clustroids, the *k* nearest points, and *k* furthest points.

The algorithm estimates the ROWSUM of *p* using the following formula:

$$\text{ROWSUM(p)} = \text{ROWSUM(c)} + \text{N}d^2(\text{p,c})$$

Where,

d(p,c) = distance between *p* and clustroid *c*.

N and ROWSUM are the values of these features before they were adjusted to account for the addition of *p*.

9.7.4 Splitting and Merging Clusters

In the last step of processing, the GRGPF algorithm splits and merges the clusters. The process of splitting and merging clusters is as follows:

Splitting Clusters

The algorithm assumes that there is a limit on the radius of a cluster. How does one define the radius of a cluster? The radius is the square root of the average square of the distance from the clustroid of the points in the cluster and uses the following formula for calculation:

$$\text{Radius} = \sqrt{ROWSUM(c)/N}$$

where,

c is the clustroid of the cluster; *N* is the number of points in the cluster

When do you decide on splitting a cluster? When the radius of a cluster grows too large, the cluster is split into two. During computation, the points of that cluster are brought into main memory and partitioned into two clusters to minimise the rowsums. After this, the cluster features for both clusters are calculated. It generates output where the leaf of the split cluster contains one more cluster to represent.

It is beneficial to manage the cluster tree like a B-tree. By doing so, it can get some space in a leaf to add one more cluster. However, if there is no room/space, then the leaf should again split into two leaves. For this splitting, it adds another pointer and more sample clustroids at the parent node. Again, it may have extra space, if not, then it must be split again. This is done to minimise the squares of the distances between the sample clustroids assigned to different nodes.

Merging Clusters

During splitting, it can so happen that the cluster-representing tree is too large to fit in main memory. In this case, the algorithm raises the limit on how large the radius of a cluster can be and then merges the pairs of the clusters.

For merging of the clusters, the algorithm selects the nearby clusters meaning the representatives of the clusters are on the same leaf or at leaves with a common parent. Alternatively, it can also merge any two clusters *C1* and *C2* into one single cluster C. The algorithm assumes that the clustroid of C will be one of the points that are as far as possible from the clustroid of *C1* or the clustroid of *C2*.

For the computation of the rowsum in C for the point *p* that is one of the *k* points in *C1* and far from the centroid of *C1*, the algorithm uses the curse of dimensionality. According to the curse of dimensionality, all angles are approximately right angles to justify the following formula:

$$\text{ROWSUMc(p)} = \text{ROWSUMc}_1\text{(p)} + \text{Nc}_2\,(\text{d}^2(\text{p, c}_1) + \text{d}^2(\text{c}_1, \text{c}_2)) + \text{ROWSUMc}_2(\text{c}_2)$$

where,

We subscript *N* and ROWSUM by the cluster to which that feature refers; c_1 and c_2 represent the clustroids of *C1* and *C2* respectively.

For this formula, the algorithm uses the following steps for calculation:

1. Now the algorithm computes the sum of the squares of the distances from *p* to all the nodes in the merged cluster C by beginning with ROWSUMc_1(p) for getting the terms for the points in the same cluster as *p*.
2. For the Nc_2 points *q* in *C2*, it considers the path from *p* to the clustroid of *C1* then to the clustroid of C2 and finally to *q*.
3. It also assumes that there is a right angle between the legs from *p* to c_1 and c_1 to c_2. In addition, there is a right angle between the shortest path from *p* to c_2 and the leg from c_2 to *q*.
4. After this, it uses the Pythagoras Theorem to justify computing the square of the length of the path to each *q* as the sum of the squares of the three legs.

The last step in merging is the computation of the features of the merged cluster. For this, the algorithm considers all points in the merged cluster that have the rowsum. It includes the centroids of the two clusters, the *k* points closest and furthest to and from the clustroids respectively for each cluster.

Now it calculates the distance from the new clustroid for each of these *4k + 1* points and selects *k* with the smallest and largest distances as the "close" and "far" points respectively. At last, it calculates the rowsums for the chosen points using the same formula that was used to calculate the rowsums for the candidate clustroids.

Check Your Understanding

1. What is GRGPF algorithm?

Ans: The GRGPF algorithm is one of the clustering algorithm that uses non-Euclidean space. Its name comes from the name of its authors V. Ganti, R. Ramakrishnan, J. Gehrke, A. Powell, and J. French.

2. How does the GRGPF algorithm initialise the clusters?

Ans: The GRGPF algorithm initialises the cluster tree by taking a main memory sample of the dataset and performing hierarchical clustering on it.

9.8 Clustering for Streams and Parallelism

The following subsections briefly explain clustering a stream and parallelism.

9.8.1 Stream-computing Model

A stream-computing model uses the stream and works like a data stream management system. What is a stream? A stream is a sequence of characters, numbers, or others.

Figure 9.21 shows a data stream system where a stream processor takes some stream inputs and generates the output stream. The standing queries answer the queries asked by the user. All these streams are stored in the Archival Storage of the system. For the processing of the stream, this model either maintains the summaries of the streams or uses a sliding window of the most recently arrived data. At present, most real applications use streams for representing the data. The image data, sensor data, web traffic, the internet are few examples of stream data.

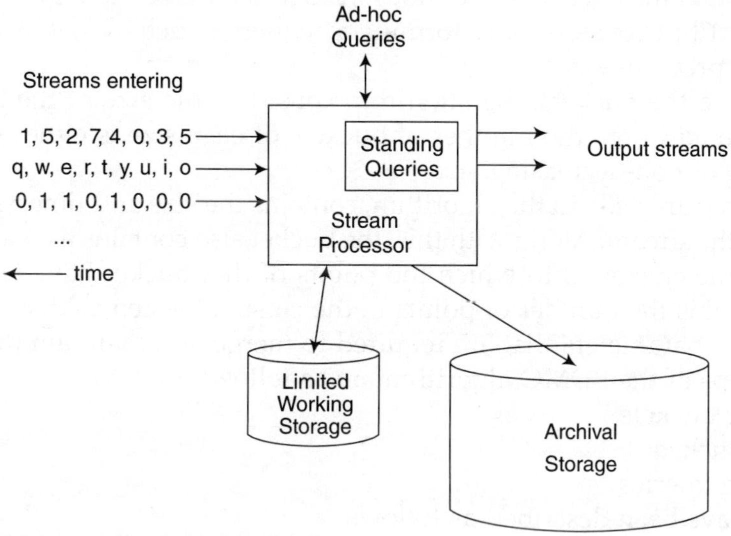

FIGURE 9.21 *Data stream management system*

With reference to clustering, a stream is nothing but a sliding window of N points. For the centroids or clustroids of the best clusters, it selects the last m points of these clusters where $m \leq N$. For clustering streams, the stream-computing model preclusters subsets of the points in the stream for getting the answer to the query *'What are the clusters of the last m points for $m \leq N$'*. In addition, the stream-computing model assumes that the statistics of the stream elements varies with time.

For getting an answer to this query, it is good to use the k-means method. This method partitions the last m points into exactly k clusters. Or we may allow the number of clusters to vary and then use a criterion to determine when to stop merging clusters into the larger clusters.

In order to find the distance space, it can use either Euclidean space or non-Euclidean space. In the Euclidean space, the distance is the centroid of the selected clusters, whereas in the non-Euclidean space, the distance is the clustroids of the selected clusters.

9.8.2 Stream-clustering Algorithm

The BDMO algorithm is one of the stream-clustering algorithms and the generalisation of the DGIM algorithm that clusters points of a slowly evolving stream. The name of the

BDMO algorithm comes from the name of its authors B. Babcock, M. Datar, R. Motwani, L.O'Callaghan.

The BDMO algorithm follows the concept of 'counting ones' method, which means that there is a window of length N on a binary stream and it counts the number of 1s that comes in the last k bits where $k \leq N$.

The BDMO algorithm uses the bucket with allowable bucket sizes that forms a sequence where each size is twice of the previous size. In the algorithm, the number of points represents the size of the bucket. It does not consider that the sequence of allowable bucket sizes starts with 1 but consider only forming a sequence such as 2, 4, 6, 8… where each size is twice the previous size.

For maintaining the buckets, the algorithm considers the size of the bucket with the power of two. In addition, the number of buckets of each size is either one or two that form a sequence of non-decreasing size.

The buckets that are used in the algorithm, contains the size and timestamp of the most recent points of the stream. Along with this, the bucket also contains a collection of records that represents the clusters into which the points of that bucket have been partitioned. This record contains the number of points in the cluster, the centroid, or clustroid of the cluster, and other parameters that are required to merge and maintain the clusters.

The major steps of the BDMO algorithm are as follows:

- Initialising buckets
- Merging buckets
- Answering queries

These steps have been described as follows.

Initialising Buckets

Initialisation of the bucket is the first step of the BDMO algorithm. The algorithm uses the smallest bucket size that is p with a power of two. It creates a new bucket with the most recent p points for p stream elements. The timestamp of the most recent point in the bucket is the timestamp of the new bucket. After this, we may choose to leave every point in a cluster by itself or perform clustering using an appropriate clustering method. For example, if k-means clustering method is used, it clusters the k points into k clusters.

For the initialisation of the bucket using selected clustering methods, it calculates the centroid or clustroids for the clusters and counts the points in each cluster. All this information is stored and becomes a record for each cluster. The algorithm also calculates the other required parameters for the merging process.

Merging Buckets

After the initialisation of the bucket, the algorithm needs to review the sequence of a bucket.

- If there happens to be a bucket with a timestamp more than N time units prior to the current time then nothing of that bucket is in the window. In such a case, the algorithm drops it from the list.

- In case we had created three buckets of size p, then we must merge the oldest two of the three buckets. In this case, the merger can create two buckets of size $2p$, *this may require us to merge* buckets of increasing sizes recursively.

For merging two consecutive buckets, the algorithm needs to perform the following steps:

1. For merging, the size of the bucket should be twice the sizes of the two buckets to be merged.
2. The timestamp of the merged bucket is the timestamp of the more recent of the two consecutive buckets.
3. In addition, it is necessary to calculate the parameters of the merged clusters.

Answering Queries

A query in the stream-computing model is a length of a suffix of the sliding window. Any algorithm takes all the clusters in all the buckets that are at least partially within the suffix and then merges them using some method. The answer of the query is the resulting clusters.

For the clustering of the streams, the stream-computing model finds out the answer to the query *'What are the clusters of the last or more recent m points in the stream for* $m \leq N$*'*. During the initialisation, the k-means method is used and for merging the buckets timestamp is used. Hence the algorithm is unable to find a set of buckets that covers the last m points.

However, we can choose the smallest set of buckets that covers the last m points and include in these buckets no more than the last $2m$ points. After this, the algorithm generates the answer in response to the query as 'the centroids or clustroids of all the points in the selected buckets'.

In addition, for getting a more accurate prediction of the query, it can assume that the points $2m$ and $m+1$ will not have different statistics from the most recent m points. In another case, if the statistics vary then reduce the error. It will follow a complex bucketing scheme that ensures to find buckets that cover at most the last $m(1+\varepsilon)$ points for any $\varepsilon > 0$.

After selecting the desired buckets, the algorithm pools all their clusters and uses some merging methods. If we are required to produce exactly k clusters then the algorithm merges the clusters with the closest centroids until it is left with only k clusters.

Now understand all the steps of the algorithm using a simple example that uses k-means method in a Euclidean space and represents the clusters by the count of their points and centroids. There is a bucket containing exactly k clusters so select point $p = k$ or $p > k$. Now cluster the p points into k clusters during bucket initialisation.

After initialisation, it is necessary to find the best match for merging between the k clusters of the first and second bucket. The best match is a match, which minimises the sum of the distances between the centroids of the matched clusters. It selects two different consecutive buckets to find each k true clusters in each of two adjacent buckets that rare in one stream.

The merging of the two clusters where each cluster is taken from each bucket sums the numbers of points in the two clusters. It generates the weighted average of the centroids of the two clusters that become the centroid of the merged cluster. The number of points in the cluster defines the weightage. Symbolically it can be defined as follows:

If there were two clusters *n1* and *n2* with centroids *c1* and *c2* respectively then the centroid of the merged cluster *c* would be as follows:

$$c = (n1c1 + n2c2) / n1 + n2$$

This centroid of the merged cluster *c* is also the answer to the query.

9.8.3 Clustering in a Parallel Environment

The simple concept of parallelism is to execute multiple processes at the same time by sharing same resources. It is possible to perform clustering and calculate the clusters in a parallel environment. For this, a simple phenomenon can be used where it is assumed that there is a huge collection of points and parallelism is needed for calculating the centroids of their clusters.

To implement such phenomenon, MapReduce method is the best option. However, most applications use only Reduce process for clustering. The MapReduce method is one of the latest programming paradigms that defines and implements the parallel distributed processing on the massive dataset. In the MapReduce programming paradigm, the Map and Reduce are two main tasks performed by the mapper and reducer respectively. The map task takes the input data as a set of key-value pairs and Reduce task produces a set of key-value pairs as the output. The detailed description of this programming paradigm is available in *Chapter 12*.

Use of MapReduce Method in Clustering

Different types of clustering algorithms are available and can be implemented with MapReduce paradigm. Most of the times, k-means clustering is used with the MapReduce framework. Use of MapReduce in data clustering helps to manage the data partition and parallel processing over the data chunks.

Any type of clustering should define both functions of the MapReduce paradigm. The MapReduce paradigm follows the concept of data partitioning and works on the keys and values.

Assuming that all data points in memory for clustering in the MapReduce paradigm are not possible, in this case, an algorithm is designed in such a way that task can be parallelised. It does not depend on other splits for any computation.

To implement the clustering in parallel environment, the MapReduce method divides the given data into chunks, clusters each chunk in parallel, and generates a single cluster. The description of both tasks is as follows:

Map Task

To start the map task, each task is assigned a subset of the points. Now the map function clusters the given points and generates a set of key-value pairs with a fixed key 1 with a value that describe one cluster in many forms such as count, centroid, or diameter of the cluster.

In simple words, the mappers do the distance computation and split out a key-value pair <centroid_id, data_point> and finds out the associativity of a data point with the cluster.

Reduce Task

Here all key-value pairs contain the same key hence only one Reduce function is used during the Reduce task. It takes the description of the clusters generated during the Map task and merges it appropriately. Now it uses a suitable clustering method to generate the output of the Reduce task.

In simple words, the Reducer work with specific cluster_id and a list of the data points associated with it. It calculates new means and writes to the new centroid file.

At last, according to the type of clustering algorithm, the paradigm needs to do a number of iterations or comparisons with the centroid in the previous iteration.

Check Your Understanding

1. What is a stream-computing model?

Ans: A stream-computing model uses the stream and works like a data stream management system.

2. What is a BDMO algorithm?

Ans: A BDMO algorithm is one of the stream-clustering algorithms and the generalisation of the DGIM algorithm that clusters points of a slowly evolving stream. The name of the BDMO algorithm comes from the names of the authors, B. Babcock, M. Datar, R. Motwani, L. O'Callaghan.

3. What is a 'counting ones' method?

Ans: The 'counting ones' method uses a window of length N on a binary stream and counts the number of 1s that come in the last k bits where $k \leq N$.

4. What is a MapReduce method?

Ans: The MapReduce method is one of the latest programming paradigms that defines and implements parallel distributed processing on massive datasets. In this method, Map and Reduce are two main tasks performed by the mapper and reducer respectively.

Case Study

Personalised Product Recommendations

Personalisation of products is similar to sales forecast. It is used to read user information, forecast the user needs, and to offer them the best products. In the process, many algorithms work together to predict the cognitive nature of customers to recommend what they need. This is also like an application for the users that can help them to identify their needs without wasting their time on the website/application.

The recommendation engine generates good revenue for a company and helps them in getting many insights on market. These days, most of the e-commerce companies have adopted this approach. Amazon, Flipkart, Snapdeal, MakeMyTrip are few examples. Recommendation is not limited ONLY to product recommendations. This mechanism can help the customers to make use of sales, discounts, etc., on anything they need.

If as a customer you placed a product in your cart, the data so generated, is used by companies to predict your requirement. Take a look at its impact.

1. ***Percentage of transaction revenue from recommendations:*** The worldwide average of website revenues generated from product recommendations is 18% as of today and likely to increase in future.
2. ***Impact on conversion rate:*** Personalisation tailors recommendations right down to the individual. It helps the retailers know the brands the customers love, the categories they shop and what they've bought or browsed in the past. The result? Higher conversion rates for the online retailers.
3. ***Placement of recommendations:*** Each recommendation has a huge impact on the customers' needs and it influences the cognitive nature of customers.
4. ***The impact of personal merchandising:*** The self-learning recommendation engine works in real-time, detecting product and customer behaviour updates as they happen and updating recommendations accordingly, ensuring a smooth, up-to-date and relevant user experience at all times.

Summary

- Clustering is a process that examines the given data and partitions it into many groups based on the similarity of data or its features.
- Data mining, information retrieval, search engines, academics, psychology and medicine, machine learning, computer graphics, pattern recognition, etc., are major application areas of clustering.
- The most common types of distance measures are Euclidean distance, Manhattan distance, Hamming distance, and Maximum norm used during clustering.

(Continued)

- R language provides a `dist()` function for measuring the distance using different types of method. The function calculates the distance and returns the distance matrix.
- Clustering strategies are the techniques that define the way in which clustering is performed on any dataset. Hierarchical and partitioning are two major and fundamental categories of the clustering strategies.
- Partitioning clustering strategy divides or partitions the dataset of *n* objects or tuples into *k* partitions of the dataset.
- The analysis and organisation of data in high-dimensional spaces (over hundreds of dimensions) that cannot fit in low-dimensional settings is called the curse of dimensionality.
- The 'curse' in the curse of dimensionality indicates that all pair of points are equally far away from one another and two vectors are mostly orthogonal.
- The angle between two vectors defines a single point or shortest angle where one vector turns around to another vector.
- The hierarchical clustering is a clustering that organises the set of nested clusters as a tree. Each cluster (node) of the tree excluding the leave nodes is the union of its sub-clusters (children) and the root of the tree is the cluster that contains all the objects.
- A Euclidean space contains two dimensions with one centre point.
- R language provides a function `hclust()` that performs hierarchical clustering on a distance matrix.
- A non-Euclidean space is space that contains more than one dimension.
- k-means algorithm is an unsupervised clustering method that assigns the different data objects into a number of clusters. It takes the input dataset (k), partitions it into a set of *n* objects, and assigns into *k* clusters.
- R language provides a function `k-means()` that performs k-means clustering on a data matrix.
- The BFR (Bradley, Fayyad, and Reina) algorithm is a variant of the k-means algorithm that performs the clustering in a high-dimensional Euclidean space.
- The discard, compressed, and retained objects or sets are used during the BFR algorithm.
- Discard set is a summary of the clusters themselves. Actually, these cluster summaries are a very essential part. However, the points that the summary represents are discarded and have no representation in main memory other than through this summary.
- A compressed set is also the summary of the clusters but it contains a set of points that are found close to one another and not close to any other cluster.
- Retained set contains points that can neither be assigned to a cluster nor are they sufficiently close to any other points that allows them to be represented by a compressed set. These points are held in main memory exactly as they appear in the input file.
- The CURE algorithm is a large-scale clustering algorithm that follows the concept of Euclidean space and does not consider the shape of clusters. The algorithm represents the clusters using a collection of representative points.
- Partitioning, hierarchical, and model-based clustering are the major categories of clustering in R.
- The GRGPF algorithm is one of the clustering algorithm that uses non Euclidean space. Its name comes from the name of authors, V. Ganti, R. Ramakrishnan, J. Gehrke, A. Powell, and J. French.
- Representing clusters, initialising the clusters, adding points in the clusters, and merging and splitting the clusters are the main steps of the GRGPF algorithm.
- The GRGPF algorithm uses the sample points for representing the clusters in the main memory.
- The GRGPF algorithm initialises the cluster tree by taking a main memory sample of the dataset and performs hierarchical clustering on it.

(Continued)

- A stream-computing model uses the stream and works like a data stream management system.
- The simple meaning of a stream is a sequence of things including characters, numbers, or others. With reference to clustering, a stream is nothing but a sliding window of *N* points.
- The image data, sensor data, web traffic, the Internet are some examples of the stream data.
- The BDMO algorithm is one of the stream-clustering algorithm and the generalisation of the DGIM algorithm that clusters points of a slowly evolving stream. The name of the BDMO algorithm comes from the name of its authors, B. Babcock, M. Datar, R. Motwani, L. O'Callaghan.
- The 'counting ones' method uses a window of length *N* on a binary stream and counts the number of 1s that comes in the last *k* bits where $k \leq N$.
- Initialising buckets, merging buckets, and answering queries are the major steps of the BDMO algorithm.
- A query in the stream-computing model is a length of a suffix of the sliding window.
- The MapReduce method is one of the latest programming paradigm that defines and implements parallel distributed processing on massive datasets. In this method, Map and Reduce are two main tasks performed by the mapper and reducer respectively.
- To implement clustering in a parallel environment, the MapReduce method divides the given data into chunks, clusters each chunk in parallel, and generates a single cluster.

Key Terms

- **BFR algorithm:** The BFR (Bradley, Fayyad, and Reina) algorithm is a variant of the k-means algorithm that performs the clustering in a high-dimensional Euclidean space.
- **Clustering:** Clustering is a process that examines the given data and partitions this data into many groups according to the similarity of the data or its features.
- **Counting ones:** The counting ones' method uses a window of length *N* on a binary stream and counts the number of 1s that come in the last *k* bits where $k \leq N$.
- **CURE algorithm:** The CURE algorithm is a large-scale clustering algorithm that follows the concept of Euclidean space and does not consider the shape of clusters.
- **Curse of dimensionality:** Analysis and organisation of data in high-dimensional spaces (over hundreds of dimensions) that cannot fit in low-dimensional settings is called the curse of dimensionality.
- **Euclidean space:** A Euclidean space contains two dimensions with one centre point.
- Hierarchical clustering: Hierarchical clustering organises a set of nested clusters as a tree.
- **k-means clustering:** k-means algorithm is an unsupervised clustering method that assigns different data objects into a number of clusters.
- **Non-Euclidean space:** A non-Euclidean space contains more than one dimension.
- **Stream-computing model:** A stream-computing model uses the stream and works like a data stream management system.

Multiple Choice Questions

1. From the given options, which of the following term defines the collection of points stored in single place?
   (a) Cluster (b) Group
   (c) Space (d) Dataset
2. From the given options, which of the following term defines the points in the Euclidean space?
   (a) Vector of real numbers (b) Vector of even numbers
   (c) Vector of decimal numbers (d) Vector of odd numbers
3. From the given options, which of the following is not a property of the distance measure?
   (a) Symmetry (b) Triangle inequality
   (c) Negative (d) Non-negative
4. From the given options, which of the following distance methods is not available in the `dist()` function?
   (a) Euclidean (b) L1 distance
   (c) Maximum (d) Manhattan
5. From the given options, which of the following function generates the distance matrix?
   (a) `plot()` (b) `dist()`
   (c) `hclust()` (d) `require()`
6. From the given options, which of the following function implements the hierarchical clustering?
   (a) `dist()` (b) `hclust()`
   (c) `k-means()` (d) `plot()`
7. From the given options, which of the following function implements the k-means clustering?
   (a) `hclust()` (b) `plot()`
   (c) `k-means()` (d) `dist()`
8. From the given options, which of the following clustering is a top-down clustering?
   (a) Agglomerative hierarchical clustering
   (b) Model-based clustering
   (c) Divisive hierarchical clustering
   (d) Grid-based clustering
9. From the given options, which of the following clustering is a bottom-up clustering?
   (a) Divisive hierarchical clustering (b) Agglomerative hierarchical clustering
   (c) Model-based clustering (d) Grid-based clustering

10. How many numbers of dimensions are used in the Euclidean space?
    (a) 1 (b) 3
    (c) 4 (d) 2
11. From the given options, which of the following method is not available in the `hclust()` function?
    (a) Average (b) Single
    (c) Mode (d) Median
12. From the given options, which of the following term defines the maximum distance between all the points and the centroid?
    (a) Diameter (b) Radius
    (c) Perimeter (d) None of the above
13. From the given options, which of the following package contains the `dist()`, `k-means()`, and `hclust()` function?
    (a) stats (b) base
    (c) forecast (d) cluster
14. From the given options, which of the following term defines the maximum distance between any two points of the cluster?
    (a) Perimeter (b) Radius
    (c) Diameter (d) None of the above
15. From the given options, which of the following algorithm is not available in the `k-means()` function?
    (a) Centre (b) Lloyd
    (c) Forgy (d) MacQueen

SHORT QUESTIONS

1. What are the different clustering strategies?
2. What is the difference between hierarchical and partitioning clustering strategies?
3. How is the efficiency of hierarchical clustering in the cluster analysis improved?
4. Explain the steps of the CURE algorithm.
5. How does the GRGPF algorithm represent clusters during the clustering process?
6. Describe the splitting and merging process of the GRGPF algorithm.
7. Explain the stream-computing model.
8. How does the BDMO algorithm initialise and merge the Buckets during clustering?

Long Questions

1. Explain the process of initialising and selecting the correct value of R in the k-means clustering.
2. Explain the `dist()` function with syntax and example.
3. Explain the `hclust()` function with syntax and example.
4. Explain the `k-means()` function with syntax and example.
5. Create a matrix and find out different distance matrix using different methods of the `dist()` function.
6. Create a matrix and implement hierarchical clustering on it.
7. Create a matrix and implement k-means clustering on it.
8. Read an appropriate built-in dataset and implement the hierarchical clustering using different methods with dendrograms.

Practical Exercises

1. Read in the data from "Cars.txt" file. The data in "Cars.txt" is as follows:

Petrol	Kilometers
1.1	60
6.5	20
4.2	40
1.5	25
7.6	15
2.0	55
3.9	39

Split the data into 3 clusters using k-means clustering. Plot the clusters for better comprehension.

Solution:

1. You can import data into the Environment as shown below. The name of the file is Cars.txt. This file contains entry for Petrol cars and its corresponding mileage in Kilometers.

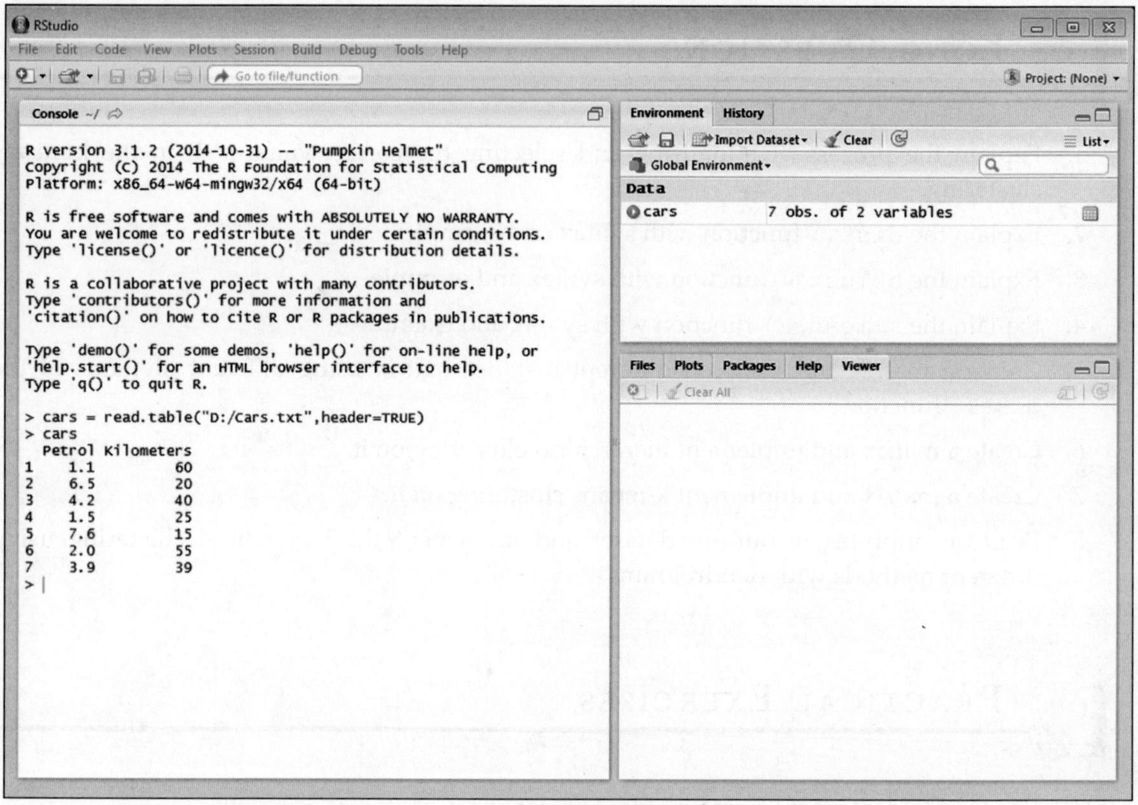

2. Apply *k*-means algorithm as shown below. The data set is split into 3 clusters and the maximum iteration is 10.

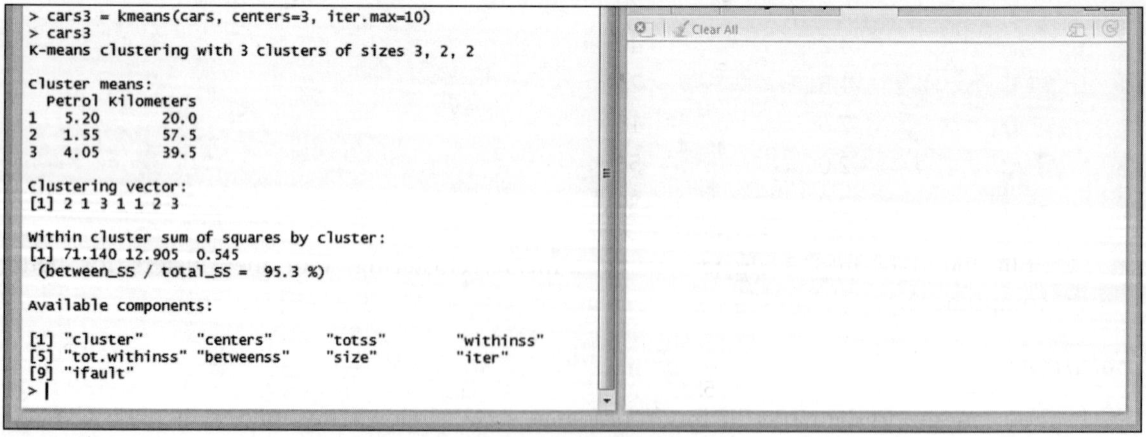

3. Plot clusters as shown below:

```
> plot(cars[cars3$cluster ==1, ], col = "red", xlim=c(min(cars[,1
]),max(cars[,1])), ylim=c(min(cars[,2]),max(cars[,2])))
>
> points(cars[cars3$cluster ==2, ], col ="blue")
>
> points(cars[cars3$cluster ==3, ], col ="green")
>
> points(cars3$centers,pch=2,col="orange")
> |
```

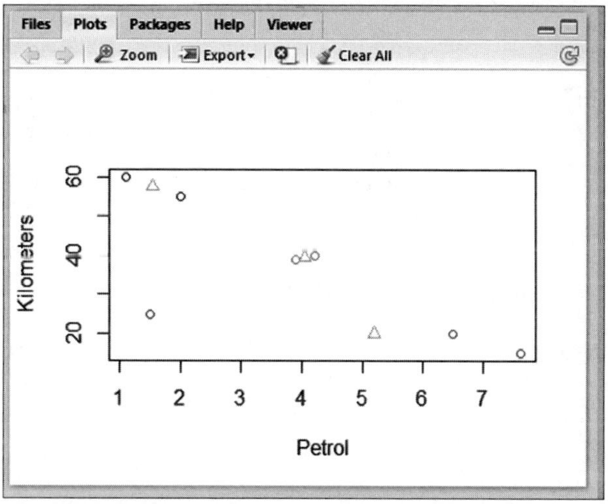

2. Consider the below data set.

Country	*Per Capita Income*	*Literacy*	*Infant mortality*	*Life Expectancy*
Brazil	10326	90	23.6	75.4
Germany	39650	99	4.08	79.4
Mozambique	830	38.7	95.9	42.1
Australia	43163	99	4.57	81.2
China	5300	90	23	73
Argentina	13308	97.2	13.4	75.3
United Kingdom	34105	99	5.01	79.4
South Africa	10600	82.4	44.8	49.3
Zambia	1000	68	92.7	42.4
Namibia	5249	85	42.3	52.9

Store it in a file, "data.txt". Read in the data into the R environment. Perform k-means clustering. Print out the result and also show it visually.

Solution:

Step 1: Read in the data from "data.csv" into the R environment.

```
> x <- read.csv("D:/data.csv", header=TRUE, row.names=1)
```

Display the content of the data frame, "x".

```
> x
               Per.Capita.Income Literacy Infant.mortality Life.Expectancy
Brazil                     10326     90.0            23.60            75.4
Germany                    39650     99.0             4.08            79.4
Mozambique                   830     38.7            95.90            42.1
Australia                  43163     99.0             4.57            81.2
China                       5300     90.0            23.00            73.0
Argentina                  13308     97.2            13.40            75.3
United Kingdom             34105     99.0             5.01            79.4
South Africa               10600     82.4            44.80            49.3
Zambia                      1000     68.0            92.70            42.4
Namibia                     5249     85.0            42.30            52.9
```

Step 2: Perform k-means clustering to form 3 clusters.

```
> km <- kmeans(x,3,15)
```

Print out the components of "km".

```
> km
K-means clustering with 3 clusters of sizes 3, 4, 3

Cluster means:
  Per.Capita.Income Literacy Infant.mortality Life.Expectancy
1          11411.33 89.86667        27.266667        66.66667
2           3094.75 70.42500        63.475000        52.60000
3          38972.67 99.00000         4.553333        80.00000

Clustering vector:
         Brazil         Germany     Mozambique          Australia            China
              1               3              2                  3                2
      Argentina United Kingdom    South Africa             Zambia          Namibia
              1               3              1                  2                2

Within cluster sum of squares by cluster:
[1]  5434630 19027221 41711855
 (between_SS / total_SS =  97.2 %)

Available components:

[1] "cluster"      "centers"      "totss"        "withinss"      "tot.withinss"
[6] "betweenss"    "size"         "iter"         "ifault"
```

Step 3: Plot the clusters.

```
> plot(x, col=km$cluster)
> points(km$centers, col = 1:3, pch = 8)
```

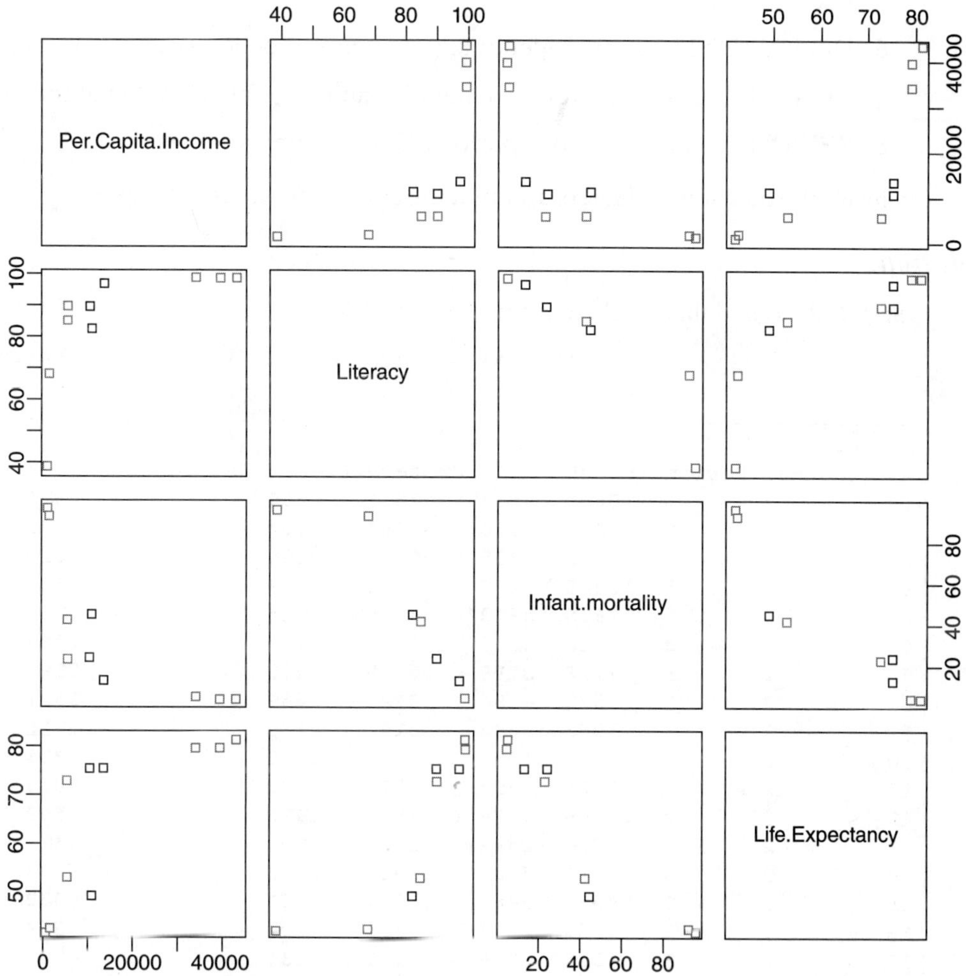

3. Consider the data available in UCI Machine learning Repository (https://archive.ics.uci.edu/ml/datasets/Wholesale+customers). The dataset is about the annual spending of customers on various items. Description of the various attributes is as follows:

Attribute Information:

1. FRESH: annual spending (m.u.) on fresh products (Continuous);
2. MILK: annual spending (m.u.) on milk products (Continuous);

3. GROCERY: annual spending (m.u.)on grocery products (Continuous);
4. FROZEN: annual spending (m.u.)on frozen products (Continuous)
5. DETERGENTS_PAPER: annual spending (m.u.) on detergents and paper products (Continuous)
6. DELICATESSEN: annual spending (m.u.) on and delicatessen products (Continuous);
7. CHANNEL: Channel - Horeca (Hotel/Restaurant/CafÃ©) or Retail channel (Nominal)
8. REGION: Region - Lisnon, Oporto or Other (Nominal)

Cluster the data into 5 clusters and plot the clusters for a visual display.

Solution:

Step 1: Read in data into R environment from "WS.csv").

```
> WholeSale <- read.csv("d:/WS.csv")
```

```
> WholeSale
   Channel Region  Fresh  Milk Grocery Frozen Detergents_Paper Delicassen
1        2      3  12669  9656    7561    214             2674       1338
2        2      3   7057  9810    9568   1762             3293       1776
3        2      3   6353  8808    7684   2405             3516       7844
4        1      3  13265  1196    4221   6404              507       1788
5        2      3  22615  5410    7198   3915             1777       5185
6        2      3   9413  8259    5126    666             1795       1451
7        2      3  12126  3199    6975    480             3140        545
8        2      3   7579  4956    9426   1669             3321       2566
9        1      3   5963  3648    6192    425             1716        750
10       2      3   6006 11093   18881   1159             7425       2098
11       2      3   3366  5403   12974   4400             5977       1744
12       2      3  13146  1124    4523   1420              549        497
13       2      3  31714 12319   11757    287             3881       2931
14       2      3  21217  6208   14982   3095             6707        602
15       2      3  24653  9465   12091    294             5058       2168
16       1      3  10253  1114    3821    397              964        412
17       2      3   1020  8816   12121    134             4508       1080
18       1      3   5876  6157    2933    839              370       4478
19       2      3  18601  6327   10099   2205             2767       3181
```

Step 2: Install packages, "ggplot2" and "ggfortify".

```
> library(ggplot2)
> library(ggfortify)
```

Step 3: Cluster the data set (columns: Fresh, Milk and Grocery) into 5 groups/cluster.

```
> km <- kmeans(WholeSale[,3:5],5)
```

```
> km
K-means clustering with 5 clusters of sizes 233, 8, 68, 22, 109

Cluster means:
      Fresh       Milk   Grocery
1  5853.605  3544.773  4476.391
2 25419.250 40750.250 48655.500
3  4643.691 12697.941 20195.191
4 50049.682  4447.409  5225.045
5 21064.431  4010.275  5303.624

Clustering vector:
  [1] 1 1 1 1 5 1 1 1 1 3 1 1 5 5 5 1 3 1 5 1 5 1 5 2 5 5 1 5 3 4 5 1 5 5 1 1 5
 [38] 5 3 4 5 5 3 3 1 3 3 2 1 3 1 1 4 3 5 1 3 1 5 1 1 2 1 3 1 3 1 5 1 1 5 5 1 5
 [75] 1 5 1 3 1 1 1 3 1 5 1 2 2 4 1 5 1 1 3 1 3 1 1 1 1 1 1 3 1 4 5 5 1 3 1 3 1
[112] 3 5 5 5 1 1 1 5 1 5 1 1 1 4 4 5 5 1 4 1 1 5 1 1 1 1 1 5 1 5 5 4 1 5 3 1 1
[149] 1 5 5 1 5 1 1 3 3 5 1 3 1 1 5 3 1 3 1 1 1 1 3 3 1 3 1 1 4 1 1 1 1 4 1 2 1
[186] 1 1 1 1 3 5 1 1 3 1 5 5 1 1 1 3 3 5 1 1 3 1 1 1 3 5 2 1 1 1 3 3 5 3 1 5 1
[223] 1 1 1 1 5 1 1 1 1 1 5 1 5 1 1 5 1 4 5 5 5 1 1 3 1 1 5 1 1 3 1 5 1 5 1 1 4
[260] 4 1 1 5 1 3 3 3 5 3 5 1 1 1 4 1 1 5 1 1 5 1 1 4 5 4 4 1 5 5 4 1 1 1 3 5 1
[297] 5 1 1 1 5 3 1 1 3 1 3 5 1 3 1 5 3 1 1 3 1 1 1 3 1 1 5 5 5 5 1 1 5 1 1 3 5
[334] 2 5 5 5 1 1 1 1 1 1 3 1 1 3 5 1 3 1 3 1 3 5 1 5 3 1 1 5 1 1 1 1 1 1 1 5 1
[371] 4 5 1 5 1 1 3 4 1 1 5 5 5 1 3 1 1 5 1 1 1 1 1 5 1 1 1 1 1 1 1 5 5 5 5 1 5
[408] 3 1 1 1 1 1 1 1 1 3 1 3 1 1 5 5 5 5 1 3 5 1 1 3 1 5 1 5 5 4 3 1 1

Within cluster sum of squares by cluster:
[1] 8208710610 8248734053 7101958937 7454062223 6263477438
 (between_SS / total_SS =  72.1 %)

Available components:

[1] "cluster"      "centers"      "totss"        "withinss"     "tot.withinss"
[6] "betweenss"    "size"         "iter"         "ifault"
```

Step 4: Plot the clusters for visual display.

```
> autoplot(km, WholeSale[,3:5], frame=T) +
labs(title="clustering wholesale data")
```

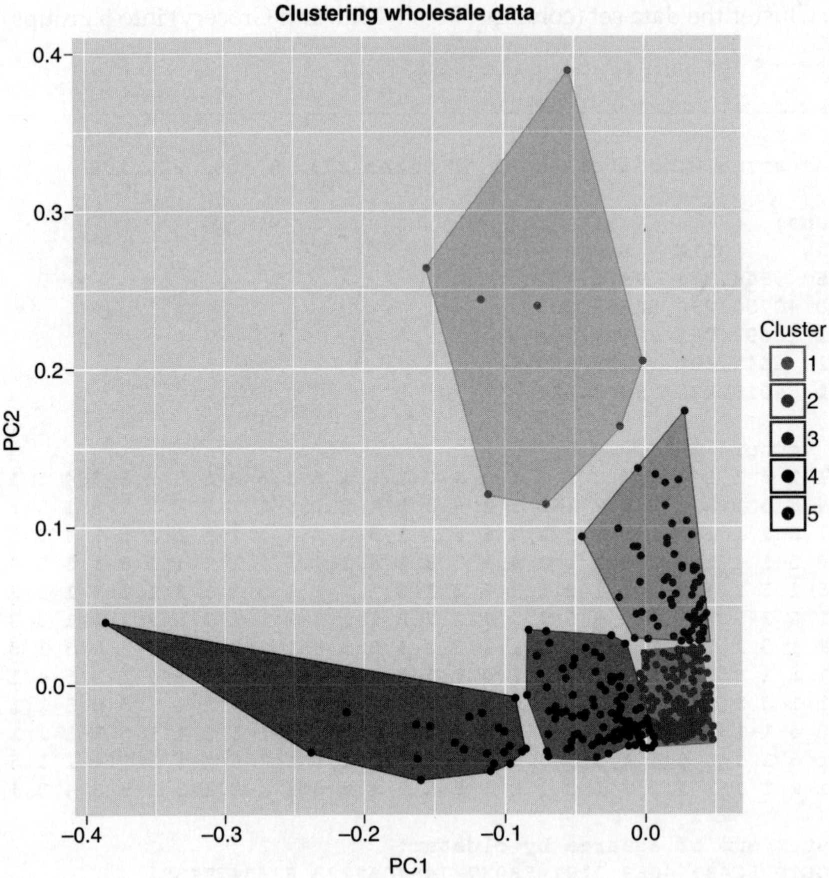

Answers to MCQs:

1. (c)	2. (a)	3. (c)	4. (b)	5. (b)	6. (b)	7. (c)
8. (c)	9. (b)	10. (d)	11. (c)	12. (b)	13. (b)	14. (c)
15. (a)						

Chapter 10

Association Rules

LEARNING OUTCOME

At the end of this chapter, you will be able to:

- Determine the association rules given the transactions and itemsets, and also evaluate the association rule using support, confidence and lift
- Implement association rule mining in R (create binary incidence matrix of the given itemsets, create itemMatrix, determine item frequencies, use `apriori()` function and `eclat()` function

10.1 Introduction

Today every field (retail, manufacturing, energy, healthcare, etc.) generates and stores a large amount of data relevant to its work and uses data mining techniques for finding the unknown and hidden patterns from this data. Big data analytics also uses data mining techniques to find hidden patterns from big data. Association rules in data mining play a major role in business analytics.

Listed below are few application areas of association rules:

- In retail, association rules help to discover purchase patterns of product items or associations between the different products.
- In the field of science, biological database uses association rules for finding patterns in biological data, discovering knowledge from agricultural database, collecting survey data from agricultural research to protein composition, etc.
- Software developers or researchers use association rules to extract knowledge from software engineering metrics in different fields of mining, such as text mining, web mining, etc.

- Other applications that use association rules include market basket analysis, studying the population and economic census, discovering data about soil and cultivation, crop production, extracting data for finding the geographical condition, etc.

The main objective of association rule is to identify a pattern among a set of items or objects in the relational database, transaction database, or any other information repository. The findings related to the co-occurrence relationship between two or more items in a database are called association. For example, consider a dataset that contains the items pen, pencil, notebook, eraser, and sharpener. The association defines the co-occurrence relationship between pen and notebook, pencil and eraser, etc.

Different algorithms are available for implementing association rules. Among all, Apriori algorithm is the most popular. For studying this algorithm, the basic knowledge of association rules is important. In this section, you will learn about the association rules, including association requirements, a database of a transaction, itemsets, form of association rules, and association techniques.

10.2 Frequent Itemset

Items and transactions (database) form a major part of association rules. An itemset is a collection of different items. For example, {pen, pencil, notebook} is an itemset. An itemset that contains items that often occur together and are associated with each other is called a frequent itemset.

Let {pen, pencil, notebook}, {pen, pencil, eraser}, {sharpener, pencil, notebook} constitute a few itemsets of the items {pen, pencil, notebook, sharpener}. In the itemsets mentioned, pencil and notebook often occur together; hence, {pencil, notebook} is an example of a frequent itemset.

Let I and T be the set of items and transactions respectively, represented as below:

$$I = \{I_1, I_2, I_3 \ldots I_m\}$$

$$T = \{T_1, T_2, T_3 \ldots T_n\},$$

where each transaction T_i is a set of items such that $T_i \subseteq I$

The transactions can be represented as follows (Table 10.1):

TABLE 10.1 Transactions and itemsets

Transaction	*Itemsets*
T_1	{pen, pencil, notebook}
T_2	{pen, pencil, eraser}
T_3	{sharpener, pencil, notebook}

Frequent itemset = {pencil, notebook}

Here, frequent itemset is identified by merely examining the occurrence of items. However, it can be calculated by using certain methods. In the next section, you will learn about these methods.

10.2.1 Association Rule

All the rules that correlate the presence of one set of items with another set of items are known as association rules. An association rule is an implication from the expression $X \rightarrow Y$, where X and Y are two disjoint itemsets and $X \subseteq I$ and $Y \subseteq I$, and $X \cap Y = \phi$.

Consider a stationery shop that contains items such as pen, pencil, notebook, sharpener, etc. A student purchases three items: pen, pencil, and notebook. Here, {pen, pencil, notebook} is a transaction. It implies that if the student purchases pen and pencil, then he or she would also purchase a notebook. An association rule from this transaction may be defined as follows:

$$\text{pen, pencil} \rightarrow \text{notebook}$$

where,

$$X = \{\text{pen, pencil}\} \text{ and } Y = \{\text{notebook}\}$$

The quality of the association rules depends on how it estimates the occurrence of items. Unexpectedness, weak and strong belief, and action belief are some subjective measures of the association rules. Also, simplicity, threshold value, support (utility), and confidence (certainty) are some of the objective measures of association rules.

10.2.2 Rule Evaluation Metrics

Rule evaluation metrics is used to measure the strength of an association rule. Support and confidence are important to rule evaluation metrics.

Support

Support is a metric that measures the usefulness of a rule using the minimum support threshold. The metric measures the number of events that have itemsets which match both sides of the implications of association rules. In addition, rules for events whose itemsets do not match both the sides sufficiently defined by a threshold value can be excluded. It determines how frequently the rule is applicable in the respective transaction set.

Let $X \rightarrow Y$ be an association rule and T be a transaction set with n being the number of transactions in T. Then, the support of this rule is the percentage of the transaction in T containing $X \cup Y$ or the estimation of the probability $Pr(X \cup Y)$. The support of rule $X \rightarrow Y$ is calculated by using the following formula:

$$\text{Support or sup} = (X \cup Y).\text{count}/n$$

If the value of Support is low, then it effectively measures the strength of the given rule.

Example

Table 10.2 represents three transactions of the itemset {pen, pencil, notebook, sharpener}.

TABLE 10.2 Transactions of the itemset {pen, pencil, notebook, sharpener}

Transactions	*Itemsets*
T_1	{pen, pencil, notebook}
T_2	{pen, pencil, eraser}
T_3	{sharpener, pencil, notebook}

The Support of the item 'pen' is calculated as follows:

$$\text{Support(Pen)} = \frac{\text{Total occurrences of pen}}{\text{Total number of transactions}}$$

$$= 2/3 = 0.66$$

$$= 60\%$$

Similarly, Support (Pencil) = 3/3 = 1 = 100%

Confidence

Confidence is a metric that measures the certainty of a rule by using threshold. It measures how often an event itemset that matches the left side of implication in the association rule also matches the right side. Rules for events whose itemsets do not sufficiently match the right side, but match the left side can be excluded. It determines the predictability of the rule.

Let $X \rightarrow Y$ be an association rule and T be a transaction set, then the confidence of this rule is the percentage of the transaction in T containing both X and Y or the estimation of the conditional probability $Pr(Y|X)$. The confidence of rule $X \rightarrow Y$ is calculated by using the following formula:

$$\text{Confidence} = \text{conf} = (X \cup Y).\text{count}/X.\text{count}$$

Or

$$\text{Confidence} = \text{conf} = \text{support}(X \cup Y)/\text{support}(X)$$

If the value of the Confidence is low for a rule, then it is unreliable to predict Y from X as there is no use of the rule with low predictability.

Consider the data (transactions and itemsets) listed in Table 10.2. Let us assume that pencil → notebook is an association rule for the transaction, then the confidence of this rule is calculated as follows:

$$\text{Confidence (pencil} \rightarrow \text{notebook)} = \frac{\text{Occurrences of (pencil, notebook)}}{\text{Occurrences of (pencil)}}$$

Or

$$\text{Confidence (pencil} \rightarrow \text{notebook)} = 2/3 = 0.66 = 60\%$$

Minimum Support and Minimum Confidence

The minimum support (minsup) and minimum confidence (minconf) is the threshold of support and confidence respectively. The goal of association rule mining is to find all the rules that fulfil the following conditions:

Support ≥ minsup threshold
Confidence ≥ minconf threshold

Few Assignments

You are the owner of a small retail shop. You would like to study what items are usually bought together. You have a set of transaction data with you as given below. Transaction with ID 1 had items A, B and E bought together. Likewise, items, A, B, D and E were purchased together in Transaction with ID 2 and so on…

Transaction ID	*Items*
1	A,B,E
2	A,B,D,E
3	B,C,D,E
4	B,D,E
5	A,B,D
6	B,E
7	A,E

Problem statement 1

Consider the itemset {B,D,E}. Determine the support count for this itemset.

Answer: The support count is 3. This is because three transactions namely, transactions 2, 3, and 4 contain the itemset, {B, D, E}.

Problem statement 2

Consider the association rule BD → E. Determine the support and confidence for this association rule.

Answer: The support for BD → E is the same as the support for {B, D, E} which is 3. This is because three transactions 2, 3, and 4 contain the itemset, {B, D, E}.

The confidence is given by the below formula:

conf. (BD → E) = support ({B,D,E}) / support ({B,D})
= 3 / 4

10.2.3 Brute-force Approach

A Brute-force approach computes the support and confidence for every possible rule for mining the association rules. Here are the steps of this method:

1. List all the possible association rules.
2. Compute the support and confidence for each rule.
3. Prune the rules that fail the minsup and minconf threshold.

The method is computationally prohibited, as there are exponentially many rules that can be extracted from a dataset after applying this method. In general, the total number of possible rules extracted from a dataset containing *d* items is represented by the following formula:

$$R = 3^d - 2^{d+1} + 1$$

In a research, it has been found that more that 80% of the rules are excluded after applying 20% minsup and 50% minconf. Hence, the method becomes expensive. To avoid this problem of needless computation, it is good to prune the rules early without having to compute their support and confidence values.

10.2.4 Two-step Approach

Due to the disadvantage of the Brute-force approach, the association rules mining algorithm uses a common method that contains two steps. It is called the two-step approach. The first step is 'frequent itemset generation' and the second step is 'rule generation'. The following subsection discusses both the steps.

1. Frequent Itemset Generation

In the first step of the two-step approach, the frequent itemset generation finds the itemsets that satisfy the minsup threshold. These itemsets are called the frequent itemsets. If a dataset contains *k* items, then it can generate upto $2^k - 1$ frequent itemsets. A lattice structure also finds out a list of all the possible itemsets. The dataset of real-life applications contains very large items.

In this case, it is difficult and time-consuming to find out frequent itemsets. Hence, a brute-force method finds out the frequent itemsets using support count for every candidate itemset. For this, each candidate itemset is compared against every transaction and if each candidate is in the transaction, then the support is incremented. This method is very expensive and complex. In this case, some of the following strategies can be used for finding frequent itemsets:

- Reduce the number of candidates using Apriori principle
- Reduce the number of transactions
- Reduce the number of comparisons using efficient data structures that store transactions or candidates.

Apriori Principle

Among the three—Apriori principle—is the best strategy and an effective method to generate the frequent itemset. According to the Apriori principle,

If an itemset is frequent, then all of its subsets must also be frequent.

The method eliminates some candidate itemsets without counting their support values. Eliminating the candidate itemsets is called pruning of itemsets. The Apriori principle uses the following property of the support measure:

$$\forall X\ Y: (X \subseteq Y) \to s(X) \geq s(Y)$$

This property is called the anti-monotone property of support, where support of an itemset never exceeds the support of its subsets. This principle need not match every candidate against every transaction.

Let {c, d, e} be a frequent itemset of the items {a, b, c, d, e}. According to the principle, any transaction that contains {c, d, e} must also contain all its subsets {c, d}, {d, e}, {c, e}, {c}, {d}, {e}. In simple words, if {c, d, e} is a frequent itemset, then all its subsets have to be frequent as well. Figure 10.1 explains this concept by selecting all the itemsets containing *c*, *d*, and *e* items. In addition, if any itemset is infrequent, then all its subsets are infrequent too. For example, let {a, b} be an infrequent itemset, then all subsets that contain *a* and *b* will also be infrequent. In Figure 10.2, all itemsets are automatically pruning the subsets containing *a* and *b*.

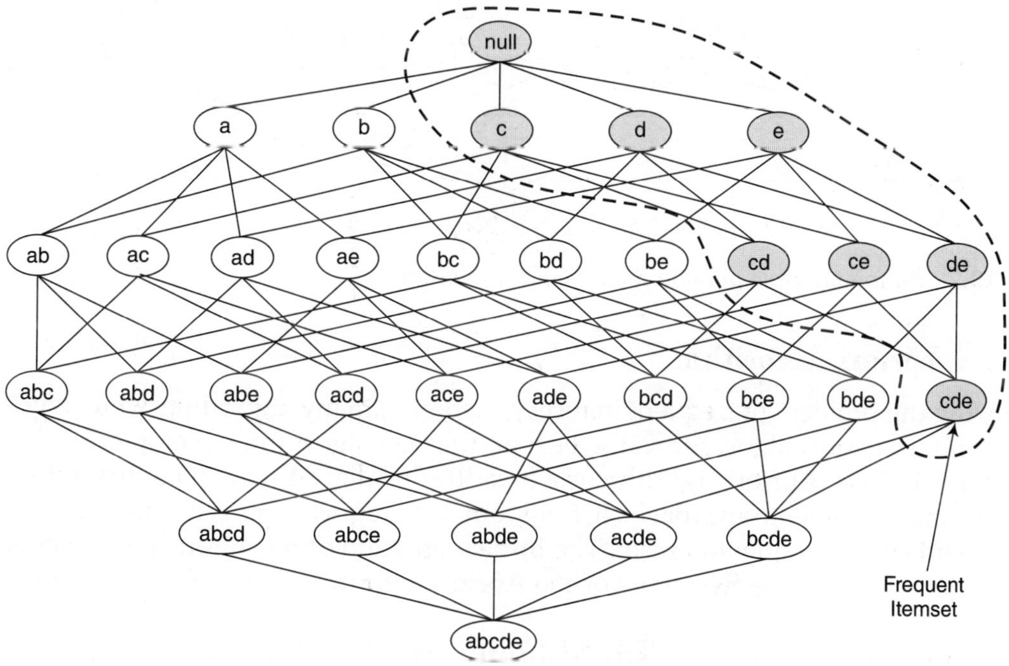

In simple words, the Apriori principle automatically prunes the candidate itemsets.

FIGURE 10.1 *Apriori principle generating frequent itemsets*

2. Rule Generation

In the second step of the two-step approach, rule generation extracts all the high-confidence rules from each frequent itemset obtained in the first step. Each rule is a binary partitioning of a frequent itemset. For each frequent *k* itemsets, $2^k - 2$ association rules can be generated by ignoring the rules containing empty antecedents or consequents ($\phi \rightarrow Y$ or $Y \rightarrow \phi$). By partitioning the itemset Y into two non-empty subsets X and $Y - X$ such that $X \rightarrow Y - X$ satisfies the confidence threshold, an association rule is extracted.

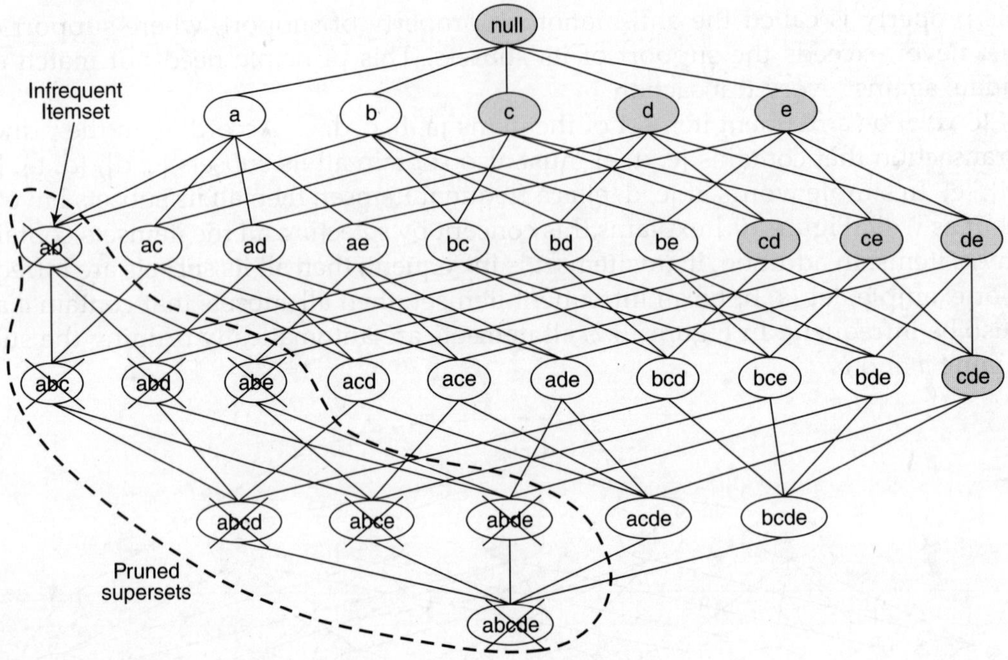

FIGURE 10.2 *Apriori principle pruning the infrequent itemsets*

10.2.5 Apriori Algorithm

For solving the problem of frequent itemset generation, many algorithms were developed. However, the Apriori algorithm is the best and fastest algorithm developed by Agarwal and Srikant in 1994. Apriori algorithm is a breadth-first algorithm that counts transactions by following a two-step approach. It finds out the frequent itemset, maximal frequent itemset, and closed frequent itemset. The implementation of the algorithm also generates the association rules. The two steps of the Apriori algorithm are explained as follows:

Step 1: Frequent Itemset Generation in Apriori Algorithm

This step generates all frequent itemsets, where a frequent itemset is an itemset that has transaction support greater than minsup. Here, the algorithm uses the Apriori principle or downward closure property for generating all frequent itemsets. According to the Apriori principle, *"If an itemset is frequent, then all of its subsets must also be frequent"*. According to the downward closure property, *"If an itemset has minimum support then all its non-empty subsets have minimum support"*. Both the properties prune a large number of infrequent itemsets.

For efficient itemset generation, the algorithm should be sorted in lexicographic order. Let {w[1], w[2], …, w[k]} represent the *k* itemsets, where w contains the item *w[1], w[2], …, w[k]* and *w[1] < w[2]< … < w[k]*. The pseudocode of the algorithm would be:

```
Apriori(T)
1.  Ck ← init-pass(T) ;                        // First pass
2.  F1 ← { f | f ∈C1 , f.count ≥minsup } // n = number of transaction
3.  for (k = 2; Fk-1 ≠ ϕ; k++) do            // subsequent passes over T
4.  Ck ← candidate-gen(Fk-1)
5.  for each transaction t ∈ T do             // scan the data once
6.  for each candidate c ∈Ck do
7.  if c is contained in t then
8.  c.count++;
9.  end
10. end
11. Fk ← { c ∈Ck |  c.count / n ≥ minsup }
12. end
13. return F ← UkFk
```

The algorithm uses a level-wise search for generating the frequent itemset and multiple passes over the data. In each pass of the algorithm, it counts the support of individual items [line 1] and determines whether each of them is frequent [line 2]. *F1* is the set of frequent 1 itemsets. In each subsequent pass *k*, it follows the following three steps:

1. It starts with the seed set of itemsets F_{k-1} found to be frequent in the $(k-1)^{th}$ pass. This seed sets generate the candidate itemsets C_k [line 4] that are possible frequent itemsets using candidate `gen()` function.
2. In the second step, the transaction database is scanned and the actual support of each candidate itemset *c* in C_k is counted [line 5 to 10].
3. At the end of the pass, the actual frequent candidate itemsets are determined.

The set of all frequent itemsets *F* is the final output of the algorithm.

Candidate `gen()` *Function*

The candidate `gen()` function is used in the Apriori algorithm that contains two steps *Join* and *Pruning* explained as follows:

1. The join step [line 2–3] joins two frequent *(k-1)* itemsets for producing a possible candidate *c* [line 6]. The two frequent itemsets f_1 and f_2 have exactly the same items except the last one [line 3–5]. The *c* is added to the set of candidates C_k [line 7].
2. The pruning step [line 8–11] determines whether all the *k-1* subsets of *c* are in F_{k-1}. If no one of them is in F_{k-1}, *c* cannot be frequent according to the downward closure property and deleted from C_k.

The pseudocode of the candidate `gen()` function is as follows:

```
candidate gen(Fk-1)
1.  Ck ← ϕ                     // initializes the set of candidates
2.  for all f1, f2∈Fk-1        // traverse all pairs of frequent itemsets
3.  with f1 ={i1, i2, …, ik-2,ik-1}
                               // differ only in the last item
4.  and f2 ={i1, i2, …, ik-2,ik-1}
5.  and ik-1 < i'k-1do          // according to the sorted order
6.  c ←{i1,…, ik-1,i'k-1}      // join the two itemsets f1 and f2
7.  Ck ← Ck ∪{c}               // add the new itemset c to the candidates
8.  For each (k-1)-subset s of c do
```

```
9.  If (s ∈F_{k-1}) then
10. delete c from C_k           // delete c from the candidates
11. end
12. end
13. return
```

Step 2: Association Rule Generation

This step generates all confidence association rules from the frequent itemsets, where confident association rules are the rules with confidence value greater than minconf. This step is an optional step as for many applications, frequent itemsets are sufficient and do not require generating the association rules.

The following formula is used to generate the rules for every frequent itemset f that contains subsets and for each subset α.

$$(f - \alpha) \rightarrow \alpha \text{ if confidence} = (f.\text{count}/(f - \alpha).\text{count}) \geq \text{minconf}$$

where,

$(f.\text{count}/(f - \alpha).\text{count})$ = support count of $f((f - \alpha))$; $f.\text{count}/n$ = support of the rule where n = number of transactions in the transaction set

This method is complex; hence, an efficient algorithm and procedure is used that generate the rules. A pseudo code of the algorithm with one item in the consequent [subset of α] is given as follows:

```
genRules(F)                         // F = set of all frequent itemsets
1. for each frequent =itemset f_k in F, k≥ 2 do
2. output every 1.item consequent rule of f_k with confidence ≥ min-
   conf and Support ← f_k.count/n
3. H_1 ← {consequents of all 1-item consequent rules derived from f_k above}
4. ap-genRules(f_k, H_1)
5. end
```

The pseudocode of the ap-genRules(f_k, H_m) procedure is as follows:

```
ap-genRules(f_k, H_m)                    // H_m = set of m-item consequents
1.  if (k > m+1) AND (H_m≠ϕ ) then
2.  H_{m+1} ← candidate-gen(H_m)
3.  for each h_{m+1} in H_{m+1} do
4.  conf ← f_k.count / (f_k - h_{m+1}).count
5.  if (conf ≥ minconf) then
6.  output the rule (f - h_{m+1}) →h_{m+1} with confidence = conf and sup-
    port = f_k.count /n
7.  else
8.  delete h_{m+1} from
9.  end
10. ap-genRules(f_k, H_m)
11. end
```

The following example uses data of Table 10.1 that represents three transactions of the itemset {pen, pencil, notebook, sharpener}. Now, the Apriori algorithm finds out the frequent itemsets with minsup 50% and minconf 50%.

Frequency of each item is given as (Tables 10.3–10.6):

TABLE 10.3 Support of each items of the given itemset

Items	*Support*
Pen	2
Pencil	3
Notebook	2
Sharpener	1

TABLE 10.4 Frequent itemset *F1* after removing items with minsup 50% = 2

Items	*Support*
Pen	2
Pencil	3
Notebook	2

TABLE 10.5 Candidate itemsets C2 – F1 x F1

Items	*Support*
Pen, Pencil	2
Pen, Notebook	1
Pencil, Notebook	2

TABLE 10.6 New frequent itemset *F2* after removing items with minsup 50% = 2

Items	*Support*
Pen, Pencil	2
Pencil, Notebook	2

After this, it cannot process as both itemsets have minsup as 2. Hence, the frequent itemset is {pen, pencil} and {pencil, notebook} for the data given in Table 10.1.

Problem statement

Consider the transactions as follows:

Transaction ID	*Items*
1	A,B,E
2	A,B,D,E
3	B,C,D,E
4	B,D,E
5	A,B,D
6	B,E
7	A,E

Find all the frequent itemsets whose counts are at least 3.

Answer:

Find all itemsets with support >= 3.

We generate the below sets, C1, C2 and C3. Remove all the sets where the support is less than 3 (the highlighted ones).

C1:

Set	Support
{A}	4
{B}	6
{C}	1
{D}	4
{E}	6

Here {C} is eliminated because its support is less than 3.

C2:

Set	Support
{A, B}	3
{A, C}	0
{A, D}	2
{A, E}	3
{B, C}	1
{B, D}	4
{B, E}	5
{C, D}	1
{C, E}	1
{D, E}	3

Here, {A, C}, {A, D}, {B, C}, {C, D} and {C, E} is eliminated because its support is less than 3.

C3:

Set	Support
{A, B, E}	2
{B, D, E}	3

Here, {A, B, E} is eliminated as its support is less than 3.

Check Your Understanding

1. What is data mining?

Ans: Data mining is a process used for finding unknown and hidden patterns from a large amount of data.

2. What are association rules?

Ans: Association rules are part of data mining used for finding patterns in data. An association rule is an implication of the expression $X \rightarrow Y$, where X and Y are two disjoint itemsets and $X \subseteq I$ and $Y \subseteq I$, and $X \cap Y = \phi$.

(Continued)

3. What is the formula for calculating support?

Ans: The Support or sup of a rule is calculated by using (X ∪ Y).count / n.

4. What is a Brute-force approach?

Ans: A Brute-force approach computes the support and confidence for every possible rule for mining the association rules.

10.3 Data Structure Overview

In the previous section, you learnt about the major theoretical concept of the association rules mining and algorithms. For the implementation of the association rules mining, users need to efficiently represent the input and output data.

R language provides packages like arules and arulesViz for implementing the association rule algorithms in R language. The arules package provides the required infrastructure that creates and manipulates the input dataset for any type of mining algorithms. It also provides features that analyse the resulting itemsets and association rules. It mainly uses the sparse matrix for representation that minimises the use of memory.

Before implementing the algorithms in R language, it is necessary to represent the input data into a well-designed structure as these algorithms contain a large amount of data. This section will describe various features of the arules package for representing data.

10.3.1 Representing Collections of Itemsets

Transaction of databases and set of associations are a main part of the association rules mining. Both use set of items means itemsets with additional information. The transaction database of the association rules mining contains the transaction id and an itemset, whereas an association rule contains at least two itemsets for left-hand side and right-hand side of the rule respectively. In both the forms of data, columns contain the items and rows contain the itemsets; hence, a matrix, sparse matrix, or binary incidence matrix is a convenient way to represent such types of data.

Here a binary incidence matrix is an effective method to represent the collection of itemsets used for transaction databases and set of associations among all three matrices. A binary incidence matrix is a type of sparse matrix that contains only two values 0 and 1 or true and false. In binary incidence matrix, columns represent items and rows represent the itemsets. The entries of the matrix represent the presence [1] and absence [0] of an item in a particular itemset.

For example, Table 10.7 represents four itemsets of a database 'stationery'.

TABLE 10.7 Itemsets of a database 'stationery'

Itemsets	*Items*
I_1	{pen, pencil, notebook}
I_2	{pencil, sharpener}
I_3	{sharpener, pencil, notebook}
I_4	{pen, notebook}

Users can represent these itemsets through a binary incidence matrix. Table 10.8 represents the corresponding binary incidence matrix of the above table. The matrix contains value 1 for the items that are in the particular itemset and 0 for those that are not in the particular itemset. For example, for the itemset I_1 = {pen, pencil, notebook}, value 1 is used to represent pen, pencil, notebook and sharpener contains 0.

TABLE 10.8 Binary incidence matrix

Itemsets	*Items*			
	Pen	*Pencil*	*Notebook*	*Sharpener*
I_1	1	1	1	0
I_2	0	1	0	1
I_3	0	1	1	1
I_4	1	0	1	0

itemMatrix class

The arules package provides a class "itemMatrix" that efficiently represents such type of set of items in the form of sparse binary matrices. The itemMatrix class is base for the itemsets, transactions, and rules of the association rule mining in R. It contains a sparse matrix representing items that can be either set of itemsets or transactions.

Since "itemMatrix" is a class, thus, an object can be created by using the new("itemMatrix",...). It is inconvenient to call it in such form, so mostly an object is created by using conversion or coercion from a matrix, data.frame, or list. Here is a basic syntax for creating an object of the "itemMatrix" class.

```
as(x, "itemMatrix")
```

where,

"*x*" can be either a matrix, data.frame, or list.

If the itemMatrix is transposed, then it represents the actual data into a binary incidence form. For this, the arules package provides a class "ngCMatrix" that represents the transposed form of the binary incidence matrix in the ItemMatrix class. The transposed form can be created by using (x, "ngCMatrix").

The "itemMatrix" class contains many methods for further representations. Table 10.9 describes few useful methods of the "itemMatrix" class:

TABLE 10.9 Values of type argument of plot command

Methods	*Description*
`dim(x)`	It returns the dimension of the itemMatrix.
`c(x)`	It combines the itemMatrix.
`dimnames(x)`	It returns the dimension names where row contains itemsetID and column contains the item names.
`Labels`	It returns the labels for the itemsets in each transaction
`nitems(x)`	It returns the number of items in the itemMatrix

The example below creates a matrix "sm" in Table 10.8 by using `matrix()` function. The function `dimnames()` sets the names of the items (Figure 10.3). In Figure 10.4, the matrix "sm" is converted to itemMatrix using the function ("sm", "itemMatrix") that represents the given data in a binary incidence matrix form.

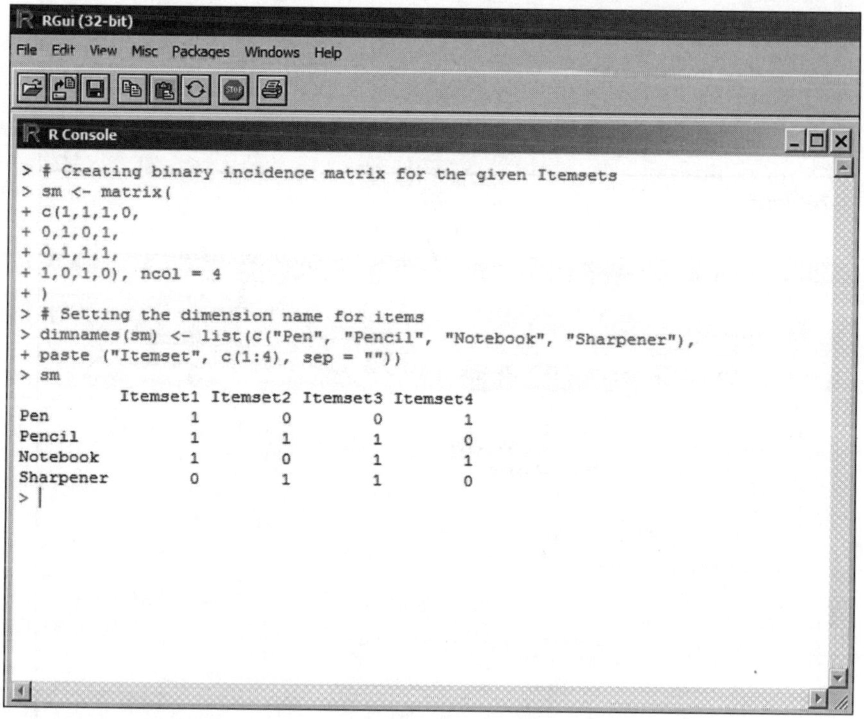

FIGURE 10.3 *Binary incidence matrix*

Figure 10.5 creates a column oriented transpose matrix using as(x, "ngCMatrix") of the matrix "sm". From the figure, the user can see that columns contain the items and rows contain the itemsets. The entries of the matrix contains '|' for the value '1' and the dot '.' for the value '0'. The `inspect()` function inspects the items of this matrix. For example, the item "Pen" is in itemset 1 and 4 and the function `inspect()` shows the same.

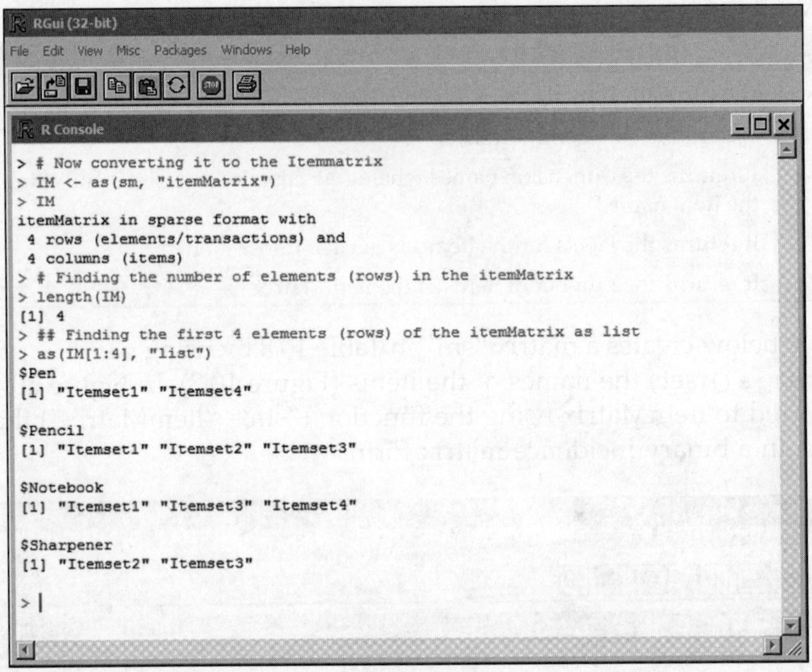

FIGURE 10.4 *itemMatrix*

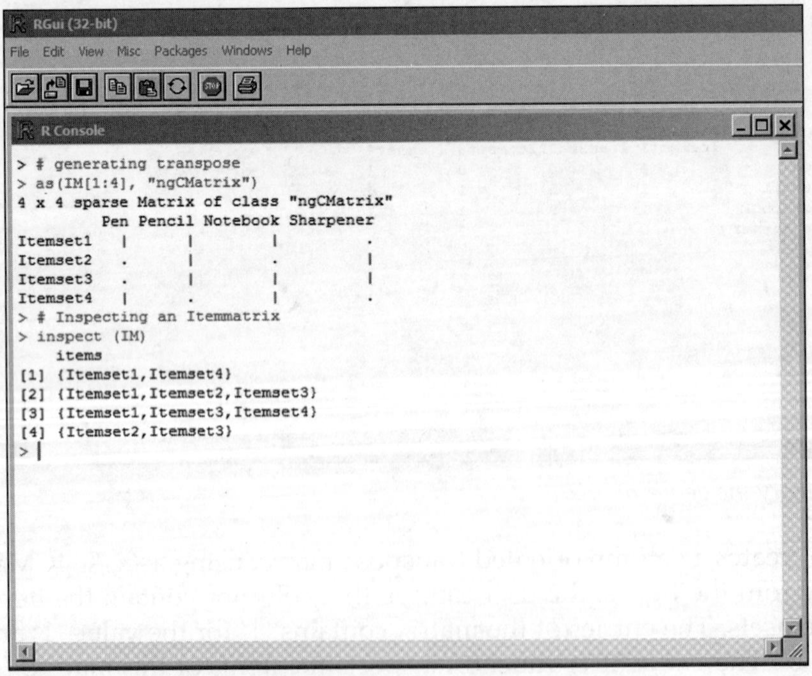

FIGURE 10.5 *itemMatrix inspection using* `inspect()`

itemFrequency() Function

The `itemFrequency()` function of the package "arules" returns the frequency or support of single items or all single items of an object of the itemMatrix. Actually, item frequencies are the column sums of the binary matrix. The basic syntax of the function `itemFrequency()` is as follows:

```
itemFrequency (x, type, …)
```

where,

"*x*" argument can be an object of itemMatrix, or transactions class or any dataset; "type" argument contains the string that specifies frequency/support in relative or absolute form. By default, it returns the relative form; the dots "…" define the other optional arguments.

In the example below, the `itemFrequency()` function returns the frequency of the itemMatrix "IM" created in the above example in both form "relative" and "absolute". The "relative" and "absolute" type returns the values in decimal points and whole number respectively (Figure 10.6).

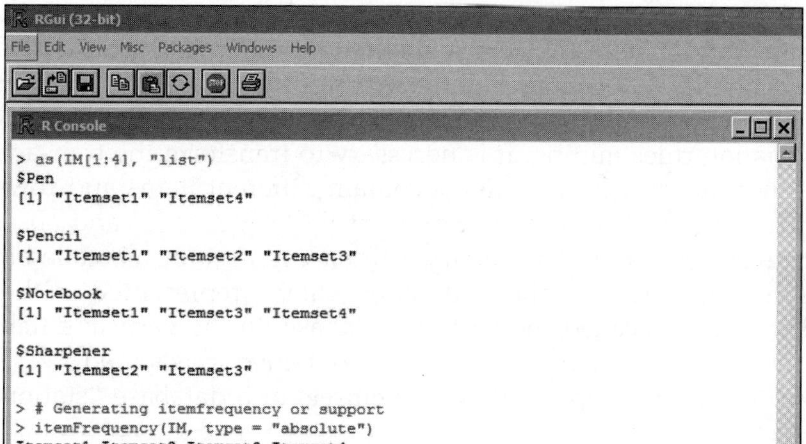

FIGURE 10.6 *Use of itemFrequency() function*

Generate Hash Tree

A hash tree is a type of data structure that stores values in the key-value pair and a type of tree, where every internal node contains the hash values. The association rules mining uses datasets that are also in the form of hash tree. Such dataset uses itemset ID and items or transaction ID and items. In the Apriori algorithm, hash tree is used for support counting. A hash tree only hashes with the candidate itemsets that belong to the same bucket instead of every candidate's itemset.

In the Apriori algorithm, candidates itemsets are stored in the form of hash tree, this means each itemset or transaction is hashed into respective buckets. Here are some steps used for support counting using hash tree:

1. Create a hash tree and hash all the candidate k itemsets to the external nodes of the tree.
2. For each transaction, generate all k items subsets of the transaction. For example, for a transaction {"a", "b", "c"}, the 2-item subsets are {"a", "b"}, {"b", "c"}, {"a", "c"}.
3. For each k item subset, hash it to an external node of the hash tree and compare it against the candidate k itemsets hashed to the same leaf node. If the k item subset matches a candidate k itemset then increment the support count of the candidate k itemset.

10.3.2 Transaction Data

All types of association rules work mostly with the transaction datasets. A transaction dataset is a collection of the transactions, where each transaction is stored in the tuple form as < transaction ID, item ID, …>. A single transaction is a group of all tuples with the same transaction ID that contains all the items of the given item ID in the tuples. For example, the transaction on the stationery items may be pen, pencil, notebook, and others.

For the association rules mining, it is necessary to transform the transaction data into a binary incidence matrix where columns contain different items and rows contain the transactions. The entries of the matrix represent the presence [1] and absence [0] of an item in a particular transaction. This binary incidence matrix form is called the horizontal database. On the other hand, if the transaction data is represented in the form of the transactions list then it is called the vertical database. In the vertical database, for each item a list of IDs of the transactions the item is contained in is stored.

For example, Table 10.10 represents four itemsets of a database "stationery" used in the previous section.

TABLE 10.10 Transactions and Itemsets for a database "Stationery"

Transactions	*Items*
T_1	{pen, pencil, notebook}
T_2	{pencil, sharpener}
T_3	{sharpener, pencil, notebook}
T_4	{pen, notebook}

Users can represent these transactions through a binary incidence matrix. Table 10.11 represents the corresponding binary incidence matrix of Table 10.10. It is a horizontal database. The matrix contains value 1 for the items that are in the particular transaction and contains 0 that are not in the particular transaction. Table 10.11 represents the horizontal database while Table 10.12 represents the vertical database.

TABLE 10.11 Horizontal database

Transactions	*Items*			
	Pen	*Pencil*	*Notebook*	*Sharpener*
T_1	1	1	1	0
T_2	0	1	0	1
T_3	0	1	1	1
T_4	1	0	1	0

TABLE 10.12 Vertical database

Items	*Transaction ID list*
Pen	T_1, T_4
Pencil	T_1, T_2, T_3
Notebook	T_1, T_3, T_4
Sharpener	T_2, T_3

Transaction Class

The arules package provides a class "transactions" that represent transaction data of the association rules. It is an extension of the itemMatrix class. Like "itemMatrix" class, an object of the "transactions" class can be created using the new ("transactions",...). An object is created by conversion from a matrix, data.frame, or list. Since, the association rule mining does not work with continuous variables and uses only items hence it is necessary to first create the data list using list, matrix, or data.frame features of R language. Here is a basic syntax for creating an object of the "transactions" class.

```
as(x, "transactions")
```

where,

"*x*" can be either a matrix, data.frame, or list.

Like "itemMatrix" class, the "transactions" class contains many methods for further representations. Table 10.13 describes some useful methods of the "transactions" class:

TABLE 10.13 Values of type argument of plot command

Methods	*Description*
`dimnames(x)`	It returns the dimension names where the row contains the transaction IDs and the column contains the item names
`labels`	It returns the labels for each transaction
`transactionInfo`	It returns information about the transaction

The example below creates a matrix "sm" of the table using `matrix()` function. The function `dimnames()` sets the names of the items (Figure 10.7). In the example the matrix "sm" is converted to transactions using function as("sm", "transactions") that represents the given data into a binary incidence matrix form (the horizontal database). Figure 10.8 describes the summary of the generated transactions "TM".

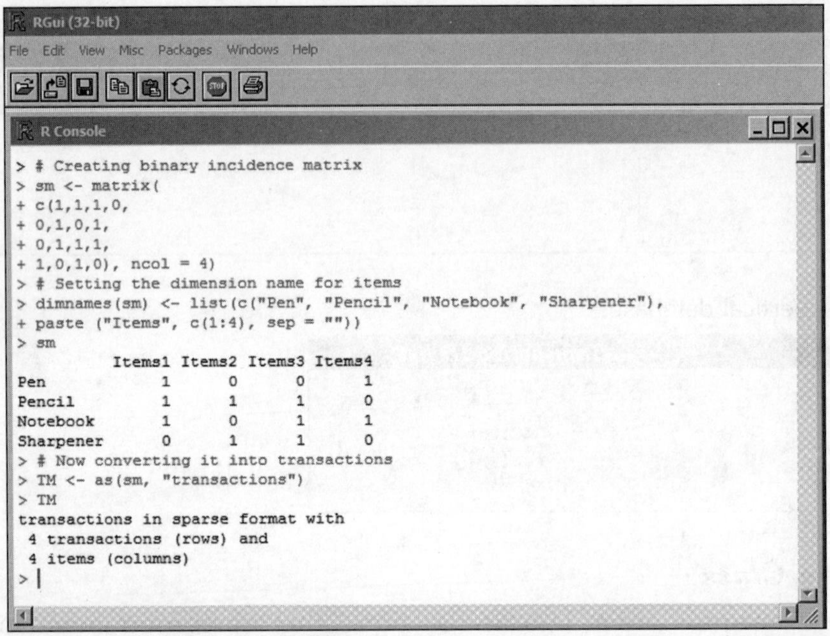

```
> # Creating binary incidence matrix
> sm <- matrix(
+ c(1,1,1,0,
+ 0,1,0,1,
+ 0,1,1,1,
+ 1,0,1,0), ncol = 4)
> # Setting the dimension name for items
> dimnames(sm) <- list(c("Pen", "Pencil", "Notebook", "Sharpener"),
+ paste ("Items", c(1:4), sep = ""))
> sm
          Items1 Items2 Items3 Items4
Pen            1      0      0      1
Pencil         1      1      1      0
Notebook       1      0      1      1
Sharpener      0      1      1      0
> # Now converting it into transactions
> TM <- as(sm, "transactions")
> TM
transactions in sparse format with
 4 transactions (rows) and
 4 items (columns)
> |
```

FIGURE 10.7 *Creating transaction using matrix*

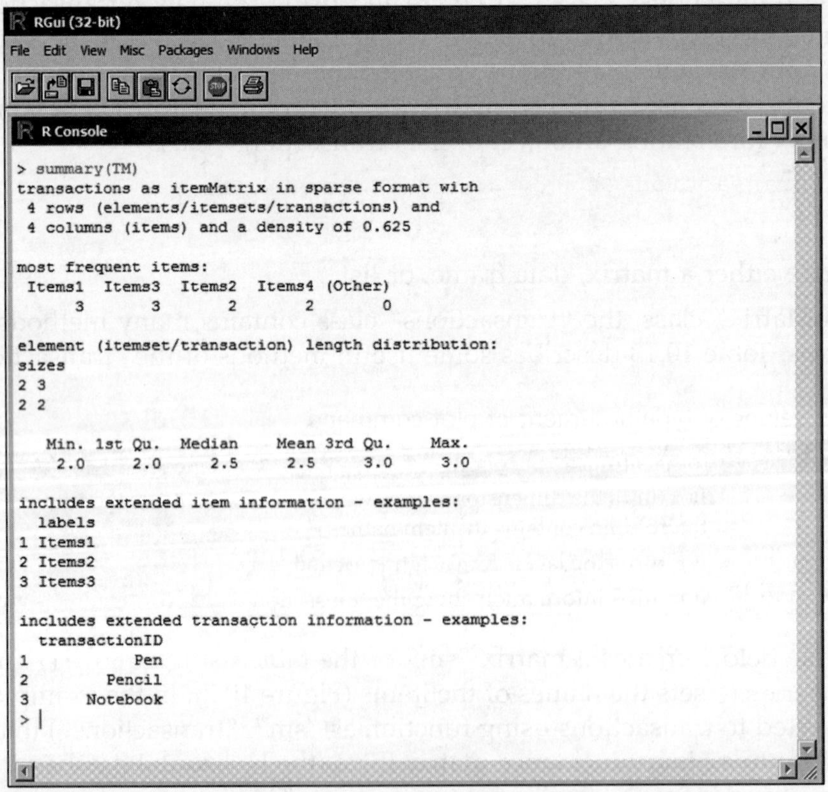

```
> summary(TM)
transactions as itemMatrix in sparse format with
 4 rows (elements/itemsets/transactions) and
 4 columns (items) and a density of 0.625

most frequent items:
 Items1  Items3  Items2  Items4 (Other)
      3       3       2       2       0

element (itemset/transaction) length distribution:
sizes
2 3
2 2

   Min. 1st Qu.  Median    Mean 3rd Qu.    Max.
    2.0     2.0     2.5     2.5     3.0     3.0

includes extended item information - examples:
  labels
1 Items1
2 Items2
3 Items3

includes extended transaction information - examples:
  transactionID
1           Pen
2        Pencil
3      Notebook
> |
```

FIGURE 10.8 *Summary of transactions*

In Figure 10.9, a transaction is created using a list. For this, the list function is used to create a list "al". Then `as(al, "transactions")` creates a transaction of this list.

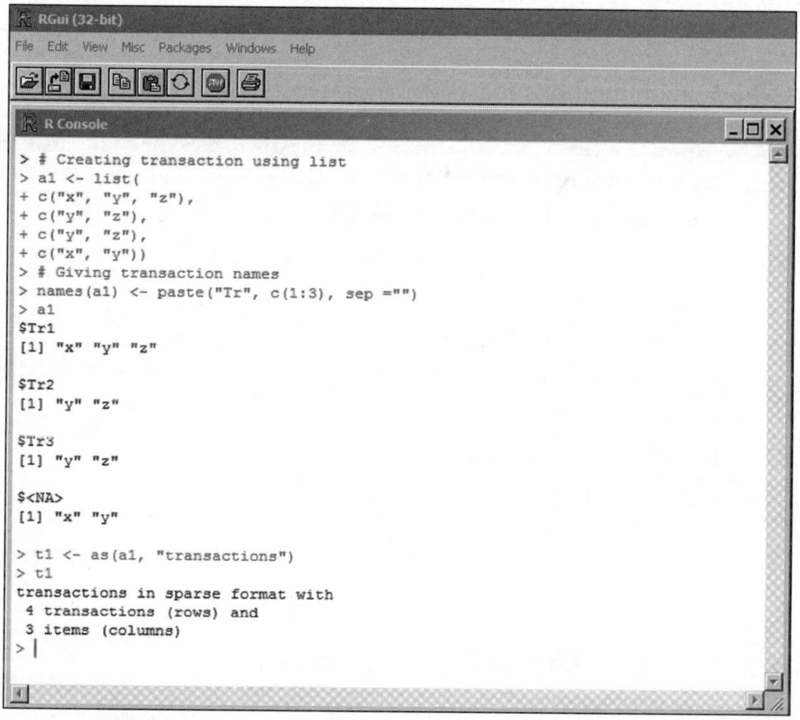

FIGURE 10.9 *Creating transaction using the list function*

10.3.3 Associations: Itemsets and Sets of Rules

In association rule mining, associations are the output of the transaction data after mining operations have been performed. Associations define the relationship between the set of itemset and a rule that has assigned some values for measuring quality. It can measure significance, such as support or interestingness such as confidence, etc.

The "arules" package provides a virtual class "associations" that is extended to mining result. For the implementation of the mining output, classes "itemsets" and "rules" are used that extend the associations class. The "itemsets" class is used for defining the frequent itemsets of their closed or maximal subsets and "rules" class is used for association rules. A brief introduction of both classes is as follows:

The "itemsets" class represents a set of itemsets and the associated quality measures. It also represents the multiset of itemsets with duplicate elements that can be removed through `unique()` function. An object of the class is created either using `new("itemsets",…)` or by calling the function `apriori()` with target parameter. Along with this, the class contains an object of the class "itemMatrix" and "tidList" that stores the items in sets of itemsets [items] and transaction ID lists [tidLists] respectively.

The "rules" class represents a set of rules. It also represents the multiset of rules with duplicate elements that can be removed through `unique()` function. An object of the class is created either using `new("rules",…)` or by calling the function `apriori()`. Along with this, the class contains an object of the class "itemMatrix" that stores the left-hand sides [lhs] and right-hand sides [rhs] of the association respectively.

Table 10.14 outlines few methods from the arules package to describe associations.

TABLE 10.14 Few common methods for describing associations in arules package

Methods	*Description*
`summary()`	It returns a short overview of the association rules and sets
`length()`	It returns the number of elements in the set
`items()`	It returns a set of items that are part of the association
`inspect()`	It displays individual associations
`sort()`	It sorts the given sets using the values of quality measures
`subset()`	It extracts the subset from the set
`union()`	It performs the union operation on the sets
`intersect()`	It performs the intersect operation on the sets
`setequal()`	It compares two sets
`match()`	It matches elements from two sets

Check Your Understanding

1. What is the arules package?

Ans: The arules package provides the required infrastructure that creates and manipulates the input dataset for any type of mining algorithm. It also provides features to analyse the resulting itemsets and association rules.

2. What is an "itemMatrix"?

Ans: The arules package provides a class "itemMatrix" that efficiently represents binary incidence matrix containing the itemsets and items.

3. What is a hash tree?

Ans: A hash tree is a type of data structure that stores values in key-value pairs and a type of tree where every internal node contains the hash values.

10.4 Mining Algorithm Interfaces

Any interface interacts with any application using some function. R language packages like "arules" and "arulesViz" provide some functions that implement the association rules mining algorithms. The Apriori algorithm is the most important algorithm of the association rules.

10.4.1 `apriori()` Function

The package "arules" provides a function `apriori()` that performs the association rule mining using Apriori algorithm. The function mines the frequent itemsets, association rules, and association hyperedges. It follows the Apriori algorithm and uses the level-wise search for frequent itemsets. The function returns the object of the classes "itemsets" and "rules". The basic syntax of the function `apriori()` is as follows:

```
apriori(data, parameter = NULL, appearance = NULL, control = NULL)
```

where,

"data" argument contains a data.frame or binary matrix that defines an object of class "transactions"; "parameter" argument contains an object of the "APparameter" class or a named list that contains the values of support, confidence, maxlen [the default values are: support = 0.1, confidence = 0.8, maxlen = 10]; "appearance" argument contains an object of the "APappearance" class or a named list that can restrict the appearance of the items; "control" argument contains an object of the "APcontrol" class or named list for controlling the performance of the algorithm.

The example given below takes the same table that was used to demonstrate "itemMatrix" and "transactions" classes. The `apriori()` function takes the object of the corresponding binary matrix and mines the frequent itemsets and association rules of the given table. Here, `apriori()` function takes no value for the parameters, support and confidence (Figure 10.10). Figure 10.11 represents the summary of the object returned by the `apriori()` function.

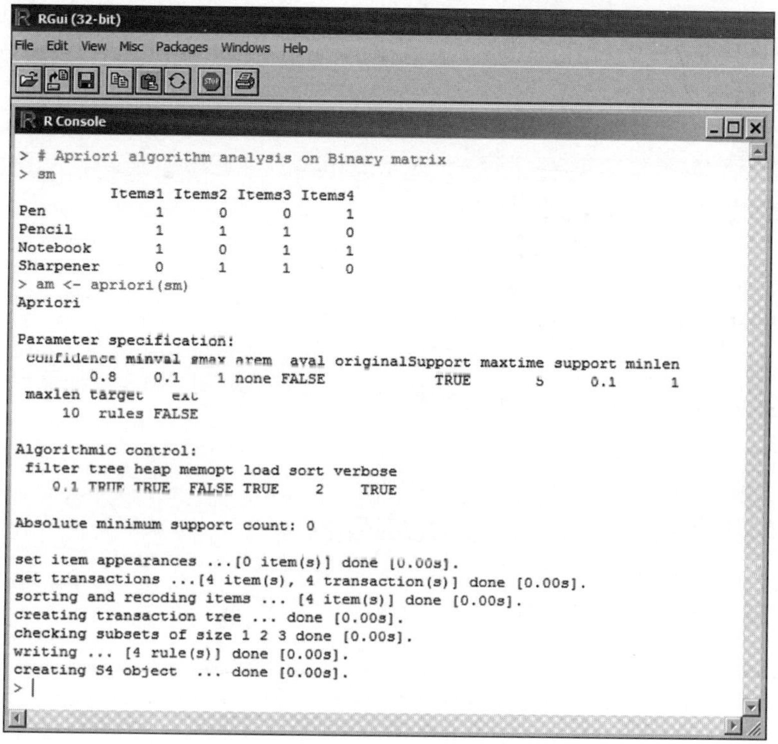

FIGURE 10.10 *Use of* `apriori()` *function to implement the Apriori algorithm*

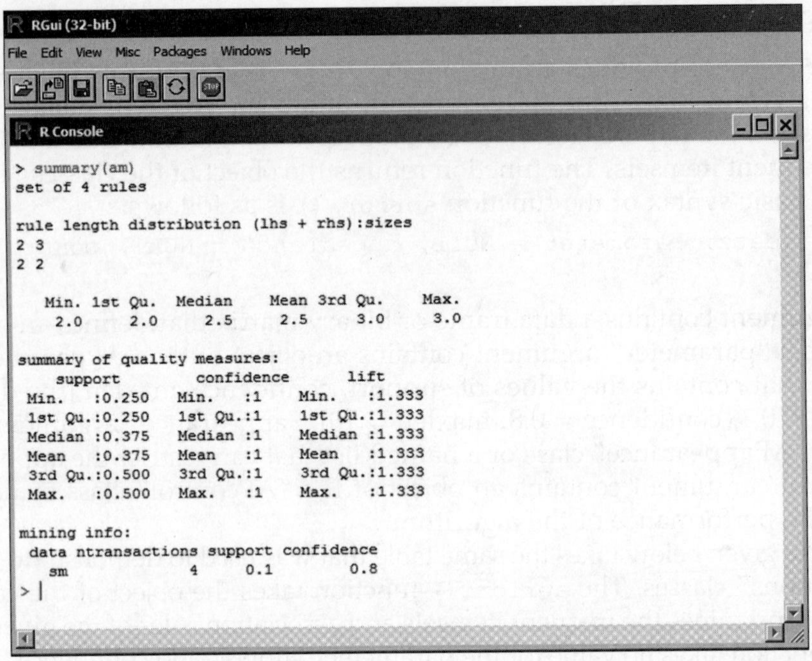

FIGURE 10.11 *Summary of* `apriori()` *function*

In Figure 10.12, the `apriori()` function implements the Apriori algorithm with support = 0.02 and confidence = 0.5 and `summary()` function provides the output of the object.

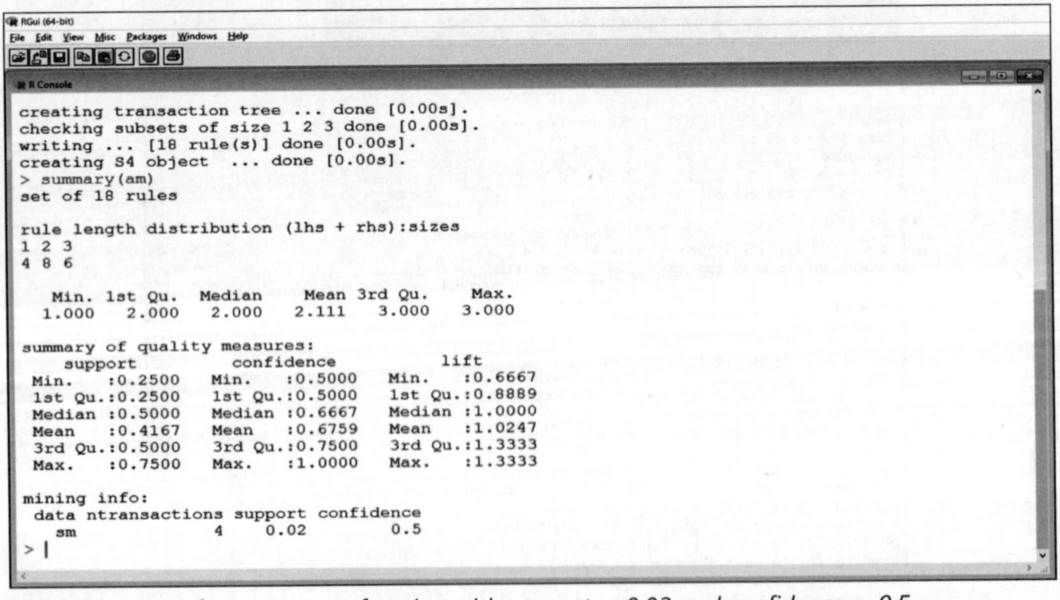

FIGURE 10.12 *Use of* `apriori()` *function with support = 0.02 and confidence = 0.5*

An example of association rule mining using "titanic" dataset. It will make use of methods such as `inspect()`, `summary()`, `union()`, `intersect()`, `setequal()`, `match()` etc.

Step 1: Load and attach the "arules" package.

```
> library(arules)
```

Step 2: Download the titanic data from: http://www.rdatamining.com/data/titanic.raw.rdata?attredirects=0&d=1

Describing the data from "titanic.raw".

```
> str(titanic.raw)
'data.frame' : 2201 obs. of 4 variables:
$ Class      : Factor w/ 4 levels "1st", "2nd", "3rd",...: 333333333 ...
$ Sex        : Factor w/ 2 levels "Female", "Male": 2 2 2 2 2 2 2 2 2 2 ...
$ Age        : Factor w/ 2 levels "Adult", "Child": 2 2 2 2 2 2 2 2 2 2 ...
$ Survived   : Factor w/ 2 levels "No", "Yes": 1 1 1 1 1 1 1 1 1 1 ...
```

Step 3: Use the apriori algorithm to mine frequent itemsets and association rules.

```
> rules <- apriori(titanic.raw)
Apriori

Parameter specification:
confidence minval smax arem aval  originalSupport maxtime support
0.8        0.1    1    none FALSE TRUE            5       0.1
minlen     maxlen target  ext
1          10     rules   FALSE

Algorithmic control:
  filter tree  heap  memopt load  sort verbose
    0.1  TRUE  TRUE  FALSE  TRUE   2    TRUE

Absolute minimum support count: 220

set item appearances ...[0 item(s)] done[0.00s].
set transactions ...[10 item(s), 2201 transaction(s)]done[0.00s].
sorting and recording items ...[9 item(s)] done[0.00s].
creating transaction tree ... done[0.00s].
checking subsets of size 1 2 3 4 done[0.00s].
writing ... [27 rule(s)] done[0.00s].
creating S4 object ... done[0.00s].
```

Step 4: Display associations and transactions in readable form (format it for online inspection).

```
> inspect(rules)
```

```
     lhs                                     rhs            support   confidence lift      count
[1]  {}                                   => {Age=Adult}    0.9504771 0.9504771  1.0000000 2092
[2]  {Class=2nd}                          => {Age=Adult}    0.1185825 0.9157895  0.9635051  261
[3]  {Class=1st}                          => {Age=Adult}    0.1449341 0.9815385  1.0326798  319
[4]  {Sex=Female}                         => {Age=Adult}    0.1930940 0.9042553  0.9513700  425
[5]  {Class=3rd}                          => {Age=Adult}    0.2848705 0.8881020  0.9343750  627
[6]  {Survived=Yes}                       => {Age=Adult}    0.2971377 0.9198312  0.9677574  654
[7]  {Class=Crew}                         => {Sex=Male}     0.3916402 0.9740113  1.2384742  862
[8]  {Class=Crew}                         => {Age=Adult}    0.4020900 1.0000000  1.0521033  885
[9]  {Survived=No}                        => {Sex=Male}     0.6197183 0.9154362  1.1639949 1364
[10] {Survived=No}                        => {Age=Adult}    0.6533394 0.9651007  1.0153856 1438
[11] {Sex=Male}                           => {Age=Adult}    0.7573830 0.9630272  1.0132040 1667
[12] {Sex=Female,Survived=Yes}            => {Age=Adult}    0.1435711 0.9186047  0.9664669  316
[13] {Class=3rd,Sex=Male}                 => {Survived=No}  0.1917310 0.8274510  1.2222950  422
[14] {Class=3rd,Survived=No}              => {Age=Adult}    0.2162653 0.9015152  0.9484870  476
[15] {Class=3rd,Sex=Male}                 => {Age=Adult}    0.2099046 0.9058824  0.9530818  462
[16] {Sex=Male,Survived=Yes}              => {Age=Adult}    0.1535666 0.9209809  0.9689670  338
[17] {Class=Crew,Survived=No}             => {Sex=Male}     0.3044071 0.9955423  1.2658514  670
[18] {Class=Crew,Survived=No}             => {Age=Adult}    0.3057701 1.0000000  1.0521033  673
[19] {Class=Crew,Sex=Male}                => {Age=Adult}    0.3916402 1.0000000  1.0521033  862
[20] {Class=Crew,Age=Adult}               => {Sex=Male}     0.3916402 0.9740113  1.2384742  862
[21] {Sex=Male,Survived=No}               => {Age=Adult}    0.6038164 0.9743402  1.0251065 1329
[22] {Age=Adult,Survived=No}              => {Sex=Male}     0.6038164 0.9242003  1.1751385 1329
[23] {Class=3rd,Sex=Male,Survived=No}     => {Age=Adult}    0.1758292 0.9170616  0.9648435  387
[24] {Class=3rd,Age=Adult,Survived=No}    => {Sex=Male}     0.1758292 0.8130252  1.0337773  387
[25] {Class=3rd,Sex=Male,Age=Adult}       => {Survived=No}  0.1758292 0.8376623  1.2373791  387
[26] {Class=Crew,Sex=Male,Survived=No}    => {Age=Adult}    0.3044071 1.0000000  1.0521033  670
[27] {Class=Crew,Age=Adult,Survived=No}   => {Sex=Male}     0.3044071 0.9955423  1.2658514  670
```

Step 5: Set rhs=c("Survived=No", "Survived=Yes") in appearance. This will ensure that only "Survived=No" and "Survived=Yes" will appear in the rhs of rules.

```
> rules <- apriori(titanic.raw, parameter = list(minlen=2, supp=0.005,
conf=0.8), appearance = list(rhs=c("Survived=No", + "Survived=Yes"),
default="lhs"), control = list(verbose=F))
```

Step 6: Display the associations for the above stated criteria.

```
> inspect(rules)
```

```
     lhs                                    rhs            support     confidence lift     count
[1]  {Class=2nd,Age=Child}               => {Survived=Yes} 0.010904134 1.0000000  3.095640  24
[2]  {Class=2nd,Sex=Female}              => {Survived=Yes} 0.042253521 0.8773585  2.715986  93
[3]  {Class=2nd,Sex=Male}                => {Survived=No}  0.069968196 0.8603352  1.270871 154
[4]  {Class=1st,Sex=Female}              => {Survived=Yes} 0.064061790 0.9724138  3.010243 141
[5]  {Class=Crew,Sex=Female}             => {Survived=Yes} 0.009086779 0.8695652  2.691861  20
[6]  {Class=3rd,Sex=Male}                => {Survived=No}  0.191731031 0.8274510  1.222295 422
[7]  {Class=2nd,Sex=Female,Age=Child}    => {Survived=Yes} 0.005906406 1.0000000  3.095640  13
[8]  {Class=2nd,Sex=Female,Age=Adult}    => {Survived=Yes} 0.036347115 0.8602151  2.662916  80
[9]  {Class=2nd,Sex=Male,Age=Adult}      => {Survived=No}  0.069968196 0.9166667  1.354083 154
[10] {Class=1st,Sex=Female,Age=Adult}    => {Survived=Yes} 0.063607451 0.9722222  3.009650 140
[11] {Class=Crew,Sex=Female,Age=Adult}   => {Survived=Yes} 0.009086779 0.8695652  2.691861  20
[12] {Class=3rd,Sex=Male,Age=Adult}      => {Survived=No}  0.175829169 0.8376623  1.237379 387
```

Step 7: Display the result summary using the `summary()` function.

```
> summary(rules)
set of 12 rules

rule  length  distribution (lhs + rhs) : sizes
3 4
6 6
   Min.    1st Qu.   Median    Mean    3rd Qu.    Max.
   3.0      3.0       3.5       3.5      4.0       4.0

summary of quality measures:
     support          confidence          lift            count
Min.   :0.005906  Min.   :0.8275  Min.   :1.222  Min.   :13.0
1st Qu.:0.010450  1st Qu.:0.8603  1st Qu.:1.333  1st Qu.:23.0
Median :0.052930  Median :0.8735  Median :2.692  Median :116.5
Mean   :0.062396  Mean   :0.9053  Mean   :2.338  Mean   :137.3
3rd Qu.:0.069968  3rd Qu.:0.9723  3rd Qu.:3.010  3rd Qu.:154.0
Max.   :0.191731  Max.   :1.0000  Max.   :3.096  Max.   :422.0

mining info:
       data   ntransactions   support   confidence
titanic.raw   2201            0.005     0.8
```

Step 8: Get the number of elements in the associations

```
> length(rules)
[1] 12
```

Step 9: Sort the associations by "lift".

```
> rules.sorted <- sort(rules, by="lift"
> inspect(rules.sorted)
```

```
     lhs                                    rhs              support     confidence lift     count
[1]  {Class=2nd,Age=Child}               => {Survived=Yes} 0.010904134 1.0000000  3.095640  24
[2]  {Class=2nd,Sex=Female,Age=Child}    => {Survived=Yes} 0.005906406 1.0000000  3.095640  13
[3]  {Class=1st,Sex=Female}              => {Survived=Yes} 0.064061790 0.9724138  3.010243 141
[4]  {Class=1st,Sex=Female,Age=Adult}    => {Survived=Yes} 0.063607451 0.9722222  3.009650 140
[5]  {Class=2nd,Sex=Female}              => {Survived=Yes} 0.042253521 0.8773585  2.715986  93
[6]  {Class=Crew,Sex=Female}             => {Survived=Yes} 0.009086779 0.8695652  2.691861  20
[7]  {Class=Crew,Sex=Female,Age=Adult}   => {Survived=Yes} 0.009086779 0.8695652  2.691861  20
[8]  {Class=2nd,Sex=Female,Age=Adult}    => {Survived=Yes} 0.036347115 0.8602151  2.662916  80
[9]  {Class=2nd,Sex=Male,Age=Adult}      => {Survived=No}  0.069968196 0.9166667  1.354083 154
[10] {Class=2nd,Sex=Male}                => {Survived=No}  0.069968196 0.8603352  1.270871 154
[11] {Class=3rd,Sex=Male,Age=Adult}      => {Survived=No}  0.175829169 0.8376623  1.237379 387
[12] {Class=3rd,Sex=Male}                => {Survived=No}  0.191731031 0.8274510  1.222295 422
```

Step 10: Set rhs=c("Survived=No") in appearance. This will ensure that only "Survived=No" will appear in the rhs of rules.

```
> rules1 <- apriori(titanic.raw,parameter = list(minlen=2,
supp=0.005, conf=0.8), + appearance = list(rhs=c("Survived=No"),
default="lhs"), control = list(verbose=F))

> inspect(rules1)
```

```
    lhs                                   rhs            support   confidence lift     count
[1] {Class=2nd,Sex=Male}               => {Survived=No} 0.0699682 0.8603352  1.270871 154
[2] {Class=3rd,Sex=Male}               => {Survived=No} 0.1917310 0.8274510  1.222295 422
[3] {Class=2nd,Sex=Male,Age=Adult}     => {Survived=No} 0.0699682 0.9166667  1.354083 154
[4] {Class=3rd,Sex=Male,Age=Adult}     => {Survived=No} 0.1758292 0.8376623  1.237379 387
```

Step 11: Set rhs=c("Survived=Yes") in appearance. This will ensure that only "Survived=Yes" will appear in the rhs of rules.

```
> rules2 <- apriori(titanic.raw,parameter = list(minlen=2,
supp=0.005, conf=0.8), + appearance = list(rhs=c("Survived=Yes"),
default="lhs"), control = list(verbose=F))

> inspect(rules2)
```

```
    lhs                                    rhs             support     confidence lift     count
[1] {Class=2nd,Age=Child}               => {Survived=Yes} 0.010904134 1.0000000  3.095640  24
[2] {Class=2nd,Sex=Female}              => {Survived=Yes} 0.042253521 0.8773585  2.715986  93
[3] {Class=1st,Sex=Female}              => {Survived=Yes} 0.064061790 0.9724138  3.010243 141
[4] {Class=Crew,Sex=Female}             => {Survived=Yes} 0.009086779 0.8695652  2.691861  20
[5] {Class=2nd,Sex=Female,Age=Child}    => {Survived=Yes} 0.005906406 1.0000000  3.095640  13
[6] {Class=2nd,Sex=Female,Age=Adult}    => {Survived=Yes} 0.036347115 0.8602151  2.662916  80
[7] {Class=1st,Sex=Female,Age=Adult}    => {Survived=Yes} 0.063607451 0.9722222  3.009650 140
[8] {Class=Crew,Sex=Female,Age=Adult}   => {Survived=Yes} 0.009086779 0.8695652  2.691861  20
```

Step 12: Run `union()` on sets of associations, "rules1" and "rules2".

```
> rules3 <-union(rules1, rules2)
> rules3
set of 12 rules
> inspect(rules3)
```

```
     lhs                                  rhs             support     confidence lift     count
[1]  {Class=2nd,Sex=Male}              => {Survived=No}  0.069968196 0.8603352  1.270871 154
[2]  {Class=3rd,Sex=Male}              => {Survived=No}  0.191731031 0.8274510  1.222295 422
[3]  {Class=2nd,Sex=Male,Age=Adult}    => {Survived=No}  0.069968196 0.9166667  1.354083 154
[4]  {Class=3rd,Sex=Male,Age=Adult}    => {Survived=No}  0.175829169 0.8376623  1.237379 387
[5]  {Class=2nd,Age=Child}             => {Survived=Yes} 0.010904134 1.0000000  3.095640  24
[6]  {Class=2nd,Sex=Female}            => {Survived=Yes} 0.042253521 0.8773585  2.715986  93
[7]  {Class=1st,Sex=Female}            => {Survived=Yes} 0.064061790 0.9724138  3.010243 141
[8]  {Class=Crew,Sex=Female}           => {Survived=Yes} 0.009086779 0.8695652  2.691861  20
[9]  {Class=2nd,Sex=Female,Age=Child}  => {Survived=Yes} 0.005906406 1.0000000  3.095640  13
[10] {Class=2nd,Sex=Female,Age=Adult}  => {Survived=Yes} 0.036347115 0.8602151  2.662916  80
[11] {Class=1st,Sex=Female,Age=Adult}  => {Survived=Yes} 0.063607451 0.9722222  3.009650 140
[12] {Class=Crew,Sex=Female,Age=Adult} => {Survived=Yes} 0.009086779 0.8695652  2.691861  20
```

Step 13: Run `intersect()` on sets of associations, "rules" and "rules1".

```
> intersectrules <- intersect(rules,rules1)
> intersectrules
set of 4 rules
> inspect(intersectrules)
```

```
    lhs                                      rhs            support   confidence lift     count
[1] {Class=2nd,Sex=Male}                  => {Survived=No} 0.0699682 0.8603352  1.270871 154
[2] {Class=3rd,Sex=Male}                  => {Survived=No} 0.1917310 0.8274510  1.222295 422
[3] {Class=2nd,Sex=Male,Age=Adult}        => {Survived=No} 0.0699682 0.9166667  1.354083 154
[4] {Class=3rd,Sex=Male,Age=Adult}        => {Survived=No} 0.1758292 0.8376623  1.237379 387
```

Step 14: Run `setequal()` on sets of associations, "rules" and "rules1".

```
> equalsets <- setequal(rules, rules1)
> equalsets
[1] FALSE
```

Step 15: Run `match()` on sets of associations, "rules" and "rules1". `match()` returns a vector of the positions of (first) matches of its first argument in its second.

```
> matchsets <- match(rules, rules1)
> matchsets
[1] NA NA  1 NA NA  2 NA NA   3 NA NA  4
```

Additional Assignments on `apriori()` Function

Exercise 1

Problem statement: Transaction data (Transaction ID and Transaction Details (the items bought together) for seven transactions is provided in the file, "trans1.csv". Analyze the data to find associations with their support, confidence and lift.

Step 1: Read data from "trans1.csv" and store it in the data frame, "transdata".

```
> transdata <- read.csv("D:/trans1.csv")
```

Print the data held in the data frame, "transdata".

```
> transdata
     Transaction.ID   Transaction.Details
1           1                 A
2           1                 B
3           1                 E
4           2                 A
5           2                 B
6           2                 D
7           2                 E
8           3                 B
9           3                 C
10          3                 D
11          3                 E
12          4                 B
13          4                 D
14          4                 E
15          5                 A
16          5                 B
17          5                 D
18          6                 B
19          6                 E
20          7                 A
21          7                 E
```

Step 2: Using the `split()` function divide the data held in "transdata$Transaction.Details" into groups defined by "transdata$Transaction.ID".

```
> AggPosData <- split(transdata$Transaction.Details,
transdata$Transaction.ID)
> AggPosData
$'1'
[1] A B E
Levels: A B C D E

$'2'
[1] A B D E
Levels: A B C D E

$'3'
[1] B C D E
Levels: A B C D E

$'4'
[1] B D E
Levels: A B C D E

$'5'
[1] A B D
Levels: A B C D E

$'6'
[1] B E
Levels: A B C D E

$'7'
[1] A E
Levels: A B C D E
```

Step 3: Use the `as()` function to coerce the data held in "AggPosData" to the class "transactions".

```
> txns <- as(AggPosData, "transactions")
> txns
Transactions in sparse format with
 7 transactions (rows) and
 5 items (columns)
```

Step 4: Use the `summary()` function to display the summary of the object, "txns".

```
> summary (txns)
transactions as itemMatrix in sparse format with
 7 rows (elements/itemsets/transactions) and
 5 columns (items) and a density of 0.6

most frequent items:
    B    E     A      D      C (Other)
    6    6     4      4      1       0
```

```
element (itemset/transaction) length distribution:
sizes
2 3 4
2 3 2

   Min.     1st Qu.   Median   Mean    3rd Qu.   Max.
   2.0      2.5       3.0      3.0     3.5       4.0

includes extended item information - examples:
 labels
1   A
2   B
3   C

includes extended transaction information - examples:
 transaction ID
1  1
2  2
3  3
```

Step 5: Use `apriori()` function to mine the data. The `apriori()` function mines frequent itemsets, association rules or association hyperedges using the Apriori algorithm. The Apriori algorithm employs level-wise search for frequent itemsets.

```
> rules <- apriori(txns,parameter=list(sup=0.3, conf=0.75))
Apriori

Parameter specification:
 confidence minval  smax  arem  aval  originalSupport  support
  0.75        0.1     1   none  FALSE       TRUE          0.3
   minlen  maxlen  target  ext
      1      10    rules  FALSE

Algorithmic control:
  filter tree  heap  memopt  load  sort  verbose
   0.1   TRUE  TRUE  FALSE   TRUE    2   TRUE

Absolute minimum support count: 2

set item appearances ...[0 item(s)] done[0.00s].
set transactions ...[5 item(s), 7 transaction(s)] done[0.00s].
sorting and recoding items ...[4 item(s)] done[0.00s].
creating transaction tree ... done[0.00s].
checking subsets of size 1 2 3 done[0.00s].
writing ... [10 rule(s)] done[0.00s].
creating S4 object ... done[0.00s].
```

Step 6: Use the `inspect()` function to inspect a set of associations or transactions or an itemMatrix.

```
> inspect(rules)
   lhs       rhs   support   confidence lift
1  {}     => {E}   0.8571429 0.8571429  1.0000000
2  {}     => {B}   0.8571429 0.8571429  1.0000000
3  {A}    => {E}   0.4285714 0.7500000  0.8750000
4  {A}    => {B}   0.4285714 0.7500000  0.8750000
5  {D}    => {E}   0.4285714 0.7500000  0.8750000
6  {D}    => {B}   0.5714286 1.0000000  1.1666667
7  {E}    => {B}   0.7142857 0.8333333  0.9722222
8  {B}    => {E}   0.7142857 0.8333333  0.9722222
9  {D,E}  => {B}   0.4285714 1.0000000  1.1666667
10 {B,D}  => {E}   0.4285714 0.7500000  0.8750000
```

Exercise 2

Problem statement: Transaction data (Transaction ID and Transaction Details (the items bought together) for five transactions is provided in the file, "trans2.csv". Analyze the data to find associations with their support, confidence and lift.

Step 1: Read data from "trans2.csv" and store it in the data frame, "transdata".

```
> transdata <- read.csv("D:/trans2.csv")
```

Print the data held in the data frame, "transdata".

```
> transdata
   Transaction.ID Transaction.Details
1  1              A
2  1              B
3  1              C
4  2              B
5  2              C
6  2              D
7  2              E
8  3              C
9  3              D
10 4              A
11 4              B
12 4              D
13 5              A
14 5              B
15 5              C
```

Step 2: Using the `split()` function divide the data held in "transdata$Transaction.Details" into groups defined by "transdata$Transaction.ID".

```
> AggPosData <- split(transdata$Transaction.Details,
transdata$Transaction.ID)
> AggPosData
$'1'
[1] A B C
Levels: A B C D E

$'2'
[1] B C D E
Levels: A B C D E

$'3'
[1] C D
Levels: A B C D E

$'4'
[1] A B D
Levels: A B C D E

$'5'
[1] A B C
Levels: A B C D E
```

Step 3: Use the `as()` function to coerce the data held in "AggPosData" to the class "transactions".

```
> txns <- as(AggPosData,"transactions")
> txns
transactions in sparse format with
 5 transactions (rows) and
 5 items (columns)
```

Step 4: Use the `summary()` function to display the summary of the object, "txns".

```
> summary(txns)
transactions as itemMatrix in sparse format with
 5 rows (elements/itemsets/transactions) and
 5 columns (items) and a density of 0.6

most frequent items:
    B    C     A     D     E   (Other)
    4    4     3     3     1      0

element (itemset/transaction) length distribution:
sizes
2 3 4
1 3 1
```

```
   Min.  1st Qu. Median   Mean  3rd Qu.  Max.
     2       3       3      3       3     4

includes extended item information - examples:
  labels
1  A
2  B
3  C

includes extended transaction information - examples:
   transactionID
1              1
2              2
3              3
```

Step 5: Use `apriori()` function to mine the data. The `apriori()` function mines frequent itemsets, association rules or association hyperedges using the Apriori algorithm. The Apriori algorithm employs level-wise search for frequent itemsets.

```
> rules <- apriori(txns, parameter = list(supp=0.2, conf=0.70))
Apriori

Parameter specification:
 confidence minval smax  arem  aval originalSupport support minlen
     0.7      0.1     1  none FALSE            TRUE     0.2      1
  maxlen    target  ext
     10      rules FALSE

Algorithmic control:
 filter  tree   heap  memopt  load   sort  verbose
   0.1   TRUE   TRUE   FALSE  TRUE     2     TRUE

Absolute minimum support count: 1

Warning in apriori(txns, parameter = list(supp = 0.2, conf = 0.7)):
 You chose a very low absolute support count of 1. You might run out
of memory! Increase minimum support.

set item appearances … [0 item(s)] done [0.00s].
set transactions …[5 item(s), 5 transaction(s)] done [0.02s].
sorting and recoding items … [5 item(s)] done [0.00s].
creating transaction tree … done [0.00s].
checking subsets of size 1 2 3 4 done [0.03s].
writing … [21 rule(s)] done [0.00s]
creating S4 object … done [0.00s]
```

Step 6: Use the `inspect()` function to inspect a set of associations or transactions or an itemMatrix.

```
> inspect(rules)
    lhs          rhs   support  confidence   lift
1   {}        => {C}    0.8        0.80     1.000000
2   {}        => {B}    0.8        0.80     1.000000
3   {E}       => {D}    0.2        1.00     1.666667
4   {E}       => {C}    0.2        1.00     1.250000
5   {E}       => {B}    0.2        1.00     1.250000
6   {A}       => {B}    0.6        1.00     1.250000
7   {B}       => {A}    0.6        0.75     1.250000
8   {C}       => {B}    0.6        0.75     0.937500
9   {B}       => {C}    0.6        0.75     0.937500
10  {D,E}     => {C}    0.2        1.00     1.250000
11  {C,E}     => {D}    0.2        1.00     1.666667
12  {D,E}     => {B}    0.2        1.00     1.250000
13  {B,E}     => {D}    0.2        1.00     1.666667
14  {C,E}     => {B}    0.2        1.00     1.250000
15  {B,E}     => {C}    0.2        1.00     1.250000
16  {A,D}     => {B}    0.2        1.00     1.250000
17  {A,C}     => {B}    0.4        1.00     1.250000
18  {C,D,E}   => {B}    0.2        1.00     1.250000
19  {B,D,E}   => {C}    0.2        1.00     1.250000
20  {B,C,E}   => {D}    0.2        1.00     1.666667
21  {B,C,D}   => {E}    0.2        1.00     5.000000
```

10.4.2 `eclat()` Function

The package "arules" provides another function `eclat()` that performs association rule mining and generates frequent itemsets. It follows the Eclat algorithm and uses simple intersection operations for frequent itemsets. The function returns the object of the class "itemsets". The basic syntax of the function `eclat()` is as follows:

```
eclat(data, parameter = NULL, control = NULL)
```

where,

"data" argument contains a data.frame or binary matrix that defines an object of class "transactions"; "parameter" argument contains an object of the class "ECparameter" or a named list that contains the values of support, maxlen [the default values are: support = 0.1, maxlen = 5]; "control" argument contains an object for controlling the performance of the algorithm

The example below takes the same table as demonstrated in "itemMatrix" and "transactions" classes. The `eclat()` function takes the object of the corresponding binary matrix with support = 0.02. It generates the frequent itemsets of the given table. Figure 10.14 represents the summary of the object as returned by the `eclat()` function.

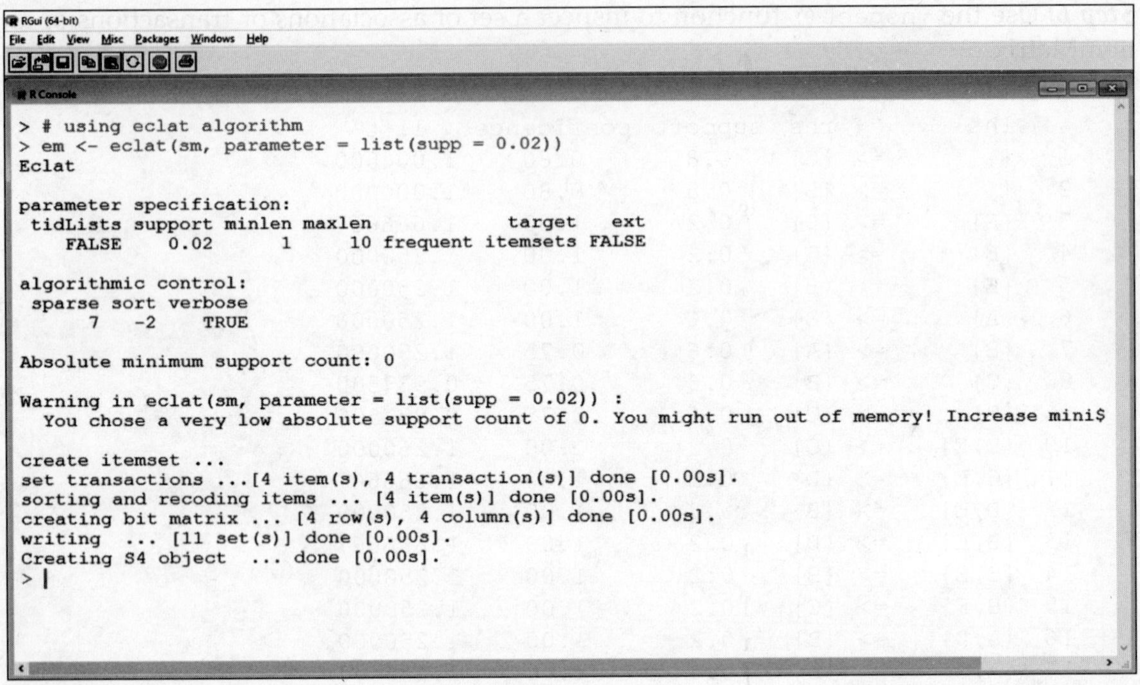

```
> # using eclat algorithm
> em <- eclat(sm, parameter = list(supp = 0.02))
Eclat

parameter specification:
 tidLists support minlen maxlen            target   ext
    FALSE    0.02      1     10 frequent itemsets FALSE

algorithmic control:
 sparse sort verbose
      7   -2    TRUE

Absolute minimum support count: 0

Warning in eclat(sm, parameter = list(supp = 0.02)) :
  You chose a very low absolute support count of 0. You might run out of memory! Increase mini$

create itemset ...
set transactions ...[4 item(s), 4 transaction(s)] done [0.00s].
sorting and recoding items ... [4 item(s)] done [0.00s].
creating bit matrix ... [4 row(s), 4 column(s)] done [0.00s].
writing  ... [11 set(s)] done [0.00s].
Creating S4 object  ... done [0.00s].
> |
```

FIGURE 10.13 *Use of* `eclat()` *function*

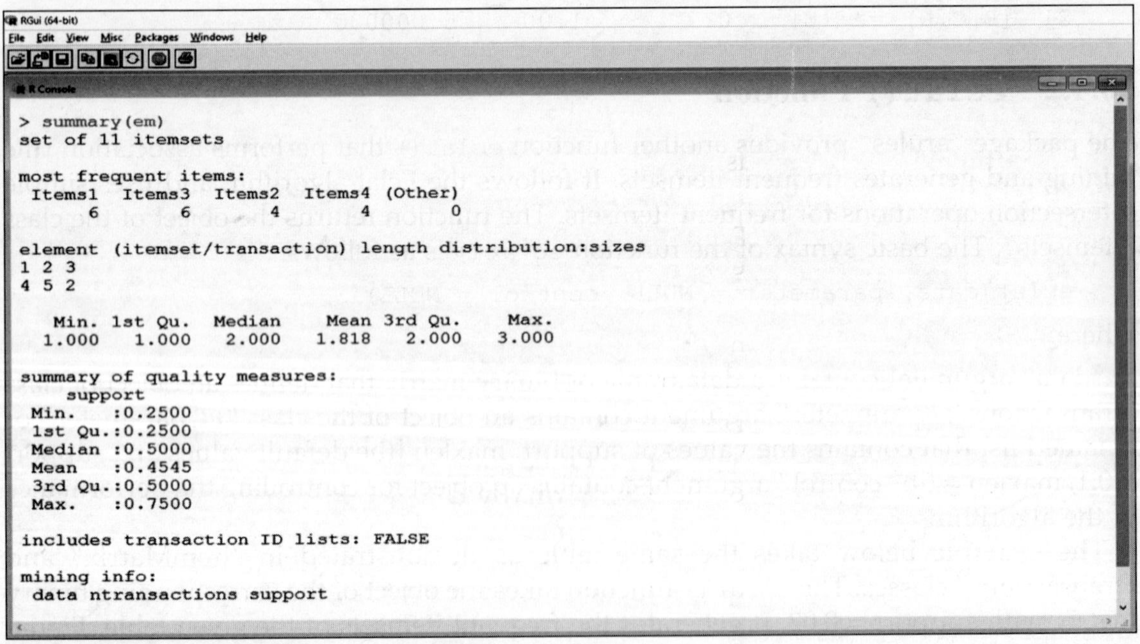

```
> summary(em)
set of 11 itemsets

most frequent items:
 Items1  Items3  Items2  Items4  (Other)
      6       6       4       4        0

element (itemset/transaction) length distribution:sizes
1 2 3
4 5 2

   Min. 1st Qu.  Median    Mean 3rd Qu.    Max.
  1.000   1.000   2.000   1.818   2.000   3.000

summary of quality measures:
    support
 Min.   :0.2500
 1st Qu.:0.2500
 Median :0.5000
 Mean   :0.4545
 3rd Qu.:0.5000
 Max.   :0.7500

includes transaction ID lists: FALSE

mining info:
 data ntransactions support
```

FIGURE 10.14 *Summary of* `eclat()` *function*

Check Your Understanding

1. What is an `apriori()` function?

Ans: The package "arules" provides a function `apriori()` that performs association rule mining using Apriori algorithm. The function mines the frequent itemsets, association rules, and association hyperedges.

2. What is an `eclat()` function?

Ans: The package "arules" provides another function `eclat()` that performs association rule mining and generates frequent itemsets. It follows the Eclat algorithm and uses simple intersection operations for frequent itemsets.

10.5 Auxiliary Functions

Implementation of any algorithm needs some auxiliary function that provides common required functionality. Here the implementation of association rules mining also needs some auxiliary functions for finding support, sample, or rules. The package "arules" provides functions for counting the support or rules. The following subsection describes these auxiliary functions.

10.5.1 Counting Support for Itemsets

It is very time-consuming to count many items for low minimum support values during mining the databases. During this process, all frequent and candidate itemsets are counted. Sometimes an application needs to mine only a single or very few itemsets and does not need to mine the whole database for all frequent itemsets.

Hence, the package "arules" provides a function `support()` that determines the support for a given set of items as an itemMatrix. It also finds the support for infrequent itemsets with a support that is too low. The basic syntax of the function `support()` is as follows:

```
support(x, transactions, type, …)
```

where,

"x" argument contains a set of itemsets for which support is to be counted; "transactions" argument contains transactions dataset; "type" argument contains the string that specifies frequency/support in relative or absolute form. By default, it returns the relative form; the dots "…" define the other optional arguments.

In the example below, the `support()` function takes a set of itemsets, "ap", i.e. an object of the `apriori()` function and a transaction dataset "TM" and returns the support of the itemset. By default, it returns the support value in a relative form. It can also return the value in absolute form (Figure 10.15).

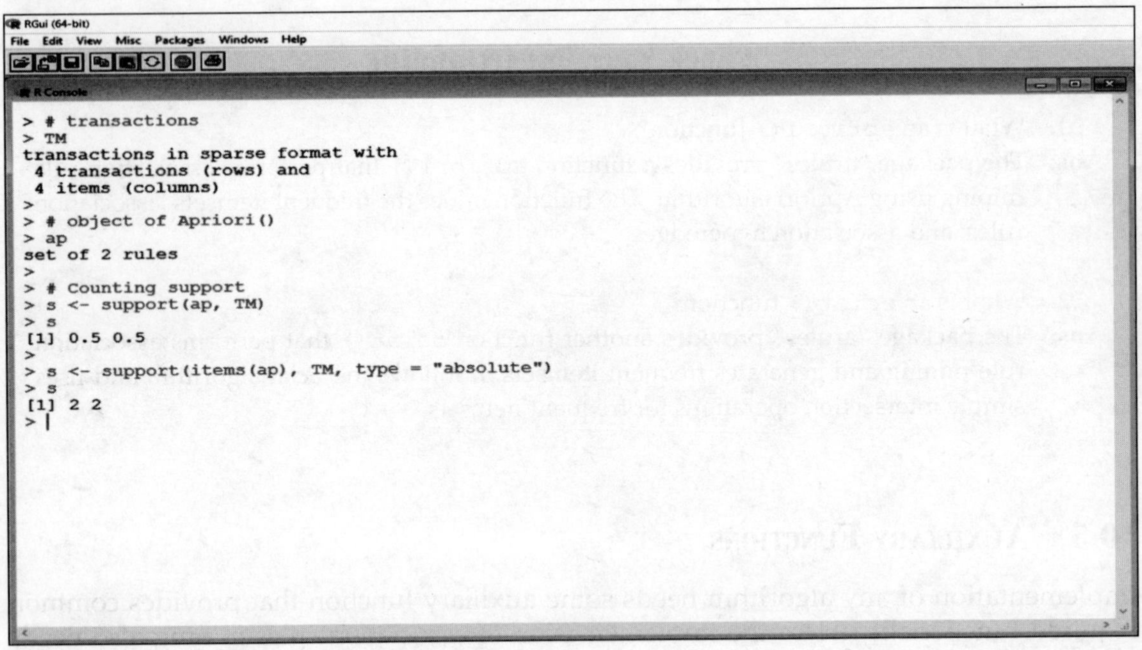

Figure 10.15 *Use of* `support()` *function*

10.5.2 Rule Induction

Sometimes only generation of rules from a set of itemsets is required. The package "arules" provides a function `ruleInduction()` that induces all rules generated by the given itemsets from a transaction dataset. The basic syntax of the function `ruleInduction()` is as follows:

```
ruleInduction(x, transactions, confidence, ...)
```

where,

"*x*" argument contains a set of itemsets for which rules are to be induced; "transactions" argument contains transactions dataset; "confidence" argument contains a numeric value for defining the minimum confidence value; the dots "..." define the other optional arguments.

In the example below, the `ruleInduction()` function takes a set of itemset, "ap" which is an object of the `apriori()` function and a transaction dataset "TM". Here the object "ap" is generated using *"ap <- apriori(TM,parameter = list(target = "closed", support = 0.02))"* where confidence is not used in the `apriori()` function. The `ruleInduction()` function returns the set of rules of the given itemset (Figure 10.16).

```
> # transactions
> TM
transactions in sparse format with
 4 transactions (rows) and
 4 items (columns)
> # object of Apriori()
> ap
set of 7 itemsets
>
> # Defining rule induction
> ri <- ruleInduction(ap, TM)
> ri
set of 4 rules
> summary(ri)
set of 4 rules

rule length distribution (lhs + rhs):sizes
2 3
2 2

   Min. 1st Qu.  Median    Mean 3rd Qu.    Max.
    2.0     2.0     2.5     2.5     3.0     3.0

summary of quality measures:
    support        confidence       lift            itemset
 Min.   :0.250   Min.   :1     Min.   :1.333   Min.   :3.00
 1st Qu.:0.250   1st Qu.:1     1st Qu.:1.333   1st Qu.:3.75
 Median :0.375   Median :1     Median :1.333   Median :5.00
 Mean   :0.375   Mean   :1     Mean   :1.333   Mean   :5.00
 3rd Qu.:0.500   3rd Qu.:1     3rd Qu.:1.333   3rd Qu.:6.25
```

FIGURE 10.16 *Use of* `ruleInduction()` *function*

In Figure 10.17, the `inspect()` function inspects these rules and displays the rules in the original form with lhs and rhs. It also provides the support and confidence values.

```
> inspect(head(ri, by = "lift"))
   lhs                  rhs       support confidence lift     itemset
1  {Items4}          => {Items1}  0.50    1          1.333333 3
4  {Items2}          => {Items3}  0.50    1          1.333333 4
7  {Items3,Items4}   => {Items1}  0.25    1          1.333333 6
12 {Items1,Items2}   => {Items3}  0.25    1          1.333333 7
>
```

FIGURE 10.17 *Inspection of rules using* `inspect()` *function*

Check Your Understanding

1. What is the `support()` function?

Ans: The package "arules" provides a function `support()` that determines the support for a set of given set of items as an itemMatrix.

2. What is the `ruleInduction()` function?

Ans: The package "arules" provides a function `ruleInduction()` that induces all rules that are generated by given itemsets from a transaction dataset.

10.6 SAMPLING FROM TRANSACTION

Any mining algorithm needs samples for mining huge databases. Business analytics also uses large databases and needs samples from these databases, as sometimes the original large database does not fit into the main memory. Sampling is a process that takes the samples from the original databases for mining of large data. The sampling process speeds up the mining with low cost. The association rules also need sampling.

For this, the package "arules" provides a function `sample()` that generates random samples and permutations from a set of transactions or associations. It takes a sample of the specified size from the elements of *x* (contains a set of transactions or associations from which a sample is required). The basic syntax of the function `sample()` is as follows:

```
sample(x, size, replace,…)
```

where,

"*x*" argument contains a set of transactions or associations from which a sample is required; "size" argument defines the sample size; "replace" argument contains the logical value that defines the replacement for the sample; the dots "…" define the other optional arguments.

In the example given below, the `sample()` function takes a built-in dataset "Mushroom" and generates 50 samples from the dataset. It returns 50 transactions [rows] and 114 items [columns].The `summary()` function generates the summary of the sample.

```
> # Sampling from a built-in dataset
> data("Mushroom")
> s <- sample(Mushroom,50)
> s
transactions in sparse format with
 50 transactions (rows) and
 114 items (columns)
> summary(s)
transactions as itemMatrix in sparse format with
 50 rows (elements/itemsets/transactions) and
 114 columns (items) and a density of 0.1919298

most frequent items:
 VeilType=partial GillAttached=free   VeilColor=white    RingNumber=one
               50                49                49                46
  GillSpace=close           (Other)
               40               860

element (itemset/transaction) length distribution:
sizes
21 22 23
16 24 10

   Min. 1st Qu.  Median    Mean 3rd Qu.    Max.
  21.00   21.00   22.00   21.88   22.00   23.00

includes extended item information - examples:
           labels variables    levels
1    Class=edible     Class    edible
```

FIGURE 10.18 *Use of* `sample()` *function*

10.7 Generating Synthetic Transaction Data

The association rules also need synthetic data. Synthetic data is data that is created on the basis of the need of an application. This data evaluates and compares different mining algorithms for measuring the behaviour of the interestingness of the rules and itemsets. The standard methods either use the simple probabilistic method or re-implements the generator.

In R language, the package "arules" provides a function `random.transactions()` that simulates random transactions datasets. It returns the object of the class "transactions". The basic syntax of the function `random.transactions()` is as follows:

```
random.transactions(nItems, nTrans, method,…)
```

where,

"nItems" argument contains an integer number that defines the number of items; "nTrans" argument contains an integer number that defines the number of transactions;

"method" argument defines the method name to be used. It can be either "independent" or "agrawal"; the dots "…" define the other optional arguments.

In the following example, the `random.transactions()` function generates a random number of transactions using 20 items and 10 transactions (Figure 10.19).

```
> # Random transactions
>
> rt <- random.transactions(nItems = 20, nTrans = 10, method = "independent")
> rt
transactions in sparse format with
 10 transactions (rows) and
 20 items (columns)
> summary(rt)
transactions as itemMatrix in sparse format with
 10 rows (elements/itemsets/transactions) and
 20 columns (items) and a density of 0.185

most frequent items:
 item12   item1   item3   item4  item19 (Other)
      4       3       3       3       3      21

element (itemset/transaction) length distribution:
sizes
1 2 3 4 5 6
1 1 2 3 2 1

   Min. 1st Qu.  Median    Mean 3rd Qu.    Max.
   1.00    3.00    4.00    3.70    4.75    6.00

includes extended item information - examples:
  labels
1  item1
2  item2
3  item3
```

FIGURE 10.19 *Use of* `random.transactions()` *function*

10.7.1 Sub, Super, Maximal and Closed Itemsets

The association rules mining require subset, superset, maximal, or closed itemsets from the given set of items. A subset contains some parts of the set and a superset contains all the sets. A maximal itemset is an itemset that does not have a proper superset of the itemset in the set of itemsets. A closed itemset is an itemset that has its own closure and does not have any superset.

In R language, the package "arules" provides functions to determine a subset, superset, maximal or closed itemsets. All these functions are very slow and consume high memory for large itemsets. The following table describes the functions. All functions need one main argument "x" that can be either set of itemsets, rules, or itemMatrix.

TABLE 10.15 Functions for finding subset, superset, maximal and closed itemsets

Method Name	*Description*
`is.subset(x)`	It finds out the subset in the associations and itemMatrix objects.
`is.superset(x)`	It finds out the superset in the associations and itemMatrix objects.
`is.maximal(x)`	It finds out the maximal itemset in the associations and itemMatrix objects.
`is.closed(x)`	It finds out the closed itemset in the associations and itemMatrix objects.

In the example given below, `is.subset()` function takes an itemMatrix, "itemM" that contains 4 itemsets. It checks the subset of each itemset and returns either a TRUE or FALSE value. For example, for the itemset "{Itemset1, Itemset3, Itemset4}", all the other itemsets return FALSE except {Itemset1, Itemset3, Itemset4} (Figure 10.20).

```
RGui (64-bit)
File Edit View Misc Packages Windows Help
R Console
> # Creating a matrix and their respective itemMatrix
> dm <- matrix(
+ c(1,1,0,0,
+ 0,1,1,1,
+ 1,1,1,1,
+ 1,1,1,0), ncol = 4)
> dimnames(dm) <-  list(c("A","B","C","D"), paste("Itemset",c(1:4), sep = ""))
> # Now finding the subset for this
> is.subset(itemM)
                                    {Itemset1,Itemset3,Itemset4}
{Itemset1,Itemset3,Itemset4}                                TRUE
{Itemset1,Itemset2,Itemset3,Itemset4}                      FALSE
{Itemset2,Itemset3,Itemset4}                               FALSE
{Itemset2,Itemset3}                                        FALSE
                                    {Itemset1,Itemset2,Itemset3,Itemset4}
{Itemset1,Itemset3,Itemset4}                                         TRUE
{Itemset1,Itemset2,Itemset3,Itemset4}                                TRUE
{Itemset2,Itemset3,Itemset4}                                         TRUE
{Itemset2,Itemset3}                                                  TRUE
                                    {Itemset2,Itemset3,Itemset4} {Itemset2,Itemset3}
{Itemset1,Itemset3,Itemset4}                               FALSE               FALSE
{Itemset1,Itemset2,Itemset3,Itemset4}                      FALSE               FALSE
{Itemset2,Itemset3,Itemset4}                                TRUE               FALSE
{Itemset2,Itemset3}                                         TRUE                TRUE
> |
```

FIGURE 10.20 *Use of `is.subset()` function*

In the example given below, `is.superset()` function takes an itemMatrix, "itemM" that contains 4 itemsets. It checks the superset of each itemset and returns either TRUE or FALSE value. For example, for the itemset "{Itemset1, Itemset3, Itemset4}", {Itemset2, Itemset3, Itemset4} and {Itemset2, Itemset3} are showing FALSE as their items are not in that itemset and they are small in size, whereas {Itemset1, Itemset2, Itemset3, Itemset4} is a superset for the "{Itemset1, Itemset3, Itemset4}". Along this, the `is.Maximal()` checks the maximal set in the given itemsets. Here, it returns TRUE for itemset {Itemset1, Itemset2, Itemset3, Itemset4} as it is the biggest in all the itemsets (Figure 10.21).

```
> # Now finding the superset for this
> is.superset(itemM)
                                          {Itemset1,Itemset3,Itemset4}
{Itemset1,Itemset3,Itemset4}                                      TRUE
{Itemset1,Itemset2,Itemset3,Itemset4}                             TRUE
{Itemset2,Itemset3,Itemset4}                                     FALSE
{Itemset2,Itemset3}                                              FALSE
                                          {Itemset1,Itemset2,Itemset3,Itemset4}
{Itemset1,Itemset3,Itemset4}                                              FALSE
{Itemset1,Itemset2,Itemset3,Itemset4}                                      TRUE
{Itemset2,Itemset3,Itemset4}                                              FALSE
{Itemset2,Itemset3}                                                       FALSE
                                          {Itemset2,Itemset3,Itemset4} {Itemset2,Itemset3}
{Itemset1,Itemset3,Itemset4}                                     FALSE               FALSE
{Itemset1,Itemset2,Itemset3,Itemset4}                             TRUE                TRUE
{Itemset2,Itemset3,Itemset4}                                      TRUE                TRUE
{Itemset2,Itemset3}                                              FALSE                TRUE
> # Now finding the maximal itemset
> is.maximal(itemM)
[1] FALSE  TRUE FALSE FALSE
> |
```

FIGURE 10.21 *Use of* `is.superset()` *and* `is.maximal()` *function*

Check Your Understanding

1. What is the `sample()` function?

Ans: The arules package provides a function `sample()` that generates random samples and permutations from a set of transactions or associations.

2. What is `random.transactions()` function?

Ans: The package "arules" provides a function `random.transactions()` that simulates random transactions datasets. It returns the object of the class "transactions".

3. What is a maximal itemset?

Ans: A maximal itemset is an itemset that has no proper superset of the itemset in the set of itemsets.

10.8 Additional Measures of Interestingness

The association rules mining needs different types of measures, such as support, confidence, list, etc., for measuring the set of itemsets and rules. For this, the package "arules" provides a function `interestMeasure()` that returns different types of interesting features from an existing set of itemsets or rules. The basic syntax of the function `interestMeasure()` is as follows:

```
interestMeasure(x, measure, transactions…)
```

where,

"x" argument contains a set of itemsets or rules for which measures need to be found; "measure" argument contains the name of measures. Table 10.16 describes few important measures that are useful for itemsets and rules respectively; "transactions" argument contains transactions dataset; the dots "…" define the other optional arguments.

TABLE 10.16 Useful measures for itemsets

Measure Name	*Range*	*Description*
Support	[0,1]	It defines the support
allConfidence	[0,1]	It defines the minimum confidence for all possible rules generated from the itemset
Cross-support ratio	[0,1]	It defines the ratio between the support of the least frequent item to the support of the most frequent item
lift	[0,∞]	It defines the probability of the itemsets over the product of the probabilities of all items in the itemset.

TABLE 10.17 Useful measures for rules

Measure Name	*Range*	*Description*
Support	[0, 1]	It defines the support.
Confidence	[0, 1]	It defines the minimum confidence for all possible rules generated from the itemset.
Certainty	[-1, 1]	It measures the variation of the probability that *Y* is a transaction when only considering transactions with *X*.
gini	[0, 1]	It measures the quadratic entropy
lift	[0, ∞]	It defines the probability of the itemsets over the product of the probabilities of all items in the itemset.
Leverage	[-1, 1]	It measures the difference of *X* and *Y* appearing together in a dataset defined as $sup(X \rightarrow Y) - sup(X)sup(Y)$
Improvement	[0, 1]	It measures the improvement of a rule by finding difference between its confidence and confidence of more general rule.

In the following example, the `interestMeasure()` function takes a set of itemset, "demoa" means an object of the `apriori()` function and a transaction dataset "itemT" and calculates the different measures of itemsets and rules such as "lift", "support", "improvement", "confidence", "oddsRatio", "leverage" (Figure 10.22, Tables 10.16 and 10.17).

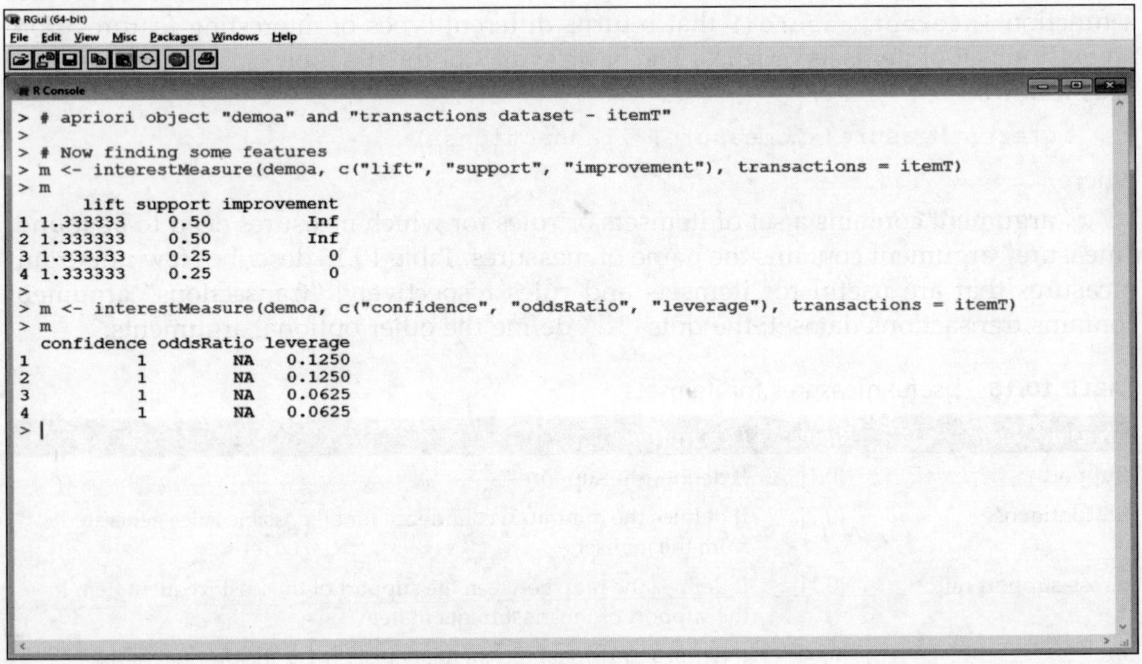

FIGURE 10.22 *Use of* `interestMeasure()` *function*

10.9 DISTANCE-BASED CLUSTERING TRANSACTION AND ASSOCIATIONS

Some applications need to calculate dissimilarities and cross-dissimilarities between transactions (itemsets) or associations (rules). Jaccard coefficient, dice coefficient, affinities between items, or simple matching coefficients are some standard methods that find out dissimilarities. In R language, the package "arules" provides a function `dissimilarity()` that calculates and returns the distances for binary data that can be either a matrix, transactions, or associations.

Distance-based clustering identifies clusters by using some distance measures. The return value of the function `dissimilarity()` is directly used by clustering methods that generate random samples and permutations from a set of transactions or associations. The basic syntax of the function `dissimilarity()` is as follows:

```
dissimilarity (x, y = NULL, method = NULL,…)
```

where,

"x" argument contains the set of elements that can be a matrix, itemMatrix, transactions, itemsets, rules; *"y"* argument contains either NULL or second set to calculate

cross-dissimilarities; method argument defines the distance measure to be used. The table describes a few methods; the dots "..." define the other optional arguments.

TABLE 10.18 Method names used in the `dissimilarity()` function

Method Name	*Description*
affinity	It calculates the average affinity distance between the items in two transactions
cosine	It calculates the cosine distance
dice	It calculates the dice coefficient
euclidean	It calculates the Euclidean distance
jaccard	It calculates the Jaccard coefficient
matching	It calculates the matching coefficient
pearson	It calculates Pearson correlation coefficient
phi	It also calculates Pearson correlation coefficient

In the example given below, the `dissimilarity()` function takes an itemMatrix, "itemM" and calculates the dissimilarities by using different methods, such as "affinity", "euclidean", "pearson". The itemMatrix has four transactions and items (Table 10.18, Figure 10.23).

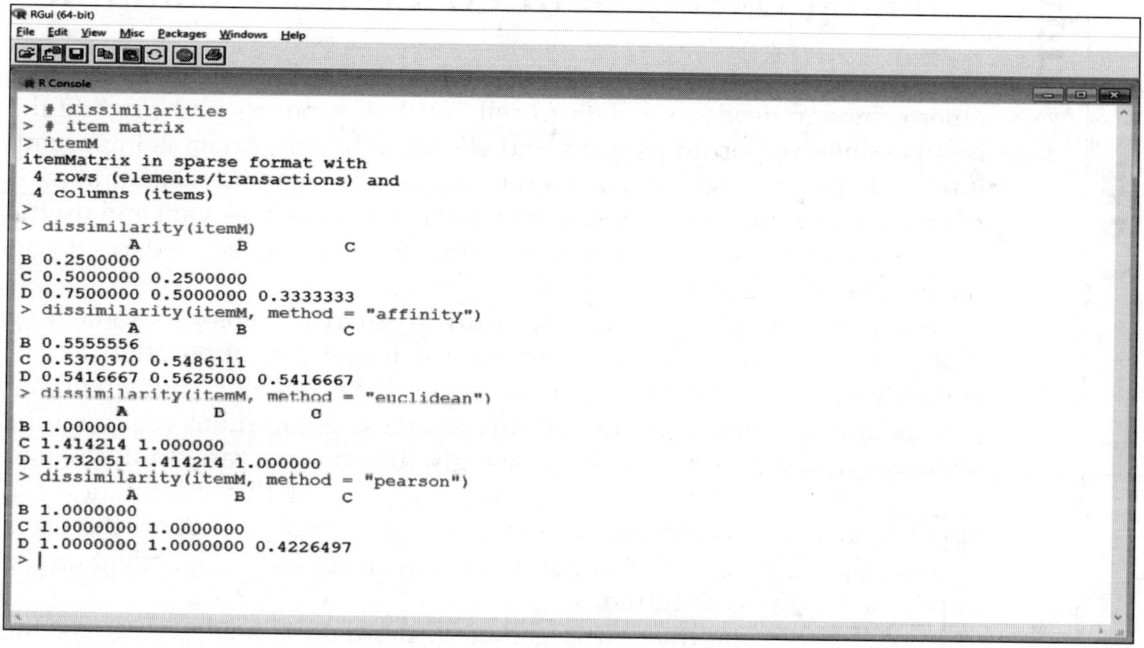

```
> # dissimilarities
> # item matrix
> itemM
itemMatrix in sparse format with
 4 rows (elements/transactions) and
 4 columns (items)
>
> dissimilarity(itemM)
          A         B         C
B 0.2500000
C 0.5000000 0.2500000
D 0.7500000 0.5000000 0.3333333
> dissimilarity(itemM, method = "affinity")
          A         B         C
B 0.5555556
C 0.5370370 0.5486111
D 0.5416667 0.5625000 0.5416667
> dissimilarity(itemM, method = "euclidean")
         A        B        C
B 1.000000
C 1.414214 1.000000
D 1.732051 1.414214 1.000000
> dissimilarity(itemM, method = "pearson")
          A         B         C
B 1.0000000
C 1.0000000 1.0000000
D 1.0000000 1.0000000 0.4226497
> |
```

FIGURE 10.23 *Use of `dissimilarity()` function*

Check Your Understanding

1. What is the `interestMeasure()` function?

Ans: The arules package provides a function `interestMeasure()` that returns different types of the interesting features from an existing set of itemsets or rules.

2. List the names of some measuring features for the set of itemsets and rules.

Ans: Support, Confidence, lift, improvement, Certainity, Leverage, gini, and cross-support ratio are some measuring features for the set of itemsets and rules.

3. What is the `dissimilarity()` function?

Ans: The package "arules" provides a function `dissimilarity()` that calculates and returns the distances for binary data that can be either a matrix, transactions, or associations.

Case Study

Making User-generated Content Valuable

User-generated content is an indispensable part of today's industry as every other company needs user data to sell and buy products and provide the best possible support to its users and clients. While user data is important, it needs to be processed to make it relevant for the company. Data mining is the most important tool to process such data and make it relevant and useful. The decision tree algorithm with the apriori algorithm can be used to support the needs of the clients.

To explain this problem, we will turn to smart technology—something that makes our lives easier. Whenever we install any application in our smartphone, we are asked for permission for the installation, but we do not pay too much attention to the information these applications require to be installed. In the process, we unknowingly disseminate varied information on maps, messages, contacts, etc. With the help of this information the application, besides collating customer data, also tries to support the users to make their life easier and at the same time makes them dependent on the application in the near future.

Once the user information is gathered, the data is analysed to get the required information so as to give the best information to the algorithm at different times. This type of analysis starts from data pre-processing steps, steps that have already been explained in Chapters 1 and 2. However, for this type of data pre-processing the information gain happens by designing

(Continued)

the decision tree at different levels—the depth decision tree or 2–10 level decision tree as well.

Each data gives a valid point of information and these points are used in designing the clusters among different types of data but they are very centric in information as they provide the information of different users according to same contents. The frequency of the matching data is processed by means of decision tree under info gain and Apriori.

It is a common experience nowadays for different applications to recommend the same item for buying from different applications or portals. Users are also able to exercise their choices when it comes to reading the news by selecting the content that is more liked. Through their preferences, they provide the application information about the cognitive behaviour of users. This allows prediction of the way a particular consumer behaves and recommendations are accordingly tweaked. Most studies of systems or online reviews so far have used only numeric information about sellers or products to examine their economic impact. The understanding that text matters has not been fully realised in electronic markets or in online communities. Insights derived from text mining of user-generated feedback can thus provide substantial benefits to businesses looking for competitive advantages.

Let us summarise some of the chief benefits of utilising user-centric data:

- It saves money: Since the users themselves provide relevant content for prediction and subsequent recommendations, user data need not be bought and efficiency in terms of time and costs is increased.
- It provides variety: By using the user data, the customer can be apprised of various new features or upgrades to the existing product. Further, the user gets to know about the discounts being offered and can avail the support extended to the end user.
- It offers a voice to the user: The company is in a position to offer individual customers different products as per individual preferences and a user can provide any specific information of the item he/she wants to use.

These benefits of user-centric data should be firmly kept in mind to make such data more predictive and relevant in our fast-paced technological era.

Summary

- Data mining is the process of finding unknown and hidden patterns from a large amount of data.
- An itemset is a collection of different items. For example, {pen, pencil, notebook} is an itemset.
- An itemset containing items that often occur together and are associated with each other are called frequent itemsets.
- Association rules are also a part of data mining used for finding patterns in data. An association rule is represented by the expression $X \rightarrow Y$, where X and Y are two disjoint itemsets and $X \subseteq I$ and $Y \subseteq I$, and $X \cap Y = \phi$.

(Continued)

- Rule evaluation metrics is used to measure the strength of an association rule. Support and Confidence are major types of rule evaluation metrics.
- Support is a metric that measures the usefulness of a rule by using the minimum support threshold. The metric measures the number of events that have such itemsets that match both sides of the implications of the association rules.
- The Support or sup of a rule is calculated using $(X \cup Y)$.count/n.
- Confidence is a metric that measures the certainty of a rule by using a threshold. It measures how often an event itemset that matches the left side of an implication in the association rule also matches the right side.
- The Confidence or conf of a rule is calculated using $(X \cup Y)$.count / X.count.
- A Brute-force approach computes the support and confidence for every possible rule for mining.
- A two-step approach uses two steps for calculating the frequent itemsets and rules where the first step is 'frequent itemset generation' and the second step is 'rule generation'.
- The frequent itemset generation finds out the itemsets that satisfy the minsup threshold. These itemsets are called the frequent itemsets. If a dataset contains *k* items then it can generate upto $2^k - 1$ frequent itemsets.
- Rule generation extracts all the high-confidence rules from each frequent itemset obtained in the first step and each rule is a binary partitioning of a frequent itemset.
- An Apriori principle is the best strategy and an effective method to generate the frequent itemset. According to the Apriori principle, *'If an itemset is frequent, then all of its subsets must also be frequent'.*
- Apriori algorithm is a breadth-first algorithm that counts transactions by following the two-step approach. It finds out the frequent itemset, maximal frequent itemset, and closed frequent itemset.
- The candidate `gen()` function is used in the Apriori algorithm that contains two steps, Join and Pruning.
- The arules package provides the required infrastructure that creates and manipulates the input dataset for any type of mining algorithms. It also provides features that analyse the resulting itemsets and association rules.
- A binary incidence matrix is a type of sparse matrix that contains only two values 0 and 1 or true and false.
- The arules package provides a class "itemMatrix" that efficiently represents the binary incidence matrix that contains the itemsets and items.
- The `itemFrequency()` function of the package "arules" returns the frequency or support of single items or all single items of an object of the itemMatrix.
- A hash tree is a type of data structure that stores values in key-value pairs and a type of tree where every internal node contains the hash values.
- A transaction dataset is a collection of transactions where each transaction is stored in the tuple form such as < transaction ID, item ID, ...>.
- The arules package provides a class, "transactions" that represents transaction data of the association rules. It is an extension of the itemMatrix class.
- The "itemsets" and "rules" are classes. The "itemsets" class is used for defining the frequent itemsets of their closed or maximal subsets and "rules" class is used for association rules.
- The `summary()`, `length()`, `sort()`, `inspect()`, `match()`, `items()`, and `union()` are some of R commands used in association rules mining.
- The package "arules" provides a function `apriori()` that performs the association rule mining using Apriori algorithm. The function mines the frequent itemsets, association rules, and association hyperedges.

(Continued)

- The package "arules" provides another function `eclat()` that performs the association rule mining and generates the frequent itemsets. It follows the Eclat algorithm and uses the simple intersection operations for frequent itemsets.
- The package "arules" provides a function `support()` that determines the support for a set of given set of items as an itemMatrix.
- The package "arules" provides a function `ruleInduction()` that induce all rules that are generated by given itemsets from a transaction dataset.
- Sampling is a process that takes the samples from the original databases for mining of large data.
- The package "arules" provides a function `sample()` that generates random samples and permutations from a set of transactions or associations.
- The package "arules" provides a function `random.transactions()` that simulates random transactions datasets. It returns the object of the class "transactions".
- A subset contains some parts of the set and a superset contains all the sets.
- A maximal itemset is an itemset that has no proper superset of the itemset in the set of itemsets.
- A closed itemset is an itemset that has own closure and does not have any superset.
- The package "arules" provides a function `interestMeasure()` that returns different types of interesting features from an existing set of itemsets or rules.
- Support, Confidence, lift, improvement, Certainty, Leverage, gini, and cross-support ratio are some measuring features for the set of itemsets and rules.
- The package "arules" provides a function `dissimilarity()` that calculates and returns the distances for binary data that can be either a matrix, transactions, or associations.
- The affinity, Euclidean, Pearson, Jaccard, cosine, dice, and phi are few methods used in `dissimilarity()` function.

KEY TERMS

- **Apriori algorithm:** Apriori algorithm is a breadth-first algorithm that counts transactions by following the two-step approach. It finds out the frequent itemset, maximal frequent itemset, and closed frequent itemset.
- **Apriori principle:** An Apriori principle is the best strategy and an effective method to generate the frequent itemset.
- **arules:** arules is a package of R language used for association rules mining.
- **Association rules:** An association rule is an implication form of the expression $X \rightarrow Y$ where X and Y are two disjoint itemsets and $X \subseteq I$ and $Y \subseteq I$, and $X \cap Y = \phi$.
- **Binary incidence matrix:** A binary incidence matrix is a type of sparse matrix that contains only two values 0 and 1 or true and false.
- **Brute-force approach:** A Brute-force approach computes the support and confidence for every possible rule for mining the association rules.
- **Confidence:** Confidence is a metric that measures the certainty of a rule by using threshold.
- **Data mining:** Data mining is the process for finding unknown and hidden patterns from a large amount of data.
- **Frequent itemsets:** An itemset containing items that often occur together and are associated with each other are called frequent itemsets.

- **Frequent itemset generation:** The frequent itemset generation finds out the itemsets that satisfy the minsup threshold. These itemsets are called the frequent itemsets.
- **Itemset:** An Itemset is a collection of different items. For example, {pen, pencil, notebook} is an itemset.
- **Rule evaluation metric:** Rule evaluation metric measures the strength of an association rule.
- **Rule generation:** Rule generation extracts all the high-confidence rules from each frequent itemset.
- **Support:** Support is a metric that measures the usefulness of a rule using the minimum support threshold.
- **Transactions:** Transactions or a transaction dataset is a collection of transactions where each transaction is stored in tuple form such as < transaction ID, item ID, ...>.

Multiple Choice Questions

1. From the given options, which of the following is a rule evaluation metric?
   (a) Frequent itemsets (b) Support
   (c) lift (d) None of the above
2. From the given options, which of the following metrics measures the certainty of a rule by using threshold?
   (a) support (b) confidence
   (c) lift (d) cross-ratio
3. How many numbers of frequent itemsets are possible of a dataset that contains k items?
   (a) $2^k - 1$ (b) 2^k
   (c) $2^k + 1$ (d) 2^{k+1}
4. From the given options, which of the following packages provides the functionality for association rules?
   (a) `arules()` (b) `ts()`
   (c) `stat()` (d) `matrix()`
5. From the given options, which of the following functions combines the item matrices?
   (a) `image()` (b) `combine()`
   (c) `c()` (d) `dim()`
6. From the given options, which of the following functions returns the dimension of an item matrix?
   (a) `dimnames()` (b) `combine()`
   (c) `c()` (d) `dim()`
7. From the given options, which of the following functions returns the frequency of itemset?
   (a) `itemFrequency()` (b) `c()`
   (c) `frequency()` (d) `dim()`

8. From the given options, which of the following functions displays the individual association of the itemsets or rules?
   (a) `image()` (b) `inspect()`
   (c) `items()` (d) `dim()`
9. From the given options, which of the following functions returns a set of items of the itemsets?
   (a) `image()` (b) `inspect()`
   (c) `items()` (d) `dim()`
10. From the given options, which of the following functions is used for calculating dissimilarities?
    (a) `interestMeasure()` (b) `random.transactions()`
    (c) `dissimilarity()` (d) `sample()`
11. From the given options, which of the following functions is used for measuring features of a set of items and rules?
    (a) `interestMeasure()` (b) `random.transactions()`
    (c) `dissimilarity()` (d) `sample()`
12. From the given options, which of the following functions is used for generating samples?
    (a) `interestMeasure()` (b) `random.transactions()`
    (c) `dissimilarity()` (d) `sample()`
13. From the given options, which of the following functions is used for creating random transactions?
    (a) `interestMeasure()` (b) `random.transactions()`
    (c) `dissimilarity()` (d) `sample()`
14. From the given options, which of the following is different from others?
    (a) support (b) matching
    (c) confidence (d) improvement
15. From the given options, which of the following is different from others?
    (a) affinity (b) Pearson
    (c) lift (d) dice

SHORT QUESTIONS

1. Briefly discuss the following with examples:
   (i) Association rule mining with its applications (ii) Frequent itemsets (iii) Association rules (iv) support (v) Confidence (vi) Brute-force approach (vii) Two-step approach (viii) Arules package
2. Write pseudocode of the Apriori algorithm.
3. What is the difference between "itemMatrix" and "transaction" class?

Long Questions

1. Explain the functions of candidate `gen()`.
2. Explain the methods of the "itemMatrix" and "transaction" classes.
3. Explain the `itemFrequency()` function with syntax and example.
4. Explain the `support()` function with syntax and example.
5. Explain the `ruleInduction()` function with syntax and example.
6. Explain the `random.transactions()` function with syntax and example.
7. Explain the `interestMeasure()` function with syntax and example.
8. Create a binary incidence matrix for a set of itemsets and convert it into transactions.
9. Create a random sample transaction dataset and implement the `apriori()` function.
10. Explain the measuring features for the set of itemsets and rules.

Practical Exercise

1. A retailer, "BigDailies" wants to cash in on their customers' buying patterns. They want to be able to enact targeted marketing campaigns for specific segments of customers. They wish to have a good inventory management system in place. They wish to learn about which items/products should be stocked up to provide ease of buying to customers, in other words enhance customer satisfaction.

   Where should they start? They have had some internal discussions with their sales and IT staff. The IT staff has been instructed to design an application that can house each customer's transaction data. They wish to have it recorded every single day for every single customer and for every transaction made. They decide to meet after a quarter (3 months) to see if there is some buying pattern.

   Presented below is a subset of the transaction data collected over a period of three months:

TABLE Sample transactional data set

Transaction ID	*Transaction details*
1	{bread, milk}
2	{bread, milk, eggs, diapers, beer}
3	{bread, milk, beer, diapers}
4	{diapers, beer}
5	{milk, bread, diapers, eggs}
6	{milk, bread, diapers, beer}

Problem statement: Determine the association rules and also find out the support and confidence of each association rule. Implement association rule mining in R (create binary incidence matrix of the given itemsets, create itemMatrix, determine item frequencies, use apriori() function with support of 0.02 and confidence of 0.5, use eclat() function with support of 0.02).

Solution:

The above table presents an interesting methodology called association analysis to discover interesting relationship in large data sets. The unveiled relationship can be presented in the form of association rules or sets of frequent items. For example, the following rule can be extracted from the above data set:

{Diapers} → {Beer}

It is pretty obvious from the above rule that a strong relationship exists between the sale of diapers and beer. Customers who pick up a pack or two of diapers also happen to pick a few cans of beers. Retailers can leverage this sort of rules to partake of the opportunity to cross-sale products to their customers.

Challenges that need to be addressed while progressing with association rule mining:

- The larger the data set, the better would be the analysis results. However, working with large transactional datasets can be and is usually computationally expensive.
- Sometimes few of the discovered patterns could be spurious or misleading as it could have happened purely by chance or fluke.

Binary representation

Let us look at how we can represent the sample data set in the Table below in binary format.

Transaction ID	*Bread*	*Milk*	*Eggs*	*Diapers*	*Beer*
1	1	1	0	0	0
2	1	1	1	1	1
3	1	1	0	1	1
4	0	0	0	1	1
5	1	1	1	1	0
6	1	1	0	1	1

Explanation of the above binary representation:

Each row of the above table represents a transaction identified by a "Transaction ID". An item (such as Bread, Milk, Eggs, Diapers and Beer) is represented by a binary variable. A value of 1 denotes the presence of the item for the said transaction. A value of zero denotes the absence of the item from the said transaction. Example: for transaction ID = 1, Bread and milk are present and are depicted by 1. Eggs, Diapers and Beer are absent from the transaction and therefore denoted by zero. The presence of the item is more important than its absence, and for the same reason an item is called as an asymmetric variable.

Itemset and Support Count

Let $I = \{i_1, i_2, i_3 \ldots. i_n\}$ be the set of all items in the market basket data set.

Let $T = \{t_1, t_2, t_3 \ldots. t_n\}$ be the set of all transactions.

Itemset: Each transaction, t_i contains a subset of items from set *I*. A collection of zero or more items is called an itemset. If an itemset contains *k* elements, it is called a *k*-item itemset. Example: the itemset {Bread, Milk, Diapers, Beer} is called a 4-item itemset.

Transaction width: Transaction width is defined as the number of items present in the transaction. A transaction t_j contains an itemset X, if X is a subset of t_j. Example transaction t_6 contains the itemset {bread, diapers} but does not contain the itemset {bread, eggs}.

Item support count: Support is an indication of how frequently the items appear in the dataset. Item support count is defined by the number of transactions that contain a particular itemset.

Item Support Count can be expressed as follows: No. of transactions that contain a particular itemset.

Example: Support Count for {Diapers, Beer} is 4.

Mathematically, the support count $\sigma(X)$, for an item set X, can be expressed as:

$$\sigma(X) = |\{t_i \mid X \subseteq t_i, t_i \in T\}|,$$

The symbol $|\cdot|$ denote the number of elements in the set.

Association rule: It is an implication rule of the form $X \to Y$ where X and Y are disjoint items, i.e. $X \cap Y = \phi$. To measure the strength of an association rule, we rely on two factors, the support and the confidence.

Support for an itemset is defined as:

$$\text{Support } (x_1, x_{2\ldots}) = \frac{\text{No. of transactions containing } (x_1, x_{2\ldots})}{\text{Total number of transactions } (n)}$$

$$\text{Support for } X \to Y = \frac{\text{No. of transactions containing } x_1, x_2 \ldots \text{ and } y_1, y_2 \ldots}{n \text{ (total number of transactions)}}$$

Example:

Support for {Milk, Diapers} → {Beer} as per the dataset in Figure 1, is as follows:

Support for {Milk, Diapers} → {Beer} = 3 /6 = 0.5.

Confidence of the rule is:

$$\text{Confidence of } ((x_1, x_2,\ldots) \text{ implies } (y_1, y_2,\ldots)) = \frac{\text{Support for } (x_1, x_2,\ldots) \text{ implies } (y_1, y_2, \ldots)}{\text{Support for } (x_1, x_2,\ldots)}$$

$$\text{Confidence of \{Milk, Diapers\}} \to \text{\{Beer\}} = \frac{\text{Support for \{Milk, Diapers\}} \to \text{\{Beer\}}}{\text{Support for \{Milk, Diapers\}}}$$

Substituting, = 0.5/Support for {Milk, Diapers}

= 0.5/0.67

= 0.7462

Implementation in R

Step 1: Creating binary incidence matrix for the given itemsets

```
> sm <- matrix ( c(1,1,0,0,0,1,1,1,1,1,1,1,0,1,1,0,0,0,1,1,1,1,1,1
,0,1,1,0,1,1), ncol=6)
> sm
     [,1]  [,2]  [,3]  [,4]  [,5]  [,6]
[1,]    1     1     1     0     1     1
[2,]    1     1     1     0     1     1
[3,]    0     1     0     0     1     0
[4,]    0     1     1     1     1     1
[5,]    0     1     1     1     0     1
```

Step 2: Setting the dimension names for items

```
> dimnames(sm) <- list(c(Bread", "Milk", "Eggs", "Diapers",
"Beer"), paste(Itemset", c(1:6), sep =""))
> sm
        Itemset1  Itemset2  Itemset3  Itemset4  Itemset5  Itemset6
Bread          1         1         1         0         1         1
Milk           1         1         1         0         1         1
Eggs           0         1         0         0         1         0
Diapers        0         1         1         1         1         1
Beer           0         1         1         1         0         1
```

Step 3: Converting to itemMatrix

```
> IM <- as(sm, "itemMatrix")
> IM
itemMatrix in sparse format with
 5 rows (elements/transactions) and
 6 columns (items)
```

Step 4: Finding the number of elements (rows) in the itemMatrix

```
> length(IM)
[1] 5
```

Step 5: Finding first 5 elements (rows) of the itemMatrix as list

```
> as(IM[1:5], "list")
$Bread
[1] "Itemset1" "Itemset2" "Itemset3" "Itemset5" "Itemset6"

$Milk
[1] "Itemset1" "Itemset2" "Itemset3" "Itemset5" "Itemset6"

$Eggs
[1] "Itemset2" "Itemset5"

$Diapers
[1] "Itemset2" "Itemset3" "Itemset4" "Itemset5" "Itemset6"

$Beer
[1] "Itemset2" "Itemset3" "Itemset4" "Itemset6"
```

Step 6: Generating transpose

```
> as(IM[1:5], "ngCMatrix")
6 x 5 sparse Matrix of class "ngCMatrix"
        Bread  Milk  Eggs Diapers Beer
Itemset1  |     |     .      .     .
Itemset2  |     |     |      |     |
Itemset3  |     |     .      |     |
Itemset4  .     .     .      |     |
Itemset5  |     |     |      |     .
Itemset6  |     |     .      |     |
```

Step 7: Inspecting an itemMatrix

```
> inspect (IM)
    items
[1] {Itemset1, Itemset2, Itemset3, Itemset5, Itemset6}
[2] {Itemset1, Itemset2, Itemset3, Itemset5, Itemset6}
[3] {Itemset2, Itemset5}
[4] {Itemset2, Itemset3, Itemset4, Itemset5, Itemset6}
[5] {Itemset2, Itemset3, Itemset4, Itemset6}
```

Step 8: Generating item frequency or support

```
> itemFrequency(IM, type="absolute")
 Itemset1  Itemset2  Itemset3  Itemset4  Itemset5  Itemset6
       2         5         4         2         4         4
> itemFrequency(IM, type="relative")
 Itemset1  Itemset2  Itemset3  Itemset4  Itemset5  Itemset6
      0.4       1.0       0.8       0.4       0.8       0.8
```

Step 9: Creating transactions using matrix

```
> TM <- as(sm, "transactions")
> TM
transactions in sparse format with
 5 transactions (rows) and
 6 items (columns)
```

Step 10: Displaying the summary of transactions

```
> summary(TM)
transactions as itemMatrix in sparse format with
 5 rows (elements/itemsets/transactions) and
 6 columns (items) and a density of 0.7

most frequent items:
 Itemset2  Itemset3  Itemset5  Itemset6  Itemset1   (Other)
        5         4         4         4         2         2

element  (itemset/transaction)  length  distribution:
sizes
2 4 5
1 1 3
```

```
Min.   1st Qu.    Median      Mean   3rd Qu.      Max.
 2.0       4.0       5.0       4.2       5.0       5.0

includes extended item information - examples:
    labels
1 Itemset1
2 Itemset2
3 Itemset3

includes extended transaction information - examples:
transactionID
1      Bread
2       Milk
3       Eggs
```

Step 11: Use of `apriori()` **function to implement the Apriori algorithm**

```
> am <- apriori(sm)
Apriori

Parameter specifications:
confidence minval  smax  arem  aval  originalSupport  maxtime support
      0.8    0.1     1  none FALSE             TRUE        5     0.1
   minlen  maxlen  target    ext
       1      10   rules  FALSE

Algorithmic control:
 filter   tree   heap   memopt   load   sort   verbose
    0.1   TRUE   TRUE    FALSE   TRUE      2      TRUE

Absolute minimum support count: 0

set item appearances …[0 item(s)] done [0.00s].
set transaction ..[6 item(s), 5 transaction(s)] done [0.00s].
sorting and recoding items … [6 item(s)] done [0.00s].
creating transaction tree … done [0.00s].
checking subsets of size 1 2 3 4 5 done [0.00s].
writing … [78 rule(s)] done [0.00s].
creating S4 object … done [0.00s].
> am
set of 78 rules
```

Step 12: Summary of `apriori()` **function**

```
> summary(am)
set of 78 rules

rule length distribution  (lhs + rhs):sizes
1   2    3    4    5
4   15   28   24   7
```

```
   Min.  1st Qu.  Median    Mean  3rd Qu.    Max
  1.000    3.000   3.000   3.192    4.000  5.000

summary of qualtity measures:
     support          confidence           lift
Min.    :0.2000  Min.    :0.8000   Min.    :1.000
1st Qu. :0.4000  1st Qu. :1.0000   1st Qu. :1.000
Median  :0.4000  Median  :1.0000   Median  :1.250
Mean    :0.4667  Mean    :0.9846   Mean    :1.154
3rd Qu. :0.6000  3rd Qu. :1.0000   3rd Qu. :1.250
Max.    :1.0000  Max.    :1.0000   Max.    :1.250

mining info:
 data ntransactions  support  confidence
   sm             5      0.1         0.8
```

Step 13: Use of apriori function with a support of 0.02 and a confidence of 0.5

```
> am <- apriori(sm, parameter=list(supp=0.02, conf=0.5))
Apriori

Parameter specification:
confidence minval  smax  arem  aval  originalSupport  maxtime support
       0.5    0.1     1  none FALSE             TRUE        5    0.02
 minlen  maxlen  target     ext
      1      10   rules   FALSE

Algorithmic control:
 filter   tree   heap   memopt   load   sort   verbose
    0.1   TRUE   TRUE    FALSE   TRUE      2      TRUE

Absolute minimum support count: 0

set item appearances ...[0 item(s)] done [0.00s].
set transactions ...[6 item(s), 5 transaction(s)] done [0.00s].
sorting and recoding items ... [6 item(s)] done [0.00s].
creating transaction tree … done [0.00s].
checking subsets of size 1 2 3 4 5 done [0.00s].
writing … [116 rule(s)] done [0.00s].
creating S4 object … done [0.00s].
```

Step 14: Summary of `apriori()` function with support = 0.02 and confidence = 0.5

```
> summary(am)
set of 116 rules

rule length distribution  (lhs + rhs):sizes
1 2    3     4     5
4 25   45    33    9
```

```
  Min.  1st Qu.  Median   Mean  3rd Qu.    Max
 1.000    2.750   3.000  3.155    4.000  5.000

summary of quality measures:
   support           confidence          lift
Min.   :0.2000  Min.      :0.500  Min.    :0.625
1st Qu.:0.4000  1st Qu.   :0.750  1st Qu. :1.000
Median :0.4000  Median    :1.000  Median  :1.250
Mean   :0.4483  Mean      :0.856  Mean    :1.137
3rd Qu.:0.6000  3rd Qu.   :1.000  3rd Qu. :1.250
Max.   :1.0000  Max.      :1.000  Max.    :1.667

mining info:
 data  ntransactions  support  confidence
   sm              5     0.02         0.5
```

Step 15: Using the `eclat()` function to generate frequent itemsets.

```
> em <- eclat(sm, parameter=list(supp=0.02))
Eclat

Parameter specification:
 tidLists  support  minlen  maxlen               target    ext
    FALSE     0.02       1      10  frequent itemsets  FALSE

Algorithmic control:
sparse sort verbose
  7    -2    TRUE

Absolute minimum support count: 0

Warning in eclat(sm, parameter = list(supp = 0.02))
 You chose a very low absolute support count of 0. You might run
out of memory! Increase minimum support.

create itemset ...
set transaction ...[6 item(s), 5 transaction(s)] done [0.00s].
sorting and recoding items … [6 item(s)] done [0.00s].
creating bit matrix … [6 row(s), 5 column(s)] done [0.00s].
writing ... [47 set(s)] done [0.00s].
Creating S4 object ... done [0.00s].
```

Step 16: Summary of `eclat()` function.

```
> summary(em)
set of 47 itemsets

most frequent items:
Itemset2 Itemset3 Itemset5 Itemset6 Itemset1  (Other)
      24       24       24       24       16       16

element (itemset/transaction) length distribution:sizes
 1  2  3  4  5
 6 14 16  9  2
```

```
 Min.   1st Qu.  Median   Mean   3rd Qu.   Max
1.000   2.000   3.000   2.723   3.000   5.000

summary of qualtity measures:
    support
Min.    : 0.2000
1st Qu. : 0.4000
Median  : 0.4000
Mean    : 0.4723
3rd Qu. : 0.6000
Max.    : 1.0000

includes transaction ID lists: FALSE

mining info:
 data  ntransactions  support
   sm              5     0.02
```

Answers to MCQs:

1. (a)	2. (b)	3. (a)	4. (a)	5. (c)	6. (d)	7. (a)
8. (b)	9. (c)	10. (c)	11. (a)	12. (d)	13. (b)	14. (b)
15. (c)						

Chapter 11

Text Mining

LEARNING OUTCOME

At the end of this chapter, you will be able to:

- Implement text mining in R
- Create a corpus and use transformation functions to remove punctuation marks, stopwords, whitespaces, numbers, etc., from it
- Create a document term matrix of the corpus and find frequent terms

11.1 Introduction

In recent years, text mining has become immensely popular in the research field. It is used for extracting interesting and non-trivial information and knowledge from different data sources. Text mining is also known as intelligent text analysis, text data mining or knowledge-discovery in text (KDT). Data mining, natural language processing (NLP), machine learning, information retrieval (IR), sentiment analysis, and knowledge management are some of the popular techniques used in text mining. Most researchers use text mining for their research work. Business analytics also uses text mining. Organisations today, have huge mounds of data and they need an efficient technique for extracting useful information from such huge volume of data. Text mining helps organisations do the same.

Pre-processing (categorisation and extraction) of document collections, storage of intermediate representations and analysis using different techniques, such as clustering, associations rules, trend analysis, visualisation of output, etc., are some necessary operations in text mining. Figure 11.1 describes the sequential operations in a text mining process. It follows the sequence of text pre-processing (syntactic/semantic text analysis), feature generation, feature selection (simple counting–statistics), text/data mining (supervised/unsupervised learning), and analysing results (making sense of data – interpretation, visualisation).

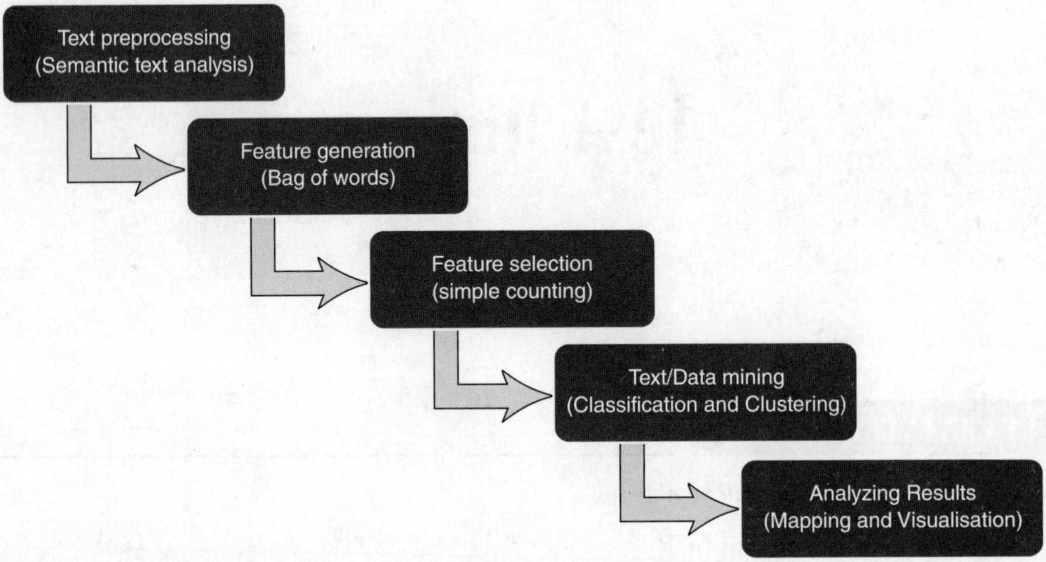

FIGURE 11.1 *Text mining process*

In the following subsections, you will learn about the basic concept of text mining.

11.2 DEFINITION OF TEXT MINING

Text mining extracts useful information from unstructured data. In unstructured data, information does not have any specific format and it contains symbols, characters, or numbers. For example, comments used on Facebook, tweets on Twitter, opinion or reviews of any products or services are few examples of unstructured data. Text mining can be used to extract useful knowledge, discover interesting patterns from unstructured data and thus support decision making.

Text mining is useful to:

- social scientists - to learn about shifting public opinion;
- marketers - to learn about consumers' opinions of products and services; and
- it has even been used to predict the direction of stock markets.

Text mining is a knowledge-intensive process where a user interacts with some text document collections using a set of analysis tools. Just like in data mining, text mining also helps to extract useful information from data sources after identification and exploration of text patterns. Here are some key elements of text mining.

11.2.1 Document Collection

Document collection is a group of text-based documents. Document collection contains from thousand to tens of millions of documents. It can either be static or dynamic. A static document collection is a document collection where initial complement of documents remains unchanged. A dynamic document collection is a document collection where documents change or are updated over time.

11.2.2 Document

A document is a group of discrete textual data within a collection. Business reports, e-mails, legal memorandums, research papers, press releases, and manuscripts are documents. There are two kinds of document—free format or semi-structured. A free format or weakly structured document is a type of document that follows some typography, layout, and makeup indicators. For example, research paper, press releases are few examples of free format document. A semi-structured document is a type of document that uses field-type metadata, such as HTML web pages, email, etc.

11.2.3 Document Features

Every document has some features or attributes that define it. The characters, words, terms, and concepts are some common features of a document. These features have been explained briefly below.

- Characters are the most important features of a document. Characters create the document. It can be individual component letter, numeric characters, special characters, etc.; spaces are the basic blocks of a document.
- Words are the second basic block element of a document. A word is a collection of characters. It can be phrases, multi-word hyphenates, multiword expressions, etc.
- Terms are single words in a document. It can also have multiword phrases that are directly selected from native document.
- Concept is a document feature generated through manual statistical method, rule-based, or hybrid categorisation methods. Any word, phrase, or expression that identifies the document is called the concept identifier, such as keyword.

11.2.4 Domain and Background Knowledge

In text mining, there are two types of knowledge—domain and background knowledge—which are available for presenting data. A domain is a specialised area of interest for which ontologies, taxonomies, and lexicons are developed. Domain includes broad areas of subject matters such as finance, international law, biology, material science, etc. Knowledge used in these domains is called domain knowledge. Background knowledge is an extension of the domain knowledge. It is used in pre-processing operations of the text mining system.

11.3 A Few Challenges in Text Mining

- Text mining deals with large datasets and encounters the usual challenges with large datasets
- Noisy data - Noisy data is often used as a synonym for corrupt data. It is data that has a considerable amount of additional meaningless information. It is data that is not easily comprehensible or understood by machines.
- Word Ambiguity and Context Sensitivity – Ambiguous words lead to vagueness and confusion. Context sensitiveness connotes "depending on context" or "depending on circumstances".

For example, Apple (the company) or apple (the fruit)

- Complex and subtle relationship between concepts in text.

For example, "AOL merges with Time-Warner" "Time-Warner is bought by AOL"

- Multilingual

11.4 Text Mining vs. Data Mining

Differences	*Data Mining*	*Text Mining*
Definition	Discovery of knowledge from structured data, i.e. data housed in structured databases or data warehouses	Discovery of knowledge from unstructured data, i.e. articles, website text, blog posts, journals, emails, memos, customer correspondence, etc.
Data representation	Straight forward	Complex
Methods	Data analysis, machine learning, statistics, neural networks	Data mining, NLP (natural language processing), information retrieval

11.5 Text Mining in R

Text mining also plays a major role in business analytics. R language provides a package "tm" for text mining. This text-mining package, "tm" provides a framework for text mining application within R. The main framework or structure for managing the documents in R language is Corpus.

Corpus represents a collection of text documents in R. It is an abstract concept with different implementations. It creates the corpora object that is held in the memory. Another class of the package is VCorpus (Volatile Corpus) that is a virtual base class. The `VCorpus` creates a volatile corpora, i.e. when the R object is destroyed, the whole corpus is lost. Here is a basic syntax of the `VCorpus` function:

```
VCorpus(x, readerControl, …) or as.VCorpus(x)
```

where,

"x" argument contains a source object or a R object for as.VCorpus(x); "readerControl" is an optional argument that contains a named list of control parameters for reading in

content from "*x*". Here one parameter is a reader that is a function for reading in and processing the format delivered by "*x*". Another parameter is language that contains a character giving the type of language. By default it is "en"; the dots, "…" define the other optional arguments of the function.

In the example given below, a number of text files ("Demo2.txt", "Demo3.txt", "DemoTM.txt", "Freqdemo.txt") are stored in a folder "tm" in "C:" drive. The "fname" object stores these files using the function file.path("C:", "tm"). The dir(fname) displays the names of all files in the folder. Now Corpus or VCorpus function represents these documents into an object, "files". Here "files" is called a Corpus. It shows that there are 4 documents in the folder "tm". The `summary()` function shows the name of each document in the folder (Figure 11.2).

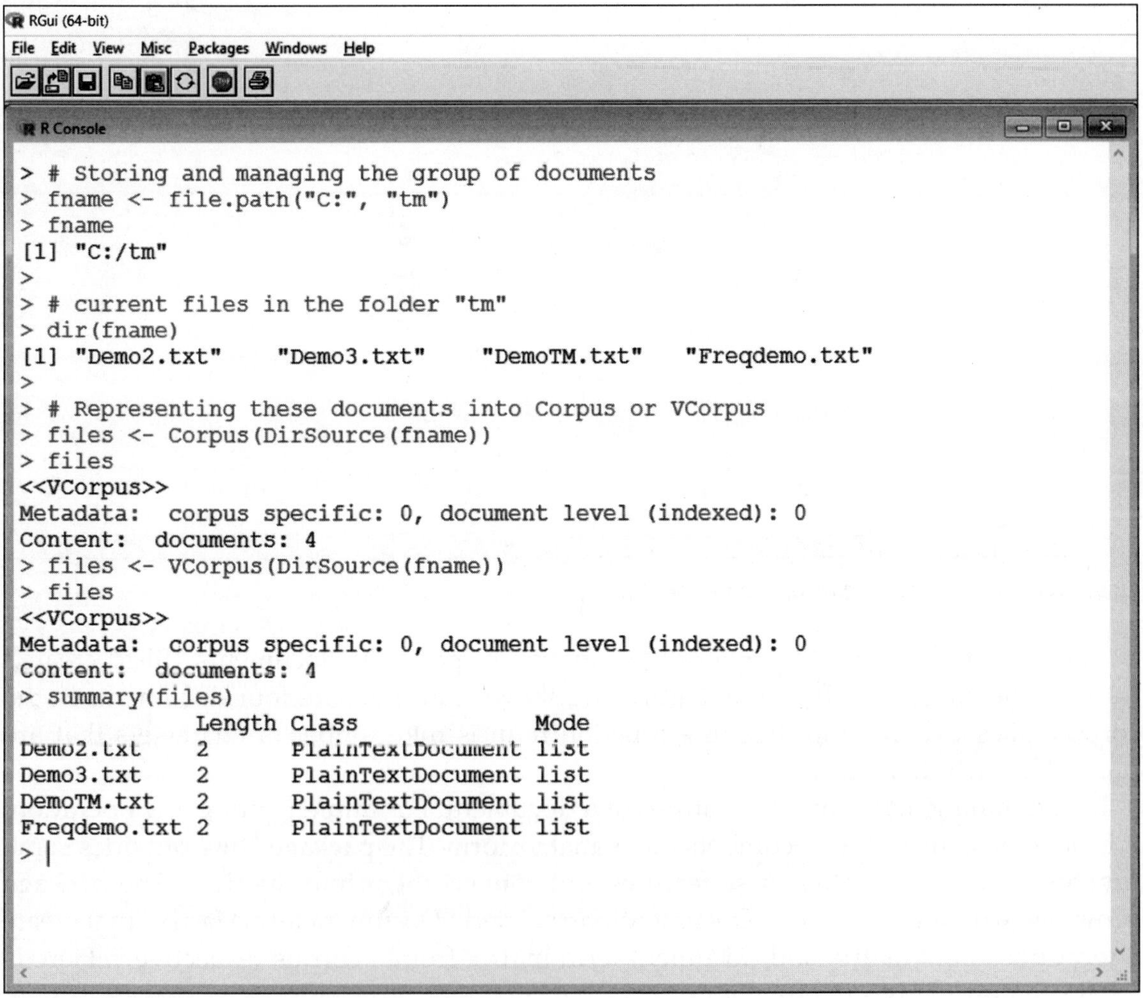

```
RGui (64-bit)
File Edit View Misc Packages Windows Help
R Console
> # Storing and managing the group of documents
> fname <- file.path("C:", "tm")
> fname
[1] "C:/tm"
>
> # current files in the folder "tm"
> dir(fname)
[1] "Demo2.txt"    "Demo3.txt"    "DemoTM.txt"    "Freqdemo.txt"
>
> # Representing these documents into Corpus or VCorpus
> files <- Corpus(DirSource(fname))
> files
<<VCorpus>>
Metadata:  corpus specific: 0, document level (indexed): 0
Content:  documents: 4
> files <- VCorpus(DirSource(fname))
> files
<<VCorpus>>
Metadata:  corpus specific: 0, document level (indexed): 0
Content:  documents: 4
> summary(files)
             Length Class             Mode
Demo2.txt    2      PlainTextDocument list
Demo3.txt    2      PlainTextDocument list
DemoTM.txt   2      PlainTextDocument list
Freqdemo.txt 2      PlainTextDocument list
> |
```

FIGURE 11.2 *Creating Corpus or documents in R*

In Figure 11.3, the `VCorpus()` function creates documents of a vector "Vfile" that contains three arbitrary sentences (Figure 11.3).

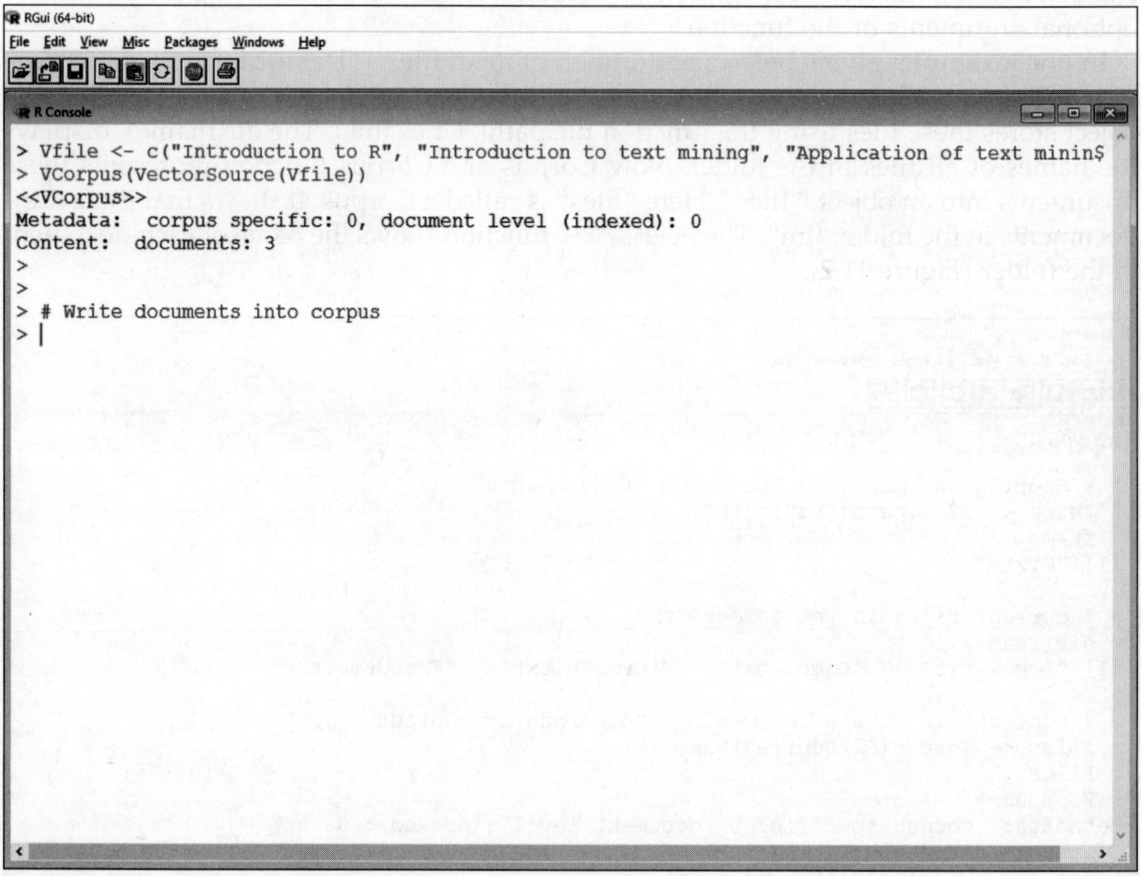

Figure 11.3 *Creating Corpus of the vector "Vfile"*

In the example below, the `inspect()` function inspects the documents "files" created through the `VCorpus()` function. Figure 11.4 shows that there are four documents in the corpus "files". Along with this, the function returns the number of characters that are present in each document.

In text mining, terms are the features of a document. For implementing any operation, it is better to convert the documents into a matrix form. The package "tm" provides some functions that can identify these features and convert them into matrices. The package provides two functions, "TermDocumentMatrix" and "DocumentTermMatrix" that create a term-document matrix and document-term matrix from a corpus respectively. Here is a basic syntax of both the functions:

```
TermDocumentMatrix(x, control)
```

or

```
DocumentTermMatrix(x, control)
```

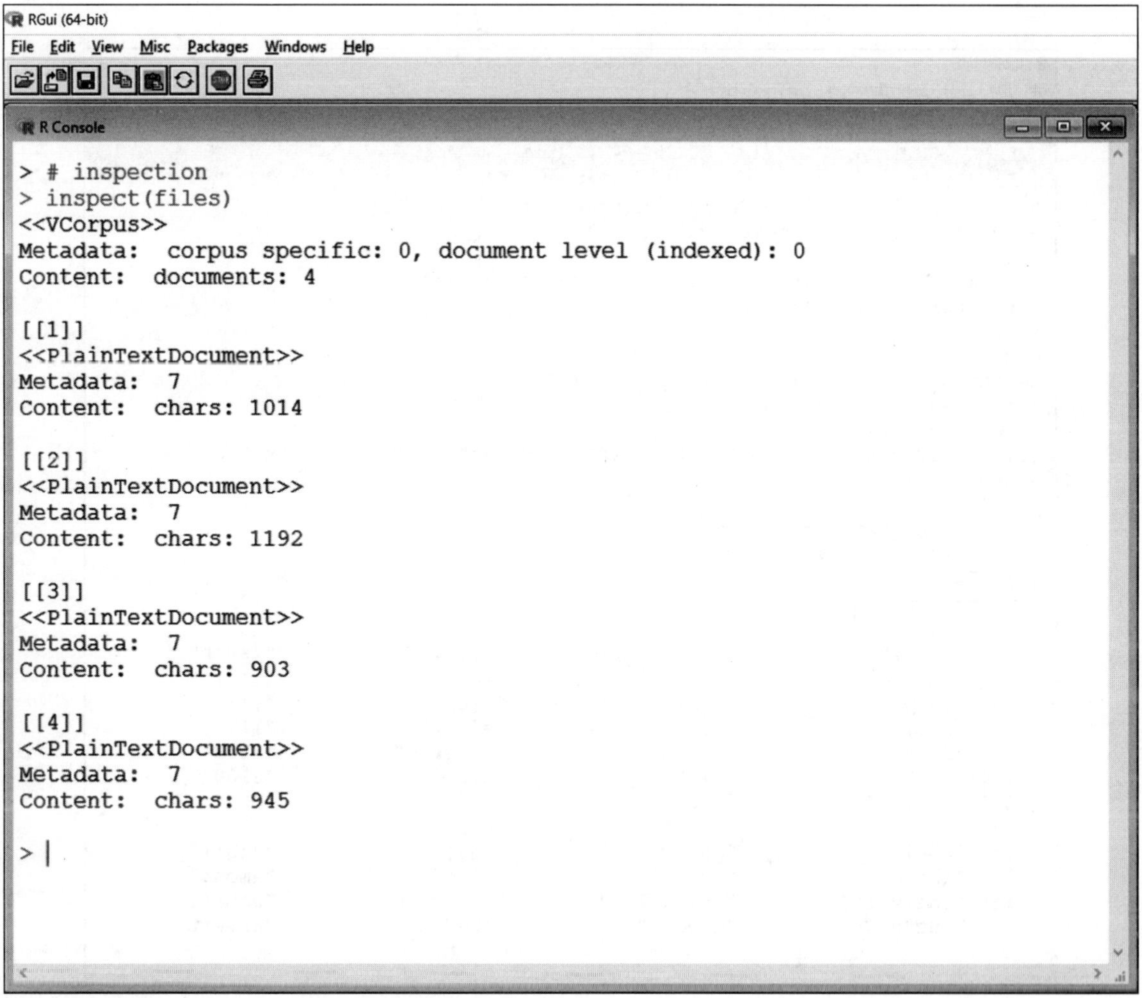

FIGURE 11.4 *Inspection of the documents using `inspect()` function*

Where,

"*x*" argument contains a Corpus; "control" is an optional argument that contains a named list of control parameters.

In the example below, the `TermDocumentMatrix()` function creates a term-document matrix "tdmfiles" of the corpus "files" (Figure 11.5). The `Docs()` function returns the number of documents of the corpus, `nTerms()` function returns the number of terms of the corpus, and `Terms()` function returns the names of each term of the corpus. In Figure 11.6, the `inspect()` function does an inspection on the object of the `TermDocumentMatrix()`.

```
> # Converting it into TermDocumentMatrix
> tdmfiles <- TermDocumentMatrix(files)
> tdmfiles
<<TermDocumentMatrix (terms: 274, documents: 4)>>
Non-/sparse entries: 325/771
Sparsity           : 70%
Maximal term length: 15
Weighting          : term frequency (tf)
> # Access Document IDs and Terms
> Docs(tdmfiles)
[1] "Demo2.txt"    "Demo3.txt"    "DemoTM.txt"   "Freqdemo.txt"
> nDocs(tdmfiles)
[1] 4
> # Finding terms of documents
> nTerms(tdmfiles)
[1] 274
> Terms(tdmfiles)
  [1] "({a2,"          "(1)"            "(2)"              "(5.2)"
  [5] "(5.3)"          "(frequent)"     "(i.e.,"           "(such"
  [9] "(we"            "?a1,"           "[categorization" "[ir],"
 [13] "[nlp],"         "{?a1,"          "{{a1,"            "{a1,"
 [17] "{a2,"           "{a8,"           "={i1,"            "1}."
 [21] "2}."            "2};"            "2}since"          "2100"
 [25] "a???"           "a?b"            "a?b,"             "a100"
 [29] "a100?;"         "a100}"          "a100}.)"          "a2,"
 [33] "a45"            "a45}"           "a50"              "a50?}."
 [37] "a50}"           "a55"            "a55}"             "a55})"
 [41] "above,"         "actual"         "also"             "among"
 [45] "analysis"       "analysis,"      "analytics"        "anb=f."
 [49] "and"            "appear"         "are"              "assert"
```

FIGURE 11.5 *Creating a term document matrix of a Corpus "files"*

In Figure 11.7, the `DocumentTermMatrix()` function creates a document-term matrix "dtmf" of the corpus "Dc". The `inspect()` function does an inspection on the object of the `DocumentTermMatrix()`.

```
> tdmf <- TermDocumentMatrix(Dc)
> tdmf
<<TermDocumentMatrix (terms: 274, documents: 4)>>
Non-/sparse entries: 325/771
Sparsity           : 70%
Maximal term length: 15
Weighting          : term frequency (tf)
> inspect(tdmf)
<<TermDocumentMatrix (terms: 274, documents: 4)>>
Non-/sparse entries: 325/771
Sparsity           : 70%
Maximal term length: 15
Weighting          : term frequency (tf)

                  Docs
Terms              Demo2.txt Demo3.txt DemoTM.txt Freqdemo.txt
  ({a2,                    0         1          0            0
  (1)                      0         1          0            0
  (2)                      0         1          0            0
  (5.2)                    0         0          0            1
  (5.3)                    0         0          0            1
  (frequent)               2         0          0            0
  (i.e.,                   0         0          0            1
  (such                    1         0          0            0
  (we                      0         1          0            0
  ?a1,                     0         1          0            0
  [categorization          0         0          1            0
  [ir],                    0         0          1            0
  [nlp],                   0         0          1            0
  {?a1,                    0         1          0            0
```

FIGURE 11.6 *Inspection of the term document matrix of a Corpus "files"*

```
> dtmf <- DocumentTermMatrix(Dc)
> dtmf
<<DocumentTermMatrix (documents: 4, terms: 274)>>
Non-/sparse entries: 325/771
Sparsity           : 70%
Maximal term length: 15
Weighting          : term frequency (tf)
> inspect(dtmf)
<<DocumentTermMatrix (documents: 4, terms: 274)>>
Non-/sparse entries: 325/771
Sparsity           : 70%
Maximal term length: 15
Weighting          : term frequency (tf)

              Terms
Docs           ({a2, (1) (2) (5.2) (5.3) (frequent) (i.e., (such (we ?a1, [categorization [ir], [nlp],
  Demo2.txt        0   0   0     0     0          2      0     1   0    0               0     0      0
  Demo3.txt        1   1   1     0     0          0      0     0   1    1               0     0      0
  DemoTM.txt       0   0   0     0     0          0      0     0   0    0               1     1      1
  Freqdemo.txt     0   0   0     1     1          0      1     0   0    0               0     0      0
              Terms
Docs           {?a1, {{a1, {a1, {a2, {a8, ={i1, 1}. 2}. 2}; 2}since 2100 a??? a?b a?b, a100 a100?; a100}
  Demo2.txt        0     0    0    0    0     0   0   0   0        0    0    0   0    0    0     0     0
  Demo3.txt        1     2    5    2    3     0   2   1   1        1    1    0   0    0    1     1     2
  DemoTM.txt       0     0    0    0    0     0   0   0   0        0    0    0   0    0    0     0     0
  Freqdemo.txt     0     0    0    0    0     1   0   0   0        0    0    1   2    1    0     0     0
              Terms
Docs           a100}.) a2, a45 a45} a50 a50?}. a50} a55 a55} a55}) above, actual also among analysis
  Demo2.txt          0   0   0    0   0      0    0   0    0     0      0      0    0     1        0
  Demo3.txt          1   9   1    2   1      1    2   1    1     1      1      1    0     0        0
```

FIGURE 11.7 *Creating a document term matrix of a Corpus "Dc"*

Additional Examples

Example 1

Objective: Create a corpus of the documents stored in folder "tm" in the "D:" drive. Create a document term matrix. Determine the number of documents, frequency of the terms in the documents, the terms in the documents, etc.

Step 1: Store a set of text files, "a1.txt", "a2.txt", "a3.txt" in a folder "tm" in the "D:" drive. Read the path of the files "D:/tm" into variable, "fname". The following are the contents in the files, "a1.txt", "a2.txt" and "a3.txt".

a1.txt
Data Analysis using R

---

a2.txt
Statistical Data Analysis

---

a3.txt
Data Analysis and Text Mining

```
> fname <- file.path("D:", "tm")
```

Step 2: Print out the value of the variable, "fname"

```
> fname
[1] "D:/tm"
```

Step 3: List out the names of the files stored in the path given by variable, "fname". It displays the names of the text files stored in "D:/tm". The `dir()` function lists the files stored in the directory/folder.

```
> dir(fname)
[1] "a1.txt" "a2.txt" "a3.txt"
```

Step 4: Create a corpus, "files" using "Corpus". Corpus are collections of documents containing (natural language) text.

```
> files <- Corpus(DirSource(fname))
```

Step 5: Print out the contents of the corpus, "files". A corpus has two types of metadata. *Corpus metadata* contains corpus specific metadata in form of tag-value pairs. *Document level metadata* contains document specific metadata but is stored in the corpus as a data frame.

```
> files
<<SimpleCorpus>>
Metadata: corpus specific: 1, document level (indexed): 0
Content:  documents: 3
```

Step 6: Create a volatile corpus, "files" using "VCorpus". A *volatile corpus* is fully kept in memory and thus all changes only affect the corresponding R object.

```
> files <- VCorpus(DirSource(fname))
```

Step 7: Print out the contents of the corpus, "files".

```
> files
<<VCorpus>>
Metadata:  corpus specific: 0, document level (indexed): 0
Content:  documents: 3
```

Step 8: List the summary as given by the `summary()` function.

```
> summary(files)
Length         Class              Mode
a1.txt 2       PlainTextDocument list
a2.txt 2       PlainTextDocument list
a3.txt 2       PlainTextDocument list
```

Step 9: Inspect the contents of the corpus, "files". The `inspect()` function display detailed information on a corpus, a term-document matrix, or a text document.

```
> inspect(files)
<<VCorpus>>
Metadata:  corpus specific: 0, document level (indexed): 0
Content:  documents: 3

[[1]]
<<PlainTextDocument>>
Metadata:  7
Content:  chars: 21

[[2]]
<<PlainTextDocument>>
Metadata:  7
Content:  chars: 25

[[3]]
<<PlainTextDocument>>
Metadata:  7
Content:  chars: 29
```

Step 10: Create a term-document matrix, "tdmfiles" using the "TermDocumentMatrix" function.

```
> tdmfiles <- TermDocumentMatrix(files)
```

Step 11: Print out the contents of the term document matrix, "tdmfiles"

```
> Docs(tdmfiles)
[1] "a1.txt" "a2.txt" "a3.txt"
```

Step 12: Print the number of documents contained in the term document matrix, "tdmfiles".

```
> nDocs(tdmfiles)
[1] 3
```

Step 13: Print the number of terms in the documents contained in the term document matrix, "tdmfiles".

```
> nTerms(tdmfiles)
[1] 7
```

Step 14: Print the terms contained in the documents of the term document matrix, "tdmfiles".

```
> Terms(tdmfiles)
[1] "analysis"   "and"     "data"    mining"   "statistical"
[6] "text"       "using"
```

Step 15: Inspect the term document matrix, "tdmfiles".

```
> inspect(tdmfiles)
<<TermDocumentMatrix  (terms: 7, documents: 3)>>
Non-/sparse entries : 11/10
Sparsity            : 48%
Maximal term length : 11
Weighting           : term frequency (tf)
Sample              :
            Docs
Terms          a1.txt   a2.txt    a3.txt
  analysis       1        1         1
  and            0        0         1
  data           1        1         1
  mining         0        0         1
  statistical    0        1         0
  text           0        0         1
  using          1        0         0
```

Step 16: Convert the text in the documents of the corpus, "files" to lowercase. The tm_map() function is an interface to apply transformation functions (also denoted as mappings) to corpora.

```
> Dc <- tm_map(files, tolower)
> Dc
<<VCorpus>>
Metadata:  corpus specific: 0, document level (indexed): 0
Content:  documents: 3
>inspect(Dc)
<<VCorpus>>
Metadata:  corpus specific: 0, document level (indexed): 0
Content:  documents: 3

[[1]]
[1] data analysis using r

[[2]]
[1] statistical data analysis

[[3]]
[1] data analysis and text mining
```

Step 17: Use the `colSums()` function to form row and column sums and means for numeric arrays (or data frames).

```
> freq <- colSums(as.matrix(tdmfiles))
```

Step 18: Find out the length of "freq".

```
> length(freq)
[1] 3
```

Step 19: Print out the contents of "freq".

```
> freq
a1.txt  a2.txt  a3.txt
     3       3       5
```

Step 20: Order the documents as per the frequency using the `order()` function. order returns a permutation which rearranges its first argument into ascending or descending order, breaking ties by further arguments.

```
> ord <- order(freq)
> ord
[1] 1 2 3
```

Step 21: Convert the term document matrix, "tdmfiles" into a matrix, "mt".

```
> mt <- as.matrix(tdmfiles)
```

Step 22: Print out the dimensions of the matrix, "mt". The matrix, "mt" has 7 rows and 3 columns.

```
> dim(mt)
[1] 7 3
```

Step 23: Print the contents of the matrix, "mt".

```
> mt
               Docs
Terms          a1.txt  a2.txt  a3.txt
  analysis          1       1       1
  and               0       0       1
  data              1       1       1
  mining            0       0       1
  statistical       0       1       0
  text              0       0       1
  using             1       0       0
```

Step 24: Write the matrix, "mt" to the file, "D:/Dtmt.csv".

```
> write.csv(mt, file= "D:/Dtmt.csv")
```

Step 25: Read the contents of the file, "D:/Dtmt.csv".

```
> read.csv("D:/Dtmt.csv")
            X  a1.txt  a2.txt  a3.txt
1    analysis       1       1       1
2         and       0       0       1
3        data       1       1       1
4      mining       0       0       1
5 statistical       0       1       0
6        text       0       0       1
7       using       1       0       0
```

Example 2:

Objective: To add a list of custom stop words to the original list of stop words. Remove these stop words from the file, "a1.txt" stored in folder, "tm1" in the "D:" drive.

Step 1: Read the contents of the file, "D:/Stop.txt" into a data frame, "stop". The file "D:/Stop.txt" has a list of custom stop words. Given below is the content of the file, "D:/Stop.txt".

Custom_Stop_Words
oh!
Hmm
OMG
Hehe
Dude

```
> stop = read.table("D:/Stop.txt", header = TRUE)
```

Step 2: Print the class of "stop" and the list of custom stop words as contained in the data frame, "stop".

```
> class(stop)
[1] "data.frame"
  Custom_Stop_Words
1              oh!
2              Hmm
3              OMG
4             Hehe
5             Dude
```

Step 3: Convert the "Custom_Stop_words" column of the data frame, "stop" into a vector, "stop_vec".

```
> stop_vec = as.vector(stop$Custom_Stop_Words)
```

Step 4: Print the class of "stop_vec".

```
> class(stop_vec)
[1] "character"
```

Step 5: Print the contents of the vector, "stop_vec".

```
> stop_vec
[1] "oh!" "Hmm" "OMG" "Hehe" "Dude"
```

Step 6: Store the path, "D:/tm1" into the variable, "fname". There is one file, "a1.txt" present in the path, "D:/tmp". Given below is the content of the file, "a1.txt" available in the path, "D:/tm1".

oh! said he
there was silence and then "Hmm"
Dude that is now how it works. Hehe Hehe
OMG is that you?

```
> fname <- file.path("D:", "tm1")
```

Step 7: Print out the contents of the variable, "fname".

```
> fname
[1] "D:/tm1"
```

Step 8: Create a corpus, "files" using the function, "Corpus".

```
> files <- Corpus(DirSource(fname))
```

Step 9: Create a document term matrix, "dtm" using the function, "DocumentTermMatrix".

```
> dtm <- DocumentTermMatrix(files)
```

Step 10: Print out the contents of the document term matrix, "dtm".

```
> dtm
<<DocumentTermMatrix (documents: 1, terms: 15)>>
Non-/sparse entries : 15/0
Sparsity            : 0%
Maximal term length : 7
Weighting           : term frequency (tf)
```

Step 11: Convert the document term matrix, "dtm" into a matrix, "dtm.mat".

```
> dtm.mat <- as.matrix(dtm)
```

Step 12: Print the contents of the matrix, "dtm.mat".

```
> dtm.mat
      Terms
Docs   and dude hehe hmm how now omg said silence that then there was works
 a1.txt 1    1    2   1   1   1   1    1       1    2    1     1   1     1
        Terms
Docs     you
 a1.txt   1
```

Step 13: Add the list of custom stop words as contained in the vector, "stop_vec" to the original list of stop words".

```
>corpus <- tm_map(files, removeWords, c(stop_vec, stopwords('english')))
```

Step 14: Again create a document term matrix, "dtm".

```
> dtm <- DocumentTermMatrix(corpus)
```

Step 15: Print the contents of the document term matrix, "dtm".

```
> dtm
<<DocumentTermMatrix  (documents: 1, terms: 4)>>
Non-/sparse entries : 4/0
Sparsity            : 0%
Maximal term length : 7
Weighting           : term frequency (tf)
```

Step 16: Convert the document term matrix, dtm" into a matrix, "dtm.mat".

```
> dtm.mat <- as.matrix(dtm)
```

Step 17: Print out the contents of the matrix, "dtm.mat". Notice that the words such as "oh!", "omg", "hmm", "hehe" and "dude" have been removed. These words were the custom stop words added to the original list of stop words.

```
> dtm.mat
        Terms
Docs      now  said  silence  works
  a1.txt   1     1        1      1
```

11.6 General Architecture of Text Mining Systems

A text mining system takes documents as input and generates patterns, associations, and trends as an output. A simple architecture of text mining system contains only input and output system. A more common function level architecture of text mining system follows some sequential processing. Figure 11.8 describes a general architecture of a text mining system that is divided into four main tasks or areas.

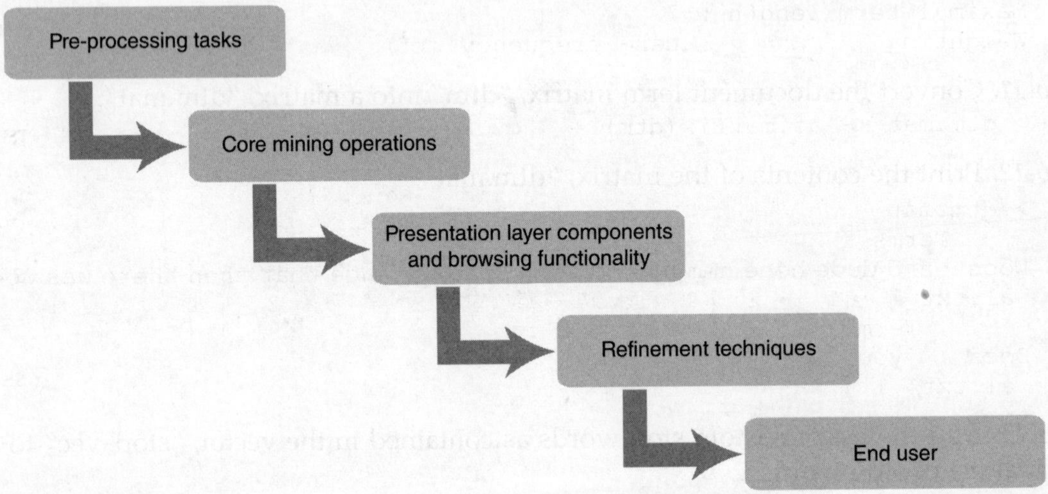

Figure 11.8 *General architecture of the text mining system*

Pre-processing tasks, core mining operations, presentation layer components and browsing functionality, and refinement techniques are the four major tasks. A brief introduction of each task is given as follows.

11.6.1 Pre-processing Tasks

Pre-processing task is the first task that includes different routines, processes, and methods necessary for preparing the input data. These convert the raw text or information collected from different data sources into a canonical format (canonicalization is a process for converting data that has more than one possible representation into a "standard", "normal", or canonical form). It is a very necessary step before applying any feature extraction methods on the document for obtaining new patterns of output.

11.6.2 Core Mining Operations

Core mining operation is the most important task of the text mining system. The pattern discovery, incremental knowledge discovery algorithms, or trend analysis are the major core mining operations. The knowledge discovery generates distribution and proportions, associations, frequent and near frequent sets.

11.6.3 Presentation Layer Components

A presentation layer component task includes some graphical interface pattern browsing functionalities and uses some query language. These tasks use some visualisation tools and user-facing query editors, optimisers. Along this, it also uses character-based tools and graphical tools that create and modify the concept of the document. It also creates and modifies the annotated profiles for specific concepts or patterns.

11.6.4 Refinement Techniques

Refinement techniques are the last processing task of the text mining system. It filters the redundant information and concept from the given input text document to generate a well-optimised output. Suppression, ordering, clustering, pruning, classification are few popular refinement techniques used in the text mining system.

A typical text mining system takes some input documents, performs pre-processing tasks on it, and extracts the features or terms. The core mining operations categorise and label these terms and features. Now the presentation layer does some browsing for finding patterns and associations. At last, using some refinement methods, unnecessary or repeated information is removed.

11.7 Pre-processing of Documents in R

During text mining, the documents may contain any type of raw data. Hence, it is very necessary to perform some pre-processing tasks on such raw data. Also, pre-processing is also the first step of text mining system. The package "tm" provides a function `tm_map()` for pre-processing of documents. This is also called transformation of documents.

The function `tm_map()` performs transformation on the corpus by modifying the documents. Since transformation functions, such as `stemDocument()`, `stopwords()`, work on single text document, thus it is good to use these functions with the function `tm_map()` that maps to all documents in a corpus. The basic syntax of the function `tm_map()` is as follows:

```
tm_map(x, fun, …)
```

where,

"x" argument contains any corpus; "fun" is a transformation function that takes a text document as input and returns a text document. Table 11.1 describes few useful transformation functions; the dots, "…" define the arguments to the fun (transformation function).

TABLE 11.1 Few useful transformation functions

Transformation Function	*Transformation Function Description*
`stripWhitespace()`	It removes the white space from the documents
`tolower()`	It converts the terms of the documents into the lower case
`stopwords()`	It removes the stop words
`stemDocument(x, language = "")`	It performs stemming on the document. For this, it is necessary to load the package "snowballs"
`removeNumbers()`	It removes the numbers from the text documents
`removePunctuation`	It removes the punctuations from the text documents

In the example below, the `tm_map()` function performs some pre-processing tasks such as removing punctuations, numbers, white space, and stemming on the documents of the corpus "Dc". Along this, the `as.matrix()` function creates a matrix from the document term matrix "dtmf". After the pre-processing of the raw data, it writes to a file. Here `write.csv()` function writes it to a file "Dtmf.csv". Figure 11.9 shows the pre-processing of the Corpus and Figure 11.10 displays the output of the file "Dtmf.csv" as `read.csv()` function reads the file.

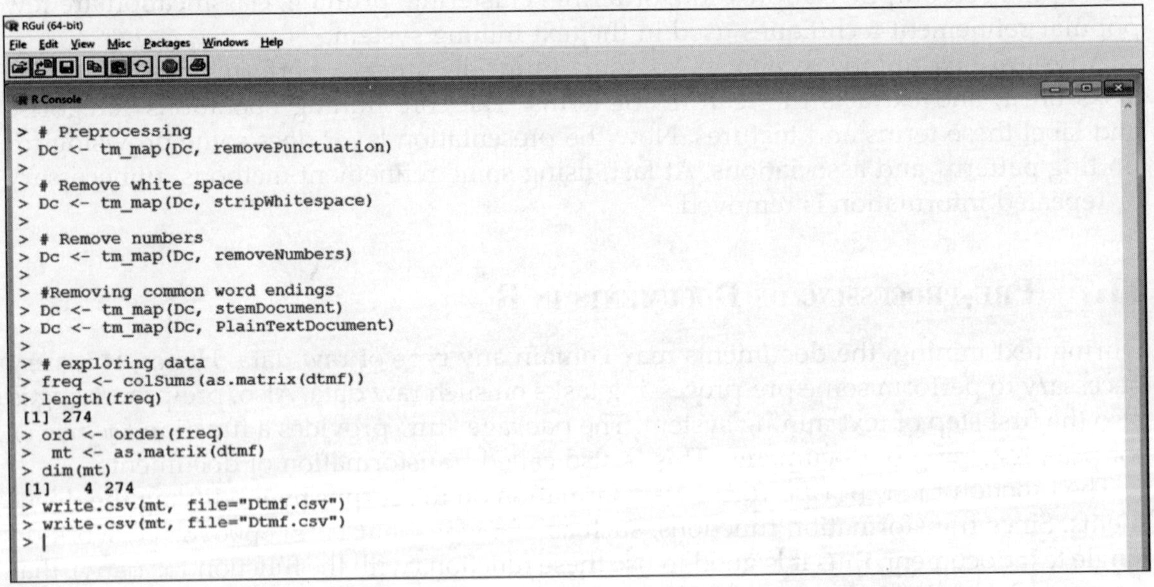


```
> # Preprocessing
> Dc <- tm_map(Dc, removePunctuation)
>
> # Remove white space
> Dc <- tm_map(Dc, stripWhitespace)
>
> # Remove numbers
> Dc <- tm_map(Dc, removeNumbers)
>
> #Removing common word endings
> Dc <- tm_map(Dc, stemDocument)
> Dc <- tm_map(Dc, PlainTextDocument)
>
> # exploring data
> freq <- colSums(as.matrix(dtmf))
> length(freq)
[1] 274
> ord <- order(freq)
>  mt <- as.matrix(dtmf)
> dim(mt)
[1]   4 274
> write.csv(mt, file="Dtmf.csv")
> write.csv(mt, file="Dtmf.csv")
> |
```

FIGURE 11.9 *Pre-processing of the Corpus*

Before pre-processing the document, term matrix of the corpus "Dc" shows 274 terms and as is evident from Figure 11.10, the generated output cannot be used for generating the frequent itemset or rules using Apriori algorithm. After the pre-processing, the document term matrix of the corpus "Dc" shows 186 terms and in the following figure, the generated output can easily be used in the mining methods. Hence, it is necessary again to create a document term or term document matrix after pre-processing of the corpus (Figure 11.11).

```
> read.csv("Dtmf.csv")
             X X..a2. X.1. X.2. X.5.2. X.5.3. X.frequent. X.i.e.. X.such X.we X.a1. X.categorization
1    Demo2.txt      0    0    0      0      0           2       0      1    0     0                0
2    Demo3.txt      1    1    1      0      0           0       0      0    1     1                0
3   DemoTM.txt      0    0    0      0      0           0       0      0    0     0                1
4 Freqdemo.txt      0    0    0      1      1           0       1      0    0     0                0
  X.ir.. X.nlp.. X..a1. X..a1..1 X.a1..1 X.a2. X.a8. X..i1. X1.. X2.. X2...1 X2.since X2100 a... a.b a.b.
1      0       0      0        0       0     0     0      0    0    0      0        0     0    0   0    0
2      0       0      1        2       5     2     3      0    2    1      1        1     1    0   0    0
3      1       1      0        0       0     0     0      0    0    0      0        0     0    0   0    0
4      0       0      0        0       0     0     0      1    0    0      0        0     0    1   2    1
  a100 a100.. a100. a100... a2. a45 a45. a50 a50... a50. a55 a55. a55.. above. actual also among analysis
1    0      0     0       0   0   0    0   0      0    0   0    0     0      0      0    0     1        0
2    1      1     2       1   9   1    2   1      1    2   1    1     1      1      1    0     0        0
3    0      0     0       0   0   0    0   0      0    0   0    0     0      0      0    1     0        1
4    0      0     0       0   0   0    0   0      0    0   0    0     0      0      0    1     0        0
  analysis. analytics anb.f. and appear are assert associated association associations associations. b..
1         0         0      0   5      2   1      0          0           0            0             1   0
2         0         0      0   4      0   2      2          0           0            0             0   0
3         2         1      0   5      0   4      0          0           0            1             0   0
4         0         0      1   5      0   0      0          1           2            0             0   1
  b... because become big both bread. business but buying called camera. can cannot card. case.
1    0       0      1   0    0      1        0   0      1      1       1   1      0     1     0
2    0       1      0   0    1      0        0   2      0      0       0   2      2     0     0
3    0       0      0   1    0      0        ?   0      0      0       0   0      0     0     1
4    1       0      0   0    1      0        0   0      0      1       0   0      0     0     0
  classification. closed clustering. collections. combined compare complete conditional confidence
1               1      0           1            0        1       0        0           0          0
2               0      3           0            0        0       1        1           0          0
3               0      0           1            1        0       0        0           0          0
```

Figure 11.10 *Reading the file Dtmf.csv*

```
> # After preprocessing of the corpus
> dtmf <- DocumentTermMatrix(Dc)
> dtmf
<<DocumentTermMatrix (documents: 4, terms: 186)>>
Non-/sparse entries: 244/500
Sparsity           : 67%
Maximal term length: 12
Weighting          : term frequency (tf)
>
> # Creating matrix
>  mt <- as.matrix(dtmf)
> mt
              Terms
Docs            abov actual also among analysi analyt anbf and appear are assert associ associat becaus becom
  character(0)     0      0    0     1       0      0    0   5      2   1      0      1        0      0     1
  character(0)     1      1    0     0       0      0    0   4      0   2      2      0        0      1     0
  character(0)     0      0    1     0       3      1    0   5      0   4      0      1        0      0     0
  character(0)     0      0    1     0       0      0    1   5      0   0      0      2        1      0     0
              Terms
Docs            big both bread busi but buy call camera can cannot card case categor classif close cluster
  character(0)    0    0     1    0   0   1    1      1   1      0    1    0       0       1     0       1
  character(0)    0    1     0    0   2   0    0      0   2      2    0    0       0       0     3       0
  character(0)    1    0     0    2   0   0    0      0   0      0    0    1       1       0     0       1
  character(0)    0    1     0    0   0   0    1      0   0      0    0    0       0       0     1       0
              Terms
Docs            collect combin compar complet condit confid confidenceab contain correl count data databas deriv
  character(0)        0      1      0       0      0      0            0       0      1     0    7       1     0
  character(0)        0      0      1       1      0      0            0       1      0     3    0       1     1
  character(0)        1      0      0       0      0      0            0       0      0     0    3       0     0
```

Figure 11.11 *Document term matrix "dtmf" of the Corpus "Dc" after the pre-processing*

11.8 Core Text Mining Operations

Core text mining operations are one of the most important tasks of the text mining system. The distribution (proportions), frequent and near frequent sets, and associations are the three main core text-mining operations. A brief introduction of each operation is given below.

11.8.1 Distribution (Proportions)

After getting the output from the pre-processing step, the core mining operations generate pattern and find out the distribution of data in the collections in the text mining system. Any text mining system uses distribution for the mining of text. This operation creates meaningful subdivisions on a single document collection for comparison purpose; it is also called the concept selection.

Table 11.2 describes some important definitions of distribution. Let D be a set of documents and K define a set of concepts.

TABLE 11.2 Few useful distributions

Distribution Name	*Definition*	*Formula*
Concept selection	Select some sub collection of the documents labelled with one or more given concepts.	D/K
Concept proportion	The proportion of a set of documents labelled with a particular concept.	$F(D,K) = \vert D/K \vert / \vert D \vert$
Conditional concept proportion	The proportion of a set of documents labelled with a particular concept, which is itself labelled with another concept.	$F(D, K1/K2) = f(D/K2, K1)$
Concept proportion distribution	The proportion of a set of documents labelled with some selected concepts.	$FK(D, x)$
Conditional concept proportion distribution	The proportion of a set of documents labelled with all the concepts in K' that are also labelled with concept x.	$FK(D, x \mid K') = FK(D/K \mid K', x)$

11.8.2 Frequent and Near Frequent Sets

A frequent concept set is another basic type of pattern obtained from a document collection. A frequent concept set is a set of concepts represented in the document collection with co-occurrences at or above a minimal support level. This minimal support level is a threshold parameter, s, i.e. all the concepts of the frequent concept set appear together in at least s documents. It comes originally from the association rules where Apriori algorithm finds out the frequent itemsets.

With reference to text mining, support is the number or percentage of documents that contains given rules. It is called co-occurrence frequency. The confidence is the percentage of the time that the rule is true. A frequent set is a query given by the conjunction of concepts of the frequent set. This frequent set is partially ordered and contains the pruning property, i.e. each subset of a frequent set is a frequent set.

11.8.3 Near Frequent Concept Set

It defines an undirected relation between two frequent sets of concepts. The degree of overlapping is used to quantify the relation. For example, according to the number of documents including all the concepts of the two concept sets defined by the distance function between the concepts sets.

In R language, the package "tm" provides a function `findFreqTerms()` that finds out the frequent terms in a document-term or term-document matrix. The basic syntax of the function `findFreqTerms()` is as follows:

```
function findFreqTerms(x, lowfreq = 0, highfreq = inf)
```

where,

"x" argument contains either term-document matrix or document-term matrix; "lowfreq" argument contains a numeric number that defines the lower frequency bound; "highfreq" argument contains a numeric number that defines the upper frequency bound.

In the example below, `findFreqTerms()` function takes a document term matrix, "dtmf" of the corpus "Dc" and returns the frequents terms. At first, it finds the frequent terms between frequencies 5 and 15. It indicates that there are only 14 terms between these frequencies. After this, it finds the frequent terms with the low frequency 10 and 1 (Figure 11.12).

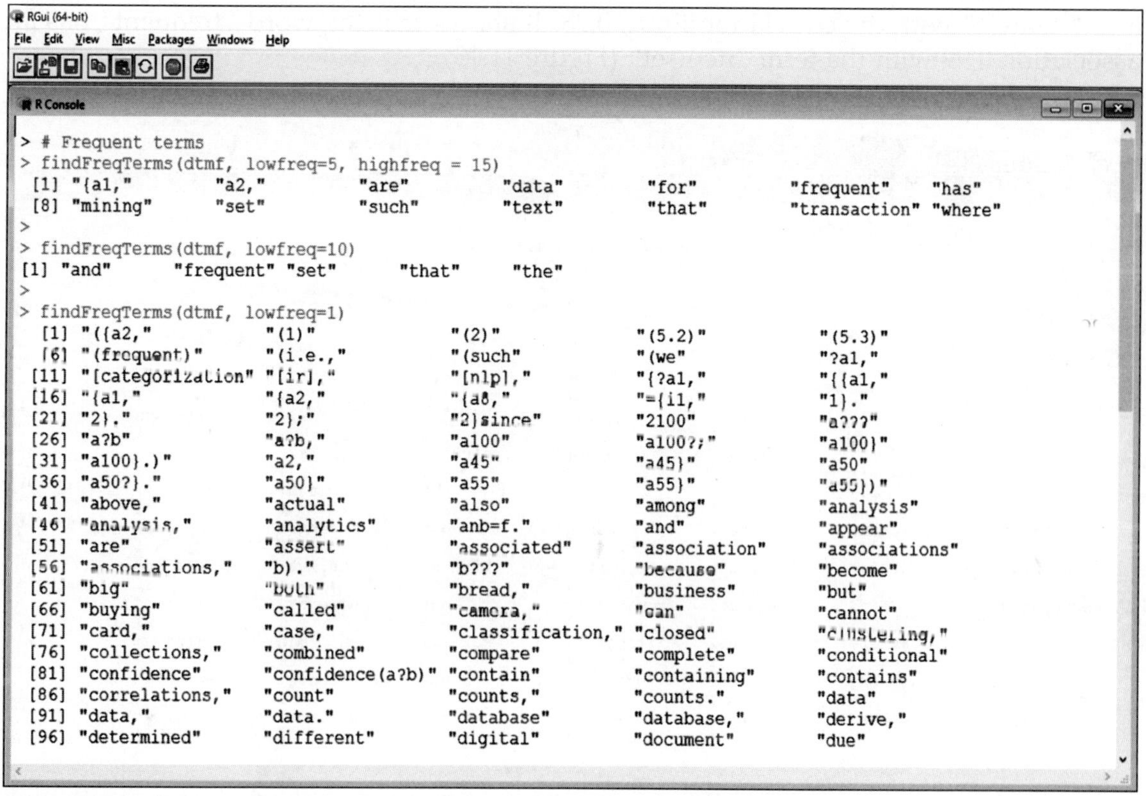

FIGURE 11.12 *Use of the `findFreqTerms()` function*

11.8.4 Associations

In the previous chapter, you learnt about the association rules generated from frequent Itemsets, relationship between two or more items, etc. With reference to text mining, association defines the direct relation between the concept and set of concepts. An association rule is an implication form of the expression $X \rightarrow Y$, where X and Y are two sets of features.

In terms of text documents, the association defines the relationship or association between two or more terms. For example, in a text file if two terms, such as "text" and "mining" come together more than once, then there is a strong association between those two terms.

In R language, the package "tm" provides a function `findAssocs()` that identifies the association between two or more terms in a document-term or term-document matrix. The basic syntax of the function `findAssocs()` is as follows:

```
function findAssocs(x, terms, corlimit)
```

where,

"x" argument contains either term-document matrix or document-term matrix; "terms" argument contains a character vector that holds the terms; "corlimit" argument contains a numeric number for the lower correlation limits of each term in the range from zero to one.

In the example below, `findAssocs()` function takes a document term matrix, "dtmf" of the corpus, "Dc" and finds out the association between the two terms "frequent" and "itemset" with the correlation limit, 0.98. It shows that the word "frequent" has an association 0.99 with the term "itemset" (Figure 11.13).

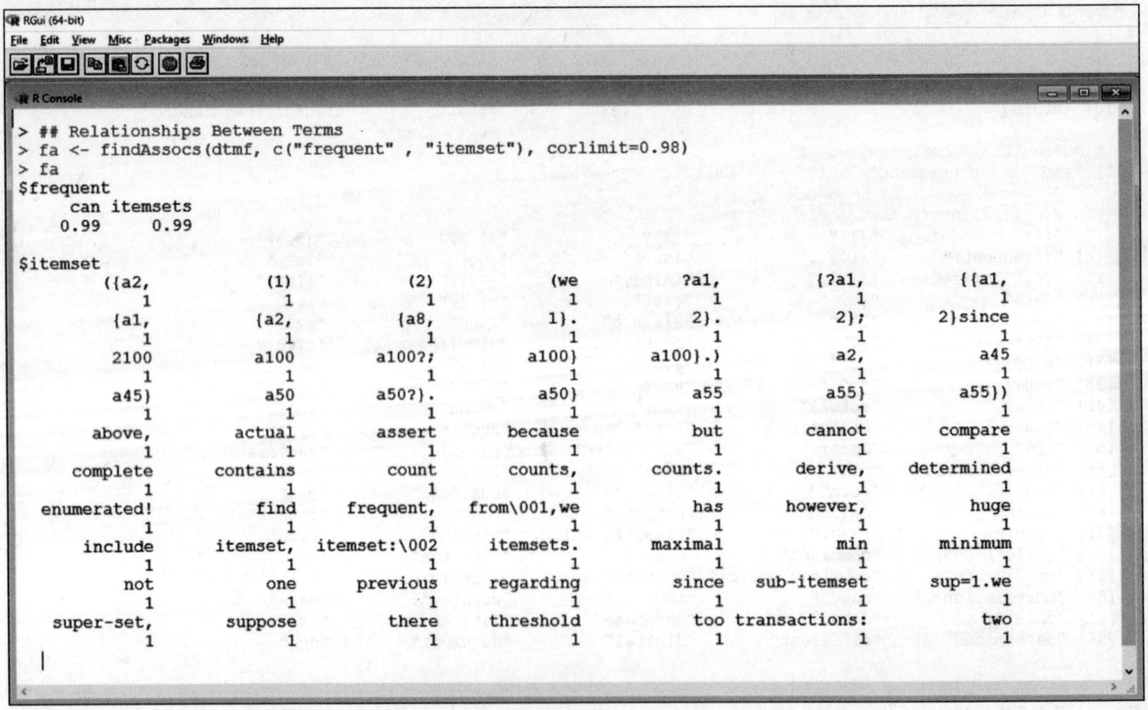

FIGURE 11.13 *Use of the `findAssocs()` function*

In the figure, `findAssocs()` is finding an association of the term "frequent" with all other terms of the corpus. The user can observe that there is less association with the words "closed" and "support" (Figure 11.14).

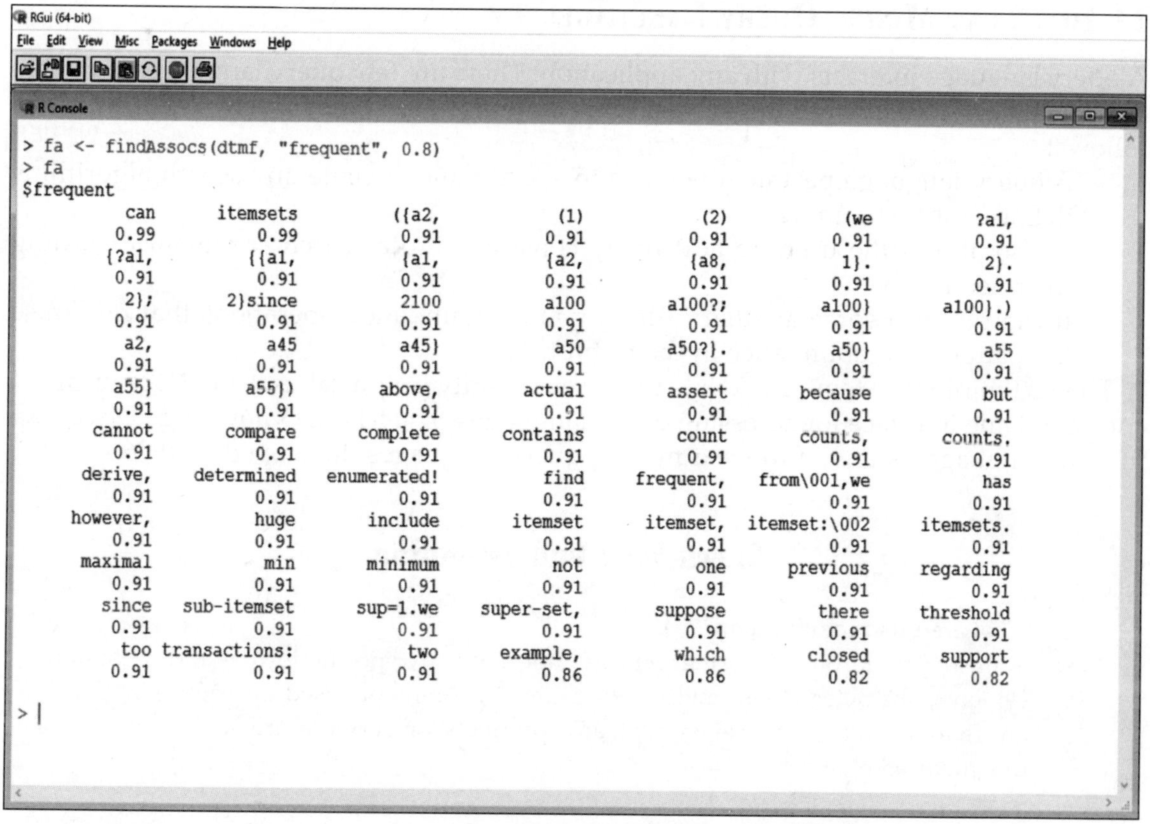

FIGURE 11.14 *Use of the* `findAssocs()` *function with only one term "frequent"*

11.9 Using Background Knowledge for Text Mining

There are two types of knowledge—domain and background knowledge—which are used in text mining. Domain knowledge defines a specific specialisation that includes ontologies, lexicons, and taxonomies, etc. In literature, background knowledge is used instead of domain knowledge. It is used in many elements of text mining system, but mostly in pre-processing operations. It plays a major role in classification and concept extraction methodologies, enhancing the core mining algorithms, and in search refinement techniques.

The constraints, attribute relationship rules, and hierarchical trees are the three main forms of background knowledge. Most data mining applications use these forms. Background knowledge is used in pre-processing operations of text mining system. It enhances the feature extraction, validation activities, develops meaningful, consistent, and normalised concept hierarchies. For developing meaningful constraints for knowledge discovery operations, background knowledge is used in text mining system.

11.10 Text Mining Query Languages

A query language interacts with any application. There are few query languages available for interaction with text mining system. This language has some objectives which are as follows:

- A query language permits the users to specify and execute any search algorithms defined for text mining.
- It also allows the users to add many constraints to a search argument regarding their need.
- It can perform some auxiliary filtering and redundancy operations that minimise the pattern overabundance in the output.

The text mining system provides either user-friendly graphical user interface or direct command line interface for accessing query languages. The KDTL (Knowledge Discovery in Text Language) is one of the text mining query languages developed in 1996.

Check Your Understanding

1. What are unstructured data?

Ans: In unstructured data, information does not have any specific format and it contains symbols, characters, or numbers. For example, comments used on Facebook, tweets on Twitter, opinion or reviews of any products or services are few examples of unstructured data.

2. What is static and dynamic document collection?

Ans: A static document collection is a document collection where initial complement of documents remains unchanged. A dynamic document collection is a document collection where documents change or are updated over time.

3. What do you mean by a freeformat or weakly structured document?

Ans: A freeformat or weakly structured document follows some typography, layout, and makeup indicators. Research paper, press release, are examples of freeformat document.

4. What are the four main components or tasks of the text mining system?

Ans: Pre-processing tasks, core mining operations, presentation layer components and browsing functionality, and refinement techniques are the four major tasks of the text mining system.

11.11 Mining Frequent Patterns, Associations, and Correlations: Basic Concepts and Methods

In this section, you will learn about the basic concepts and methods of frequent patterns, associations, and correlations that are an important part of text mining. The main objective behind the development of frequent mining is to identify the inherent patterns in data, i.e. which products are often purchased by customers, what is the subsequent purchase pattern after purchasing some products, etc.

Market basket analysis, catalogue design, web log analysis, cross-marketing, sale campaign analysis, and DNA sequence analysis are some applications of frequent patterns. Market basket analysis is one of the most famous applications of frequent pattern.

11.11.1 Basic Concepts

Frequent pattern is a major concept in text mining. It helps researchers in finding associations, correlations, distributions, clustering, classification, etc., in mining tasks.

1. ***Frequent pattern:*** A frequent pattern is a type of pattern that frequently occurs in a dataset. These patterns can be any itemsets, subsequences, or substructures. For example, a set of items such as petrol, car, bike, tyre, etc., appear together in a dataset. A frequent itemset is a set of items that frequently occur together in a dataset.
2. ***Frequent sequential pattern:*** A frequent sequential pattern is a frequent pattern that frequently occurs in a serial manner in a dataset. It follows the concept of subsequence, i.e. one-by-one. For example: first a car is purchased, then petrol, tyre, and so on are bought in a sequential manner.
3. **Frequent structured pattern:** A frequent structured pattern is a frequent pattern that is constructed from a dataset that often occurs frequently. It follows the concept of substructure, i.e. hierarchical form, such as subgraphs, sub lattices, subtrees, etc.

11.11.2 Market Basket Analysis: A Motivating Example

Market basket analysis is a common and classic example of frequent itemset mining. The main objective is to identify the associations and correlations among a set of items. Market basket analysis process analyses the buying behaviours of customers for identifying the associations and correlations between different items purchased or placed in their "shopping baskets". This process of identifying associations helps a business organisation to develop an effective marketing strategy. Through this, they identify the frequent items purchased by the customers together.

Figure 11.15 provides an example of the market basket analysis. In the figure, each customer has his or her own basket where he or she places items as per their needs. For example, one customer picks and places milk, bread, and cereal in the basket, another customer places milk, bread, and butter in the basket and so on. In simple words, each basket contains some items that are related to each other and a market analyst finds out the frequent items from looking into these different shopping baskets.

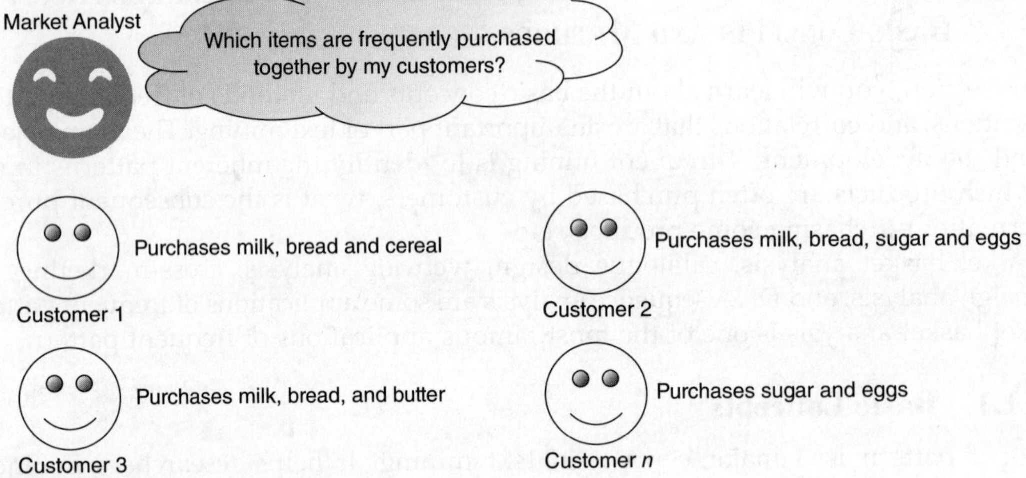

FIGURE 11.15 *Market basket analysis*

Here, each item can be represented by a Boolean variable that represents the presence or absence of that item, and each basket represents a Boolean vector of values that are assigned to these Boolean variables. These Boolean vectors are analysed for finding the buying pattern of the customers and items that are frequently associated or purchased together. These patterns can be represented by association rules. The Support and Confidence are two metrics that measures a rule's interestingness. Here is a brief introduction of few basic terms that are used in next subsections as follow:

Let $I = \{I_1, I_2, I_3 \dots I_m\}$ = a universal set of items

$D = \{T_1, T_2, T_3 \dots T_n\}$ = a set of all transaction in a given time where each transaction T_i is a set of items such that $T_i \subseteq I$

$A \subseteq T$ is an itemset and $|A| = k$ then it is called k itemset.

Occurrence frequency = Number of transactions that contain the itemset. It is also called the frequency, count, support count, or absolute support of an itemset.

11.11.3 Association Rule

An association rule correlates the presence of one set of items with another set of items. An association rule is an implication form of the expression $X \rightarrow Y$, where X and Y are two disjoint itemsets and $X \subseteq I$ and $Y \subseteq I$, and $X \cap Y = \phi$.

Support

Support is a metric that measures the usefulness of an association rule by using the minimum support threshold. The metric measures the number of events with such itemsets that match both sides of the implications of the association rules.

Let $X \rightarrow Y$ be an association rule and D be a transaction set. Let n be the number of transactions in D. Then the support of this rule is the percentage of the transactions in D

containing $X \cup Y$ or the estimation of the probability $Pr(X \cup Y)$. The support of the rule $X \rightarrow Y$ is calculated using the following formula:

Support or sup = $(X \cup Y)$.count/n or transactions that contain X and $Y / |D|$

Confidence

Confidence is a metric that measures the certainty of an association rule by using threshold. It measures how often an event itemset that matches the left side of implication in the association rule also matches the right side.

Let $X \rightarrow Y$ be an association rule and D be a transaction set. Then the confidence of this rule is the percentage of the transactions in D containing both X and Y or the estimation of the conditional probability $Pr(Y \mid X)$. The confidence of rule $X \rightarrow Y$ is calculated using the following formula:

Confidence or conf = $(X \cup Y)$.count/X.count

Or

Confidence or conf = transactions that contain both X and Y/transactions that contain X

Or

Confidence or conf = support$(X \cup Y)$/support(X)

11.12 Frequent Itemsets, Closed Itemsets and Association Rules

In this section, you will learn about frequent itemsets, closed itemsets, and association rules.

11.12.1 Frequent Itemset

An itemset that contains items that often occur together and are associated with each other is called frequent itemset. The support of that itemset is greater than the minimum support threshold. A minimum support threshold defines the relative support of itemset. L_k represents the set of frequent k itemsets.

11.12.2 Closed Itemset

An itemset is a closed itemset in a dataset if there does not exist a proper super itemset. If Q is a closed itemset in D, then there is an itemset R such that $Q \subseteq R \subseteq D$, where the Support count(Q) = Support count(R).

An itemset is a closed frequent itemset in a dataset if it is closed and frequent. For example, if Q is a closed and also a frequent itemset in D then Q is a closed frequent itemset. An itemset is a maximal frequent itemset in a dataset if it is frequent and there is no super itemset on this.

11.12.3 Association Rule Mining

An association rule is an implication form of the expression $X \rightarrow Y$, where X and Y are two disjoint itemsets and $X \subseteq I$ and $Y \subseteq I$, and $X \cap Y = \phi$.

For any two itemsets X and Y, if Support $(X \rightarrow Y)$ is at least a minimum support threshold and confidence $(X \rightarrow Y)$ is at least minimum confidence threshold, then the association rule $(X \rightarrow Y)$ is called a strong association rule.

The association rules mining two steps approach for mining:

1. The first step is "frequent itemset generation" that finds out all frequent itemsets. Each of these itemsets will occur at least as frequently as a predetermined minimum support count.
2. The second step is "rule generation" that generates strong association rules from the frequent itemsets. These rules will have to satisfy minimum support and minimum confidence.

Check Your Understanding

1. What is a frequent pattern?

Ans: A frequent pattern is a type of pattern that frequently occurs in a data set. These patterns can be any itemsets, subsequences, or substructures.

2. What is market basket analysis?

Ans: Market basket analysis is a common and classic example of frequent itemset mining. The main objective is to find out the associations and correlations among a set of items.

3. What is occurrence frequency?

Ans: Occurrence frequency is the number of transactions in the itemset. It is also called frequency, count, support count, or absolute support of an itemset.

11.13 Frequent Itemsets: Mining Methods

In this section, you will learn about the basic mining methods of frequent patterns, associations, and correlations used for text mining. The main aim of the mining method is to generate frequent itemsets and association rules.

11.13.1 Apriori Algorithm: Finding Frequent Itemsets

The Apriori algorithm is seminal algorithm developed by Agarwal and Srikant in 1994 for mining the frequent itemsets. Apriori algorithm is a breadth-first algorithm that counts transactions by following two-step approach and follows the concept of the Apriori principle. The Apriori principle is the best strategy and an effective method to generate frequent itemset. According to the Apriori principle, *if an itemset is frequent, then all of its subsets must also be frequent.*

The Apriori principle eliminates some candidate itemsets without counting their support values. Elimination of candidate itemsets is called the pruning of itemsets. The Apriori principle uses the following property of the support measure:

$$\forall\ X\ Y: (X \subseteq Y) \text{->} s(X) \geq s(Y)$$

This property is called the anti-monotone property of support, where support of an itemset never exceeds the support of its subsets. The principle does not require matching every candidate against every transaction.

The Apriori algorithm identifies the frequent itemset, maximal frequent itemset, and closed frequent itemset. The implementation of the algorithm also generates the association rules. In this section, the Apriori algorithm generates all frequent itemsets, where a frequent itemset is an itemset that has transaction support greater than minsup.

For efficient itemset generation, the algorithm should be sorted in lexicographic order. Let $\{w[1], w[2], \ldots, w[k]\}$ is representing k itemsets and w contains the item $w[1], w[2], \ldots, w[k]$ where $w[1] < w[2] < \ldots < w[k]$. The pseudocode of the algorithm is as follows:

```
Apriori(T)
1.  Ck ← init-pass(T) ; // First pass
2.  F1  ← { f | f ∈C1 , f.count ≥minsup } // n = number of transaction
3.  for (k = 2; Fk-1 ≠ ϕ; k++) do          // subsequent passess over T
4.  Ck ← candidate-gen(Fk-1)
5.  for each transaction t  ∈ T do          // scan the data once
6.  for each candidate c ∈Ck do
7.  if c is contained in t then
8.  c.count++;
9.  end
10. end
11. Fk  ← { c ∈Ck |  c.count / n ≥ minsup }
12. end
13. return F ← UkFk
```

The algorithm uses a level-wise search for generating the frequent itemset and multiple passes over the data. In each pass of the algorithm, it counts the supports of individual items [line 1] and determines whether each of them is frequent [line 2]. *F*1 is the set of frequent 1-itemsets. In each subsequent pass *k*, it follows the following three steps:

1. It starts with the seed set of itemsets $F_{k\text{-}1}$ found to be frequent in the $(k\text{-}1)^{th}$ pass. These seed sets generate the candidate itemsets C_k [line 4] that are possible frequent itemsets using candidate `gen()` function
2. In the second step, the transaction database scanned and the actual support of each candidate itemset *c* in C_k is counted [line 5 to 10].
3. At the end of the pass, it determines the actual frequent candidate itemsets.

The set of all frequent itemsets *F* is the final output of the algorithm.

Candidate gen() Function

The candidate `gen()` function is used in the Apriori algorithm that contains two steps Join and Pruning. They are as follows:

1. The Join step [line 2–3] joins two frequent *(k-1)* itemsets for producing a possible candidate *c* [line 6]. The two frequent itemsets f_1 and f_2 have exactly the same items except the last one [line 3–5]. The *c* is added to the set of candidates C_k [line 7].
2. The pruning step [line 8–11] determines whether all the *k*-1 subsets of *c* are in F_{k-1}. If no one of them is in F_{k-1}, *c* cannot be frequent according to the downward closure property and deleted from C_k.

The pseudocode of the candidate `gen()` function is as follows:

```
candidate gen(Fk-1)
1.  Ck ← ϕ                              // initialises the set of candidates
2.  for all f1, f2∈Fk-1           // traverse all pairs of frequent itemsets
3.  with f1 ={i1, i2, …, ik-2,ik-1}        // differ only in the last item
4.  and f2 ={i1, i2, …, ik-2,ik-1}
5.  and ik-1 < i'k-1do                   // according to the sorted order
6.  c ←{i1,…, ik-1,i'k-1}               // join the two itemsets f1 and f2
7.  Ck ← Ck ∪{c}                  // add the new itemset c to the candidates
8.  For each (k-1)-subset s of c do
9.  If (s ∉Fk-1) then
10. delete c from Ck                      // delete c from the candidates
11. end
12. end
13. return
```

Consider the below example. Table 11.3 represents four transactions of the itemset {A, B, C, D}. The Apriori algorithm determines the frequent itemsets with min. sup. = 50% and min. conf. = 50%.

TABLE 11.3 Demo items

Transactions	*Items*
T_1	{ A, B, C, D}
T_2	{ A, B}
T_3	{ A, B,C }
T_4	{ B, C }

Let us determine the frequency of each item as per the above table.

Frequency of Items

Items	*Support*
A	3
B	4
C	3
D	1

Determine the frequent itemset—F1 after removing items with min. sup. = 50% = 2.

Items	*Support*
A	3
B	4
C	3

Generate the candidate itemsets C2 – *F*1 X *F*1.

Items	*Support*
A, B	3
A, C	2
B, C	3

Here, there is no itemset with min. sup. = 50% = 2 hence go on to generate the new candidate Itemsets.

Items	*Support*
A, B, C	2

After this, it cannot further process. Hence, the frequent itemset is {A, B, C} for the given Table 11.3.

Implementation of Corpus Using `apriori ()` *function of the "arules" Package*

In the example below, the `apriori()` function of the "arules" package takes the matrix "mt" (created in above examples) of the corpus "Dc" with support 0.98 and returns an object. This object is used for finding the different correlation values in the further section.

11.13.2 Generating Association Rules from Frequent Itemsets

After generating the frequent itemsets from the transactions in a database, it is time to generate all confidence association rules from the frequent itemsets, where a confident association rule is a rule with confidence greater than minconf. This step is an optional step as for many application frequent itemsets are sufficient and does not require generating the association rules.

The following formula is used to generate the rules for every frequent itemset f that contains subsets and for each subset α:

$$(f - \alpha) \rightarrow \alpha \text{ if confidence} = (f.\text{count}/(f - \alpha).\text{count}) \geq \text{minconf}$$

Where,

$$(f.\text{count}/(f - \alpha).\text{count}) = \text{support count of } f((f - \alpha))$$

f.count / n = support of the rule where n = number of transactions in the transaction set

This method is complex, hence an efficient algorithm and procedure is used that generates the rules. Given below is the pseudocode of the algorithm with one item in the consequent (subset of α):

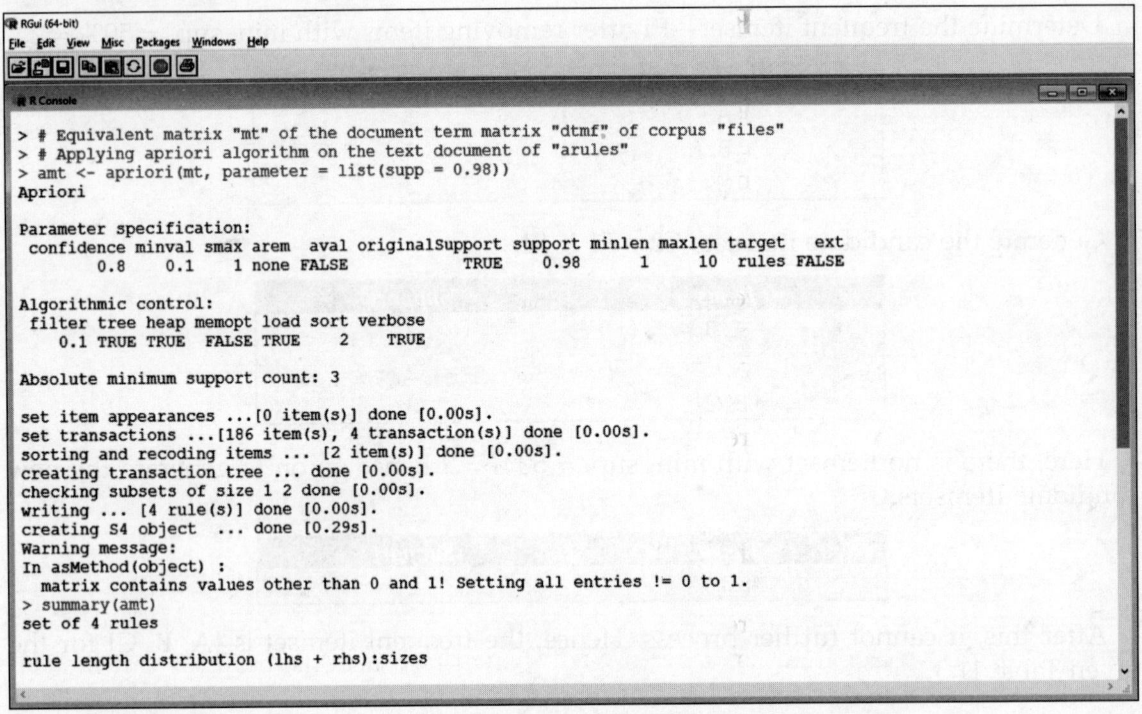

FIGURE 11.16 *Implementation of the Apriori algorithm on text documents (Corpus)*

```
genRules(F)     // F = set of all frequent itemsets
1. for each frequent =itemset fk in F, k≥ 2 do
2. output every 1.item consequent rule of fk with confidence ≥ minconf and
   Support ← fk.count / n
3. H1 ←  {consequents of all 1-item consequent rules derived from fk
   above}
4. ap-genRules(fk, H1)
5. end
```

The pseudocode of the ap-genRules(f_k, H_m) procedure is as follows:

```
ap-genRules(fk, Hm)                    // Hm = set of m-item consequents
1. if (k > m+1) AND (Hm≠ϕ ) then
2.  Hm+1 ← candidate-gen(Hm)
3.  for each hm+1 in Hm+1 do
4.  conf ← fk.count / (fk - hm+1).count
5.  if (conf ≥ minconf) then
6.  output the rule (f - hm+1) →hm+1 with confidence = conf and
support = fk.count /n
7.  else
8.  delete hm+1
9.  end
10. ap-genRules(fk, Hm)
11. end
```

11.13.3 Improving the Efficiency of Apriori

Several variations are proposed that could improve the efficiency of Apriori-based mining. Hash-based techniques, transaction reduction partitioning, sampling, and dynamic itemset counting are some methods to improve the efficiency of Apriori. Here is a brief introduction to each of these methods.

Hash-based Techniques

Hash-based techniques reduce the size of the candidate k itemset C_k for $k > 1$. A hash technique uses key-value concept. Hence, it can be applied to the candidate itemsets. For example, during scanning each transaction in the database for generating the frequent 1-itemsets [F_1] from the candidate 1-itemsets in C_1, the user can generate all hash table structure and increase the corresponding bucket counts.

Transaction Reduction

Transaction reduction method reduces the number of transactions during scanning in further iterations. For example, if a transaction does not contain any frequent k itemsets, then it cannot contain any frequent $(k+1)$ itemsets. Hence, such transactions can be removed from further iterations. By removing such transactions, the user can increase the efficiency of the Apriori.

Partitioning

Partitioning method partitions the data for finding candidate itemsets. For this, it uses two phases. It can be applied where two database scan needs to generate the frequent itemsets. The two phases are as follows:

1. In phase 1, it subdivides the transactions of the dataset D into n non-overlapping partitions. For each partition, local frequent itemsets are found by means of all frequent itemsets within that partition. It is repeated for every partition. The transaction ID of the transactions for each itemset is recorded into a special data structure. It easily finds out the local frequent k itemsets for $k = 1, 2 \ldots$ in one scan of the database.
2. In phase 2, a second scan of the database D is completed in which the actual support of each candidate is assessed for finding the global frequent itemsets.

Sampling

Sampling method generates a random sample and mines on a subset of a given dataset. It searches the frequent itemsets in the subset instead of the whole database. The user is required to select a sample size that fits into the main memory so frequent itemsets get in one scan of the transactions. Sometimes, it uses a lower support threshold than minimum support for finding frequent itemsets to avoid the problem of missing the global frequent itemsets.

Dynamic Itemset Counting

Dynamic itemset counting method adds the candidate itemsets at different points during a scan. It is suitable for the database where it is partitioned into blocks using some start points. These start points help in adding the new candidate itemsets.

11.13.4 A Pattern-growth Approach for Mining Frequent Itemsets

The Apriori algorithm has many advantages and a few drawbacks as well. The Apriori algorithm needs to generate a large number of candidate sets and repeatedly scan the database to check the candidates for pattern matching. Sometimes, this process becomes very complex and time-consuming particularly when there is a need to find a frequent pattern of size 100. Hence, to overcome this problem, another method is introduced for mining the frequent itemsets that does not use candidate generation. This method is called the frequent-pattern growth or FP tree.

Frequent pattern growth follows a divide-and-conquer technique that first compresses the database, representing the frequent items into a frequent-pattern tree that retains the itemset association information. After this, it divides the compressed database into a set of conditional databases where each database is associated with one frequent item or pattern fragment and then it mines each such database separately.

The method transforms from finding the long frequent patterns to searching the shorter patterns recursively and concatenating the suffix. Least frequent items are used as suffix. The method reduces the search costs but for larger databases, it does not produce a realistic answer. It is an efficient method for mining the long and short frequent patterns.

The FP growth algorithm mines the frequent itemsets using an FP-tree by pattern fragment growth. It takes the transaction database and the minimum support count threshold as input and generates the complete set of frequent patterns as an output. The algorithm follows the following steps:

1. Scan the transaction database once and collect the set of frequent items *F* and their support counts. For this, sort *F* in descending order of support count as the list of frequent items *L*.
2. Now create the root of an FP-tree and label it as "null". Now for each transaction Trans in *D* do the following:

   Select and sort the frequent items in Trans according to the order of *L*. Let the sorted frequent item list in Trans be [p | P] where p is the first element and P is the remaining list.

   Call insert_tree ([p | P], T) which is performed as follows: if *T* has a child *N* such that N.item-name = p.item-name then increment N's count by 1 else create a new node *N* and let its count be 1, its parent link be linked to *T* and its node-link to the nodes with the same item-name via the node-link structure. If *P* is nonempty, call insert_tree(P, N) recursively.

3. Now call procedure FP-growth (Tree, null) for mining the FP tree.

```
Procedure: FP-growth(Tree,α)
1. if Tree contains a single path P then
2. for each combination(β)of the nodes in the path P
3. generate pattern β U α with support count = minimum support
   of nodes in β.
4. else for each  aᵢ in the header of Tree {
5. generate pattern β = aᵢ U α with support count = aᵢ.support
   count;
6. construct β's conditional pattern base and then β's condi-
   tional FP_tree Treeβ;
6. if Treeβ≠□
7. call FP_growth(Treeβ, β)
```

11.13.5 Mining Frequent Itemsets Using Vertical Data Format

The Apriori algorithm and the FP-growth method uses a horizontal data format where a set of transactions are stored in the TID-itemset format [TID:itemset]. The vertical data format is another method for mining frequent itemsets, where sets of transactions are stored as items-TID set format [items:TID set]. Here items are the names of the items and TID is a set of transaction identifiers that contains items. The Eclat algorithm uses the vertical data format.

Tables 11.4 and 11.5 represent the horizontal database and the vertical database of Table 11.3 "Demoitems" respectively in the form of binary incidence matrix. A binary incidence matrix uses two values either a one or a zero. In simple words, the matrix uses value 1 for items that are in the particular itemset or transaction and value 0 for items that are not in the particular itemset.

TABLE 11.4 Horizontal database

Transactions	*Items*			
	A	*B*	*C*	*D*
T_1	1	1	1	1
T_2	1	1	0	0
T_3	1	1	1	0
T_4	0	1	1	0

TABLE 11.5 Vertical database

Items	*Transaction ID List*
A	T_1, T_2, T_3
B	T_1, T_2, T_3, T_4
C	T_1, T_3, T_4
D	T_1

The vertical data format transforms the horizontal formatted dataset into a vertical dataset format after scanning for mining the dataset. Here, the support count of an itemset is the length of the transaction ID set of the itemset. It starts with $k = 1$, then uses the frequent k itemsets to construct the candidate $(k+1)$ itemsets. It is repeated with k incremented by 1 each time until no frequent itemsets can be found.

This method efficiently generates the candidate $(k+1)$ itemsets from the frequent k itemsets as compared to the Apriori algorithm with no need to scan the dataset for finding the support $(k+1)$ itemsets. There is only one drawback of the method and that is it takes more memory space and computation time for storing and executing the transaction-id sets.

11.13.6 Mining Closed and Max Patterns

An itemset is a closed pattern if it is frequent and there are no super-patterns with the same support, whereas an itemset is a max pattern if it is frequent and there are no frequent super patterns. Mining such types of patterns is also a critical task as both are sub-patterns of a long pattern. However, it is good to mine a set of closed frequent itemsets instead of a set of all frequent itemsets.

To mine such closed or max frequent itemsets, the simplest method is to first mine the complete set of frequent itemsets and then remove every frequent itemset (subset) that carries the same support or greater support respectively. This method becomes expensive and complex when the lengths of the frequent itemsets are too long.

In such situations, another simple method is to search the closed or max itemsets directly during the mining process. It needs to prune the search space as soon as closed or max itemsets are found. Itemmerging, Sub-itemset pruning, and Itemskipping are few pruning techniques. Here is an introduction to these pruning techniques.

Itemmerging

Itemmerging method merges the frequent itemsets. If every transaction contains a frequent itemset X and another itemset Y but not any proper superset of Y, then $X \cup Y$ will design a frequent closed itemset that does not require searching for any itemset that contains X but no Y.

Sub-itemset Pruning

Sub-itemset pruning technique prunes the sub-itemsets. If a frequent itemset X is a proper subset of an already found frequent closed itemset Y and support count(X) = support count(Y) then X and all of X's descendants in the set enumeration tree cannot be frequent closed itemsets and it is easily pruned.

Item Skipping

Item skipping pruning technique skips the itemsets. If in-depth first mining of closed itemsets is done at each level, there will be a prefix itemset X associated with a header table and a projected database and a local frequent item p that has the same support in several header tables at different levels then it will prune frequent item p from the header tables at higher levels.

Whenever these pruning techniques are applied, it is necessary to check the following conditions:

- A superset checking that checks if the new frequent itemset is a superset of some already found closed itemsets with the same support.
- A subset checking that checks if the new frequent itemset is a subset of an already found closed itemset with the same support.

Check Your Understanding

1. What is Apriori algorithm?

Ans: Apriori algorithm is a seminal algorithm developed by Agarwal and Srikant in 1994 for mining the frequent itemsets.

2. What are hash-based techniques?

Ans: Hash-based techniques reduce the size of the candidate k itemset C_k for $k > 1$. A hash technique uses key-value concept hence it can also be applied to the candidate itemsets.

3. What is dynamic itemset counting?

Ans: Dynamic itemset counting method adds the candidate itemsets at different points during a scan. It is suitable for the database where it is partitioned into blocks using some start points.

4. What pruning techniques are used for mining a closed pattern?

Ans: Itemmerging, sub-itemset pruning, and item skipping, are few pruning techniques used for mining the closed pattern.

11.14 Pattern Evaluation Methods

Association rules mining follows the concept of support-confidence and uses minimum support and confidence threshold. It generates different numbers of the rules. However, sometimes, it does not create an effective output when mining is done with low support threshold or done for long patterns. In this case, strong association rules become uninteresting and misleading for the users. The next section discusses it.

11.14.1 Strong Rules are not Necessarily Interesting

For some application, the support-confidence framework does not give an interesting result or a strong association rule. Unexpectedness, weak and strong belief, and action belief are some subjective measures of the association rules. The support (utility), confidence (certainty), and few others are objective measures of the association rules. Different users judge the rules using some subjective measures where the output of each user differs from the others. However, the objective measures use statistics data that may generate the same output. In this case, it may be true that strong rules are not necessarily interesting and present a misleading rule in front of the user.

For example, consider transactions of items (pen and notebook) and assume nearly 10,000 such transactions are analysed. Further assume that your analysis reveals that 6,000 customer transactions include pens whereas 7,500 customer transactions include notebooks, and 4,000 customer transactions include both. Proceeding with 30% minimum support and 60% minimum confidence, a strong association rule is discovered student(A,"Pen") → student(A, "notebook"). It generates the support 40% and confidence 66% that satisfy the minimum support and confidence. Although it is a strong rule but also a misleading association rule as probability of purchasing notebook is 75% that is far greater than 66%. It means the purchase of the pen and notebook is negatively associated with the purchase of these items and decreases the likelihood of purchasing other items.

After analysing this example, it can be concluded that the confidence of a rule can be deceiving in that it is only an estimate of the conditional probability of itemset Y given itemset X. Since it does not measure the real strength of the rule hence strong rules are not always necessarily interesting.

11.14.2 From Association Analysis to Correlation Analysis

Correlation is another objective measure for finding the association rules in data mining. To improve the efficiency of the support and confidence measures, the correlation measure is augmented to the support-confidence framework for the association rules. The new augmented form of the rule is as follows:

$$X \rightarrow Y \text{ [support, confidence, correlation]}$$

This is a correlation rule that measures support, confidence, and correlation between itemsets X and Y. There are different types of correlation measures that are available and measures the correlation but for pattern evaluation mostly lift, Chi-squared (χ^2), allConfidence, and cosine measures are used. Here is a brief introduction to all the correlation measures as follows:

Lift

Lift is a simple correlation measure where the occurrence of itemset X is independent of the occurrence of itemset Y if $Pr(X \cup Y) = Pr(X)Pr(Y)$ otherwise itemsets X and Y are dependent and correlated events. For the occurrence of itemset X and Y, the following formula calculates the lift.

$$\text{Lift}(X, Y) = \text{Pr}(X \cup Y) \; / \; \text{Pr}(X)\text{Pr}(Y)$$

If the formula generates the output less than 1 then the occurrence of X is negatively correlated with the occurrence of Y. In another case, if it generates the output greater than 1 then the occurrence of X is positively correlated with the occurrence of Y. If it generates the output equal to 1 then X and Y are independent and there is no correlation between them.

Chi-squared

Chi-squared (χ^2) is another correlation measure that takes the squared difference between the observed and expected value and adds it to all slots of the contingency table. The following formula calculates the correlation using χ^2 as follows:

$$\chi^2 = \sum \frac{(\text{observed} - \text{expected})^2}{\text{expected}}$$

all_confidence

The all_confidence is another correlation measure that measures the correlation between the itemsets. For an itemset X, the following formula calculates the all_confidence as follows:

$$\text{all\_confidence}(X) \text{ or all\_conf}(X) = \text{sup}(X)/\text{max\_item\_sup}(X)$$

or

$$\text{all\_conf}(X) = \text{sup}(X)\ /\text{max}\{\ \text{sup}(i_j)\ \mid \text{ for all } i_j \text{ belongs to } X)$$

where,

max{ sup(i_j) | for all i_j belongs to X) is a maximum (single) item support of all the items in X. Due to this, it is called the max_item_sup of the itemset X.

The all_confidence of X is a minimal confidence among the set of rules $i_j \rightarrow X \rightarrow i_j$.

Cosine

Cosine is another horizontal lift measure for finding the correlation between the itemsets. The following formula calculates the cosine measure of two itemset X and Y:

$$\text{cosine}(X, Y) = \frac{\Pr(X \cup Y)}{\sqrt{\Pr\Pr(Y)}}$$

or

$$\text{cosine}(X, Y) = \frac{\text{sup}(X \cup Y)}{\sqrt{\text{sup}(X)\text{sup}(Y)}}$$

11.14.3 A Comparison of Pattern Evaluation Measures

In the above section, you learnt about the different pattern evaluation measures for measuring the performance of the frequency pattern. All four-correlation measures lift,

Chi-squared, allConfidence, and cosine give good output for an independent case. As compared to allConfidence and cosine, lift and Chi-squared give poor output for the associations.

Amongst allConfidence and cosine measures, cosine gives a better result compared to allConfidence as cosine considers the support of both itemsets, whereas allConfidence considers only the maximal support of itemset. Along with this, sometimes a null transaction (that does not contain any items) may also affect the performance of all the measures.

In the example below (Figure 11.17), the `interestMeasure()` function takes the object of `apriori()` and transactions dataset of the corpus "Dc" and returns the values of different correlation measures such as lift, Chi-squared (χ^2), allConfidence, and cosine. Since it is a dummy corpus, hence it does not give appropriate values for the measures. In the previous chapter, this was discussed in detail.

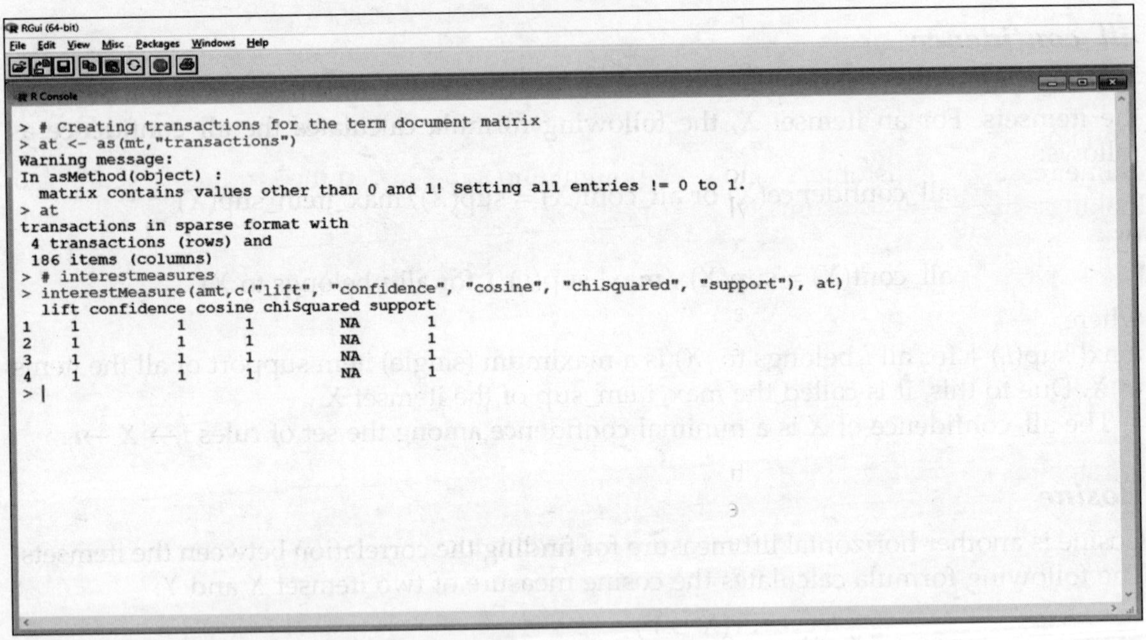

FIGURE 11.17 *Comparison between the pattern evaluation measures*

Check Your Understanding

1. What is correlation?

Ans: Correlation is another objective measure for finding the association rules in data mining.

(Continued)

2. What is the lift?

Ans: Lift is a simple correlation measure where the occurrence of itemset X is independent of the occurrence of itemset Y *if* $Pr(X \cup Y) = Pr(X)Pr(Y)$ otherwise itemsets X and Y are dependent and correlated events.

3. What is Chi-squared ?

Ans: Chi-squared (χ^2) is another correlation measure that takes the squared difference between the observed and expected value and adds it to all slots of the contingency table.

11.15 Sentiment Analysis

Sentiment analysis is also referred to as emotion AI or opinion mining or subjectivity analysis.

Picture this...

You have decided to buy a new cellphone, iPhone 6s Plus. You have been reading a lot of online reviews of customers who have bought and experienced the product. You are also looking at discussion forums where experts are comparing this model of the cellphone with cellphones of similar genre. This is today where more than 80% of the customers research the product before buying, thanks to the World Wide Web. They read the posts from unknown buyers. However, this was not always the case. A decade or two earlier, we checked with our friend, relative and family before buying an expensive product.

11.15.1 What Purpose does Sentiment Analysis Serve?

It helps to comprehend the attitude of a speaker or a writer with respect to some topic. The attitude may be their judgment or evaluation, their affective state (the emotional state of the writer or speaker), their reaction to an event, incident, interaction, document, etc., or the intended emotional communication.

11.15.2 What Does it Use?

It uses the following:

- Text analysis
- Natural language processing
- Computational linguistics
- Biometrics

11.15.3 What is the Input to Sentiment Analysis?

The input to sentiment analysis is the voice of customer data such as survey, blog posts, reviews, tweets, social media, internet discussion groups, online reviews, etc.

11.15.4 How does Sentiment Analysis Work?

- Classifying the polarity of the given text—determine whether the expressed opinion is positive, negative or neutral
- Classifying the given text into one of the two classes—objective, subjective
- Feature/aspect based sentiment

Sentiment = Holder + Target + Polarity

Holder here is the person who expresses the sentiment.
Target is about whom the sentiment/opinion is expressed.
Polarity is the nature of the sentiment: positive, negative or neutral

Example:

The games on iPhone 6s Plus has piqued the interest of the customers
Holder in the above example is the user or the reviewer
Target is iPhone 6s Plus
Polarity is positive

Case Study

Credit Card Spending by Customer Groups can be Identified by using Business Needs

Big data is the collection and cross-referencing of large numbers and varieties of data sets that allows organisations to identify patterns and categories of cardholders through a multitude of attributes and variables.

Every time customers use their cards, big data suggests the products that can be offered to the customers. These days many credit card users receive calls from different companies offering them new credit cards as per their needs and expenses on the existing cards. This information is gathered on the basis of available data provided by vendors.

There are quite a few options available to customers to choose from. Sometimes customers even switch their existing credit card companies. But competition may not always work in the best interests of consumers. It also involves bank's profit. Competition may also be focused on particular features of credit cards that may not represent long-term value or sustainability. Those paying interest on balances may be paying more than they realise or expect. Some consumers use up their credit limits quickly or repeatedly make minimum payments without considering how they will repay their credit card debt. A proportion of consumers may also be over-borrowing and taking on too much debt, and there are signs that some issuers may profit

(Continued)

Case Study

more from higher risk borrowers (by which we mean customers at greater risk of credit default).

With the launch of this credit card market study, we intend to build up a detailed picture of the market and assess the potential identified issues. We plan to focus on credit card services offered to retail consumers by credit card providers, including banks, mono-line issuers and their affinity and co-brand partners.

While mass marketing continues to dominate most retailers' advertising budgets, one-to-one marketing is growing rapidly too. In this case study, you will learn how to improve performance by communicating directly with customers and delighting them with relevant offers. Personalised communication is becoming a norm. Shoppers now expect retailers to provide them with product information and promotional offers that match their needs and desires. They count on you to know their likes, dislikes and preferred communication method—mobile device, email or print media.

On the surface, generating customer-specific offers and communications seems like an unnerving task for many retailers, but like many business problems, when broken into manageable pieces, each process step or analytical procedure is attainable. First, let's assume you have assembled promotions that you intend to extend as a group of offers (commonly called "offer bank") to individual customers. Each offer should have a business goal or objective, such as:

- Category void for cross or up-selling of a particular product or product group
- Basket builder to increase the customer's basket size
- Trip builder to create an additional trip or visit to the store or an additional e-commerce session
- Reward to offer an incentive to loyal customers

Summary

- Text mining extracts useful information from unstructured data.
- In unstructured data, information does not have any form obtained from natural language. For example, comments used on Facebook, tweets in Twitter, opinions or reviews of any products or services are examples of unstructured data.
- Sequential operations of the text mining process include text pre-processing, feature generation, feature selection, text/data mining and analysing results.
- A document collection is a group of text-based documents and a major element of text mining. A document collection can contain from thousands to tens of millions of documents.
- A static document collection is a document collection where initial complement of documents remains unchanged.

(Continued)

- A dynamic document collection is a document collection where documents change or are updated over time.
- A document is a group of discrete textual data within a collection and another major element of text mining. The business report, e-mail, legal memorandum, research paper, press release, manuscript are few examples of the document.
- A freeformat or weakly structured document is a type of document that follows some typography, layout, and makeup indicators. For example, research paper, press release are examples of freeformat document.
- A semi-structured document is a type of document that uses field-type metadata. For example, HTML web pages, email, etc.
- The characters, words, terms, and concepts are some common features of the document.
- A term is a document feature that defines single words or multiword phrases in the document.
- A term is a document feature that is generated through manual statistical method, rule-based, or hybrid categorisation methods.
- A domain is a specialised area of interest for which ontologies, taxonomies, and lexicons are developed.
- Domain includes the broad areas of the subject matters such as finance, international law, biology, material science and the knowledge used in these domains is called domain knowledge.
- The background knowledge is an extension of the domain knowledge. It is used in the pre-processing operation of the text mining system.
- R language provides a package "tm" that provides a framework for text mining application within R. The main framework or structure for managing the documents in the R language is Corpus.
- A Corpus represents a collection of text documents in R. It is an abstract concept but several different implementations exist.
- The VCorpus (Volatile Corpus) creates a volatile corpora meaning when the R object is destroyed then whole corpus is gone.
- The package "tm" provides the functions `TermDocumentMatrix()` and `DocumentTermMatrix()` that creates a term-document matrix and document-term matrix from a corpus respectively.
- A text mining system takes documents as an input and generates the patterns, associations, trends as an output.
- Pre-processing tasks, core mining operations, presentation layer components and browsing functionality, and refinement techniques are the four major tasks of the text mining system.
- Pre-processing tasks converts the raw text or information collected from different data sources into a canonical format.
- Refinement techniques filter the redundant information and concept from the given input text document to generate a well-optimised output. Suppression, ordering, clustering, pruning, classification are few popular refinement techniques used in the text mining system.
- The function `tm_map()` of the package "tm" performs the transformation on the corpus by modifying the documents.
- The distribution (proportions), frequent and near frequent sets, and associations are the three main core text-mining operations.
- The distribution operation creates meaningful subdivisions on a single document collection for comparison purpose; it is also called the concept selection.
- A frequent concept set is a set of concepts represented in the document collection with co-occurrences at or above a minimal support level.

(Continued)

- The package "tm" provides a function `findFreqTerms()` that finds out the frequent terms in a document-term or term-document matrix.
- In terms of text documents, an association defines the relationship or association between two or more terms. For example, in a text file if two terms such as "text" and "mining" occur together more than once then there is a strong association between those two terms.
- The package "tm" provides a function `findAssocs()` that determines the associations between two or more terms in a document-term or term-document matrix.
- The constraints, attribute relationship rules, and hierarchical trees are three main forms of the background knowledge.
- The KDTL (Knowledge Discovery in Text Language) is one of the text mining query language developed in 1996.
- A frequent pattern is a type of pattern that frequently occurs in a data set. These patterns can be any itemsets, subsequences, or substructures.
- Market basket analysis, catalogue design, web log analysis, cross-marketing, sales campaign analysis, and DNA sequence analysis are few applications of the frequent patterns.
- Market basket analysis is a common and classic example of frequent itemset mining. The main objective is to determine the associations and correlations among a set of items.
- The occurrence frequency is the number of transactions in the itemset. It is also called frequency, count, support count, or absolute support of an itemset.
- An association rule correlates the presence of one set of items with another set of items.
- Support is a metric that measures the usefulness of an association rule using the minimum support threshold.
- Confidence is a metric that measures the certainty of an association rule by using threshold.
- A frequent itemset contains items that often occur together and are associated with each other. In a frequent itemset, the support of that itemset is greater than the minimum support threshold.
- An itemset is a closed frequent itemset in a dataset if it is closed and frequent.
- The Apriori algorithm is a seminal algorithm developed by Agarwal and Srikant in 1994 for mining the frequent itemsets.
- Hash-based techniques, transaction reduction partitioning, sampling, and dynamic itemset counting are few methods to improve the efficiency of the Apriori algorithm.
- Hash-based techniques reduce the size of the candidate *k* itemset C_k for $k > 1$. A hash technique uses key-value concept hence it can also apply to the candidate itemsets.
- Transaction reduction method reduces the number of transactions during scanning in further iterations.
- Partitioning method partitions the data for finding candidates itemsets. For this, it uses two phases and it can be applied where two database scan needs to generate the frequent itemsets.
- Sampling method generates a random sample and mines on a subset of a given dataset. It searches the frequent itemsets in the subset instead of the whole database.
- Dynamic itemset counting method adds the candidate itemsets at different points during a scan. It is suitable for a database that is partitioned into blocks by using some start points.
- FP-growth follows a divide-and-conquer technique for mining frequent itemsets.
- The vertical data format is another method for mining the frequent itemsets, where a set of transactions are stored as items-TID set format [items:TID set].
- Itemmerging, Sub-itemset pruning, and Item skipping are few pruning techniques used for mining closed patterns.

(Continued)

- Correlation is another objective measure for finding the association rules in data mining.
- Lift is a simple correlation measure, where the occurrence of itemset *X* is independent of the occurrence of itemset *Y* if $Pr(X \cup Y) = Pr(X)Pr(Y)$ otherwise itemsets *X* and *Y* are dependent and correlated events.
- Chi-squared (χ^2) is another correlation measure that takes the squared difference between the observed and expected value and adds it to all slots of the contingency table.

Key Terms

- **Apriori algorithm:** The Apriori algorithm is a seminal algorithm developed by Agarwal and Srikant in 1994 for mining frequent itemsets.
- **Chi-squared:** Chi-squared (χ^2) is another correlation measure that takes the squared difference between the observed and expected value and adds it to all slots of the contingency table.
- **Confidence:** Confidence is a metric that measures the certainty of an association rule by using threshold.
- **Corpus:** Corpus represents a collection of text documents in R. It is an abstract concept. However, there are different implementations.
- **Correlation:** Correlation is another objective measure for finding the association rules in data mining.
- **Document:** A document is a group of discrete textual data within a document collection.
- **Document collection:** A document collection is a group of text-based documents.
- **Domain:** A domain is a specialised area of interest for which ontologies, taxonomies, and lexicons are developed.
- **FP-growth:** The FP-growth follows a divide-and-conquer technique for mining frequent itemsets.
- **Frequent concept set:** A frequent concept set is a set of concepts represented in the document collection with co-occurrences at or above a minimal support level.
- **Frequent pattern:** A frequent pattern is a type of pattern that frequently occurs in a data set.
- **KDTL:** The KDTL (Knowledge Discovery in Text Language) is one of the text mining query languages developed in 1996.
- **Lift:** Lift is a simple correlation measure where the occurrence of itemset *X* is independent of the occurrence of itemset *Y* if $Pr(X \cup Y) = Pr(X)Pr(Y)$.
- **Market basket analysis:** Market basket analysis is a common and classic example of frequent itemset mining.
- **Occurrence frequency:** The occurrence frequency is the number of transactions in an itemset.
- **Support:** Support is a metric that measures the usefulness of an association rule by using the minimum support threshold.
- **tm:** R language provides a package "tm" that provides a framework for text mining application within R.
- **Term:** A term is a document feature that defines single words or multiword phrases in the document.
- **Text mining:** Text mining extracts useful information from unstructured data.
- **Unstructured data:** In unstructured data, information does not have any form obtained from natural language.
- **VCorpus:** VCorpus (Volatile Corpus) creates a volatile corpora i.e., when the R object is destroyed, then the whole corpus is lost.
- **Vertical data format:** The vertical data format is another method for mining frequent itemsets, where a set of transactions are stored as items-TID set format [items:TID set].

Multiple Choice Questions

1. From the given options, which of the following is an example of weakly structured document?
   (a) E-mail (b) Research paper
   (c) HTML web page (d) Message
2. From the given options, which of the following is an example of semi-structured document?
   (a) E-mail (b) Research paper
   (c) Press-release (d) Report
3. From the given options, which of the following is not a feature of a document?
   (a) Document collection (b) Term
   (c) Concept (d) Word
4. From the given options, which of the following represents a collection of text documents in R?
   (a) Document collection (b) Corpus
   (c) File (d) Document features
5. From the given options, which of the following functions returns the number of documents of the corpus?
   (a) `Docs()` (b) `nTerms()`
   (c) `Terms()` (d) `DocumentTermMatrix`
6. From the given options, which of the following functions returns the number of terms of the corpus?
   (a) `Docs()` (b) `nTerms()`
   (c) `Terms()` (d) `DocumentTermMatrix`
7. From the given options, which of the following functions returns the terms of the corpus?
   (a) `Docs()` (b) `nTerms()`
   (c) `Terms()` (d) `DocumentTermMatrix`
8. From the given options, which of the following functions creates the document term matrix of the corpus?
   (a) `Docs()` (b) `nTerms()`
   (c) `Terms()` (d) `DocumentTermMatrix`
9. From the given options, which of the following functions finds the frequent terms of corpus in R?
   (a) `nTerms()` (b) `tm_map()`
   (c) `findFreqTerms()` (d) `findAssocs()`
10. From the given options, which of the following functions finds an association between terms of corpus in R?
    (a) `nTerms()` (b) `tm_map()`
    (c) `findFreqTerms()` (d) `findAssocs()`

11. From the given options, which of the following functions performs pre-processing of text documents of the corpus in R?
    (a) `nTerms()` (b) `tm_map()`
    (c) `findFreqTerms()` (d) `findAssocs()`
12. From the given options, which of the following functions removes white spaces of a text document of the corpus in R?
    (a) `nTerms()` (b) `tm_map()`
    (c) `stemDocument ()` (d) `stripWhitespace()`
13. From the given options, which of the following functions contains the parameter "terms"?
    (a) `nTerms()` (b) `findAssocs()`
    (c) `findFreqTerms()` (d) `tm_map()`
14. From the given options, which of the following methods improves the efficiency of the Apriori algorithm?
    (a) Transaction reduction (b) Itemmerging
    (c) Item skipping (d) Sub-itemset pruning
15. From the given options, which of the following pruning techniques is used during mining of closed pattern?
    (a) Item skipping (b) dynamic itemset counting
    (c) Item generation (d) Sampling
16. In which year was the Apriori algorithm developed?
    (a) 1996 (b) 1994
    (c) 1995 (d) 1997
17. In which year was the KDTL text mining query language developed?
    (a) 1996 (b) 1994
    (c) 1995 (d) 1997
18. From the given options, which of the following is not a core text mining operation?
    (a) Distribution (b) Frequent and near frequent sets
    (c) Associations (d) Refinement techniques
19. From the given options, which of the following is not a component of the text mining system?
    (a) Presentation layer components (b) Text document query language
    (c) Core text mining operations (d) Pre-processing task
20. From the given options, which of the following document features defines single words or multiword phrases in a document?
    (a) Characters (b) Terms
    (c) Words (d) Concept

Long Questions

1. What is text mining? Explain with its applications.
2. Explain the sequential process of the text mining process.
3. Define document collection, document, and document features.
4. Define Corpus and VCorpus.
5. Explain the `TermDocumentMatrix()` function with syntax and an example.
6. Explain the `DocumentTermMatrix()` function with syntax and an example.
7. Explain the `tm_map()` function with syntax and an example.
8. Explain the `findFreqTerms()` function with syntax and an example.
9. Explain the `findAssocs()` function with syntax and an example.
10. Write a note on the market basket analysis.
11. Explain the methods used to improve efficiency of the Apriori algorithm.
12. Explain the FP-Growth method.
13. What are the types of pruning techniques used for mining closed patterns?
14. Create a corpus from some documents and create its document term matrix.
15. Create a corpus from some documents and perform the pre-processing operations on it.
16. Create a corpus from some documents and create its matrix and transactions. Also, find out the different correlation measures.

Practical Exercises

1. Create a text file, "EnglishText.txt" in "D:/tm2" folder and copy the below lines into it:

   Excerpts from Martin Luther King's I have a dream speech August 28 1963

   This will be the day when all of God's children will be able to sing with new meaning, "My country 'tis of thee, sweet land of liberty, of thee I sing. Land where my fathers died, land of the Pilgrims' pride, from every mountainside, let freedom ring."

   And if America is to be a great nation, this must become true. So let freedom ring from the prodigious hilltops of New Hampshire. Let freedom ring from the mighty mountains of New York. Let freedom ring from the heightening Alleghenies of Pennsylvania.

   Let freedom ring from the snow-capped Rockies of Colorado. Let freedom ring from the curvaceous slopes of California. But not only that; let freedom ring from the Stone Mountain of Georgia. Let freedom ring from Lookout Mountain of Tennessee.

Let freedom ring from every hill and molehill of Mississippi. From every mountainside, let freedom ring.

And when this happens, and when we allow freedom ring, when we let it ring from every village and every hamlet, from every state and every city, we will be able to speed up that day when all of God's children, black men and white men, Jews and gentiles, Protestants and Catholics, will be able to join hands and sing in the words of the old Negro spiritual, "Free at last! Free at last! Thank God Almighty, we are free at last!"

Create a corpus and use transformation functions to remove punctuation marks, stopwords, whitespaces, numbers, etc., from the extract.

Solution:

Step 1: Create a file, "EnglishText.txt" in the folder "tm2" in the "D:" drive.

```
> fname <- file.path("D:", "tm2")
> fname
[1] "D:/tm2"
```

Step 2: Create a corpus, "corpus"

```
> corpus <- Corpus(DirSource(fname))
> inspect(corpus)
<<SimpleCorpus>>
Metadata:  corpus specific: 1, document level (indexed): 0
Content:  documents: 1

Excerpts from Martin Luther King's I have a dream speech August
28 1963\nThis will be the day when all of God's children will be
able to sing with new meaning, "My co$
```

Step 3: Remove punctuation marks from the corpus. The same is evident from inspecting the corpus, "corpus".

```
> corpus <- tm_map(corpus, removePunctuation)
> inspect(corpus)
<<SimpleCorpus>>
Metadata:  corpus specific: 1, document level (indexed): 0
Content:  documents: 1

Excerpts from Martin Luther Kings I have a dream speech August
28 1963\nThis will be the day when all of Gods children will be
able to sing with new meaning My countr$
```

Step 4: Remove numbers from the corpus. The same is evident from inspecting the corpus, "corpus".

```
> corpus <- tm_map(corpus, removeNumbers)
> inspect(corpus)
<<SimpleCorpus>>
```

```
Metadata:  corpus specific: 1, document level (indexed): 0
Content:  documents: 1

Excerpts from Martin Luther King I have a dream speech August \
nThis will be the day when all of Gods children will be able to
sing with new meaning My country tis$
```

Step 5: Remove stopwords from the corpus. The same is evident from inspecting the corpus, "corpus".

```
> corpus <- tm_map(corpus, removeWords, stopwords('English'))
> inspect(corpus)
<<SimpleCorpus>>
Metadata:  corpus specific: 1, document level (indexed): 0
Content:  documents: 1

Excerpts  Martin Luther King I  dream speech August This will
day  Gods children will  able  sing  new meaning My country tis
thee sweet land  liberty  thee I $
```

2. Create a document term matrix of the above corpus and find the frequent terms between frequencies 5 and 15.

Solution:

Step 1: Create a document term matrix, "dtm" from the corpus, "corpus".

```
> dtm <- DocumentTermMatrix(corpus)
```

Step 2: Determine the terms that have frequency in the range of 5 to 15.

```
> findFreqTerms(dtm, lowfreq=5, highfreq=15)
[1]  "every"  "freedom"  "let"    "ring"
```

Step 3: Determine the terms that have a frequency of 10.

```
> findFreqTerms(dtm, lowfreq=10)
[1]  "freedom"  "let"    "ring"
```

Step 4: Determine the terms that have a frequency of 1.

```
> findFreqTerms(dtm, lowfreq=1)
 [1] "able" "alleghenies" "allow" "almighty" "america" "and"
     "august" "become" "black" "but"
[11] "california" "catholics" "children" "city" "colorado"
     "country" "curvaceous" "day" "died" "dream"
[21] "every" "excerpts" "fathers" "free" "freedom" "from" "gen-
     tiles" "georgia" "god" "gods"
[31] "great" "hamlet" "hampshire" "hands" "happens" "heighten-
     ing" "hill" "hilltops" "jews" "join"
[41] "kings" "land" "last" "let" "liberty" "lookout" "luther"
     "martin" "meaning" "men"
```

```
[51] "mighty" "missisippi" "molehill" "mountain" "mountains"
     "mountainside" "must" "nation" "negro" "new"
[61] "old" "pennsylvania" "pilgrims" "pride" "prodigious" "prot-
     estants" "ring" "rockies" "sing" "slopes"
[71] "snowcapped" "speech" "speed" "spiritual" "state" "stone"
     "sweet" "tennessee" "thank" "thee"
[81] "this" "tis" "true" "village" "white" "will" "words" "york"
```

Answers to MCQs:

1. (b)	2. (a)	3. (a)	4. (b)	5. (a)	6. (b)	7. (c)
8. (d)	9. (c)	10. (d)	11. (b)	12. (d)	13. (b)	14. (a)
15. (a)	16. (b)	17. (a)	18. (d)	19. (b)	20. (b)	

Chapter 12

Parallel Computing with R

LEARNING OUTCOME

At the end of this chapter, you will be able to:

- Perform parallel computing in R using the 'doParallel' and 'foreach' package
- Use the '`benchmark()`' function to compare the performance of single and parallel execution of the foreach loop

12.1 Introduction

Parallel computing is the simultaneous use of multiple compute resources for solving any complex problem. Parallel computing refers to the division of a problem into discrete parts where each part further gets divided into a series of instructions. All these parts and their respective instructions run concurrently on different processors. Due to this simultaneous execution of different instructions, parallel computing is used to simulate, model and solve complex and real world problems (Figure 12.1).

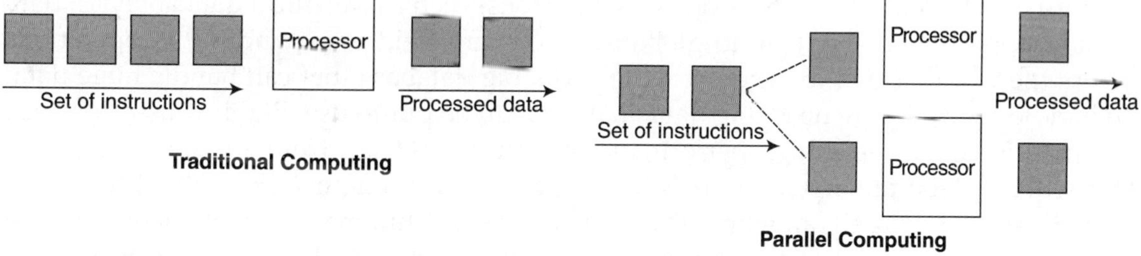

Figure 12.1 *Traditional vs. parallel computing*

Parallel computing is best used in image modelling of different situations like weather, galaxy formation, climate change and so on. Every field, including science, engineering, business industries and others are using parallel computing for solving their complex problems. It saves time and increases the performance of their working. The field of big data, data mining and databases also use parallel computing.

Parallel computing uses different hardware tools and software concepts for concurrent execution. The hardware tools include multi-processors and multi-core computers (distributed computers) containing multiple processing elements within a single machine. This multi-core computer can be homogeneous or heterogeneous. The software concepts include Shared memory, Pthreads, Open Multi-Processing (OpenMP), Message Passing Interface (MPI), Distributed memory, and Parallel Virtual Machine (PVM).

R language is a free and open-source software language with multiple packages that support statistical computing with graphics features. R is also a highly productive language as it provides domain-specific packages with high-level expressiveness features. R language has packages that support parallel computing. In the next subsection, you will learn about parallel computing with R.

12.2 Introduction of R Tool Libraries

R language provides different packages for parallel computation. R packages have a special property of high reusability. These features are used in high-performance computing. Different repositories provide packages for parallel computing. The Comprehensive R Archive Network (CRAN) is one of the repositories of R that defines different packages group-wise for high-performance computing in their task view. Users can use the weblink for checking a list of packages available for parallel computing within R. https://cran.r-project.org/web/views/HighPerformanceComputing.html

Since different methodologies are used to implement parallel computing, R language also divides their available packages of parallel computing into some groups. Each group contains many packages to implement parallel computing. Table 12.1 highlights the different packages of each group.

12.2.1 Motivation of Empowering R with HPC

R language efficiently executes small computations, such as statistical data analysis, data mining applications, etc. Due to globalisation, every field is expanding its operations across the world. This expansion would need a big database that can handle huge data. To handle such a future need, big data analytics can be put to use. Big data uses complex computations to achieve high-performance computing (HPC). Here are some highlights that will help you understand why R language should be empowered with HPC.

- R is a script-based language. The analysis-based solutions do not efficiently handle large-scale computation. These solutions can be calculated in a few hours or days.

TABLE 12.1 R packages associated with high performance computing

Parallel Computing Concept	*Related Packages*
Explicit Parallelism (the programmer is responsible for (almost) every aspect of the parallelization problem such as partitioning the program into processes, mapping of these processes onto the processors and their synchronization	Rmpi Snow pdbMPI snowfall foreach
Implicit Parallelism (Wherein the compiler or interpreter can recognize opportunities for parallelization and implement them without being told to do so	pnmath romp Rdsm Rhpc
Grid Computing (Is a computer network where in each computer's resources (processing power, memory, and data storage) is shared with every other computer in the system. Authorized users can leverage the same for their requirements)	multiR
Random Numbers	rlecuyer doRNG
Hadoop	RHIPE rmr toaster

If the size of data increases, the execution time also increases. Complexity involved in the computation of big data motivates developers to provide features or packages that can perform HPC.

- Sometimes R language abruptly stops the current execution of data that contains a lot of information. This happens due to insufficient computational resources like system memory. This is another reason why R is developed with HPC.
- Although R language comes with a high-level expressiveness feature, it is still unable to perform the fine-grained control that provides a high-level coding development environment.
- The runtime environment efficiently implements coding and simplifies coding development. To simplify the process, additional time and resources are required to do the computation. Hence, to reduce the time and utilisation effort, developers develop HPC with R.
- The design of the R framework is inspired from the 90s and it uses a single thread execution mode. Due to this, R language specification and implementation cannot utilise the modern computer infrastructure like parallel coprocessors, multiple cores, or multi-node computing clusters. Hence, it is necessary to enable R language with HPC.

The main aim to empower R with HPC is to scale up the processing of the R language so that it efficiently implements the parallelism and reduces the computation time.

Check Your Understanding

1. What do you understand by parallel computing?

Ans: Parallel computing is a type of computing that uses more than one resource for solving any complex problem. It refers to the division of a problem into discrete parts where each part further gets divided into a series of instructions.

2. What are the types of software concepts used in parallel computing?

Ans: The software concepts include Shared memory, Pthreads, Open Multi-Processing (OpenMP), Message Passing Interface (MPI), Distributed memory, and Parallel Virtual Machine (PVM).

3. What is the need to empower R language with high-performance computing (HPC)?

Ans: The main motivations to empower R language with high-performance computing are as follows:

- No efficient packages available to address the computation complexity of big data.
- Insufficient computational resources.
- The design and implementation of R language.
- To reduce the time and efficient utilisation of resources.
- Unable to utilise the modern computer infrastructure like parallel coprocessors.

12.3 Opportunities in HPC to Empower R

At present, there are many methods available in HPC that can easily empower R. It is possible due to continuous development in the parallel, distributed, grid, or cloud computing technologies. In addition, increasing computation demand is also forcing to develop new technologies. An effective utilisation of these technologies in R can also give high-performance computing in business analytics.

R language uses the available parallel computing technologies. In the following subsections, you will learn about parallel computation within a single node and multiple nodes.

12.3.1 Parallel Computation within a Single Node

When multiple processing units, including hosts CPUs, threads, or other units, are simultaneously executed within a single computer system, then this single computer system becomes a single node. The single node parallelism is executed within a single computer. In a single computer, multiple processing units like host CPUs, processing cores, or co-processing cards share memory to implement the single node parallelism. To implement parallel processing within a single node, two methods are available namely:

- Increase the number of CPUs within a node
- Use the add-on processing devices

Out of the two methods, developers prefer the first method. Developers host multiple identical CPUs with the help of additional sockets in a single node. There are multiple processing cores or components that read and execute instructions within each CPU of a single node. In addition, all these multiple processing cores are independent of each other. A normal commercial computer has 8 to 16 cores. A single node can extend up to 72 processing cores according to the capability of multiple CPUs.

The second method uses add-on processing devices like an accelerator card to implement parallel processing within a single node. These accelerator card coprocessors contain many cores that run with lower frequency to provide high performance per chip. These cards are also available in on-board memory units and processing units and they can directly access data from this on-board memory. For example, GPGPU (general-purpose computing on graphics processing units) is one of the graphics card used as an add-on processing device. This card performs parallel processing on the graphic processing units using vector computations.

12.3.2 Multi-node Parallelism Support

Single-node parallelism is easy to implement with a low cost; however, it has limited use in research analysis work. To overcome such limitations, multi-node parallelism has been developed. The multi-node parallelism uses more than one computer system, called a cluster, to implement parallel processing. Just like single-node parallelism, there are two methods in multi-node parallelism as well.

- Use the traditional high-performance computing clusters
- Use MapReduce programming paradigm

Message Passing Interface

The first method uses traditional high-performance computing clusters to implement parallel processing. Here, a cluster is a group of interconnected computers that shares the available resources. This individual single computer, also called node, has its own memory. In these clusters, all the nodes are connected through more than one high-performance switches. These switches provide high-performance communication between two nodes. For establishing this communication, the most-widely used method is *message passing interface*.

Message passing interface is a portable message-passing system that works on different types of parallel computers. The system provides an environment where programs run parallel and communicate with each other by passing messages. MPI also follows the concept of master-slave or client-server system, where master system controls the cluster and slave system performs computation and responds to the requests of the master.

MPI also provides library routines that contain the syntax and semantics to design and implement the message passing programs in various computer programming languages, such as C, C++, Java, and others. The MPI interface comes with many features, such as synchronisation, virtual topology, language-specific syntax, and communication functionality between a set of processes that are mapped to other nodes. For performing parallel computing, MPI sends codes to multiple processors. The current computers or laptops have multiple cores that share memory. Each core uses the shared memory.

To implement MPI on a system, some message-passing programs are required. These programs are called 'mpirun/mpiexec' that work with the processes (tasks) and every core is assigned to a single process. These cores obtain maximum performance using the agents that start the MPI programs. MPICH2 and OpenMPI are some examples of open source implementation of the MPI. OpenMPI is one of the open source MPI programs. It is used for the distributed memory model implementation. It is possible to execute multiple threads on a single core computer using these programs.

MapReduce Programming Paradigm

The MapReduce programming paradigm is a new programming paradigm developed by Google. This programming paradigm is specially designed for parallel distributed processing of a large set of data to divide it into small regular-sized data. Parallel or distributed processing system is a powerful framework that uses distributed processing to process any large data.

This paradigm collects and stores data from different distributed nodes and performs computation on each local node. After computation on each local node, the collected output is transferred. In simple words, it converts a large dataset into a set of tuples, and combines and reduces these tuples into a smaller set of tuples. In MapReduce, these tuples are known as key-value pairs that are collected, sorted, and processed. The MapReduce framework operates on these key-value pairs.

Due to the small size of tuples, it efficiently handles any big data and scales the data over multiple nodes. This scaling feature can scale an application to execute over thousands of machines in a cluster. Due to this scalability feature, the MapReduce paradigm has become popular for big data analytics. Hadoop and Spark are few examples of implementation of MapReduce programming. Section 12.3.3 explains the MapReduce paradigm in Hadoop.

MapReduce Algorithm

Map and Reduce are two main steps in MapReduce programming performed by a mapper and reducer respectively. The map process views the input as a set of key-value pair and the process produces a set of key-value pairs as an output. You will learn about each step of the MapReduce algorithm in the subsection that follows.

Map process In this step, the master node of the distributed system takes the input data that is delegated into key-value pairs and divides it into fragments that are assigned to map tasks. Now, each computing cluster of the system is assigned to a number of map tasks. These clusters distribute these map tasks among their nodes. Some intermediate key-value pairs are also generated during the key-value pairs processing. According to their key-values, these intermediate key-value pairs are sorted. After this, it is further divided into a set of fragments.

In Figure 12.2, the input pairs are divided into different fragments. The `map()` function of the map process assigns a single map task to each single input pair that generates an output fragment. In simple words, the `map()` function generates a new output list.

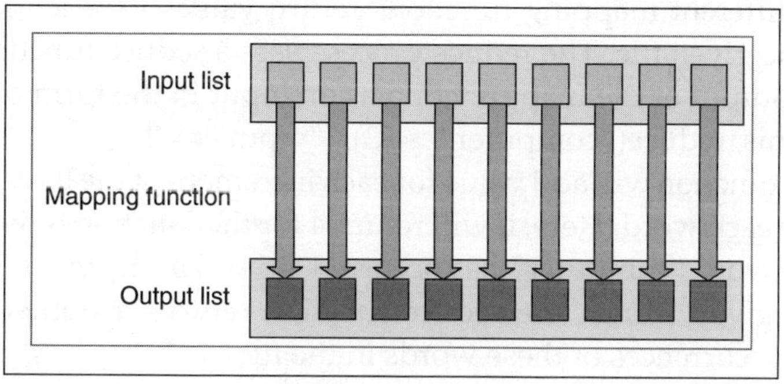

FIGURE 12.2 *Map process*

Reduce Process In this step, each reduce task is assigned to a fragment that processes it and generates the output into key-value pairs. Like map task, reduce task is distributed to each node in the cluster. At last, the final output is sent to the master node of the system.

In Figure 12.3, the reduce process takes the new output list as an input list and reduces it to the input values. It produces an aggregated value output.

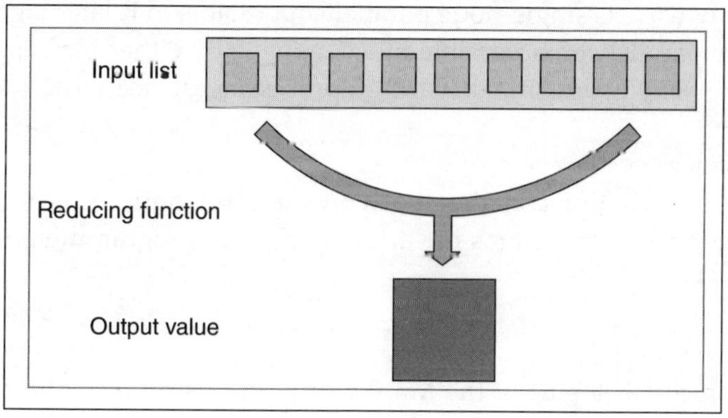

FIGURE 12.3 *Reduce process*

MapReduce Algorithm Example

Let us assume that there is a big file that contains a large amount of information about a computer system. Here is some information on the file.

"Computer is an electronic device. The input devices, output devices, and CPU are major parts of a computer system. Charles Babbage is the father of computers. The computer takes inputs from the input devices and generates the output on the output devices…."

The MapReduce algorithm will find out the number of occurrences of specific words in the file by using the following steps:

1. The map process uses different mapping functions for looping each word. For example, the `map()` function returns a key value for the key word "computer".
2. Similarly, different mapping functions return values for each key that are actual words in the given file. The reduce process uses a reduce function that accepts the generated output of the map function as an input in the form of key-value pair. It looks like this, reduce("computer" >= 3), ("input" >=2).
3. The reduce function will add value for each increment of the loop and return a single number for each word. Here, it will return 4 for the function reduce("computer" >= 3) since the word "computer" has occurred 4 times in the given lines.
4. For all the given words, the reduce function returns a numeric number for the number of occurrences of these words in the file.

Check Your Understanding

1. What do you mean by single-node parallelism?

Ans: Single-node parallelism uses multiple processing cores within a single computer system.

2. In how many ways is single-node parallelism possible in R language?

Ans: Single-node parallelism is possible in R language by either increasing the number of CPUs within a node or using the add-on processing devices.

3. What does message library routine refer to?

Ans: Message library routine contains the syntax and semantics to design and implement the message passing programs in various computer programming languages, such as C, C++ and Java.

4. What is Map process?

Ans: The Map process is a part of the MapReduce. In this process, the master node of the distributed system takes the input data that is delegated into key-value pairs and divides it into fragments that are assigned to map tasks.

12.4 Support for Parallelism in R

The previous section explained the scope of parallelism in R. Further, you will learn how R language supports parallelism. To support parallelism, R language provides different packages. The following subsections will explain these packages.

12.4.1 Support for Parallel Execution within a Single Node in R

Single node parallelism uses multiple processing cores within a single computer system. R language provides packages that support single-node parallelism. Multicore was the first package of R language that implemented multiple cores on systems. These days, Multicore package has been replaced by the package "parallel", "doParallel" and "foreach" also performs single-node parallelism. Here is an introduction to the packages.

parallel

The package "parallel" was introduced in R 2.14.0 to replace the packages "multicore" and "snow". It was introduced to mainly perform the random-number generation. It also performs other parallel applications, such as vector/matrix operations, bootstrapping, linear system solver, etc. Another new feature of this package is that it also performs forking. Forking is a method for creating additional processing threads and generating additional worker threads that run on different processing cores.

Nowadays, every physical CPU contains more than two cores for processing. Some CPUs use their built-in multicore for parallel computing and some operating systems, such as Windows follow the concept of logical CPUs that extend the number of cores. Users can use the function `detectCores()` for finding the number of available cores in a CPU.

The `mclapply()` function of the "parallel" package does the single-node parallelism. It can increase the number of cores in a CPU. The `lapply()` function of the "base" package can be used in place of `mclapply()` function, if it is not supported. `mclapply()` is a parallelized version of `lapply()`, it returns a list of the same length as *x*, each element of which is the result of applying FUN to the corresponding element of *x*.

The function follows the concept of forking. Hence, it is not available on Windows unless mc.cores = 1. The basic syntax of the function `mclapply()` is as follows:

```
mclapply(x, FUN, mc.cores,…)
```

where,

"*x*" argument contains either atomic or list vector or expressions vectors (for class object use as.list for conversion object); "FUN" argument defines the definition of the function applied to each element of *x*; "mc.cores" is an optional argument that defines the number of cores to use, i.e. at most how many child processes will be run simultaneously. It must be at least one, and parallelization requires at least two cores; the dots "…" define the other optional arguments.

Single-node Parallelism using mclapply()

In the following example, a function "DemoFunc" is applied on the function `mclapply()`, where *x* is a list [1:5] and mc.cores is 1. Windows does not support more than 1. For the operating system Unix, Linux, value of the mc.cores can be greater than 1 as they support forking (Figure 12.4).

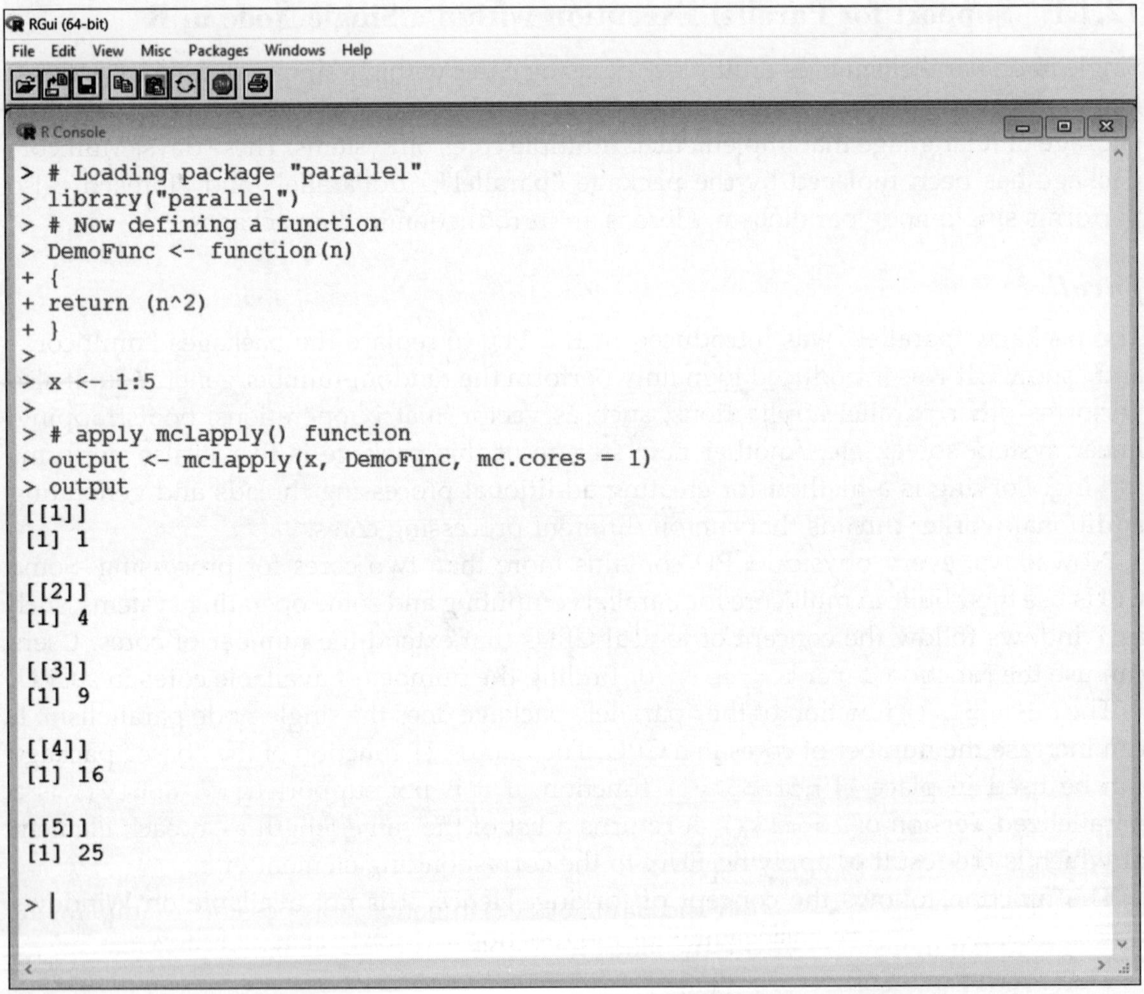

Figure 12.4 *Use of parallel package*

Single-node Parallelism in Windows Operating System using Clusters

Since Windows operating system does not work on forking, it is not possible to use more than 1 in the mc.cores argument of the `mclapply()` function. If more than 1 is used in Windows, then it will show an error. Figure 12.5 shows an example where value 8 is taken in mc.cores. As explained earlier, it shows an error.

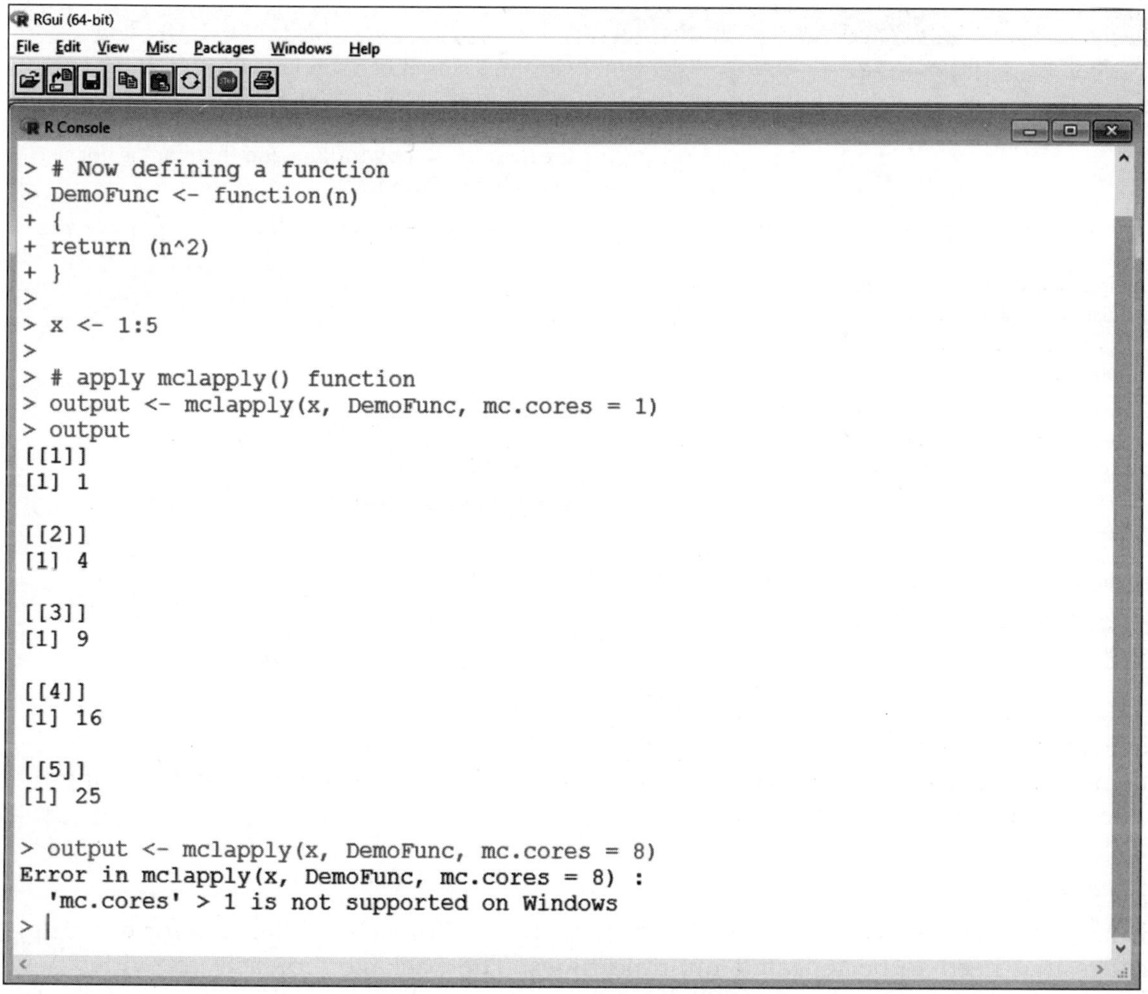

FIGURE 12.5 *Trying multiple core in Windows*

There are many options available to implement single node parallelism in Windows. With the help of clusters function and `parLapply()` function, it is possible to implement single node parallelism. Here are the steps for implementing single-node parallelism:

1. Create clusters of child processes using `makeCluster()`
2. Load the necessary R packages on the `parLapply()`
3. Copy the necessary R objects to the cluster
4. Distribute work to the cluster using `clusterExport()`
5. Stop the cluster using `stopCluster()`

By following the above steps, implementation of any other parallel applications like bootstrapping or random number generation is also possible.

Function syntax	*Details*
`makeCluster(spec, type, …)`	Creates a cluster of a supported type. Default type is "PSOCK". It calls the makePSOCKcluster. Type "Fork" calls makeForkCluster. makeForkCluster creates a cluster by forking and therefore is not available for Windows.
`parLapply(cl = NULL, X, fun, ...)` where cl is an object of class "cluster". If NULL, use the registered default cluster. X is a vector (atomic or list) fun is a function	Is a parallel version of lapply
`clusterExport(cl = NULL, varlist, envir = .GlobalEnv)` where cl is an object of class "cluster". If NULL, use the registered default cluster. varlist is a character vector of names of objects to export. envir is environment from which to export variables	clusterExport assigns the values on the master R process of the variables named in varlist to variables of the same names in the global environment of each node
`stopCluster(cl = NULL)` where cl is an object of class "cluster"	Shut down the cluster

In Figure 12.6, `makeCluster()` function creates a cluster "cl". The package "Matrix" is loaded on the function `parLapply()` and copied. Then, the cluster is distributed by using the function `clusterExport()`. The `parLapply()` function is used for doing the calculation. Then, the cluster is stopped.

foreach

R language provides many looping facilities, such as foreach, while, etc., for executing codes that need to be repeated multiple times. The package "foreach" provides new looping facility and supports parallel execution. In simple words, this package executes repeated operations on multiple cores or processors on a single node or multiple nodes. Before implementing single mode parallelism, here are some important points on the package foreach.

- The package foreach uses "%do%" or "%dopar%" binary operators that execute code repeatedly.
- It provides combined feature that converts a list into a matrix.

To implement single-node parallelism by using the foreach package, it is necessary to use parallel backend, such as doParallel, doMC, etc. These parallel backend, execute foreach loops parallelly. To use this parallel backend, it is necessary to register it even when "%dopar%" binary operator is used. This parallel backend acts as an interface between foreach and parallel package.

`makeCluster()` and `stopCluster()` can also be used for defining the number of cores in the parallel backend.

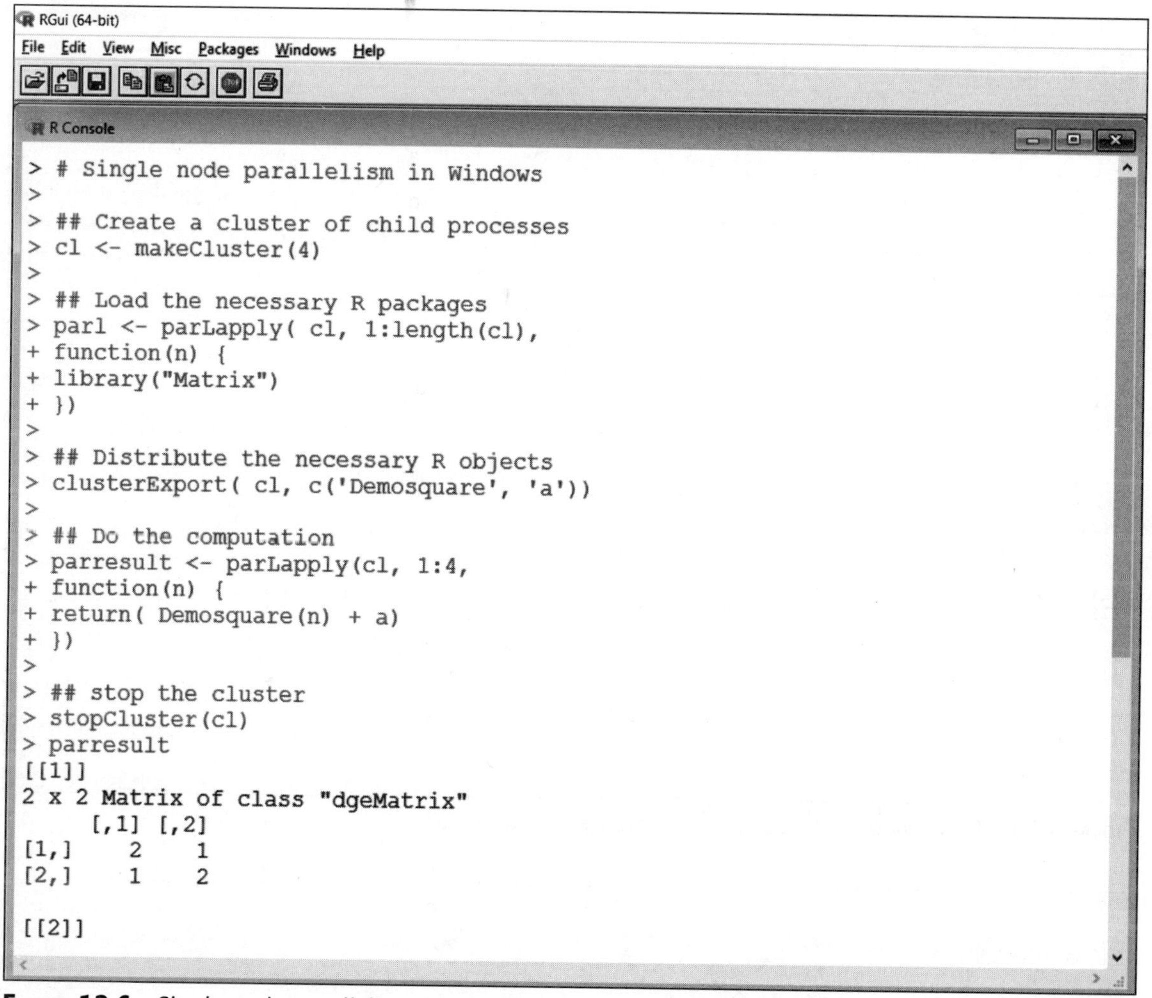

FIGURE 12.6 *Single node parallelism in Windows*

Example 1

In this example, parallel computing of a function "sqr" is carried out to calculate the square of a number. After loading the foreach and doParallel packages, register the four doParallel packages by using `registerDoParallel()`. Then, the `foreach()` function does parallel execution of the function. By default, it returns the output in the form of a list. By using the option ".combine = c/cbind", the output can be converted into columns or a matrix (Figure 12.7).

Example 2

In this example, parallel computing of a function "cube" is carried out to calculate the cube of a number. After loading the foreach and doParallel packages, `makeCluster()` creates a cluster "cl" that contains 8 clusters. It is then passed to the `registerDoParallel()` function. Then, the `foreach()` function does parallel execution of the function "cube". After this, stopCluster stops the cluster (Figure 12.8).

```
> library(foreach)
> library(doParallel)
>
> registerDoParallel(4)
>
> # Define the function
> sqr <- function(N) {
+ N ^ 2
+ }
>
> # Define foreach
> foreach(n = 1:5) %dopar% sqr(n)
[[1]]
[1] 1

[[2]]
[1] 4

[[3]]
[1] 9

[[4]]
[1] 16

[[5]]
[1] 25

> foreach(n = 1:5, .combine = 'c') %dopar% sqr(n)
[1]  1  4  9 16 25
> |
```

FIGURE 12.7 *Single-node parallelism using foreach and doParallel*

```
> library(foreach)
> library(doParallel)
>
> cl <- makeCluster(8)
> registerDoParallel(cl)
>
> cube <- function(N) {
+ N^3
+ }
>
> # apply foreach
> foreach(n = 1:5, .combine = 'c') %dopar% cube(n)
[1]   1   8  27  64 125
>
> stopCluster(cl)
> |
```

FIGURE 12.8 *foreach and doParallel using clusters*

Example 3

In this example, we execute the code sequentially using "%do%" and then in parallel using "%doPar%" and compare the execution time (for sequential and parallel execution).

Step 1: Load the "doParallel" package.

```
> library(doParallel)
Loading required package: foreach
foreach: simple, scalable parallel programming from Revolution Analytics
Use Revolution R for scalability, fault tolerance and more.
http://www.revolutionanalytics.com
Loading required package: iterators
Loading required package: parallel
```

Step 2: Execute the sequential "foreach" loop. The below code calculates the sum of hyperbolic tangent function results.

```
> system.time(foreach(i=1:10000) %do% sum(tanh(1:i)))
   user  system elapsed
   6.13    0.02    6.99
```

Step 3: Change "%do%" to "%dopar%" to execute the code in parallel.

```
> system.time(foreach(i=1:10000)  %dopar% sum(tanh(1:i)))
   user  system elapsed
   6.09    0.00    6.13
Warning message:
executing %dopar% sequentially: no parallel backend registered
```

However, it may respond with a warning message which indicates that the loop ran sequentially. This happens if we run "%dopar%" for the first time. To counter this, register parallel backend and run the code in parallel. The execution time is much lower this time. If the backend is registered without any parameters, by default it creates three workers on a Windows platform and on a Unix platform, half the number of cores approximately.

```
> registerDoParallel()
> system.time(foreach(i=1:10000) %dopar% sum(tanh(1:i)))
   user  system elapsed
   2.31    0.06   11.62
```

Step 4: Check the number of workers with `getDoParWorkers()`.

```
> getDoParWorkers()
[1] 3
```

Step 5: Perform sequential execution of the code and observe the execution time.

```
> registerDoSEQ()
> getDoParWorkers()
[1] 1
> system.time(foreach(i=1:10000) %do% sum(tanh(1:i)))
   user  system elapsed
   6.24    0.02    6.33
```

Step 6: Explicitly set the number of workers and execute the code in parallel. Observe the execution time.

```
> registerDoParallel(cores=2)
> getDoParWorkers()
[1] 2
> system.time(foreach(i=1:10000) %dopar% sum(tanh(1:i)))
   user  system  elapsed
   2.23    0.03    13.94
```

Step 7: Create a computational cluster manually. Once the code has been executed, unregister the cluster by calling the `stopCluster()` function.

```
> cl <- makeCluster(2)
> registerDoParallel(cl)
> system.time(foreach(i=1:10000) %dopar% sum(tanh(1:i)))
   user  system  elapsed
   2.12    0.01    13.98
> stopCluster(cl)
```

Comparison between Single and Parallel Execution

By using the `benchmark()` function of "rbenchmark" parallel, it is possible to compare the performance of single and parallel execution of the foreach loop. The `benchmark()` function is based on all around system.time that evaluates any expression. It generates the output into a data frame and returns many values, such as counts of replications, environment, relative, etc. The replication defines the number of times an expression needs to be evaluated, environment defines where the expression runs, elapsed defines the execution time, etc.

Figure 12.9 compares the two expressions of the foreach package. The first expression is based on single execution, whereas the second expression is based on parallel execution of more than one process. For single execution, the package has an elapsed time 0.53, whereas the parallel execution of five processes has an elapsed time 1.01 that indicates that parallel execution takes less time compared to the single execution.

12.4.2 Support for Parallel Execution over Multiple Nodes with Message Passing Interface

The multi-node parallelism uses computing clusters to implement parallel computing. R language provides different packages that support multi-node parallelism by using MPI. Section 12.2 described the basic concept of MPI that provides a portable interface to obtain HPC using high-performance message passing operations. The Rmpi, SNOW (Simple Network of Workstations), and pbdR are few popular packages of R that implement multi-node parallelism through MPI. You will learn about these packages in this section.

Rmpi

Rmpi is one of the user-developed parallel packages of R language. Actually, Rmpi is an interface or wrapper to use MPI for parallel computing using R. It follows the master/slave paradigm. Hao Yu developed this package. It supports all types of operating systems.

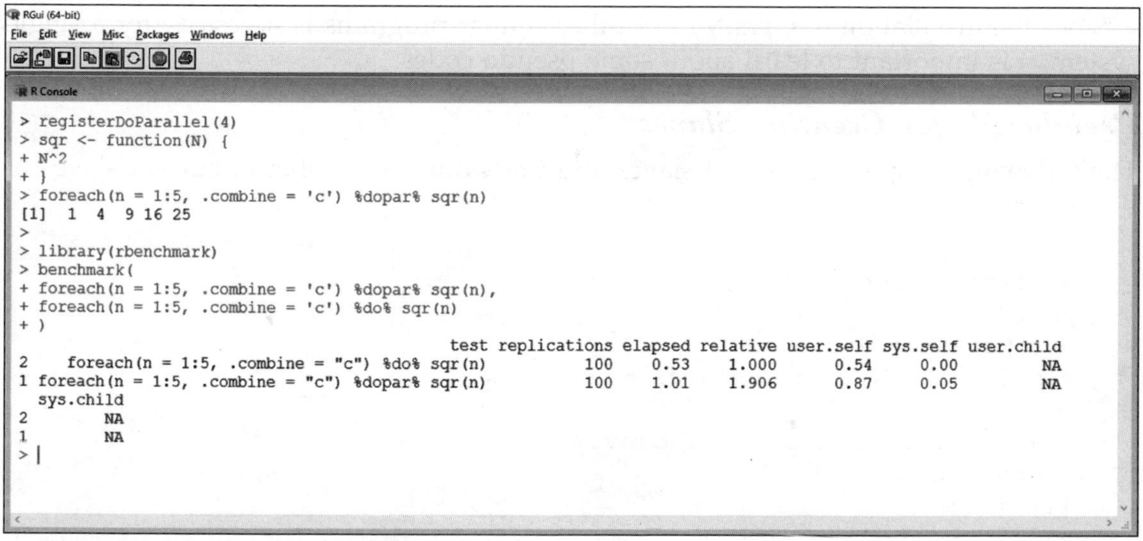

```
> registerDoParallel(4)
> sqr <- function(N) {
+ N^2
+ }
> foreach(n = 1:5, .combine = 'c') %dopar% sqr(n)
[1]  1  4  9 16 25
>
> library(rbenchmark)
> benchmark(
+ foreach(n = 1:5, .combine = 'c') %dopar% sqr(n),
+ foreach(n = 1:5, .combine = 'c') %do% sqr(n)
+ )
                                              test replications elapsed relative user.self sys.self user.child
2   foreach(n = 1:5, .combine = "c") %do% sqr(n)          100    0.53    1.000      0.54     0.00         NA
1 foreach(n = 1:5, .combine = "c") %dopar% sqr(n)          100    1.01    1.906      0.87     0.05         NA
  sys.child
2        NA
1        NA
> |
```

FIGURE 12.9 `benchmark()` *function*

The package supports the OpenMPI or MPICH2 message passing programs. For performing parallel processing on a single system, it is necessary to install such message passing programs. Without this, it is not possible to perform parallel execution on a single machine.

The Rmpi package contains many functions. Table 12.2 below lists some useful functions of the package for parallel computing.

TABLE 12.2 Some useful functions of Rmpi package

Function Name	*Function Description*
`mpi.universe.size()`	It returns the total number of available CPUs in a cluster
`mpi.comm.size()`	It returns the number of processes
`mpi.comm.rank()`	It returns the rank of a process. By default, rank of the master is 0 and rank of slave is 1 to the number of slaves
`mpi.spawn.Rslaves(nslaves = mpi.universe.size(), root = 0)`	It spawns the R slaves
`mpi.bcast.cmd(cmd = ...)`	It transmits or executes the commands from master to all R slaves
`mpi.remote.exec(cmd = ...)`	It remotely executes the commands on R slaves and returns all executed results back to masters
`mpi.bcast.Robj2slave(obj, all = FALSE)`	It transmits or broadcasts an R object from the master to all slaves
`mpi.bcast.Rfunc2slave(obj)`	It transmits functions of all masters to slaves
`mpi.bcast.Robj(obj, root =0)`	It collects the object of each member of the specified member by the argument root
`mpi.send.Robj(obj, destination, tag)`	It sends objects to the destination
`mpi.recv.Robj(mpi.any.resource(), mpi.any.tag())`	It sends objects to the destination
`mpi.close.Rslaves(dellog = FALSE)`	It shuts down all R slaves without deleting the current log files of the slaves
`mpi.exit()`	It terminates the MPI execution environment and detaches the library Rmpi

Since the installation of OpenMPI or other similar programs is necessary for a single system, it is important to learn about some pseudo codes.

Pseudocode for Creating Slaves

The following sample code sets 4 slaves and finds out the number of current slaves of the system.

```
> # Loading library
>  library(Rmpi)
>
> # Creating 4 slaves
> mpi.spawn.Rslaves(nslaves = 4)
>
> # getting the number of slaves
> mpi.comm.size()
[1] 4
>
> # return the rank
> mpi.comm.rank()
[1] 0
>
> # terminate execution
> mpi.exit()
```

Pseudocode for Message Passing

The following sample code defines a function for message passing, where one slave sends the message to the next slave.

```
msgmpi <- function() {

# find out the rank of first slave [Sender slave]
ranks <- mpi.comm.rank()

# find out the rank of second slave [receiver slave]
rankr <- (ranks + 1) %% mpi.comm.rank()
rankr <- rankr + (rankr  == 0)

# Now send a message to the receiver
mpi.send.Robj(paste ("Sender ---", ranks), dest = rankr, tag =
ranks)

# Now receiver is receiving the message
recv.msg <- mpi.recv.Robj(mpi.any.source(), mpi.any.tag())
recv.tag <- mpi.get.sourcetag()
paste(" Receiver received message----",  "recv.msg", "recv.tag[1]",
sep = "")
}
```

SNOW

Simple network of workstations or SNOW is another R package that provides features of simple parallel computing on a network of workstations. The package hides the communication details and provides an abstraction layer. It uses many communication methods sockets, MPI, Parallel Virtual Machine (PVM) via rpmv package, and NetWorkSpaces (NWS) for doing parallel computing. It gives the best output, along with the Rmpi package.

Like the Rmpi package, it follows the master/slave paradigm. In this paradigm, a master R process uses the function `makeCluster()` for starting a cluster of worker processes. Then, it uses some functions, such as `clusterApply()` for executing the R codes on the worker process and returns the results back to the master.

The package provides many functions for the cluster, parallel programming, and random number generation. Users can view the complete list of functions of the package "SNOW" from the following link—https://cran.r-project.org/web/packages/SNOW/index.html.

Table 12.3 describes some useful functions of the package for parallel computing. All functions take a cluster object 'cl'. "*x*" argument defines the matrix object, "*X*" argument defines the array object and the "fun" argument defines the function definition in the functions.

TABLE 12.3 Some useful functions of SNOW package used in parallel processing

Function Name	*Function Description*
`makeCluster(n, …)`	It creates the clusters according to the given value *n* in the function
`makeCluster()`	It stops the current cluster
`clusterExport(cl, val,…)`	It assigns the global value in the global environment of each node
`parLapply(cl, x, fun,…)`	It is a parallel version of the `lapply()` function that returns a list of the same length as *x* where each element is the result of applying fun to the corresponding element of *x*
`parSapply(cl, X, fun,…)`	It is a parallel version of the `sapply()` function that returns a vector
`parApply(cl, X, fun,…)`	It is a parallel version of the `apply()` function that returns a vector after applying fun
`parRapply(cl, x, fun,…)`	It is parallel rows apply function for a given matrix
`parCapply(cl, x, fun,…)`	It is parallel columns apply function for a given matrix
`parMM(cl, A, B…)`	It is parallel matrix multiply function that multiplies two given matrices *A* and *B*

The following example creates 4 clusters by using the `makeCluster(4)` function. A function "Demofunction" adds three numbers that are passed to the function `clusterExport()`. Then, individual values of a, b, c are assigned into a data frame "df". The `parRapply()` function performs parallel execution of the function and returns the output list. It is necessary to stop the cluster by using `stopCluster()` function (Figure 12.10).

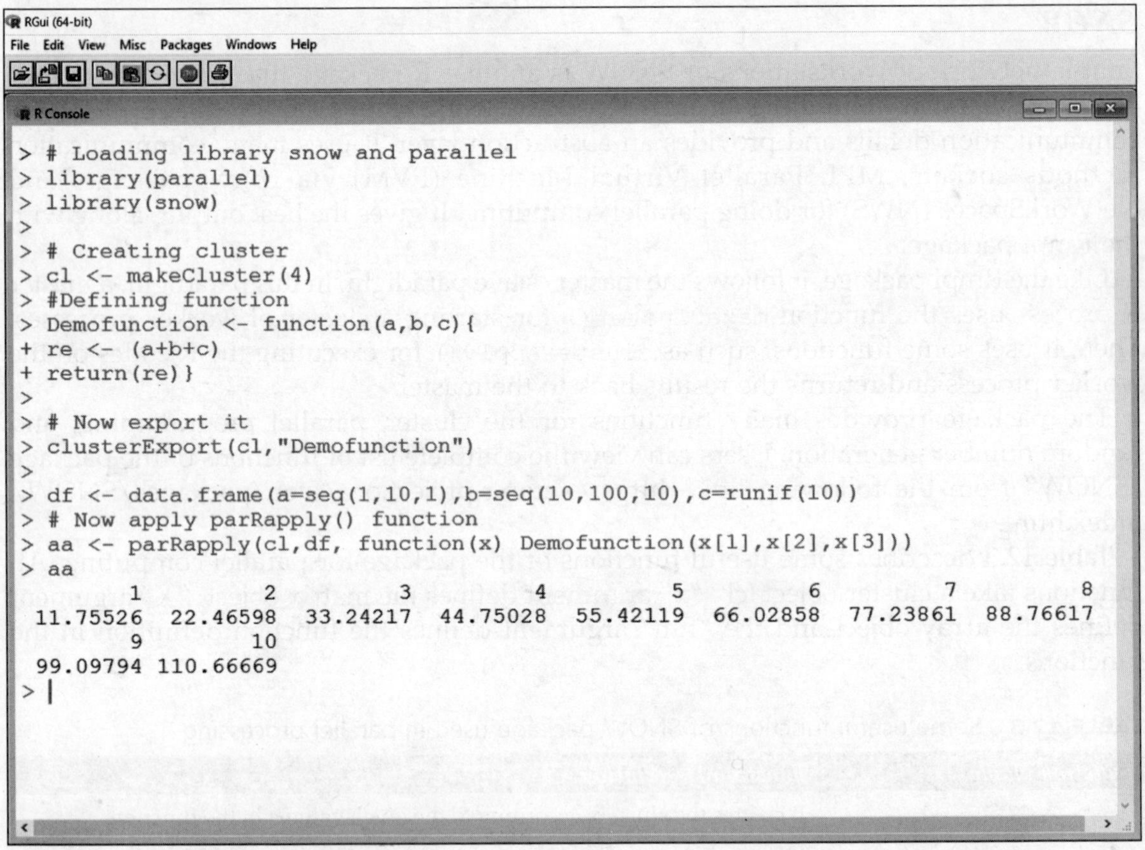

FIGURE 12.10 *Example of SNOW package*

pbdR

Programming with big data in R or pbdR is a series of R packages that contains many other individual packages. It provides an environment for mathematics and statistical computing with big data through high-performance statistical computation. It follows the concept of MPI for communication that provides the flexibility during big analytics. pbdR contains the following packages:

- pbdMPI: The package is designed for MPI communication. It provides S4 classes that directly interface MPI that supports the single program multiple data (SPMD). For batch parallel execution, it is the best option.
- pbdSLAP: The package is designed for scalable linear packages such as PBLAS, BLACS, and ScaLAPAC.
- pbdBASE: The package provides the core classes and methods for distributed data types.
- pbdDMAT: The package provides classes for distributed dense matrices for programming with big data.

- pbdNCDF4: The package allows multiple processes to write to the same file without any manual synchronisation. It supports the terabyte-sized files.

The basic concept of pbdMPI package uses two functions. The first function is comm. size() that returns the number of processes and the second function is comm.rank() that returns the rank of a process. Like, snow and Rmpi packages, this package also needs the installation of the message passing program like OpenMPI or other similar programs.

Pseudocode for Calculating Pie of Multiple Processes

The following sample code is calculating pie [π] of multiple processes:

```
> #  Loading library
>  library(pbdMPI)
>  init()
>
> # initialize value
> np <- 1000000
>
> # defining function
> Demopi <- function(n) {
> + as.integer ((n[, 1] ^ 2 + x [, 2] ^ 2) <= 1)
> + }
>
> # function that calculates pi
>  calp <- function(np) {
>  + mt <- matrix(runif(np * 2), np, 2)
>  + p <- Demopi(mt)
> + return (sum(p))
> + }
>
> # Now call the calp() for each process
> pr <- calp(np)
>
> # Now use reduce() to total across processes
> pr <- reduce(pr, op = "sum")
> api <-  4 *pr / (comm.size() * np)
>
> # Release the memory
> finalize()
```

12.4.3 Packages Utilising Other Distributed Systems

The packages explained in the previous sections significantly manage data parallel problems. It is also possible to solve such problems independently on different subsets of data by using distributed programming. In distributed programming, big data is broken into different chunks and each chunk is then executed in parallel. The distributed system is the system where a number of computers are distributed and a high-speed network is used for communication among these computers. This system follows the concept of distributed programming and uses some programming paradigm.

MapReduce is one of the programming paradigms that has been briefly explained in Section 12.2. At present, Hadoop and Spark are the two most popular distributed systems for big data analytics that use the concept of MapReduce programming paradigm.

Cloud systems are also a type of distributed system, where cloud is also a group of distributed computers connected through high-speed network that use the Internet for working. This system uses distributed processing for computing and users need to pay as per their usage only. It is one of the biggest advantages of this system. Different cloud service providers provide these services. Amazon's EC2 and Google's Cloud are the most popular systems.

It is very efficient to use such systems in R language for analysing big data. It improves the throughput of processing big data analytics problems. The CRAN task view and other depositories define packages for such systems. Here is a brief introduction of these systems and their respective available packages.

Hadoop

Hadoop is an open-source distributed system for distributed processing of huge data on computer clusters. In 2005, Doug Cutting and Mike Cafarella developed it under the terms of Apache License. Hadoop provides a distributed environment across clusters of computers through simple programming models. It scales up from the single server to thousands of servers with local computation and storage. Hadoop's modules automatically handle any hardware failure of individual machines within the framework.

Here are some of the best features of Hadoop:

- The most important and powerful feature of Hadoop is "Hadoop Streaming" that follows the concept of MapReduce programming paradigm. It permits users to create and execute the Map and Reduce process with any executable script as the mapper and/or the reducer respectively. For this, it is necessary that both the mapper and the reducer should be executable, where the mapper reads the input from any standard input and sends the output to any standard output.
- Highly scalable storage platform of the Hadoop System stores and distributes very big data across hundreds of inexpensive parallel servers. Due to this, every business is trying to use this system for their benefit.
- The affordable cost of Hadoop is also attracting organisations. It is very expensive for any organisation to store huge data in traditional ways. By using Hadoop, organisations easily can reduce their storage cost.
- The flexibility and usability features of Hadoop permit users to store structured and unstructured data.

Due to all these features, not only organisations, but other fields like research are also using Hadoop for different purposes, for example, log processing, data warehousing, recommendation systems, market campaign analysis and fraud detection, etc. The "Hadoop Streaming" feature is used for generating reports to find answers to any historical queries.

R language provides many packages for Hadoop, such as RHIPE, RHadoop, toaster, HistrogramTools, and RProtoBuf.

R Package—"rmr2" of the "RHadoop"

Revolution analytics developed a group of packages namely RHadoop. RHadoop is an open source package that permits users to manage and analyse data with Hadoop by using Hadoop streaming. It contains the following packages:

- rhdfs: It provides connectivity to the Hadoop Distributed File System [HDFS] where the user performs any operations in HDFS from within R.
- rhbase: It provides connectivity to the HBASE distributed database using the Thrift server where the user performs any operations in HBASE from within R.
- rmr2: It provides functionality for statistical analysis through Hadoop MapReduce functionality on a Hadoop cluster.
- Plyrmr: It provides functionality for common data manipulation operations.
- Ravro: It provides functionality to read and write the avro files from local and HDFS file system.

In all the packages, the rmr2 package is a good option for big data analysis in Hadoop system. It provides flexibility and allows integration within the R environment. `mapreduce()` is one of the core functions of the package used for writing custom MapReduce algorithms. The MapReduce algorithm uses key-value pairs, where the map() function takes key-value pairs as input and the `reduce()` function generates output as key-value pairs.

Let "k" and "v" be the key and value matrix respectively. The rmr2 package provides a function `keyval()` that generates a list from the output key and value matrices. For this, the key should be a matrix with a column and the same number of rows as the value matrix. Along this, each matrix of the key matrix is matched with a row of the value matrix. Here is a general syntax of the `map()` or `reduce()` function:

```
map = function (k, v)
{
        key  = ...
        val  = ...
        return(keyval(key, val))
}
```

To execute this function, it is necessary that Hadoop is running on the current system. Here is a pseudocode for a `mapreduce()` function that counts words of any given text. For the function, input should be text and the output will be a list with each word along with its number of occurrences.

```
mapreduce(
{
 in <- read.csv("Demo.csv"),
 out <- read.csv("DemoOut.csv"),
 map =  function (k, v)
 {
        key  = v
        n =  dim(v)[1]
        val = matrix( data = 1, nrow = n, ncol = 1)
        return(keyval(key, val))
 }
     reduce = function ( k, v)
 {
        key  = k[1, 1]
        val = sum(k[, 2])
        n =  dim(v)[1]
              return(keyval(key, val))
 }
 )
```

Spark

Spark or Apache Spark is another open source system after Hadoop. The cluster-computing framework of Spark is simple, sophisticated and easy to use. In 2009, it was originally developed in AMPLab at UC Berkeley and in 2010, it was available as an open source Apache project. It uses MapReduce technology for big data analytics and provides many advantages compared to Hadoop. Here are some features of Spark.

- Spark does not use Hadoop YARN for functioning. It uses its own streaming API and independent processes for continuous batch processing on a very short interval. It is faster than Hadoop in some cases. Spark does not have its own distributed storage system. Most of the big data analytics prefer Spark over Hadoop.
- The major difference between Spark and Hadoop is that Spark runs in-memory on the cluster and does not require two-stage MapReduce paradigm like Hadoop. Due to this in-memory feature, it can repeatedly access the same data with much speed. It also runs as a standalone or top of a Hadoop cluster from where it can directly access the data. The in-memory feature of Spark gives better performance for machine learning algorithms.
- The streaming feature of Spark is making the processing of big data analytics very simple. It permits the user to pass data through various software functions that give instance data analytics output. Due to this, the developers use it for graph processing that easily maps the data relationship among different real world entities.
- For the processing of plain data, Spark is the best option since it supports different machine-learning algorithms and processes graphs. It permits the user to use a single platform for everything instead of dividing it into many tasks. As compared to Hadoop, Spark is more costly as Hadoop provides the service-offering feature.

Some of the other features include lazy optimisation of big data queries and higher level API. It optimises the data processing steps and gives a better performance compared to other big data technologies.

R Package—"SparkR"

R language provides package "SparkR" for establishing a connection between Spark and R. SparkR is a lightweight frontend or R API that helps in using Apache Spark from R language. Spark1.4 introduced R API with SparkDataFrame. SparkDataFrame is like a table in a relational database or a data frame in R where data is organised into named columns. Some of the features of this package are as follows:

- It provides distributed data frame implementation that supports many operations on large datasets, such as selection, grouping, aggregation, filtering, and any other statistical or analytical functions.
- Users can create SparkR data frame from the local R data frames or from any other Spark data source HDFS, JSON, Hive, or Parquet.
- It also supports mixing-in SQL queries and converting these query output to and from data frames.

Installation and proper environment setting of Spark in the current system is necessary for running different functions of the package "SparkR". Table 12.4 lists some major functions of SparkR packages that are used for creating a data frame and starting a session with Spark. Users can view the complete list of functions of the package SparkR at the following link—https://spark.apache.org/docs/1.6.0/api/R/.

TABLE 12.4 Major functions of SparkR

Function	*Description*
`sparkR.session()`	The function creates a SparkR session that connects the R programs to a Spark cluster. The user can pass the application names and spark package dependency in this function
`sparkR.init()`	The function creates a SparkR context that also connects the R programs to a Spark cluster

`createDataFrame(sqlcontext, data,…)`
`as.DataFrame(sqlcontext, data,…)`
 	
`Where`
`Sqlcontext is any sql database object`
`data is any dataset`
	The function converts an R data frame or list into DataFrame

`read.df()`	The function creates SparkDataFrame from data sources

Here is a sample code (not executable) where package SparkR starts a session with Spark within R. It converts a dataset into a data frame and creates a new data frame.

```
> # Starting a session with Spark
> sc1 <- sparkR.init()
>
> # Creating session with SQL
> sqlcontext1 <- sparkRSQL.init()
>
> # Converting a dataset into data frame
> df <- as.DataFrame(sqlContext, dataset)
>
> # Creating a new data frame
> ddf <- createDataFrame(sqlContext, dataset)
>
> # Closing a session
> End()
```

Google Cloud

Google Cloud is a famous cloud-computing platform for storing large unstructured data. Google developed it in 2011. The cloud platform follows the concept of distributed processing, as the cloud is a group of computers connected via high-speed networks. Here are some major features of the Google Cloud as follows:

- Cloud storage permits world-wide storage and retrieval of a large amount of data at any time. Along with the storage, it also provides services, such as serving website content, distributing large data, storing data for archival and disaster recovery, or allowing direct downloading of data.
- The impressive network performance of Google Cloud is attracting different organisations. It is to be noted that Google Cloud uses its own fibre network instead of the public network. In Google Cloud, each instance is attached to a single network that spans all regions without using virtual private network or any gateway.
- By providing BigQuery and Google Cloud Dataflow, it offers different big data solution in the big data analytics. The user can run the SQL queries using BigQuery on huge data and can use the Google Cloud Dataflow for creating, monitoring, and gleaning from a data processing pipeline.
- Another major tool Cloud Debugger permits the user to assess, evaluate, and debug the code in the production. It will help the developers during the development of the code as they can set a point on a certain line of code and at any time server request hits that line of code.

Due to the different features of Google Cloud, it is playing a major role in big data analytics and data mining applications. Business analytics uses this during research work to obtain a high-performance output. For this, they also use various available tools of the Google cloud platform.

R Package—"googleCloudStorageR"

R language provides the package "googleCloudStorageR" for supporting an interaction with Google Cloud Storage API in R language. This interface is a part of the "cloudyr" project. To work with the Google cloud storage, users need to open a paid account in Google cloud platform and grant an authentication. Here, the account is called a bucket.

If a user opens a bucket, then he or she receives an access key ID and secret access key for working. All packages of the "cloudyr" project need the key ID and secret access key in the environment variables. Also, the user needs to use `Sys.setenv()` or any other functions for setting the environments.

Table 12.5 describes some major functions of "googleCloudStorageR" package used for creating a data frame and starting a session with Spark. The user can view a complete list of functions of the package "googleCloudStorageR" from the following link—https://cran.r-project.org/web/packages/googleCloudStorageR/index.html.

TABLE 12.5 Major functions of the googleCloudStorageR

Function	*Description*
`gcs_auth(new_user = FALSE, no_auto = FALSE)` where, new_user argument defines the user name if TRUE then re-authenticate via Google login screen; no_auto is an optional argument when TRUE then ignore the auto-authentication settings	The function authenticates each session using R with Google Cloud storage
`gcs_create_bucket(name, projectID, …)` where, name argument defines the name of the bucket; projectID argument defines the valid ID of the Google Project	The function creates a new bucket in the current project
`gcs_get_bucket(name, …)` where, name argument defines the name of the bucket	The function returns the information of the given bucket
`gcs_get_global_bucket(name, …)` where, name argument defines the name of the bucket	The function returns the information of the global bucket
`gcs_list_buckets(projectID, …)` where, projectID argument defines the name of the project that contains buckets to list	The function returns the list of the buckets of a particular project
`gcs_upload(file, ….)` where, File argument contains the name of the file to be uploaded	The function uploads any arbitrary file on the google cloud storage. The file size should be less than 5 MB

Here is a sample code (not executable) where package googleCloudStorageR starts a session with Google Cloud Storage within R. It also explains some functions with examples.

```
> # Setting system environment
>  Sys.setenv("GCS_ClIENT_ID" = "Demokey",
                    "GCS_ClIENT_SECRET" = "DemoSecretkey",
                    "GCS_DEFALULT_BUCKET" = "DefaultBucket",
                    "GCS_AUTH_FILE = " …/ file name")
>
> # loading package
> library(googleCloudStorageR)
>
> # Getting authentication
> gcs_auth()
>
> # checking default bucket
> gcs_get_global_bucket()
[1] "DefaultBucket"
>
> # Uploading a file onto cloud
> write.csv(dataset, file = filename)
> gcs_upload(filename)
```

Amazon EC2

Amazon E2C or Amazon Elastic Compute Cloud is a type of web service that provides distributed computing capacity in the Amazon Web Services (AWS) cloud. It is specially designed for implementing cloud computing. Cloud computing is a type of distributed computing where different computers are connected by using a high-speed Internetwork and it uses the Internet for providing services. The "pay per use" is one of the most important characteristics of the cloud services through which it has become popular for big data analytics. Here are some of the features of Amazon E2C:

- The simple web interface permits the users to obtain, configure, and control the computing resources and run on the computing environment of Amazon. It provides many services, such as simple mail services, content delivery network services, etc. Due to this, it has become a market leader in the cloud computing market. The content delivery network services are not available in Google Cloud.
- The free Usage Tier permits to use micro-Windows instances in the Amazon, which is not available in Google Cloud. It saves time to obtain and start any new server instances in few minutes.
- The customised networking equipment and corresponding protocols permit the developers to build failure resilient applications. The developers separate them from common failure through Amazon EC2.

Amazon EC2 provides a better performance as compared to Google Cloud. Google Cloud is a public cloud that sometimes creates problems. Amazon EC2 provides more number of services as compared to Google Cloud with excellent quality. It is giving a tough competition to Google Cloud. The specific tools for media transcoding and streaming, remote windows desktops, managed directory service, relational and NoSQL databases are some examples of the exclusive services of Amazon EC2.

R package—"segue"

R language provides a package "segue" for implementing parallel processing on Amazon EC2. The package "segue" runs on Mac or Linux operating system, but not on Windows. It is pronounced as "sey-gwey" or "seg-wey".

The segue package contains one main function `lapply()` for parallel processing of the Elastic Map Reduce (EMR) engine, known as `emrlapply()`. It uses Hadoop streaming to implement simple parallel computation with a fast and easy setup on Amazon's EMR. For using the Segue, it is necessary to have an account on Amazon Web Services and an activated Elastic Map Reduce service.

Check Your Understanding

1. List the names of some available R packages for single-node parallelism.

Ans: The names of some available R packages for single-node parallelism are as follow:
- parallel
- foreach with doParallel

2. What is forking?

Ans: Forking is a method for creating additional processing threads and generating additional worker threads that run on different processing cores.

3. How many types of operators are used by 'foreach' package?

Ans: The 'foreach' package uses "%do%" or "%dopar%" binary operators that execute code repeatedly.

4. What is the use of the `makeCluster()` function?

Ans: The `makeCluster()` function creates the clusters according to the given value *n* in the function.

5. What is Hadoop?

Ans: Hadoop is an open-source distributed system for doing distributed processing of huge data on computer clusters. In 2005, Doug Cutting and Mike Cafarella developed it under the terms of the Apache License.

12.5 Comparison of Parallel Packages in R

The above section explained some parallel packages of R language. Each package has specific features and is built for some specific purpose. Fault tolerance defines continued operations even on the failure of some slaves. Load balancing is a parameter that spreads the loading of tasks among resources to obtain optimal resources utilisation. Only snowFT and biopara support fault tolerance, where Rmpi, snow, snowFT, and biopara support load balancing.

Usability is another feature that describes how easily software can be deployed to obtain a goal. For example, foreach, snow, pbdMPI, Rmpi, googleCloudStorageR, spark have a complete list of the API whereas rmr or segue has no complete API.

The performance of the packages depends on the design and efficient implementation, technology, or hardware factors. Hence, a benchmark is used to assess the performance of the parallel packages using different metrics. For this, R language provides a package "rbenchmark". The package "rbenchmark" contains only a single function `benchmark()` for evaluating the performance of parallel packages in R. Table 12.6 shows a comparison between some major parallel packages in R

TABLE 12.6 Parallel packages in R

Package Name	*Version*	*Features*	*Technology*	*Download Link/Document Link*
parallel	NA	• Replaces multicore and snow • Simple parallel processing • Efficient and ease of use	Clustering	https://stat.ethz.ch/R-manual/R-devel/library/parallel/doc/parallel.pdf
foreach	1.4.3	• Uses looping for parallel processing • Enhances the doMC, doParallel, RUnit • Efficient and ease of use	Looing constructs	https://cran.r-project.org/web/packages/foreach/index.html
doparallel	1.0.10	• Enhances RUnit • Foreach parallel adaptor	Parallel processing	https://cran.r-project.org/web/packages/doParallel/index.html
Rmpi	0.6-6	• Interface to MPI APIs • Not very efficient, low error, provide satisfied output • Highly developed	MPI implementation	https://cran.r-project.org/web/packages/Rmpi/index.html
snow	0.4-1	• Defines simple parallel processing • Efficient, compatible with other packages, low errors • Provide satisfied output, Highly developed	MPI implementation	https://cran.r-project.org/web/packages/snow/index.html
pbdMPI	0.3-2	• Interface to MPI as based on SPMD • Simple but not efficient • Provides satisfied output and developing	MPI implementation	https://cran.r-project.org/web/packages/pbdMPI/index.html

Check Your Understanding

1. What is fault tolerance?

Ans: Fault tolerance defines continued operations even on the failure of some slaves.

2. What is rbenchmark?

Ans: rbenchmark is a package of the R language that provides the function `benchmark()`.

Case Study

Sales Forecasting

Today household products are sold by deploying sales forecast and using events, exhibitions, sales, etc. Retailers use location details to influence the supply chain. But, sometimes it is not that simple for retailers to handle the demand chain. In such cases, they hire professionals to help them forecast sales by using historical data or predicting cognitive behaviour of customers depending upon their location. In order to ensure good sale even in bad markets, retail store network needs to understand the condition of the market. Sales forecast is the process of making customers happy. There are many companies from local market to e-commerce too which use this technology. These days most of the companies use parallel computing with the help of big data. Hadoop, MapReduce, Spark, Machine Learning, and Cognitive Intelligence (computing), etc., are some of the technologies that are used by companies.

Hadoop, MapReduce, and Spark are the latest software that are used to handle such problems. However, there are some new technologies that are used to minimise the effort in computing the results for sales forecast. Retail market depends heavily on future sales trends to increase revenue and satisfy customers. These days, we have technology to predict sales for every 10–15 days with nearly 98% accuracy.

In this case study, you will learn about Spark that is being used from past 2 years in the market. It is the most useful optimisation tool used for parallel computing. Spark engine runs on Hadoop, Mesos, and Standalone or in the cloud environment. Depending upon the size of the database, it can be performed on HDFS, Cassandra, HBase and EC3. The best thing about Spark is its Fault Tolerance property with packages of Java, Python, and R.

For forecasting sales and understanding cognitive nature of customers, many companies use a cluster of techniques. Take a look at an example.

(Continued)

Case Study

Input from UX/UI includes:

```
# if "Nearest neighbor clustering" is selected, cluster.
method="single"
# if "Fathest neighbor clustering" is selected, cluster.
method="complete"
# if "Average clustering" is selected, cluster.
method="average"
# only one of the three options can be, and must be, se-
lected
# Here, as an example, suppose "Average clustering" is se-
lected, I set cluster.method="average"
# This needs to be changed, depending on the selection
from UX/UI

cluster.method="average"

png("test.png",width=800,height=600)

options(bitmapType="cairo")
require("XLConnect")
wb <- loadWorkbook("example_data.xlsx")
df1 <- readWorksheet(wb, sheet ="sheet1")

#extracting ID
id=df1[,1]
df1=df1[,-1,drop=FALSE]

#keep only numeric columns
#categorical columns will be ingnored
df1 <- df1[sapply(df1,is.numeric)]

n.col=ncol(df1)
if (n.col<2) plot(0,pch="",ylab="",xlab="",axes=FALSE,main
="Error: at least 2 numeric variables are required.")

if (n.col>1)
{
 df1=as.matrix(df1)
 rownames(df1)=id
 d <- dist(df1, method = "euclidean")
 fit <- hclust(d, method=cluster.method)
 plot(fit,ylab="Distance",xlab="Sample ID",sub="")
}

dev.off()
```

(Continued)

Case Study

The output depends on the files users want to use. Big data provides many exciting opportunities for discovering knowledge that might be relevant to this task in unconventional ways. However, it also raises important questions of theory and method. On the theoretical side, there are questions about what the value of data known today might be for what might be happening around now (nowcasting) or to what might happen months or years later (forecasting). On the method side, there is the need to avoid drawing unreliable conclusions, and to find ways to reduce the dimensionality of the information in big data in ways which enable it to be turned into meaningful knowledge.

These days many companies and even e-commerce sites use graph theory. They implement the basis of user information under the mean of their choice they like or dislike. This also helps them in understanding the new trends in the market, sales and discount they need to offer to customers for gaining their interest. Implementing graph mining can help retailers maintain their most important customers. This also helps them to approach a new customer through the shortest path. It is like a stock market share which we can sell to users. Many international banks are reading information of users to offer them different kinds of credit cards and policies on the basis of their needs.

Some of the techniques to do this are Bayesian techniques: Kalman filtering, spike-and-slab regression, and model averaging, significance testing (forward and backward stepwise regression, Gets); information criteria; principle component and factor models (e.g. Stock and Watson) and Lasso, ridge regression and other penalised regression models.

Another important approach is directed algorithmic text analysis (DATA). The approach is based on searching particular terms in textual databases. Textual data is more comparative in nature. It involves mutual indexing and referring information to another node. However, in contrast to the econometric approaches, this methodology is based upon a theory of human cognitive, behaviour changes as per the radical uncertainty. The search is directed by the theory. This direction dramatically reduces the dimensionality of the search under graph search engine as they look forward for the shortest path to get valuable insights by the customer to hit the right users to complete their needs in the market.

Summary

- The simple concept of parallel computing is that it divides a problem into discrete parts, where each part is further divided into a series of instructions.
- Image modelling of different situations, such as weather, galaxy formation, climate change, etc., data mining applications, big data analytics, database applications are few of the major applications where parallel computing can be applied.

(Continued)

- Different hardware tools, such as the multiprocessors and multicore computers (distributed computers) containing multiple processing elements within a single machine are used in parallel computing. This multi-core computer can be homogeneous or heterogeneous.
- CRAN or Comprehensive R Archive Network (CRAN) is one of the repositories of R language that defines different packages group wise for high-performance computing in their task view.
- The main motivations that empower R language with high-performance computing (HPC) are no efficient packages available for the computation complexity of the big data, insufficient computational resources, the design, and implementation of R language, to reduce the time and efficient utilisation of resources, unable to utilise the modern computer infrastructure like parallel coprocessors.
- When multiple processing units including hosts CPUs, threads, or other units simultaneous execute within a single computer system then this single computer system becomes a single node.
- The MPI or message passing interface is a portable message-passing system that works on different types of parallel computers. The system provides an environment where programs run in parallel and communicate with each other by passing messages to each other.
- The message library routine contains the syntax and semantics to design and implement the message passing programs in various computer programming languages like C, C++, Java, and others.
- The MapReduce programming paradigm is a new programming paradigm developed by Google. This programming paradigm is specially designed for parallel or distributed processing of large set of data into small regular-sized data.
- Parallel and foreach with doParallel are the names of some available R packages for the single-node parallelism.
- Rmpi, SNOW, pbdR are the names of some available R packages for the multi-node parallelism.
- Forking is a method for creating additional processing threads and generating additional worker threads that run on different processing cores.
- The function `detectCores()` finds out the number of available cores of the current CPU.
- The `mclapply()` function of the "parallel" package does the single node parallelism. The function can increase the number of cores in the CPU
- The "foreach" is a package of the R language that provides new looping facility and supports parallel execution.
- The "foreach" package uses "%do%" or "%dopar%" binary operators that execute code repeatedly.
- The package "foreach" provides .combine feature that converts the list into a matrix.
- The `registerDoParallel()` function registers the doParallel packages in R environment.
- The SNOW (Simple Network of Workstations) is an R package that provides the feature of the simple parallel computing on a network of workstations.
- The pbdR is a series of R packages that contains many other individual packages. It provides an environment for mathematics and statistical computing with Big Data through high-performance statistical computation.
- Hadoop is an open-source distributed system for doing distributed processing of huge data on computer clusters. In 2005, Doug Cutting and Mike Cafarella developed it under the terms of the Apache License.
- The RHadoop is an open source package that permits user to manage and analyse the data with Hadoop using Hadoop streaming.
- The RHadoop contains the packages rhdfs, rhbase, rmr2, plyrmr, and ravro .
- The `mapreduce()` is one of the core function of the package rmr2 used for writing custom MapReduce algorithms.

(Continued)

- Spark or Apache Spark is an open source system with cluster-computing framework.
- A SparkDataFrame is like a table in a relational database or a data frame in R where data is organised into named columns.
- R language provides package "googleCloudStorageR" for interaction with Google Cloud Storage API in R language.
- Amazon E2C is a type of web service that provides distributed computing capacity in the Amazon Web Services [AWS] cloud.
- R language provides a package "segue" for implementing parallel processing on Amazon EC2. The package "segue" runs on Mac or Linux operating system but not on windows.
- Usability is another feature that describes how easily software can be deployed to obtain a goal.
- A benchmark is used to assess the performance of parallel packages using different metrics.

Key Terms

- **Amazon E2C:** Amazon E2C is a type of web service that provides the distributed computing capacity in the Amazon Web Services (AWS) cloud.
- **Benchmark:** Benchmark is used to assess the performance of parallel packages using different metrics.
- **Big data:** Big data is a type of data that contains huge information. It is a directory that contains the installed packages.
- **Cloud:** A cloud is a group of distributed computers connected via high-speed networks.
- **Cloud computing:** Cloud computing is a type of distributed computing where computers are connected via high-speed networks.
- **Cluster:** A cluster is a group of interconnected computers that share available resources.
- **CRAN:** CRAN or Comprehensive R Archive Network (CRAN) is one of the repositories of R language that defines different packages group-wise for high-performance computing in their task view.
- **Distributed computing:** Distributed computing is a type of computing where computers are connected via a high-speed network and share resources.
- **Fault tolerance:** Fault tolerance defines the continued operations even on the failure of some slaves.
- **Google Cloud:** Google Cloud is a famous cloud-computing platform for storing large unstructured data.
- **Grid computing:** Grid computing is a type of distributed computing where multiple computers share resources.
- **Hadoop:** Hadoop is an open-source distributed system used for distributed processing of huge data on computer clusters.
- **High-performance computing:** High-performance computing is a type of computing that supports parallel processing to obtain an efficient and reliable output.
- **Load balancing:** Load balancing is a parameter that spreads the loading of tasks among resources to obtain optimal resources utilisation.
- **Map:** Map is a process that takes input data delegated into key-value pairs and divides it into fragments assigned to map tasks.
- **MapReduce:** The MapReduce programming paradigm is a new programming paradigm developed by Google that divides a large set of data into small regular-sized data.

- **MPI:** MPI or message passing interface is a portable message-passing system that works on different types of parallel computers.
- **OpenMPI:** OpenMPI is a message-passing program used for implementing MPI.
- **Parallel computing:** Parallel computing divides a problem into discrete parts, where each part is further divided into a series of instructions.
- **rbenchmark:** rbenchmark is a package of R language that provides the function `benchmark()`.
- **Reduce:** Reduce is a process that generates an output into key-value pairs after grouping.
- **Spark:** Spark or Apache Spark is an open source system with cluster-computing framework.
- **SparkDataFrame:** SparkDataFrame is like a table in a relational database or a data frame in R, where data is organised into named columns.
- **Usability:** Usability is another feature that describes how easily software can be deployed to obtain a goal.

Multiple Choice Questions

1. From the given options, find the odd one out.
   (a) Multi-processors (b) Multi-core computers
   (c) Pthreads (d) CPU
2. From the given options, find the odd one out.
   (a) Shared memory (b) MPI
   (c) Pthreads (d) CPU
3. From the given options, which of the following packages is used for explicit parallelism?
   (a) SNOW (b) Pnmath
   (c) Romp (d) Rdsm
4. From the given options, which of the following packages is used for implicit parallelism?
   (a) Rhpc (b) pdbMPI
   (c) foreach (d) Rmpi
5. From the given options, which of the following packages is used for grid computing?
   (a) SNOW (b) multiR
   (c) Rmpi (d) Rdsm
6. From the given options, which of the following packages is used for Hadoop?
   (a) Rmpi (b) pdbR
   (c) foreach (d) RHIPE
7. From the given options, which of the following packages supports single-node parallelism?
   (a) parallel (b) sparkR
   (c) Rmpi (d) rmr2
8. From the given options, which of the following packages is defined for Amazon EC2?
   (a) segue (b) sparkR
   (c) googleCloudStorageR (d) RHIPE

9. From the given options, which of the following packages contains the binary operators?
   (a) Parallel (b) sparkR
   (c) foreach (d) rmr2
10. From the given options, which of the following packages contains the `mclapply()` function?
   (a) Segue (b) SNOW
   (c) parallel (d) RHIPE
11. From the given options, which of the following functions returns the number of processes?
   (a) `comm.size()` (b) `comm.rank()`
   (c) `makeCluster()` (d) `install.packages()`
12. From the given options, which of the following packages contains the function `comm.rank()`?
   (a) Rmpi (b) pdbR
   (c) foreach (d) SNOW
13. From the given options, which of the following packages contains the function `parMM()`?
   (a) Rmpi (b) pdbR
   (c) foreach (d) SNOW
14. From the given options, which of the following packages contains the function .combine feature?
   (a) Rmpi (b) pdbR
   (c) foreach (d) SNOW
15. From the given options, which of the following packages contain the function `read.df()`?
   (a) Rmpi (b) sparkR
   (c) segue (d) rmr2
16. From the given options, which of the following packages contain the function `gcs_auth()`?
   (a) segue (b) rmr2
   (c) googleCloudStorage2 (d) Rmpi

SHORT QUESTIONS

1. What are the advantages and applications of parallel processing?
2. What are the hardware tools and software concepts used in parallel processing?
3. What are the reasons to empower R with high-performance computing?
4. What is the difference between single and multi-node parallelism?
5. How are single-node parallelism and multi-node parallelism in R implemented?
6. What is the difference between Map and Reduce process?
7. How is the single-node parallelism implemented in Windows?

Long Questions

1. Explain the working of message passing interface mechanism.
2. Explain the MapReduce programming paradigm.
3. Why is support forking not supported by Windows. Explain.
4. Explain the Rmpi package and its functions.
5. Explain the functions of SNOW package. How is parallel processing implemented by using the SNOW package? Give an example.
6. What is the pbdR package and rmr2 package?
7. Write a note on the functioning of sparkR package.
8. What is the googleCloudStorageR package?
9. Write about the functions of the googleCloudStorageR package.
10. Explain some performance metrics that compare the packages of R.

Practical Exercises

1. What will be the output of the following syntax?

```
lapply( 2:5, function(x) c(x, x^2, x^3))
```

Solution:

```
> lapply(2:5, function(x) c(x, x^2, x^3))
[[1]]
[1] 2 4 8

[[2]]
[1] 3 9 27

[[3]]
[1] 4 16 64

[[4]]
[1] 5 25 125
```

2. What will be the output of the following function?

```
lapply(1:3/2, round, digits = 3)
```

Solution:

```
> lapply(1:3/2, round, digits=3)
[[1]]
[1] 0.5

[[2]]
[1] 1

[[3]]
[1] 1.5
```

3. Determine the number of cores in the system (hint: use `detectCores()`) and use it to create a cluster (hint: use `makeCluster()`). What will be the output of running the below code?

```
library(parallel)
# calculate the number of cores
no_cores <- detectCores() -1
cl <- makeCluster(no cores)
# call the parallel version of lapply(), parLapply
parLapply(cl, 2:4, function(exponent) 2^ exponent)
```

Solution:

```
> library(parallel)
> # Calculate the number of cores
> no_cores <- detectCores() - 1
> no_cores
[1] 1
> # Initiate cluster
> cl <- makeCluster(no_cores)
> cl
socket cluster with 1 nodes on host 'localhost'
> # call the parallel version of lapply(), parLapply
> parLapply(cl, 2:4,
+            function(exponent)
|              2^exponent)
[[1]]
[1] 4

[[2]]
[1] 8

[[3]]
[1] 16

> # stop the cluster
> stopCluster(cl)
```

4. What will be the output of the following code?

```
library(doParallel)
no_cores <- detectCores() - 1
cl <- makeCluster(no_cores)
registerDoParallel(cl)
base <- 3
foreach(exponent = 2:4, .combine = c) %dopar% base^exponent
foreach(exponent = 2:4, .combine = rbind) %dopar% base^exponent
foreach(exponent = 2:4, .combine = list, .multicombine = TRUE)
%dopar% base^exponent
```

Solution:

```
> library(doParallel)
Loading required package: iterators
Loading required package: parallel
> no_cores <- detectCores() - 1
> cl<-makeCluster(no_cores)
> registerDoParallel(cl)

> base <- 3
> foreach(exponent = 2:4,
+          .combine = c)    %dopar%
+   base^exponent
[1]   9  27  81

>foreach(exponent = 2:4,
+          .combine = rbind)   %dopar%
+   base^exponent
         [,1]
result.1   9
result.2  27
result.3  81

> foreach(exponent = 2:4,
+          .combine = list,
+          .multicombine = TRUE)   %dopar%
+   base^exponent
[[1]]
[1] 9

[[2]]
[1] 27

[[3]]
[1] 81
```

5. What will be the output of the following code?

```
x <- 1:100
x
y  = Map({function(a) a *3}, x)
unlist(y)
x = seq(1,20,2)
x
Reduce(function(x , y) x+y, x)
```

Solution:

```
> x <- 1:100
> x
  [1]   1   2   3   4   5   6   7   8   9  10  11  12  13  14  15  16  17  18
 [19]  19  20  21  22  23  24  25  26  27  28  29  30  31  32  33  34  35  36
 [37]  37  38  39  40  41  42  43  44  45  46  47  48  49  50  51  52  53  54
 [55]  55  56  57  58  59  60  61  62  63  64  65  66  67  68  69  70  71  72
 [73]  73  74  75  76  77  78  79  80  81  82  83  84  85  86  87  88  89  90
 [91]  91  92  93  94  95  96  97  98  99 100
> y = Map({function(a) a *3}, x)
> unlist(y)
  [1}   3   6   9  12  15  18  21  24  27  30  33  36  39  42  45  48  51  54
 [19]  57  60  63  66  69  72  75  78  81  84  87  90  93  96  99 102 105 108
 [37] 111 114 117 120 123 126 129 132 135 138 141 144 147 150 153 156 159 162
 [55] 165 168 171 174 177 180 183 186 189 192 195 198 201 207 207 210 213 216
 [73] 219 222 225 228 231 234 237 240 243 246 249 252 255 258 261 264 267 270
 [91] 273 276 279 282 285 288 291 294 297 300
> x = seq(1,20,2)
> x
 [1]   1  3  5  7  9 11 13 15 17 19
> Reduce(function(x, y) x+y, x)
[1] 100
```

Answers to MCQs:

1 (c) 2. (d) 3. (a) 4. (a) 5. (b) 6. (d) 7 (a)
8. (a) 9. (c) 10. (c) 11. (a) 12. (b) 13. (d) 14. (c)
15. (b) 16. (c)